Web Developer's SECRETS®

Web Developer's SECRETS®

by Harold Davis

IDG Books Worldwide, Inc.
An International Data Group Company

Foster City, CA ♦ Chicago, IL ♦ Indianapolis, IN ♦ Southlake, TX

Web Developer's SECRETS®

Published by
IDG Books Worldwide, Inc.
An International Data Group Company
919 E. Hillsdale Blvd.
Suite 400
Foster City, CA 94404
http://www.idgbooks.com (IDG Books Worldwide Web site)

Library of Congress Catalog Card No.: 96-80030

ISBN: 0-7645-8015-9

Printed in the United States of America

10 9 8 7 6 5 4 3 2 1

1B/RV/QV/ZX/FC

Distributed in the United States by IDG Books Worldwide, Inc.

Distributed by Macmillan Canada for Canada; by Transworld Publishers Limited in the United Kingdom and Europe; by WoodsLane Pty. Ltd. for Australia; by WoodsLane Enterprises Ltd. for New Zealand; by Longman Singapore Publishers Ltd. for Singapore, Malaysia, Thailand, and Indonesia; by Simron Pty. Ltd. for South Africa; by Toppan Company Ltd. for Japan; by Distribuidora Cuspide for Argentina; by Livraria Cultura for Brazil; by Ediciencia S.A. for Ecuador; by Addison-Wesley Publishing Company for Korea; by Ediciones ZETA S.C.R. Ltda. for Peru; by WS Computer Publishing Company, Inc., for the Philippines; by Unalis Corporation for Taiwan; by Contemporanea de Ediciones for Venezuela. Authorized Sales Agent: Anthony Rudkin Associates for the Middle East and North Africa.

For general information on IDG Books Worldwide's books in the U.S., please call our Consumer Customer Service department at 800-762-2974. For reseller information, including discounts and premium sales, please call our Reseller Customer Service department at 800-434-3422.

For information on where to purchase IDG Books Worldwide's books outside the U.S., please contact our International Sales department at 415-655-3023 or fax 415-655-3299.

For information on foreign language translations, please contact our Foreign & Subsidiary Rights department at 415-655-3021 or fax 415-655-3281.

For sales inquiries and special prices for bulk quantities, please contact our Sales department at 415-655-3200 or write to the address above.

For information on using IDG Books Worldwide's books in the classroom or for ordering examination copies, please contact our Educational Sales department at 800-434-2086 or fax 817-251-8174.

For press review copies, author interviews, or other publicity information, please contact our Public Relations department at 415-655-3000 or fax 415-655-3299.

For authorization to photocopy items for corporate, personal, or educational use, please contact Copyright Clearance Center, 222 Rosewood Drive, Danvers, MA 01923, or fax 508-750-4470.

ABOUT IDG BOOKS WORLDWIDE

Welcome to the world of IDG Books Worldwide.

IDG Books Worldwide, Inc., is a subsidiary of International Data Group, the world's largest publisher of computer-related information and the leading global provider of information services on information technology. IDG was founded more than 25 years ago and now employs more than 8,500 people worldwide. IDG publishes more than 275 computer publications in over 75 countries (see listing below). More than 60 million people read one or more IDG publications each month.

Launched in 1990, IDG Books Worldwide is today the #1 publisher of best-selling computer books in the United States. We are proud to have received eight awards from the Computer Press Association in recognition of editorial excellence and three from *Computer Currents*' First Annual Readers' Choice Awards. Our best-selling *...For Dummies®* series has more than 30 million copies in print with translations in 30 languages. IDG Books Worldwide, through a joint venture with IDG's Hi-Tech Beijing, became the first U.S. publisher to publish a computer book in the People's Republic of China. In record time, IDG Books Worldwide has become the first choice for millions of readers around the world who want to learn how to better manage their businesses.

Our mission is simple: Every one of our books is designed to bring extra value and skill-building instructions to the reader. Our books are written by experts who understand and care about our readers. The knowledge base of our editorial staff comes from years of experience in publishing, education, and journalism — experience we use to produce books for the '90s. In short, we care about books, so we attract the best people. We devote special attention to details such as audience, interior design, use of icons, and illustrations. And because we use an efficient process of authoring, editing, and desktop publishing our books electronically, we can spend more time ensuring superior content and spend less time on the technicalities of making books.

You can count on our commitment to deliver high-quality books at competitive prices on topics you want to read about. At IDG Books Worldwide, we continue in the IDG tradition of delivering quality for more than 25 years. You'll find no better book on a subject than one from IDG Books Worldwide.

John Kilcullen
CEO
IDG Books Worldwide, Inc.

Steven Berkowitz
President and Publisher
IDG Books Worldwide, Inc.

Eighth Annual Computer Press Awards 1992

Ninth Annual Computer Press Awards 1993

Tenth Annual Computer Press Awards 1994

Eleventh Annual Computer Press Awards 1995

IDG Books Worldwide, Inc., is a subsidiary of International Data Group, the world's largest publisher of computer-related information and the leading global provider of information services on information technology. International Data Group publishes over 275 computer publications in over 75 countries. Sixty million people read one or more International Data Group publications each month. International Data Group's publications include: **ARGENTINA:** Buyer's Guide, Computerworld Argentina, PC World Argentina; **AUSTRALIA:** Australian Macworld, Australian PC World, Australian Reseller News, Computerworld, IT Casebook, Network World, Publish, Webmaster; **AUSTRIA:** Computerwelt Osterreich, Networks Austria, PC Tip Austria; **BANGLADESH:** PC World Bangladesh; **BELARUS:** PC World Belarus; **BELGIUM:** Data News; **BRAZIL:** Annuário de Informática, Computerworld, Connections, Macworld, PC Player, PC World, Publish, Reseller News, Supergamepower; **BULGARIA:** Computerworld Bulgaria, Network World Bulgaria, PC & MacWorld Bulgaria; **CANADA:** CIO Canada, Client/Server World, ComputerWorld Canada, InfoWorld Canada, NetworkWorld Canada, WebWorld; **CHILE:** Computerworld Chile, PC World Chile; **COLOMBIA:** Computerworld Colombia, PC World Colombia; **COSTA RICA:** PC World Centro America; **THE CZECH AND SLOVAK REPUBLICS:** Computerworld Czechoslovakia, Macworld Czech Republic, PC World Czechoslovakia; **DENMARK:** Communications World Danmark, Computerworld Danmark, Macworld Danmark, PC World Danmark, Techworld Denmark; **DOMINICAN REPUBLIC:** PC World Republica Dominicana; **ECUADOR:** PC World Ecuador; **EGYPT:** Computerworld Middle East, PC World Middle East; **EL SALVADOR:** PC World Centro America; **FINLAND:** MikroPC, Tietoverkko, Tietoviikko; **FRANCE:** Distributique, Hebdo, Info PC, Le Monde Informatique, Macworld, Reseaux & Telecoms, WebMaster France; **GERMANY:** Computer Partner, Computerwoche, Computerwoche Extra, Computerwoche FOCUS, Global Online, Macwelt, PC Welt; **GREECE:** Amiga Computing, GamePro Greece, Multimedia World; **GUATEMALA:** PC World Centro America; **HONDURAS:** PC World Centro America; **HONG KONG:** Computerworld Hong Kong, PC World Hong Kong, Publish in Asia; **HUNGARY:** ABCD CD-ROM, Computerworld Szamitastechnika, Internetto online Magazine, PC World Hungary, PC-X Magazin Hungary; **ICELAND:** Tolvuheimur PC World Island; **INDIA:** Information Communications World, Information Systems Computerworld, PC World India, Publish in Asia; **INDONESIA:** InfoKomputer PC World, Komputek Computerworld, Publish in Asia; **IRELAND:** ComputerScope, PC Live!; **ISRAEL:** Macworld Israel, People & Computers/Computerworld; **ITALY:** Computerworld Italia, Macworld Italia, Networking Italia, PC World Italia; **JAPAN:** DTP World, Macworld Japan, Nikkei Personal Computing, OS/2 World Japan, SunWorld Japan, Windows NT World, Windows World Japan; **KENYA:** PC World East African; **KOREA:** Hi-Tech Information, Macworld Korea, PC World Korea; **MACEDONIA:** PC World Macedonia; **MALAYSIA:** Computerworld Malaysia, PC World Malaysia, Publish in Asia; **MALTA:** PC World Malta; **MEXICO:** Computerworld Mexico, PC World Mexico; **MYANMAR:** PC World Myanmar; **NETHERLANDS:** Computer! Totaal, LAN Internetworking Magazine, LAN World Buyers Guide, Macworld Netherlands, Net, WebWereld; **NEW ZEALAND:** Absolute Beginners Guide and Plain & Simple Series, Computer Buyer, Computer Industry Directory, Computerworld New Zealand, MTB, Network World, PC World New Zealand; **NICARAGUA:** PC World Centro America; **NORWAY:** Computerworld Norge, CW Rapport, Datamagasinet, Financial Rapport, Kursguide Norge, Macworld Norge, Multimediaworld Norge, PC World Ekspress Norge, PC World Nettverk, PC World Norge, PC World ProduktGuide Norge; **PAKISTAN:** Computerworld Pakistan; **PANAMA:** PC World Panama; **PEOPLE'S REPUBLIC OF CHINA:** China Computer Users, China Computerworld, China InfoWorld, China Telecom World Weekly, Computer & Communication, Electronic Design China, Electronics Today, Electronics Weekly, Game Software, PC World China, Popular Computer Week, Software Weekly, Software World, Telecom World; **PERU:** Computerworld Peru, PC World Profesional Peru, PC World SoHo Peru; **PHILIPPINES:** Click!, Computerworld Philippines, PC World Philippines, Publish in Asia; **POLAND:** Computerworld Poland, Computerworld Special Report Poland, Cyber, Macworld Poland, Networld Poland, PC World Komputer; **PORTUGAL:** Cerebro/PC World, Computerworld/Correio Informático, Dealer World Portugal, Mac*In/PC*In Portugal, Multimedia World; **PUERTO RICO:** PC World Puerto Rico; **ROMANIA:** Computerworld Romania, PC World Romania, Telecom Romania; **RUSSIA:** Computerworld Russia, Mir PK, Publish, Seti; **SINGAPORE:** Computerworld Singapore, PC World Singapore, Publish in Asia; **SLOVENIA:** Monitor; **SOUTH AFRICA:** Computing SA, Network World SA, Software World SA; **SPAIN:** Communicaciones World España, Computerworld España, Dealer World España, Macworld España, PC World España; **SRI LANKA:** Infolink PC World; **SWEDEN:** CAP&Design, Computer Sweden, Corporate Computing Sweden, Internetworld Sweden, it.branschen, Macworld Sweden, MaxiData Sweden, MikroDatorn, Nätverk & Kommunikation, PC World Sweden, PCaktiv, Windows World Sweden; **SWITZERLAND:** Computerworld Schweiz, Macworld Schweiz, PCtip; **TAIWAN:** Computerworld Taiwan, Macworld Taiwan, NEW ViSiON/Publish, PC World Taiwan, Windows World Taiwan; **THAILAND:** Publish in Asia, Thai Computerworld; **TURKEY:** Computerworld Turkiye, Macworld Turkiye, Network World Turkiye, PC World Turkiye; **UKRAINE:** Computerworld Kiev, Multimedia World Ukraine, PC World Ukraine; **UNITED KINGDOM:** Acorn User UK, Amiga Action UK, Amiga Computing UK, Apple Talk UK, Computing, Macworld, Parents and Computers UK, PC Advisor, PC Home, PSX Pro, The WEB; **UNITED STATES:** Cable in the Classroom, CIO Magazine, Computerworld, DOS World, Federal Computer Week, GamePro Magazine, InfoWorld, I-Way, Macworld, Network World, PC Games, PC World, Publish, Video Event, THE WEB Magazine, and WebMaster; online webzines: JavaWorld, NetscapeWorld, and SunWorld Online; **URUGUAY:** InfoWorld Uruguay; **VENEZUELA:** Computerworld Venezuela, PC World Venezuela; and **VIETNAM:** PC World Vietnam.

3/24/97

Credits

Acquisitions Editor
Greg Croy

Development Editors
Deborah Craig
Stefan Grünwedel

Technical Editor
Hussein Kanji

Copy Editor
Deborah Craig

Project Coordinators
Susan Parini
Ben Schroeter

Book Design
Liew Design

Graphics and Production Specialists
Tom Debolski
Ed Penslien
Christopher Pimentel
Dina F Quan
Andreas F. Schueller

Quality Control Specialist
Mick Arellano

Proofreader
Christine Sabooni

Indexer
Nancy Anderman Guenther

About the Author

Harold Davis is a programmer, author, Webmaster, graphic designer, and photographer. He is the author of many books, with topics ranging from advanced software development to art and photography. His computer titles include the best-selling *Visual Basic SECRETS* (from IDG Books Worldwide), *Delphi Power Toolkit,* and *Peter Norton's Guide to Visual Basic 4 for Windows 95.* He has also written *The Photographer's Publishing Handbook* and *Publishing Your Art As Cards, Posters & Calendars.*

As a principal of Evolution Software, Inc., he has developed software for numerous clients, including Chase Manhattan Bank, PaperDirect, J. P. Morgan, and Viacom International.

Davis is the creator of the well-known Wilderness Studio fine art poster series. His photographs are distributed on CD-ROM by Corel Corporation.

He holds a B.A. in Computer Science and Mathematics from New York University and a J.D. from Rutgers Law School.

In his spare time, he enjoys backpacking and scuba diving with his wife and coconspirator, Phyllis.

This book is dedicated to all those whose imagination, creativity, skill, and hard work have made the Web so exciting.

Preface

May you live in interesting times.

— Chinese proverb

This fabled Chinese curse — or blessing — is very apt to the situation currently confronting developers at all levels who wish to write web applications, or just keep up with the shifting focus of software development. There is no doubt that the ability to create applications that can be distributed over the Web (or via *intranets*, which are private webs) presents a tremendous opportunity for both individual programmers and corporate information science departments.

A whole new generation of programmers has come of age, speaking the development languages of the Web: *Hypertext Markup Language* (HTML) and Java. In addition, Microsoft has focused on web development, with OLE-based ActiveX controls as a cornerstone of its web development effort.

No developer can afford to ignore the opportunities presented by the Web. With some 50,000 new Internet domains being added every month, there are myriad career opportunities available for programmers who understand the secrets of web development. In addition, web development presents the opportunity to learn a revolutionary kind of cross-platform development, in which the browser is the client. There is absolutely no doubt that web development will be important and exciting for some time to come.

However, along with opportunity, ferment, and excitement has come confusion. Programmers whose skill sets were honed before the web revolution have legitimate concerns about learning the new techniques they need to keep current. In my experience, published information at the developer level about web applications tends to be both vague and hard to find. *Web Developer's SECRETS* is the book that I wish I had been able to read when I first started learning about programming on the Web. For the first time in one book, *Web Developer's SECRETS* provides the insights, techniques, and tools that developers need in order to understand this significant area.

I stated earlier, and it bears repetition, that the native languages of the Web are HTML and Java, for reasons — which may already be clear to you — that I will discuss in Chapter 1. It is also the case that server-side web development has a strong UNIX bias. This has made it particularly difficult to find sophisticated information targeted at Windows web development — the primary subject of *Web Developer's SECRETS*.

When you get right down to it, the course of future web development is unclear and fragmented. Will ActiveX conquer the Web? Will Navigator come to include cross-platform OLE support? Will the mass of Visual Basic programmers learn to love Java and start churning out Java applets? Will Windows web servers gain ground as opposed to UNIX web servers? Which of the myriad Windows web server packages is best?

In *Web Developer's SECRETS,* I try, as far as is possible, to take a neutral position on all these questions. It is my job to tell you the truth about all available technologies and to show you the secrets of using them in your web applications.

Who Should Read This Book

Web Developer's SECRETS is intended to be read by a wide range of developers and those involved with Web site design. However, as the term "developer" implies, I do expect that you will have some familiarity with basic programming concepts (and at least know what the Web is).

Experienced web developers will find inside secrets they need to make their web applications truly awesome. Programmers who started before there was a "Generation X" will learn how to leverage their programming skills into the ability to create dynamic and sophisticated web applications.

This book contains a great deal of information on a variety of topics you need to know about to create great web applications, including

- Web page design
- Web site design
- Scripting languages — JavaScript and VBScript — on the Web
- Using ActiveX controls and Java applets in web applications
- Web development, Internet programming, and client/server development
- Java programming
- Creating ActiveX controls
- Using specific development tools — such as Microsoft's ActiveX Control Pad included on the companion CD-ROM
- CGI programming on the Windows NT platform
- Server-side programming with Internet Information Server

Web Developer's SECRETS will be useful and interesting to readers who find themselves anywhere on the following spectrum:

- Those who want to better understand the Web, web development concepts, and how the various technologies fit together
- Web masters, and mistresses, and those responsible for the design of HTML pages and sites who would like to be able to create more

impressive sites and effectively use programs they have created as part of their Web sites

- Internet developers who would like to harness the power of up-and-coming web technologies
- Those who would like to make more effective use of web scripting techniques
- Developers who would like to better harness the power of executables in web development projects
- Anyone who would like to put up her own web server or Web site
- Programmers interested in making effective use of Java applets
- All those who have heard about ActiveX controls and want to know exactly what they are and how to use them in web applications
- Developers who would like to create their own ActiveX controls, using either Visual C++ or Microsoft's Java development environment, Visual J++

This Book's Overall Structure

Web Developer's SECRETS is divided into four parts:

- Part I, "Creating Web Content," covers the basics of HTML design and web content creation in a structured fashion geared for programmers.
- Part II, "Scripting Languages on the Web," explains how to use JavaScript and VBScript to add dynamic and interactive content to web applications.
- Part III, "Adding Executable Content," covers using and creating executable code modules — ActiveX controls and Java applets — on the Web.
- Part IV, "Client and Server on the Web," provides the specific information you will need to create server-side web programs

How to Use This Book

It's important to bear in mind that web development — like the Web itself — can aptly be termed *seamless*. One thing always seems to lead to another that eventually leads back to the first thing. Therefore, I'd encourage you to jump in at any place in this book that interests you. You can always "link" back to pick up information you missed.

My approach in *Web Developer's SECRETS* is practical: I'll show you how to do jazzy things with Web pages and Web sites and how to create sophisticated real-world web applications. I include background and theoretical information only to the extent that you will need it to understand the sample projects that I develop and the technology that I show you how to use. I've always learned best by seeing actual examples, and I assume that what applies to me also applies to you.

Each chapter starts with an introduction and concludes with a summary that describe and list the most important topics covered in the chapter. You can use these previews and summaries to quickly identify the chapters that contain information you need.

Icons and Conventions

The cute little icons you'll find in the margins have specific meanings:

Hot Web Tip Readers primarily interested in learning ways to dress-up their Web pages or increase the functionality of web applications should look for this icon.

Inside Scoop Text accompanied by the "Inside Scoop" icon includes information that is essential either to understanding a technology or to making it work (or both).

Warning The "Warning" icon flags areas that involve potential development problems, for example, where programs are buggy or product documentation is inaccurate.

URL This icon indicates that the text contains a URL, or *Universal Resource Locator* — in other words, a specific Web address that can be used to find in-depth, up-to-date information on specific topics.

A Note on HTML Styles

Web Developer's SECRETS is a book about Web programming — but the prevailing language of the Web, HTML, is hardly a programming language at all. Many hard-core programmer types feel that HTML is too easy to understand to be considered "code." Because HTML is a markup language rather than a programming language, there is some truth to this — although as HTML gets further and further extended, in some respects it has grown quite complex. And it is certainly difficult to decipher when it hasn't been formatted with ease of reading in mind.

To make the HTML in *Web Developer's SECRETS* easier to read, I have taken a nonstandard approach to formatting it. HTML tags are presented in uppercase. Indentation has been used where possible. Tag attributes are referred to in the text, in bold, as **parameters**.

I don't mean to imply that you should format your own HTML in this fashion. In fact, if you use a program such as FrontPage that generates HTML for you, you won't be able as a practical matter to do so. These are not the conventions that most HTML front ends follow.

In general, Web development is still in its infancy — and highly anarchic. There are no generally accepted conventions about how to format HTML (or other Web code). Except for situations where doing so makes the code highly unreadable, and except for the HTML conventions that I've just described, I've tried to follow the formatting conventions of the Web language or program that the text is discussing.

Acknowledgments

While writing *Web Developer's SECRETS* I have sometimes felt like Captain Ahab. Like Ahab's whale Moby Dick, World Wide Web development is a fast moving, and very, very large target.

A book that has such huge ambitions could never truly be the work of one person. Many others have helped me. The fabulous crew at IDG Books Worldwide has included Walter Bruce, Greg Croy, Stefan Grünwedel, and John Osborn.

Deborah Craig edited this book. Her editorial skills, and general all-round good sense, place her in a class by herself. I couldn't ask for a better editor.

Matt Wagner stood by me when the going got rough on *Web Developer's SECRETS*. For a while, it looked as though the whale was going to win. Thank you, Matt, for hanging in there.

Personally speaking, I would never have been able to complete this book without the help and support of my own true love, Phyllis.

I'd also like to put in a good word — in alphabetical order — for Audrey, Eunice, Hacker, and (not least) Snapper.

My father, Martin Davis, first taught me to program. He also mentioned recursive functions, the Fibonacci series, compilers, and Boolean logic. Without him, this book wouldn't exist.

This book also wouldn't exist without my grandmother, Virginia Whiteford Palmer. As they say, everything is always up to date in Kansas City.

Contents at a Glance

Contents

Part I

Creating Web Content

Chapter 1

An Overview of Web Concepts

"I can't explain myself, I'm afraid, sir, because I'm not myself, you see."

— Alice in Lewis Carroll's Alice in Wonderland

Like Alice, many normally well-informed developers — and those involved with software technology — are not themselves when it comes to the Internet and the Web. The three primary reasons for this confusion are change, rate of change, and jargon.

The business of creating applications for the Web represents a tremendous change in the way developers think and work, and the tools they use. This kind of change has been termed a *paradigm shift*. It is hard enough to take by itself. In this case, it has happened from left field and with blinding speed. In the space of a few months the entire orientation of software development has shifted.

This paradigm shift and change of orientation has to do with the new focus on developing programs (web applications) that are independent of specific operating systems. Web development tends to treat the entire universe as one connected network. This is a very different way of thinking about software development than creating programs that are meant to be run on one machine under a specific operating system. The purpose of *Web Developer's SECRETS* is to help you deal with these momentous changes by explaining the new technologies.

The rate of change — and constant barrage of new information — is so dizzying that it's hard to keep on top of web development issues. (The opposite of shooting fish in a barrel, keeping up in this field is like trying to shoot flying barrels of fish located on the far side of the moon from earth with a peashooter.)

While I'm on the topic of how quickly web development is moving, I'd like to clearly and loudly note that there is no sign of this rate of change slowing down. The key players in the Internet development tools arena, including Microsoft and Netscape, are doing their best to compress development cycles as much as possible. This means that an accelerated rate of change in web development is — at least for the foreseeable future — a given. I have made every effort to explain the most up-to-date technologies available throughout *Web Developer's SECRETS*. The best way to make sure that information is current is to check the Web pages of the software vendor responsible for the product. Where appropriate, I list the URL (*Universal Resource Locator*, or Web address) for vendors whose products are discussed in this book.

The third cause of confusion is jargon. Web development is drowning in a sea — actually, a vast ocean — of jargon. This syndrome, which I call "the attack of the acronyms," is understandable in a field still in ferment, a field which is far from consensus on standards, methods, and tools. However, the confusion caused by the attack of the buzzwords can be cured. Stripped of their opaque linguistic exterior, most web development concepts are really quite straightforward.

Some of the more important web development concepts are clarified in the remainder of this chapter. Obviously, not all web concepts can be covered in a few pages. However, after reading the next few pages you will have a good general feeling for the most important of these concepts and should have banished the attack of the acronyms in the process. With the conceptual framework behind you, you can get to work with practical examples of creating web applications.

The Internet and Intranets

The *Internet* is a vast global collection of networks of computers. These networks communicate with each other using the *TCP/IP protocol,* which is described in a moment. No one knows exactly how many independent networks make up the Internet or how many individual computers (*nodes*) are connected at any given time. It is estimated that at least 100,000 networks are part of the Internet. These networks range in size from tiny — for example, my network has three nodes attached to the Internet via a Microsoft NT server — to gigantic, with thousands of nodes.

You may be interested to know that these 100,000 (or more) interconnected networks include at least 200,000 World Wide Web sites and 20 million or so Web pages. There are 418,089 registered Internet domains, of which 212,693 have associated Web sites. Some 25 million users surf these pages and sites. Obviously, these numbers will be larger by the time you read this book.

These statistics about the Internet and the Web come from I/PRO's CyberAtlas Web site, *http://www.cyberatlas.com*. The CyberAtlas site is intended as an Internet research guide; I/PRO is setting itself up to be a Nielsen-like rating service for the Internet.

An *intranet* is a private Internet, meaning a network that communicates using the TCP/IP protocol. It's typical for technically savvy corporations to set up their own intranet for internal purposes such as scheduling and collaborative work flow.

For the convenience of the internal users, intranets are often connected to the Internet. In this case, firewall software generally controls what comes in from the Internet and addresses security concerns.

Because developing for a private intranet is in many ways similar to developing for the public Internet, a new term, *I-Net*, which covers both, is starting to be used.

Protocols

A *protocol* is a definition of the form of the data that is moved between devices. Protocols do not involve the contents of a communication — that is, the actual data. A protocol is merely the form in which the communication is transmitted. To decode (understand) the communication, a receiving device must know the protocol with which it was transmitted. In other words, the receiving device must have something like a decoding manual that contains codes and their meanings as well as a set of rules. Think of kids with their "Super Spy" book containing secret codes.

A *protocol stack* is a layered collection of protocols, with each layer intended to perform a different function. (Most protocols, such as TCP/IP, are actually protocol stacks — that is, collections of protocols with different purposes.)

In a protocol stack, different layers, or levels, have logically distinct functions. For example, the top-level protocol usually handles transmission and receipt of data by applications (such as a web browser). An intermediate level protocol handles moving chunks of information from one point to another on the network. (With TCP/IP this is handled by the Internet Protocol.) At the lowest level, a protocol ensures that data moves correctly across the physical circuits and hardware.

TCP/IP

TCP/IP, shorthand for *Transmission Control Protocol/Internet Protocol*, is a collection of protocols. (It's named after two of the most important members in that collection.) TCP/IP is the protocol that Internet devices use to communicate. As mentioned, the IP protocol handles networking issues. As its name implies, TCP manages the transmission of data from one point to another on the Internet (and thus is one step up the protocol stack from IP).

Both Windows 95 and Windows NT ship with 32-bit TCP/IP drivers.

The Web

The *World Wide Web,* or Web, is a collection of devices connected using TCP/IP, whose upper-level communication is achieved using HTTP, *Hypertext Transfer Protocol*. HTTP is used to transmit and receive *Web pages* written in HTML, *Hypertext Markup Language*.

HTML is an ASCII text-based tagged markup language. (It's a derivative of SGML, *Standard Generalized Markup Language.*) The key characteristic of a markup language is that it consists of standard text interspersed with formatting commands indicated with brackets, such as <I'm a markup command>. These markup commands are called *tags*.

You should know that HTML does not function like a page layout program such as PageMaker. HTML tags merely identify what an element of an HTML document is, not how it should be displayed. A given HTML page will display differently in different browsers. (For more information on this topic, see Chapter 4, "Different Browsers for Different Folk.")

A *web browser* is a program designed to decode HTML-based Web pages and render them in a way that is attractive to the viewer.

For example, Listing 1-1 consists of HTML tags and text.

Listing 1-1: A pretty boring Web page

```
<HTML>
<HEAD>
<TITLE>Not a Very Exciting Web Page!</TITLE>
</HEAD>
<BODY>
<H1>
Hi! I'm a heading!
</H1>
<P>
This is definitely
<BR>
A pretty
<STRONG>
boring
</STRONG>
<BR>
web page.
</BODY>
</HTML>
```

When a web browser such as Internet Explorer decodes the HTML code contained in Listing 1-1, the user will see a display like that shown in Figure 1-1.

Chapter 2, "Using HTML Tags to Design Web Pages," covers the structure, syntax, and formatting of HTML documents in detail.

In the meantime, you probably know that you can add hypertext links to Web pages created using HTML. *Hypertext links* are used to jump to related text. You can jump within a document, to a document on the active system, or — provided that the computer is connected to the Web — to any Web page available on the Web.

Obviously, the ability to navigate using hypertext links is fundamental to the Web and to the look and feel of Web pages. For example, you could add a hyperlink to the HTML page shown in Figure 1-1:

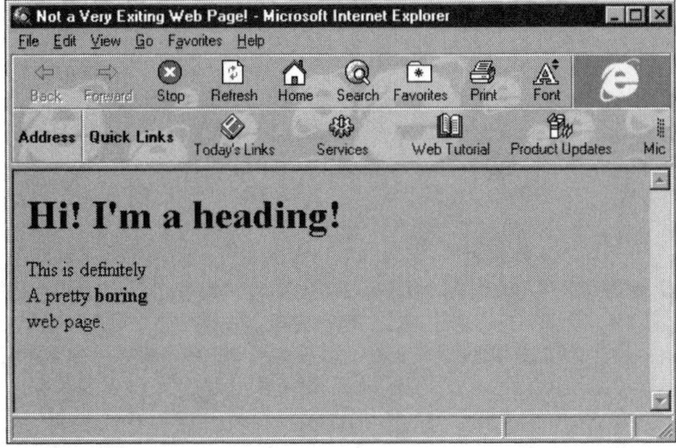

Figure 1-1: Here's the pretty boring Web page displayed in Internet Explorer.

```
...
<BR>
But you can always add links to better ones:
<A HREF="http://www.microsoft.com/workshop">
Microsoft's Internet Developer Toolbox
</A>
...
```

If you use your browser to open the page containing the hyperlink, the link appears underlined, as shown in Figure 1-2.

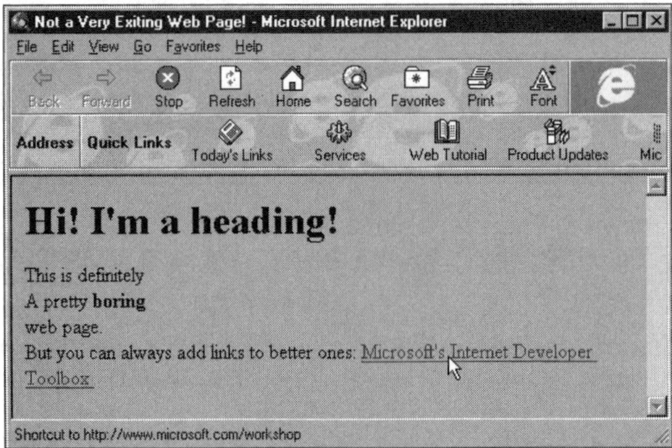

Figure 1-2: It's easy to add hyperlinks to HTML documents.

Assuming that the user's system is connected to the Internet (for example, with a dial-up account) and the specified URL is a valid, connected Web location, when the user clicks on the hyperlink, she will be "transported" to the specified page. ("Beam me up, Scotty; there's a hyperlink here!")

Note that the first part of the hyperlink, *http://*, specifies that the connection is being made using HTTP.

In some important respects, HTML is a rather crude standard. The situation is comparable to the evolution of standards for fax transmissions: The standard is in such widespread use that everyone must use it, regardless of its technical merits.

For one thing, HTML is conceptually a document formatting system, not a programming environment in which you can easily place executable commands. (Nor is it — as I mentioned — a page description system, such as PageMaker, which would easily allow you to precisely place elements.) For another, there really is no one HTML standard. The truth is that the major Internet vendors — Microsoft and Netscape — are each extending standardized HTML in their own way. In addition, many browsers do not support recent HTML extensions. The bottom line is that proprietary tags — tags implemented in only one browser — do not necessarily behave gracefully when interpreted by another browser. Extensions of one sort or another to different browsers then become necessary to completely support web applications, and the same HTML page looks and acts differently in different browsers. This means that the developer must make choices and accept trade-offs in terms of which browsers are supported, a topic covered in Chapter 4.

HTML may be a pain, but it is our pain. Its universal acceptance as the rails on which the web locomotive runs means that all web applications must be grounded in HTML, even if they ultimately soar far beyond HTML.

Internet Explorer and Netscape Navigator

In *Web Developer's SECRETS*, I generally assume that you are running Microsoft's Internet Explorer version 3.0 or later, or Netscape's Navigator version 2.0 or later. With either browser, you can duplicate most of the functionality explained in this book.

You can download the latest version of Internet Explorer from *http://www.microsoft.com/ie/*. You can download Navigator from *http://www.netscape.com*.

Obviously, choice of browser is like freedom of religion: each to her own. However, Explorer and Navigator are the two most widely used and powerful browsers on the Web. They both run Java applets and JavaScript. Explorer has native support for ActiveX; if you wish to use ActiveX controls using Netscape's Navigator, you need a *plug-in* (or extension to Navigator) that supports ActiveX, to some extent.

You'll find further information about the ActiveX Plug-in for the Netscape browser at *http://www.ncompass.com*.

As mentioned, as a developer you have to design applications with multiple possible browsers in mind (or make the conscious decision to drop users of certain browsers). This important topic is discussed in detail in Chapter 4.

Web Servers, Addresses, and Applications

The IP protocol uses an addressing scheme to identify particular nodes on the Internet. An IP address is made up of four numbers, each between 0 and 255 and each separated by a period. For example, the IP address of a Web site might be 204.71.18.55.

Because numeric IP addresses are notoriously hard to remember, each IP address can also have a name. For example: *http://www.bearhome.com* is somewhat easier to remember than 204.71.18.55, right?

Names are *resolved* into numerical IP addresses using a service called *Domain Name System* (DNS). DNS is a distributed database containing IP addresses and domain names for all registered Internet servers. (Internet servers are also called *hosts*, or *gateways*.)

The Internet Network Information Center (InterNIC) maintains DNS and administers IP addresses and domain names. You can find out more about registering domain names (and obtaining IP addresses) on InterNIC's Web site, *http://www.internic.net*.

Parsing Domain Names

Although the rules for naming a domain have yet to be completely codified, the final word in a domain name represents what is called the *top-level domain*. Within the United States, by convention the top-level domain identifies the kind of organization that owns the domain name: .com means a business; .edu means a school; .gov means government; .net means a network; and .org means a noncategorized institution. Outside the United States, the top-level domain tends to identify the country of the organization (.ca stands for Canada, .fr stands for France, and so on).

Sockets

Socket is a term for the combination of an IP address and an IP *port*. An IP port identifies an application running on a server. WinSock (Windows Socket) is the implementation of Internet sockets designed for the Windows operating systems.

An Internet server (also called a host, or a gateway) is identified by its IP address. There are no limits to the number of possible IP ports. (In serial communication, by contrast, there is a four port maximum.)

For a client computer to execute an application on a server that it is connected to using TCP/IP, the client needs to know

- The server's IP address
- The application's IP port

Fortunately, all World Wide Web servers communicate on IP port 80. This means that it is easy for client applications — such as web browsers — to jump from web server to web server. Each server answers at port 80. All the browser needs to know is the server's IP address; once it is connected it can use HTTP to communicate with the server.

Web Servers

A *web server* is software installed on an Internet node that manages services when it is accessed. For example, a web server handles dispatching requested HTML documents to browsers. There are many commercially available web server packages, including products from Microsoft, Netscape, O'Reilly, and Process Software. Microsoft's Internet Information Server is designed to run on NT Server 4.0 and can be downloaded from Microsoft's Web site.

The seldom openly acknowledged truth is that programming for each web server is somewhat different. Hooks, mechanisms, and programming languages that easily speak to each other just differ from web server program to web server program. For more information on this, see Part IV, "Client and Server on the Web."

Web Applications

Earlier in this chapter I raised the question of how web applications get executed. Because HTML is a stream of text, what are the mechanisms for telling a browser, "it's time to start taking programmatic actions?" The term "programmatic actions" is shorthand for a wide variety of activities, including retrieving information from a database, downloading files, accepting user input in a form, and starting an animation.

There is a three-tiered response to this question:

- At the simplest level, using appropriate tags, you can embed scripting commands in an HTML file. Browsers that "speak" the scripting language can then decode the commands and execute them. This topic is covered in Part II, "Scripting Languages on the Web."
- You can embed executables — ActiveX controls and Java applets — in a web application. When an event such as a scripting command triggers an embedded executable, it "does its thing," whatever that may be. This topic is covered in Part III, "Adding Executable Content."

- The HTML page being browsed — think of it as the client — sends information to the web server, which processes the information and sends HTML back to the browser. This topic is covered in Part IV.

How Java Works

Java is a programming language that lets you create executable content that will run on remote systems across the Web regardless of what operating system the remote computer is using. From the very beginning, Java was intended to be a language that was independent of hardware (meaning the processor) and the operating system. How can this *platform independence* be achieved?

Java source code is compiled into platform-independent binary code sometimes called Java *byte code*. As Gertrude Stein might have said, "Java byte code is Java byte code is Java byte code." This is true whether you are running a Windows, Mac, or UNIX computer so long as the user has a browser that "understands" Java. This is extremely important for developers who want to create a single cross-platform (for example, Mac, UNIX, and Windows) code base.

The next step is to include a Java byte code interpreter in the environment where the Java program will be run. This environment is usually a browser such as Netscape's Navigator or Microsoft's Internet Explorer. A slight variant to the interpreter is the *just-in-time Java compiler* included in Explorer.

The Java byte code is downloaded from the host Web page to the remote browser. At this point the interpreter embedded in the browser, sometimes called a Java *virtual machine*, causes execution of the Java applet.

ActiveX Controls

ActiveX controls do not share Java applets' revolutionary platform independence. "We have met the enemy and he is us," as Walt Kelley's character Pogo said. Plain and simple, ActiveX controls are *OLE controls* (also known as OCXs). OCXs are components created using the *Component Object Model* (COM) specification. For more details on how ActiveX controls are internally implemented and created, see Part III of this book. ActiveX controls are downloaded fully compiled to a target machine (if they do not already exist on the target). They are then registered and executed normally.

Although the ActiveX technology seems to miss the point of platform-independent web development, there are some advantages to using it, particularly when all your targets are Windows machines. These advantages include

- The ability to integrate with the Windows operating system
- The availablility of an existing, tested base of components
- The ability to create and manipulate ActiveX controls in well-known and familiar programming environments

In addition, Microsoft has UNIX and Mac ActiveX SDKs (software development kits) in the works. As these become reality, ActiveX will become cross-platform — and enable development more fully in the spirit of the Web.

Server-Side Programming

One of the most common methods of executing commands is to use *Common Gateway Interface (CGI)* scripts or programs that are executed on the server side. Basically, CGI script commands included in an HTML page can easily send information entered in an HTML *form* in a browser to a web server program when a web browser encounters the <POST> or <GET> tag. (HTML forms are explained in Chapter 2.) The server program then processes the information. This processing might involve database access. When the processing is complete, the server program prepares an HTML document, which is then displayed in the browser.

An alternative web server program model is the ISAPI (Internet Server Application Programming Interface) used by Microsoft's Internet Information Server. The ISAPI are routines contained in a library, OLESAPI.DLL, that comes with Internet Information Server. Essentially, OLESAPI lets you call methods of in-process OLE servers — written in a Windows programming language such as Visual Basic or C++. Once these server programs start executing, they can process entries in an HTML form and return HTML text to a browser. For more information, see Chapter 22, "The Internet Server API (ISAPI) and Active Server Pages (ASP)."

As mentioned, the programming for each server has its own methodology and quirks. Expect to learn a new way of doing things for each server package out there.

Learning More

Far and away the best place to get timely information about web development topics is on the Web itself. I'll use the URL icon to indicate Web site URLs that are important to developers. I'll let you know about sites that are important to web developers as I go along, but here are a few for starters.

Microsoft's primary sites for web developers are Microsoft's "Developer's Only" and "Internet Developer Toolbox":

- *http://www.microsoft.com/devonly*
- *http://www.microsoft.com/workshop*

Netscape is at *http://www.netscape.com*. Netscape's site contains a wealth of information about Java script and web development. For example,

Netscape's resource page, which contains links to JavaScript language description and tutorial pages, is at *http://www.netscape.com/comprod/products/navigator/version_2.0/script/script_info/index.html*.

A site that bills itself as "Web Designer's Paradise" — and contains an incredible array of web development tools ready for downloading — is at *http://www.desktoppublishing.com/webparadise.html.*

Summary

This chapter covered much of the preliminary and overview information you'll need to know before jumping into the vast topic of web development, including

- An overview of important Internet concepts, including protocols, TCP/IP, domain names, sockets, HTML, browsers, and the Web
- An overview of web development and server concepts, including scripting, ActiveX controls, Java, and server-side programming
- Where to go for more information

Chapter 2

Using HTML Tags to Design Web Pages

"An idea is a greater monument than a cathedral."

— Thomas Hardy

Creating HTML Web pages is neither rocket science nor brain surgery. Hundreds of thousands of people with no background in programming have created their own pages, some of them using graphical tools provided by on-line services such as CompuServe and America Online, or semi-WYSIWYG tools such as Microsoft's FrontPage.

However, HTML Web page design is one of those things that is easy to do poorly, but surprisingly difficult to do well. In particular, hard-core programmer-types should note that success with HTML is more a design activity than a coding activity. Any web developer worth her or his salt must live, eat, and breath HTML. HTML's lack of high-level interface design capability makes this task more difficult, but not less important.

In this chapter I will

- Show you how to create well-designed Web pages
- Explain the structure of an HTML document
- Define the syntax and meaning of HTML tags that you are likely to use
- Discuss the trade-offs involved in various HTML design choices
- Provide tricks and secrets that experienced web mistresses use to create award-winning HTML pages

HTML Editing Tools

HTML editing tools take either a WYSIWYG or a text-and-tag based approach. Currently, only a few tools let you see the finished appearance of your HTML page (in other words, is WYSIWYG) and also allow sufficient access to the underlying tags.

For a programmer, the WYSIWYG tools generally do not supply sufficient control over the underlying HTML document. But the text editing tools do not provide a preview of the visual impact of changes to HTML tags, meaning that you have to go back and forth between editor and browser. The user interface of the editing tools can also be a little daunting in comparison to what they accomplish; it's probably easier to type in a simple tag than to figure out a three-level deep menu structure that does the same thing.

The truth is that there is not currently one tool for generating HTML that is up to snuff for developers. The best strategy seems to be to mix and match different tools and to create much of your HTML code in a simple text editor such as Notepad (shown in Figure 2-1), using a browser to view your work. This approach, at least, has the advantage of teaching you "low-level" HTML from the start.

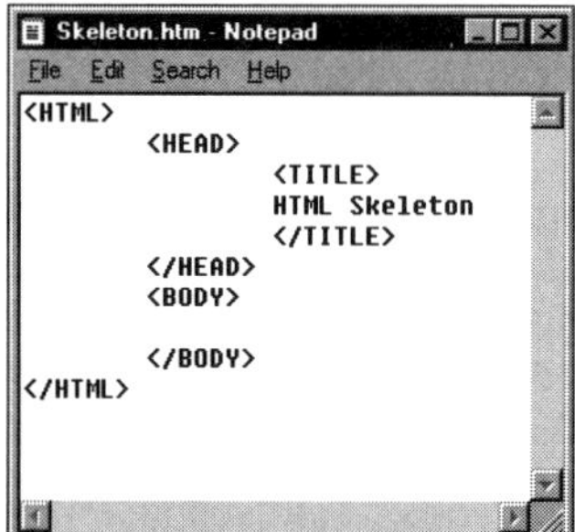

Figure 2-1: You can use Notepad, or any simple text editor, to create and modify HTML documents.

Earning honorable mention as "tools that I have found helpful for handling some of the grunt work of Web page design" are Sausage Software's HotDog 32 and Q&D Software Development's WebMania! 1.5.

You can download a trial version of HotDog from Sausage's site, *http://www.sausage.com*. WebMania!, written by Dave Verschleiser, is shareware, available for downloading at *http://www.q-d.com*.

The site Web Designer's Paradise (*http://www.desktoppublishing.com/webparadise.html*) mentioned earlier includes links to myriad useful web development tools. These tools are most relevant to HTML page work, as opposed to executable programming.

One more HTML editing tool that you should know about is Microsoft's *ActiveX Control Pad*. The companion CD-ROM to *Web Developer's SECRETS* includes a copy of this program for your use. This HTML editor is best used to add ActiveX functionality to HTML pages and to work with Microsoft's HTML Layout control. It is essential for these purposes, although it lacks many features that you would wish for in an HTML editor. The ActiveX Control Pad is covered in Chapter 10, "Doing it with VBScript," and Chapter 11, "VB Script and ActiveX."

Although HTML code is simple conceptually to a developer used to working in a complex programming language, it can rapidly become impossible to read. It is therefore important to write HTML that combats this opaqueness factor. You should use plenty of comments. In addition, indenting nested structures — such as lists and framesets — will save you much time in the long run. Another good habit is to always create the "close bracket" tag before entering the contents of the tag. For example, after you've inserted a <BODY> tag, be sure to enter a </BODY> tag before getting to work on the contents of the document.

HTML Standards

HTML standards. What HTML standards? Seriously, folks, take my HTML standards.... Okay. So HTML is actually a young, living, eating, breathing, and changing language — already in its third iteration. Any "standards" are constantly changing.

Generally, *Web Developer's SECRETS* assumes that you are creating web applications for browsers that speak HTML 3, such as the latest versions of Explorer and Navigator. Perhaps you've included a text-only version of your site to accommodate users who don't have HTML 3 browsers.

The truth is that even two HTML 3 browsers — for example, Explorer and Navigator — do not decode identical HTML pages in precisely the same way. These differences, how they appear in the browser, and strategies for dealing with them are discussed in Chapter 4, "Different Browsers for Different Folk." (Also see the following sidebar, "If You Can't Beat HTML, Join HTML.")

As developers, we should primarily be concerned with the commercial implementations of HTML, not with some theoretical standard that is constantly changing.

If you are interested in the "official" HTML standards, World Wide Web Consortium — also known as W3C — is the organization charged with standardizing web technology.

According to the W3C Web site, *http://www.w3.org*, "[t]he World Wide Web Consortium exists to realize the full potential of the Web.... The W3C is an industry consortium which seeks to promote standards for the evolution of the Web and interoperability between WWW products by producing specifications and reference software. Although W3C is funded by industrial members, it is vendor-neutral, and its products are freely available to all."

W3C delegates the job of formulating changes to HTML standards to the Internet Engineering Task Force (IETF). The URL for the IETF is *http://www.ietf.org*.

The IETF is the protocol engineering and development arm of the Internet and is responsible for general technology definition. (In other words, its theoretical purview goes far beyond HTML.) The IETF articulates proposed changes to standards using documents — available on the IETF site — known as *Requests for Comments* (RFCs). As the term implies, RFCs are circulated on the Internet for feedback.

The IETF describes itself as a "large open international community of network designers, operators, vendors, and researchers concerned with the evolution of the Internet architecture and the smooth operation of the Internet. It is open to any interested individual."

The Structure of an HTML Document

An HTML document is made up of normal ASCII text, with markup tags indicated using angular brackets (<TAG>). HTML documents are case-insensitive: It doesn't matter — other than from the viewpoint of clarity and aesthetics — whether you capitalize your HTML tags. <TITLE> is read the same way as <Title>, <tItle> and <title>. Bear in mind, however, that JavaScript commands, which may be embedded in your HTML pages, are extremely, and annoyingly, case sensitive.

In *Web Developer's SECRETS*, I use all uppercase for tags to set them apart from the actual content of the HTML documents. It is also often helpful for clarity's sake to put each tag on a line of its own, although <LI> and <TD> tags, indicating list items and table cells respectively, should not be followed by a space or a carriage return.

A slash following the opening bracket in a tag (</TAG>) indicates the end of the text being marked by the tag. In addition, some tags can include parameters and values. The syntax for this is

```
<TAG Parameter1=value ... ParameterN=value> </TAG>
```

For example, the <BODY> tag often includes parameters and values that set the colors of text and background in a web document. (The <BODY> tag is discussed in detail later in this chapter.)

As shown in Listing 2-1, a bare bones "skeleton" of an HTML document begins with an <HTML> tag and concludes with an </HTML> tag.

Listing 2-1: The HTML "skeleton"

```
<HTML>
   <HEAD>
      <TITLE>
      HTML Skeleton
      </TITLE>
   </HEAD>
   <BODY>

   </BODY>
</HTML>
```

If You Can't Beat HTML, Join HTML

Because of my extensive visual arts background, my tendency is to try to fully control the Web pages I design. This means viewing my pages under various browsers, preparing alternative versions of my sites, and stretching the design capabilities of HTML. Obviously, choosing which browser(s) to design a site for involves complex trade-offs that you must carefully consider, perhaps in conjunction with the client who has commissioned the site. These issues are discussed in more detail in Chapter 4.

It is crucial to understand that HTML is not intended for the jobs of design and visual layout. Like markup languages in general, HTML is intended to *structure* a document, not lay it out. Structuring a document means specifying the role of each content element in a document, *not* specifying how that element should be displayed. The theory is that it is then entirely up to each browser to decide how to deal with (display) a given element once the kind of element has been made known to the browser.

Going with this HTML flow is certainly the path of least resistance. If you do, your HTML pages will more universally display appropriately, which is the point of HTML, after all. But some of us are just not prepared to give up this much control! In its short leap from infancy to, well, toddlerhood, the Web has evolved from a way to access text-based information toward a way to provide the user with a multimedia experience. Developers who aspire to create Web pages that provide this experience will find it necessary to push the limit of the HTML envelope, and break the spirit — if not the letter — of HTML.

Inside Scoop

Although the <HTML> tag is required for adherence to HTML standards, most browsers can read HTML documents that omit the <HTML></HTML> tags without a problem.

Within the <HTML> </HTML> tags lie a head section, denoted with the <HEAD> and </HEAD> tags, and a body section, denoted with the <BODY> and </BODY> tags.

The head section may contain a number of things, although none of them are mandatory. (Although it's not required, you will rarely see an HTML document without a title.) Generally, JavaScript routines are placed in the head section. That way the routines are loaded before any possible call to them.

Every HTML document is supposed to include a title, placed in the head section between the <TITLE> and </TITLE> tags. Typically, browsers display the document's title in the browser's title bar. Meaningful titles are preferred, but not mandatory.

The content of the HTML page itself goes between the <BODY> and </BODY> tags. Of course, a wide range of content can go into a Web page. This content is identifaed to a browser through use of the tags explained in this chapter.

Using Comments

As in any development environment, it's important to add comments to your HTML code so you and others can easily to tell what it's supposed to do.But commenting HTML seems to be rare. Perhaps this is because web designers feel that HTML is self-explanatory. However, I know from personal experience that complex HTML documents can be difficult to decipher. (It's along the lines of reading your own handwriting after using the computer for too long.) So be kind to whomever will be maintaining your HTML pages — which may amount to being kind to your future self — and use plenty of pithy but well-conceived comments.

Comments, which are not displayed by browsers, are any text included between <!-- and --> tags. For example:

```
<!--
I am a comment!
-->
```

is a comment. Any HTML line that begins with two slashes is also considered a comment:

```
// I'm a comment, too!
```

The astute reader may have noted that I said comments "are not displayed by browsers," which is different from saying that comments have no impact on a browser.

In fact, comments in HTML have an important role beyond that of documentation.

If you embed a JavaScript routine or function within a comment, it is appropriately processed by a JavaScript-capable browser and ignored by other browsers. This is sometimes called code "hiding." If you don't embed the script within comments, browsers that don't "speak" JavaScript will include the text of the comment in the displayed page — a horrific result. (Note that the same principle applies to other web scripting languages, such as VB Script.)

Here's how this works. The HTML page whose code is shown in Listing 2-2 includes a JavaScript function, Presto, that displays an Alert when the page loads. (An Alert is JavaScript's, and Java's, equivalent to Visual Basic's Message Box. Adding exciting JavaScript interactivity and effects to your Web pages is discussed in Chapter 8, "JavaScript Applications.") Figure 2-2 shows the results of opening the page in Navigator.

Listing 2-2: JavaScript Alert on load, without "hiding" code

```
<HTML>
   <HEAD>
      <TITLE>Alert</TITLE>

      <SCRIPT Language="JavaScript">
      function presto(){
         alert("Presto pop, alert box!")
      }
      </SCRIPT>
```

```
   </HEAD>
   <BODY onLoad="presto()">
    This is a test!
   </BODY>
</HTML>
```

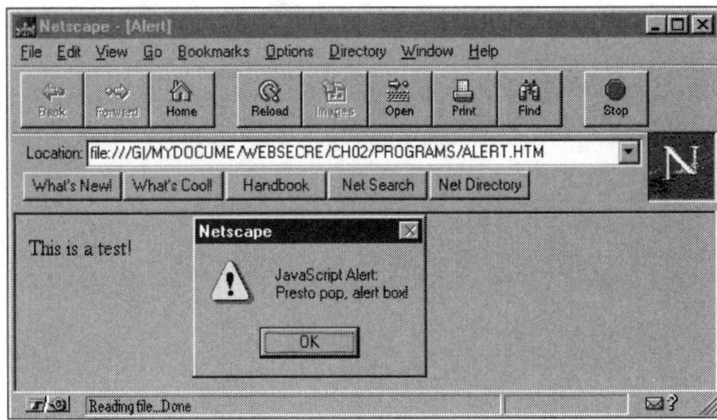

Figure 2-2: You can use JavaScript to display an Alert when an HTML page is loaded.

The problem with this HTML page occurs when it's loaded by a browser that cannot interpret JavaScript. Figure 2-3 shows the same HTML page loaded in an older version of Mosaic. As you can see, the JavaScript code is displayed as though it were part of the document itself. Not what you wanted!

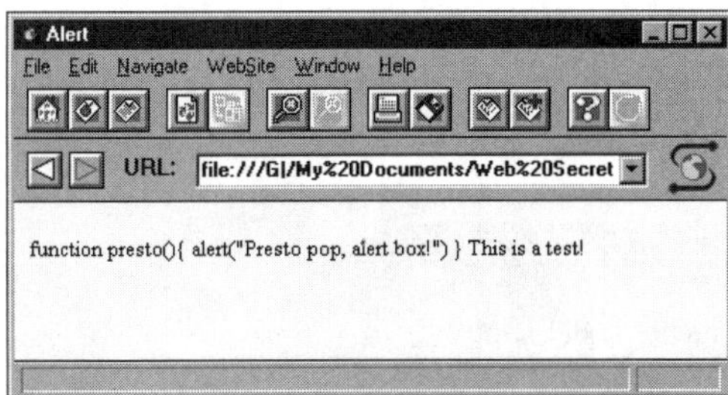

Figure 2-3: Unprotected JavaScript code displays as literal HTML text in older browsers.

Ignore Those <COMMENT> </COMMENT> Tags

You may occasionally see comments included between <COMMENT> and </COMMENT> tags. Personally, I think this is an attractive idea, as it is more "English" to me than exclamation points, dashes, and slashes. However, the <COMMENT></COMMENT> tags are only supported by Explorer, so you shouldn't use them.

The answer is to embed the JavaScript within comments, as shown in Listing 2-3.

Listing 2-3: JavaScript Alert on load, with comments used to hide code

```
<HTML>
   <HEAD>
      <TITLE>Alert</TITLE>

      <SCRIPT Language="JavaScript">
      <!-- The comment begins...
      function presto(){
         alert("Presto pop, alert box!")
      }
      // the comment ends-->
      </SCRIPT>

      </HEAD>
      <BODY onLoad="presto()">
      This is a test!
   </BODY>
</HTML>
```

Browsers with JavaScript capability will read this HTML code correctly. And older browsers will ignore everything between the comments; this achieves the desired result, as shown in Figure 2-4.

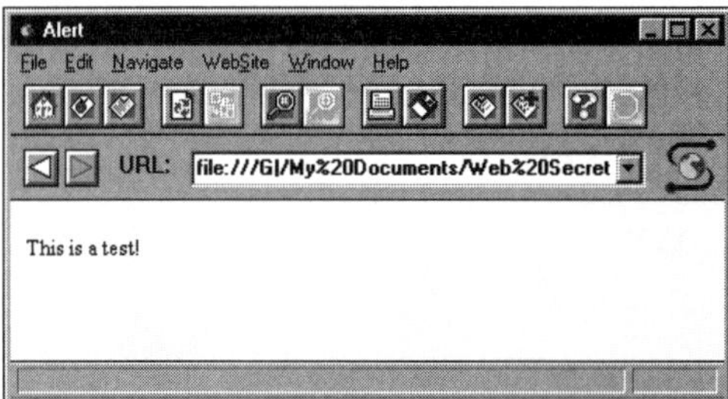

Figure 2-4: Older browsers ignore JavaScript commands hidden within comments.

There are two ways of concluding the comment that "hides" the scripting commands. As in Listing 2-3, you can conclude with a comment line indicated by double slashes (//) that ends with a close comment (->). Alternatively, you can simply include a comment at the end of the script code. Non-JavaScript browsers will ignore the start of the final comment because they think it is part of the original comment. Note that if you use this style you can place the </SCRIPT> tag on the same line as the end of the JavaScript code.

Here's an example of the alternative method:

```
<SCRIPT Language="JavaScript">
   <!-- The comment begins...
```

```
function presto(){
alert("Presto pop, alert box!")} <!-- end o'comment--></SCRIPT>
```

HTML Limitations

Some formatting features are not currently available in any commercially supported versions of HTML.

Some features *not* available include

- The ability to position HTML document elements on a grid without workarounds
- Footnotes and end notes
- Automatic table of contents and index generation
- Tabs (for setting spaces between words)

The <BODY> Tag

The <BODY> tag encloses the body of the HTML document. In other words, the actual page content goes between the <BODY> and </BODY> tags, as you saw earlier. <BODY> is an important tag because every HTML document includes it, and because the <BODY> parameters play an important role in determining the look and feel of a Web page and site. (By the way, as with all HTML tags, the use of any parameter is technically entirely optional.) These parameters fall into three categories:

- Color specification of an element of the page
- Microsoft Internet Explorer page layout
- Specification of a background image for a page

You can also use the <BODY> tag to add JavaScript code to the load and unload events of the browser window object. You do this by assigning a JavaScript routine name to the <BODY> tag's **onLoad** and **onUnload** parameters. For example:

```
<BODY onLoad="HelloWorld()" onUnload="GoodnightGracie()"> </BODY>
```

The HelloWorld function would run when the page was opened, and the GoodnightGracie function when the page was closed.

For more information on adding JavaScript routines to your HTML pages, see Chapter 8.

I'll show you an example of actual use of the <BODY> tag to specify colors and background after I've covered some preliminaries. In the meantime, Table 2-1 explains the meaning and use of each <BODY> tag formatting parameter.

Table 2-1 <BODY> Tag Formatting Parameters

Parameter	*Purpose*	*Comments*
alink	Sets the color of the text that is an *active*, or currently selected, link.	For more information on links, see the section "Hyperlinks" later in this chapter.
bgcolor	Sets the background color of an HTML page.	If a background image is also specified using the **background** parameter, the image takes precedence over the **bgcolor** background. You will not see the color specified by the **bgcolor** tag unless the image is largely transparent.
link	Sets the color of the text of a link that is not currently selected and has not yet been visited.	For more information on links, see the section "Hyperlinks" later in this chapter.
text	Sets the color of the normal text (for example, text not used for a link) in an HTML page.	
vlink	Sets the color of *visited* links — that is, links that the user has previously activated.	For more information on links, see the section "Hyperlinks" later in this chapter.
bgproperties	When set equal to *fixed*, its only possible value, causes the image specified in the **background** not to scroll.	Only works with Explorer. Used to create "watermark" effects.
leftmargin	Indents the HTML page by the specified number of pixels from the left border of the browser window.	Only works with Explorer.
topmargin	Indents the HTML page by the specified number of pixels from the top border of the browser window.	Only works with Explorer.
background	Lets you specify a background image by setting the parameter equal to the URL of a graphics file.	Background images on the Web are normally contained in .gif files (.Jpeg files are also possible). For more information, see Chapter 3, "Graphics on the Web." See the following note on using URLs that are relative to your site's domain name.

It's a good idea to set up a standard scheme of color choices for the parameters of the <BODY> tag and apply these to each Web page on a site. This helps to give all the pages on the site a common look and feel.

Identifying the Location of Local Files

How do you identify the *path,* or relative location, of a local file in your Web site? When specifying a URL from within a Web page — for example, when adding a textured background to the page — you could simply place all files in your domain's root directory and identify them by name only:

```
<BODY Background="texture.gif"> </BODY>
```

This strategy works but is highly inelegant and confusing enough to be impractical on a complex site that has many files of a variety of types.

You cannot specify a relative file location using DOS directory conventions. If you try to do so, it may work locally, but many browsers will not find the specified path.

The answer is to specify the URL of the web domain followed by a directory structure entered using TCP/IP, and UNIX, conventions, *not* DOS/Windows conventions. This will work:

```
<BODY Background="http://www.bearhome.com/images/texture.gif">
</BODY>
```

These paths — and any variations of them — will not:

```
<BODY Background="http://www.bearhome.com\images\texture.gif">
</BODY>

<BODY Background="www.bearhome.com\images\texture.gif"> </BODY>

<BODY Background="images\texture.gif"> </BODY>

<BODY Background="C:\...\images\texture.gif"> </BODY>
```

Note that if you enter URL paths correctly you will be unable to browse your Web sites locally without a TCP/IP connection set up to the web domain. This makes adding and verifying URLs a multistep process in which you must add URLs using an editor and then check them over the Web using a browser.

Specifying Colors on the Web

Specifying the colors of page elements on the Web is not a pretty picture. Officially speaking, HTML standards have no provision for specifying color. The official position is that HTML style sheets, when they are implemented on the Web, will allow you to do this.

As a practical matter, most web browsers accept two different methods of color specification: using an English word descriptive of the color and using a hexadecimal hash code that translates into a red, green, blue (RGB) triplet.

Using English to Specify Color

Obviously, compared to hexadecimal code, English is, well, more like a language that humans understand. An advantage to using color words rather than hex codes is that the intended meaning is clearer. (Although after you've been working on the Web for a while, you'll pretty much have internalized that magenta is the same as #FF00FF.)

The problem with using descriptive color words is that each browser "understands" a different list of words, although primary colors, such as red, green, blue, yellow, and so on are pretty safe across the web universe. To be absolutely safe, you'll have to check the documentation of all target browsers, or stick with the hex equivalents. In general, browsers ignore descriptive color words they do not understand, so the consequences of getting this wrong are not catastrophic.

Note that, for reasons that elude me, even hex colors are not rendered in a precisely identical fashion from browser to browser (although they are pretty close).

Netscape Navigator supports several hundred color names, including all common ones. The partial list that follows contains some interesting ones (note that Explorer's color name capability, while overlapping to some degree, is not identical). Very poetic, I'd say, but not terribly practical in terms of browser-independent color designation. Also, using color names rather than hexadecimal color equivalents may cause dithering.

antiquewhite	blanchedalmond	cornsilk
darksalmon	forestgreen	goldenrod
hotpink	khaki	lavender
mistyrose	navy	orchid
papayawhip	seashell	thistle
violet	wheat	whitesmoke

For the record, here's an example of using the **vlink** parameter set to papayawhip. This tag sets all links that have been used to papayawhip — whatever that may be — to the user's browser:

```
<BODY  vlink="papayawhip">...</BODY>
```

Under Navigator this is rendered as a white with a little splash of pink in it. The color comes out as sort of a pink under Explorer 3.0. My own feeling is that a color named papayawhip should be yellowish, like the meat of a whupped papaya. You can readily see the problems with these descriptive color words.

Understanding Hex Color Notation

You can specify a color as a six-digit hexadecimal triplet, where the first two hex digits represent the red component of an RGB value, the second two hex digits represent the green component, and the final two hex digits are the blue component.

RGB values are used to specify colors that appear on monitors. They are not the same as the CMYK designation system used to specify process colors for reflective (printed) art such as books. The differences between RGB and CMYK, and related issues, are discussed further in Chapter 3.

The range of each hexadecimal pair in the RGB color triplet is from 00 to FF. This translates in decimal to a range of 0 to 255. 00 turns the component color completely off; FF (255) turns it completely on. You can produce bright blue by turning the red and green triplets off and amplifying the blue all the way: 0000FF.

Remember the old kindergarten cliché about black being "the absence of color"? Well, in hex RGB notation it's true: 000000 is black and FFFFFF is white.

To use hexadecimal color notation, you're supposed to add a hash symbol (#), and put the expression in quotes. For example,

```
<BODY text="#0000FF"> ... </BODY>
```

sets all text that is not used as a link in a given document to bright blue. For all you cowgirls and web mistresses out there, the truth is that you can leave off the quotes and hash symbol. Most browsers will decode the naked hex just fine.

Table 2-2 shows a number of the basic colors in RGB hexadecimal hash notation.

Table 2-2 Commonly Used RGB Color Triplets in Hexadecimal Hash Notation and Their Color Equivalents

Hex RGB Equivalent	*Color*
FF0000	bright red
FF9900	orange
FFFF00	bright yellow
FFFFCC	light yellow
FF00FF	magenta
FFFFFF	white
00FF00	green
00FFFF	cyan
663300	brown
0000FF	bright blue
6699CC	light blue
000000	black

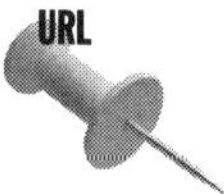

The URL *http://www.bga.com/~rlp/dwp/palette/palette.html* features a display map of colors on the Web that, when clicked, provide the RGB hexadecimal triplet for the color selected.

This site also includes a JavaScript program that displays the appearance of text and background for any RGB triplets that are input and generates the appropriate <BODY> tag.

Here is a use of the <BODY> tag that provides a pleasing combination of colors:

```
<BODY bgcolor="#FFFFCC" text="#993300" link="#0000FF"
vlink="#339900">
...
</BODY>
```

This produces a Web page with a creamy yellow background, maroon text, and blue links that become forest green once they have been accessed.

Text and Content Tags

You can use tags within the body of an HTML document — meaning between a <BODY> and a </BODY> tag — to identify the function of text and content elements to the browser so that the browser can format the element appropriately.

These tags fall into two categories: text markup tags and content and flow tags. Note that this chapter does not attempt to cover all HTML tags — that would be the subject of another, entire book — but only covers the ones that are likely to be most important to web developers. Also, other portions of this book include information on additional HTML functionality:

- Chapter 3 covers adding graphics to Web pages.
- Chapter 5, "Multimedia and Sound on the Web," describes adding multimedia and sound.
- Part III explains how to add executable content — Java applets and ActiveX controls.

Text Markup Tags

Table 2-3 shows some of the more commonly used text markup tags and their meanings.

Table 2-3 Common Text Markup Tags

Tag	*Meaning*
<B>...</B>	Boldfaces enclosed text.
<BIG>...</BIG>	No, not a movie staring Tom Hanks; <BIG> increases font size of enclosed text (not available for all browsers).

Tag	***Meaning***
<BLINK>...</BLINK>	Causes enclosed text to blink; implementation varies browser to browser; use of this tag can be extremely offensive to users.
<CITE>...</CITE>	Formats enclosed text as a citation.
<CODE>...</CODE>	Formats enclosed text as a code sample.
<EM>...</EM>	Formats enclosed text with emphasis.
<I>...</I>	Italicizes enclosed text.
<SMALL>...</SMALL>	Down Igor, yes I know; if I can make text bigger, I can also make it smaller.
<STRIKE>...</STRIKE>	Puts line through enclosed text (strikeout text).
<STRONG>...</STRONG>	Gives a strong emphasis to enclosed text.
_{...} and ^{...}	Formats enclosed text as subscript or superscript, respectively.
<TT>...</TT>	Places enclosed text in monospaced font.

Listing 2-4 shows how to use the text tags included in Table 2-3.

Listing 2-4: Using text tags

```
<HTML>
   <HEAD>
      <TITLE>
         Tag Demo
      </TITLE>
   </HEAD>
   <BODY>
    It's easy to create
    <B>ransom <BIG>note</BIG></B>
    <BLINK>effects</BLINK>.
    I can give you many citations for this, including
    <CITE>Web Developer's SECRETS by Harold Davis</CITE>
    <CODE>onClick="window.status='';"</CODE>
    <I>But if you give your </I>text too much <EM>emphasis</EM>
    it is sure to look <STRIKE>not very good</STRIKE>.
    As <SMALL>Yoda</SMALL> would say,
    <STRONG>Don't design your web page; be your web page!</STRONG>
    And somehow get <TT>monospaced fonts</TT>,
    <SUB>Subscripts</SUB> and
    <SUP>Superscripts</SUP> into this!
   </BODY>
</HTML>
```

The HTML page created in Listing 2-4 is shown in Figure 2-5 (note that the effect of the <BLINK> tag cannot be displayed on a printed page).

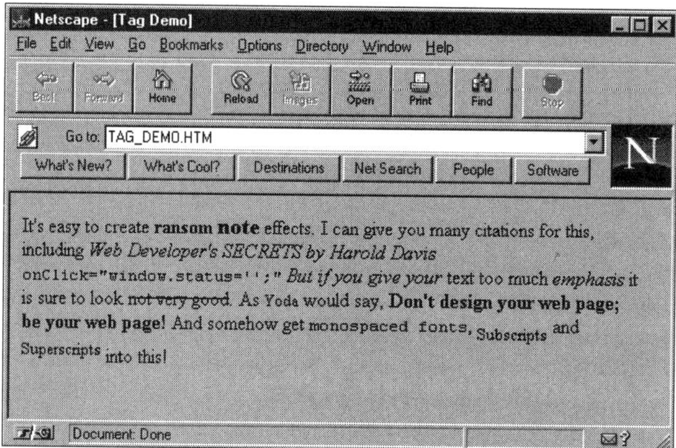

Figure 2-5: You can use text tags to indicate the purpose of HTML document elements so that a browser can display it accordingly.

Lists

Lists are a useful way to present hierarchical information (and so much of life is hierarchical, isn't it?). Kidding aside, HTML provides a very effective tool set for organizing list information on your Web sites in a way that is helpful to your users. As an example, lists are often effectively used to contain menus to linked topics.

Although there are some specialized kinds of lists, and quite a few formatting options, there are two basic kinds of lists:

- Unordered lists, specified by the <UL>...</UL> tags
- Ordered lists, specified by the <OL>...</OL> tags

Unordered lists consist of items that, hopefully, have no obvious precedence, and are indicated using bullets. Ordered lists, on the other hand, contain a numerical designation for each item in the list. You can nest either kind of list.

Within either type of list, you indicate list items with the <LI> tag. Although the official syntax of the list item tag is <LI>*list item*</LI>, it is conventional — and acceptable to all browsers that I know of — to omit the final </LI>. Listing 2-5 demonstrates the syntax for unordered lists and shows nested lists.

Listing 2-5: An unordered list

```
<HTML>
   <HEAD>
      <TITLE>
      List Demo
      </TITLE>
   </HEAD>
   <BODY>
```

```
        An unordered list of citizens of Narnia:
        <UL>
        <LI>LIONS
        <LI>BEARS - Marshals of the Lists
        <LI>TALKING MICE
           <UL>
           <LI>Reepacheep
           <LI>Torroweep
           </UL>
        <LI>CHILDREN OF ADAM
           <UL>
           <LI>Girls
              <UL>
              <LI>Lucy
              <LI>Polly
              </UL>
           <LI>Boys
              <UL>
              <LI>Eustace
              <LI>Caspian
              <LI>Digby
              </UL>
           </UL>
        </UL>
   </BODY>
</HTML>
```

The five unordered lists in this HTML code are displayed as shown in Figure 2-6.

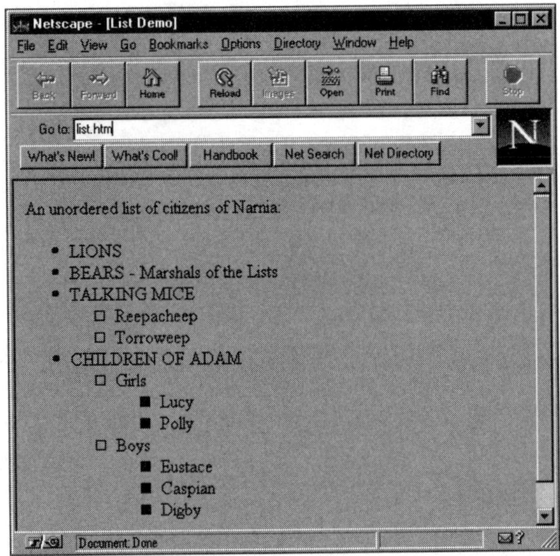

Figure 2-6: You use the <UL>...</UL> tags to create unordered lists.

Ordered lists work much like unordered lists, but you create them using the <OL>...</OL> tags. It's worth noting that <OL> tags can include a **type** parameter that changes the style of the numbered list. (If you leave the **type** parameter off, the list uses standard Arabic numerals.) Table 2-4 lists the possible values for the **type** parameter.

Table 2-4 Values for the type Parameter of the <OL> Tag

Type Value	*Meaning*
A	Capital letters
a	Lowercase letters
I	Capital Roman numerals
i	Lowercase Roman numerals
1	Arabic numerals

The HTML code in Listing 2-6 demonstrates a simple, nested, ordered list, with the results shown in Figure 2-7.

Listing 2-6: A nested, ordered list

```
...
Mythological characters:
<OL type="A">
    <LI>Greek
    <OL type="1">
        <LI>Gods
        <LI>Humans
        <OL type="a">
            <LI>Aristophanes
            <LI>Hercules
            <LI>Theseus
        </OL>
        <LI>Animals
        <OL type="i">
            <LI>Minotaur
        </OL>
    </OL>
    <LI>Roman
    <LI>Norse
</OL>
...
```

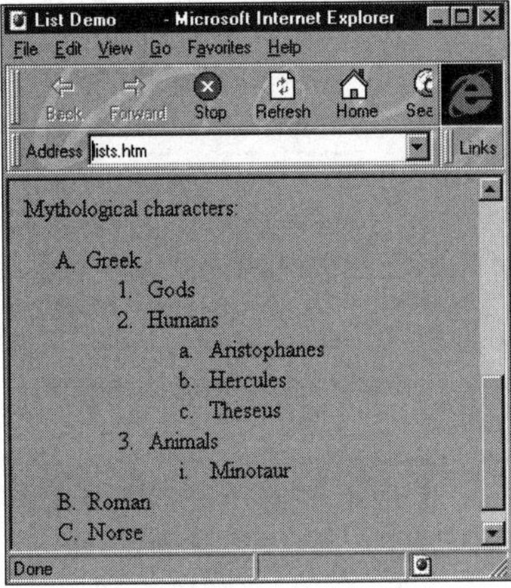

Figure 2-7: It's easy to organize material using nested, ordered lists.

Content and Flow Tags

Many tags control the content and appearance of an HTML page without being directly related to the text contained in the page. Table 2-5 lists the content and flow tags most often used by web developers. (Note that many of these tags have parameters that affect their function; by and large I have not noted parameters and acceptable values.)

Table 2-5 Content and Flow Tags

Tag	*Meaning*
<ADDRESS>...</ADDRESS>	Formats an address.
<BLOCKQUOTE>...</BLOCKQUOTE>	Formats a quotation.
 	Line Break; **Clear** parameter causes the browser to break and resume after any in-line images.
<CENTER>...</CENTER>	Centers the enclosed contents.
<FONT>...</FONT>	Sets the typeface, color, and size for the enclosed text.
<H*n*>...</H*n*>	Makes the enclosed text a heading of level *n*, where *n* is between 1 and 6.
<HR>	Inserts a horizontal rule.

(continued)

Table 2-5 (Continued)

Tag	Meaning
<IMG>	Inserts an in-line image into an HTML page. Can be used in combination with the <A>...</A> tag to designate a hyperlink (see the section "Hyperlinks" later in this chapter). Chapter 3 covers adding images to HTML applications.
<NOBR>...</NOBR>	Does not allow a line break on material within the tags.
<P>	New paragraph. Technically, paragraphs should end with </P>, but most HTML authors don't bother. Multiple <P> tags are treated as equivalent to one <P> tag.

Listing 2-7 demonstrates some uses for these content and flow tags. Note that you can use the <FONT>...</FONT> tags to create drop-cap and other typographic effects (the **size** parameter of the tag is, by default, on a scale of 1 to 7, relative to a normal font size of 3).

You'll learn how to use the <IMG> tag as part of the anchor for a hyperlink in the next section of this chapter, "Hyperlinks." For more information on graphics files, see Chapter 3.

Listing 2-7: Sample HTML page using content and flow tags

```
<HTML>
   <HEAD>
      <TITLE>
      Content and Flow Tags
      </TITLE>
   </HEAD>
   <BODY>
   <IMG src="benjerry2b.gif" alt="Hobbits like Ben&Jerry's ice
    cream!" align = "right">
   <ADDRESS>
   Mr. Bilbo Baggins<BR>
   1 Bagshot Row<BR>
   Bag End, Hobbiton, The Shire
   </ADDRESS>

   <HR>
   <CENTER>
    <FONT Size=7>
     W <!—Drop Cap effect—>
    </FONT>
    hen Mr. Bilbo Baggins of Bag End announced that he would
    shortly be celebrating his eleventy-first birthday with a
    party of special magnificence, there was much talk and
    excitement in Hobbiton.
```

```
        <HR>
        <H1>"They" said:</H1>
        <BLOCKQUOTE>
        It will have to be paid for.
        </BLOCKQUOTE>
        <H2>"They" also said:</H2>
        <BLOCKQUOTE>
        It isn't natural, and trouble will come of it!
        </BLOCKQUOTE><P>
        Twelve more years passed. The history and character of
        <NOBR>Mr. Bilbo Baggins</NOBR>
        became once again the chief topic of conversation.
    </CENTER>
    </BODY>
</HTML>
```

Figure 2-8 shows the sample content and flow HTML page.

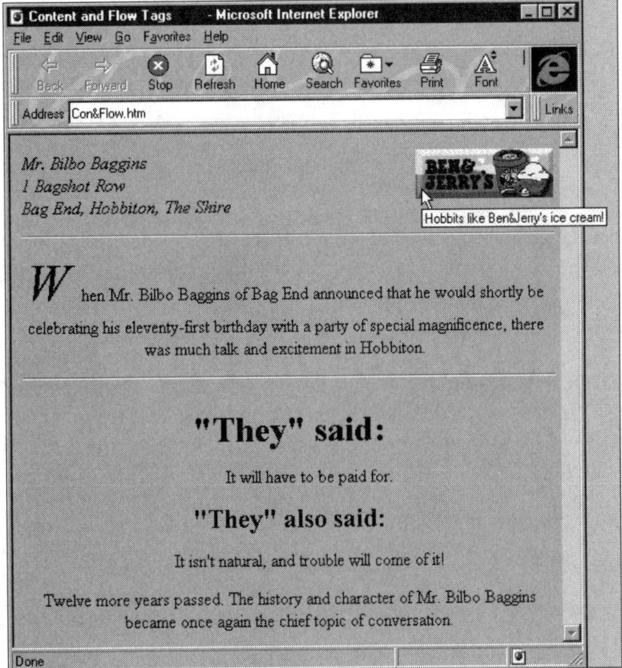

Figure 2-8: It's easy to use content and flow tags to format an HTML page.

Hyperlinks

Hyperlinks are what make the Web go round. (Remember, hyperlinks are the mechanism that lets users jump within an HTML document, to another local HTML document, or to an HTML document located at another web domain.) These connections are what give the Web its special flavor by allowing Web site designers and content providers to include sites published by others as an apparently seamless part of their own sites. Hyperlinks also provide an intuitively obvious and universally understood method for web navigation.

As you probably know, it is extremely easy to add simple hyperlinks to an HTML document. You use the <A>...</A> tags (the "A" is short for "anchor") to create links, and to create a target for a link within an HTML page. Although you can combine these two functions, for the sake of clarity it's better to use each anchor tag for only one purpose.

You can add a target location for linking using the **name** parameter of the <A> tag. This is analogous to adding a label to a line of code so that you can pass control to the code line using a "GoTo" statement. For example, suppose you wanted to add a link to the HTML page whose code appears in Listing 2-7 so that a user could click on the "Mr. Bilbo Baggins" at the top of the page and jump to the "history and character of Mr. Bilbo Baggins" at the bottom of the page (see Figure 2-8). To do this, first use an <A> tag to name the link target "bilbo":

```
The history and character of <A name="bilbo">Mr. Bilbo Baggins</A>
```

Next, use the **href** parameter of the <A> tag to establish a hyperlink anchored around the first occurrence of the name Bilbo Baggins:

```
<A href="#bilbo">Mr. Bilbo Baggins</A><BR>
1 Bagshot Row<BR>
```

There is nothing to stop you — unless the target page and link do not exist — from linking to a named reference on another page or site, for example:

```
<A href="http://www.middleearth.org/baggins.html#bilbo">Mr. Bilbo
Baggins</A><BR>
```

I recommend that you specify all local files within the **href** parameter of the <A> tag using the full URL and web directory notation; for more information, see the section "Identifying the Location of Local Files" earlier in this chapter.

Here's an example of a hyperlink to another domain:

```
Hobbits like <A href="http://www.bearhome.com">bears</A>.
```

Generally, it is simplest to create the text that you want and then add the <A> tags with links around the text.

It is easy to create an image that triggers a jump. Simply place the <IMG> tag within the <A> tag. For example, the following HTML code causes the Ben&Jerry's .gif file shown in Figure 2-8 to trigger a jump to Ben&Jerry's home page:

```
<A href="http://www.benjerry.com">
<IMG src="benjerry2b.gif" alt="Hobbits like Ben&Jerry's ice cream!"
align = "right">
</A>
```

By the way, clickable *image maps* — images that contains a number of different hyperlinks — have become the standard for sophisticated Web pages. I'll show you how to create them in Chapter 3.

Tables

Tables are important in and of themselves since so much information is, after all, best presented in tabular form. However, you can place anything — including text, images, Java applets, and ActiveX controls — in a table.

The ability to position elements makes tables significant in HTML coding because you can use them to assign a location to page elements in a quasi-grid fashion. This bears repeating because it is so important. Using tables with invisible borders, you can approximate a layout grid in HTML — at least for browsers such as Navigator and Explorer that "speak" tables.

Although there are many possible formatting parameters, the basic structure of a table is straightforward; it's contained between a <TABLE> and a </TABLE> tag.

Rows are contained between <TR> and </TR> tags. <TH>...</TH> indicates a table column head and <TD>...</TD> tags indicate normal table cells.

Here's an example of a basic table with three rows, including one made up of column headers:

```
<TABLE>

<!—Header Row—>
<TR><TH>Noise</TH><TH>by</TH><TH>Pooh</TH><TH>Oh</TH><TH>the</TH>
</TR>

<!—First Row of table body—>
<TR><TD>butterflies</TD><TD>are</TD><TD>flying</TD><TD>Now</TD>
<TD>the</TD></TR>

<!—Second and last row of table body—>
<TR><TD>winter</TD><TD>days</TD><TD>are</TD><TD>dying</TD>
<TD>and</TD></TR>

</TABLE>
```

This table is shown in Figure 2-9.

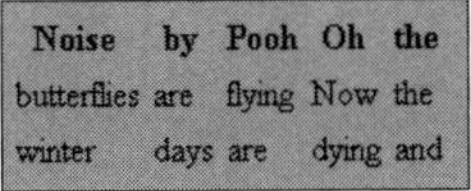

Noise	by	Pooh	Oh	the
butterflies	are	flying	Now	the
winter	days	are	dying	and

Figure 2-9: Here's a three-row table with no border.

To add a border, you use the **border** parameter as part of the <TABLE> tag, as shown in Figure 2-10:

```
<TABLE border>...</TABLE>
```

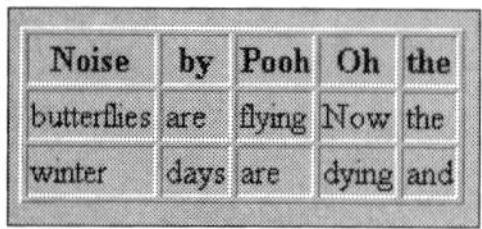

Noise	by	Pooh	Oh	the
butterflies	are	flying	Now	the
winter	days	are	dying	and

Figure 2-10: It's easy to add borders to HTML tables.

You can use the **colspan** parameter with a <TH> or <TD> tag to allow a row to fill more than one column, as shown in Figure 2-11:

```
<TR><TH Colspan=5>Noise, by Pooh</TH></TR>
```

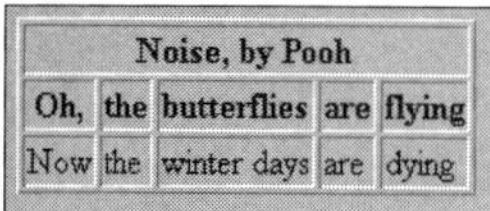

Noise, by Pooh				
Oh,	the	butterflies	are	flying
Now	the	winter days	are	dying

Figure 2-11: You can use the **colspan** parameter to span more than one column.

A related parameter, **rowspan**, causes the contents to take up any number of rows, with the exact dimensions depending on the specific contents.

Perhaps most significantly, you can specify the exact dimensions of the table in pixels with the <TABLE> **width** and **height** parameters. This allows you to set up a virtual grid, if the table is borderless.

To set the Pooh table to 500×200 pixels, as shown in Figure 2-12, modify the <TABLE> tag:

```
<TABLE border width=500 height=200>
```

Noise, by Pooh				
Oh,	the	butterflies	are	flying
Now	the	winter days	are	dying

Figure 2-12: You can use the **border** parameter to specify the exact dimensions of a table, in pixels.

You can place any element you'd like, including graphics, in a table cell. To add the Ben & Jerry's button, with a hyperlink to that triumphantly superb ice cream maker, you'd use the following HTML code, with the results displayed in Figure 2-13:

```
...
<TABLE>
...
<TR>
...
<TH align="center">
<A href="http://www.benjerry.com">
<IMG src="benjerry2b.gif">
</A>
</TH>
...
</TR>
...
</TABLE>
...
```

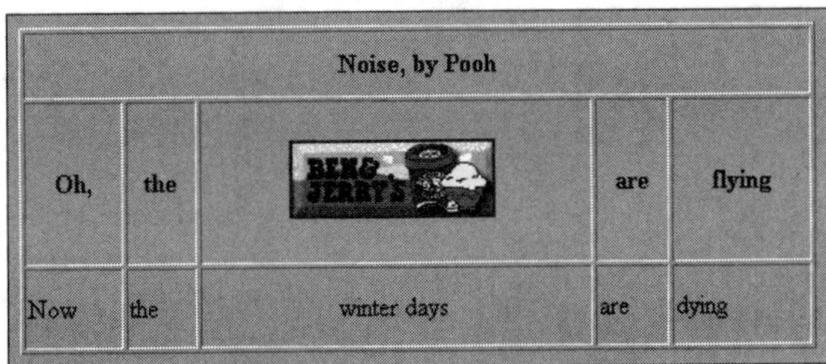

Noise, by Pooh				
Oh,	the	BEN & JERRY'S	are	flying
Now	the	winter days	are	dying

Figure 2-13: Tables provide the web developer with an unofficial way to precisely position graphics.

Frames

Frames are a mechanism for one HTML document to include a number of separate HTML pages. This can be a particularly effective way to present dynamic content in part of the browser window while keeping the rest of the display static. For example, the InvestorsEdge site, *http://www.investorsedge.com*, shown in Figure 2-14, uses the frame in the lower-left corner to present scrolling, dynamic stock quotes.

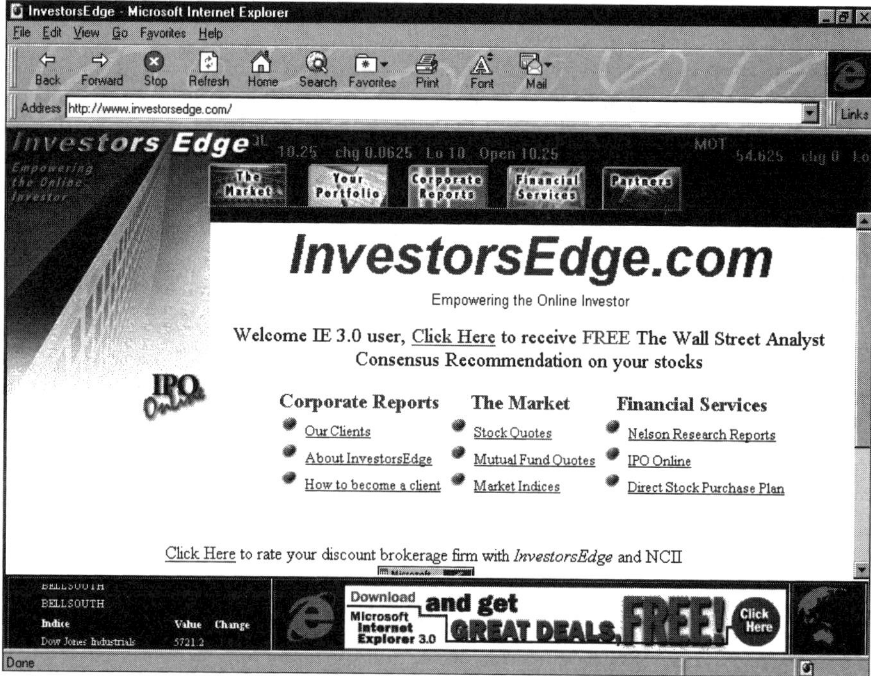

Figure 2-14: Sophisticated Web sites such as InvestorsEdge use frames to display dynamic motion.

But be careful: Generally a frame that is only a portion of a window should not include hyperlinks, because a linked document will only display in the portion of the browser available to the frame.

Another note of caution: sites that include too many frames scrolling this way and that can look very gadgety. Beware of including too many frames in one display.

The syntax of creating frames is quite simple:

- A frameset holds a collection of frames, which are contained within <FRAME>...</FRAME> tags.
- You indicate framesets with the <FRAMESET>...</FRAMESET> tags.
- You use the parameters of the frameset tag to define the initial number of rows and columns (made up of frames) within the frameset.
- You can nest one frameset within another.
- You use the <NOFRAMES>...</NOFRAMES> tag to provide a viable display — usually with a link to the first document in the frameset — for older browsers that do not support frames.

For example, Listing 2-8 shows how to create three frames in one column and two rows, based on the HTML documents developed earlier in this chapter, as shown in Figure 2-15.

Listing 2-8: HTML page that uses frames in one column and two rows to display three different HTML documents

```
<HTML>
<HEAD>
<TITLE>Frameses</TITLE>
</HEAD>
<BODY>
<FRAMESET COLS="40%,*">
   <FRAME SRC="lists.htm">
   <FRAMESET ROWS="57%,*">
      <FRAME SRC="Con&Flow.htm"
    NAME = "bilbo" SCROLLING = "auto"
    MARGINWIDTH=1 MARGINHEIGHT=1 NORESIZE>

    <FRAME SRC="table.htm" NAME = "table"
    SCROLLING = "auto" MARGINWIDTH=1
    MARGINHEIGHT=1 NORESIZE>

   </FRAMESET>
   <NOFRAMES>
   Since your browser cannot read frames, <A href="Con&Flow.htm">
   click here<A>!
   </NOFRAMES>
</FRAMESET>
</BODY>
</HTML>
```

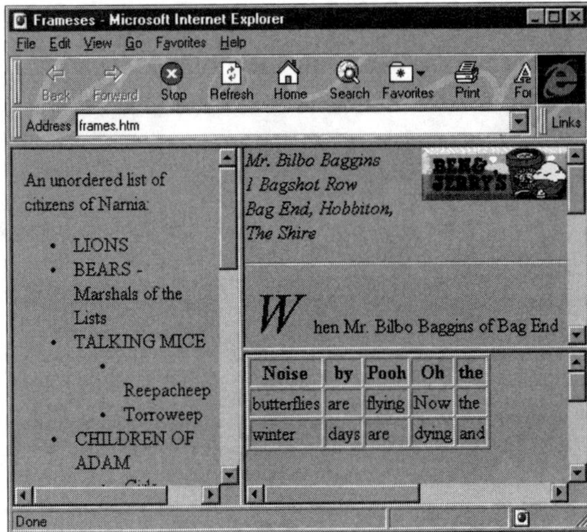

Figure 2-15: You can use frames to display multiple HTML documents.

Creating Interactive Documents with Frames

You can use frames to create interactive documents in which user input in one frame is used to write the HTML that is displayed in another frame. As a simple example, I've created a frameset document containing two frames, in.htm (the input document) and out.htm (the output document). When the frameset document is run in a browser, it displays the input document and updates — and displays — the output document based on user input, as shown in Figure 2-16.

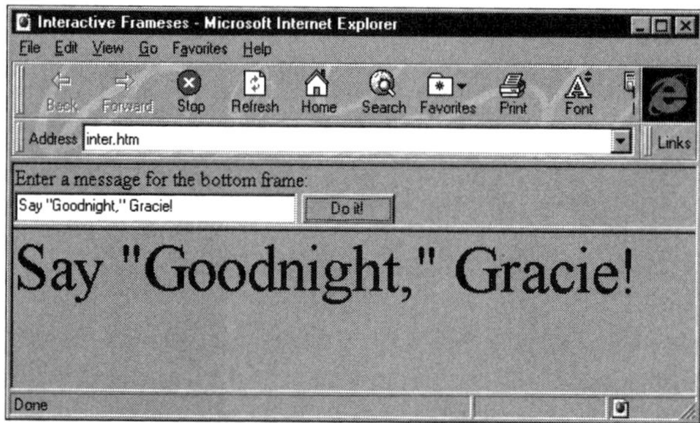

Figure 2-16: You can use frames to create interactive browser displays.

Here's the code for the frameset document:

```
<HTML>
<HEAD>

   <TITLE>Interactive Frameses</TITLE>
</HEAD>
<BODY>
<FRAMESET ROWS="28%,*">
      <FRAME SRC="in.htm"
      NAME = "in" SCROLLING = "auto"
      MARGINWIDTH=1 MARGINHEIGHT=1 NORESIZE>

      <FRAME SRC="out.htm" NAME = "out"
      SCROLLING = "auto" MARGINWIDTH=1
      MARGINHEIGHT=1 NORESIZE>
</FRAMESET>
   <NOFRAMES>
   Since your browser cannot read frames, <A href="in.htm">
   click here<A>!
   </NOFRAMES>
</BODY>
</HTML>
```

Note that for the interactive feature of in.htm to run without error, a skeleton version of out.htm must actually exist on the path specified in the frameset document. Here's the — pretty basic — HTML for out.htm:

```
<HTML>
   <BODY>

   </BODY>
</HTML>
```

In.htm runs up a text input and a button and uses a JavaScript routine (the function is named MakeOut) to write the required HTML to out.htm:

```
<HTML>
   <HEAD>
      <TITLE>
      Interactive Input!
      </TITLE>
   <SCRIPT language="JavaScript">
   <!--hide script
   function MakeOut(msg) {
      var gt = unescape("%3E");
      parent.out.document.open();
      parent.out.document.open();
      parent.out.document.write("<HTML" + gt);
      parent.out.document.write("<BODY" + gt);
      parent.out.document.write("<FONT size=7" + gt);
      parent.out.document.write(msg);
      parent.out.document.write("</FONT" + gt);
      parent.out.document.write("</BODY" + gt);
      parent.out.document.write("</HTML" + gt);
      parent.out.document.close();
   }

   // decloak script -->
   </SCRIPT>

   </HEAD>
   <BODY>
   Enter a message for the bottom frame: <BR>
   <INPUT type="TEXT" size=40 name="txtMessage"
      value='Say "Goodnight," Gracie'>
   <INPUT type="Button" value="Do it!"
onClick="MakeOut(txtMessage.value);">
   </BODY>
</HTML>
```

You can use frames to write whatever HTML you want to a frame document, without any server-side processing being required.

Inside Scoop

You cannot include a "greater than" character (>) within a script without closing the comment that hides the scripting from nonscript aware browsers. Therefore, use the unescape function, built into JavaScript, to convert the hex value for > (3E) and fool those silly browsers:

```
var gt = unescape("%3E");
```

This is analogous to embedding the quote character in a quote-delimited string by using a conversion function to convert the ASCII equivalent of the quote (34).

Mac and Windows (but not UNIX) browsers will not open a document window without two calls to the document.open method. Therefore, always call the method twice:

```
parent.out.document.open();
parent.out.document.open();
```

Forms

In the interactive frames example I just showed you, JavaScript text and button objects are used to store and manipulate user input. HTML forms are "parents" to objects such as text and buttons; the concept will be immediately apparent to anyone who has used a Windows graphical programming environment, which is based around forms (also called "windows").

Using forms means that an entire grouping of objects can be referred to — and values passed — using the form name. For example, if you are passing the values of three text inputs to a function in a button click event, you can simplify matters by merely passing as a parameter the name of the form that "owns" the text objects.

In addition to being used with script functions, forms are commonly used to pass user input values for server-side processing. This will be explained in detail in Part V, "Client and Server on the Web."

I'll be going into detail about JavaScript objects and their properties, methods, and events in Chapters 7 and 8.

In the meantime, you should know that <INPUT> objects are built into HTML and can be used as form elements. The syntax is to use the <INPUT> tag with a **type** parameter, for example:

```
<INPUT type="password" name="txtPassword" value="swordfish">
```

The following are possible <INPUT> type values:

- "button" (appears on the screen as a push button)
- "checkbox" (appears on the screen as a check box)
- "hidden" (does not appear on the screen, used for internal value storage)
- "password" (appears as a text input with characters replaced by asterisks for security reasons)
- "radio" (member of an option button array)
- "reset" (a push button used to clear or reset a form)

- "submit" (a push button used to submit the values in a form to a server program)
- "text" (a single-line text box available for user input)
- "textarea" (a multiline text box available for user input)

In addition, you should know that the options array, consisting of option objects designated with an <OPTION> tag, appears on the screen as a drop-down list of choices.

Forms are covered in detail in Chapter 8 and in Part IV. In the meantime, just to show you how forms work using a simple example, here's how you'd rewrite the frames example from the previous section using forms.

Keeping the frameset document and out.htm unchanged, here's the input form revised to accept the values of an entire form as one parameter:

```
<HTML>
   <HEAD>
      <TITLE>
      Interactive Input!
      </TITLE>
   <SCRIPT language="JavaScript">
   <!--hide script
   function MakeOut(form) {
      var gt = unescape("%3E");
      parent.out.document.open();
      parent.out.document.open();
      parent.out.document.write("<HTML" + gt);
      parent.out.document.write("<BODY" + gt);
      parent.out.document.write("<FONT size=7" + gt);
      parent.out.document.write(form.txtMessage.value);
      parent.out.document.write("</FONT" + gt);
      parent.out.document.write("<BR" + gt);
      parent.out.document.write(form.txtMsg2.value);
      parent.out.document.write("</BODY" + gt);
      parent.out.document.write("</HTML" + gt);
      parent.out.document.close();
   }

   // decloak script -->
   </SCRIPT>

   </HEAD>
   <BODY>
   Enter a message for the bottom frame: <BR>
   <FORM name="myform">
   <INPUT type="TEXT" size=40 name="txtMessage"
    value='Say "Goodnight," Gracie'><BR>
   <INPUT type="TEXT" size=40 name="txtMsg2"
    value='"Goodnight, Gracie!"'>
   <INPUT type="Button" value="Do it!" onClick="MakeOut(myform);">
   </FORM>
   </BODY>
</HTML>
```

Figure 2-17 shows the results.

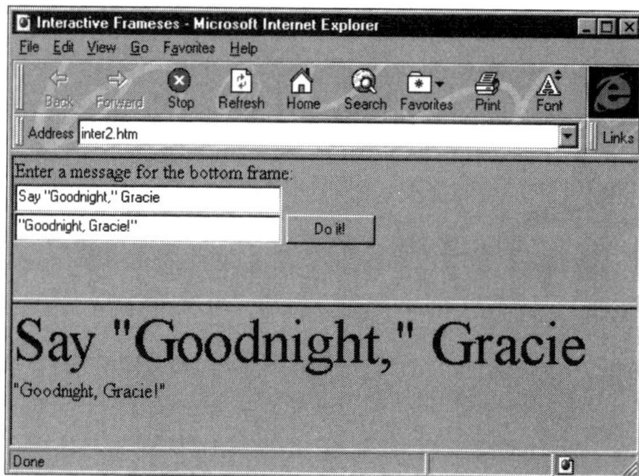

Figure 2-17: You can use forms to pass multiple <INPUT> values to a JavaScript function (or server-side program).

Adding Executable Content

Many of the most exciting things happening in Web development involve downloading executable content to browsers. This topic is covered in detail in Part III. But, until you get there, here's a sneak preview to give you an idea of what's in store!

You can include executable code blocks in HTML by using the <APPLET> tag for Java applets and the <OBJECT> tag for ActiveX controls.

If the applet or ActiveX control has a visible interface within the browser, you have to take care to position its tag carefully, perhaps using an invisible table as described earlier in this chapter under "Tables." Adding executable content — Java applets and ActiveX controls — is covered in depth in Part III.

ActiveX Controls

You place ActiveX controls on an HTML page using the <OBJECT> tag, and identify them using the control's *CLSID*. CLSIDs, or Class ID's, are theoretically unique numerical identifiers for each registered OLE control. The ActiveX Control Pad — available on the *Web Developer's SECRETS* companion CD-ROM — is designed to let you place and refer to ActiveX controls without having to deal with CLSIDs.

You can add a command button to an HTML page using the following HTML code:

```
<OBJECT ID="CommandButton1" WIDTH=96 HEIGHT=32
 CLASSID="CLSID:D7053240-CE69-11CD-A777-00DD01143C57">
    <PARAM NAME="Caption" VALUE="YES">
    <PARAM NAME="Size" VALUE="2540;847">
    <PARAM NAME="FontCharSet" VALUE="0">
    <PARAM NAME="FontPitchAndFamily" VALUE="2">
    <PARAM NAME="ParagraphAlign" VALUE="3">
    <PARAM NAME="FontWeight" VALUE="0">
</OBJECT>
```

There are a couple of interesting things to note about this code. First, you set the properties of the ActiveX control (that is, the command button) using HTML tags. For example, the button's caption reads "YES." Second, to insert the control, you need to know its CLSID. You can obtain this information manually from the local system registry or by using tools such as Microsoft's ActiveX Control Pad, which is discussed in detail in the next chapter.

Suppose you want something to happen when a user clicks on the button. In event-driven programming terminology, this means putting code in the command button's click event.

Here's how you would add a line of VBScript code to an HTML document that displays a message box when the button is clicked:

```
<SCRIPT LANGUAGE="VBScript">
Sub CommandButton1_Click()
    MsgBox "This is a trivial example!",vbInformation,"GADZOOKS!"
End Sub
</SCRIPT>
```

As you can see, inserting ActiveX controls in a web document, and then causing the code in the control to be invoked, is pretty simple.

Java Applets

Java *applets* are executable programs written in Java source code. They are compiled into Java byte code and are then embedded in an HTML Web page and interpreted by the browser at runtime. (As you probably know, you can also create stand-alone Java applications that are not connected to a Web page provided that you have access to a run-time Java interpreter. These executables are termed *Java applications* rather than Java applets.)

A number of programming environments available from companies including Borland, Microsoft, and Symantec feature tools for creating and editing Java code, class frameworks and code libraries, and Java compilers and debuggers. Microsoft's Visual J++ is discussed in Chapters 14 and 15.

Java applets are perhaps easier to understand in the context of an actual example. (For source code and project files, consult the Programs\Ch02\Java directory of the companion CD-ROM.) I'll explain the steps involved in creating, compiling, and running a Java applet that initializes with a button and a label from a Web page. As shown in Figure 2-18, when the user clicks the button, the caption in the label changes to read "Now you've done it!"

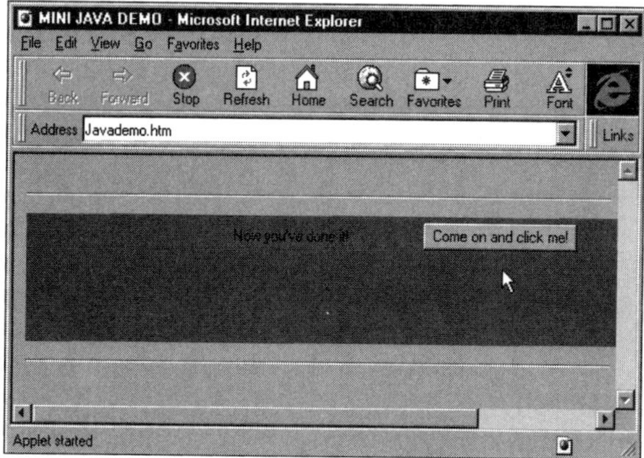

Figure 2-18: Here's a simple Java applet running in a Java-enabled browser (Internet Explorer).

The Applet's Source Code

Here is the Java source code for the simple applet shown in Figure 2-18, with one button and one label (the label's caption changes when the button is clicked):

Listing 2-9: Java source code for a simple applet

```
import java.applet.*;
import java.awt.*;
/** Author: Harold Davis
*/
class HelloWorld extends Applet {
   Label helloLabel = new Label("Mine eyes have seen the glory!");
   Button clickButt = new Button("Come on and click me!");
   public void init() {
        setBackground(Color.red);
           add(helloLabel);
           add(clickButt);

   }
   public boolean action(Event evt, Object what){
      String buttString = new String("Come on and click me!");
         if (buttString.equals(what)) {
            helloLabel.setText("Now you've done it!");
            return true;
         }
         return false;
     }
}
```

You can add the HTML code shown in Listing 2-10 to the body of a Web page to run the applet.

Listing 2-10: Running a Java applet from a Web page

```
<APPLET
code=HelloWorld
width=600
height=100>
</APPLET>
```

The **width** and **height** parameters of the Applet tag determine the size of the Java applet on the Web page; the value of the **code** parameter is the name of the Java class that is being executed.

Note that the compiled module containing the Java class — in this case, HelloWorld.class — must be where the web browser can find it, either at a specified location or in the same directory as the Web HTML page that invokes the applet.

Understanding the Simple Applet Code

It's worth taking the time to understand the Java source code for the simple applet just presented (see Listing 2-9 and Figure 2-18). Obviously, this is a minimal applet. Readers who are familiar with Java will no doubt find it comprehensible enough, but others may need to take a bit of time to get in the spirit of Java.

As mentioned, the first two lines of code

```
import java.applet.*;
import java.awt.*;
```

add the applet framework and the Abstract Windowing Toolkit (AWT). The next code block creates a class extended with the addition of a label and a button:

```
class HelloWorld extends Applet {
   Label helloLabel = new Label("Mine eyes have seen the glory!");
   Button clickButt = new Button("Come on and click me!");
```

Next, code is added to the HelloWorld's init event. This code is fired when the applet is downloaded from a web server (or opened locally in a web browser). In this case, the code displays the button and label and sets the background color of the applet to red:

```
public void init() {
   setBackground(Color.red);
   add(helloLabel);
   add(clickButt);

    }
```

The final part of the applet calls an action method. All components that are part of the AWT inherit an action method. In the case of a button, action is called when the button is clicked. The applet checks whether the button was clicked, and, if it was, changes the label caption:

```
public boolean action(Event evt, Object what){
   String buttString = new String("Come on and click me!");
      if (buttString.equals(what)) {
           helloLabel.setText("Now you've done it!");
            return true;
      }
      return false;
}
```

Optimizing Pages for Loading Speed

It's critical to optimize your pages so they load as quickly as possible. You can't expect many users to accept lengthy download times passively (that Stop button is always available). A rule of thumb is that it takes about one second for 1K of browser file size (based on normal dial-up phone connections for the browser at 28.8kps or less). This means that if you don't want users to pass away from boredom while your pages load, you should keep file sizes small. The worst offenders are graphic files. Try to keep graphics less than 10K in size (for each individual graphic). In any event, don't exceed 60K (one minute load time) for any individual graphic and 90K (one and a half minute load time) for the aggregate file size on a page. (Chapter 3 discusses techniques for minimizing the size of graphics.)

Do test your pages under actual conditions, with various browsers.

Summary

This chapter covered a lot of material involving basic Web page construction. HTML is not the world's most powerful programming environment. It lacks even the most rudimentary page layout facility: the ability to place elements precisely on a grid. The fact is that HTML was never intended as a programming environment, nor as a page layout system.

To provide today's web users with the rich, interactive, multimedia experience that they have come to expect, you'll have to understand HTML in detail and learn to use techniques and extensions that allow you to overcome its inherent limitations.

This chapter included information on the following facets of HTML web development:

- HTML editing tools
- HTML standards
- The structure of an HTML document
- Commenting an HTML document
- The <BODY> tag
- Color specification
- Text markup tags
- Content and flow markup tags
- Lists
- Hyperlinks
- Tables
- Frames
- Forms
- Adding ActiveX controls and Java Applets to HTML forms

Chapter 3

Graphics on the Web

"One picture is worth a thousand words."

The apparent meaning of this well-known aphorism, coined by printer Fred Barnard, is that pictures convey more than words. Barnard called it a Chinese proverb, which it wasn't, since he coined the phrase. This suggests an additional meaning: that pictures are not always what they seem.

Much of the appeal of the Web is due to the strongly visual orientation of popular Web sites. In a sense, this is paradoxical: HTML provides neither a visual editing environment nor a conceptual framework that is intended to foster precise design work. In addition, developers who come to web projects with a programming background do not necessarily understand visual design techniques and priorities.

The fact is, however, that effectively designed and implemented graphics are a necessary — but not sufficient — perquisite for professional Web sites. A chapter on graphics that covers design practice and techniques may be a bit unusual in a book targeted at developers and programmers. It's included here because Web site designers and developers absolutely must make effective use of graphics on the Web.

This chapter contains information on the tools and techniques you need to create and manipulate graphics on the Web. Perhaps even more importantly, I've included advice, techniques, and secrets to help you design Web pages with visual "attitude."

Graphic File Formats for the Web

Most graphic files on the Web are in one of two formats: Gifs (.gif files) and Jpegs (.jpg files). Both formats are designed to compress the size of the file relative to the amount of image information included, which minimizes download time.

Gifs

"Gif," usually pronounced like the first three letters in the word "gift," is short for "Graphics Interchange Format." This format was originally developed by the pioneer on-line service CompuServe and is still sometimes referred to as "CompuServe Gif." (It appears this way on Photoshop's and CorelDraw's drop-down file list.)

Gifs use 8-bit LZW (Limpel-Ziv and Welch) compression and are not quite as high in image quality as Jpegs, which are compressed using a 24-bit LZW algorithm. (File compression algorithms use repeating patterns of bits within binary files to delete redundant information, thus making a file smaller in size without removing any of its "content.")

Because Gifs only store up to 8 bits of color depth information per pixel, they work best for images that do not need high color resolution, such as line art and relatively simple graphics. The good news about Gifs is that they are smaller in file size than Jpegs. However, when you need photographic depth and quality, you should use the Jpeg format.

There are two varieties of Gifs. The Gif87a format is a plain vanilla Gif. The Gif89a format — sometimes called "transparent Gif" — is a subset of the Gif specification that allows the file to include extra information, in particular information specifying that certain areas of the image are transparent, or invisible.

"Interlaced" Gifs appear on the Web in discrete chunks, starting at low resolution and eventually resolving to their full resolution. Such Gifs seem to load faster than noninterlaced Gifs, where you must wait for the whole thing to download before you see anything.

Inside Scoop

Gif file compression works using a scheme that counts pixel change along a horizontal axis. This means that if large parts of your image do not involve horizontal pixel change, comparatively large images will squash way down in size. Conversely, if there is a great deal of horizontal pixel change, much smaller images will Gif-up to be pretty big.

Saving Gifs as 8-bit Graphics

To save an image as a Gif file, you first have to take it down to 8-bit color, assuming it was originally created in a higher color resolution.

Follow these steps to convert an image to an 8-bit Gif in Photoshop:

1. With the image open, from the Mode menu select Indexed Color.
2. In the Indexed Color dialog, with 8 bits/pixel selected (the default), click on OK (see Figure 3-1).

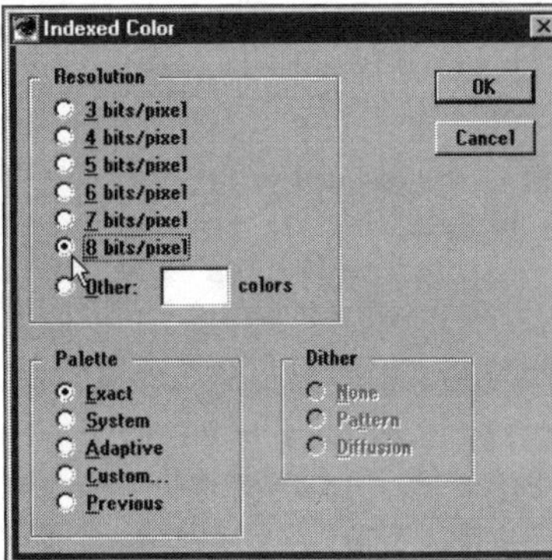

Figure 3-1: You can use the Indexed Color dialog in Photoshop to reduce the color depth of an image to 8 bits per pixel (as required by the Gif format).

3. From the File menu, choose Save a Copy from the File menu and then choose CompuServe GIF from the drop-down list in the Save File As dialog box that appears.

Jpegs

Jpeg is usually pronounced like the letter "j" followed by the word "peg" (as in "peg leg"). The acronym is short for "Joint Photographic Experts Group." As the name implies, this format is designed for use with photographs and photographic quality images. In general, Jpegs produce a more subtle rendering than Gifs. For example, images with soft edges and blurred shadows appear richer and deeper when they have been saved in Jpeg format. Like Gifs, Jpegs can be used to create mapped graphics, hot spots, and all kinds of nifty web features.

Gif Files and the Unisys LZW Patent

In 1987 CompuServe created a specification document for Gif files. It based the format on the LZW compression algorithm and released the specification "for use in computer software without royalties, or licensing restrictions."

There was just one problem with this. CompuServe either didn't know or didn't care that the LZW compression algorithm was the subject of a patent that had been owned by Unisys since 1985.

Unisys seems to have waited to attempt to collect licensing fees until the Gif format was widely in use. Making up for lost time, toward the end of 1994 Unisys announced that they would attempt to collect licensing fees from the publishers of any product that reads or writes graphic files that use LZW compression.

As a practical matter, Unisys is not trying to collect licensing fees from people who create graphics using LZW, only from tool vendors that enable people to create those graphics. You are safe in continuing to put Gifs up on the Web.

Jpeg compression works so well for photographs because its internal compression algorithms are optimized to do so (unlike those used by LZW and other schemes).

When naming graphics that are to be part of your Web site, it is important to keep the file name and extension lowercase. For example, use mypic.gif and thispic.jpg, not mypic.Gif or thispic.JPG. This is because mixed-case file names and extensions are not universally recognized in UNIX. If you don't keep all file names and extensions lowercase, some browsers may not be able to find the files.

Tools for Creating and Editing Graphic Files

To create and edit graphics for the Web, you need a good drawing program (such as CorelDraw), a photographic manipulation program (such as Photoshop), and some specialized utilities.

You need a drawing program to create and manipulate line drawings and illustrations. You can do this using basic tools such as the Paint accessory that ships with Windows, but for even reasonably sophisticated work you need a program along the lines of CorelDraw. (Other possibilities are CorelDraw's competition: Illustrator and Freehand. In addition, Corel Corporation publishes Corel Xara, a graphics package particularly intended for web graphic manipulation.)

A photo manipulation program lets you change color properties so as to minimize load time and improve the appearance of the image on the Web. In addition, you can use the filters built into these programs to quickly generate "awesome" effects. (I'll bet it took the impressionists more time to paint their paintings than it takes you to use Photoshop's "pointillism" filter.) Adobe's Photoshop is the best choice in this category, but it is an expensive program with a steep learning curve. Other possibilities include Corel's PhotoPaint and Macromedia's xRes 2.

In addition to these generic tools, you need a tool for mapping images (see the section "Mapping an Image" later in this chapter), and a tool to help with aspects of Gif file creation — such as creating an animated Gif — that are specific to the Web (see "Using the Gif Construction Set" and "Creating a Continuously Looping Gif" later in this chapter).

Creating Web Graphics in CorelDraw

Before you even open CorelDraw — or any other illustration program — you should conceptualize what the graphic needs to do. (Personally, I find that low technology such as pencil and paper works best for this.)

Before running the program, you should know the answers to these questions:

- Is the purpose of the graphic simply to emphasize something?
- Are you going to use the graphic for mapping or as a button?
- How will the image integrate with the Web page and Web site as a whole?

The first step in the illustration program is to create the "base" image you are going to use. This means either opening a piece of clip art and manipulating it to suit your needs or drawing the image from scratch. It's important to realize that this is where control of the number of colors in your image starts.

You may be interested to know that CorelDraw 7 includes Netscape and Explorer color palettes.

At this point, decide what kind of overall color scheme you will be using. Is the image subtle — made up of pastels and creams? Or, is it bold and fiery — composed of bright colors?

Web imagery, although designed to minimize load time, should neither be boring nor flat. Techniques that help to create exciting texture and dimensionality in CorelDraw include adding pattern and gradient fills, blends, extrusions, shadows, and blurs.

CorelDraw's native file format (.cdr) is not supported by Photoshop. Consequently, you have to export the image in a format that Photoshop recognizes. The best choices are .gif, .eps, .jpg, .tif, and .bmp.

I recommend the .jpg format, even if you will ultimately be saving the file as a Gif. Set the Quality Factor in the JPEG Export dialog to High Quality, as shown in Figure 3-2.

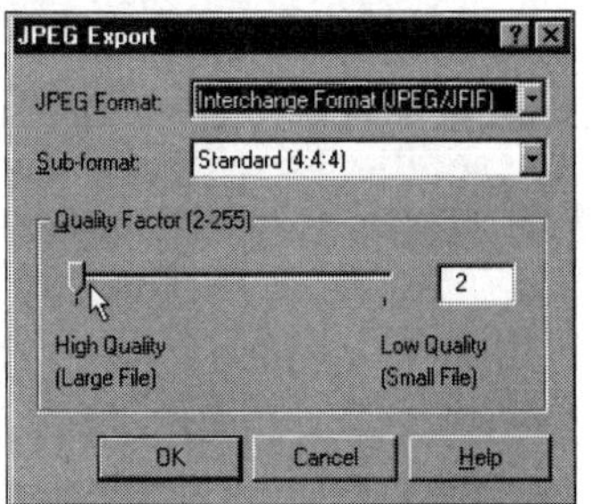

Figure 3-2: You use CorelDraw's JPEG Export dialog to make sure your graphic is exported with as much information as possible.

Although setting the High Quality option produces a larger file, you can edit the image in Photoshop and save it with fewer colors to reduce the size.

When you export an image from CorelDraw, the Bitmap Export dialog shown in Figure 3-3 appears. You can use this dialog to set the number of colors, the size, and the resolution of the exported image. It's very important to set the resolution to 72 dots per inch (dpi). This is often the maximum monitor resolution, so from the viewpoint of web graphics any greater resolution simply adds file size for no reason. Selecting a greater dpi will not improve the quality of the image viewed on a monitor.

Also make sure that Identical Values is checked. This sets the vertical and horizontal resolutions to the same size, ensuring that the image isn't distorted.

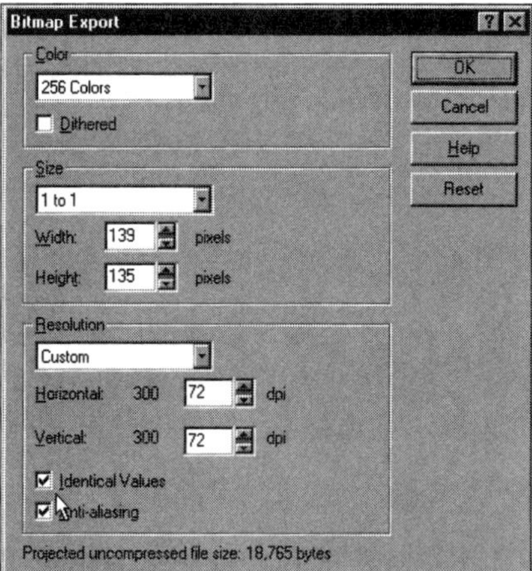

Figure 3-3: You use CorelDraw's Bitmap Export dialog to set the color, size, and resolution of an image.

If your image consists of several objects, make sure that you group them together before exporting. Otherwise the image will not export from CorelDraw correctly.

Using Photoshop to Manipulate and Create Web Graphics

The primary reason for editing an image in Photoshop is that CorelDraw, when it exports the image, will only save it in 16 or 256 colors, and nothing in between. For instance, the ideal compromise between file size and image appearance might be 90 colors. In addition, having an image open in Photoshop allows you to employ all the marvelous filters, plug-ins, and tools available in Photoshop.

Follow these steps to save an image in Photoshop with the fewest colors possible:

1. On the Mode menu, make sure that RGB Color is selected.
2. Return to the Mode menu and select Indexed Color to open the Indexed Color dialog.
3. If Photoshop brings up a dialog asking if you want to flatten layers, click on OK.
4. In the Resolution frame, select Other, which usually has a default value of 256 colors. For starters, halve the value to 128 as shown in Figure 3-4.

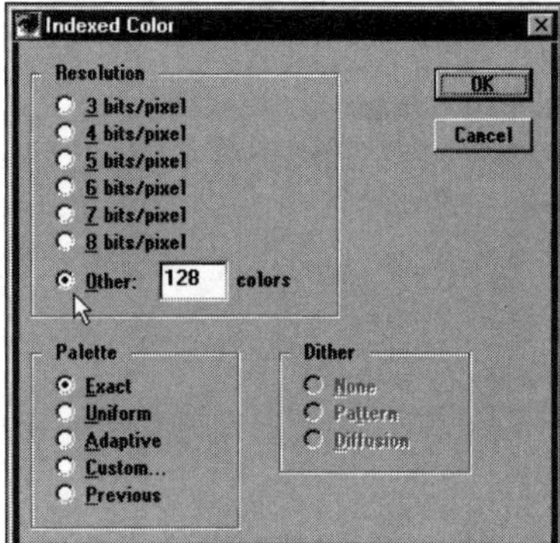

Figure 3-4: You use Photoshop's Indexed Color dialog to reduce the number of colors to the minimum that still gives a visually pleasing effect.

5. Click on OK. Look at the image as it appears on the screen. Is it still acceptable? If so, try decreasing the number of colors by selecting Undo Mode Change from the Edit menu (the keyboard equivalent is Ctrl+Z) and repeating Steps 2 through 4 with fewer colors. If the image is not acceptable, try increasing the colors using the same technique.

Photoshop's artistic possibilities are endless — and the subject of numerous good books. Some Photoshop effects that work particularly well, and without much effort, on the Web include lighting effects, textures, and Gaussian blurs.

Figure 3-5 shows an example of an image that uses a Gaussian blurred shadow to make a pleasing web graphic. (You can find Bucklin Hill Farm's Web page at *http://www.bearhome.com/bucklin/bucklin.htm*.)

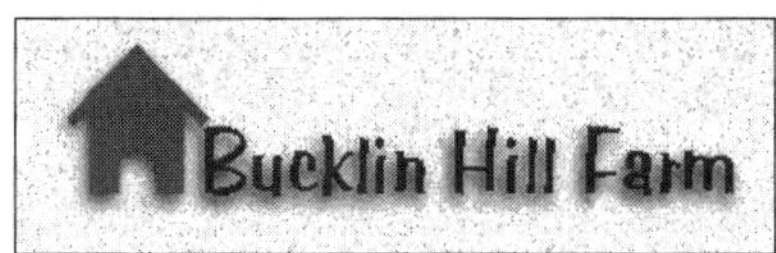

Figure 3-5: The graphic for Bucklin Hill Farm's page was created in CorelDraw and manipulated in Photoshop using a Gaussian blur for the shadow.

Photoshop and Transparent Gifs

To use Photoshop to produce transparent Gifs, you need Adobe's GIF89a Export plug-in, which you can download from Adobe at *http://www.adobe.com/prodindex/photoshop/main.html*.

Creating a Background

You create a tiled background on a Web page using the **background** parameter of the <BODY> tag. (See the section "The <BODY> Tag" in Chapter 2, "Using HTML Tags to Design Web Pages.")

When you use the URL of a graphics file as the argument of the **background** parameter, the graphics file is tiled to become the entire background of the Web page. If you specify a background graphic in the <BODY> tag, the tiled background graphic supersedes a color specified using the <BODY> tag's **bgcolor** parameter (if this parameter is used).

Here's an example of using the <BODY> tag to add a tiled background, assuming the URL points to an actual file:

```
<BODY background="http://www.bearhome.com/images/confetti.gif">
```

A background graphic file is almost the first thing to load in an HTML page. (It loads right after anything that has been placed in the <HEAD> </HEAD> section, such as a title or JavaScript code.) Background graphics not only have to load, they also have to "replicate" as they tile. This means that any file used in a background must be tiny. You can use the techniques outlined earlier in this chapter to ensure that a background Gif is never larger than 3K in file size (1K to 2K is better).

Used effectively, background graphics can easily produce "awesome" Web pages. When designing your background, make sure you consider the contrast between foreground elements and the background. You don't want a visually complicated background that competes with the content on your page. Nor do you want page elements to become hard to read because they are similar in color to the background. In other words, there is a reason that backgrounds are called "backgrounds." They should contrast to some extent with the other elements on your pages, but, for the most part, they should quietly fade into the, well, background.

Although all background images added using the <BODY> tag are, technically speaking, tiled to fill the entire client area of the browser window, you can use two very different design approaches. One is to produce an image that is intended to appear as a seamless background. With this kind of image it is not necessarily apparent that the graphic has been tiled. In the next section, "Quickly Creating a Textured Background," I'll show you one technique for creating a background that is seamless and does not appear to have been tiled.

A visually opposite approach is to create a graphic that works well obviously tiled. This "wallpaper" effect has been used with excellent visual results at least since the days of M.C.Escher and Andy Warhol. See "Creating a Tiled 'Wallpaper' Effect" for an example.

Remember, with design, less is often more. Often a simple, solid background color will do just fine. Adding a complex background image may add nothing to your Web page design.

Quickly Creating a Textured Background

For this example, I'm going to use Photoshop to create a textured background.

Use the following steps to quickly and easily create attractive textured backgrounds:

1. Select New from Photoshop's File menu.
2. In the New dialog, select pixels as the unit of measure, and set the Width and Height to 50 pixels each, as shown in Figure 3-6. Make sure that resolution is set to 72 pixels/inch as described earlier in this chapter and that Mode is set to RGB Color.

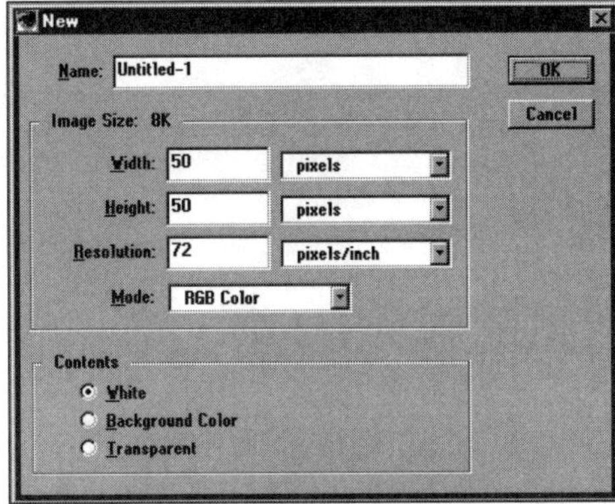

Figure 3-6: You use the New dialog to set the size, resolution, and color mode of a new graphic.

3. Click on OK. A 50×50 pixel screen, called a *canvas,* appears in its own window.
4. Make sure that the Swatches Palette is visible. If not, display it by selecting Palettes from the Windows menu and then selecting Show Swatches from the submenu.
5. On the Swatch Palette, pick your favorite color. Backgrounds work best with light colors. When your mouse pointer passes over the Swatches Palette, it changes into an "eye-dropper" shape. Place this eye-dropper over the color you want to select and click. This color becomes your foreground color and is displayed on the Photoshop toolbar.
6. Select the Paint Bucket tool from the Photoshop toolbar, as shown in Figure 3-7. Your mouse pointer will turn into a little paint bucket when it is positioned over the canvas area.

Figure 3-7: You use Photoshop's Paint Bucket tool to fill an area with color.

7. Click on the canvas. Boom! The canvas is filled with the color you selected.
8. In the Filter menu, click on Noise and then select Add Noise from the submenu. You'll see the Add Noise dialog, as shown in Figure 3-8.

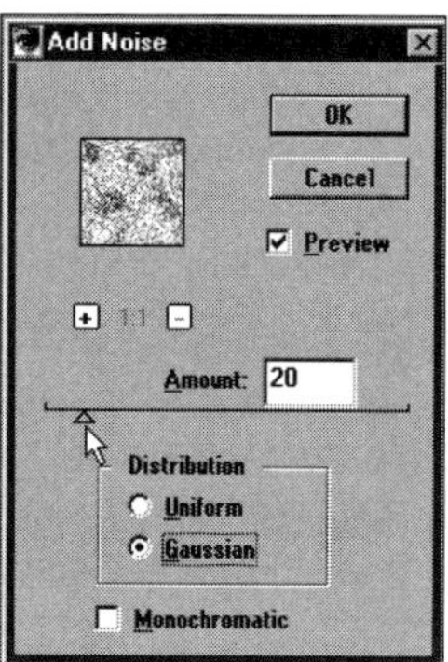

Figure 3-8: You can use Photoshop's Noise dialog to add interesting textures to a solid fill.

9. More "noise" means a more speckled, colorful background; less "noise" means a more solid, uniform fill. If Uniform is selected under Distribution, 20 is a good Noise value to try. Gaussian distribution produces a different visual result; the noise is distributed in a way that results in a more active texture. If the Monochromatic check box is selected, the noise added to the background image will be in the same color spectrum as the original fill. When you are happy with the look you have achieved in the preview window, click on OK.
10. Change the mode to Indexed Color and reduce the number of colors as far as possible, as described earlier in "Using Photoshop to Manipulate and Create Web Graphics." You should be able to reduce a tiled background to fewer than ten colors.
11. Save the image as a CompuServe. Gif using the Save As item on the File menu.

This sounds complex, but it's not really that difficult after you've run through the steps once.

An alternative to adding noise is to use the "Pixelate" submenu of the Filter menu. Most of the items on this submenu produce interesting effects when used in a background. I particularly recommend Pointillize.

Creating a Tiled "Wallpaper" Effect

Figure 3-9 shows a simple Gif of a bear I created in Photoshop by drawing a bold red line around a clip art bear. (Actually, the bear is a lowercase letter "b" from Monotype's Monkey Business MT font displayed in Photoshop at 75 points.)

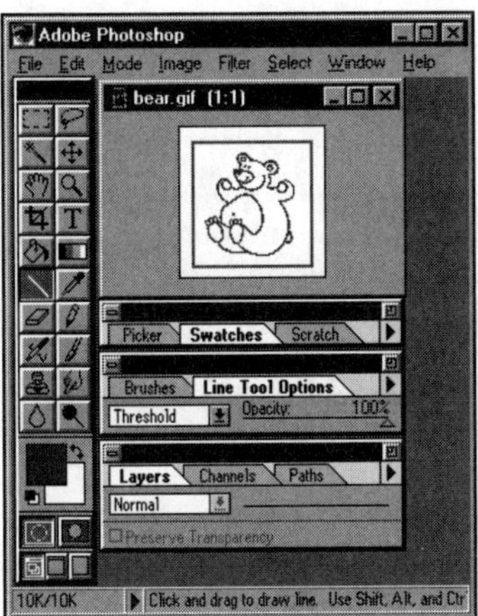

Figure 3-9: It's easy to create images that will produce backgrounds with a tiled wallpaper appearance.

I saved my bear as a small-sized Gif file named bear.gif using the techniques described earlier in this chapter. Now I can turn it into a tiled background in the standard way:

```
<HTML>
   <HEAD>
      <TITLE>Tiled Bear Background</TITLE>
   </HEAD>
   <BODY background="bear.gif">
   </BODY>
</HTML>
```

The result, assuming you can "bear" it, appears in Figure 3-10.

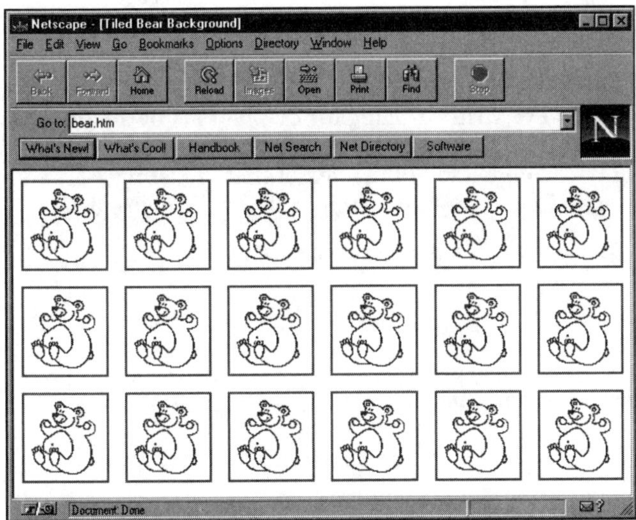

Figure 3-10: Is it a bear, or a Campbell's soup can? The tiled wallpaper effect has been popular at least since the time of Andy Warhol and Pop art.

Placing and Aligning Imagery

HTML has no direct tools for precisely placing graphics on the page. (To find out why, see the sidebar "If You Can't Beat HTML, Join HTML," in Chapter 2.) Nevertheless, there are techniques for precisely locating graphics — together with related text — on a Web page. The most common approach is to place the graphics within tables and then position and size them using the align, width, and height parameters of the <IMG> tag.

The use of these tags is easier to understand in the context of an example. But first, take a look at the possible values of the **align** parameter, which are listed in Table 3-1.

Table 3-1 The <IMG> Tag Align Parameter

Value	***Syntax***	***Description***
top	<IMG src="myfile.gif" align = top>	Aligns text to the top of the image.
bottom	<IMG src="myfile.gif" align = bottom>	Aligns text to the bottom of the image. Note that this is the default, meaning that not including an align parameter has the same effect as setting its value to bottom.
middle	<IMG src="myfile.gif" align = middle>	Aligns text to the middle of the image.
left	<IMG src="myfile.gif" align = left>	Aligns the image to the left side of the page.
right	<IMG src="myfile.gif" align = right>	Aligns the image to the right side of the page.

Now for a real-world example. Suppose I'd like my Web site to include a catalog of books I've written, using for display Gifs of the book covers. As it happens, each of the Gifs is different in size. If I just plunk the Gifs into the page, using HTML code along the lines of that in Listing 3-1, I will get the disorganized and unharmonious results shown in Figure 3-11.

Listing 3-1: The way not to create a catalog page

```
...
<IMG src="http://www.bearhome.com/books/vb4s.gif">

<I>Visual Basic 4 SECRETS<I> is an intermediate/advanced book in the
premier "Secrets" series.
...
<IMG src="http://www.bearhome.com/books/delphipt.gif">

<I>Delphi Power Toolkit</I> was written by Harold Davis. This is an
intermediate to advanced level book containing
```

```
cutting-edge tools and techniques for programmers. The book includes
a companion CD-ROM. 750 pages, 1995, $49.95, ISBN 1-56604-292-5,
published by <A href="http://www.vmedia.com/delphi.html">Ventana
Communications</A>.
...

<IMG src="http://www.bearhome.com/books/norton.gif">

<I>Peter Norton's Guide to Visual Basic 4 for Windows 95</I> was
written by Harold & Phyllis
Davis. This is a beginner
to intermediate text written in the user-friendly style of Peter
Norton. 918 pages, $39.99, 1995, ISBN 0-672-30615-8, published by
<A HREF="http://www.mcp.com">Sams/Macmillan</A>.

<HR>
...
```

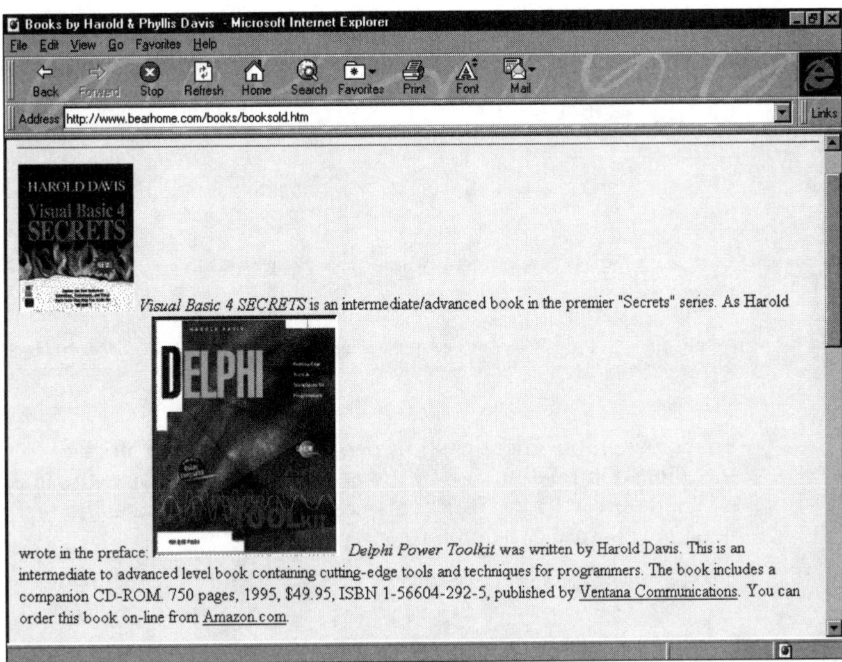

Figure 3-11: Images that are not placed carefully produce sloppy looking Web pages.

Let's straighten out this situation right away! A good first step is to make all the images on the page the same size. This is easy to do using the **width** and **height** parameters of the <IMG> tag. But first you have to know what size to standardize on, expressed in pixels.

In this example, I've decided to make all the book cover images the same size as the *Visual Basic 4 SECRETS* Gif. There are any number of good ways to determine the dimensions of this graphic in pixels. (No, Igor; down, Igor. I am not going to make you count pixels!) You can use the Photoshop's Image Size dialog to determine this information, as shown in Figure 3-12.

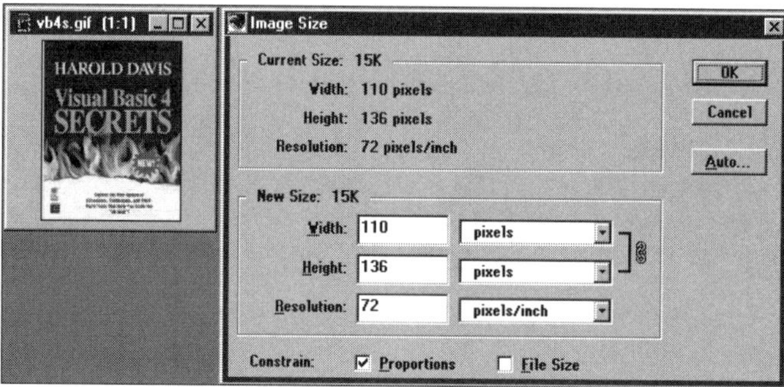

Figure 3-12: Most graphics programs such as Photoshop (shown here) let you determine the dimensions, in pixels, of a graphic.

Once you've found the dimensions, it's easy to set the sizes of all images on the page so they are the same:

```
...
<IMG src="http://www.bearhome.com/books/vb4s.gif" width=110
height=136>
...
<IMG src="http://www.bearhome.com/books/delphipt.gif" width=110
height=136>
...
<IMG src="http://www.bearhome.com/books/norton.gif" width=110
height=136>
...
```

That's better, but there is still work to be done. Each block of text should be top aligned in relationship to the appropriate image, and the images should be lined up vertically. To do this, you can put the image and text for each book in separate two-column, one-row tables:

```
<TABLE cellpadding=10>
   <TR>
      <TD align=top>
         <IMG src="myfile.gif" width=110 height=136>
      </TD>
      <TD align=top>
         Descriptive Text
      </TD>
   </TR>
</TABLE>
```

Listing 3-2 contains the HTML code for the revised page. As shown in Figure 3-13, this works much better.

Listing 3-2: Using tables to create an organized catalog page with precisely placed graphics

```
...
<!-************************************->

<TABLE cellpadding=10>
<TR>
<TD align=top>

<IMG src="http://www.bearhome.com/books/vb4s.gif" width=110
height=136>
</TD>
<TD align=top>
<I>Visual Basic 4 SECRETS</I> is an intermediate/advanced book in the
premier "Secrets" series. As  Harold wrote in the preface:

"Programming is - at its best - one part art, one part science, and
one part lore. As programming languages go, Visual Basic is
extremely easy to program, but only up to a certain point. Learning
the secrets that lie beyond that point, sometimes referred to
by developers as the "VB Wall," is a matter of obtaining access to
the secrets included in <EM>Visual Basic 4 SECRETS<EM>.
...
</TD>
</TR>

</TABLE>
<HR>

<!-************************************->

<TABLE cellpadding=10>
<TR>
<TD align=top>

<IMG src="http://www.bearhome.com/books/delphipt.gif" width=110
height=136>
</TD>
<TD align=top>
<I>Delphi Power Toolkit</I> was written by Harold Davis. This is an
intermediate to advanced level book containing
cutting-edge tools and techniques for programmers. The book includes
a companion CD-ROM. 750 pages, 1995, $49.95, ISBN 1-56604-292-5,
published by <A HREF="http://www.vmedia.com/delphi.html">Ventana
Communications</A>.
...
</TD>
</TR>
</TABLE>
<HR>
<!-************************************->
<TABLE cellpadding=10>
```

(continued)

Listing 3-2: ***(Continued)***

```
<TD align=top>
<IMG src="http://www.bearhome.com/books/norton.gif" width=110
height=136>
</TD>
<TD align=top>
<I>Peter Norton's Guide to Visual Basic 4 for Windows 95</I> was
written by Harold & Phyllis Davis. This is a beginner
to intermediate text written in the user-friendly style of Peter
Norton. 918 pages, $39.99, 1995, ISBN 0-672-30615-8, published by
<A href="http://www.mcp.com">Sams/Macmillan</A>.
...
</TD>
</TR>
</TABLE>
<HR>
<!—***********************************—>
...
```

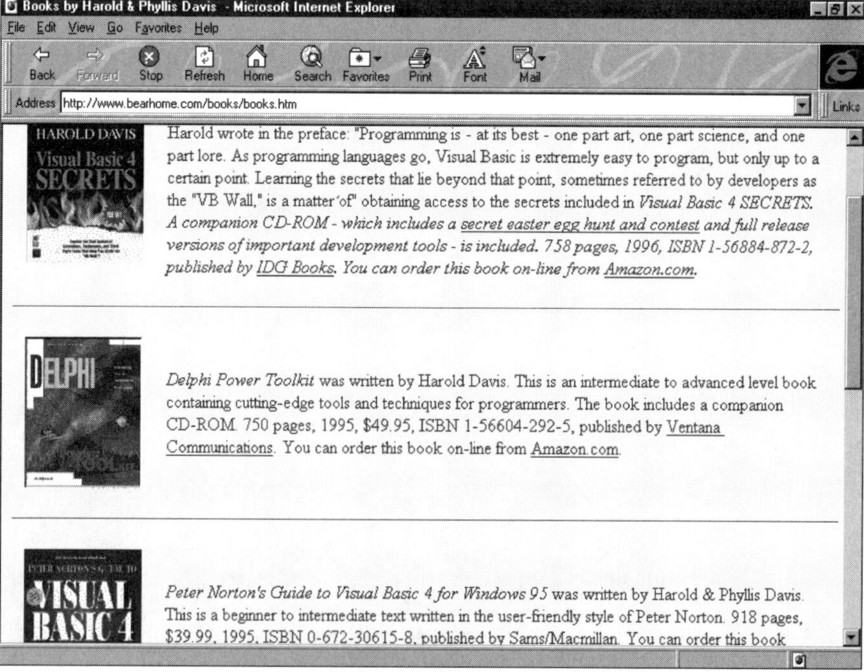

Figure 3-13: You use tables to precisely place graphics and text in Web pages.

You use the **cellpadding** parameter of the <TABLE> tag to place a blank area of the indicated number of pixels between the contents of a table's cell and the column and row borders of the table. Alternatively, you can add space around images using the **hspace** and **vspace** parameters of the <IMG> tag; these parameters add horizontal and vertical space around an image.

The HTML Layout Control

Microsoft's HTML Layout control allows precise grid placement, with some limitations. This ActiveX control does allow WYSIWYG page element editing, meaning that you don't need to resort to HTML magic to locate graphics. It is discussed further in Chapter 11, "VBScript and ActiveX."

There are some other important image placement techniques you should know about. You can use blank images to hold areas of a page empty; this lets you precisely position adjoining page elements. (Images used in this way are sometimes called "spacers.") To successfully use an image this way, you need to create the graphic file so it either matches the background of the page or is transparent.

You can create transparent Gifs using a Photoshop GIF89a plug-in, available for downloading from *http://www.adobe.com/prodindex/photoshop/main.html*. Many programs besides Photoshop support the Gif89a format, including Alchemy Mindwork's Gif Construction Set, which you can find at *http://www.mindworks.com/alchemy/alchemy.html*.

Style Sheets and Internet Explorer

Internet Explorer versions 3.0 and later support a fairly sophisticated implementation of the "style sheet" concept familiar to users of word processing and desktop publishing programs — that is, a way of reusing a set of formatting commands. This feature is supported by IE in two ways:

- You can format an entire HTML page by placing parameters and values within <STYLE></STYLE> tags. This kind of style sheet is called a STYLE block. The <STYLE></STYLE> section goes before the <BODY> tag.
- You can assign a **style** parameter in-line to a specific tag. You can add style information to content contained in a tag within the <SPAN> block, for example:

```
<SPAN style="font-size: 14pt"><IMG src="my.gif"></SPAN>
```

Obviously, the fact that styles are only fully implemented by Explorer is a grave drawback to using them widely. However, if you are prepared to deal with this — either by creating parallel versions of your Web pages or by requiring the use of Explorer — there are many advantages.

These advantages include the ability to define one look and feel for all HTML documents on a site, controlled by the <STYLE></STYLE> section copied from document to document. In addition, you can use **style** parameters to set the exact placement of HTML elements such as text and graphics.

For example, Listing 3-3 shows an HTML page using styles.

Listing 3-3: A page with <STYLE>!

```
<HTML>
   <HEAD>
      <TITLE>
      I've got Style
      </TITLE>
   </HEAD>
   <STYLE>
      H1 {font: 14pt Arial bold}
   </STYLE>
   <BODY>
      <H1>14 is nice</H1>
      <P style="font-size: 30pt">Bigger is nicer!</P>
<SPAN STYLE="margin-left: 3.5in">
         <IMG src="bear.gif">
      </SPAN>
   </BODY>
</HTML>
```

The <STYLE> section before the body of the document sets global options for <H1> text. The in-line **style** parameters in the document set the font size of a paragraph of text and the exact position from the left margin of the bear.gif graphic. Figure 3-14 shows the results.

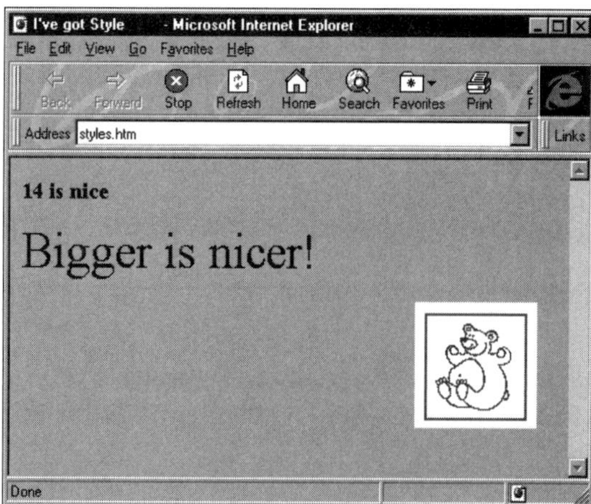

Figure 3-14: You can use Internet Explorer's <STYLE> tag and **style** parameter to precisely control the appearance of HTML documents under IE.

For full documentation on using the <STYLE> tag and parameter, check Microsoft's Web site at *http://www.microsoft.com/author/newhtml/default.htm*.

By the way, there is no requirement that the URL for a graphic on one of your pages be physically included on your site. It's pretty common to reference graphics located elsewhere, although this practice can add to load time.

As an example, the Yahoo! search site encourages sites that wish to link with Yahoo! to include the following HTML code in their pages:

Listing 3-4: Adding a graphical link to Yahoo to your site

```
<!— Begin Yahoo Search Form —>
<FORM METHOD="GET" ACTION="http://search.yahoo.com/bin/search">
   <TABLE>
   <TR>
   <TD>
      <A HREF="http://www.yahoo.com">
      <IMG SRC="http://www.yahoo.com/images/doyou.gif"
         BORDER="0"></A>
   </TD>
   <TD>
<INPUT SIZE="20" NAME="p">
      <INPUT TYPE="SUBMIT" VALUE="Search">
      <A HREF="http://www.yahoo.com/search.html">
         <SMALL>options</SMALL></A>
   </TD>
   </TR>
   </TABLE>
</FORM>
<!— End Yahoo Search Form —>
```

Figure 3-15 shows the results of including the doyou.gif file, which is physically located on the Yahoo! site, in a "foreign" site.

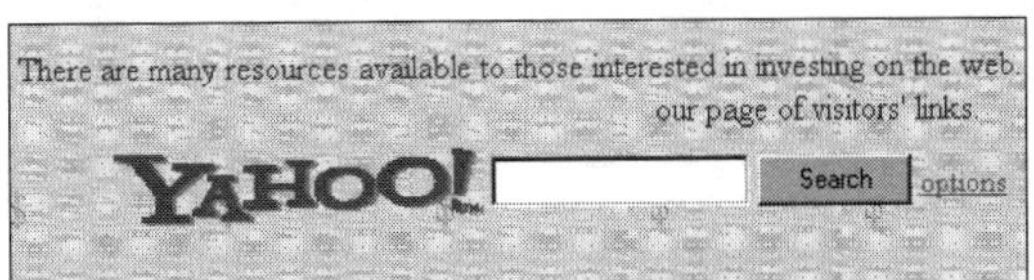

Figure 3-15: Your Web pages can include graphics even when the graphics file is physically located on another site. (Here is Yahoo!'s doyou.gif and search form. Text and artwork copyright 1996 by Yahoo!, Inc. All rights reserved. Yahoo! logo is a trademark of Yahoo, Inc.)

Mapping an Image

Clickable image maps are used to set portions of an image as links. These image maps use a coordinate system that corresponds to specific areas on a graphic. That way, a user can click on different parts of a graphic to access different links. Images that provide this linking facility are a jazzier way for users to navigate than straight text links and have become pretty much *de rigeur* for sophisticated Web sites. Figure 3-16 shows an image that has been mapped to provide clickable links along the left side of the bearhome.com home page. (The "image" in this case is the script list along the left side of Figure 3-16; the mouse pointer is aimed at one of the image-mapped links.)

The phrase "to map an image" means to create the HTML tags that contain the coordinate system and links required to create clickable links within an image.

Strongly consider letting users whose browsers do not support client-side maps navigate your site. A text-only version of your site is an easy, fail-safe, and elegant way to do this.

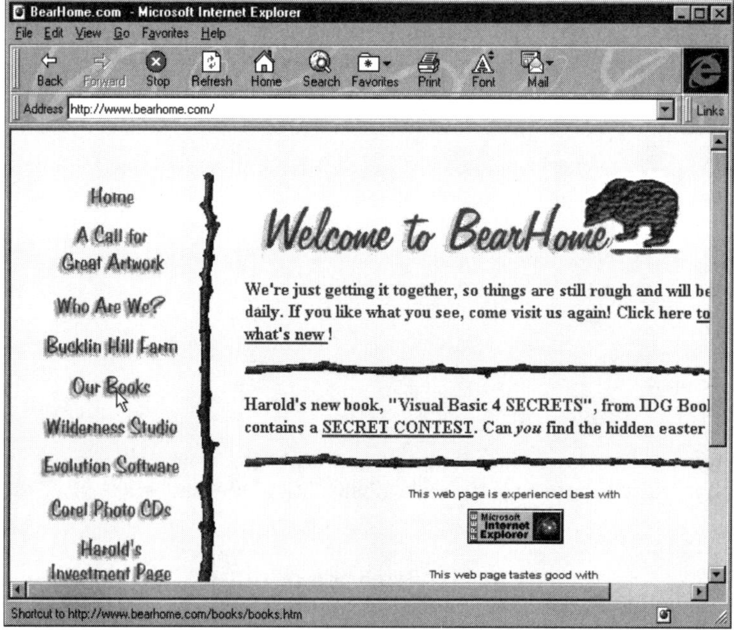

Figure 3-16: Modern Web site design practically requires the use of images that have been mapped to provide clickable links; here's the bearhome.com home page with a mapped image along its left side.

Creating Client-Side Image Maps

You indicate a client-side map by adding the **usemap** parameter to an <IMG> tag. You set the **usemap** parameter equal to the name of the map, where the map name is preceded by the pound hash symbol and enclosed in quotes, for example:

```
<IMG src="image.gif" usemap="#map1">
```

You may wish to organize complex Web sites by placing maps in a particular location and calling them by full URL:

```
<IMG src="image.gif"usemap="http://www.bearhome.com/maps/map.htm#map1">
```

Placing maps in a separate location helps to ease site maintenance chores, particularly when the same image is mapped in a number of different pages. If the links change, you only need to edit the referenced file, not the map contained in each page.

You create the maps themselves by using <AREA> tags between <MAP> and </MAP> tags. You specify the name of the map within the <MAP> tag:

```
<MAP name="Map1">
...
<AREA> tags
...
</MAP>
```

<AREA> tags can contain the parameters described in Table 3-2. Table 3-3 shows the arguments required for shapes other than rect.

Server-Side Versus Client-Side Maps

Server-side maps are map files that are processed by the web server; client-side maps are embedded in HTML pages and are processed directly by the browser (the client). Server-side maps are indicated with the **ismap** parameter within the <IMG> tag, while client-side maps are specified with the **usemap** parameter within the <IMG> tag. (You specify the map itself using the <MAP> and <AREA> tags, as explained in the text.)

In olden days, in the early years of the World Wide Web — that is, up until a year or so ago — you had to use server-side maps because there was no client-side browser support for image maps. This has changed, however, and browsers that even roughly support HTML 3.0 include an implementation of client-side mapping.

While you say "ismap" and I say "usemap," there are a number of reasons why you should use client-side maps rather than server-side maps. These include performance advantages to client-side processing — that is, less information going back and forth across the Web. In addition, there is no one standardized way to locate server-side map files. If you wish to speak "ismap," you'll have to check the documentation for the particular server your Web site is using.

Note that you can include **ismap** (server-side) and **usemap** (client-side) parameters in a single <IMG> tag. When you do this, the browser invokes the usemap client-side map if possible. When the browser cannot decode client-side maps, it invokes the server-side ismap file.

Table 3-2 <AREA> Tag Parameters

Parameter	*Values*	*Comments*
shape	circ, circle, poly, polygon, rect, rectangle. For example, shape="rect"	Rect and rectangle are equivalent, as are circ and circle, and poly and polygon. Because rect is the only universally accepted value for the shape parameter, it is safest to stick with it. After all, you can approximate any shape using rectangles.
coords	A sequence of ordered pairs of coordinates. You specify the coordinates in pixels measured from the upper-left corner of the image. For example, a rect requires two ordered pairs: coords="x1,y1,x2,y2"	The required number of pairs depends on the specified shape. Note that portions of graphics specified in different <AREA> tags can overlap; in this case the one that is sequentially first contains the link chosen by the browser.
href	"URL"	Note that the URL is evaluated relative to the map file, which may be different from the file containing the clickable image.
nohref		If present, this parameter tells the browser to take no action if the image is clicked within the <AREA> tag.

Table 3-3 Coordinate Notation for <AREA> Shapes Other Than rect

Shape	*Coordinates*
CIRC	Takes three coordinates: centerx, centery, and radius.
POLY	Takes three or more pairs of coordinates denoting a polygonal region.

As an example, here's the HTML code for the map for the clickable image shown along the left-hand side of Figure 3-16:

```
...
<img src="http://www.bearhome.com/home.gif" width=150 height=450
valign=top border=0 usemap="#home">
...
<map name=home>
   <area shape = rect coords="1,  15, 150,  47"
      href="http://www.bearhome.com">
   <area shape = rect coords="1,  48, 150, 107"
      href="http://www.bearhome.com/phyllis/art.htm">
```

```
   <area shape = rect coords="1, 108, 150, 147"
      href="http://www.bearhome.com/WhoAreWe/WhoAreWe.htm">
   <area shape = rect coords="1, 148, 150, 183"
      href="http://www.bearhome.com/bucklin/bucklin.htm">
   <area shape = rect coords="1, 184, 150, 217"
      href="http://www.bearhome.com/books/books.htm">
   <area shape = rect coords="1, 218, 150, 255"
      href="http://www.bearhome.com/wilder/wilder.htm">
   <area shape = rect coords="1, 256, 150, 291"
      href="http://www.bearhome.com/evolu/evolu.htm">
   <area shape = rect coords="1, 292, 150, 330"
      href="http://www.bearhome.com/harold/corel.htm">
   <area shape = rect coords="1, 331, 150, 385"
      href="http://www.bearhome.com/harold/invest.htm">
   <area shape = rect coords="1, 386, 150, 435"
      href="http://www.bearhome.com/phyllis/slim.htm">
</map>
...
```

To work out the coordinates for an area map, all you really need is the ability to accurately determine dimensions of portions of the image in pixels. If you want to be a macha web cowgirl you can do this just fine with a program that gives you image dimensions in pixels, such as the Windows Paint applet or Photoshop. (You'll also need a pencil and paper, plenty of time, and, to really be a cowgirl, a horse.)

It's probably easier to use one of the many tools for creating area maps. Figure 3-17 shows the graphic used in the preceding example as it is mapped in an excellent utility program called Map This! You can download a copy of Map This! from *http://galadriel.ecaetc.ohio-state.edu/tc/mt*.

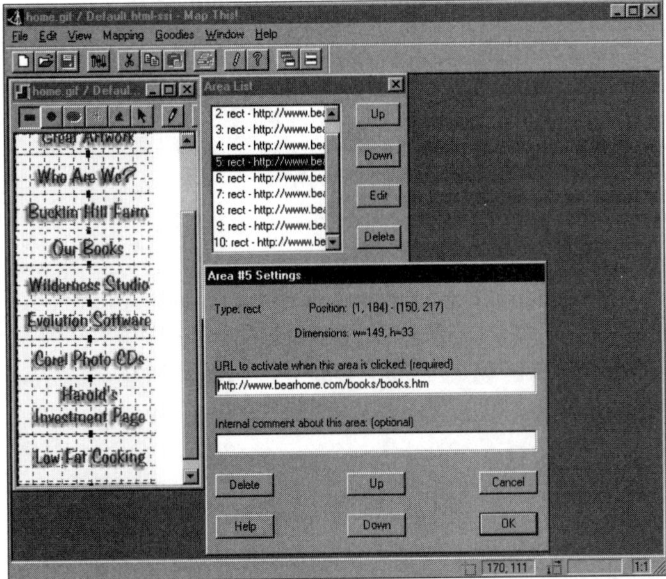

Figure 3-17: It's easy to create image maps using tools such as Map This!

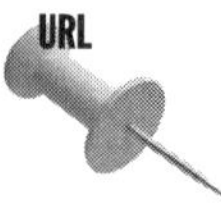

There are many mapping resources on the Web Paradise site, *http://desktoppublishing.com/webparadise.html*. Besides Map This!, another popular mapping program is Mapedit, available from *http://www.boutell.com/mapedit*.

Using the Gif Construction Set

Gif Construction Set for Windows (Gifcon32) is one of the best programs used to create animated Gifs.

This excellent program — practically required for creating graphics used on the Web — is shareware created by Alchemy Mindworks of Ontario, Canada. I encourage you to register your copy of the program after you discover how useful it is; the small fee is certainly worth it.

Alchemy Mindworks' homepage is *http://www.mindworks.com/alchemy/alchemy.html*. You'll find much useful material at this site, including the most recent version of the GIF Construction Set.

Gifcon32 is a collection of utilities that allow you to work with Gif files easily. Among other things, Gifcon32 can

- Create continuously looping Gif animations.
- Create interlaced Gif files — that is, Gifs that load in chunks rather than all at once. The advantage of interlaced Gifs is that the user knows something is happening (she doesn't assume the program is hung up), even if an entire file hasn't loaded yet.
- Create transparent Gif files.
- Add, edit, and delete comment blocks within a Gif.
- Add text to images.
- Create multiple-image Gif files.
- Display Gif files.
- Create Gifs that include fades and transitions.
- Create animated marquee banners.

Although Gifcon32 may be best known for its ability to easily create continuously looping Gifs (*animated Gifs*), it has many other uses. For example, Figure 3-18 shows how you would use Gifcon32 to create a moving banner.

You can easily add a banner made this way to an HTML file using the <IMG> tag, for example:

```
<IMG src="road.gif">
```

The resulting banner will run continuously across the top of a Web page as long as it is open, as shown in Figure 3-19.

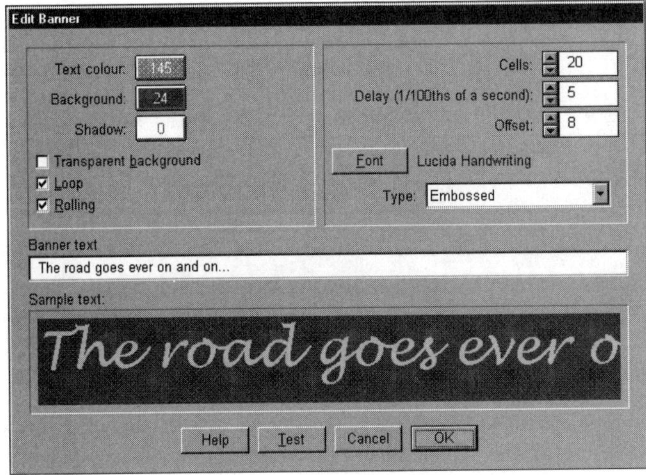

Figure 3-18: Gifcon32 provides tools for creating animated banners and marquees that you can save as Gifs.

Figure 3-19: Using Gifcon32, it's easy to create animated banners that go on and on and on.

Creating a Continuously Looping Gif

You've almost certainly seen examples of animated Gifs that loop continuously — for example, the logos for Navigator 3.0 and Explorer 3.0.

A site located in New Zealand called "The Clip Art Universe," *http://www.nzwwa.com/mirror/clipart/index.html*, provides lots of free clip art for Web pages, including a number of hot animated Gifs, as shown in Figure 3-20. (Unfortunately, the Figure is still — so it doesn't really show the way these puppies wiggle!) These files are not copyrighted and you can use them freely. (Maybe I should move to New Zealand. It has always seemed like a place that has it all: beautiful mountains, rugged coastline. Add to that copyright-free animated Gifs! I'm going!) By the way, the easiest way to copy an animated Gif to your system is to simply drag it from the Web page in your browser to your desktop.

A great way to get others to add links to your site is to make a cool animated Gif available, with the proviso that it can only be used to link to your site.

In the next section I'll show you how to use the Gifcon32 Wizard to create your own continuously looping Gifs.

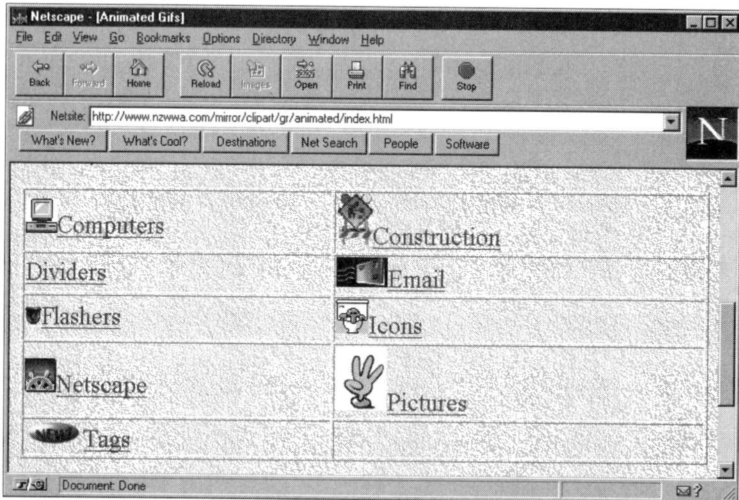

Figure 3-20: New Zealand's Clip Art Universe is a good source of royalty-free animated Gifs.

Using the Animation Wizard

The Gifcon32 Animation Wizard steps you through the required choices for making a continuously looping animation, as shown in Figure 3-21.

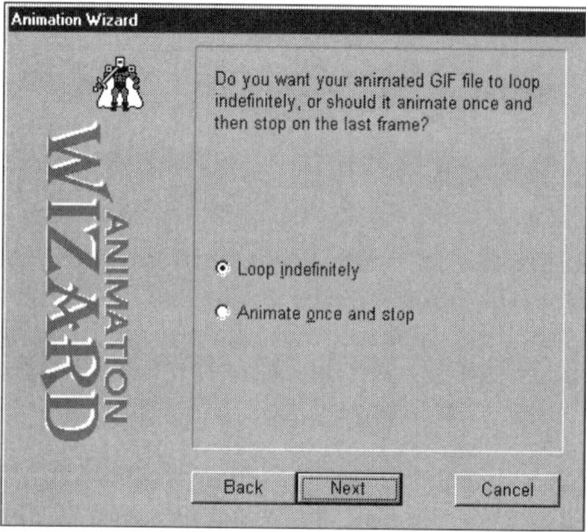

Figure 3-21: Gifcon32's Animation Wizard makes it easy to create complex animated Gifs.

When the Animation Wizard completes its process, it will have assembled an animated Gif in the Gif89a format, which internally is represented in a kind of macro language, as shown in Figure 3-22. Note that it is perfectly possible to use the insertion commands included in Gifcon32 to put together an animated Gif without using the Animation Wizard, although this is a little tricky.

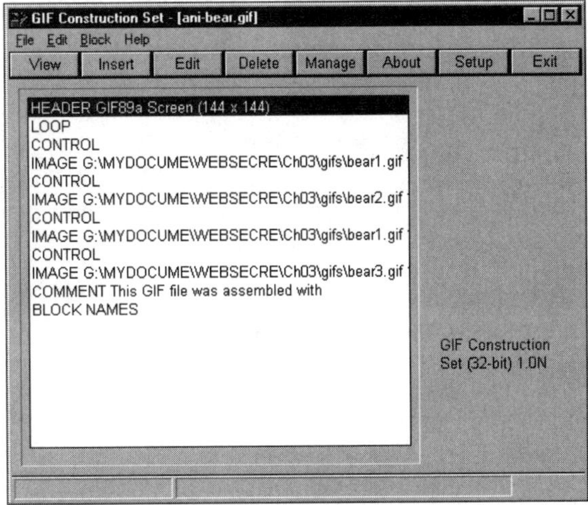

Figure 3-22: The internal structure of an animated Gif89a file appears as a macro language.

As you can see from the code in Figure 3-22, an animated Gif is made up of a number of separate graphics pasted together with simple commands. The "combination" Gif made up of all the others pasted together is, of course, also a Gif file. When you place it in an HTML page and view it with a browser capable of handling animated Gifs — such as Explorer 3.0 and Navigator 3.0 — it will dance on and on, all day and night, without needing any gas, as shown in Figure 3-23. (You'll need to bring this bear up in your browser to really see him dance.)

Figure 3-23: Animated Gifs keep on going, and going, and going....

Effective Use of Graphics on the Web

Using graphics effectively on the Web means balancing many competing values. It requires judgment calls. It's deceptively simple — there's no great skill involved in plopping a graphic on a Web page — and dismayingly complex — check the source code of Web pages whose visual effects you appreciate. There is no doubt that designing great Web pages is one of the true art forms at the end of the second millennia.

You should consider the following important issues as you make your Web page design choices:

- Size, size, size. Keep web graphics small in file size.
- Avoid clutter. Just because you can do something doesn't mean you should.
- Consider maintenance issues when you add imagery to your site.
- A Web page should be designed to be an experience, not a smorgasbord. Graphics should help to direct the flow of traffic on a site.
- As Yoda might have said, don't design your Web site, be your Web site.
- Like life itself, designing a Web site means giving up control. Ultimately, you cannot control all aspects of your user's web experience.

The Key Characteristics of Many Successful Web Sites Have Nothing to Do with Graphics

The key characteristics of many of the most successful Web sites have nothing to do with the visual appearance of the site. Many of the most successful sites are popular because they take advantage of the strengths of the Web by

- Involving users as participants who help to create and expand the site
- Taking advantage of the Web's ability to deliver up-to-the-minute information that can be configured to the particular requirements of each individual user
- Extending capabilities beyond the borders of the site itself, turning related portions of the Web into a "virtual" site that includes more features than would be possible in any one site

For these sites, the key issue of graphic design is to make sure that the visuals do not get in the way of the purpose of the site.

Summary

This chapter provided information about many of the tools and techniques that you will need to create inspirational Web sites. Topics covered included

- Understanding graphic file formats on the Web
- Using Gifs
- Reducing image file size
- Creating and editing images
- Using CorelDraw to create art for the Web
- Using Photoshop to manipulate art for the Web
- Creating backgrounds
- Creating tiled and patterned backgrounds easily
- Placing and aligning images
- Organizing a catalog of images
- Using style sheets and Internet Explorer
- Creating image maps
- Using the Gif Construction Set
- Creating an animated Gif
- Using graphics effectively on the Web

Chapter 4

Different Browsers for Different Folk

"Oh what a tangled web we weave!"

— Sir Walter Scott

The *New Yorker* once printed a cartoon which showed a dog at a computer monitor, presumably surfing the World Wide Web, bragging to his canine companions about his supposed anonymity. The line read, "On the Internet, nobody knows you're a dog."

It turns out, in fact, that not only do many Web sites know that you are a dog, they know exactly what kind of dog you are, what you had for dinner, and which sites you've visited recently. Well, maybe not quite. (Malamute mutt, kibbles, leather_puppy_toys.com — we don't think so!) But you can obtain a fair amount of information about browsers of your sites — and, conversely, browsers that are aware of privacy issues have techniques for hiding their identities. Things are not always what they seem.

From the viewpoint of an application running on a web server, the question is what you know — or don't know — about those browsing your applications (the "client" browser). Sure, you can ask the client to fill out an HTML form and tell you about herself, but many users will not stop to fill out a form (or provide truthful information). What useful information can you gather whether or not the user wants you to?

Obviously, gathering information about people "whether they like it or not" raises troubling ethical issues — largely depending on the context in which the information is gathered and what is done with it. Those responsible for development on the Web would do well to ponder issues of personal privacy with great care. However, these issues represent a big topic — one far beyond the scope of *Web Developer's SECRETS.*

In addition, some information you want to know — such as persistent state data related to the client's previous stops at your site — may not be known to the client. This becomes important in situations such as a catalog site, when the browser may make a partial selection, link to another site, and then come back to the catalog site.

Web applications must often know how to hand off persistent state information to a browser and also how to decode persistent information that is being stored on the client browser's system.

This chapter details practical issues involved in obtaining and handling information disclosed when a browser opens an HTML page that is part of your application. It also looks at some of the privacy issues involved and describes how to maintain your anonymity on the Web, if you're inclined to do so. Finally, the chapter shows you how to easily web-enable generic Windows applications.

The Browser Wars

Any two browsers have numerous superficial and substantive differences. Features that are intended to accomplish the same goal may, in fact, function differently in the two browsers. These differences can have to do with minor shifts in the final appearance of a Web page, but they can also extend to whole areas of vastly different functionality.

In particular, the latest versions of Netscape's Navigator and Microsoft's Internet Explorer do not support the same feature set and implement the shared features in different ways. Currently Explorer emulates all HTML features included in Navigator and then adds some of its own, such as the implementation of styles discussed in Chapter 3, "Graphics on the Web." It would take a book the length of *War and Peace* to detail these differences. What is worse is that they will change with the next release of each publisher's browser.

I could make strenuous editorial noises about the morality and sanity of browser publishers intentionally deviating from agreed-upon standards. To outgun their opposition, these publishers are making life much more difficult for all web developers. Those who create Web pages, sites, and applications need them to work as universally as possible. In fact, the universality of HTTP and HTML 1.0 is what got the Web started in the first place. Now, rivalry — the browser wars — is threatening the homogenous development environment that is the Web.

Much more could be said on this topic, but I will refrain! Software publishers take note: If the shoe fits, wear it.

There is no entirely sane way to handle this situation. It's a case of pay your money and take your chances. You should bear in mind, however, that a lowest common denominator text-only version of a Web page will work in any browser. (For more insight into going with the HTML flow in this way, see the sidebar "If You Can't Beat HTML, Join HTML," in Chapter 2, "Using HTML Tags to Design Web Pages.") If you are going to take advantage of "advanced" browser features, it's a good idea make a text-only version of your site available too.

Here are some possible ways to play this situation:

- You can write a version of your HTML pages for every known browser. Using the techniques outlined later in this chapter, you can detect which browser is being used and switch to the appropriate set of pages, but this is by no means a foolproof or trivial job.
- You can write your pages for one particular browser and warn users that this is the case. If you want to make your pages available to users not using "your" browser, provide a text-only alternative.
- You can create pages and check that they function and look good — albeit somewhat different — in Navigator and Explorer, the two most popular browsers. Provide a text-only version for users who don't have browsers with the advanced features of Navigator and Explorer.

My preference leans toward the last option. I'll show you a nifty way to implement this option in the next section of this chapter.

Handling Differences between Browsers

Obviously, one fairly easy way to handle differences between browsers is to provide a Web site start-up page with links to several options. For instance, these could be "Click here for Text Only" and "Click Here for Navigator and Explorer." A variant of this would be to provide a default start-up page that is one or the other, with a link for the alternative. An example of this is the Web page with all kinds of whiz bang graphics including frames and a link captioned "If your browser doesn't support frames, click here for an all text version."

Here is a more elegant way to handle this situation. Let's assume you have written two versions of your Web site. I'll call one the "advanced" version; it is designed to work in the 2.0 or later version of Navigator and 3.0 or later version of Explorer. The second version of your Web site is text-only and can be handled by all browsers. The browsers that the "advanced" version was written for understand JavaScript; text-only browsers do not.

The solution is to create a text-only start-up page that includes a JavaScript function that automatically boots "advanced" browsers into the "advanced" version. I'll use an example to show you how to do this.

Here's the HTML for the text-only start-up page:

```
<HTML>
   <HEAD>
      <TITLE>
      TEXT ONLY
      </TITLE>
   </HEAD>
   <BODY>
   <H1>
      Look at me!<BR>
      I'm text only...
   </H1>
```

```
   </BODY>
</HTML>
```

I'll use something similar to create a placeholder for the "advanced" page:

```
<HTML>
   <HEAD>
      <TITLE>
      Advanced
      </TITLE>
   </HEAD>
   <BODY>
   <H1>
   I'm as advanced as can be;<BR>
   Navigator and Explorer are<BR>
   for me, you see!
   </H1>
   </BODY>
</HTML>
```

Figure 4-1 shows the two pages in appropriate browsers.

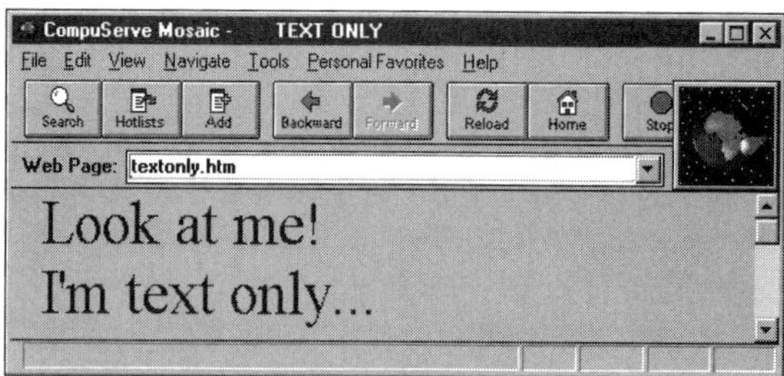

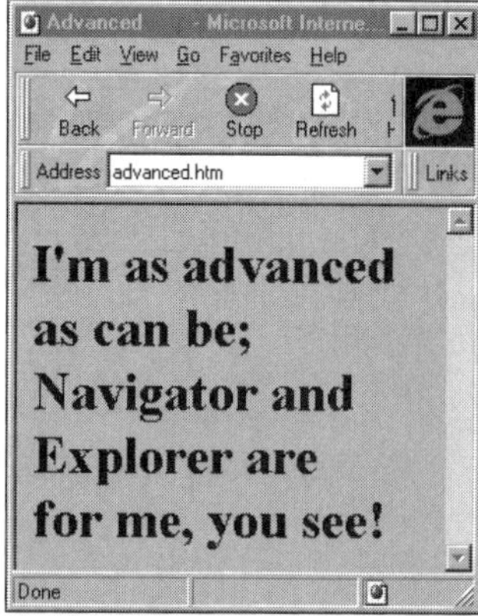

Figure 4-1: An elegant way to provide a text-only alternative is to add a JavaScript function that automatically loads pages with advanced features when viewed by a browser that understands JavaScript.

If you add a one-line JavaScript function, and a call to it in the <BODY> onLoad event, as shown in Listing 4-1, non-JavaScript browsers will stay on the text-only page, while "advanced" browsers will automatically be transported to the correct page, right away.

Listing 4-1: Using JavaScript to change documents automatically

```
<HTML>
   <HEAD>
      <TITLE>
      TEXT ONLY
      </TITLE>
      <SCRIPT Lang="JavaScript">
      <!-
      function movePage(){
      window.location.href="advanced.htm";
      return;
      }
     //->
     </SCRIPT>
   </HEAD>
   <BODY onLoad="movePage();">
   <H1>
      Look at me!<BR>
      I'm text only...</H1>
   </BODY>
</HTML>
```

If you use this technique, it's absolutely essential to practice code-hiding because the text-only page is *intended* for browsers that don't "speak" JavaScript. (For more information on this technique, see the "Comments" section in Chapter 2.)

Creating an Automatic "We've Moved" Page

The technique for creating a "we've moved" page is pretty much the same as the one for automatically changing documents, with the addition of a countdown mechanism. If you don't include a countdown delay, the message with the new URL goes by too fast for people to make a note of it.

To start at the beginning, another perfectly viable option is to simply put up a static "we've moved" page containing the new information and a link. This page could contain HTML code along these lines:

```
...
Evolution Software has moved...<HR>
The new location is
<A href="http://www.bearhome.com/evolu/evolu.htm">
http://www.bearhome.com/evolu/evolu.htm</A><HR>
Please make a note of our new URL and change any applicable links.
...
```

This approach is quite acceptable, but not particularly exciting. Listing 4-2 shows how to add an automatic jump to the new page from the "we've moved" page shown in Figure 4-2 with a one minute delay so that users can note the new URL.

Listing 4-2: A "we've moved" page that jumps to the new location after 60 seconds

```
<HTML>
   <HEAD>
      <TITLE>
      We Moved!
      </TITLE>
      <SCRIPT Lang="JavaScript">
      <!-
      function moved(){
         window.location.href=
         "http://www.bearhome.com/evolu/evolu.htm";
         return;
      }
     //->
     </SCRIPT>
   </HEAD>
   <BODY onLoad="setTimeout('moved();',60000);">
   <CENTER>
   <H1>
      Evolution Software has moved...<HR>
      The new location is
      <A href="http://www.bearhome.com/evolu/evolu.htm">
      http://www.bearhome.com/evolu/evolu.htm</A><HR></H1><H3>
      Please make a note of our new URL and change any
      applicable links. This page will automatically transfer
      you to the new location in one minute!
     </H3>
   </CENTER>
   </BODY>
</HTML>
```

The "we've moved" page uses the JavaScript setTimeout method of the Window object. This method delays execution of the expression that is the first argument of the method for the number of milliseconds in the second argument. JavaScript expressions are string literals. The call to the setTimeout method in the <BODY> tag involves using a JavaScript string literal within a string literal:

```
<BODY onLoad="setTimeout('moved();',60000);">
```

You do this using single quotation marks to embed an expression within another expression.

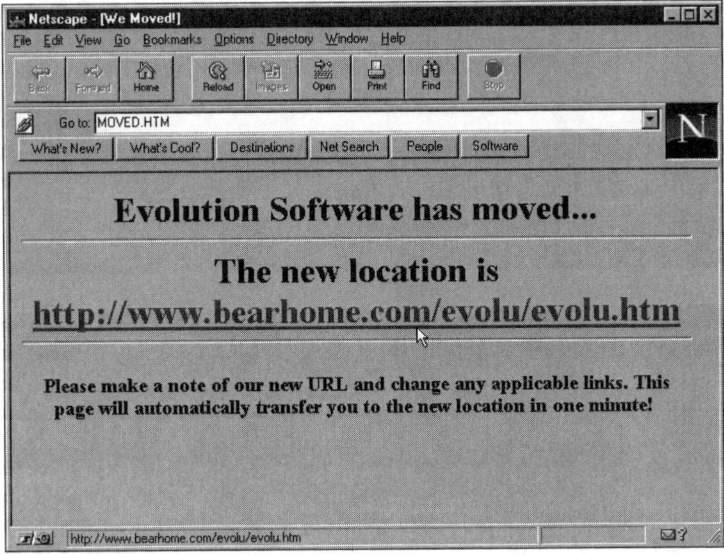

Figure 4-2: It's easy to create a "we've moved" page that automatically jumps to the new URL after a specified delay.

Obtaining Information about Client Browsers

Obtaining information about those browsing your site — without users providing the information voluntarily by filling out a form — involves server-side programming, which is discussed in detail in Part IV, "Client and Server on the Web."

Servers obtain information about client browsers in two fashions:

- Analysis of the HTTP header of the client browser
- Use of UNIX finger and whois commands

The latter is beyond the scope of *Web Developer's SECRETS*. In a moment, I'll give you the gist of using information available to the server without going too far into the nuts and bolts of server-side programming. But first, the easy way.

The Referrer Property

This section shows you how to use the JavaScript document object's referrer property to find the URL of the document that called the current document. In other words, this property tells you where your visitors were immediately before they linked to your site.

You can use the JavaScript document object's write method to place the contents of the referrer property in the HTML page:

```
...
Thank you for visiting from
<SCRIPT Language="JavaScript">
<!- hide that code
   document.write(document.referrer)
// ->
</SCRIPT>
...
```

Although this seems to work fine for Navigator 2.0, results with other, later browsers are unpredictable. Often, the referrer property holds the current URL rather than the previous URL.

Properties of the Navigator Object

One of the easiest ways to obtain information about a JavaScript-enabled browser is to read the values of the properties of the Navigator 3.0 object. Listing 4-3 contains the code for an HTML page that displays these properties, as shown in Figure 4-3. Table 4-1 shows the comparable information for Internet Explorer 3.0.

Listing 4-3: Obtaining the values of the Navigator object properties

```
<HTML>
   <HEAD>
      <TITLE>
       Navigator Object Properties
      </TITLE>
   </HEAD>
   <BODY>
   <H2>
   <CENTER>
   <SCRIPT Language="JavaScript">
   <!-hide me

   document.write("Browser code name: " + navigator.appCodeName);
   document.write("<BR>");
   document.write("Browser name: " + navigator.appName);
   document.write("<BR>");
   document.write("Browser version: " + navigator.appVersion);
   document.write("<BR>");
   document.write("User agent header: " + navigator.userAgent);
   document.write("<BR>");
   //->
   </SCRIPT>
   </H2>
   </CENTER>
   </BODY>
</HTML>
```

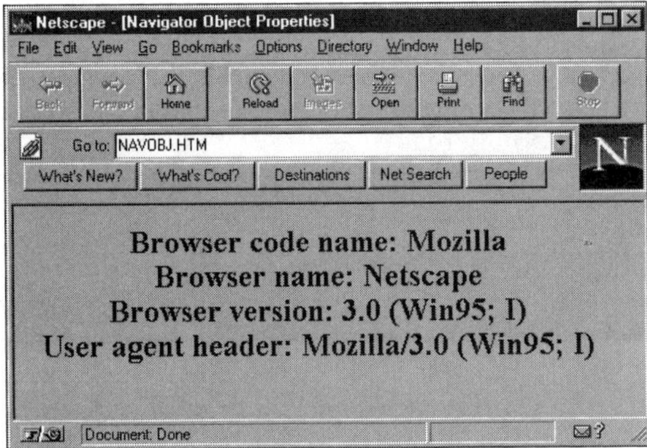

Figure 4-3: You can use the JavaScript Navigator object to obtain browser information.

Table 4-1 Navigator Object Version Information for Explorer 3.0

Category	***Contains***
Browser code name	Mozilla
Browser name	Microsoft Internet Explorer
Browser version	2.0 (compatible; MSIE 3.0A; Windows 95)
User agent header	Mozilla/2.0 (compatible; MSIE 3.0A; Windows 95)

What is this with "Mozilla," anyhow? Mozilla is the code name for Netscape Navigator. In its version information Explorer is to some extent pretending to be Navigator. Perhaps the word "Mozilla" is a cross between "Microsoft" and "Godzilla." Be that as it may be, it is easy to use the navigator.appname property to branch depending on which browser is being used.

Using CGI to Obtain Client Information

CGI (Common Gateway Interface) scripts are programs residing on a server that process inputs from an HTML form. The input is a text file saved on the server with specific standardized characteristics. The output is HTML code sent back to the browser. You can use a CGI program to send client browser information available to the server back to the browser.

Actually, a great deal of information about browsers "hitting" a site is available to any server software. To verify this, just open the server's access log. The CGI programming trick is in sending the information back to the browser on demand, not in obtaining the information (which is generally available on the server as CGI environment variables).

To return to the browser information about the browser that is readily available to the server, nothing really needs to be input via the CGI script. Rather, the call to the CGI script simply invokes a program that returns HTML code, including available information, to the browser.

The mechanisms and facilities for handling CGI scripts vary from server to server. I'll show you how to work with a number of different servers in Part V of this book. For now, to give you a feeling for this process, I'll demonstrate how to write a simple Visual Basic program that uses O'Reilly WebSite's Windows CGI scripting facilities. (You can download WebSite from *http://www.website.ora.com/*.)

First, to call the CGI script, create a form with a Submit <INPUT> as part of an HTML form:

```
<FORM ACTION="/cgi-win/whoru.exe" METHOD="post">
   Enough about us! What about you?
   <INPUT Type="Submit">
</FORM>
```

This causes the CGI program whoRU.exe to be executed on the server when the user clicks on the Submit Query button (see Figure 4-4).

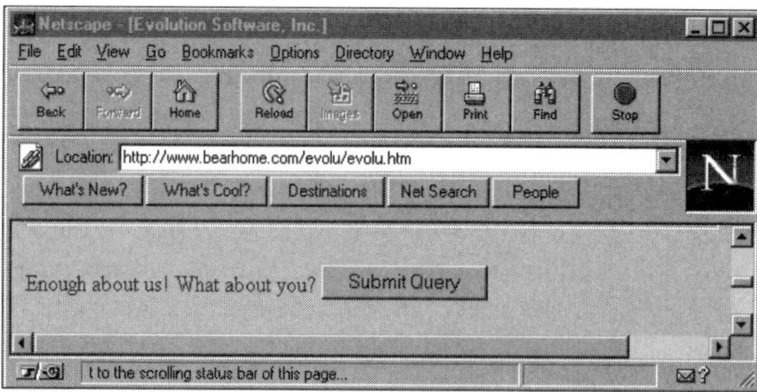

Figure 4-4: HTML forms are used to execute CGI scripts.

O'Reilly provides a code module, CGI32.bas, that you must include in Windows CGI Visual Basic programs that run with their server. Projects that include CGI32.bas are set to start from a Sub Main( ). Program flow is then sent to routines created for each project, Inter_Main and CGI_Main.

Inter_Main is called when the CGI program has been executed directly rather than invoked by the server:

```
Public Sub Inter_Main()
   MsgBox "This CGI program is not meant for direct execution!", _
```

```
      vbInformation, "BearHome.com"
End Sub
```

Assuming the CGI program has been correctly invoked, control branches to CGI_Main. CGI_Main determines the request method from the HTML form (usually this will be POST) and directs execution accordingly:

```
Public Sub CGI_Main()
   If CGI_RequestMethod = "POST" Then
      SendWhoRU
      Beep
   Else
      Exit Sub
   End If
End Sub
```

SendWhoRU uses constants built into the O'Reilly CGI32.bas module to construct HTML code that is sent back to the browser:

```
Public Sub SendWhoRU()
   Dim Quote As String
   Const Terminator = "</BODY></HTML>"
   Quote = Chr(34)

   Send ("Content-type: text/html")
   Send ("")
   Send ("<HTML><HEAD>")
   Send ("<TITLE> We know who you are...</TITLE>")
   Send ("</HEAD><BODY><CENTER><H2>")
   Send ("Here is some of what we know about you:")
   Send ("<BR>")
   Send ("You are using the following protocol: " _
      & CGI_RequestProtocol)
   Send ("<BR>")
   If CGI_From <> "" Then
      Send ("Your e-mail address: " & CGI_From)
   Else
      Send ("Your e-mail address is not available!")
   End If
   Send ("<BR>")
   Send ("Your Hostname: " & CGI_RemoteHost)
   Send ("<BR>")
   Send ("Your Remote Host IP: " & CGI_RemoteAddr)
   Send ("</CENTER></H2>")
   Send ("Return to <A href=" & Quote & _
      "http://www.bearhome.com/evolu/evolu.htm" _
      & Quote & ">" & "Evolution Software" & "</A>")
   Send (Terminator)
End Sub
```

The results are shown in Figure 4-5.

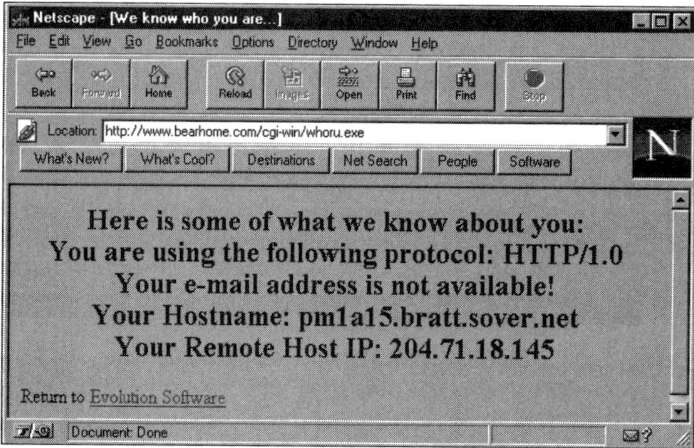

Figure 4-5: It's easy to use O'Reilly Web Site global variables to obtain information about visitors to a site.

A good question is: Where are these global variables coming from? If you look inside CGI32.bas, you'll find — and, by now, this should not come as a great surprise — that the CGI environment variables are set pretty simply by parsing the browser's HTTP header.

As I've mentioned, when you get around to actually wiring a heavy-duty Web site, you'll probably want to heavily use server-side programming. The exact form that this will take depends on the server being run and its operating system. (Windows 95 and Windows NT server programming is covered in Part IV of this book.)

In the meantime, it makes sense to understand what CGI environment variables are generally available. Table 4-2 shows the available CGI environment variables as they have been prepared for use with Visual Basic by O'Reilly Web Site.

Table 4-2 CGI Environment Variables

Variable Name	*Description*	*Visual Basic Data Type*
CGI_ServerSoftware	Name and version of the server software	String
CGI_ServerAdmin	E-mail address of the server's administrator	String
CGI_Version	The CGI version to which the server complies — for example, CGI/1.2	String
CGI_GMTOffset	Number of seconds from Greenwich Mean Time	Variant

Variable Name	*Description*	*Visual Basic Data Type*
CGI_RequestProtocol	Name and revision of protocol used by browser — HTTP/1.0	String
CGI_Referer	URL that referred to the CGI script	String
CGI_From	E-mail address of the user — usually not available because not supplied by the browser	String
CGI_RemoteHost	Host name of remote host running browser	String
CGI_RemoteAddr	IP address of remote host running the browser	String
CGI_AcceptTypes	CGI accept types	Tuple
CGI_NumAcceptTypes	Number of CGI accept types	Integer
CGI_ExecutablePath	Path of CGI program being executed	String
CGI_LogicalPath	Logical path	String
CGI_PhysicalPath	Physical path	String
CGI_RequestMethod	Method with which the CGI request was made — for example, GET, POST, or HEAD	String
CGI_ServerPort	Port number associated with the request	Integer
CGI_ServerName	Server host name for the request	String
CGI_QueryString	Encoded portion of the CGI URL after the ?, containing GET data or query string	String
CGI_ContentFile	Full path name of the file containing POST data	String
CGI_ContentType	MIME content type of requests with POST data	String
CGI_ContentLength	Length of attached data in bytes	Long
CGI_FormTuples	Name=value pairs supplied by the form	Tuple
CGI_NumFormTuples	Number of name=value pairs	Integer
CGI_HugeTuples	Large name=value pairs	Huge tuple
CGI_NumHugeTuples	Number of huge tuples	Integer

(continued)

Table 4-2 (Continued)

Variable Name	*Description*	*Visual Basic Data Type*
CGI_AuthUser	Name of authorized user	String
CGI_AuthPass	Password of authorized user, if enabled	String
CGI_AuthType	Authorization method	String
CGI_AuthRealm	Realm of authorized user	String
CGI_ExtraHeaders	"Extra" headers supplied by the browser	Tuple
CGI_NumExtraHeaders	Number of extra headers	Integer
CGI_OutputFile	Full path name of CGI program's output	String
CGI_DebugMode	CGI server tracing flag	Integer

Cookies

A *cookie* is an entry in a text file residing on the browser's local hard drive. Cookies are a property of the JavaScript document object, and, as I'll show you, you can easily use JavaScript to read, write, and delete cookies.

Cookies are used to maintain persistent state information between browsers and sites. This is important because users can easily link off a site but then return later to complete a transaction. In this situation, cookies provide a kind of memory, stored on the user's local hard drive, so that the user does not have to start from scratch. In addition, cookies can be used for communication between documents that "know" of the existence of the cookie.

If your browser is set to notify you before accepting cookies, you'll get a message like the one shown in Figure 4-6 before a browser writes a cookie to your local system. (You'll learn how to have your browser notify you about cookies in the section "Hiding Personal Information When You Browse" later in this chapter.)

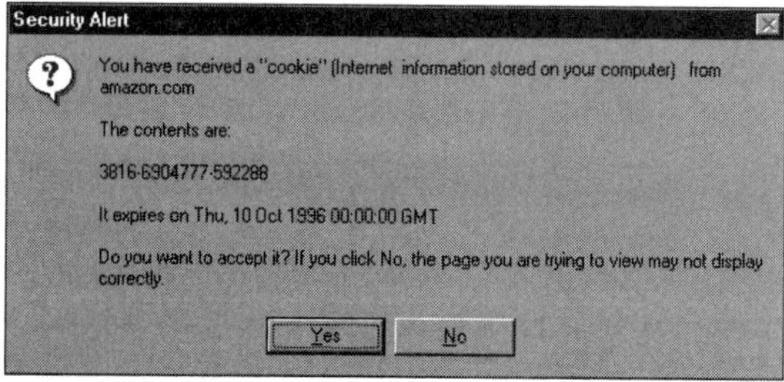

Figure 4-6: You can configure your browser to warn you before accepting cookies.

Cookie File Locations

When programming with cookies, you don't really need to know where they are stored. However, when working with cookies you may wish to examine the actual contents of a cookie file in a text editor. In this case, you need to know that Navigator and Explorer handle cookie storage differently.

The location of cookies stored for the two different browsers can be found as the value of a Registry key. For Explorer, the key is "Cookie" found under *HKEY_LOCAL_MACHINE\Software\Microsoft\...Internet Settings\Special Paths*. By default, the value associated with the Microsoft cookie key is windows\cookies. Each cookie is stored as an independent text file in the cookies directory.

Navigator handles things differently. The location of the file cookie.txt is the value of the "Cookie File" key found under *HKEY_LOCAL_MACHINE\Software\Netscape Navigator*. All cookies given to Navigator are concatenated within the one file cookie.txt.

Form of a Cookie Entry

Cookie entries are stored as delimited strings. In the Netscape universe, the delimiters between each cookie parameter are semicolons (;). End-of-cookie is indicated with a line break. In the Microsoft universe, each cookie has its own one-line text file. ASCII character 10 (line feed) is used as the internal delimiter.

In the Navigator notation, a full cookie entry with each key equal to a parameter value looks like this:

```
NAME=VALUE; expires=DATE; path=PATH; domain=DOMAIN_NAME; secure
```

Name, the name given to the particular cookie, is required, as is the corresponding value. The remaining entries are optional. The value of the expires entry is the date on which the cookie will no longer be kept on the system. If an expires value is not provided, the cookie is only valid for the current session. The path and domain entries are used to specify which URLs can access the cookie. Secure is a Boolean value that should be set to True when a secure connection is being used.

The Bill Dortch Cookie Functions

Bill Dortch has written a number of JavaScript functions for standardized handling of reading, writing, editing, and deleting cookies. Mr. Dortch has released his cookie functions into the public domain. The full text of the Dortch cookie functions, along with documentation and examples, is on the *Web Developer's SECRETS* companion CD-ROM in the Chapter 4\Programs directory, saved as dortch.htm. Please be sure to take a look at the complete dortch.htm file, as it contains some detailed information that I haven't included here.

You can download the latest versions of the Dortch functions from *http://www.hidaho.com/cookies/cookie.txt.*

Listing 4-4 shows the functions themselves, which should be included in the <HEAD> portion of an HTML document:

Listing 4-4: The Dortch cookie functions

```
<SCRIPT language="JavaScript">
<!— begin cookie functions
// "Internal" function to return the decoded value of a cookie
function getCookieVal (offset) {
   var endstr = document.cookie.indexOf (";", offset);
   if (endstr == -1)
      endstr = document.cookie.length;
   return unescape(document.cookie.substring(offset, endstr));
}
//  Function to return the value of the cookie specified by "name".
function GetCookie (name) {
   var arg = name + "=";
   var alen = arg.length;
   var clen = document.cookie.length;
   var i = 0;
   while (i < clen) {
     var j = i + alen;
     if (document.cookie.substring(i, j) == arg)
        return getCookieVal (j);
     i = document.cookie.indexOf(" ", i) + 1;
     if (i == 0) break;
   }
   return null;
}
//  Function to create or update a cookie.
function SetCookie (name,value,expires,path,domain,secure) {
   document.cookie = name + "=" + escape (value) +
     ((expires) ? "; expires=" + expires.toGMTString() : "") +
     ((path) ? "; path=" + path : "") +
     ((domain) ? "; domain=" + domain : "") +
     ((secure) ? "; secure" : "");
}
//  Function to delete a cookie.
function DeleteCookie (name,path,domain) {
   if (GetCookie(name)) {
      document.cookie = name + "=" +
      ((path) ? "; path=" + path : "") +
      ((domain) ? "; domain=" + domain : "") +
      "; expires=Thu, 01-Jan-70 00:00:01 GMT";
   }
}
// end o' script —>
</SCRIPT>
```

A Cookie Monster: A Cookie Example

One use of cookies that you've almost certainly seen is to maintain personalized Web pages. In this example — saved as cookie.htm in the Chapter 4\Programs directory of the companion CD-ROM — I'll show you how to create a basic personalized start-up page. You could easily expand this example to create a true user-configurable custom start-up page.

The standard JavaScript cookie methods do not work with Internet Explorer except across a TCP/IP network. In other words, for cookies to work with Explorer, the cookie page has to be loaded on a web. To test your cookies with Explorer, you'll have to work with a web server; otherwise these cookies will give you indigestion.

The example assumes that the Dortch cookie functions are loaded in the head of the HTML page. The first time the page is opened — or if no value is stored in the User_Name cookie — the user is asked to personalize the page, as shown in Figure 4-7.

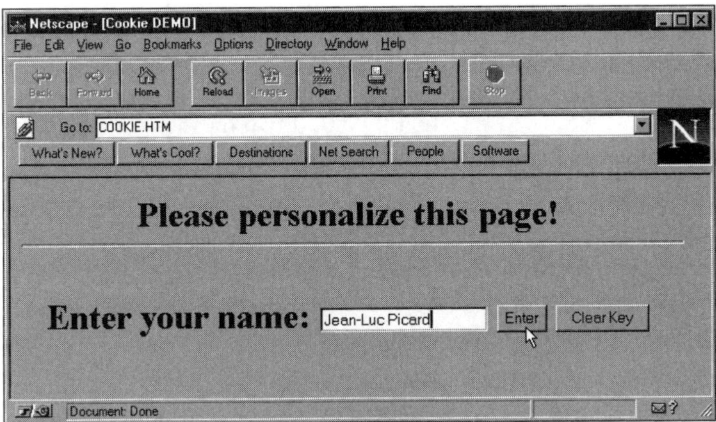

Figure 4-7: The first time the page is opened, the user is asked to customize it.

Here is the code that checks for a cookie value. If it is not present, the user is asked to personalize the page:

```
<SCRIPT Language=JavaScript>
   <!—Hide me
   var thisCookie;
   thisCookie = GetCookie("User_Name");
   if (thisCookie != null)
      document.write("Hello there, " + thisCookie + "!")
   else
      document.write("Please personalize this page!");
   //—release me —>
</SCRIPT>
```

If the User_Name cookie does contain a value, the script displays it on the page, as shown in Figure 4-8.

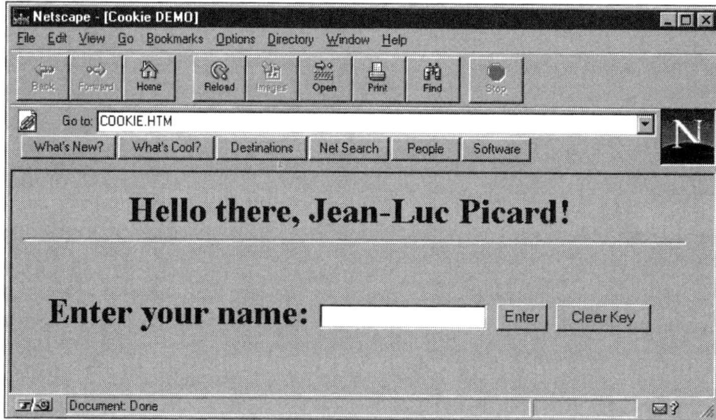

Figure 4-8: Cookies are used to retain an HTML page's persistent state data.

The actual code that calls the Dortch functions to set the cookie is contained in a form with an <INPUT> text field and two buttons, one for adding the cookie and one for deleting it:

```
<FORM Name="form">
   Enter your name:
   <INPUT Type="text" Name="txtName" MaxLength=40>
   <INPUT Type="button" Value="Enter" Name="btnSaveVariable"
       OnClick="var expdate = new Date (); var thisName;
       thisName = form.txtName.value;
       expdate.setTime (expdate.getTime() + (24 * 60 * 60 * 1000));
       SetCookie('User_Name',thisName, expdate);">
   <INPUT Type="button" Value="Clear Key" Name="btnKillVariable"
       OnClick="DeleteCookie('User_Name');form.txtName.value='';">
</FORM>
```

This code may look a little confusing, until you remember that the entire literal string expression that is the argument of a JavaScript button's OnClick handler can be made up of numerous JavaScript statements delimited with semicolons.

The JavaScript date object passed to the cookie function has a value that is 24 hours from the present. This means that the cookie expires — will be deleted — in 24 hours. After the user has entered a value for the cookie, the new value will appear whenever the page is reloaded.

Hiding Personal Information When You Browse

For those who are not thrilled about revealing their identities to sites they browse, I'm including a brief discussion about the other side of the coin, or cookie, on how to hide your identity. Anonymity is a thrilling facet of the World Wide Web. Thrilling means dangerous, but it can be both good and bad. With anonymity — and electronic cash — it's potentially easier to launder drug money and organize neo-Nazis. That's an example of the bad. An example of the good is that in an era rightfully afraid of the control of government and special interests, information and opinions can flow freely without fear of attribution or retribution. Suppression of opinions and information about corruption is much harder in a world in which anonymous access to the Internet and World Wide Web is widely available. This in keeping with the philosophy behind the First Amendment to the United States constitution. There is a reason why contemporary totalitarian societies such as Vietnam and China are barring their citizens from open access to the Web. In other words, ethical reasons why you might wish to maintain your anonymity go far beyond a desire to hide your visits to the Latex and Long Legs Web site.

The first thing you should understand is that entries in InterNIC's DNS database are a matter of public record. (For more information on InterNIC, see Chapter 1, or browse their site, *http://www.internic.net.*) This means that with the IP for the browser you are using — included as part of the HTTP header every time you link to a Web site — any server can do a reverse look-up on the DNS database. How much information this discloses depends on a number of factors. For one thing, if you are using a dial-up connection, the IP belongs to your ISP (Internet Service Provider), not you. The information obtained will be that of the ISP, not yours, and their configuration may determine how much of your information is being released. Other factors in determining how much information you are revealing include

- The browser you are using and how it is configured
- The presence or absence of a firewall or other security software

For a look at what information about you is easily available to Web sites, browse the Center for Democracy & Technology's demonstration site: *http://www.13x.com/cgi-bin/cdt/snoop.pl.* If you are browsing directly from an Internet domain, you may also want to have a look at what is included for your domain in the DNS database. To do this, use the WhoIs service at InterNIC's site.

Obviously, you can hide your information from sites by establishing a false identity one way or another: for example, by opening an account with an ISP just for anonymous surfing. You can also configure your browser for safety and to warn you when it is offered a cookie. (It is then your choice if you wish to accept the sweet treat.)

To configure your browser for safety, with Internet Explorer, open the Explorer property sheet and choose the High option in the Safety Level dialog on the Security tab (Figure 4-9). Next, on the Advanced tab, make sure that Warn Before Sending Over an Open Connection, Always, and Warn Before Accepting Cookies are checked, as shown in Figure 4-10.

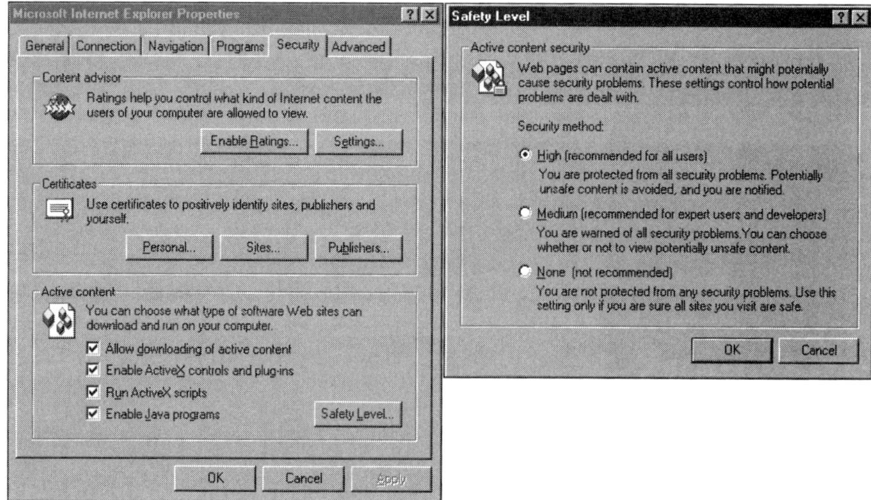

Figure 4-9: It's easy to configure Internet Explorer for security.

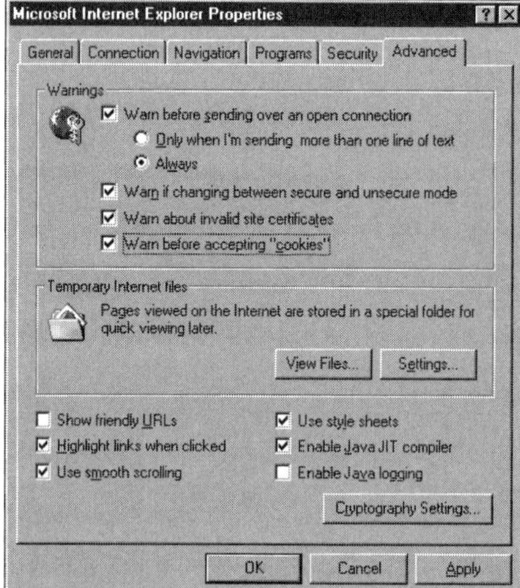

Figure 4-10: It's a good idea to configure Explorer to let you know when you are sending information over an open connection, and to give you the opportunity to decline cookies.

The same kinds of security settings are available on Navigator's Options menu. To set Navigator to warn you before accepting a cookie, choose Options and then choose Network Preferences. On the Protocols tab, make sure that Accepting a Cookie is checked, as shown in Figure 4-11.

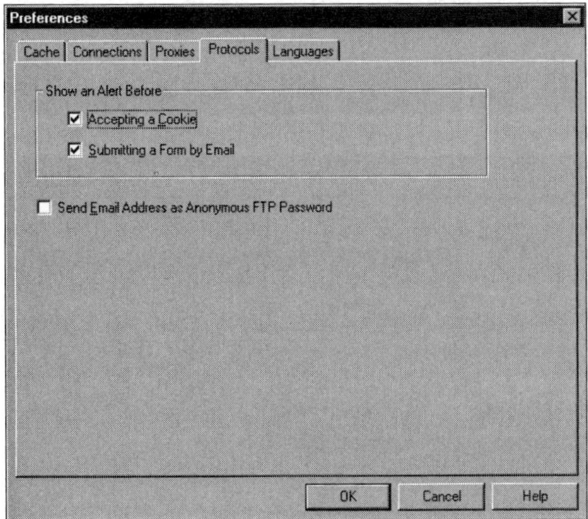

Figure 4-11: You configure Navigator's security options using the various tabs in the Preferences dialog, which you reach via the Options menu.

Don't check the Send Email Address as Anonymous FTP Password check box. If you do, a site may be able to read its FTP logs to find your e-mail address.

As a side note, you should consider all e-mail sent over the Internet as potentially insecure. Use encryption for anything sensitive.

It's fairly easy to see how you could set up an HTTP server with some kind of unrevealing identity. Each time you browsed into this server, it could replace your header information with its own, thus enabling you to hide your identity. Fortunately, you don't have to go to the trouble of setting up this kind of "proxy" server. (The term *proxy server* normally applies to an Internet server that acts as a security buffer between an internal network and the Internet.)

There's a site that allows anyone to practice anonymous surfing at *http://www.anonymizer.com*. The Anonymizer site acts as a buffer between you and HTML documents you retrieve. When you want to retrieve a document whose URL is *http://www.xxx.com*, you place your request to *http://www.anonymizer.com:8080/http://www.xxx.com*. You can do this using links at the Anonymizer site, or by "prepending" the anonymizer URL, as in the preceding example. The Anonymizer server retrieves the document, without revealing your identity, and sends it back to you.

Adding Your Own Browsers to Visual Basic and Delphi Applications

You can use the 32-bit Webster OCX to quickly add quite extensive web browsing capability to a program created in languages — such as Visual Basic, Delphi, and VC++ — that can be extended using OLE controls. You can download a demonstration version of the Webster control from *http://www.saxsoft.com.*

One good use for a browser such as Webster within your applications is to add it to your application's Help menu. You can set the browser to open a particular URL for specific technical support.

To add the Webster to an application after it has been installed on your system, add it to your toolbox of custom controls. (In Visual Basic, this means making sure that it is checked in the Custom Tools dialog.) Next, select the Webster and draw it on your form, as shown in Figure 4-12.

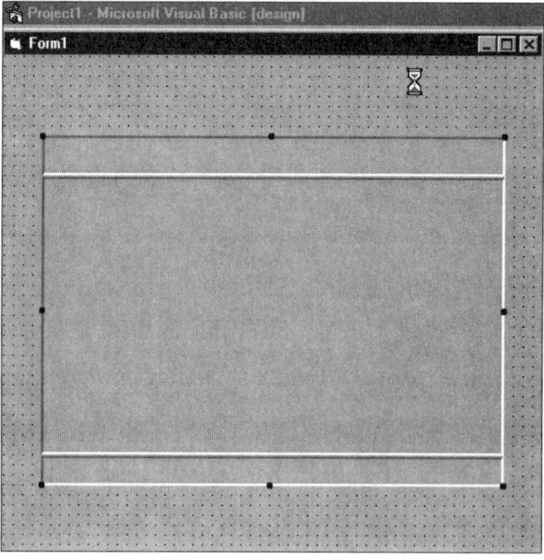

Figure 4-12: You can add a browser to your applications simply by drawing the Webster on a form.

That's really all there is to it, although you can configure and extend the Webster in many ways.

To set it to always connect to a particular URL, set the Webster's PageURL property. For example:

```
Private Sub Form_Load()
   Webster1.PageURL = "http://www.bearhome.com"
End Sub
```

This results in a connection to the specified URL — assuming the system can be connected to the remote server and page specified — when the form containing the Webster is loaded, as shown in Figure 4-13.

Figure 4-13: You can easily use the Webster OCX to add a browser that jumps to a specified location to any application.

Summary

As they used to say, "war is unhealthy for children and other living things." Clearly, the browser wars make life more complicated for developers — none of whom are children, anyhow, at least in theory.

As if life weren't already complex enough on the World Wide Web! You'll need every trick in the book — that is, in *Web Developer's SECRETS* — to successfully cope with issues of varying browser feature implementations. Another can of worms that will take all the development smarts you've got is coping with obtaining information about client browsers and maintaining persistent state information.

This chapter has provided a starting place on these issues, with practical technical examples of how to overcome obstacles. Topics covered included

- The browser wars
- Handling browser differences
- Creating a page that automatically loads text-only or Java-enabled HTML
- Creating an automatic "we've moved" page

- Obtaining information about client browsers
- The Navigator object
- Using CGI to obtain information about the browser from the server
- Cookies
- The Dortch cookie functions
- Creating a user-configurable start-up page
- Hiding personal information when you browse
- Using the Webster to add a browser to your applications

Chapter 5

Multimedia and Sound on the Web

"I got rhythm, I got music, I got my computer. Who could ask for anything more?"

— with apologies to Ira Gershwin

The World Wide Web is moving from infancy to toddlerhood. As this transformation takes place, Web sites are positioning themselves to provide experiences rather than to provide text-based reference material (such as technical documentation).

As human beings facing the rushing onset of the second millennium in contemporary society, we tend to have sophisticated expectations about what it means "to experience." We experience things with multiple senses, including those of sight, sound, touch, and smell. Our sensory expectations have been raised from that of brute animals by all kinds of experiences, including watching movies, driving a car on a freeway, playing with computers, and walking down city streets.

While "touchies" and "smellies" are out of the question for the Web — at least for the time being — there is no doubt that movies and television have influenced our expectations for visual stimuli. Movies are vivid, realistic, fast-paced, and can portray their internal worlds with great visual depth. As the Web becomes an experiential and recreational media, web developers must create sites that live up to this comparison. It also might be noted that from the beginning the Web has conceptually borrowed from the realm of science fiction: Web experiences not only must rival — and, in time, surpass — movies, they also must do so in a "jacked-in," cyber-punk, "cool" fashion.

As far as sound goes, the aural experience on the Web is in competition with excellent stereos playing superbly engineered audio CDs — if not with music being performed live. This is a competition that the Web cannot win, yet.

Unfortunately, sound and video on the Web, like the shadows on the wall of Plato's cave, are pale and unsatisfactory representations of the real thing at this point. Although there are many technical reasons for this, it boils down to two problems: the nature of HTML, and bandwidth.

Regarding the former, HTML was originally intended to enable the presentation of text-based content. For further discussion of the issues involved, see the sidebar "If You Can't Beat HTML, Join HTML," in Chapter 2, "Using HTML Tags to Design Web Pages." However, HTML we can kludge around. Bandwidth we cannot to any significant degree, although see the section "Streaming" later in this chapter. (Streaming is a technique for compressing and splitting up multimedia and sound into packets, sending it across the Internet, and recombining it at the other end.)

If the three secrets of retailing are "location, location, location," the three secrets of a satisfactory web experience are "bandwidth, bandwidth, bandwidth."

The fact is that most users are connected using 28.8 Kbps dial-up modems (or with even slower connections). Even if you have awesome bandwidth for your web server — and many servers do not — your users are trying to cram vast amounts of content (satisfying sound and multimedia files are huge) into tiny pipelines. No wonder some users who feel it is more like "wading" than "surfing" the Web have dubbed it the "World Wide Wait."

No doubt the bandwidth situation will ease in the near future. But until it does, developers have to be thoughtful and resourceful to provide multimedia experiences on their Web sites.

Cheap Thrills

Some of the easiest ways to give your sites that multimedia look and feel are to use sophisticated web graphics and HTML techniques. You'll find a great deal of information on these topics in Chapters 2 and 3 of this book.

Animated Gifs turn out to be particularly versatile (see "Creating a Continuously Looping Gif" in Chapter 3 for instructions on how to create one). They have the advantage of being completely encapsulated and identical in appearance in any advanced browser. One effective use of animated Gifs is to create a virtual multimedia slide show. In this case, the HTML page is made up of a number of animated Gifs positioned using the <IMG> tag. Each animated Gif consists of an image, such as a photograph, that fades in and out on a timed basis.

A site that uses this technique very effectively is *http://www.menuez.com*, which displays photographer Doug Menuez's images of the dawn of the digital age.

Another option is to create animated Gifs that consist of text that fades in and out.

You can easily embed multimedia content in an HTML page by creating an appropriate Java or ActiveX application. For more information, see Part III, "Adding Executable Content."

Another relevant technique that you can use to add multimedia effects is called "server push." In server push, the web server software is responsible

The <META> Tag

The <META> tag contains no content. You place it in the header section of an HTML document; it contains keyword equals value pairs. You use the **URL** parameter with the <META> tag to specify the location of a client pull document under Navigator.

for creating animation effects by changing specific images that are part of the client's screen. This is accomplished using a program (such as a CGI script) and is completely dependent on the particular server being used (for the details see Part IV, "Client and Server on the Web").

In contrast to server push, the "client pull" technique uses the <META> tag in an HTML document header to automate changing pages — in theory, creating an animation effect. This technique is Navigator specific, but results are erratic no matter what browser is used. Too many bandwidth factors are at issue to predict the effect with accuracy. Usually, client pull animations are not seamless, meaning that viewers see at least a flash of Web page.

Animation Secrets with Explorer

A number of techniques specific to Explorer can help give those who browse your site using this browser a multimedia experience.

Scrolling Title

Listing 5-1 demonstrates how to give the impression of a scrolling title under Explorer. The user will first see an "H" on the title bar of her browser, followed by an "HA," and so on. Note that you'll need to play with the number of repetitions of each scroll position. It's a good idea to add a few more of each intermediate step than in the example, which was abbreviated in the interest of not taking up the entire text of *Web Developer's SECRETS.*

Listing 5-1: Scrolling document title under Explorer

```
<HTML>
<HEAD>
   <TITLE>H</TITLE>
   <TITLE>H</TITLE>
   <TITLE>H</TITLE>
   <TITLE>H</TITLE>
   <TITLE>H</TITLE>
   <TITLE>H</TITLE>
   <TITLE>H</TITLE>
   <TITLE>H</TITLE>
   <TITLE>HA</TITLE>
   <TITLE>HA</TITLE>
   <TITLE>HA</TITLE>
   <TITLE>HA</TITLE>
```

```
    <TITLE>HA</TITLE>
    <TITLE>HA</TITLE>
    <TITLE>HA</TITLE>
    <TITLE>HA</TITLE>
    <TITLE>HAR</TITLE>
    <TITLE>HAR</TITLE>
    <TITLE>HAR</TITLE>
    <TITLE>HAR</TITLE>
    <TITLE>HAR</TITLE>
    <TITLE>HAR</TITLE>
    <TITLE>HAR</TITLE>
    <TITLE>HAR</TITLE>
    <TITLE>HARO</TITLE>
    <TITLE>HARO</TITLE>
    <TITLE>HARO</TITLE>
    <TITLE>HARO</TITLE>
    <TITLE>HARO</TITLE>
    <TITLE>HARO</TITLE>
    <TITLE>HARO</TITLE>
    <TITLE>HARO</TITLE>
    <TITLE>HAROL</TITLE>
    <TITLE>HAROL</TITLE>
    <TITLE>HAROL</TITLE>
    <TITLE>HAROL</TITLE>
    <TITLE>HAROL</TITLE>
    <TITLE>HAROL</TITLE>
    <TITLE>HAROL</TITLE>
    <TITLE>HAROL</TITLE>
    <TITLE>HAROLD</TITLE>
</HEAD>
<BODY>
</BODY>
</HTML>
```

The <MARQUEE> Tag

You can use the <MARQUEE> tag, which is Explorer specific, to configure a scrolling marquee — like that of a movie — on a Web page. For example, the HTML code shown in Listing 5-2 produces a marquee that has been frozen in time in Figure 5-1.

Listing 5-2: Using the <MARQUEE> tag

```
<HTML>
    <HEAD>
        <TITLE>
        Marquee
        </TITLE>
    </HEAD>
    <BODY>
        <H1>
        <MARQUEE bgcolor=red loop=infinite height=100 width="50%">
        The road goes ever on and on...
        </MARQUEE>
        </H1>
    </BODY>
</HTML>
```

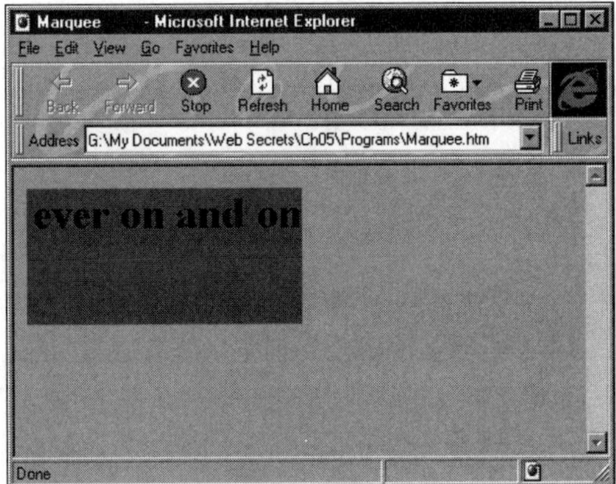

Figure 5-1: You can't see it in this static figure, but the <MARQUEE> tag creates a scrolling effect for Explorer users.

Note that you cannot include images within the scrolling marquee text; in addition, text formatting must take place outside the <MARQUEE> tag (in the example, the <H1>...</H1> tags sandwich the <MARQUEE>, not the other way around).

Borrowing Bandwidth

Suppose you don't have the bandwidth, or correct server software, to play a sound or multimedia file from your server. (Playing a sound or multimedia file from your server is sometimes called "serving up.") One rather sneaky alternative is to "borrow" bandwidth by embedding a reference to a file on someone else's server in your HTML page.

For example, *http://www.mission.apple.com* is the URL for Apple Computer's rather elaborate Mission Impossible web adventure game. Web URLs are read from right to left, with the right-hand side being the uppermost domain name. Thus, "mission.apple.com" is beneath the "apple.com" domain.

If you include the following HTML code in your page, the Mission Impossible theme will play on your site, but off Apple's RealAudio server:

```
<EMBED src="http://www.mission.apple.com/realaudio/homecut.rpm"
height=33 width=30 controls="PlayButton" autostart=true>
```

To test this in a browser, I've added this to *http://www.bearhome.com/evolu/evolu.htm*. Note that you'll need to be able to play RealAudio files — a facility included in Explorer 3.0. Navigator users can download a RealAudio player from *http://www.realaudio.com* and must correctly configure the .rpm file type as a Mime extension in Navigator's Helpers dialog (choose Options, Preferences).

Audio File Formats

Table 5-1 shows common audio file formats found on the Web. The size and quality of compressed sound files varies tremendously, so you'll have to experiment to find out what sounds (and compresses) best.

Table 5-1 Audio File Formats on the Web

File Extension	*Comments*
.au	Also called μ-law (pronounced "mew-law") files, .au files are the native UNIX sound format. (The "SAT for Geeks" analogy is that ".au is to UNIX as .wav is to Windows.") You'll see a lot of .au files on the Web because of the Web's UNIX roots. These files are generally considered lower quality than the other sound formats.
.aif	The native sound format for the MAC is — you guessed it — the Audio Interchange File Format. Generally, AIFF files are saved with the .aif extension. This is a high-quality, flexible format.
.mid	.mid files are created using the Musical Instrument Digital Interface, a language that lets synthesizers and computers communicate with one another. You cannot create a .mid file using a microphone. (Later in this section you'll learn about Music Sculptor, a program that creates a MIDI interface with a virtual keyboard on your PC.) On systems with a sound card that uses wavetable digitized instruments, .mid files can sound great; conversely, they can sound terrible on systems with inadequate audio components. .mid files tend to be very small in size compared to other audio formats.
.mpg	.mpg files are in the extremely high-quality MPEG format. To create such files you need hardware that is not part of a normal personal computer, such as high-end video editing equipment.
.ra, .ram, .rpm	.ra, .ram, and .rpm are Progressive Networks' proprietary RealAudio file formats. To serve up these files you must license the RealAudio server (see the section "Streaming" later in this chapter) or borrow someone else's server (see "Borrowing Bandwidth" earlier in the chapter).
.wav	.wav is the native sound file format for the Windows OS (it was developed by Microsoft and IBM). It is a high-quality, flexible format comparable to AIFF.

Generally, you'll need "helper" applications to hear sounds that are not native to your platform (although Internet Explorer does a good job of including intrinsic support for many different kinds of sound files). It's pretty common practice, therefore, to include links to sites from which these "helpers" can be downloaded.

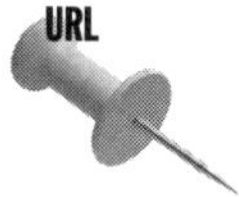

A good source for Windows media players and conversion utilities is Tom's Multimedia World, *http://www.geocities.com/SiliconValley/Park/4059/*. And who is Tom, anyway? Turns out he's a gifted teenager. Well, you know to whom the future belongs....

Particularly recommended is Wham, which plays — and allows you to edit — most audio file formats.

Also of note, and downloadable from the Tom's Multimedia World site, is Music Sculptor. This program installs a virtual keyboard on your computer, allowing you to create MIDI files without external hardware.

As you probably know, there are oodles of sound files floating around the Web for the grabbing. The "pure of heart" will understand that just because you can grab a sound file off the Web doesn't mean you are necessarily licensed to use it on your site (or anywhere). Be sure to check for licensing information on Web sites that offer sound and multimedia goodies.

An extraordinary resource for classical MIDI renditions is the Classical MIDI Archives, located at *http://www.prs.net/midi.html* (see Figure 5-2).

You'll find 1,000 .wav files on tap at *http://www.aristosoft.com/asoft.htm*. This archive includes sound bytes of the voices of past and present officers of the starship Enterprise, as well as the winding down monologue of that digital maniac, HAL2000.

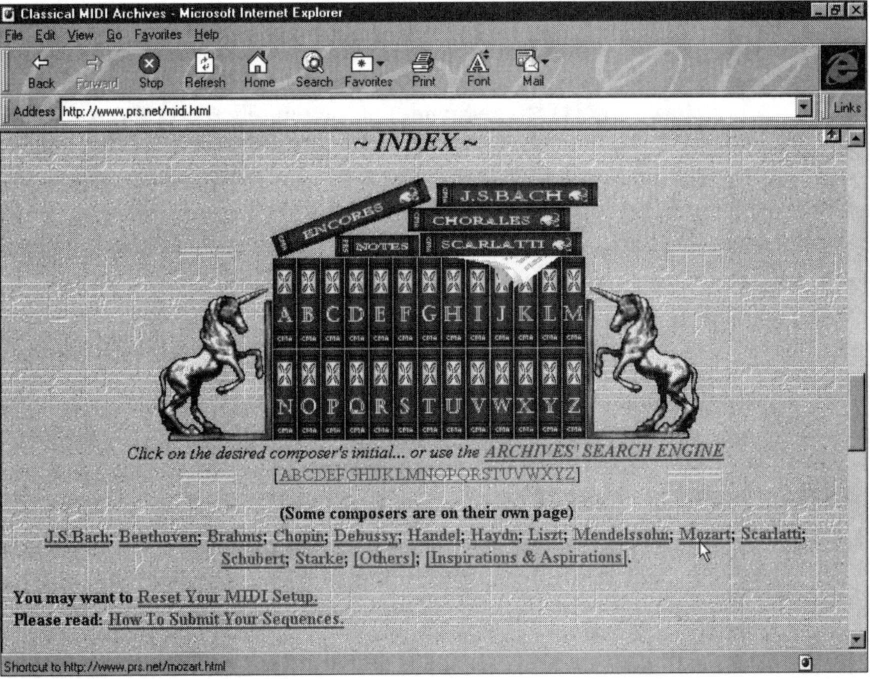

Figure 5-2: You name it, if it's classical you can probably find it at the Classical MIDI archives (copyright 1996 PRS Corporation — by permission).

Including Sounds on Web Pages

Sound files are included as hyperlinks in HTML pages. This means including the location of the sound file as the argument of the **href** parameter of the <A> tag. For example:

```
<A href="quit.wav">Play Goodbye</A>
```

If you wish, you can include an icon in the link in the normal fashion:

```
<A href="quit.wav">
<IMG src="goodbye.gif">
Play Goodbye</A>
```

It's normal Web etiquette to include information on file size if the sound in question is large. Users should have the option of not downloading something if it will take too long. For example:

```
<A href="quit.wav">
<IMG src="goodbye.gif">
Play Goodbye</A><BR>
Sultry Goodbye<BR>
33K Wav File<BR>
```

The <BGSOUND> Tag

An important HTML extension, unfortunately restricted to Explorer, is the <BGSOUND> tag. This tag automatically plays a sound in the background when the HTML document is loaded in Explorer. It represents the easiest and cleanest way of integrating audio into Web pages.

Here's an example:

```
<BGSOUND src="reggae.mid" loop=infinite>
```

If the **loop** parameter is set to infinite, the sound keeps playing in the background as long as the document is open. You can also set **loop** to an integer value representing the number of times the sound will play.

Video File Formats

The story with video is much the same as the story with sound on the Web. There are a few different video formats that have roughly comparable functionality and features. Explorer has more video integration than Navigator, but one way or another you need an application that can play the video file on the browser's system. And — even more with video than with sound files — there is currently only a fraction of the bandwidth available that it would take to truly bring the movies to the Web. A moving picture may be worth a thousand words, but not when it's downloading at 14.4 Kbps.

Table 5-2 lists the video formats commonly used on the Web.

Table 5-2 Video File Formats on the Web

File Extension	*Comments*
.avi	AVI is the native video file format for Windows. A player is included with Windows 95 and Windows NT. Players are available for UNIX and Mac.
.dir, .dcr, .dxr, .fgd	Macromedia Director streaming Shockwave files; see the later section "Streaming."
.mov, .qt	QuickTime, created by Apple Computer, is the native video format of the Mac. Players are available for Windows and UNIX; Windows users will need to install the QuickTime runtime library.
.mpg	MPEG video is related to the MPEG audio standard discussed earlier. MPEG2 is the highest quality of the video standards but is generally not appropriate for real-time web use because of bandwidth constraints.

QuickTime is available as a plug-in for Navigator and as a Windows run-time library. For more information, browse *http://www.quicktime.apple.com*. For general information and links about QuickTime, check out *http://www.astro.nwu.edu/lentz/mac/qt/*.

You can find MPEG resources, tips, and viewers at *http://www.mpeg.org/index.html/*. The movie "Toy Story" was created using MPEG. You can have a look at some clips on the Web at *http://www.disney.com/toystory/*.

Rene Guerror's "List of Internet Tools, Browsers and Viewers" contains a comprehensive catalog of video viewers ready for download (as well as information on the fraternity Mr. Guerror belongs to). His URL is *http://pilot.msu.edu/user/heinric6/tools.htm*.

Including Video on Web Pages

You include video files in Web pages the same way you include sound files — that is, using the **href** parameter of an anchor tag. There are two caveats:

- Always include links to appropriate viewers.
- Don't ever, ever start a video file download without warning the user about the size of the file.

Most quality video is simply too large to be handled in any way other than downloading "on the side" and playing off a local hard drive.

Streaming

Streaming is a technique that has been developed for delivering continuous video and high-quality sound over the Web. So you don't have to wait for an entire, huge file to download, streamed files are sent down — and played — a piece at a time. However, streaming is still not a panacea for slothful sluggishness and general molasses-type speed of sound and video on the Web. As Macromedia's documentation notes:

"Delivery speed limits the size of movies because most users will wait only a brief time for a movie to download. Within the next few years, new technologies will dramatically increase access speeds to the Internet. As the new technologies become widely available, the limits imposed by the current technology will no longer be an issue."

The sooner the better, say I! In the meantime, if you wish to stream your video or sound so that it appears continuous to browsers, you'll have to use special platform extensions.

Macromedia's Shockwave is the leading platform for the delivery of streaming multimedia on the Web. For more information, browse *http://www.macromediea.com/shockwave/*.

Progressive Network's RealAudio technology can serve up continuous streamed FM-quality sound. For more information, visit *http://www.realaudio.com*.

Note that in either case you have to have plenty of bandwidth at the server end, install proprietary server software to serve up the stream, and make players available for the different browsers. (Normally, players are available for free download, while servers must be licensed.) That exception is if you steal that bandwidth, as I showed you how to do earlier in this chapter in the section on "Borrowing Bandwidth."

Summary

Full-featured rich audio and video are not yet ready for prime time on the Web. But it's only a matter of time and bandwidth. As the Web continues to move from an information-based medium to an experience-based medium, multimedia delivery will become more and more important.

In the meantime, as a web developer, you need to understand the available options, and work arounds.

This chapter included material on

- Producing multimedia-like effects without using video
- Borrowing bandwidth
- The <BGSOUND> tag
- Sound file types on the Web
- Video file types on the Web
- Including sound and video in web applications
- Streaming multimedia from a server

Chapter 6

Adding the Third Dimension Using Virtual Reality

"Between two worlds life hovers like a star,
'Twixt night and morn, upon the horizon's verge."

— George Gordon, Lord Byron (from *Don Juan*)

The topic of "adding the third dimension" can be as prosaic as adding video to a Web site (see Chapter 5, "Multimedia and Sound on the Web"). You can also use three-dimensional rendering to make complex technical visuals clearer. But the truly exciting aspect of adding the third dimension to the Web lies in the concept of *virtual reality*. Virtual reality is the stuff of dreams and science fiction, cyberpunk and William Gibson, and the holodeck suite on the Starship Enterprise. Conceptually, virtual reality has nothing to do with three-dimensional rendering — other than the fact that it is difficult to induce the illusion of reality without the presence of three dimensions. The concept behind virtual reality "worlds" is that users interact with them as though they were interacting with a "real world" they could move around and manipulate. Obviously, virtual reality has not yet come of age on the Web. But it is only a matter of time.

Fully functional VRML (Virtual Reality Modeling Language) worlds do exist on the Web. For example, Figure 6-1 shows a scene from a virtual reality murder mystery game (*http://www.murdermystery.com*). How much the user can manipulate a given VRML world varies, but all VRML implementations attempt to convey an experience that feels much closer to three-dimensional living than normally viewing a computer screen.

Today, collaborative games give users the chance to play against each other, or in teams, strung across the Web. Some sites are virtual worlds in which browsers can pick an *avatar* to represent themselves and interact with other avatars.

Inside Scoop

VRML is a text-based markup language used to represent virtual worlds that has now entered its second generation. The basic difference between VRML 1.0 and VRML 2.0 is that VRML 1.0 describes a static three-dimensional world. VRML 2.0 worlds are interactive, permitting users to manipulate the objects in them.

Figure 6-1: In virtual reality worlds, the user can manipulate the scenes she is viewing. (Site shown reproduced with the permission of Murder Mystery Weekend, Inc.)

You can think of VRML as a three-dimensional version of HTML. VRML files can be viewed in special browsers — or in HTML browsers, such as the latest versions of Netscape's Navigator and Microsoft's Internet Explorer, equipped with VRML extensions.

Developers should be interested in virtual reality. In the future, the ability to browse VRML sites may well be as important as the ability to browse HTML is today. Do not underestimate how quickly virtual reality worlds may become a widespread component on the Web.

I truly believe that, within ten years, users will be "jacked-in" to the Web using a VR headset, surfing virtual reality sites that have a high degree of verisimilitude.

Applications such as technical equipment training can make good use of VRML. Three-dimensional tools vendors have realized that top corporations are open to creating virtual worlds — as long as the term "virtual reality," which seems too frivolous for corporate use, is avoided. Corporate applications that make use of virtual reality today include

- Three-dimensional design (such as viewing an airplane, automobile, or factory before it is built)
- Three-dimensional interfaces that allow users to more quickly assimilate complex data

- Training systems
- Technical support (allowing demonstrations of how things are physically done)
- Applications that allow users to "try" before they buy on the Web — for example, examining the way furniture would look in a room

Silicon Graphics (SGI)

Developers at Silicon Graphics Incorporated (SGI) are largely responsible for the emergence of virtual reality languages. SGI's Web site, located at *http//www.sgi.com*, features a great deal of information about virtual reality, as well as a changing gallery of visuals created using virtual reality techniques.

SGI's Open Inventor — a language that is used to describe three-dimensional objects — helped lead to the creation of VRML 1.0. SGI's continued work in the virtual reality area includes their Onyx RealityEngine. Although you can experience "worlds" created with the Onyx RealityEngine using some standard Web browsers (and extensions), you cannot use this virtual reality authoring system under Windows.

Moving Worlds is SGI's extension to VRML 1.0 that was adapted as one of the primary roots of VRML 2.0.

CosmoPlayer is SGI's VRML 2.0 client for Windows 95 and Windows NT. You can download it from *http://vrml.sgi.com/cosmoplayer/*. There's information on the Cosmo VRML 2.0 SDK at *http://www.sgi.com/products/cosmo3D.*

VRML Resources

So far as there is a standards organization for VRML, it is the VRML Architecture Group (VAG). VAG is responsible for soliciting specification proposals and for polling the VRML community in order to achieve a consensus.

The best sources for in-depth information on virtual reality and VRML include

- The VRML Repository, which is maintained by the San Diego SuperComputer Center, *http:/sdsc.edu/vrml/*.
- The VRML Forum, *http://vag.vrml.org/www-vrml/*.
- Netscape's site, *http://www.netscape.com*. Netscape appears to have a substantial interest in bringing virtual worlds to the Web. Their site contains a great deal of information on VRML, including guides and introductions. The best bet is to search their site for "VRML."

Embedding VRML Files into Web Pages

VRML files have an extension of .wrl — for example, *startrek.wrl*. (Mnemonically, .wrl is short for "world." You may also see .wrz virtual reality files, which are compressed .wrl files that virtual reality players can decompress automatically.)

Once you have created and saved your virtual VRML world, you can include it in an HTML page using the **src** parameter of the <EMBED> tag. For example:

```
<EMBED src="startrek.wrl" width=200 height=240>
```

Using <EMBED> is much like using the <IMG> tag to include an image in a Web page.

The alternative to embedding the .wrl virtual world file is, of course, to browse (or "play") it directly in a VRML player (or a browser equipped with a VRML plug-in).

The Structure of a VRML Document

Just as HTML pages are structured text meant to be "played" in an HTML browser, VRML pages are text files that can be decoded by a virtual reality browser.

Every VRML 2.0 file begins with a line that identifies the document as VRML 2.0:

```
#VRML V2.0 utf8
```

This indicates that the document is a version 2.0 VRML file using UTF-8 text string encoding as specified by the ISO 10646 standard. (The UTF-8 standard is a variant of Unicode.)

You'll find more information on UTF-8 encoding at *http://www.iso.ch/cate/d18741.html*.

Here's the first line of a VRML 1.0 file:

```
#VRML V1.0 ascii
```

Although UTF-8 encoding is less familiar than ASCII text encoding, the first 128 ASCII characters can be used transparently under UTF-8.

Understanding VRML 1.0 Code

VRML objects are called *nodes*. There are 36 kinds of nodes in VRML 1.0, generally organized into three groups. Hierarchically arranged nodes make up a *scene graph*. The appearance of nodes in a scene graph is called a *state*.

Comments in VRML

Lines beginning with a pound symbol (#) are comments in VRML 1.0 and VRML 2.0. Except for file headers, VRML players ignore everything in the line following the #.

Table 6-1 shows the overall categories of nodes available in VRML 1.0. Most but not all kinds of nodes fall into these categories.

Table 6-1 Types of VRML Nodes

Node Type	*What It's Used For*
Shape nodes	Used to describe actual geometry
Property nodes	Used to modify geometry
Grouping nodes	Cause groups of objects — defined with shape and property nodes — to be modified as one object

Each node can have up to four pieces of information associated with it:

- The node type
- The node name
- A set of fields
- Sub (or child) nodes

The Separator Node

The most important grouping node is the separator node. Separator nodes are used to encapsulate the modifying effect of property nodes. In other words, shape nodes within a separator node can be modified by a property node within that separator, but shapes external to the separator cannot.

The syntax of a separator node is

```
Separator {
    encapsulated nodes
}
```

VRML Units of Measure

Table 6-2 shows the units of measurement available in VRML 1.0.

Table 6-2 VRML Units of Measurement

Thing Being Measured	*Unit*
Distance and size	Meters, using a 3-D coordinate system.
Angles	Radians (1 radian is approximately 57 degrees). For example, *cutOffAngle 0.348.*
Other things *shininess 0.2.*	Percentage, expressed as a fraction of 1. For example,

Predefined Shapes

Predefined VRML shape nodes are called *primitives*. There are four primitives: cube, sphere, cone, and cylinder. You don't need to use VRML code to list parameters and values for primitives. Default values are assumed for any primitive parameter that you omit. Listing 6-1 shows the defaults.

Listing 6-1: Default parameters and values for VRML primitives

```
#VRML V1.0 ascii
Separator {
   Cube {
      width   2
      height  2
      depth   2
   }
   Sphere {
      radius 1
   }
   Cone {
      parts           ALL
      bottomRadius    1
      height          2
   }
   Cylinder {
      parts           ALL
      radius          1
      height          2
   }
}
```

The **parts** parameter determines which part of the shape is displayed. A cone can have **parts** values of ALL, SIDES, or BOTTOM. A cylinder supports parts values of ALL, SIDES, BOTTOM, or TOP.

Other Shapes

There are other shape nodes to create scenes, including

- AsciiText
- IndexedFaceSet
- IndexLineSet
- PointSet

Material

Shapes not only have to be outlined, they must also be filled-in — that is, they must have "material." The material property node specifies the color properties of shapes. You can specify four types of color using an RGB color notation. You specify each RGB triplet on a scale between 0 and 1. The color types are

- ambientColor
- diffuseColor
- specularColor
- emissiveColor

In addition, you can specify shininess and transparency (using a 0 to 1 scale).

For example, the following VRML code specifies a blue cone (as shown in black and white in Figure 6-2):

```
#VRML V1.0 ascii
Separator {
   Material {
      emissiveColor   0 0 1 #blue
      shininess        0.2
      transparency    0
   }
   Cone {
      parts        SIDES
      bottomRadius 3
      height 6
   }
}
```

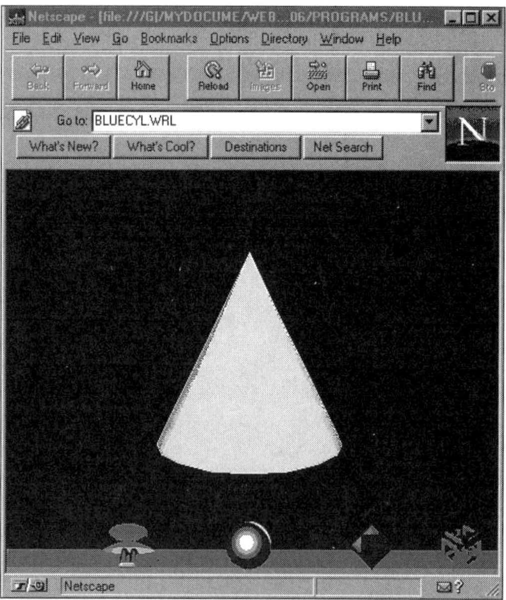

Figure 6-2: You use material nodes to "fill-in" the appearance of shapes.

Textures

The easiest way to apply texture to the surface of a shape is to use a Texture2 node, which wraps a VRML shape in a texture contained in a referenced file. For example, the following VRML code creates a cube with argyle-patterned sides (using the argyle.bmp bitmap file that ships with Windows):

```
#VRML V1.0 ascii
Separator {
   Texture2 {
      filename "argyle.bmp"
   }
   Cube {
      width   4
      height  4
      depth   4
   }

}
```

Just as it is best to add images to an HTML file with a full URL, it's a good idea to add patterns to virtual reality nodes using the file's HTTP identifier — for example, *http://www.myserver.com/argyle.bmp*.

Transformations and Translations

Translation nodes translate an object along an axis. Rotation nodes rotate an object along an axis. Scale nodes scale an object. For example, the following

VRML code produces a sideways cone sitting on top of an upright cone (an effect kind of like a 1950's automotive side mirror, as shown in Figure 6-3):

```
#VRML V1.0 ascii
Separator {
   Translation {
      translation 0 -2 0
   }
   Cone {
      parts          ALL
      bottomRadius   1
      height         3
   }
}
Separator {
   Rotation {
      rotation 0 0 1 1.4
   }
   Cone {
      parts          ALL
      bottomRadius   2
      height         4
   }
}
```

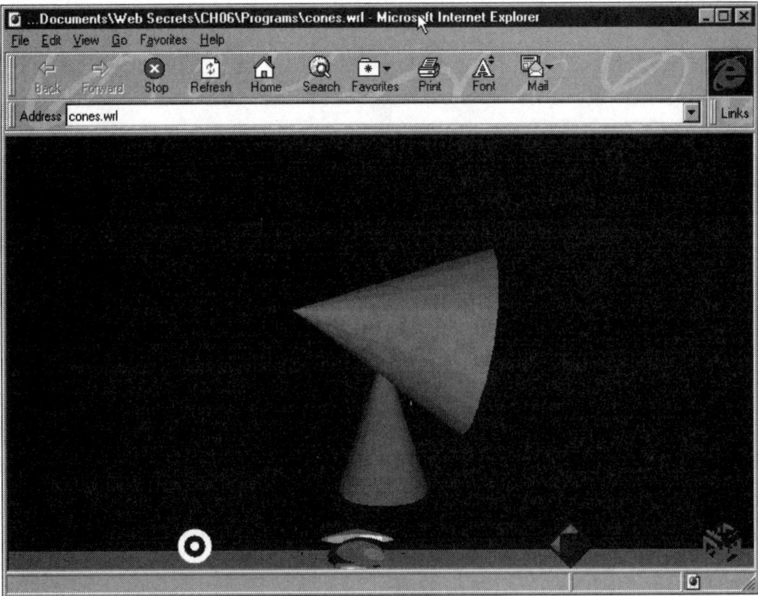

Figure 6-3: You can use translation and rotation nodes to orient VRML objects.

You can combine translation, rotation, and scaling in one Transform node. As a matter of VRML code style, and in the interest of clarity, it is often better to stick to individual-purpose nodes than to combine transformations in one transform.

Instancing Nodes

You can name and define groups of nodes. This technique lets you reuse nodes that you create, potentially saving you a great deal of time. Virtual worlds of even moderate complexity contain many nodes, which are often quite similar. By building a world from blocks used repeatedly, you can make complex virtual worlds somewhat manageable.

The syntax of instancing and then reusing a group of nodes goes like this:

```
# First define it
DEF myInstance
Separator {
   Group of Nodes
}
#Then use it
Separator {
   USE myInstance
}
```

Inlines

You can use the WWWInline node to let one virtual world include another virtual world. As an example, consider a virtual world gallery with pictures on the wall. As the user gets closer, the pictures acquire more definition. Finally, the user goes through the picture, which is now a WWWInline node, and into another world.

Property Nodes

Property nodes tell shapes how to draw themselves. Texture2 and translations, described earlier, are property nodes, as are the lighting nodes described next.

One property node you should know about is the Info node, which you can use to provide custom information to the virtual reality player. For example, if you define an Info node named Viewer, SGI's CosmoPlayer will launch the world that includes the node in the viewer specified by the node. This code launches the world in Examiner mode (rather than Walk mode):

```
#VRML V1.0 ascii
Separator {
   DEF Viewer Info {
      string "examiner"
   }
nodes
}
```

Lights and Cameras

Lights and cameras are very important property nodes used to create illumination sources and viewpoints.

Lights

"Let there be light," in the words of the Old Testament. Without light, there are no worlds to explore, virtual or otherwise.

By default, VRML players will add a light source. Usually, this will be a DirectionalLight from straight ahead (think of it as the keyboard's viewpoint). But in any but the simplest VRML scenarios, you will want to provide your own light sources.

The VRML light nodes are DirectionalLight, PointLight, and SpotLight. For example, DirectionalLight creates a light source that illuminates shapes that are hierarchically in its range. The DirectionalLight node that follows illuminates the two cones created earlier in this chapter along the X axis of the world, as shown in Figure 6-4.

```
#VRML V1.0 ascii
Separator {
   DirectionalLight {
       on                TRUE
       intensity         1
       color             1 1 1
       direction         0 0 -1
   }
   Separator {
      Translation {
         translation 0 -2 0
      }
      Cone {
         parts           ALL
         bottomRadius    1
         height          3
      }

   }
   Separator {
      Rotation {
         rotation 0 0 1 1.4
      }
      Cone {
         parts           ALL
         bottomRadius    2
         height          4
      }
   }
}
```

Figure 6-4: You can use light nodes to determine how your "worlds" are illuminated.

Cameras

A *viewpoint* is the position from which a virtual world is seen. (Horrors! A definition of a technical term that is intuitively obvious!) A viewpoint is defined by *a scene graph*, which, as you'll recall from the beginning of this chapter, is a hierarchical collection of nodes.

The simple examples in this chapter have presented virtual worlds from the default viewpoint, also called the *entry view*. The entry view is the appearance of a world as it is rendered in a VRML player if no viewpoint has been defined. To get other views, you would have to use the VRML player's tools to manually "walk" around the world.

Although two camera nodes — PerspectiveCamera and OrthographicCamera — are included in the VRML 1.0 specification, only one, PerspectiveCamera, is generally recognized by VRML players.

Listing 6-2 shows how to use a Switch node to add front, back, side, top, and bottom viewpoints to the two cones shown earlier in the chapter (Figures 6-3, 6-4).

Inside Scoop

The Switch node, a grouping node, is used for flow control. It is the VRML analog to a Select...Case statement.

When the file shown in Listing 6-2 is viewed in a VRML player, the mechanism for switching viewpoints will show the predefined viewpoints included in the Switch statement. (In CosmoPlayer, there is a context menu for switching viewpoints.)

Figure 6-5 shows the bottom view of the two cones. To get there, as you'll find out if you click between viewpoints, brings "action" to lights and camera!

Listing 6-2: Switching viewpoints

```
#VRML V1.0 ascii
Separator {
   Separator { # viewpoints
    DEF Cameras Switch {
        whichChild  0
        DEF "Front" PerspectiveCamera {
            position    0 0 7
        }
        DEF "Back" PerspectiveCamera {
            position    0 0 -7
            orientation 0 1 0   3.14
        }
        DEF "Side" PerspectiveCamera {
            position    7 0 0
            orientation 0 1 0   1.57
        }
        DEF "Top" PerspectiveCamera {
            position    0 10 0
            orientation 1 0 0   -1.57
        }
        DEF "Bottom" PerspectiveCamera {
```

```
            position    0 -10 0
            orientation 1 0 0   1.57
        }
    }
  }
  Separator {
     Translation {
        translation 0 -2 0
     }
     Cone {
        parts           ALL
        bottomRadius    1
        height          3
     }

  }
  Separator {
     Rotation {
        rotation 0 0 1 1.4
     }
     Cone {
     parts          ALL
     bottomRadius   2
     height         4
     }
  }
}
```

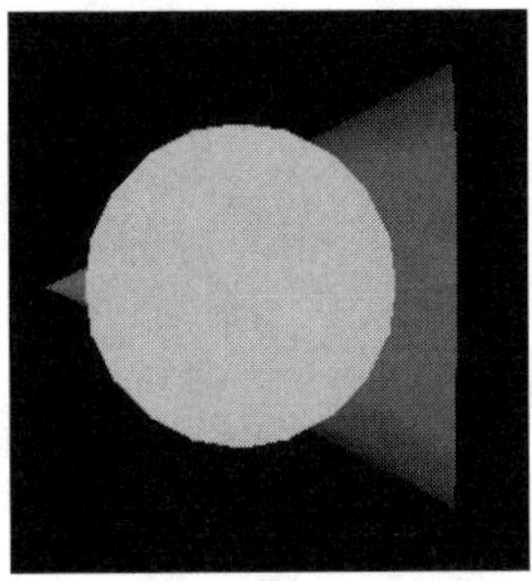

Figure 6-5: A "bottom" viewpoint has been added to the two cones.

Level of Detail

You use the Level of Detail (LOD) node to specify a set of ranges and child nodes. If the user is far away from a virtual object you can have it display as a primitive (for example, a cube). As the user gets closer to the object, you can have more detail and texture appear (this is often accomplished using the WWWInline node).

LOD nodes implemented in this fashion are used to reflect hierarchies within worlds. The objects in the room are presented schematically (using VRML primitives). As the user gets close to each object in the room, the object takes on individuality and definition.

VRML 2.0

VRML 2.0 is an extension of VRML 1.0 in the sense that VRML 2.0 players are designed to play VRML 1.0 files, and more. Most importantly, VRML provides the possibility of dynamism: user interaction with the virtual objects.

There is a fair amount of new object terminology in VRML 2.0 compared to VRML 1.0, although the basic structure has conceptually stayed the same. (For details, refer to the VRML Repository mentioned early in this chapter; it's at *http:/sdsc.edu/vrml.*)

Web developers will want to know that *program scripts*, written in Java, JavaScript, and other languages, can be added to VRML 2.0 worlds.

Adding JavaScript Functions to VRML 2.0 Files

It's easiest to see how this works with JavaScript. JavaScript functions are called when a *script node* receives an event. (This is analogous to adding a JavaScript function call to an HTML event, such as the <Body onLoad> event.) The script node specifies a URL containing the JavaScript code.

In some cases, JavaScript functions can edit nodes. You can use this feature to create dynamic worlds, with changes brought about by the user (through events she has triggered).

Summary

Virtual worlds are fun to create, using VRML, and fun to play with. Although the course of life in today's virtual worlds can be a bit bumpy, there is no doubt that they are an important part of the future on the Web.

Considering that the Web as we know it is only a few years old, it's reasonable to assume that virtual worlds will become common in the next few years. It's also pretty reasonable to assume that VRML will be as important to virtual worlds on the Web as HTML is to today's two-dimensional sites. In other words, VRML is an important technology helping to shape the future of the Web.

This chapter has given you enough information to get a feeling for how VRML works. In addition, it has explained

- Where to find more information on VRML
- How to obtain CosmoPlayer, SGI's VRML 2.0 32-bit Windows client
- How to create simple worlds of your own
- How to embed virtual reality files in Web pages
- The structure of a VRML document
- Commonly used VRML nodes
- How to group VRML nodes
- VRML 2.0 extensions

Chapter 7

FrontPage 97 for Developers

"Roses and raindrops and whiskers on kittens,
Door bells and sleigh bells and warm woolen mittens,
Bright paper packages tied up with string,
These are a few of my favorite things."

— Rogers & Hammerstein, *The Sound of Music*

FrontPage 97 is web publishing software that combines a WYSIWYG ("what you see is what you get") HTML editor with Web site maintenance tools. In other words, FrontPage allows Web authors to easily create and maintain entire Web sites and also to design individual Web pages. This extremely powerful set of programs is published by Microsoft, based on software originally acquired from Vermeer Technologies, Inc.

In this chapter I'll explain how FrontPage works. Next, I'll explore advanced features that developers should know about. Topics covered in this chapter include

- An introduction to FrontPage 97 Explorer and Editor
- Understanding the FrontPage Server Extensions
- Using the FrontPage 97 Software Developer's Kit (SDK)
- Customizing FrontPage 97
- Creating your own FrontPage 97 WebBots

Introducing FrontPage 97

Technically, the FrontPage suite of programs consists of a number of OLE client/server applications. The server portion of FrontPage is known as the FrontPage Server Extensions and is explained in the next section of this chapter. In addition to the FrontPage Server Extensions, the suite includes a Personal Web Server application. The primary purpose of the Personal Web Server is to let you create and browse a Web site on a single computer. In other words, it is intended as an authoring aid rather than a production Web server.

The FrontPage 97 client applications are described further in this section. They consist of

- FrontPage 97 Explorer
- FrontPage 97 Editor
- To Do List

You can use ActiveX programming techniques to customize the FrontPage 97 client programs. Applications that customize the FrontPage clients use FrontPage OLE automation APIs to interact with these programs, as described later in this chapter.

Figure 7-1 shows the FrontPage 97 architecture in overview.

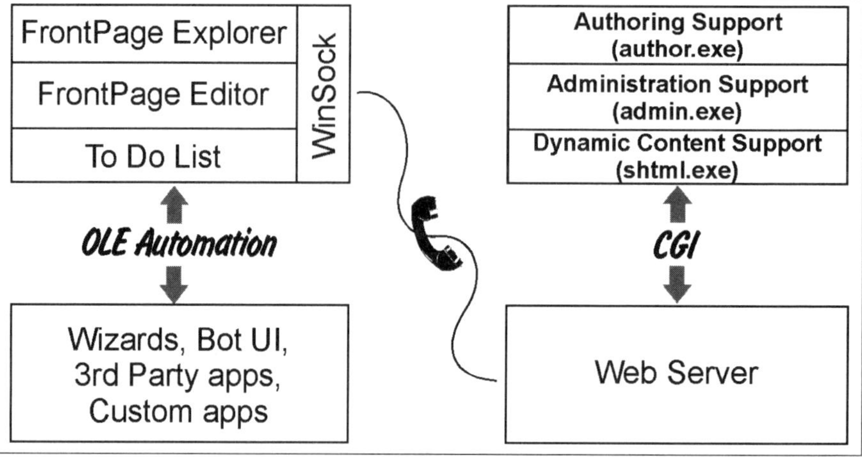

Figure 7-1: FrontPage 97 includes server applications — the FrontPage Server Extensions — and client applications — Explorer, Editor, and To Do List.

FrontPage 97 Explorer

The FrontPage 97 Explorer is used to provide an overview of the user's Web site, as shown in Figures 7-2 and 7-3. (In FrontPage 97 parlance, a Web site is called "a Web.")

FrontPage 97 Explorer shows two views of a Web site:

- Folder view shows the directory and file structure of the Web site (Figure 7-2).
- Hyperlink view shows the structure of the links in the Web site (Figure 7-3).

No matter which view you select, FrontPage 97 Explorer automatically updates the picture of your Web site in real time as you make changes. This is a great convenience and saves a great deal of time.

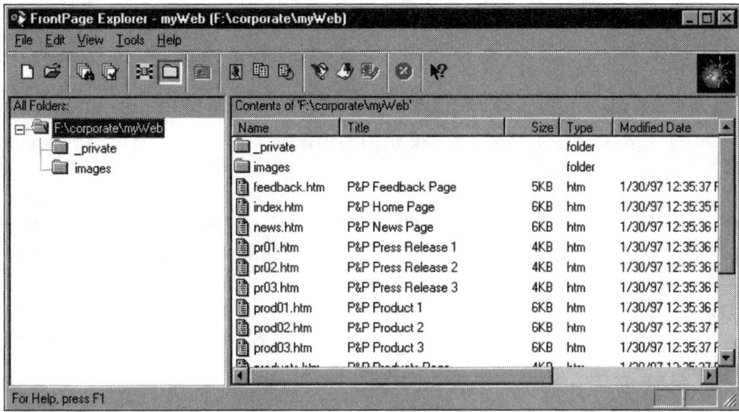

Figure 7-2: In Folder view, FrontPage 97 Explorer shows the directory and file structure of a Web site.

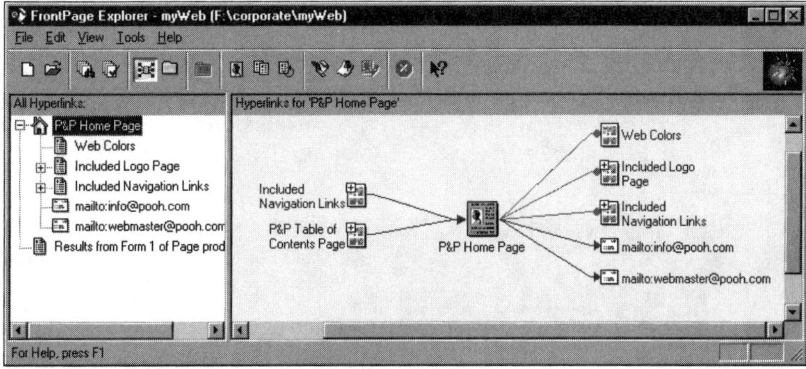

Figure 7-3: In Hyperlink view, FrontPage 97 Explorer shows the links contained in a Web site.

Using FrontPage 97 Explorer you can

- Show all the hyperlinks in a Web site
- Automatically fix links to a Web page when that document is moved or renamed
- Verify that all internal and external hyperlinks are valid
- Fix all occurrences of a specific broken link
- Use Wizards to easily create new Web sites based on templates

Conceptually, you can think of FrontPage 97 Explorer as treating an entire Web site as one extended "document" in some respects. This means that you can use Explorer's tools to perform an operation on an entire Web site at once. For example, you can use Explorer to spell check an entire Web site in one fell swoop.

In addition, FrontPage 97 Explorer includes site administration tools, as outlined next.

Site Administration

FrontPage 97 Explorer allows you to perform important overall site administration tasks.

You can use the Copy Web command to copy an entire Web site — including all Web pages and image files — from a local computer to a computer used to host a Web site. This command works in both directions: You can copy the Web site from a host back to a local computer. This feature is a great convenience when you are maintaining a Web site that is hosted remotely by an Internet Service Provider (ISP).

ISPs usually have higher speed connections to the Internet than individuals or small businesses. It usually makes sense to place Web sites on a computer maintained by an ISP rather than paying for a high-speed Internet hookup. ISPs that perform this service are said to be "hosting" the Web site. A Web host is sometimes referred to in FrontPage 97 documentation as a Web Presence Provider (WPP).

The other primary administrative task that can be accomplished in FrontPage 97 Explorer is setting permissions to access and change elements of a FrontPage 97 Web. To open the Permissions dialog, shown in Figure 7-4, choose Permissions from the Tools menu.

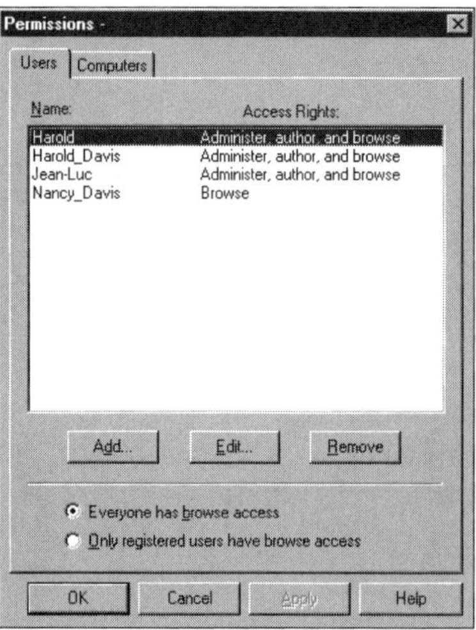

Figure 7-4: You can use the Permissions dialog to establish access rights to elements of a FrontPage Web.

It's important to understand that a FrontPage Web can be accessed in two ways: locally, using a file structure saved on a local hard drive, and across the Internet using TCP/IP protocols. The Permissions dialog is only available for FrontPage 97 Webs that have been opened in the latter fashion — that is, using Internet access.

Using the Permissions dialog, you can control

- The list of *end users*—that is, people who are allowed to browse the FrontPage Web
- *Authors*, those who can add, delete, and change elements of the FrontPage Web
- *Administrators*, people who can add and delete end users, authors, and other administrators

FrontPage 97 Editor

The FrontPage 97 Editor is a WYSIWYG Web page editor. As you can see from Figure 7-5, FrontPage 97 Editor looks a lot like Microsoft Word — with perhaps a bit of Internet Explorer thrown in. In fact, the FrontPage 97 Editor is well integrated in many ways with the Office 97 suite.

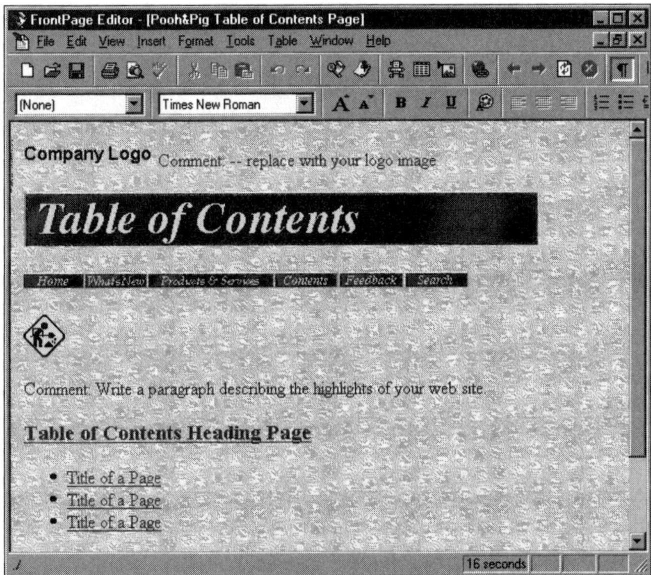

Figure 7-5: You can use the FrontPage 97 Editor to edit individual Web pages.

The real point of the FrontPage 97 Editor is that it lets you do advanced Web page design without bothering with HTML codes. Of course, if you want to get down and dirty with HTML, you can: by selecting HTML from the View menu. Figure 7-6 shows the straight HTML editor that opens when you make this selection.

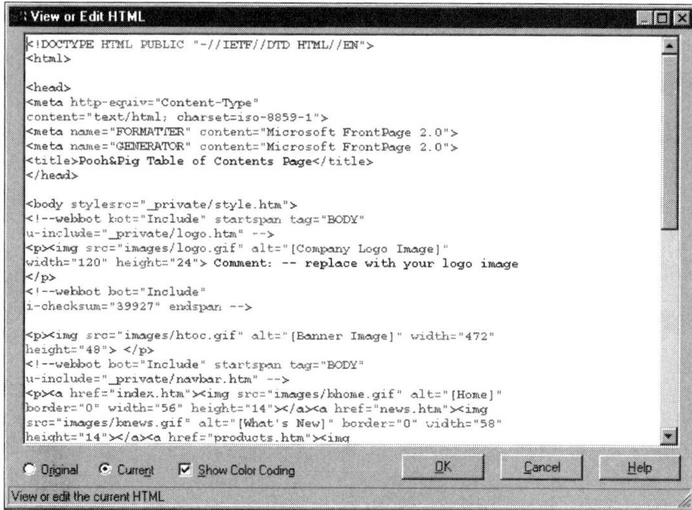

Figure 7-6: You can use the View or Edit HTML dialog to edit a Web page's straight HTML code.

Although a Web page in FrontPage 97 looks pretty close to the way it will look in a Web browser, you may wish to get an even closer look. By selecting Preview in Browser from the Editor's File menu, you can look at your Web page in any browser installed on your system. Using the Preview in Browser dialog — shown in Figure 7-7 — you can even select the screen resolution for the browser preview.

Facilities in the FrontPage 97 Editor allow you to

- Quickly insert and format text (a selection of fonts that were created with the Web in mind comes with FrontPage)
- Create a consistent look throughout a Web site
- Easily insert graphics using the library of images that comes with FrontPage (or your own images)
- Create and manipulate frames using a special Wizard
- Add a consistent toolbar across all pages in a FrontPage Web (the graphic for the toolbar can be created once and referred to in each page that uses the toolbar)
- Easily create custom image maps and hot spots
- Add colored or tiled backgrounds
- Add sounds or multimedia clips
- Implement marquees
- Quickly create and format tables (included nested tables)

- Insert Active content, meaning WebBots (described in a moment), ActiveX controls, VBScript, JavaScript, and Java applets
- And pretty much anything else you can dream of

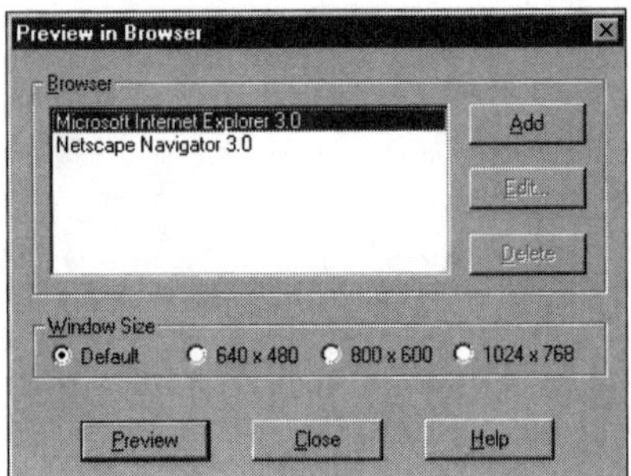

Figure 7-7: Using the Preview in Browser dialog, you can view a Web page in any installed browser at a variety of resolutions.

For a good introduction to using FrontPage 97 to design Web pages and sites, take a look at *FrontPage 97: Visual Quickstart Guide* by Phyllis Davis from Peachpit Press.

Wizards and WebBots

Wizards and WebBots, and bright colored backgrounds, these are a few of my favorite things. (Also, snitzels, packages tied with string, and the rest of it....)

Wizards

Wizards are ActiveX component applications that guide users through a set of tasks using the familiar Wizard interface.

Web Wizards are Wizards relating to a FrontPage 97 Web site as a whole — such as the Wizard that helps you to create a new Web site based upon a particular style.

Page Wizards are Wizards that help users achieve tasks related to a single Web page. Page Wizards are opened in the FrontPage 97 Editor. For example, the Frequently Asked Questions (FAQ) Page Wizard helps users create a standardized FAQ sheet.

Although FrontPage comes with a great many Wizards, you might want to create a custom Wizard. Custom Wizards could be used by a group that is collaboratively working on Web site design and maintenance. Later in this chapter, under "Writing Applications to Customize FrontPage 97," I'll show you how to create your own Wizards.

WebBots

WebBots are programs that users can add to a Web page using the FrontPage Editor. Often, WebBots are used to include expanded content in a Web page.

You open the Insert WebBot Component dialog — shown in Figure 7-8 — by choosing WebBot from the Editor's Insert menu.

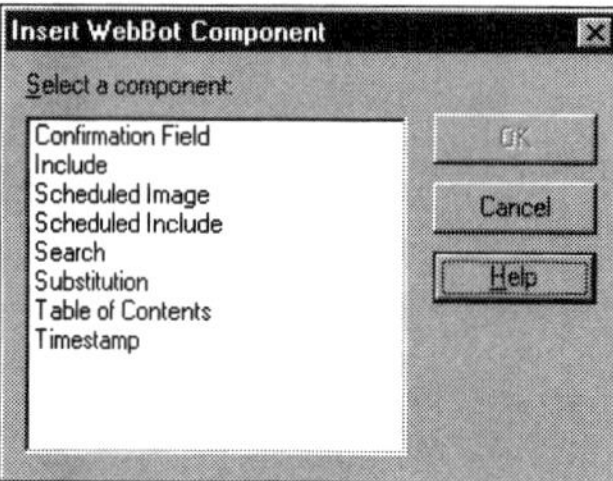

Figure 7-8: FrontPage 97 comes with a number of WebBots, which are programs that you can add to a Web page.

The WebBot components listed in Figure 7-8 are all installed when you install FrontPage 97. They are

- Confirmation Field, which echoes data entered in a form field, and is intended to let users validate information they have entered.
- Include, which includes the contents of another Web page in the current page.
- Scheduled Image, which shows an image on a page, but only during a specified time period.
- Scheduled Include, which includes the contents of another Web page for the time period specified.
- Search, which returns a page providing full text-searching capability on your FrontPage Web. This WebBot component returns a page with hyperlinks to all pages matching the search criteria.
- Substitution, which expends to the value of a Web configuration or Page configuration variable.
- Table of Contents, which generates a TOC for your FrontPage Web, with hyperlinks to each page. The best part about this WebBot component is that it automatically updates the TOC when the contents of the Web changes.
- Timestamp, which expands to display the time and date the Web page it is on was last modified.

The specific action that the WebBot performs is specified using a WebBot Component Property dialog. Figure 7-9 shows the Properties dialog for a Scheduled Image component.

Using a programming language such as Visual Basic or Visual C++, it's quite easy to create your own FrontPage 97 WebBot components. I'll show you how to do this, and provide an example, later in this chapter in the section "Writing Applications to Customize FrontPage 97."

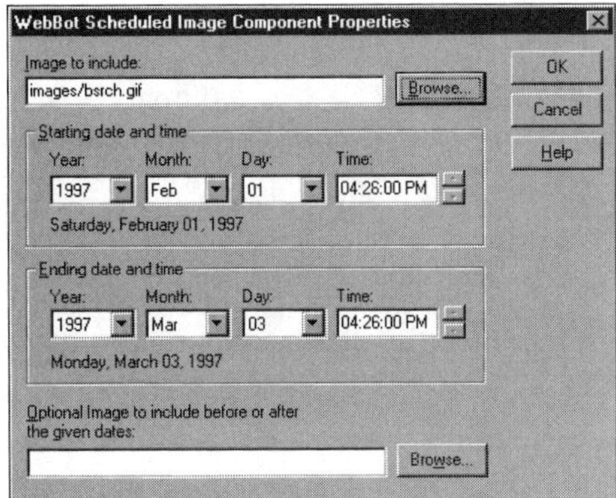

Figure 7-9: You can set the properties of a WebBot Component using the WebBot Component Properties dialog.

To Do List

The FrontPage To Do List is technically a separate ActiveX component application from either the FrontPage 97 Explorer or Editor. It maintains a list of items that must be completed before a Web site is finished. Figure 7-10 shows the initial To Do List generated for a Web created using New Web Wizard.

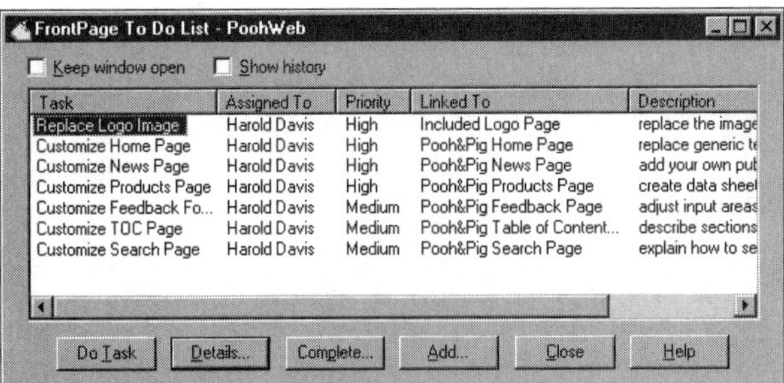

Figure 7-10: The FrontPage 97 To Do List includes items that you should take care of before your Web site is ready for prime time.

You can gain access to the To Do List from either the Explorer or Editor. In either case, you can manually add items to the list.

Inside Scoop

You can also programmatically manipulate To Do List items.

The FrontPage Server Extensions

The FrontPage Server Extensions consist of three compiled CGI programs — Author.Exe, Admin.Exe, and Shtml.Exe — placed in a specific directory structure on the web server.

You can download the latest version of the FrontPage Server Extensions from *http://www.microsoft.com/frontpage/*.

Table 7-1 shows the area of functionality of the three programs included in the Extensions.

Table 7-1 Purpose of Server Extension Programs

Program	*Purpose*
Author.Exe	Authoring, meaning uploading and downloading Web pages, updating the To Do List.
Admin.Exe	Administration, such as setting user, author, and administrator permissions.
Shtml.Exe	Dynamic content, such as WebBot components. ("Shtml" is short for "Smart HTML," FrontPage's name for HTML pages that contain WebBots.

FrontPage 97 Webs will not work correctly with servers that don't have the FrontPage Server Extensions installed.

The FrontPage Server Extensions are automatically installed when you install FrontPage Personal Web Server or Windows 95 Personal Web Server. The FrontPage Server Extensions can be installed with most commercial Web server software running under either Windows or UNIX, although in some cases it may take a little tweaking.

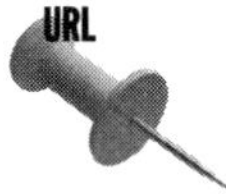

The FrontPage Web site, *http://www.microsoft.com/frontpage/*, maintains a comprehensive list of Independent Service Providers (ISPs) that host Web sites and support the FrontPage Server Extensions.

Writing Applications to Customize FrontPage 97

The FrontPage 97 Software Developer's Kit (SDK) contains tools and information that will help you customize FrontPage 97.

For example, Webtpml.Exe (Web Template Maker) is a Visual Basic program — complete with source code — located in the SDK's utility\webtmpl folder. This program allows you to make a template from an existing FrontPage

Web. Once the template has been created, users can create new Webs based on it. (Note that a FrontPage user can easily create a page template by saving a Web page as a template. But the FrontPage user has no tools without the SDK for creating a template for an entire Web.) Developers will probably be most interested in the ability to create Wizards and WebBots.

Creating Custom Wizards

FrontPage Wizards come in two flavors: Page Wizards typically load a page into the FrontPage Editor and Web Wizards typically load Web pages into FrontPage Explorer.

The Visual Basic 5 project saved on the companion CD-ROM as Animal.Vbp shows how to create a simple Page Wizard. I call it the "Animal" Wizard. All it does is create a Web page based on some user input.

Many of the utility routines used in the Animal Wizard are included in a file named Wizutil.Bas, which is provided by Microsoft as part of the FrontPage 97 SDK.

You open Page Wizards by choosing New from the FrontPage 97 Editor File menu. When the Editor loads, it reads templates and Wizards from folders beneath the FrontPage\Pages directory.

Each folder that has a .Tem extension becomes a template, and each folder that has a .Wiz extension becomes a Wizard. So the first step in creating the Animal Wizard is to create a folder named Pages\Animal.Wiz.

Both .Tem and .Wiz folders should contain a file with the same name as the folder and an .Inf extension. (For our Animal Wizard example, this file would be named Animal.Inf.) These Inf files are ASCII text files in the standard private profile (.Ini) format. They contain a title and description for the related template or Wizard, formatted as follows:

```
[info]
title=
decription=
```

In the case of a template, the folder — in addition to the Inf file — contains an HTML page, named like the folder in which it is contained. This HTML page is used as the template for new pages based on it. For example, the agenda template that ships with FrontPage 97 is located in a folder name Agenda.Tem that contains two files, Agenda.Inf and Agenda.Htm.

Wizard folders contain an executable rather than an HTML file. The executable includes the code that actually creates the Wizard's interface and interacts with FrontPage. Thus, the Animal Wizard is located in a folder named Animal.Wiz and contains two files, Animal.Exe and Animal.Inf. Although Animal.Exe is a compiled stand-alone Visual Basic 5 program, you could write a FrontPage Wizard in a number of other languages, including Delphi and Visual C++.

Animal.Inf contains the title and description of the Wizard:

```
[info]
title=Animal Page Wizard
description=Create an Animalistic welcome page for your Web. After
all, the talking animals of Oz and Narnia belong on the Web. Right?
```

Assuming that a program named Animal.Exe exists in the correct location (as described earlier), when you choose New from the FrontPage Editor's File menu, you'll find the Animal Page Wizard in the list of Templates and Wizards, along with the description from its Inf file, as shown in Figure 7-11.

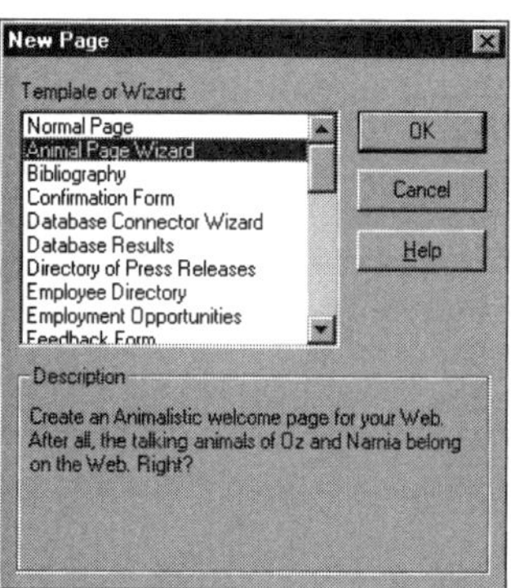

Figure 7-11: Page Wizard names and descriptions are retrieved from their Inf files.

The Animal Wizard consists of three panels. The first (Figure 7-12) is a welcome screen. The next Wizard panel solicits information about the appearance and contents of the page that is to be created, as shown in Figure 7-13. The final panel asks for a page title and name (URL), as shown in Figure 7-14.

When the user clicks on the Finish button on the final Wizard panel (shown in Figure 7-14), the Wizard creates a page based on the user's choices, as shown in Figure 7-15.

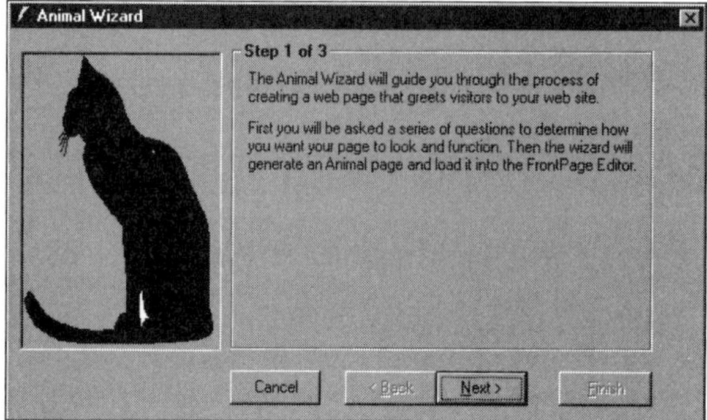

Figure 7-12: For many custom Wizards, the first panel is a welcome screen.

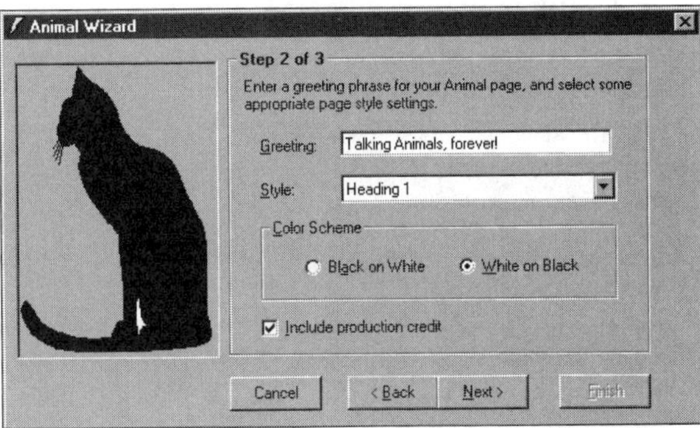

Figure 7-13: The second panel of the Animal Wizard is used to enter information about the page that will be created.

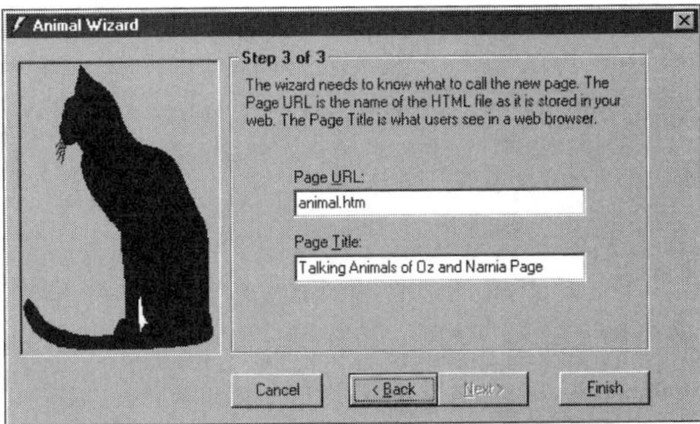

Figure 7-14: The third, and final, Wizard panel is used to name the page.

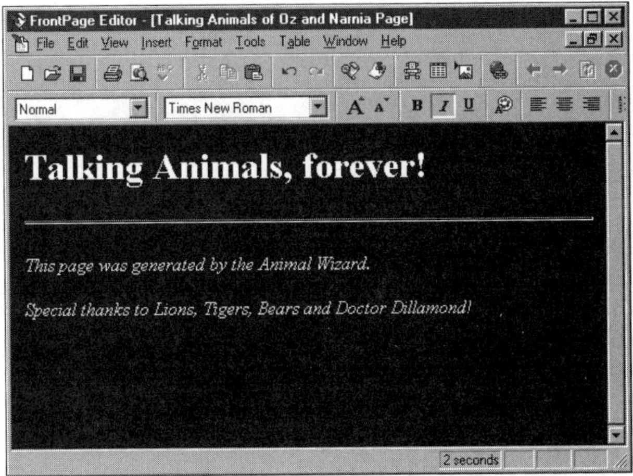

Figure 7-15: The Animal Wizard creates a Web page in the FrontPage 97 Editor using the user's choices in the Wizard.

When the time comes to save the page that the Animal Wizard has created in Front Page, the Page Title and URL selected in the Wizard are provided as default names, as shown in Figure 7-16.

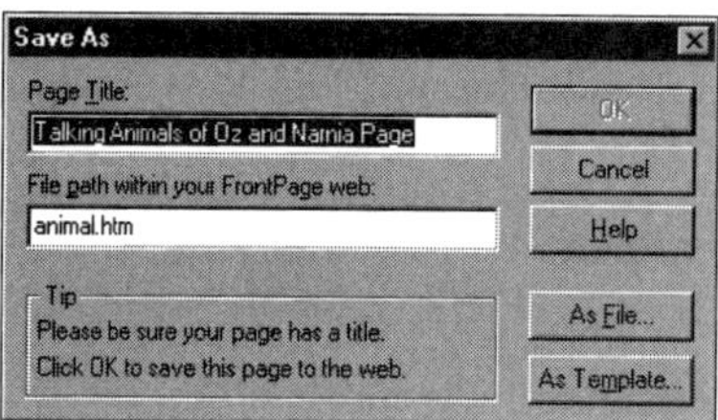

Figure 7-16: FrontPage retains names given the page created by the custom Wizard.

Besides the code in the Wizutil.Bas file, all the code to make the Animal Wizard work is contained in a VB form module saved as Animal.Frm.

The Wizard interface is contained in a single Visual Basic form, even though it seems to the user as though three panels are involved.

This form steps through the Wizard dialog pages using a control array of Frame objects called grpPage. At runtime the array is moved to match the location and size of grpPage(0). Only one frame in the array is visible at a time:

```
grpPage(CurPage).Visible = True
```

When the user moves forwards and backwards through the Wizard panels, all the frames except the current one — grpPage(CurPage) — are set so they are not visible.

The details of making a Wizard interface functional in Visual Basic are, unfortunately, beyond the scope of this book. However, they are explained in detail in another book of mine, *Visual Basic 5 SECRETS*, also available from IDG Books.

The Wizard is initialized using a series of utility procedures called in the form load event:

```
Private Sub Form_Load()
   ...
   GetFrontPageInfo
   GetWizardInfo
   LoadSettings
   ...
End Sub
```

GetFrontPageInfo is used to retrieve information about the current FrontPage installation:

```
Public Sub GetFrontPageInfo()
   FrontPageRootDir = GetIniValue(FrontPageIniName, _
      FrontPageSection, FrontPageRootKey)
   FrontPageDataDir = FrontPageRootDir & "\data"
   FrontPageTempDir = FrontPageRootDir & "\temp"
```

```
    FrontPageWebsDir = FrontPageRootDir & "\webs"
    FrontPagePagesDir = FrontPageRootDir & "\pages"
    FrontPageServerRoot = GetIniValue(FrontPageIniName, _
        FrontPageSection, FrontPagePWSKey)
    FrontPageServerHost = GetIniValue(FrontPageIniName, _
        FrontPageSection, FrontPageHostKey)
End Sub
```

Persistent state information for FrontPage Wizards is stored in Ini files with the same name as the Wizard executable — for example, Animal.Ini. These files should be placed in the FrontPage\Data directory.

GetWizardInfo determines if such a file exists

```
...
If Len(FrontPageDataDir) > 0 Then
    WizardIniFile = FrontPageDataDir & "\" & App.EXEName & ".ini"
Else
    ' use wizard dir; better than nothing
    WizardIniFile = App.path & "\" & App.EXEName & ".ini"
End If
WizardHasPreviousSettings = FileExists(WizardIniFile)
...
```

If there is an Ini file, LoadSettings populates the Wizard accordingly:

```
...
' retrieve any previous values
If WizardHasPreviousSettings Then
    txtGreeting = GetIniString("Greeting")
    cmbStyle.ListIndex = GetIniInt("Style")
    optBW = GetIniBool("BlackOnWhite")
    optWB = GetIniBool("WhiteOnBlack")
    chkCredit = GetIniInt("IncludeCredits")
End If
...
```

A procedure named GeneratePage handles the work of actually creating the Web page. GeneratePage is called from the click event handler of the Wizard's Finish button and uses the variable values as entered by the Wizard user to generate an HTML page:

```
Public Sub GeneratePage(pagefile As String)
    Dim fn As Integer
    Dim nl As String
    Dim tag As String
    nl = Chr$(10)
    fn = FreeFile

    On Error GoTo BadFile
    Open pagefile For Output As #fn

    Print #fn, "<HTML>"
    Print #fn, "<HEAD>"
    Print #fn, "<TITLE>" & txtTitle & "</TITLE>"
    Print #fn, "</HEAD>"
    If optBW Then
```

```
      Print #fn, "<BODY BGCOLOR=#ffffff TEXT=#000000>"
   Else
      Print #fn, "<BODY BGCOLOR=#000000 TEXT=#ffffff>"
   End If
   tag = "H" & (cmbStyle.ListIndex + 1)   ' H1, H2, or H3
   Print #fn, "<" & tag & ">" & txtGreeting & "</" & tag & ">"
   If chkCredit Then
      Print #fn, "<HR>"
      Print #fn, "<P><EM>This page was generated by the Animal" & _
         "Wizard.</EM></P>"
   End If
   Print #fn, "</BODY>"
   Print #fn, "</HTML>"
   Close #fn
BadFile:
   Exit Sub
End Sub
```

GeneratePage saves the HTML it has created in a file, internally saved in a variable named pagefile. Finally, a new document based on the saved HTML file is created in the FrontPage Editor:

```
...
Set editor = CreateObject(FrontPageEditorID)
Set newdoc = editor.vtiOpenWebPage(pagefile, txtURL, "", "")
...
```

You'll find the complete Animal Wizard code on the *Web Developer's SECRETS* companion CD-ROM. In general, it's not that difficult a matter to modify the Visual Basic sample code available in the FrontPage SDK to create Wizards with tremendous capabilities.

Custom WebBot Components

In addition to using the WebBot components that ship with FrontPage 97, you can create custom WebBot components. The easiest way to do this is to start with the samples that ship with the FrontPage SDK.

WebBot components can be implemented in C/C++, Perl, or TCL. The *Web Developer's Secrets* companion CD-ROM includes a Visual C++ source code project named Quote.Mdp and related files for a sample WebBot component. This WebBot has no great functionality. It simply appends text entered in the custom WebBot property YourQuote to the string "Talking Animals say, thanks for saying:", and returns the expanded string.

Once it is installed, the Quote WebBot component appears in the FrontPage Insert WebBot component dialog as the Animal QuoteBot (see Figure 7-17).

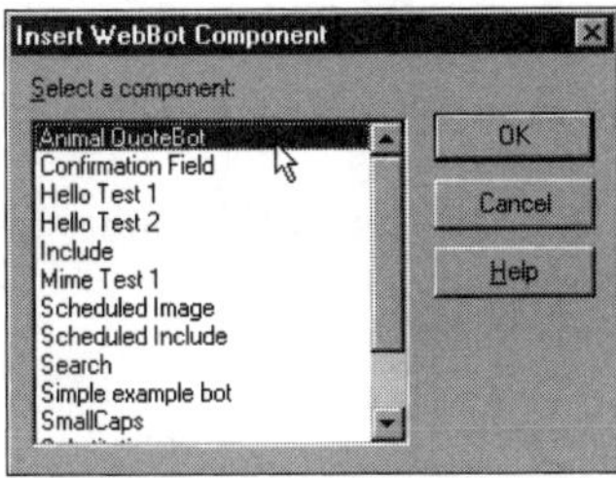

Figure 7-17: Installed custom WebBot components appear in FrontPage Editor's Insert WebBot component dialog.

WebBot components consist of three parts:

- An interface for editing the WebBot's properties
- A placeholder — sometimes called a *presentation* — in the FrontPage Editor
- Executable code that performs the WebBot's tasks

Generally, there are two kinds of WebBots:

- *Insert* WebBot components that replace themselves with HTML
- *Form* WebBot components that handle the submission of HTML form data (these components essentially wrap the functionality of CGI programs)

Each custom FrontPage WebBot library must be created in its own folder under the Bots folder. If the Bots directory does not exist, you must create it under the FrontPage root folder — for example, C:\Program Files\Microsoft FrontPage\Bots.

FrontPage does not load new custom WebBots until you choose Recalculate Hyperlinks from the FrontPage Explorer Tools menu. Choose Recalculate Hyperlinks as a final step after you have created a new WebBot component to make it appear in the FrontPage Editor interface.

The sample WebBot component consists of three files (in addition to the VC++ source code):

- Quote.Inf, the component description file
- Quote.Htm, the component template file
- Quote.Dll, the component implementation file.

To try out this WebBot component, you should copy these three files to the FrontPage\Bots directory as described earlier.

Note that a given WebBot component directory can contain more than one WebBot component; also, a component implementation file can, in fact, be a library of WebBot components.

The component description (Inf) file identifies the name, type, and capabilities of components in the directory, and identifies the component's template and implementation files. This information is used by FrontPage to construct its list of WebBot components and also is downloaded to FrontPage clients that access a FrontPage Web using the custom components.

Inf files are in standard private profile format. Here's the Quote.Inf file:

```
;Quote.INF

[info]
list=Quote
clientarchitectures=All
vendor=Evolution Software
contact=http://www.bearhome.com
version=0.1
serverbinding=dll
servermodule=quote.dll
clientbinding=BTL
clientmodule=quote.htm

[Quote]
name=Animal QuoteBot
description=DLL (C++) QuoteBot Component
type=insert
```

If this description file contained information on more than one component, each component would be included in the value of the list argument, and each would have its own section.

The component template file is an HTML document that provides a placeholder for the WebBot component and provides property variable information for FrontPage's generic WebBot Component Properties dialog shown in Figure 7-18. (For information on creating custom WebBot property dialogs, see the FrontPage 97 SDK.)

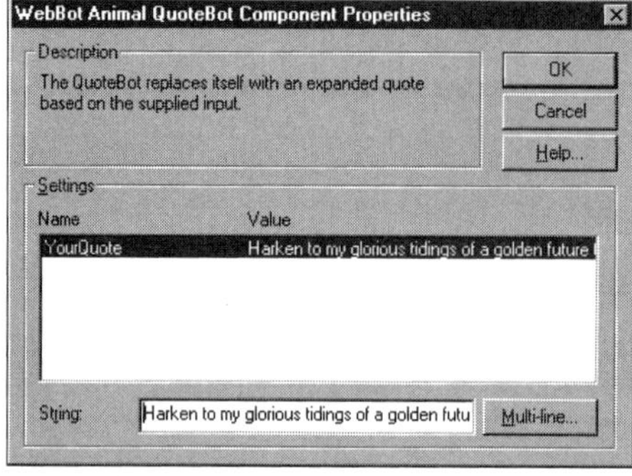

Figure 7-18: WebBot component variables included in the WebBot Component Properties dialog depend on the contents of the WebBot's template file.

The Animal Quote WebBot has one property variable — sometimes called an attribute — a string named YourQuote. Here's the contents of the component's template file, Quote.Htm:

```
<!—WEBBOT BOT=Quote
Tag=H2
PREVIEW="&lt;H2&gt;Placeholder for the QuoteBot!&lt;/h2&gt;"
DESCR="The QuoteBot replaces itself with an expanded quote based on
the supplied input."
HELP="Enter whatever text you would like."
S-YourQuote
—>
```

Inside Scoop

The WebBot is placed in the FrontPage Web page using a special tag, WEBBOT, embedded in a comment, so that it will not appear unexpanded in browsers. In previous editions of FrontPage, this tag was VERMEER.

The line

```
S-YourQuote
```

means that the WebBot has an attribute named YourQuote of type string. Table 7-2 shows the types of attributes available and how they are abbreviated in the template file.

Table 7-2 User-Editable WebBot Component Attributes

Parameter Type	*Abbreviation*
Boolean	B
Color	C
Date	D
Integer	I
String	S
URL	U

The DESCR and HELP fields are used to complete the WebBot Component Properties dialog, and the contents of the PREVIEW field determines how the WebBot looks in the FrontPage Editor, as shown in Figure 7-19.

To see what the WebBot component has really done, you need to use a browser (and not FrontPage Editor) to look at the Web page it's on. Figure 7-20 shows the Animal Quote WebBot in Navigator.

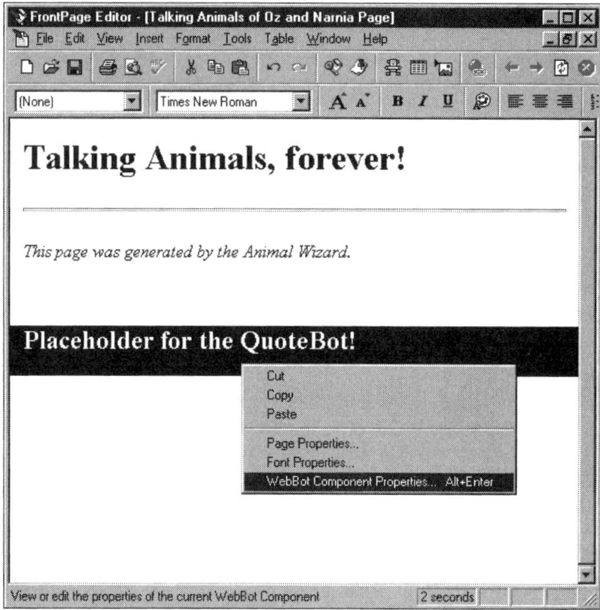

Figure 7-19: The WebBot component's template file provides a placeholder for the WebBot in the FrontPage Editor.

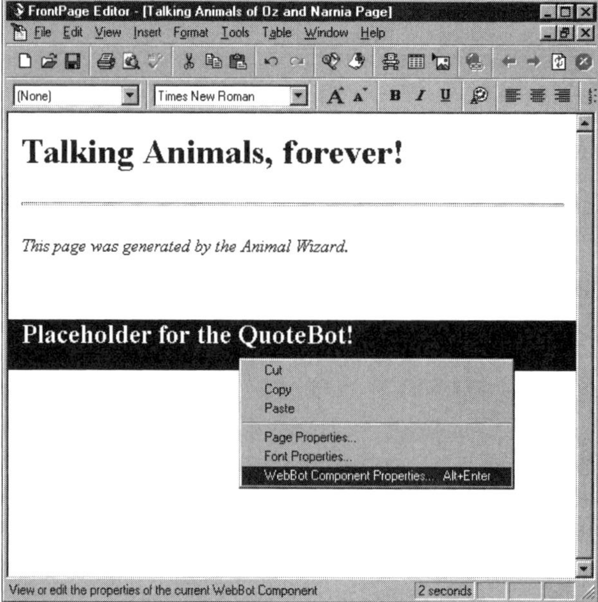

Figure 7-20: WebBot components do not expand until they are viewed in a Web browser.

Listing 7-1 contains the source code for the custom component implementation file.

Listing 7-1: A simple custom WebBot implementation file

```
/*
 * File: Quote.Cpp
 * DLL Custom WebBot Example
 *
 */

#include "stdio.h"
#include "../webbot.h"

////////////////////
// BOT: Quote

BeginWebBot(Quote,ret,bot,cgi,form)
{
     const char* value;
     value = bot.GetValue("YourQuote");
     ret.Append("Talking Animals say, thanks for saying: ");
     ret.Append(value);
}
EndWebBot
```

Note that you must include the file webbot.h, the definition header for custom WebBots. This file is distributed with the FrontPage SDK.

To create an implementation for a customized WebBot component using Visual C++ based on the QuoteBot (or on one of the samples that comes with the SDK), you should take these steps:

1. Create a folder named bots below the main folder for FrontPage. By default this main folder is C:\Program Files\Microsoft FrontPage.
2. Create a folder in the bots directory based on the name for your new custom component. All custom component folders go below the bots folder. Copy the QuoteBot or one of the WebBot samples from the SDK into the folder. Copy the file webbot.h into the bots directory, where it can be accessed by all custom WebBot implementations.
3. Start Microsoft Visual C++. From the File menu, choose New, and then choose Project Workspace. From the New Project Workspace dialog, choose Dynamic-Link Library. Click on the Browse button next to the Location field, and select the bots folder. Put your new component's internal name (*botname*) in the Project Name field and click on Create.
4. Open a C++ source file such as Quote.Cpp, and save it into your project as *botname*.cpp. You may need to use the Insert..Files into Project option. Modify the source code for the module so it uses the internal name for your component.
5. Select the Win32 Release target from the drop-down menu on the toolbar. Open the Build Settings property sheet. Go to the Link tab (you may have to scroll to the right to find it). Change the Output file name

from Release/*botname*.dll to *botname*.dll. Now use the menu option Build *botname*.dll.

6. Create the component description file (*botname*.inf) and the component template file (*botname*.htm), as described earlier in this chapter.
7. From the FrontPage Explorer's Tools menu, choose Recalculate Hyperlinks. Your component should now show up in the FrontPage Editor's Insert : WebBot Component dialog.

Summary

FrontPage 97 represents a uniquely powerful way for users to create and design Web pages and Web presences without having to understand the underlying HTML code. Because FrontPage is so easy to use, and its interface is similar to that of the popular Office 97 applications, FrontPage 97 will undoubtedly acquire legions of loyal users. For many of them, a FrontPage Web will be *the* Web.

As I've shown you in this chapter, with the aid of the materials included in the FrontPage 97 SDK, the FrontPage interface is highly customizable. You can create your own FrontPage Wizards and WebBots and distribute them to end users. From a developer's viewpoint — for example, in the context of corporate Web development in which FrontPage represents a corporate standard — this represents a tremendous opportunity to aid end users in their tasks.

Topics covered in this chapter included

- Introducing FrontPage 97
- Understanding FrontPage 97 Editor and Explorer
- Using the FrontPage 97 interface
- Using FrontPage 97 Wizards and WebBots
- FrontPage 97 Site Administration
- How the FrontPage applications work together
- Understanding the FrontPage 97 Server Extensions
- Creating a custom Page Wizard
- Creating custom WebBot components

Part II

Scripting Languages on the Web

Chapter 8

Understanding JavaScript

"The Eagle has landed."

— Neil Armstrong
upon reaching the moon, July 20, 1969

Scripting languages — also known as *macro languages* — are the easiest and best way to implement client-side programming on the Web. They are a great tool for creating awesome interactive and dynamic Web pages. JavaScript, you might say, is "good to the last drop."

Obviously, there are pros and cons to using a client programming solution. A great advantage is how easy it is to do. However, a drawback (one that you should always have in mind) is that your naked source code is available for the world to see. This means, as only one example, that JavaScript is an inappropriate way to implement passwords and other security measures. Client-side programs, such as those written in JavaScript, are simply not reliable enough for mission critical applications.

JavaScript and VBScript have become the dominant web scripting languages. Although JavaScript bears some relationship to Java, the correspondence is loose, and has more to do with software politics than technology. However, JScript, a version of JavaScript, is interpreted by Explorer, thus making JavaScript the closest thing there is to a universal scripting language on the Web since it will execute in both Explorer and Navigator. VBScript, which is a kind of watered-down Visual Basic, does not execute in Navigator. But the combination of ActiveX and VBScript lets you easily create powerful and dynamic web solutions — either for intranets (where the client software can be specified) or on the Web — only targeting Explorer users. VBScript and JavaScript are compared in more detail in Chapter 10, "Doing it with VBScript."

The purpose of Part II of *Web Developer's SECRETS* is to show you how to use both of these scripting languages — JavaScript and VBScript — as powerful components of web development.

JavaScript and Java

JavaScript is a scripting language; Java is a full-fledged programming language. The JavaScript language resembles Java, but without Java's strict variable typing and type checking (and without Java's full object orientation). JavaScript variables are not declared as a particular type. They are *implicitly typed* by the interpreter, depending on the type of the values loaded into the variable. (In some languages, variables of this sort are known as *variant*.) JavaScript's statement syntax and control flow constructions resemble Java's. (Much as instant freeze-dried coffee resembles real coffee....)

Before you can execute a Java program, it must be compiled. The Java source code that is compiled consists exclusively of a system of classes and methods. Java's requirements for declaring classes, writing methods, dealing with object hierarchies, and strict typing make programming in Java conceptually challenging but a pleasure to work in from the viewpoint of an object-oriented programmer. In contrast, JavaScript is a run-time system based on a small number of data types representing numeric, Boolean, and string values. It's a language that you can work in quite informally, on an ad hoc basis and in an intuitive way, without worrying about data types or objects and inheritance.

JavaScript can work with Java applets that have exposed properties. JavaScript statements can get and set the exposed properties. You can use this feature to dynamically query the state or alter the performance of a Java applet or plug-in. For more information on this topic, see Chapter 17, "Java Development and the Web." In other words, in the language of an S.A.T. question, "JavaScript is to Java as VBScript is to ActiveX."

Table 8-1 lists some of the main differences between JavaScript and Java.

Table 8-1 JavaScript Versus Java

JavaScript	*Java*
Interpreted by client (for example, the browser). JavaScript is not compiled.	Compiled into Java byte code before execution.
Object-based. JavaScript uses built-in objects, but has no facilities for classes or inheritance.	Highly object oriented. Applets consist of object classes that are capable of full inheritance.
Code integrated with, and embedded in, HTML (in Navigator 3.0, can be in external .js files).	Applets are completely distinct from HTML (although they can be accessed from HTML pages).
Variable data types not declared (loose typing).	Variable data types must be declared (strict typing).

JavaScript	*Java*
Dynamic binding. Object references checked only at runtime.	Static binding. Object references must exist when the source code is compiled.
No local disk access.	No local disk access.

JavaScript: The Language

JavaScript is a living and rapidly changing language. Be sure to check the Netscape site for up-to-the-minute information about the current iteration of JavaScript.

JavaScript Information

Netscape is the keeper of the JavaScript flame, and the best source of information on JavaScript. JavaScript (as implemented in Navigator version 2.0) documentation can be found at *www.netscape.com/eng/mozilla/2.0/handbook/javascript/@srindex.html.*

JavaScript 1.1 (as implemented in Navigator version 3.0) documentation can be found at *www.netscape.com/eng/mozilla/3.0/handbook/javascript/@srindex.html.*

External Script Files

New to JavaScript Version 1.1 — supported by Navigator 3.0 but not Explorer 3.0 — are external JavaScript files. Being able to encapsulate script code in files separate from HTML code helps minimize maintenance problems and encourages reuse of JavaScript code. As this feature becomes widely used on the Web, it's fairly likely that future versions of Explorer will adopt it as well.

Here's how this works. You place the JavaScript code in an external file, which must have the .js extension. You place a reference to the external file in an HTML document, using the **src** parameter of the <SCRIPT> tag. When Navigator hits the <SCRIPT> tag, the JavaScript code in the external file is executed.

Suppose an external script file that shows a JavaScript alert box is created. The file could be named alert.js. It contains only one line of code:

```
alert("Wake up and smell the coffee!")
```

Every time Navigator hits a reference to alert.js in the **src** parameter of an HTML file's <SCRIPT> tag, the alert box opens. The simple example HTML file in Listing 8-1 shows the alert box immediately after loading (as shown in Figure 8-1):

Listing 8-1: Executing an external script file

```
<HTML>
   <HEAD>
      <TITLE>
      Handy-dandy JavaScript Test
      </TITLE>
   </HEAD>
   <BODY>
   <SCRIPT src="alert.js"></SCRIPT>
   </BODY>
</HTML>
```

Figure 8-1: The contents of an external .js file are executed when Navigator encounters a reference to the file in a <SCRIPT> tag.

JavaScript Identifiers

This section explains how JavaScript variables can be named, what values can be put in the variables, and how literals are treated.

Always Practice JavaScript Code Hiding

Your Mama says, "always wear waterproof shoes in the rain, and always practice JavaScript code hiding." Listen to your Mama!

If you do not use HTML comments to hide embedded JavaScript code, your naked code will display as part of your HTML pages in older, non-JavaScript aware browsers. For more details, see the section on "Comments" in Chapter 2, "Using HTML Tags to Design Web Pages."

Variable Naming

Variables, which are used to hold values, are referenced by their names. JavaScript variable names are case sensitive, meaning that myVariable will not be recognized as equivalent to Myvariable.

In addition, the following variable naming rules apply:

- A JavaScript variable name must start with a letter or underscore (_)
- Subsequent characters can include digits (0 through 9) as well as letters

The Scope of JavaScript Variables

The scope of a variable determines which functions and routines can access the variable. In JavaScript, variables can be scoped in two ways:

- Variables have a global scope — meaning they can be accessed by any JavaScript function included as part of the HTML page — when they are declared using the **var** keyword outside a function, or when they are declared implicitly inside a function by assigning a value to the variable.
- Variables have a local scope — meaning they can only be used within the current function — when they are declared using the **var** keyword inside a function.

The following JavaScript snippet shows two global variables and one local variable:

```
...
var imaGlobal
function doSomething() {
    var imaLocal
    imaGlobal2 = "Enterprise"
    ...
}
...
```

It's good programming practice to declare global variables at the beginning of your JavaScript code. Getting in the habit of always explicitly declaring variables saves time and trouble in the long run.

JavaScript Variable Values

You can assign the following kinds of values to JavaScript variables:

- Numbers, such as 42 or 1.0012. No distinction is made between variables that contain integer and real values.
- Boolean values, either True or False.
- Strings, such as "Jean-Luc Picard".
- Null, a special keyword denoting a null value.

The Date Object

You've probably noticed that JavaScript doesn't have many data types. In particular, it has no date type. However, the date object and its built-in functions allow you to manipulate dates.

The internal representation of the JavaScript date object is in milliseconds from midnight on December 31, 1969 (1/1/70, 00:00:00). This rather odd way of keeping track of dates clearly creates large internal numbers quickly. As a consequence, JavaScript 1.0 (as implemented in Navigator 2.0) has no way to handle dates after December 31, 1999 entered in the date object. (Presumably, there is also a maximum date value in JavaScript 1.1; you can use the demonstration program to find it for yourself using trial and error.)

To test this — and see how the JavaScript date object works — try running the following JavaScript function in Navigator 2.0. Enter a date after the year 2000, and watch the error messages fly (see Figure 8-2)!

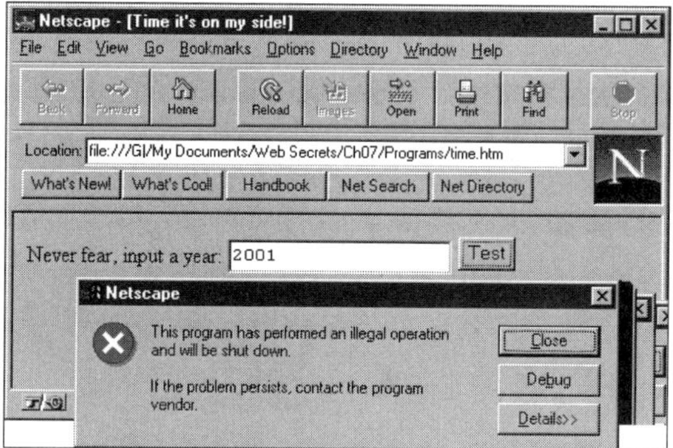

Figure 8-2: Entering dates after the year 2000 in JavaScript's date object causes protection faults in Navigator 2.0.

```
<HTML>
   <HEAD>
      <TITLE>
      Time it's on my side!

      </TITLE>
   <SCRIPT Language = "JavaScript">
   <!-- Hide that code
   function testTime(year){
      testDate = new Date();
      testDate.setTime(Date.parse("January 1," + year));
      alert ("Milliseconds since January 1, 1970: " +
         testDate.getTime());
   }
```

```
    // release me -->
    </SCRIPT>
    </HEAD>
    <BODY>
    <Form Name = "form">
    Never fear, input a year:
    <INPUT Type=text Name="txtYear" MaxLength=4>
    <INPUT Type="button" Value="Test"
       OnClick="testTime(form.txtYear.value)">
    </Form>
    </BODY>
</HTML>
```

Type Conversion

JavaScript is a loosely typed language. This means that you do not have to specify the type of a variable when you declare it. Variables are automatically converted to reflect the type of the values stored in them during the course of script execution. In other words, you are given enough rope to hang yourself.

For example, a variable declared

```
var myVar = 3.1415
```

could later be assigned a string value:

```
myVar = "Pi in the sky"
```

If in doubt, JavaScript converts numeric values to strings, rather than the other way round. If you enter the following JavaScript assignments:

```
x = "The answer is " + 42
y = 42 + " is the answer."
```

x evaluates to "The answer is 42" and y evaluates to "42 is the answer."

Table 8-2 shows important JavaScript functions for manipulating strings and numbers.

Table 8-2 JavaScript Conversion Functions

Function Name	*What it Does*
eval	Evaluates a string representing literals and variables, converting it to a number. For example, eval("21 + (42/2)" would return a value of 42.
parseInt	Converts a string to an integer of the specified base, if possible.
parseFloat	Converts a string to a floating-point number, if possible.

Literals

In contrast to variables, literals are fixed values used in your JavaScript programs. For example:

```
"Starship Enterprise"
42
1000.123
```

Integers

Integers can be expressed in decimal (base 10), hexadecimal (base 16), or octal (base 8). A decimal integer consists of a sequence of digits without a leading zero (0). A leading 0 (zero) means an Integer is expressed using octal notation; a leading 0x (or 0X) means hexadecimal. Hexadecimal integers can include digits (0 through 9) and the letters a–f and A–F. Octal integers can include only the digits 0 through 7.

Floating-Point Numbers

Floating-point numbers can be expressed either in decimal notation (an integer followed by a decimal point followed by another integer) or in scientific notation (an exponent is indicated by an "e" or "E" followed by an integer). A floating-point number must have at least one digit, plus either a decimal point or "e" (or "E"). For example:

```
1.1
-2E16
3.4e-2
6.789
```

Booleans

The Boolean type has two literal values: True and False. For example:

```
Flag = True;
```

Strings

Strings consist of zero or more characters delimited by double (") or single (') quotes. For example:

```
"The Cat in the Hat is back."
'Make it so!'
```

Both the beginning and the ending quote character must be the same. For example,

```
'Not a valid string"
```

will give the JavaScript interpreter hiccups.

Table 8-3 describes special characters that can be embedded in a string.

Table 8-3 JavaScript Special Characters

Character	*Meaning*
\b	backspace
\f	form feed
\n	new line character
\r	carriage return
\t	tab character

You can insert quotes in strings by preceding the quote character with a backslash (\) (sometimes called *escaping* the quotes). For example:

```
var theQuote = "I said \"Make it so,\" so, make it so!"
document.write (theQuote)
```

would display the following expression:

```
I said "Make it so," so, make it so!
```

Operators

JavaScript has arithmetic, string, and logical operators. There are both binary and unary operators. A binary operator requires two operands, one before the operator and one after the operator, for example, 20 + 22 and x * y.

You may be a little less used to unary operators, which require a single operand, either before or after the operator — for example, x++ and ++x. (For an explanation of ++, see increment operator in the next section.)

Arithmetic Operators

JavaScript has some arithmetic operators in addition to the standard arithmetic operators, as shown in Table 8-4.

Table 8-4 JavaScript Arithmetic Operators (Other than Standard Arithmetic Operators)

Operator	*What it Does*
%	Modulus operator. X % Y returns X modulo Y.
++	Increment operator. Adds one to the operand. If the increment operator is used as a *prefix* (++X), the operator returns the value after incrementing. If it is used as a *postfix* (X++), the value returned is before incrementing.

(continued)

Table 8-4 (Continued)

Operator	What it Does
++	If X = 7 the statement Y = X++ causes X to equal 8 and Y to equal 7; however, Y = ++X causes both X and Y to have a value of 8.
--	Decrement Operator. Subtracts one from the operand and returns a value. The rules for postfix and prefix returns work the same as the increment operator. Note that some older browsers see the decrement operator as the end of a comment; JavaScript code that has been protected with code hiding is potentially vulnerable to this problem. See Chapter 2 for more information on code hiding.

In addition, JavaScript has a full complement of bitwise operators, which operate on the individual bit values of operands.

Boolean Operators

Table 8-5 shows the JavaScript Boolean operators.

Table 8-5 JavaScript Boolean Operators

Operator	Meaning
&&	And
||	Or
!	Not

Incomplete Boolean Evaluation

JavaScript Boolean expressions are evaluated from left to right and tested for possible "incomplete" evaluation using the following rule:

- False && anything is always evaluated to false
- True || anything is short-circuit evaluated to true.

Although the rules of logic imply that these "short-circuit" evaluations will always be correct, programmers must take care, because any effects of code to the right of the Boolean operator will not be triggered. (Advanced compiled languages generally let developers turn incomplete Boolean evaluation on and off.)

Comparison Operators

JavaScript supports standard comparison operators, for both numbers and strings, as shown in Table 8-6. A comparison operator compares its operands and returns a logical value based on whether or not the resulting comparison is true. Comparison of strings is based on a dictionary ordering of the strings.

Table 8-6 JavaScript Comparison Operators

Operator	Meaning
==	equal
>	greater than
>=	greater than or equal
<	less than
<=	less than or equal
!=	not equal

Concatenation Operator

The familiar concatenation operator (+) glues two strings together. For example, "Make" + " it so!" returns the string "Make it so!"

JavaScript also includes a shorthand assignment operator (+=), which you can use to concatenate strings by concatenating a new string value to the contents of an existing string. For example, if the variable myString contains the value "cat," the expression

```
myString += "atonic"
```

evaluates to "catatonic" and assigns this value to myString.

Assignment Operators

An assignment operator assigns a value to its left operand based on the value of its right operand. In addition to the standard assignment operator, =, which assigns the value on the right of the equal sign to the variable on the left, JavaScript includes some shorthand assignment operators:

- x += y means x = x + y
- x -= y means x = x - y
- x *= y means x = x * y
- x /= y means x = x / y
- x %= y means x = x % y

Operator Precedence

Operator precedence means the order in which operators are applied when evaluating an expression. You can tell the JavaScript interpreter to evaluate part of an expression first by enclosing it within parentheses. In the absence of parentheses, evaluation order is roughly what you're probably used to. The following JavaScript operators are shown in order of precedence, with highest precedence first:

- Negation, increment, decrement
- Multiply, divide, modulo
- Addition, subtraction
- Comparison
- Logical And
- Logical Or
- Assignment

Conditional Expressions

A conditional expression has one of two values based on a condition. The syntax is

```
(condition) ? val1 : val2
```

If the condition is true, the expression has the value of val1. Otherwise it has the value of val2. For example:

```
status = (age >= 21) ? "adult" : "minor"
```

This statement assigns the value "adult" to the variable status if age is 21 or greater. Otherwise, it assigns the value "minor" to status.

JavaScript Statements

In JavaScript, execution is controlled by flow control statements pretty much along the lines of what you would expect. But there are fewer statements available than in many programming languages.

JavaScript is, after all, an interpreted *scripting* language. You aren't limited by the lack of extensive flow control — for instance, although JavaScript doesn't currently implement case (and switch) statements, you can achieve the same results in alternate ways.

In some cases, such as writing multiple if statements since there is no switch statement available — you may have to work in less than elegant ways with the statements it does have.

You separate multiple JavaScript statements with semicolons (;).

JavaScript Comments

There are two ways of including comments in JavaScript code. Anything on a line following a double-slash (//) is a comment. And comments that span multiple lines are preceded by a /* and terminated by a */. Here are two examples:

```
// I'm a comment
/* I'm a
   multiline
   comment */
```

If Statements

The if statement is the only conditional statement in JavaScript:

```
if (condition) {
   first set of statements
   }
else {
   second set of statements
}
```

The condition can be anything that JavaScript can evaluate to true or false. Which set of statements is executed depends on the evaluation. The first set of statements is executed if the condition evaluates to true and the second set of statements is executed if the condition evaluates to false.

Loop Statements

JavaScript supports for and while loops. The syntax of these statements is roughly comparable to that used in Java and C++.

Break and continue are used in conjunction with for and while loops. The break statement terminates the current for or while loop and passes control to the next executable statement following the loop. The continue statement halts execution of the block of statements in a loop and continues execution of the loop with the next iteration.

For Loop

A for loop repeats until the specified condition evaluates to false. The syntax is

```
for (initial expression; condition; increment expression) {
   loop statements
}
```

When JavaScript encounters a for loop, the initial expression is executed. The loop statements are executed as long as *condition* evaluates to true. The *increment expression* is executed on each pass through the loop.

The howMany function in Listing 8-2 uses a for loop to determine how many options the user selected, as shown in Figure 8-3.

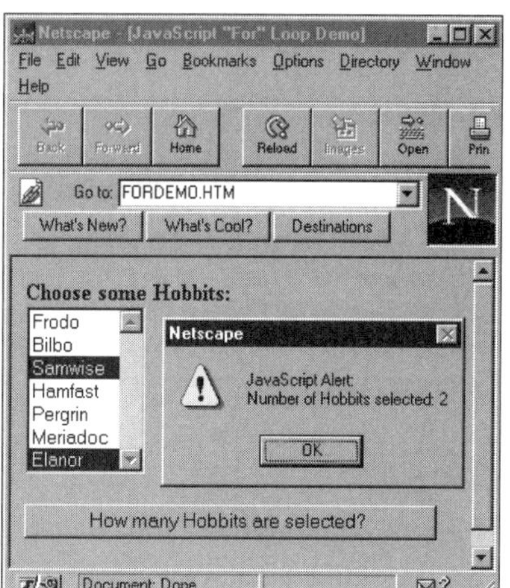

Figure 8-3: You can use a JavaScript for loop to determine the number of options selected by the user.

Listing 8-2: Using a JavaScript for loop to determine how many options were selected

```
<HTML>
   <HEAD>
      <TITLE>
      JavaScript "For" Loop Demo
      </TITLE>
   <SCRIPT Language="JavaScript">
   <!-- Hide that code...
      function howMany(selectObject) {
         var numberSelected=0
         for (i=0; i < selectObject.options.length; i++) {
            if (selectObject.options[i].selected==true)
            numberSelected++
         }
         return numberSelected
      }
   // ...Release me-->
   </SCRIPT>
   </HEAD>
   <BODY>
   <FORM NAME="myForm">
   <P><B>
   Choose some Hobbits:
   </B><BR>
   <SELECT NAME="hobbitNames" MULTIPLE>
      <OPTION SELECTED> Frodo
      <OPTION> Bilbo
      <OPTION> Samwise
      <OPTION> Hamfast
      <OPTION> Pergrin
```

```
      <OPTION> Meriadoc
      <OPTION> Elanor
   </SELECT>
   <P>
   <INPUT TYPE="button" VALUE="How many Hobbits are selected?"
      onClick="alert ('Number of Hobbits selected: ' +
      howMany(document.myForm.hobbitNames))">
   </FORM>
   </BODY>
</HTML>
```

While Loop

You can use the JavaScript while statement to repeat a group of statements as long as a condition evaluates to true. Here's the syntax:

```
while (condition) {
   statements
}
I'm the statement after the loop!
```

When the condition becomes false, the statements within the loop stop executing and control passes to the statement following the loop. When programming with while loops in JavaScript — as in other environments — be sure that the condition evaluates to false at some point, or your loop will continue forever.

Functions

The function is the fundamental building block of JavaScript. Using functions in JavaScript code is essentially a two-step process. First the function must be defined — usually in the <HEAD> section of the HTML page. In and of itself, defining a function does nothing. The second step is to actually cause the function to be executed.

If you try to execute a function before the JavaScript interpreter has parsed its definition, you will get an error message. This means that it is important to understand the order of processing, as described later in this chapter under "Processing Order." Note also that methods you define for objects are simply functions (see the upcoming section "JavaScript Objects").

A function definition is as follows:

```
function myFunc (arg1,...,argn) {
   all my statements
}
```

You can use the optional keyword return to return a function value. Statements in a function can include other function calls, as well as recursive calls to the function itself.

For example, here is the definition of a function named printMeBold that adds some HTML tags to a string and displays the results in the current document:

```
function printMeBold(theString) {
   document.write("<HR><P><B>" + theString + "</B>")
}
```

You could define the printMeBold function in the <HEAD> section of an HTML document and execute it at the beginning of the body section (with the results shown in Figure 8-4):

```
<HTML>
   <HEAD>
      <TITLE>
      Print Me Bold!
      </TITLE>
   <SCRIPT Language="JavaScript">
   <!--Hide that code..
   function printMeBold(theString) {
      document.write("<HR><P><B>" + theString + "</B><HR>")
   }
   //release me -->
   </SCRIPT>
   </HEAD>
   <BODY>
   <SCRIPT Language="JavaScript">
   <!--Hide that code..
   printMeBold("Rings of Power are VERY dangerous!");
   //release me -->
   </SCRIPT>
   </BODY>
</HTML>
```

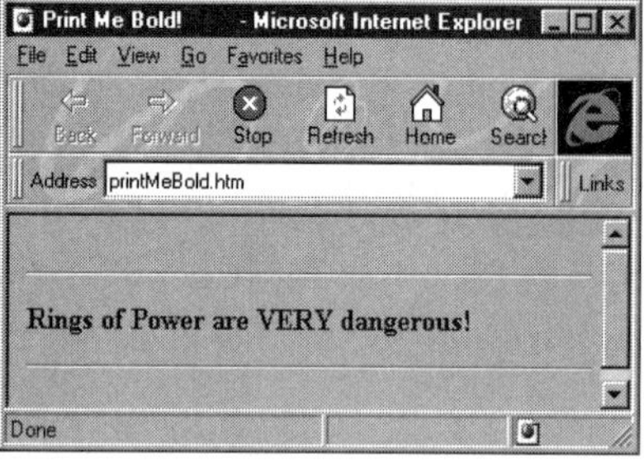

Figure 8-4: JavaScript functions, which can display HTML text in the current document, must be both defined and executed.

The Function Arguments Array

The arguments of a JavaScript function are stored in an array. This means that within a function, you can access the parameters passed to it — for example,

```
myFunction.arguments[i]
```

where i is the number of the argument, counting from zero. (The first argument passed to myFunction is myFunction.arguments[0].)

You can call a function with more arguments than it is formally defined to accept using the arguments array of the function. This approach is extremely useful when you don't know in advance the number of arguments you will be passing to a function. You can then use the argument.length property of the function to determine the total number of arguments that were actually passed to the function.

For example, the following function

```
function paras() {
   document.write("<P>")
   for (var i = 0; i < paras.arguments.length; i++)
      document.write(paras.arguments[i]+"<P>"
}
```

will insert an HTML paragraph tag (<P>) in the current document, followed by as many text strings as you'd like. It will place a <P> tag in the document after each text string.

You can pass any number of arguments you'd like to this function; if you called it with five,

```
paras("Well, Hello", "Dolly, It's", "Nice To", "Have You",
   "Back Again!");
```

the HTML it writes will be on five lines, as shown in Figure 8-5.

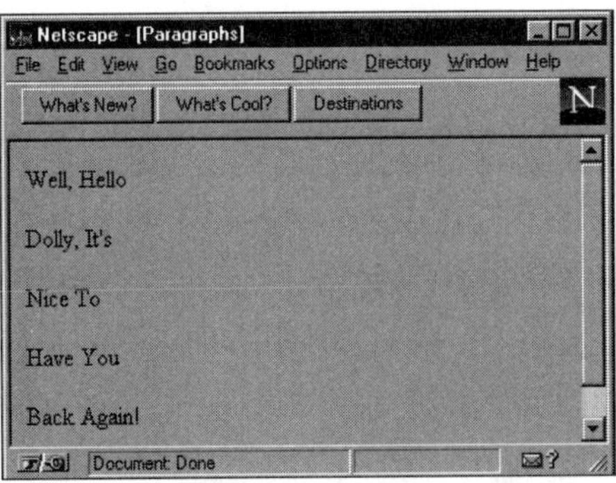

Figure 8-5: JavaScript functions can be called with a variable number of arguments.

Processing Order

It's important to understand the order in which Navigator and Explorer process JavaScript code included in HTML documents. When the JavaScript interpreter hits a function definition, it evaluates — or *parses* — the function and stores the evaluation for future use when the function is invoked (that is, called). Because JavaScript functions must be defined before they can be executed, if you inadvertently attempt to execute an undefined function, you'll end up with an embarrassing error message.

Defining all your functions in the <HEAD> section of your HTML document ensures that they will be evaluated before they are invoked. Otherwise, the user might perform some action while the page is still loading that triggers an event handler and calls an undefined function, leading to an error.

The term *layout* describes the process a browser uses to transform HTML code to the graphical display on screen. Generally, layout is performed from the top to the bottom of an HTML document.

Consistent with this top-to-bottom layout approach, JavaScript functions placed in the <HEAD> section are evaluated before any of the <BODY> content of the HTML page is parsed. Scripts placed within <SCRIPT> tags in the body of the HTML page are evaluated after the page loads in the order of their location, top to bottom.

Because of this "top-down" behavior, JavaScript code can only reference HTML items that it has already encountered. For instance, if you placed a form with some <INPUT> objects in an HTML page, you could reference the form and its objects after (below) its definition, but not before it.

It's also important to understand that once *layout has occurred* — think of it as, "the eagle has landed," meaning that the page has completely loaded and is displayed — you can no longer change the page's properties or appearance using code.

JavaScript Objects

You can think of objects simply as named containers for values. JavaScript objects have properties that are JavaScript variables. These properties can, themselves, be other objects. Functions associated with an object are known as the object's methods.

Manipulating Objects

JavaScript has several statements, keywords, and operators that you can use to manipulate objects.

You use the for...in statement to automatically step through all the properties of an object. Each property in the object is referenced using its index number. For example, the following JavaScript function will display all the properties of the current Navigator document object, as shown in Figure 8-6.

```
<HTML>
   <HEAD>
      <TITLE>
      The Eagle Has Landed
```

```
        </TITLE>

    </HEAD>
    <BODY>
    <SCRIPT Language="JavaScript">
    <!--Hide that code
    for (i in window.document) {
        document.write("Document Property(" + i + "): " +
            window.document[i] + "<BR>")
    }
    //release me -->
    </SCRIPT>
    </BODY>
</HTML>
```

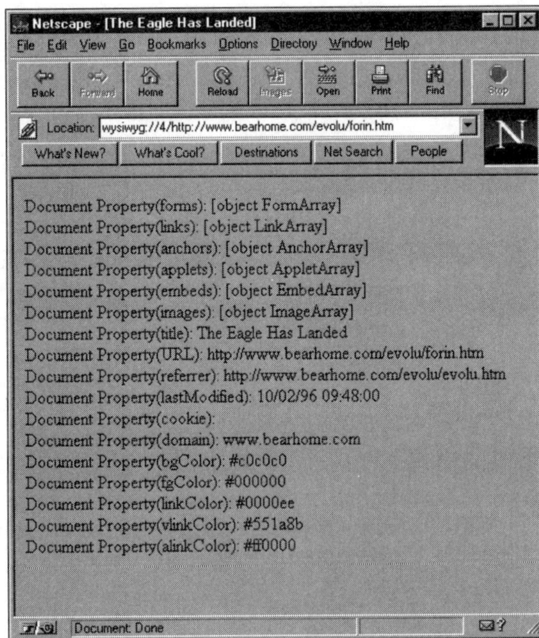

Figure 8-6: You can use the JavaScript for...in statement to cycle through all the properties of an object, such as Navigator's built-in Document object.

Note that this use of the for...in statement will probably be of more practical use for manipulating (and recovering) property information from objects that you have defined rather than from built-in objects.

You use the new statement to create an instance of a user-defined object type.

Creating an object in JavaScript involves two steps:

1. Define the object using a function for the object type that specifies the object's name, properties, and methods.
2. Create an instance of the object (also known as *instantiation*) using the new statement.

The this keyword is used to refer to the current object and is usually part of a user-defined object definition.

For example, suppose you wanted to define a starship object with two properties: captain and description. The following function could define this object:

```
function starship (captain, description){
   this.captain = captain;
   this.description = description;
}
```

You could instantiate the starship object using the new statement:

```
enterprise1 = new starship("Kirk", "Run like a pirate ship")
enterprise2 = new starship("Picard", "Run by committee")
voyager = new starship("Janeway", "On its own")
```

You access and set object properties using the familiar dot operator:

```
myVar = voyager.captain
enterprise2.description = "Maybe Ryker will take command!"
```

Alternately, you can refer to object properties using an array notation:

```
enterprise2["captain"] = "Picard"
enterprise2["description"] = "Run by committee"
```

Objects can, themselves, be properties. You'd reference the property of an object that is itself a property using the dot operator hierarchically, for example:

```
enterprise.engine.warp_coil.revision
```

You create an object method by assigning a function as the value of an object parameter. For example:

```
this.makeitso = warp_speed();
```

Of course, you'll need to define the function warp_speed() as well as reference it.

Because objects can be passed as parameters, using the this keyword to refer to the current object can be very useful. For example, a validation function could be called in the onChange event of a text input object. The validation function would then be called using the this keyword. Note that this example uses a generalized function, with only the alerts customized for the specific numeric range (13 through 19 inclusive, as shown in Figure 8-7):

```
<HTML>
   <HEAD>
      <TITLE>
      Validate
      </TITLE>
      <SCRIPT Language="JavaScript">
      <!--Hide that code...
      function validate(obj, lowval, hival) {
         if ((obj.value < lowval) || (obj.value > hival))
            alert("Not a Teen!")
         else
            alert("Teenager! A target! Teenager!")
      }
      //Release me...-->
      </SCRIPT>
   </HEAD>
   <BODY>
  <FORM>
  <B>Are you a teenager? Enter a number greater
      than 12 and less than 20:</B>
  <INPUT TYPE = "text" NAME = "age" SIZE = 3
      onChange="validate(this, 13, 19)">
   </FORM>
   </BODY>
</HTML>
```

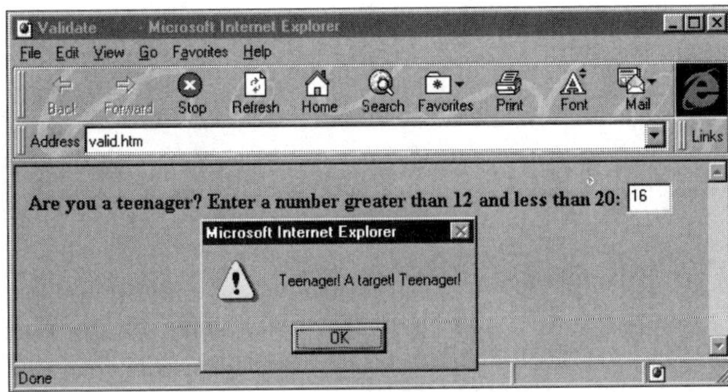

Figure 8-7: The current object can be referred to — and passed as a parameter — using the this keyword.

A final JavaScript object statement is with, which allows shorthand references to an object. Within the set of statements "owned" by the with statement, any property reference that does not specify an object is assumed to belong to the default object. For example:

```
with enterprise2 {
   captain = "Ryker"
   description = "I don't think so!"
   ...
}
```

Navigator Objects

When a page is loaded in a JavaScript-aware browser, a number of objects are created that correspond to the page, its contents, and other related information.

You should know that Explorer's implementation of JavaScript does not completely support the Navigator object hierarchy. It's important to carefully test JavaScript routines on both browsers.

Each page generates the following objects:

- Window, the top-level object, containing properties that apply to the entire window. There is also a window object for each for "child window" in a frames document.
- Location, containing properties of the current URL.
- History, containing properties representing URLs the user has previously visited.
- Document, containing properties for content in the current document, such as title, background color, and forms.

The Window Object

The Window object is the "parent" object for all other objects that involve the currently loaded document in the browser. The Window object name is optional, meaning that

```
window.document.write...
```

has the same effect as

```
document.write...
```

The Window object has a number of methods that create new windows and pop-up dialogs, as shown in Table 8-7.

Table 8-7 The Window Object's Methods

Method	*What it Does*
alert	Opens an alert pop-up
close	Closes a browser window
confirm	Opens a confirm pop-up
open	Opens a browser window

Window Properties

The Window object stores property values for all the frames in a frameset. The frames are stored in the frames array. The frames array contains an entry for each child frame in a window. For more on manipulating frames using JavaScript, see Chapter 9, "JavaScript Applications."

The window.status property enables you to set the message in the status bar at the bottom of the browser window.

The Form Object

Navigator creates a Form object for each form in a document. Forms can be named, for example:

```
<FORM NAME="thisForm">
<INPUT TYPE="text" NAME="theText" onChange="...">
...
</FORM>
```

This code creates a JavaScript object named thisForm that includes a text object named theText. Its properties can be referenced:

```
document.thisForm.theText.value
```

The forms in a document are stored in an array named forms. The first form (based on page load order and therefore the topmost in the page) is forms[0], the second is forms[1], and so on. So the preceding references could also be

```
document.forms[0].theText.value
```

The elements in a form — such as text fields, radio buttons, and so on — are also stored in an elements array.

The Document Object

The document object is probably the most useful browser object. The document.write and document.writeln methods can generate HTML on the fly. You use these methods to dynamically display text to the user.

The only difference between write and writeln is that writeln adds a carriage return at the end of the line.

The document object also has onLoad and onUnload event handlers that you can use to execute functions when a user first loads a page and when a user exits a page. To do this, place a function call in the document's <BODY> tag, for example:

```
<BODY onLoad="DoStuff()" onUnload="DoExitStuff()">
```

There is only one document object for an HTML page loaded in a browser, and it is the ancestor for all the form, link, and anchor objects included in the page.

The properties of the document object depend largely on what is in the HTML page. Form and control objects are only created if they exist in the HTML page; only if they are created do they become properties of the document object.

For example, if your page includes a form named thisForm, the corresponding document object will include an object named document.thisForm. (This object will not exist if thisForm does not exist.)

Browser Object Hierarchy

Browser objects in Navigator exist in a hierarchy that reflects the hierarchical structure of an HTML page itself. You cannot subclass these objects; essentially, JavaScript operates on instances of the objects rather than the underlying object classes. It is still useful to fully understand the hierarchy.

The navigator object is at the top of this hierarchy. The window object is a descendant of the navigator object that describes the currently loaded HTML document. Beneath the window object are the frames, location, history, and document objects.

The subobjects of the document object depend on the make-up of the actual loaded HTML page, but can include forms, links, and anchors arrays of objects.

Form objects can include text fields, text area, check box, password, radio, select, button, submit, and reset objects.

To refer to properties of an object, you must specify the object name and all its ancestors other than the window object. For example:

```
document.thisForm.thisText.value
```

Built-In JavaScript Objects

The JavaScript Language contains the following built-in objects:

- String object
- Math object
- Date object

These objects and their properties and methods are built into the language. In addition, JavaScript includes a number of built-in functions.

The String Object

When you assign a string to a variable or property, you create a string object. Strings themselves are also string objects. For example, the statement

```
theString = "Make it so!"
```

creates a string object called theString. “Make it so!” is also a string object.

The string object has 19 (very useful) methods that you can use to return manipulated versions of the string or to format the string in HTML.

For example, given the example value of theString, the statements

```
theString.toUpperCase()
"Make it so!".toUpperCase()
```

both return MAKE IT SO!

The Math Object

The Math object has properties and methods corresponding to mathematical constants and functions. These include trigonometric, logarithmic, exponential, and other functions.

The Date Object

JavaScript does not have a date data type. However, the date object and its methods enable you to work with dates and times in your applications. The date object has a large number of methods for setting, getting, and manipulating dates. It does not have any properties.

The date object stores dates as the number of milliseconds since January 1, 1970 00:00:00. Although the JavaScript problem with dates greater than the year 2000 has been resolved in version 1.1, you still cannot currently work with dates prior to 1/1/70.

For an example of how to use the date object, see the discussion of dates in the section “JavaScript Variable Values” earlier in this chapter.

Built-In Functions

JavaScript built-in functions include

- escape, which converts nonalphanumeric characters to their hex equivalents
- eval, which evaluates the passed expression or executes the passed statements
- parseInt, which parses its first argument, a string, and attempts to return an integer of the specified base
- parseFloat, which parses its argument, a string, and attempts to return a floating-point number

Using the eval Function

The eval function can provide a really easy way to evaluate complex user input and handle other computation tasks. For example, you could use the following function to compute the value of an expression entered by the user:

```
function compute(obj) {
   obj.result.value = eval(obj.expr.value)
}
```

Here's the form that accepts the user's input, applies the compute function, and displays the result, as shown in Figure 8-8:

```
<FORM NAME="evalform">
   Enter an expression: <INPUT TYPE=text NAME="expr" SIZE=20 >
   <BR>
   And your answer is: <INPUT TYPE=text NAME="result" SIZE=20 >
   <BR>
   <INPUT TYPE="button" VALUE="Evaluate"
      onClick="compute(this.form)">
</FORM>
```

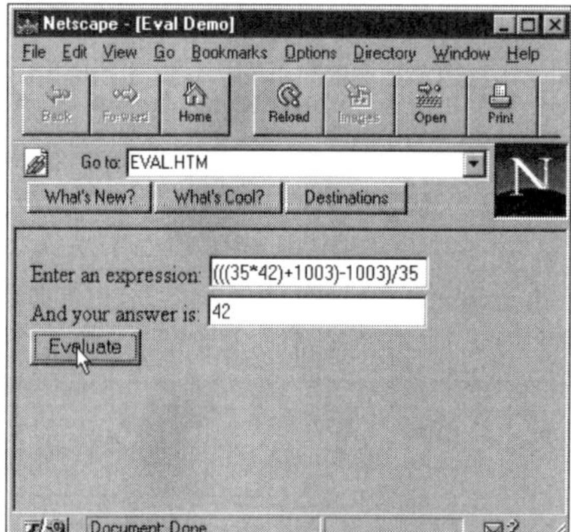

Figure 8-8: You can use the JavaScript eval function to quickly generate computational results.

JavaScript Events

JavaScript applications are essentially event-driven, meaning that code is executed in response to a browser event — such as loading an HTML document — or, more usually, in response to something the user does. An example of an event caused by the user is clicking a button.

Event handlers are embedded in documents as attributes of HTML tags to which you assign JavaScript code to execute. The general syntax is

```
<TAG eventHandler="JavaScript Code">
```

where TAG is some HTML tag and eventHandler is the name of the event handler. Here are some examples:

```
<INPUT TYPE="button" VALUE="Click Here"
    onClick="doSomething()">
<BODY onLoad="doSomethingElse()">
<BODY onUnload="doSomething();doSomethingElse()">
```

You can include an arbitrary number of JavaScript statements within the event handler assignment (separated by semicolons, with all statements delimited by a set of quotes). But if you use this approach your code rapidly becomes confusing to read. It's better programming practice to limit each event handler to a single function call (which, itself, can contain as much code as needed). This improves code clarity and modularity.

Table 8-8 shows which events apply to which HTML document objects.

Table 8-8 JavaScript Events and HTML Document Objects

Events	***HTML Objects***
onLoad, onUnload	User loads or unloads a page in the browser, event handler added to the <BODY> tag
onFocus, onBlur, onChange (the Blur event is fired when an object loses focus)	Text, text areas, selections
onClick	Buttons, radio buttons, check boxes, submit buttons, reset buttons, links
onSelect	Text fields, text areas
onSubmit	Fired when a form is submitted
onMouseOver	Links

Summary

This chapter has covered a great deal of the nitty-gritty details that you need to know to use JavaScript in a sophisticated fashion and to take advantage of its object-aware architecture.

Topics covered included

- JavaScript compared to Java
- Where to get more information about JavaScript
- External JavaScript (.Js) files
- JavaScript identifiers

- Type conversion and assignments
- JavaScript operators and statements
- JavaScript functions
- Functions and optional arguments
- JavaScript processing order
- Understanding JavaScript objects
- Creating your own JavaScript objects
- Using built-in browser objects
- Using JavaScript built-in objects and functions
- JavaScript events

Chapter 9

JavaScript Applications

"Coffee: black as hell, strong as death, sweet as love."

— Turkish proverb

Adding JavaScript executable functions to an HTML page is an excellent way to create dynamic web applications that interact with the user. You can also use JavaScript programs to accomplish tasks such as validating user form input, provided that security is not a concern.

The traditional way — that is, without JavaScript — to handle these kinds of jobs was to write a CGI script. The user's action in submitting a form sends a trigger to the server, which executes the CGI program. The CGI program produces, as output, HTML code, which is sent to the user's browser. (For more information on CGI scripting in the Windows environment, see Chapter 21, "CGI Scripting.")

The advantages of using JavaScript as opposed to CGI include

- Taking advantage of the client's processor (and not, therefore, overloading the server)
- Avoiding slowdowns through multiple sends across the Net (and issues involving the clogging of the Web itself)
- Avoiding problems with different CGI requirements on different servers

In addition, some servers — particularly those provided by web hosting services — simply do not allow CGI scripting.

Manipulating Windows

As I mentioned in Chapter 8, "Understanding JavaScript," you can open a window using the window object's open method. The following JavaScript code will open two new windows in Navigator, one containing *randomo.htm*, and the other *http://www.bearhome.com*.

```
<SCRIPT Language="JavaScript">
   <!--
   myWindow = window.open("randomo.htm")
```

```
   nextwin = window.open("http://www.bearhome.com")
   //-->
</SCRIPT>
```

The first window has been named myWindow, the second nextwin.

As usual on the Web, some caveats apply. First, the browser must be able to find the file or location specified. Next, Explorer's implementation of JavaScript does not support the open method of the window object, so this will not work for Explorer users. Finally, it's good practice to call the window.open method twice; some browsers require this.

Windows can have two names. For example

```
myWindow = window.open("randomo.htm", "random");
```

You use the first name, myWindow, when referring to the window's properties, methods, and objects; you use the second name, random, when referring to the window as the target of a form submit or hypertext link.

Windows don't have to have names. But if you want to refer to a window from another window — for example, when using frames — the window must have a name.

When opening a window, you can specify its height, width, and whether it contains a toolbar, location field, or scroll bars. The following statement creates a window with a toolbar and scroll bars, as shown in Figure 9-1:

```
nextwin = window.open("http://www.bearhome.com,"
    toolbar=1,scrollbars=1)
```

Figure 9-1: You can specify the attributes of a window when using the open method.

Closing a Window

You use the window.close method to close a window. Each of the following statements closes the current window:

```
window.close()
self.close()
myWindow.close() //closes a window named myWindow
close()          //Don't use in event handler
```

Note that you should not use close()in an event handler, as it will not work.

Window manipulation functions — such as those used to close windows — come into their own in applications that use frames dynamically.

Navigating between Windows

Many Navigator windows can be open at the same time. The user can move among these windows by clicking them to give them focus or by using Navigator's Window menu.

You can give focus to a window — make the window active — in code by giving focus to an object in the window or by specifying the window as the target of a hypertext link that the user can select. (Changing an object's values in a second window does not by itself change the focus.)

Suppose you created a window with the following statement:

```
bearWin = window.open("bear.htm", "bear");
```

The following statement gives focus to a text object named bearName in a form named theForm in the window named bearWin. Because the text object is gaining focus, bearWin also gains focus and becomes the active window.

```
bearWin.document.theForm.bearName.focus()
```

Here's how you'd give focus to another window using a hyperlink that the user clicks on:

```
<A href="bear.htm" target="bear2"> Load a bear text into window2</A>
```

This statement specifies bear2 as the target of a hypertext link. When the user clicks on the link, focus switches to bear2. If bear2 does not exist, it is created. Note that you specify the document using its hypertext name, not its JavaScript variable name.

Frames

Many of the most impressive dynamic JavaScript effects make use of frames. (Using HTML tags to create and manage frames was covered in Chapter 2 under "Creating Interactive Documents with Frames.") Using frames, you can have user actions in one part of the browser window change the contents of another part of the window (actually, another frame). To create these dynamic effects, you will probably find yourself using JavaScript code and the Navigator object hierarchy.

The general note of caution that applies to much web design applies here: Just because you can do it doesn't mean you should. Some of the worst HTML pages make extensive use of interactive frames. These pages can appear busy and gadgety and be very difficult for users.

Using the Status Bar

This example shows you how to add a scrolling status bar to an application. The user enters text and clicks on the Do it! button; the user's text scrolls across the status bar (see Figure 9-2).

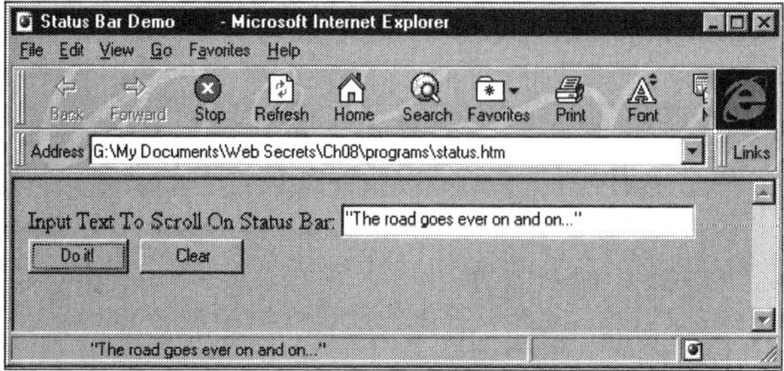

Figure 9-2: You can use JavaScript to add a scrolling status bar or marquee.

Obviously, the example would be simpler if the text string that scrolled was a literal supplied by the programmer rather than chosen by the user. Also, you could apply the same scrolling technique to a text field, creating a marquee effect within an HTML page.

The status bar is written to be setting the value of the window object's status property:

```
window.status = "This is status bar text!"
```

The underlying logic of the scrolling function isn't that complicated (see the example in Listing 9-1 later in this section). Spaces — presumably roughly matching the length of the status bar — are concatenated at the beginning of the text that will scroll. (The example does this by setting the variable winLength to 120.)

The text — with only blanks visible — is written to the status bar. After an interval (in the example, 20 milliseconds set by the variable speed) the text is written to the status bar again, only with one less leading blank.

Eventually, the text comes into view on the status bar and appears to be moving from left to right.

The setTimeout method of the window object is used to time the status bar redraws. setTimeout works by executing the command that is the first parameter passed to it after the delay specified in the second parameter. The setTimeout method also returns an option ID that can be used as an argument to the window.clearTimeout method to halt further setTimeout executions.

When there are no more spaces in front of the text being written to the status bar, a substring of the message is displayed, moving one character to the right each time. Finally, the string appears to have vanished off the left edge of the screen and the process starts over from the beginning.

Here's the form that allows the user to enter text for the scrolling status bar:

```
<FORM name="thisForm">
Input Text To Scroll On Status Bar:
   <INPUT type="TEXT" SIZE=45 name="txtStatus" value='"The road goes
      ever on and on..."'>
   <INPUT type="Button" value="Do it!" onClick="doIt()">
   <INPUT type="Button" value="Clear" onClick="clearIt()">
</FORM>
```

Listing 9-1 shows the scroll function, which takes care of the actual status bar display, as well as the functions that send the user's input to the scroll function and clear the status bar.

Listing 9-1: A user-configurable scrolling status bar

```
<SCRIPT Language="JavaScript">
<!--Hide that code
var winLength = 120;      //start scrolling after 120 spaces
var speed = 20;           //milliseconds between updates
var msg = "Add your own text to the status bar!"
var timeoutID;            //holds timerID for clearTimeout method
function scroll(count){
   var out = " ";
   var cmd = "scroll(";
   if (count <= winLength && 0 < count){      //pad the front
      var c = 0;                               //with count spaces
      for (c = 0; c < count; c++){
         out += " ";
      }
      out += msg;                              //add the text to the pad
      }
   else if (count<=0){                         //no more leading blanks
      if (-count < msg.length)
         out += msg.substring(-count,msg.length);
      else                                     //reset count
         count = winLength + 1;
   }
```

```
    window.status = out;                        //show to status bar
    count --;                                   //decrement count
    cmd += count + ")";                         //construct call to
                                                //scroll function
    timeoutID=window.setTimeout(cmd,speed);     //recursive call
}
function doIt(){
    msg=document.thisForm.txtStatus.value;
    window.clearTimeout(timeoutID);
    window.setTimeout("scroll(winLength)", speed);
}
function clearIt(){
    document.thisForm.txtStatus.value="";
    window.clearTimeout(timeoutID);
    window.status="";
}
// release me-->
</SCRIPT>
```

Creating a Game

Games are lots of fun, and we like fun. So do Web surfers. Games are a good way to attract users to your Web sites — and to practice JavaScript programming techniques.

Random Number Generation

Generally, games involve random number generation. This is because, by definition, a game involves something besides an intellectual puzzle. This "something" is often competition.

If the computer competes with the user, random number generation is required to keep the game interesting. Without it, the computer, which knows all the user's inputs, would win all the time, or play in a predictable pattern.

If the "competition" is a "deck" of cards — or, as in the example later in this chapter, a clenched fist containing rock, scissors, or paper — random number generation is required to mimic the real-world behavior of the object in question.

When it is called, the random method of JavaScript's Math object produces a "random" number, expressed as a decimal fraction, between 0 and 1. For example, the following line of JavaScript code prints a randomly generated number when the HTML page it is in is loaded:

```
<SCRIPT language="JavaScript">
//Displays a random number between 0 and 1
document.write("The random number is " + Math.random())
</SCRIPT>
```

The word "random" is in quotes in the preceding paragraph because there is no such thing as a function (or method) that truly generates random numbers. A well-chosen random number generation function — such as the one in JavaScript — will, however, satisfy various statistical tests for randomness.

Not all JavaScript-aware browsers include the random method of the Math object (although current Windows versions of Navigator and Explorer do).

If you wish to include random number generation and bypass the generator included in JavaScript — thereby circumventing any possible problems with browsers that don't recognize JavaScript's random method — you can write your own function easily. For more information on appropriate schemes, see *http://csepls.phy.ornl.gov:80/rn/rn.html*, which contains technical information about random number generation techniques.

Rock, Scissors, Paper

Perhaps you remember from childhood the game "rock, scissors, paper." The rules are very simple. Two entities, usually children, throw down a hand at the same time. Each hand can be in one of three positions: a fist, representing rock; two fingers, mimicking scissors; and palm down, meaning paper. The victor is determined by comparing the positions of the two childrens' hands as follows:

- Rock smashes scissors (meaning rock wins)
- Scissors cut paper (meaning scissors wins)
- Paper covers rock (meaning paper wins)

In this section, I'll show you how to create a simulation of the "rock, scissors, paper" game using JavaScript. The user competes against the computer, whose position is determined through random number generation (see Figure 9-3).

First, create the interface using a form and radio buttons:

```
...
<H2>
   Play "Rocks, Scissors and Paper" the JavaScript way!
</H2>
<UL>

   <LI>Rock smashes scissors!
   <LI>Scissors cut paper!
   <LI>Paper covers rock!
</UL>
<FORM name="gameForm">
<P>Make a choice:
<BR>
<INPUT type="radio" name="game" value="Rock"
```

```
   checked><STRONG>Rock</STRONG><BR>
<INPUT type="radio" name="game"
   value="Paper"><STRONG>Paper</STRONG><BR>
<INPUT type="radio" name="game"
   value="Scissors"><STRONG>Scissors</STRONG>
<P>
<BR>
<INPUT type="button" name="play" value="Play" onClick="shakeIt()">
...
```

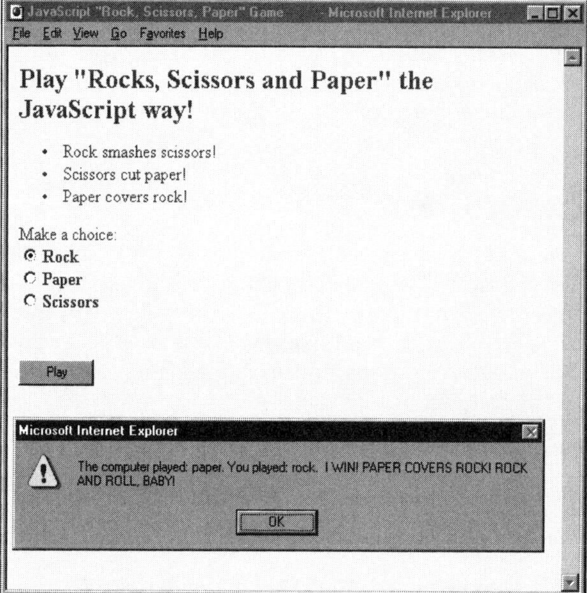

Figure 9-3: It's time to rock and roll with rocks, scissors, and paper!

The form elements can be referred to in JavaScript functions using the form object — named gameForm — of the document object. Radio buttons can be referenced using their array element, for example:

```
document.gameForm.game[0]
```

The actual start of play is initiated in the onClick event of the input button named play by calling a function named shakeIt():

```
function shakeIt(){
   randGen = Math.random();
   if (randGen <= .33)
      computerPlay = "rock"
   if ((randGen >.33) && (randGen <= .66))
      computerPlay = "scissors"
   if (randGen > .66)
```

```
      computerPlay = "paper"
   if (document.gameForm.game[0].checked)
      myPlay = "rock"
   if (document.gameForm.game[1].checked)
      myPlay = "paper"
   if (document.gameForm.game[2].checked)
      myPlay = "scissors"
   alert ("The computer played: " + computerPlay +
      ". You played: " + myPlay + ".  " +
      whoWon(computerPlay,myPlay))
}
```

This function is pretty straightforward. First, it calls the Math.random method and determines the computer's play based on the result. Next, it determines the user's play. Finally, it calls a function named whoWon — passing whoWon the plays of the computer and the user — and displays an alert box with the results.

The whoWon function is responsible for comparing plays, determining the victor, and returning an appropriate message:

```
function whoWon (iplay, uplay) {
   // "I" am the computer
   if (iplay == uplay)

      return "IT'S A TIE! TRY AGAIN, ENTITY?"
   if (iplay == "rock") {
      if (uplay == "scissors")
         return "I WIN! ROCK SMASHES SCISSORS! COMPUTERS FOREVER!"
      else
         return "YOU WIN. Paper covers rock." +
         " Paltry human, how did you beat me?"

   }
   if (iplay == "scissors") {
      if (uplay == "paper")
         return "I WIN! SCISSORS CUT PAPER! CHIPS BEAT BRAINS!"
      else
         return "YOU WIN. Rock smashes scissors." +
         " Frail human, would you like to try again?"
   }
   if (iplay == "paper") {
      if (uplay == "rock")
         return "I WIN! PAPER COVERS ROCK! ROCK AND ROLL, BABY!"
      else
         return "YOU WIN. Scissors cut paper." +
         " Oh, vain flesh and bone entity, I'll get you next time!"
   }
}
```

Listing 9-2 contains the complete code for the rock, scissors, paper game.

Listing 9-2: "Rock, scissors, paper" the JavaScript way!

```
<HTML>

<!--  JavaScript Rock, Scissors, Paper by Harold Davis -->
   <HEAD>
   <TITLE>
      JavaScript "Rock, Scissors, Paper" Game
   </TITLE>
   <SCRIPT Language="JavaScript">
   <!--Hide that code...
   function whoWon (iplay, uplay) {
      // "I" am the computer
      if (iplay == uplay)

         return "IT'S A TIE! TRY AGAIN, ENTITY?"
      if (iplay == "rock") {
         if (uplay == "scissors")
            return "I WIN! ROCK SMASHES SCISSORS! COMPUTERS
               FOREVER!"
         else
            return "YOU WIN. Paper covers rock. Paltry human, how
               did you beat me?"

      }
      if (iplay == "scissors") {
         if (uplay == "paper")
            return "I WIN! SCISSORS CUT PAPER! CHIPS BEAT BRAINS!"
         else
            return "YOU WIN. Rock smashes scissors. Frail human,
               would you like to try again?"
      }
      if (iplay == "paper") {
         if (uplay == "rock")
            return "I WIN! PAPER COVERS ROCK! ROCK AND ROLL, BABY!"
         else
            return "YOU WIN. Scissors cut paper. Oh, vain flesh and
               bone entity, I'll get you next time!"
      }
   }
   function shakeIt(){
      randGen = Math.random();
      if (randGen <= .33)
         computerPlay = "rock"
      if ((randGen >.33) && (randGen <= .66))
         computerPlay = "scissors"
      if (randGen > .66)
         computerPlay = "paper"
      if (document.gameForm.game[0].checked)
         myPlay = "rock"
      if (document.gameForm.game[1].checked)
         myPlay = "paper"
      if (document.gameForm.game[2].checked)
```

```
         myPlay = "scissors"
      alert ("The computer played: " + computerPlay +
         ". You played: " + myPlay + ".  " +
               whoWon(computerPlay,myPlay))
   }
   //release me -->
   </SCRIPT>
   </HEAD>
   <BODY>
   <H2>
   Play "Rocks, Scissors and Paper" the JavaScript way!
   </H2>
   <UL>

      <LI>Rock smashes scissors!
      <LI>Scissors cut paper!
      <LI>Paper covers rock!
   </UL>
   <FORM name="gameForm">
   <P>Make a choice:
   <BR>
   <INPUT type="radio" name="game" value="Rock"
      checked><STRONG>Rock</STRONG><BR>
   <INPUT type="radio" name="game"
      value="Paper"><STRONG>Paper</STRONG><BR>
   <INPUT type="radio" name="game"
      value="Scissors"><STRONG>Scissors</STRONG>
   <P>
   <BR>
   <BR>
   <INPUT type="button" name="play" value="Play"
      onClick="shakeIt()">
   </FORM>
   </BODY>
</HTML>
```

Creating Arrays

As you probably know, an *array* is a series of variables with the same name that use an index or indices. JavaScript has no array data type, which would be a serious limitation to its capabilities, except that it is pretty easy to define your own array object type, as follows:

```
function MakeArray(n) {
   this.length = n;
   for (var i = 1; i <= n; i++) {
     this[i] = 0 }
     return this
}
```

This code defines an array object (think of it as a template for actual arrays) with a first property, length, that contains the number of elements in a specific instance of the array. Length is the zero element of the array and contains the number of elements in it. The remaining elements in the array have an index from one up to the number of elements in the array; these elements are initialized to zero.

You create an actual array using the new keyword, specifying the number of elements in the array. For example,

```
hobbits = new MakeArray(8);
```

creates an array called hobbits with eight elements, and initializes the elements to zero.

To populate an array, simply assign values to its elements, as you would in a programming language that had a built-in array data type. For example:

```
hobbit[1] = "Frodo Baggins";
hobbit[2] = "Meriadoc Brandybuck";
hobbit[3] = "Samwise Gamgee";
...
```

The elements of arrays can themselves be objects. Suppose you define an object as follows:

```
function nice_hobbit(fname, lname, home) {
   this.fname = fname;
   this.lname = lname;
   this.home = home;
}
```

You could define an array of the nice_hobbit objects as follows:

```
hobbit = new MakeArray(3);
hobbit[1] = new nice_hobbit("Frodo", "Baggins", "Bag End");
hobbit[2] = new nice_hobbit("Meriadoc", "Brandybuck", "Buckland");
hobbit[3] = new nice_hobbit("Samwise", "Gamgee", "Bagshot Row");
```

To display the objects in this array as shown in Figure 9-4, use the show_props function:

```
function show_props(obj, obj_name) {
    var result = ""
    for (var i in obj)
        result += obj_name + "." + i + " = " + obj[i] + "\n"
    return result;
}
```

called as follows:

```
for (var n =1; n <= 3; n++) {
   document.write(show_props(hobbit[n], "hobbit") + " ");
}
```

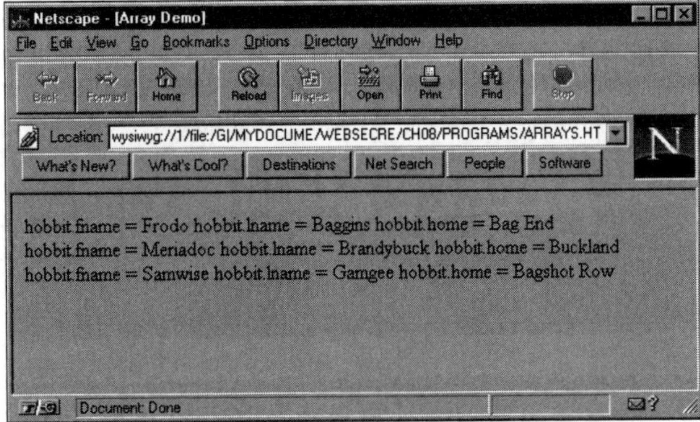

Figure 9-4: It's easy to define instances of JavaScript objects that behave like arrays.

Listing 9-3 shows the complete code that generates and displays the array shown in Figure 9-4.

Listing 9-3: Creating and displaying an array of objects

```
<HTML>
   <HEAD>
   <TITLE>
      Array Demo
   </TITLE>
   <SCRIPT Language="JavaScript">
   <!--Hide that code
   function MakeArray(n) {
      this.length = n;
      for (var i = 1; i <= n; i++) {
        this[i] = 0 }
        return this
   }
   function nice_hobbit(fname, lname, home) {
      this.fname = fname;
      this.lname = lname;
      this.home = home;
   }

   function show_props(obj, obj_name) {
      var result = ""
      for (var i in obj)
          result += obj_name + "." + i + " = " + obj[i] + "\n"
      return result;
   }

   //release me-->
   </SCRIPT>
   </HEAD>
```

```
    <BODY>
    <SCRIPT Language="JavaScript">
    <!--Hide that code
    hobbit = new MakeArray(3);
    hobbit[1] = new nice_hobbit("Frodo", "Baggins", "Bag End");
    hobbit[2] = new nice_hobbit("Meriadoc", "Brandybuck", "Buckland
       Hall");
    hobbit[3] = new nice_hobbit("Samwise", "Gamgee", "Bagshot Row");
    for (var n =1; n <= 3; n++) {
         document.write(show_props(hobbit[n], "hobbit") + " ");
         document.write("<BR>");
    }
    //release me-->
    </SCRIPT>
    </BODY>
</HTML>
```

Validating Forms

JavaScript functions are the best way to validate forms used for user input provided that security is not involved. Using JavaScript as opposed to server-side programming for this purpose has the bandwidth advantages mentioned at the beginning of this chapter, and some user interface pluses, as well. Validation can be performed essentially as the user enters input, rather than after the entire form — which has been submitted to the server — has been processed.

I don't know about you, but I find it really irritating to enter personal information in a Web form, submit it to the server, and have it bounce back to me later because I omitted a required field. You can easily use JavaScript functions to avoid this kind of thing.

For example, take the form requesting first name, last name, and profession shown in Figure 9-5. Imagine it were much longer, with many more required entries. Wouldn't it be a total pain to complete everything except one field, submit the form, and have it bounce back to you, unprocessed?

Here's a function that tests whether an entry is empty:

```
function validate(obj){
   if (obj.value == ""){
      alert ("You cannot leave " + obj.name + " field empty. " +
         "Please enter something, however vacuous!");
   }
}
```

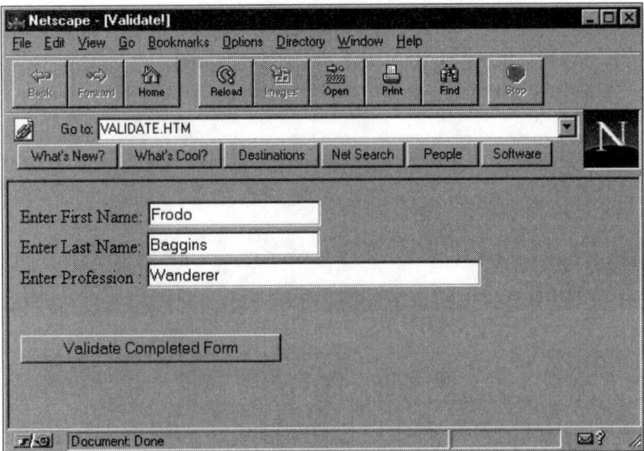

Figure 9-5: JavaScript should be used to validate forms on the fly.

You could call the validate function from the onBlur event of a text input object. The onBlur event is termed the *lost focus* event in many languages; it is fired when the object loses focus, usually because the user has tabbed to another control:

```
<INPUT type="text" size=20 name="First_Name"
onBlur="validate(this);">
```

Note that the this keyword is used to refer to the current text object when the validate function is called.

Now, when the user leaves a text field without having entered anything, she is warned with an alert message like the one shown in Figure 9-6.

You might even like to do more processing than merely testing for empty fields. For example, you might want the entry of certain text to produce special responses. This code shows another alert box when someone enters "Java Programmer" in the Profession text input, as shown in Figure 9-7.

```
if (obj.name=="Profession"){
   if (obj.value.toUpperCase()  == "JAVA PROGRAMMER")
      alert(obj.value.toUpperCase() + ", We've got work for you!");
}
```

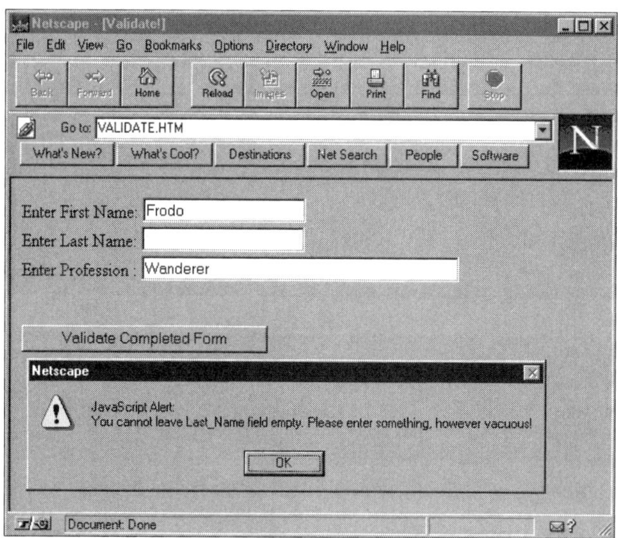

Figure 9-6: You can use a validate function to check for required entries.

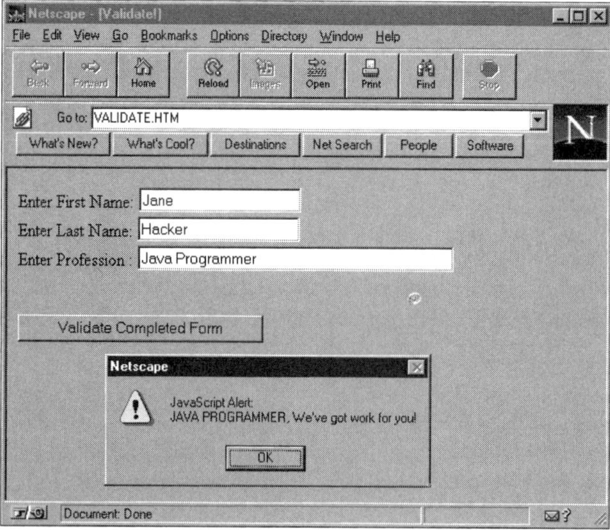

Figure 9-7: You can also use a validate function to specially process particular entries.

Another excellent approach is to validate each text field after the user has completed the information, but before server processing. If the text inputs were contained in a form called thisForm, you could write a function that cycled through all the elements of thisForm and called the validate function for text inputs:

```
function complete(){
   for (i in document.thisForm.elements){
      if (document.thisForm.elements[i].type == "text")
         validate(document.thisForm.elements[i]);
      else
         break
   }
}
```

Listing 9-4 shows the complete HTML and JavaScript code for the validation example demonstrated in this section.

Listing 9-4: Validating inputs in text fields

```
<HTML>
   <HEAD>
      <TITLE>
      Validate!
      </TITLE>
   </HEAD>
   <SCRIPT Language="JavaScript">
   <!--Hide that code
   function validate(obj){
      if (obj.value == ""){
         alert ("You cannot leave " + obj.name + " field empty. " +
            "Please enter something, however vacuous!");
      }
      if (obj.name=="Profession"){
         if (obj.value.toUpperCase()  == "JAVA PROGRAMMER")
            alert(obj.value.toUpperCase() + ", We've got work for
               you!");
      }
   }
   function complete(){
      for (i in document.thisForm.elements){
         if (document.thisForm.elements[i].type == "text")
            validate(document.thisForm.elements[i]);
         else
            break
      }
   }
   //release me -->
   </SCRIPT>
   <BODY>
   <FORM name="thisForm">
      Enter First Name:
      <INPUT type="text" size=20 name="First_Name"
         onBlur="validate(this);">
      <BR>
      Enter Last Name:
      <INPUT type="text" size=20 name="Last_Name"
```

```
            onBlur="validate(this);">
        <BR>
        Enter Profession :
        <INPUT type="text" size=40 name="Profession"
            onBlur="validate(this);">
        <P>
        <BR>
        <INPUT type="button" value="Validate Completed Form"
             onClick="complete();">
    </FORM>
    </BODY>
</HTML>
```

Summary

JavaScript is like the scrawny, eighty-pound weakling on the beach. At first blush it seems like the language can't win. But as you get to know JavaScript, it becomes clear just how much you can do with it. Before you know it, the erstwhile scrawny weakling in some circumstances has more potential than those big bully server-side solutions.

This chapter discussed further material related to JavaScript's object structure and to creating JavaScript applications. Topics covered included

- Manipulating Navigator windows
- Moving between windows
- Creating a scrolling status bar
- Creating games
- Building a working version of "Rocks, Scissors, Paper"
- Creating and working with arrays
- Validating forms

Chapter 10

Doing It with VBScript

"Onward and upward through the fog...."

— Folk saying from the 1960s

The purpose of this chapter is to help familiarize you with the VBScript language and to start you on the path of creating VBScript/ActiveX Web applications. In a nutshell, VBScript is to Explorer is to Visual Basic as JavaScript is to Navigator is to Java. Using VBScript, you can create executable scripts that are part of an HTML page. These scripts will be run when they are encountered by a VBScript-aware browser.

You can use VBScript commands to manipulate Explorer objects, such as HTML document windows, in much the same way that you can use JavaScript to manipulate Navigator objects. In addition — and potentially of very great significance — you can use VBScript to manipulate the exposed events, methods, and properties of ActiveX objects.

If you have experience programming in Visual Basic — or even if you don't — you'll find the "Visual Basic lite" syntax of VBScript very intuitive and easy to pick up.

Netscape Navigator and VBScript

Unfortunately, all is not perfect in cyberspace. Navigator, which is statistically the dominant web browser, does not support — and has no announced intention of supporting — either VBScript or the ActiveX technology. VBScript and ActiveX, of course, are fully supported by Internet Explorer.

NCompass's ActiveX plug-in for Netscape, available from *http://www.ncompass.com,* solves this problem for Netscape users to some degree. Before assuming that a VBScript/ActiveX web application will run using Navigator and the NCompass plug-in, you should test it thoroughly. Quite of bit of VBScript/ActiveX technology does not seem to work very well in Navigator, even extended with the NCompass ActiveX plug-in.

If you want to take advantage of the "golly, gee whiz" potential of VBScript and ActiveX on the Web, this leaves essentially two alternatives:

1. Forget about users who don't run Explorer. Provide a link on your site so that those who wish to do so can download Explorer.
2. Write two versions of your web application, one for users who have a VBScript/ActiveX browser and one for users who don't.

These issues — and techniques for dealing with them — are discussed in more detail in Chapter 4, "Different Browsers for Different Folk."

"Hello World" á la VBScript

To begin to get a feeling for VBScript, why not start with the traditional "Hello, World"? Listing 10-1 uses VBScript to display the text "Hello, World!" in HTML's <H1> style in a Web page and to open a VB-style message box when the page loads (see Figure 10-1).

Listing 10-1: "Hello, World" à la VBScript

```
<HTML>
   <HEAD>
      <SCRIPT Language="VBScript">
      <!--Hide that code
      Sub window_onLoad()
           MsgBox "This is VBSCRIPT!", 64, "I think I can..."
      end sub
      //release me-->
      </SCRIPT>
      <TITLE>
         Hello, World!
      </TITLE>
   </HEAD>
<BODY>
   <SCRIPT Language="VBScript">
   <!--Hide that code
      window.document.write "<H1>Hello, World!</H1>"
   //release me-->
   </SCRIPT>
</BODY>
</HTML>
```

The VBScript code in Listing 10-1 has some similarities with JavaScript, as well as some differences:

- It's as important to use code hiding in VBScript as in JavaScript.
- Unlike JavaScript, VBScript lets you access document event handlers implicitly, without putting function calls in the <BODY> tag.

Figure 10-1: You can use VBScript to write HTML to a document and to add executable statements to browser events.

- Like JavaScript, VBScript supports a write method for the document object, which is beneath the window object in the browser hierarchy. It's really annoying that the syntax of statements is just slightly different in the two languages. If this were not the case, you could write one body of code, leave off the **language** parameter in the <SCRIPT> tag, and have it work in both web clients. Alas!
- VBScript's MsgBox statement will be very familiar to Visual Basic programmers. It is easier to use and more flexible than JavaScript's alert function. Note that the second parameter of the MsgBox statement, 64, is a constant — familiar from Visual Basic 3 — representing the information icon. "New" Visual Basic 4-style constants — for example, vbInformation in place of 64 — will not work with VBScript.

Using ActiveX Controls: An Overview

Much of the power, grace, and style of VBScript comes from its ability to interact with ActiveX controls. The next two chapters describe more advanced issues of VBScript and ActiveX interaction, but for now, here's what you need to know:

- Before you can use ActiveX controls in a web application, you need to download them and register them on the local (target) machine.
- ActiveX controls are then referenced in VBScript code using their CLSID, or class ID, a theoretically unique hexadecimal identifier that can be found in the Windows Registry.
- Two Microsoft-provided tools — the ActiveX Control Pad and the HTML Layout Control — greatly simplify the process of referencing ActiveX controls, manipulating them, and laying out HTML pages that include ActiveX controls and VBScript.

Manual ActiveX Control Registration

To manually register 32-bit ActiveX controls (Ocxs) on a local system, you need the utility program Regsvr32.Exe. This program is quite likely on your system already; if not, you can find it on the Visual Basic product CD-ROM or you can also get it by contacting Microsoft. Just copy the OCX into the destination location and then run Regocx32.Exe with the full path of the OCX as an argument. You'll then find entries for the ActiveX control in the Windows Registry.

This process can, of course, be automated as part of a download and install routine, although usually you would use the Internet Component Download service outlined in the next section. For example, executing the following statement

```
regsvr32 c:\windows\system\grid32.ocx
```

would produce a Registry entry along the lines of the one shown in Figure 10-2.

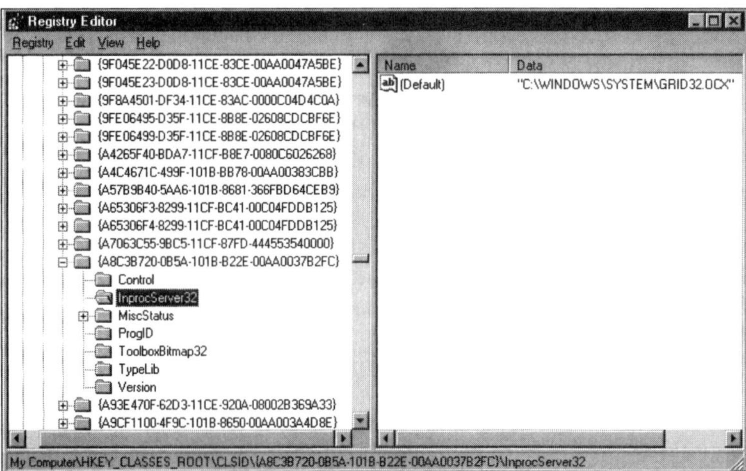

Figure 10-2: ActiveX controls that are properly installed can be found in the Windows Registry.

By the way, if you want to manually unregister an ActiveX control, run Regsvr32.Exe with the /u flag:

```
regsvr32 /u c:\windows\system\grid32.ocx
```

Downloading Internet ActiveX Controls

ActiveX controls run, in-process, on the local machine. This raises a number of questions, including

- Security. These are executables with complete access to local system resources. What if the author has intentionally or unintentionally created a monster program with destructive tendencies?
- How do they get to the local machine?

You use the Internet Component Download service to handle these matters. I'll discuss it in detail in Chapter 12, "Using ActiveX in Web Applications." For now, it's important that you have an overview of the process.

When Explorer hits an <OBJECT> tag in an HTML tag, it knows to load an ActiveX control. The **classid** parameter of the <OBJECT> tag specifies which ActiveX control to load; the **codebase** parameter is a URL specifying where to find the control if it is not already present on the local system. Explorer passes the classid and code URL arguments to an Application Programming Interface (API) function, CoGetClassObjectFromURL. CoGetClassObjectFromURL is responsible for downloading, verifying, and installing controls across the Web. Table 10-1 shows the kinds of files that can be downloaded using CoGetClassObjectFromURL.

Table 10-1 Types of Files Downloadable Across the Web

File Type	*Comments*
Ocx, dynamic link library (Dll)	A single file download is the most straightforward, but not appropriate in cross-platform situations or where more than one file is required.
Cab	Cab (or cabinet) files are Microsoft's compressed file libraries. You'll find tools for compressing and decompressing Cab files as part of the ActiveX SDK (and a number of other SDKs).
Inf	Inf files are text files in private profile format (such as .Ini files) that function as installation scripts. An Inf file can be used to point to multiple Cab files, depending on the target system's operating system.

Part of the Internet Component Download service involves CoGetClassObjectFromURL calling two other API functions, WinVerifyTrust and ICodeInstall, to complete the process. For more details, consult Chapter 12.

Using the ActiveX Control Pad for Scripting

Microsoft's ActiveX Control Pad is an HTML editing tool — with a big difference. A copy of the ActiveX Control Pad is ready to install and use on the *Web Developer's SECRETS* companion CD-ROM.

Although you can use the ActiveX Control Pad to lay out HTML code — it features an HTML visual design tool, the HTML Layout control — the main thrust of this tool is to help you add ActiveX controls and scripts to Web pages. Note that ActiveX Control Pad contains no way to display Web pages created or edited using it. You have to open the page in Explorer to see what you've done!

You can use the ActiveX Control Pad to add either JavaScript or VBScript code to an HTML page. VBScript is Explorer's native language and seems to work better with it and with ActiveX. However, the choice is yours. The only limitation is that "or" is exclusive: You cannot use both languages in the same HTML page constructed by the ActiveX Control Pad.

If you use a straight text editor to create your HTML pages, you can include both JavaScript and VBScript in the same HTML document.

To specify which scripting language you will use, open the ActiveX Control Pad's Tools menu, choose Options, and then choose Script from the sub-menu that appears. Choose either Visual Basic Scripting Edition or JavaScript, as shown in Figure 10-3.

Figure 10-3: Using the ActiveX Control Pad, you can use either JavaScript or VBScript for a given HTML page.

VBScript is the default language for the ActiveX Control Pad. In this and the next three chapters — which cover VBScript and the ActiveX technology — it's assumed unless otherwise specified that VBScript is used for scripting functionality.

When you start the ActiveX Control Pad, by default it opens a new HTML page for editing (see Figure 10-4).

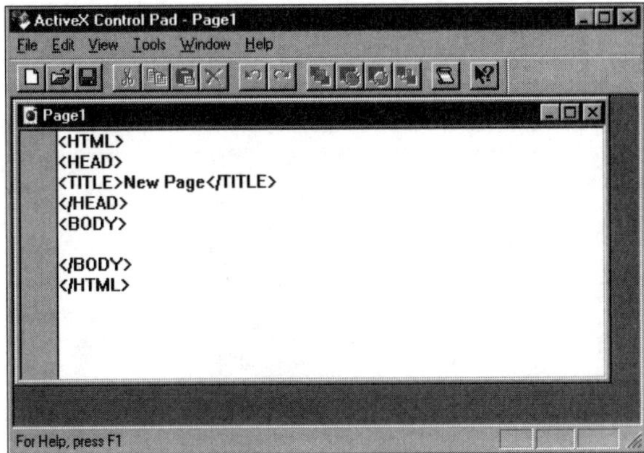

Figure 10-4: By default, the ActiveX Control Pad opens a new HTML page for editing.

If you wish, you can now open an existing HTML page for modifications. Figure 10-5 shows the VBScript "Hello, World" page opened. Once you open a new or existing HTML page in the ActiveX Control Pad, you can do a number of different things to it, including

- Directly edit the HTML code
- Insert an ActiveX control into the HTML page
- Create and insert an HTML Layout Control, which contains a number of ActiveX controls and is stored in a separate file with an .Alx extension
- Create or edit script commands

If you look carefully at the left margin of the Hello.Htm file shown in Figure 10-5, you'll see icons that look like little scrolled pieces of paper (Figure 10-6). This is the Script Wizard icon, which you use to start the Script Wizard. (You can also start the Script Wizard by using a toolbar button or the Tools menu.) Figure 10-7 shows the Script Wizard.

The Script Wizard provides several views. In List View, you can use the Script Wizard to assign simple actions to events using a "point-and-click" approach. In Code View, you can create custom scripts and assign them to an event handler. The Script Wizard then inserts the appropriate <SCRIPT> tag into HTML.

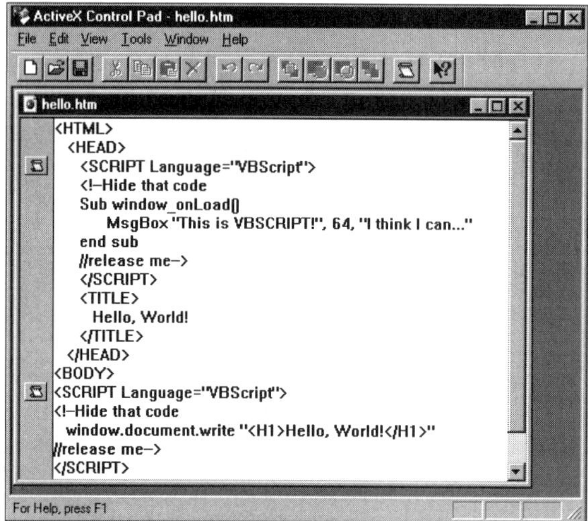

Figure 10-5: You can open existing HTML files for modifications in the ActiveX Control Pad.

Figure 10-6: When the Script Wizard icon appears in the margin of an HTML page, clicking on the icon starts the Script Wizard with the related code open.

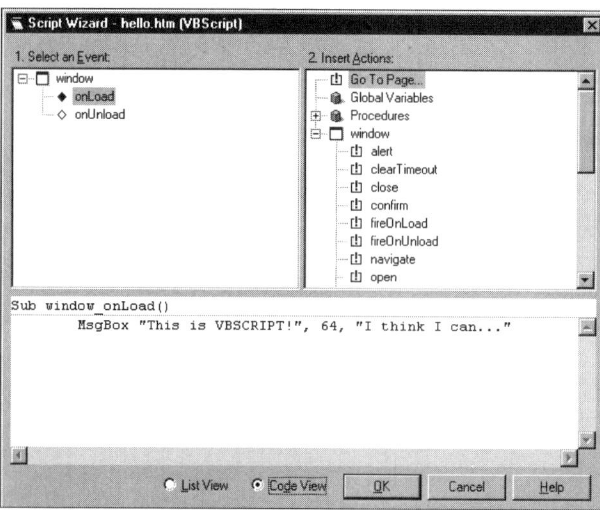

Figure 10-7: You use the Script Wizard to add VBScript to an HTML page (Code View shown).

Using the Script Wizard in List View

In List View, you can create event handlers that perform these actions:

- Call an object's method, or a procedure, provided that the method takes no parameters *or* has the same number and names of parameters as the calling event handle
- Invoke Go To Page, Hide or Show Control, or Bring to Front/Send to Back actions
- Assign a value to an object's property or to a global variable

For example, suppose you have an HTML page containing a label and a command button (using the *intrinsic* ActiveX controls bundled with Internet Explorer). You can add the controls to the HTML page by choosing Insert ActiveX Control from the Edit menu in the ActiveX Control Pad. The Edit ActiveX facility brings up a Properties window, and a way to visually edit the physical location of controls, as shown in Figure 10-8.

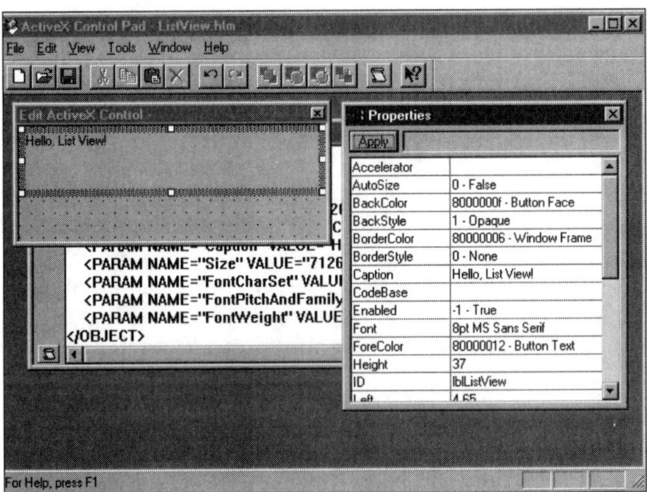

Figure 10-8: You can visually edit the location and size of ActiveX controls and can use the Properties window to set object properties.

If you set the label's caption to "Hello, List View!" in the Properties window, users will see this text when the HTML page is open. You can use the ID property of the control to give the control a name, lblListView, that scripts included in the HTML page can use to reference it. Note that object properties are written to the underlying HTML code by including a <PARAM> tag within the control's <OBJECT> tag for each property.

Next, open the Script Wizard and select the Click event of the command button in the Event pane (on the left in Figure 10-9). The Event pane shows a hierarchical view of all the objects and events that you can script.

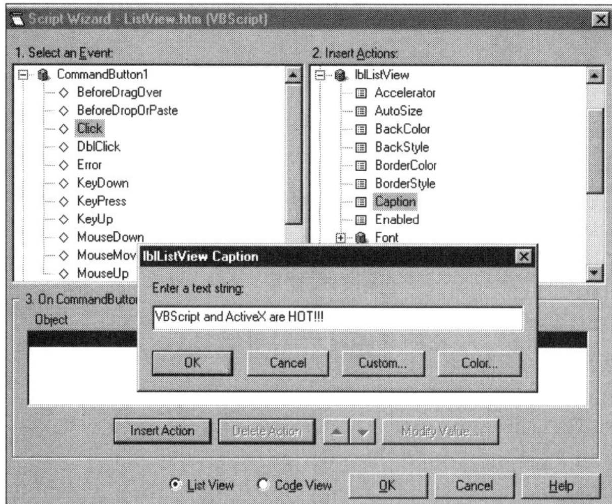

Figure 10-9: In List View, the Script Wizard takes care of code generation.

The Action pane (on the right, Figure 10-9) shows the actions and properties you can use in the event handler, as well as the global variables and procedures defined for the page. The icons in this pane represent different types of actions, properties, and objects. Once you've specified a value for the property, the Script Wizard adds that property to the list in the Script pane.

In the Action pane, select lblListView's caption property. In the Object pane (the bottom pane shown in Figure 10-9), click on Insert Action (or double-click on the caption property). The type of dialog box you'll see and the values you can select depend on the type of property you've double-clicked. When you double-click on an action, the Script Wizard adds that action to the list in the Script pane. A dialog box opens, requesting a string value for the label's caption property. Enter **VBScript and ActiveX are HOT!!!** — since they are — and click on OK. Click on OK to exit the Script Wizard.

If you save the HTML page and open it in Explorer, clicking on the command button changes the label caption, as shown in Figure 10-10.

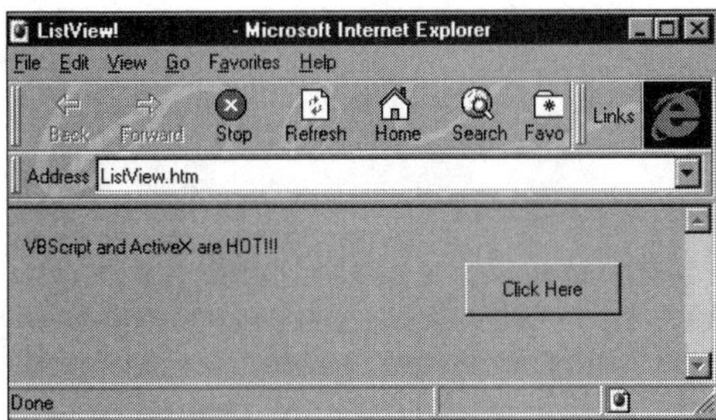

Figure 10-10: The Script Wizard makes it easy to create dynamic web applications.

Here's the underlying HTML code for the sample application:

```
<HTML>
<HEAD>
<TITLE>ListView!</TITLE>
   <OBJECT ID="lblListView" WIDTH=269 HEIGHT=49
   CLASSID="CLSID:978C9E23-D4B0-11CE-BF2D-00AA003F40D0">

      <PARAM NAME="Caption" VALUE="Hello, List View!">
      <PARAM NAME="Size" VALUE="7126;1305">
      <PARAM NAME="FontCharSet" VALUE="0">
      <PARAM NAME="FontPitchAndFamily" VALUE="2">
      <PARAM NAME="FontWeight" VALUE="0">
   </OBJECT>
   <SCRIPT LANGUAGE="VBScript">
   <!--
   Sub CommandButton1_Click()
      lblListView.Caption = "VBScript and ActiveX are HOT!!!"
   end sub
   -->
   </SCRIPT>
   <OBJECT ID="CommandButton1" WIDTH=96 HEIGHT=32
   CLASSID="CLSID:D7053240-CE610-11CD-A777-00DD01143C57">
      <PARAM NAME="ForeColor" VALUE="2147483669">
      <PARAM NAME="Caption" VALUE="Click Here">
      <PARAM NAME="Size" VALUE="2540;846">
      <PARAM NAME="FontCharSet" VALUE="0">
      <PARAM NAME="FontPitchAndFamily" VALUE="2">
      <PARAM NAME="ParagraphAlign" VALUE="3">
      <PARAM NAME="FontWeight" VALUE="0">
   </OBJECT>
</HEAD>
<BODY>
</BODY>
</HTML>
```

A good strategy is to use the ActiveX Control Pad to get your application started. Then, finish it up by modifying the HTML code by hand.

Using Code View

Using the Script Wizard Code View, you can create any VBScript code that you'd like and associate it with any available event handler. Note that the Script Wizard automatically generates the Sub and End Sub statements for event handlers. This can be a little confusing: If you enter your own End Sub code manually to close a routine, an End Sub statement will be placed in the HTML code twice. This will cause an error.

Using the Script Pane

You can script multiple actions for any given event, and they'll be executed in the order in which they appear in the list in the Script pane. You can use the Up and Down Arrows to reorder the actions in the list and the Insert Action and Delete Action buttons to add or remove actions from the list. If you specified a value for a property, you can edit it by selecting that property and clicking on the Modify Value button.

In the Event pane, if you click an event handler that's associated with a custom action — for example, a script that contains an if statement — a message in the Script pane will advise you to switch to Code View to edit the action because you cannot modify "custom" event code in List View.

Adding a Hyperlink Jump to an Event

You can easily add a hyperlink to an event. First select the event, as described earlier. Next, in the Action pane, double-click on Go To Page. Finally, if you're in List View, enter the URL for the jump destination page in the Go To Page dialog box, and click on OK. Alternatively, if you're in Code View, type the URL of the jump destination page for the window.location.href property in the Script pane. For example, in a command button double-click event, type

```
Sub CommandButton1_DblClick(Cancel)
   Window.location.href = "http://www.bearhome.com"
End Sub
```

The VBScript Language

Microsoft Visual Basic Scripting Edition — VBScript for short — is a language in the Basic family. In fact, it is an abridged sibling of two other VB languages: Visual Basic for Applications, which is used as a macro language in many of Microsoft's applications; and Visual Basic, the stand-alone programming environment.

Most developers will probably have at least a passing familiarity with some version of Basic. You likely have some experience with Visual Basic, which is the world's best-selling programming language. But even if you don't have a background in Basic, or in VB, VBScript is pretty easy to use. Despite its ease of use, it packs a wallop. This is not your father's scripting language.

For reference information on VBScript, check Microsoft's site, at *http://www.microsoft.com/vbscript/*.

Comments

To include comments in VBScript you use either the Rem keyword or a single apostrophe ('). The remainder of a line that starts with an apostrophe, or Rem, is a comment. If the line begins with a VBScript statement, it must be separated from the Rem keyword with a colon. For example

```
' I'm a comment
Dim bigDough ' holds maximum money
Rem Must consider taxes
bigDough = bigDough - taxes : Rem those taxes!
```

Using Variables in VBScript

There is only one variable type in VBScript: variant. Table 10-2 shows the different kinds of information that can be stored in VBScript variant variables.

Table 10-2 Kinds of Information Contained in VBScript Variant Variables

Subtype	*Meaning*
Boolean	Contains either True or False. The keyword True evaluates to -1; False evaluates to 0.
Byte	Contains an integer in the range 0 to 255.
Integer	Contains an integer in the range -32,768 to 32,767.
Long	Contains an integer in the range -2,147,483,648 to 2,147,483,647.
Single	Contains a single-precision, floating-point number.
Double	Contains a double-precision, floating-point number.
Date	Contains a number that represents a date between January 1, 100 and December 31, 9999.
String	Contains a variable-length string that can be up to approximately 2 billion characters in length.

(continued)

Table 10-2 (Continued)

Subtype	*Meaning*
Object	Contains an object.
Error	Contains an error number.

VBScript will treat the contents of a variant variable appropriately, depending on the data assigned to the variable. (To treat a number as a string, enclose it within quotes.) There are also a great many conversion functions available for explicit subtype conversions.

Arrays

You create arrays in VBScript simply by declaring them with parentheses. For example, the following script creates a one-dimensional array with 20 elements and assigns a value of Smeagol to the second element in the array:

```
<SCRIPT LANGUAGE="VBScript">
<!--
   Dim myArray(20)
   myArray(1) = "Smeagol" 'First element of an array is always 0
-->
</SCRIPT>
```

It's easy to create and manipulate *dynamic arrays* — that is, arrays whose number of elements fluctuates during the execution of a script. You declare them, using Dim or the ReDim keyword, without elements. Next, you initialize them with a specific number of elements using ReDim. You assign and manipulate values of elements.

You can change the number of elements on the fly using ReDim. If you use the Preserve keyword with ReDim, existing elements are saved. Alas, without it they are not preserved.

To create an array, give it 20 elements, and resize it to add 5 more elements while preserving the values of the original 20 elements, you'd write VBScript code along these lines:

```
<SCRIPT LANGUAGE="VBScript">
<!--
   Dim myArray()               ' Declare it
   ...
   ReDim myArray(20)           ' initialize with 20 elements
   ...                         ' do things
   ReDim Preserve myArray(25)  ' more elements, good
-->
</SCRIPT>
```

Variable Names

Variable names must begin with an alphabetic character. They cannot contain embedded periods, must be less than 255 characters long, and must be unique in the scope in which they are declared.

Declaring Variables

You declare variables using the Dim statement. You can declare multiple variables using one Dim statement if you separate them by commas. For example:

```
Dim myString
Dim Frodo, Bilbo, Samwise
```

You can also declare variables implicitly, by simply assigning them values. It is better coding practice, however, to declare all variables explicitly. This can be enforced by placing the statement

```
Option Explicit
```

as the first line of VBScript code in an HTML document.

Variable Scope

Variables declared — explicitly or implicitly — within a procedure are limited in scope and lifetime to the procedure. Variables declared outside a procedure are global to the script in which they are declared and persist as long as the script is running.

Limitation on the Number of Variables

There is a limit of 127 variables allowed per VBScript procedure (arrays count as a single variable). In addition, each script can have no more than 127 "script-level" variables.

Constants

There is no explicit syntax for declaring a constant in VBScript. Of course, you can declare a variable (using the Dim statement), assign a fixed value — such as a number, string, or date/time literal — and use the variable as a constant in the remainder of your script.

To distinguish variables that will be used as constants, Microsoft recommends naming them using uppercase and underscores, as in

```
Dim MAX_POSS_VALUE, PSEUDO_CONSTANT_STR
MAX_POSS_VALUE = 1012
PSEUDO_CONSTANT_STR = "I don't change!"
```

Literals

You assign string literals by enclosing the string within quotation (") marks. You assign date/time literals by enclosing the value within pound signs (#). For example

```
Dim DueDate, myString
DueDate  = #4-25-98#
myString = "I'm a string - and proud of it!"
```

Operators

Table 10-3 shows the operators used in VBScript.

Table 10-3 VBScript Operators

Operator	*Meaning*	*Operator Category*
^	Exponentiation	Arithmetic
-	Negation	Arithmetic
*	Multiplication	Arithmetic
/	Division	Arithmetic
\	Integer division	Arithmetic
Mod	Modulo	Arithmetic
+	Addition	Arithmetic
-	Minus	Arithmetic
&	String concatenation	String
=	Equals	Comparison
<>	Does not equal	Comparison
<	Less than	Comparison
>	Greater than	Comparison
<=	Less than or equal	Comparison
>=	Greater than or equal	Comparison
Is	Comparisons using Is are True if two object references point to the same object	Object Reference
Not	Logical negation	Logical
And	Conjunction	Logical
Or	Disjunction	Logical
Xor	Exclusive or	Logical

Operator	Meaning	Operator Category
Eqv	Equivalence	Logical
Imp	Evaluates to True if the statement (A implies B) is True	Logical

Operator Precedence

You can use parentheses to set the order of expression evaluation; operations within parentheses are always performed before those outside the parentheses. Otherwise, arithmetic operators are evaluated before comparison operators, which are evaluated before logical operators. Comparison operators have equal precedence — that is, they are evaluated form left to right in the order in which they are encountered. Arithmetic and logical operators are evaluated in the order in which they are shown in Table 10-3. The string concatenation operator is evaluated after arithmetic operators and before comparison operators.

Flow Control Statements

VBScript supports a rich vocabulary of flow control statements, including

- If...Then...Else
- Do...Loop
- While...Wend
- For...Next

VBScript does not support Visual Basic's Select...Case statement. If you're modifying VB code to run as VBScript, be sure to substitute logically equivalent flow control statements for any Select...Case statements in your original code.

VBScript statements, and variables, are completely case insensitive, thank goodness! In other words, it has the same impact as IF and If. And VBScript will recognize a variable you call "MyString" as the same one as "myString."

If Statements

Here's an example of a simple If statement that changes the properties of a label when a button is clicked, provided that a check box is checked (as shown in Figure 10-11):

```
<SCRIPT LANGUAGE="VBScript">
<!--
Sub CommandButton1_Click()
If CheckBox1.Value = true then
   lblFun.BackColor = &H000000FF
```

```
    lblFun.ForeColor = &H00FFFFFF
    lblFun.Font.Bold = True
    lblFun.Font.Size = 20
    lblFun.Caption = "I got Text!"
end if
end sub
-->
</SCRIPT>
```

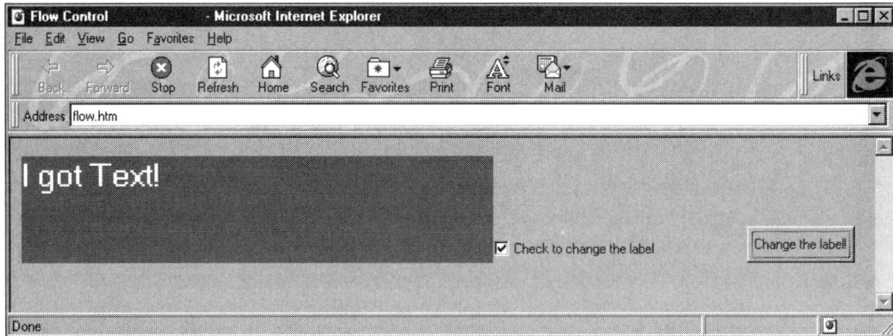

Figure 10-11: You can use VBScript flow control statements to control the Web user interface.

Looping

Figure 10-12 shows the results of placing the number of Xs in a label that are specified with a For loop.

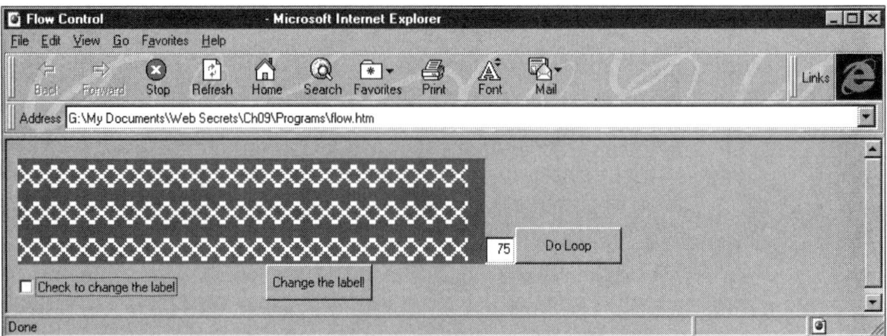

Figure 10-12: VBScript has extremely flexible looping statements.

Here's the For loop code:

```
<SCRIPT LANGUAGE="VBScript">
<!--
Sub cmdLoop_Click()
   Dim myString
   myString = ""
   For i = 1 to TextBox1.text
      mystring = mystring + "X"
   Next
   lblFun.caption = myString
end sub
-->
</SCRIPT>
```

As production code, of course this would not do: There is no validation checking that TextBox1.text is a number (let alone a reasonable number).

You could, of course, have achieved the same effect with a Do loop, for example:

```
Sub cmdLoop_Click()
   Dim myString
   myString = ""
   i = 1
   Do
      mystring = mystring + "X"
      i = i + 1
   Loop Until i = TextBox1.text
   lblFun.caption = myString
end sub
```

VBScript looping statements contain a great deal of functionality and flexibility not covered here due to space limitations. I'll use variations in examples as I go along (and you can look up the syntax of the statements on Microsoft's Web site).

Procedures and Functions

VBScript procedures, or subroutines, are a series of statements surrounded by Sub and End Sub statements.

Functions are a series of statements delimited by the Function and End Function keywords. Functions return a value, which is assigned to the function name. For example:

```
Function Add2Nums (nOne, nTwo)
   Add2Nums = nOne + nTwo
End Function
```

Functions must be used on the right side of a variable assignment, or in an expression. Here are a couple of examples:

```
Sum = Add2Nums (40,2)
MsgBox "The sum of 40 and 2 is " & Add2Nums (40,2)
```

You can call subroutines just using the procedure's name, along with any arguments. Alternatively, you can call them using the Call statement. If mySub (arg1, arg2) is a subroutine, here are examples of calling it:

```
mySub firstarg, secondarg
call mySub (First, Second)
```

Like JavaScript functions, VBScript procedures and functions need to be declared before they can be invoked. All procedures and functions should therefore go in the <HEAD> section of your HTML documents.

Summary

VBScript is a stripped-down version of Visual Basic for Applications, which itself is a stripped-down version of Visual Basic. Compared to Visual Basic, VBScript lacks the stand-alone integrated development environment. Variable typing is limited. A few significant parts of the syntax are missing, along with the ability to create stand-alone executables and OLE servers. However, VBScript still packs plenty of punch and is remarkably easy to use.

JavaScript and VBScript are roughly comparable in capabilities, although quite different in flavor. Which you prefer to work with is a matter of taste. Pretty clearly, most things you can do in one, you can do in the other.

For my money, I think VBScript is somewhat more powerful — for example, in its inclusion of arrays — and less fussy — for instance, in the case insensitivity of statements. Be that as it may, probably the most radical thing about VBScript is its integration with ActiveX. This combination produces a truly awesome potential for creating web applications that really sing and dance the cha-cha — provided client browser software can "read" ActiveX. In the next few chapters explore further how to put the VBScript language and the ActiveX technology together.

This chapter has covered

- Navigator and VBScript
- Creating a "Hello, World" application using VBScript
- An overview of using ActiveX controls
- Downloading and registering ActiveX controls
- An introduction to the ActiveX Control Pad
- The VBScript language, including comments, variables, statements, operators, operator precedence, and flow control

Chapter 11

VBScript and ActiveX

"Science is all metaphor."

— Timothy Leary

Chapter 10, "Doing It with VBScript," was an introduction to VBScript's place in the universe and to VBScript as a programming language. This chapter picks up where Chapter 10 left off. I'll show you how to start adding dynamic ActiveX controls to your Web pages.

VBScript comes into its own when VBScript procedures interact with ActiveX controls. I'll demonstrate how to quickly and easily use VBScript in this fashion to make interactive and awesome Web pages.

Using the HTML Layout Control

Chapter 10 discussed the basics of using Microsoft's ActiveX Control Pad. (There's a copy of the ActiveX Control Pad program on the companion CD-ROM to this book.)

ActiveX Control Pad ships with an extremely important ActiveX control — the HTML Layout control, sometimes simply called the Layout control. The Layout control allows you to visually position ActiveX controls precisely on a Web page. It's like a container's container: Its purpose in life is to hold a basket of ActiveX controls (which are, of course, themselves, code containers).

Inserting a Layout Control

The Layout control's editing environment is reminiscent of Visual Basic. For example, you use a Properties window to set ActiveX control properties. (You can also do this, perhaps dynamically in response to user action, using VBScript code.)

You can use the ActiveX Control Pad to insert as many Layout controls as you want in an HTML page. (In turn, each Layout control can contain numerous ActiveX controls.) By the way, the content of a Layout control is often referred to as a *layout*.

Although you may never need to directly edit the ASCII file "behind" a Layout control, you should know that every Layout control corresponds to an Alx file. These are text files using extensions to HTML — such as the <DIV> tag — to hold positioning and control information for the contents of the Layout control.

In the ActiveX Control Pad, you insert a Layout control by choosing Insert HTML Layout from the Edit menu. Before the Layout control is created, you must provide a location and name for its Alx file. Somewhat oddly, you do this with the Windows common File Open dialog, rather than the File Save dialog. After you've given the Alx file a name, the Layout control's development environment opens (see the section "Using the Layout Control's Development Environment" later in this chapter).

Let's skip ahead for a moment to the way the Layout control is inserted in the underlying HTML code. Here's a sample HTML page containing one Layout control:

```
<HTML>
  <HEAD>
  <TITLE>Layout Demo</TITLE>
  <OBJECT CLASSID="CLSID:812AE312-8B8E-11CF-93C8-00AA00C08FDF"
  ID="layout_alx" STYLE="LEFT:0;TOP:0"
  CODEBASE="http://www.activex.microsoft.com/controls/mspert10.cab">
  <PARAM NAME="ALXPATH" REF VALUE="layout.alx">
  </OBJECT>
  </HEAD>
  <BODY>
  </BODY>
</HTML>
```

It's worth noting that — depending on the contents of the Layout control and related Alx file — this HTML page might be chock-full of objects, although the official body of the document is empty.

For every inserted Layout control, there are two parts of this HTML code that you will probably end up editing by hand. These are

- The value assigned to the ALXPATH property of the Layout control
- The value assigned to the **Codebase** parameter of the <OBJECT> tag

In HTML, you indicate the properties of ActiveX controls using the <PARAM> tag. Each **name** parameter of the <PARAM> tag corresponds to a control property. For example,

```
<PARAM NAME="ALXPATH" REF VALUE="layout.alx">
```

really references the ALXPATH property of the referenced control (as specified in the <OBJECT> tag).

You will probably want to edit the value of the ALXPATH property by hand, because, as originally set in the ActiveX Control Pad, it will be hard coded to a specific local location, for example, C:\webstuff\layouts\layout.alx.

As you complete work on your HTML page — and the included Layout control and attached Alx file — you'll want to move the files into the location specified by your web server software and other HTML documents that are part of your site. If you place the Alx file in the same directory as the HTML page it is part of, you can name it without a path — for example, layout.alx. Otherwise, you'll want to use TCP/IP locating conventions — for example, http://www.mywebsite.com/layouts/layout.alx.

Using the Codebase Parameter

You use the **Codebase** parameter of the <OBJECT> tag to specify the location of a control's code. Automatic download code for all the controls intrinsic to the Layout control — these controls are roughly comparable to the Visual Basic starter set, which is described under "Intrinsic Controls," later in the chapter — is included in one compressed library file, mspert10.cab. (For an explanation of .cab files, see "Downloading Internet ActiveX Controls" in Chapter 9.)

Code specified in the **Codebase** parameter is only downloaded and installed if it isn't present on the local machine. When dealing with the Layout control's intrinsic controls, you only need to specify the **Codebase** parameter the first time one of the intrinsic controls is invoked. One download works for all the controls.

The URL that you should specify for the intrinsic controls is *http://activex.microsoft.com/controls/mspert10.cab*. Alternatively, according to Microsoft, you can copy mspert10.cab from the location just shown to your local server, and then specify the location on your server in the **Codebase** parameter. For example, this might be *http://www.myownserver.com/controls/mspert10.cab.*

Listing 11-1 shows an HTML page that invokes a Layout control, using the correct **Codebase** URL for the intrinsic controls library:

Listing 11-1: Using the Codebase parameter

```
<HTML>
<HEAD>
<TITLE>Layout Demo
<OBJECT CLASSID="CLSID:812AE312-8B8E-11CF-93C8-00AA00C08FDF"
ID="layout_alx" STYLE="LEFT:0;TOP:0"
CODEBASE="http://www.activex.microsoft.com/controls/mspert10.cab">
<PARAM NAME="ALXPATH" REF VALUE="layout.alx">
</OBJECT>
</TITLE>
</HEAD>
<BODY>

</BODY>
</HTML>
```

The Layout Control from an HTML Page in ActiveX Control Pad

When you add a Layout to an HTML page in the ActiveX Control Pad, you'll see the Edits HTML Layout icon in the left margin, as shown in Figure 11-1. (This icon appears to represent objects on a field, as opposed to embedded VBScript code, which is represented by the Code Wizard's scroll icon.) To change the contents of a Layout control — for example, by adding or moving a control, or changing a property — open the Layout control's development environment by clicking on the Edits HTML Layout icon.

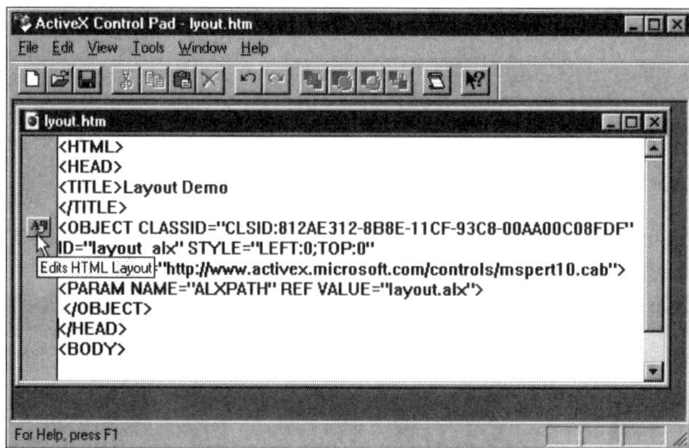

Figure 11-1: To change the contents of a Layout, click on the Edit HTML Layout button in the left margin.

Using the Layout Control's Development Environment

With a Layout open, you'll see a visual development environment, as shown in Figure 11-2. This is a serious visual development environment that features a Toolbox of available ActiveX controls and a Properties window for setting the properties of controls. You can also click on the Code Wizard button (remember, it looks like a scroll) to edit VBScript code.

Perhaps the most serious failing of the Layout control's development environment is its lack of debugging capabilities. If you've done something wrong in a script, you won't know it until you run the application in Explorer. When it hits the offending code, Explorer will show a (usually cryptic) error message with the line number of the error. 102, 103, 104 ... counting line numbers in a text file gets old quickly.

Inside Scoop

To help prevent bugs arising from typographic errors, it's an excellent idea to require explicit variable declarations by including the statement "Option Explicit" as the first line in all of your scripts.

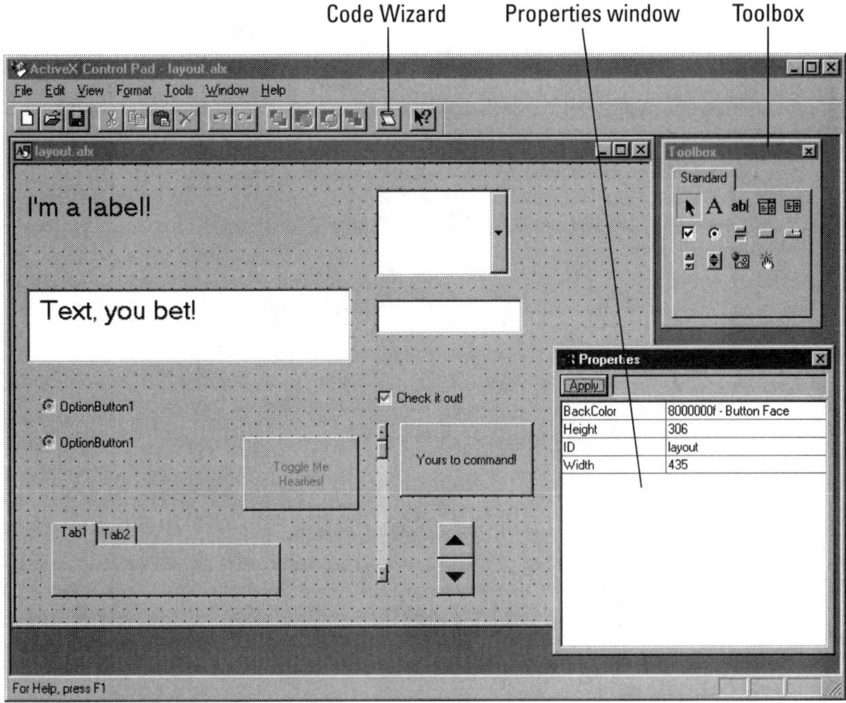

Figure 11-2: The Layout editing environment includes a Toolbox of controls and a Properties window.

If you don't see the Properties window, make sure that it is checked on the Layout's View menu.

When you first open a Layout, the Properties window shows the properties of the Layout itself (Figures 11-2 and 11-3). There are four Layout properties that you can change in the Properties window: Height, Width, ID, and BackColor.

ID is the control's *name*; you can use the string entered as a value for an object's ID in code to dynamically change properties and invoke methods. When necessary, you can invoke a further dialog to set a property by clicking on the button with three dots to the right of the Apply field, as shown in Figure 11-3. (This process will be very familiar to users of other Microsoft development tools.) For example, Figure 11-3 shows using the common color dialog to set the Layout's BackColor property.

Of course, most controls have more properties you can set than the Layout control. To change the properties of a control that you have placed on a Layout, first make the control active by selecting it. The Properties window will list those properties you can change. (For example, Figure 11-4 shows the Properties window with a text box active.) Select the property whose value you wish to change, and enter the new value in the field at the top of the Properties window. Click on the Apply button to make the change.

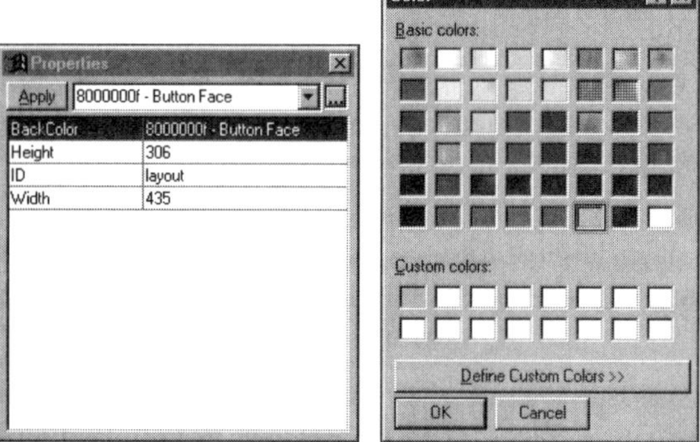

Figure 11-3: You can usually invoke common dialogs when needed to set object properties.

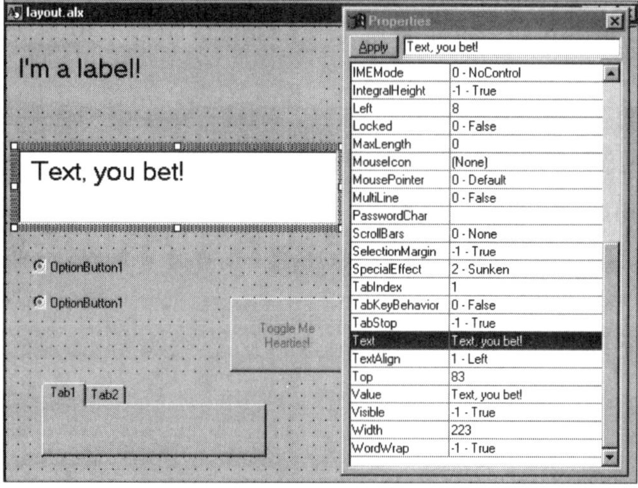

Figure 11-4: The Properties window displays properties for the currently selected control.

Intrinsic Controls

By default, the *intrinsic* ActiveX controls — those that come with the Layout control — are displayed in the Toolbox the first time you open a Layout. I'll show you in a moment how to add and remove ActiveX controls from the Toolbox. Figure 11-5 shows a Web page that contains almost all the intrinsic controls.

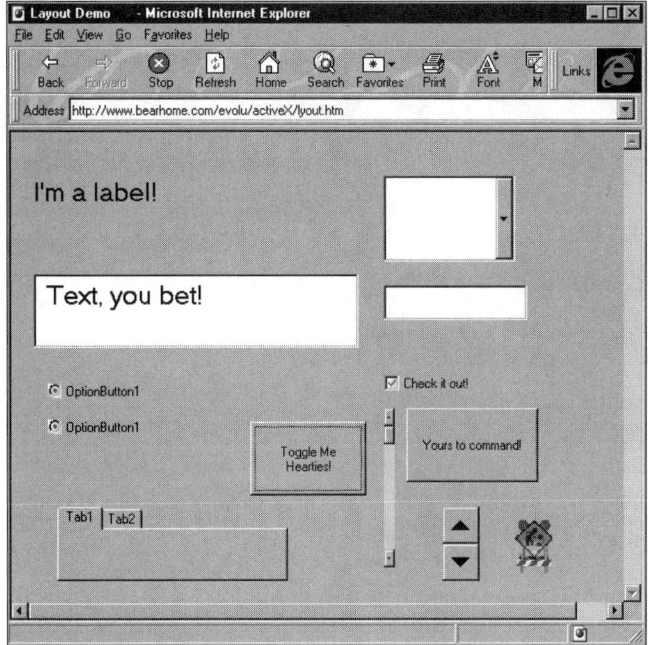

Figure 11-5: You can display the intrinsic ActiveX controls as part of a Web page simply by adding them to a Layout.

Table 11-1 lists the objects that appear by default in the Layout Toolbox, in the order in which they typically appear (other than the selector, these objects are all the intrinsic controls).

Adding Additional Controls

To add an additional control, right-click on an empty part of the Layout Toolbox. Select Additional Controls from the pop-up menu. You'll see the Additional Controls dialog, as shown in Figure 11-6.

You can use the Additional Controls dialog to add to your Toolbox any ActiveX control (or, as they used to be known, OCX) that is registered on your system. You can also add insertable OLE objects — for example, a Microsoft Excel chart. Note that if Selected Items Only is checked, you will only see those controls already selected in the Toolbox.

Working with nonintrinsic ActiveX controls is explored in detail in Chapter 12, "Using ActiveX in Web Applications."

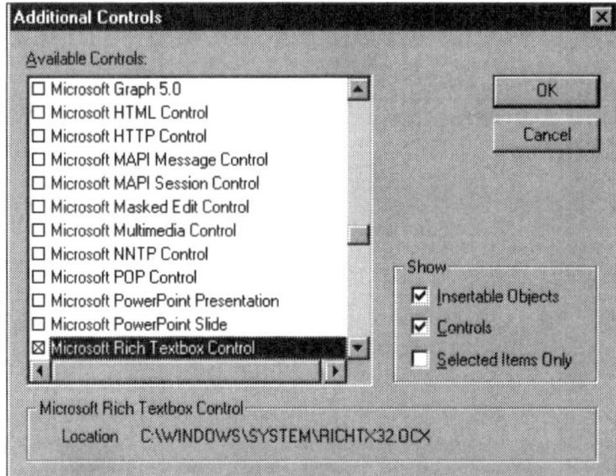

Figure 11-6: You can use the Additional Controls dialog to add ActiveX controls to your Toolbox.

Table 11-1 HTML Layout Intrinsic Controls

Object	*Formal Name (as it Appears in the Additional Controls Dialog)*
Selector	The selector is an arrow used for selecting controls (making them active) on the Layout
Label	Microsoft Forms 2.0 Label
TextBox	Microsoft Forms 2.0 TextBox
ComboBox	Microsoft Forms 2.0 ComboBox
ListBox	Microsoft Forms 2.0 ListBox
OptionButton	Microsoft Forms 2.0 Microsoft Forms 2.0 OptionButton
CheckBox	Microsoft Forms 2.0 CheckBox
ToggleButton	Microsoft Forms 2.0 ToggleButton
CommandButton	Microsoft Forms 2.0 CommandButton
TabStrip	Microsoft Forms 2.0 TabStrip
ScrollBar	Microsoft Forms 2.0 ScrollBar
SpinButton	Microsoft Forms 2.0 SpinButton
ISImage	Microsoft ActiveX Image Control 1.0
ISHotSpot	Microsoft ActiveX Hot Spot Control 1.0

Sophisticated Programming Using VBScript and ActiveX

VBScript, combined with ActiveX, is a rich and sophisticated programming environment in which you can do just about anything. In particular, almost anything you can do in the full version of Visual Basic you can do in VBScript/ActiveX — and put it right up on the Web. Only in the area of object-oriented programming (OOP) will it possibly let you down.

The principles of sound code architecture and construction are beyond the scope of *Web Developer's SECRETS,* as is the information you need to become a Visual Basic guru. I'll cover various advanced topics as I go along. For example, Chapter 12 shows you how to use VBScript to manipulate the information stored in SQL databases.

In addition, there are many good sources of information on coding practices and on Visual Basic. On the topic of software construction, I recommend Steve McConnell's *Code Complete* (Microsoft Press, 1993). For how to use Visual Basic in a sophisticated fashion, I suggest — with all due modesty — my own *Visual Basic 5 Secrets* (IDG Books, 1997).

Scripting with Intrinsic ActiveX Controls

Programming using the Layout control has more of the flavor of conventional software development than of Web development. If you've worked in any Windows development environment — particularly Visual Basic — you should be able to pick it right up.

Inside Scoop

Be *very* cautious about editing VBScript code contained in an Alx file directly using a text editor while it is open in a layout in the ActiveX Control Pad. If you are like me, you'll often want to edit your VBScript directly without using the Code Wizard tool in the ActiveX Control Pad. This is all very well and good. The problem is that if you edit an Alx file whose related Layout is open, even if you have saved your work, when you close the Layout in the ActiveX Control Pad, it may manually overwrite any code changes. Also, be careful of having multiple copies of an Alx file open in Notepad. Forewarned is forearmed on this one.

Labels

Figure 11-7 shows an ActiveX Web page containing four intrinsic ActiveX controls: two command buttons, a label, and a text box. When the Add Date & Time! button is clicked, the current date and time are concatenated to the end of the label's caption. The user can enter any text she likes in the text box. When the Apply New Text label is clicked, the text property of the text box is assigned to the caption property of the label.

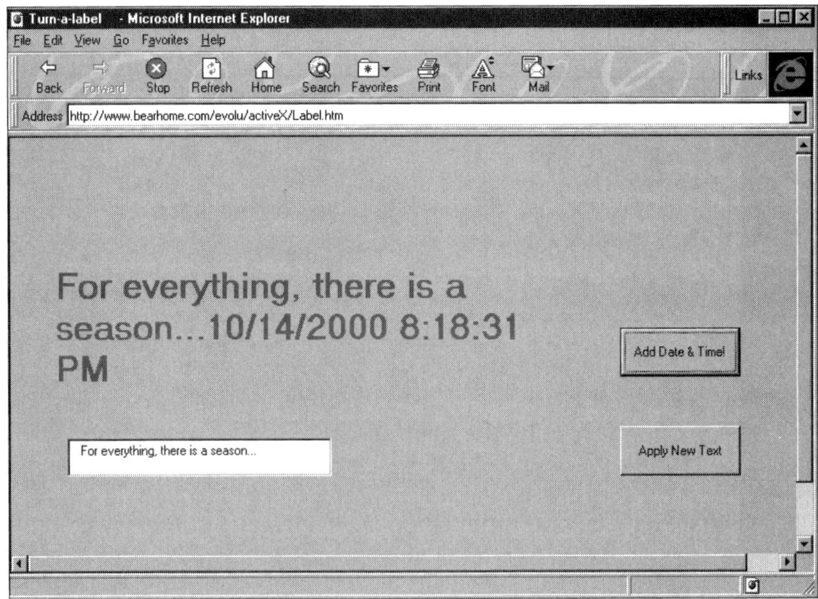

Figure 11-7: It's easy to manipulate label controls using VBScript.

This is clearly neither rocket science nor brain surgery, but it does help to show how VBScript works — and how easy it is to use.

Here's the underlying script for the project:

```
<SCRIPT LANGUAGE="VBScript">
<!--
Sub cmdApply_Click()
   Label1 = TextBox1      ' Uses default control properties
end sub

Sub cmdDate_Click()
   Label1 = Label1 & Now  ' Use the Now function to read current
                          ' date & time using system format
end sub
//-->
</SCRIPT>
```

It's worth noting that this code uses a kind of shorthand. Each control has a default property. If no property is referenced, VBScript assumes the default. Caption is the default property of a Label control and Text is the default property of a Textbox control. Hence the statement

```
Label1 = TextBox1
```

is actually assigning the contents of TextBox1's Text property to Label1's caption.

If you're curious about the relativity of time on the Web you may be interested to know that the time and date returned by VBScript's Now function (and other time and date routines) is that of the local machine (for example, the client browser), not the server.

Changing Mouse Pointers

My next demonstration involves somewhat more sophisticated programming techniques. When a user browsing this Web page clicks the Change Mouse Pointer button, a new, randomly generated mouse pointer is selected (based on the constants 1 through 15, all of which are acceptable values for the MousePointer property). Figure 11-8 shows a Lady dinosaur selected, which is a representation of the hourglass icon under an NT 4.0 scheme. (Go figure. Is this gender bias, or what?)

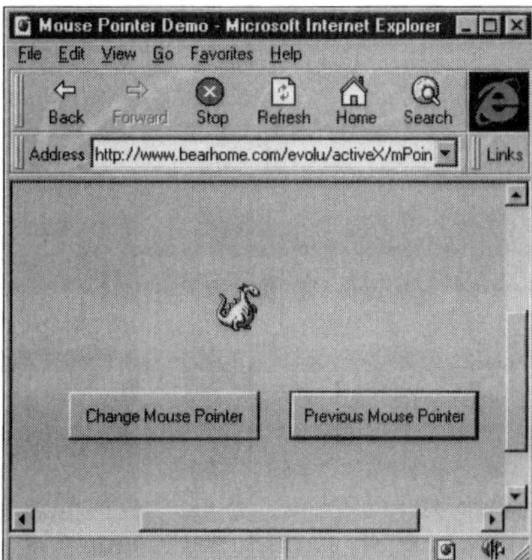

Figure 11-8: Changing the MousePointer property of the active control changes the cursor that appears on the screen.

Clicking on the Previous Mouse Pointer button restores the previous mouse pointer.

Because you have no idea how many new mouse pointers will be selected, you can provide infinite restoration of pointer capability using a stack data structure. You can use VBScript's powerful ability to dynamically redimension arrays to implement the stack. (For a full explanation of this technique, see Chapter 13, "Secrets of Good Programming Practice," in *Visual Basic 5 SECRETS*.)

The script first declares two global variables — one an array to contain the stack, the other to hold the top of the stack — and two procedures. PushStack places a new value on the stack. PopStack retrieves the previous value from the stack. PushStack and PopStack are shown in Listing 11-2.

Listing 11-2: Implementing a stack as a VBScript array

```
<SCRIPT LANGUAGE="VBScript">
<!--
Option Explicit
Dim MStack()              'Mouse Stack
Dim StackTop              'Top of the Stack

Sub PushStack(NewMouseValue)
   If StackTop = UBound(MStack) Then
      ReDim Preserve MStack(UBound(MStack) + 1)
   End If
   StackTop = StackTop + 1
   MStack(StackTop) = Label1.MousePointer
   Label1.MousePointer = NewMouseValue
   CommandButton1.MousePointer = NewMouseValue
   CommandButton2.MousePointer = NewMouseValue
End sub

Sub PopStack()
   If StackTop >= 0 Then
      Label1.MousePointer = MStack(StackTop)
      CommandButton1.MousePointer = MStack(StackTop)
      CommandButton2.MousePointer = MStack(StackTop)
      StackTop = StackTop - 1
      If StackTop > 0 Then
         ReDim Preserve MStack(UBound(MStack) - 1)
      End If
   End If
End sub
...
```

The Layout control is named mpoint. Note that the MousePointer property is changed for Label1, not mpoint. In mpoint's OnLoad event, Label1 is set to the size of mpoint so that it will appear to occupy the entire layout (Labels have a MousePointer property, while Layouts do not). In addition, the MousePointer properties for the command buttons are set, so that an unpleasant effect is not created when the mouse is passed over the buttons. Finally, the stack is initialized:

```
...
Sub mpoint_OnLoad()
   Label1.height = mpoint.height
   Label1.width = mpoint.width
   ReDim MStack(10)
   StackTop = -1
end sub
...
```

All that remains is to implement click procedures that push the stack with a new value (to display a new mouse pointer) and pop the stack to restore the previous pointer.

```
...
Sub CommandButton1_Click()
   PushStack Rnd*15  'New Mouse Pointer
```

```
end sub

Sub CommandButton2_Click()
   PopStack           'Previous Mouse Pointer
end sub
-->
</SCRIPT>
```

Drag and Drop

Drag and drop — giving the user the ability to visually edit data by moving it around — is an important component of the functionality of Windows applications. Drag and drop is easy to implement on the Web using VBScript and ActiveX.

Figure 11-9 shows an ActiveX Web page with text boxes whose contents can be dragged to a combo box, a button, labels, or the other text boxes. Selected text from the combo box can also be dragged and dropped. In addition, when the word "click" is dragged onto the button or the word "doubleclick" is dragged onto the combo box, special messages are displayed.

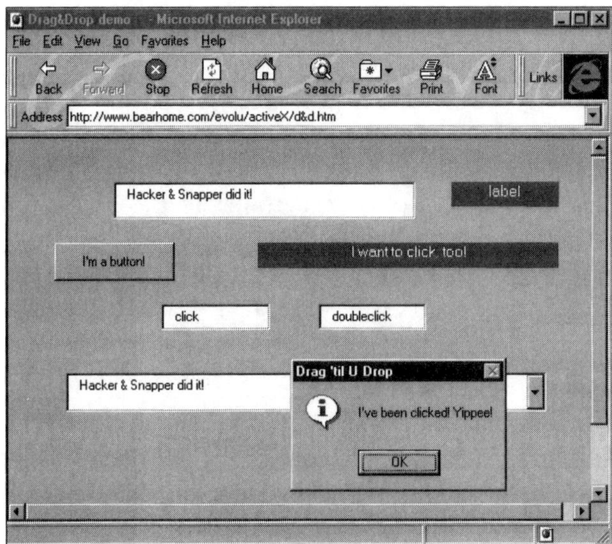

Figure 11-9: Using VBScript and the intrinsic controls, it's easy to implement drag and drop on the Web.

Not surprisingly, there are two parts to a drag-and-drop operation: dragging and dropping. Text that is selected in a text box or combo box can be dragged, provided that the control's DragBehavior property is set to enabled (the default is disabled). The easiest way to set this property is in the Layout environment using the Properties window. You can also set it in code using object.property syntax, for example:

```
ComboBox1.DragBehavior = 1 'enabled
```

Note, however, that there is no easy way to explicitly change the DragBehavior parameter in an Alx file. As an object parameter, DragBehavior resides in the rather opaquely named VariousPropertyBits parameter. Don't even think about trying to edit VariousPropertyBits manually! Here's an example:

```
<OBJECT ID="TextBox1"
   CLASSID="CLSID:8BD21D10-EC42-11CE-9E0D-00AA006002F3"
      STYLE="TOP:17pt;LEFT:66pt;WIDTH:206pt;HEIGHT:25pt;
      TABINDEX:0;ZINDEX:0;">
   <PARAM NAME="VariousPropertyBits" VALUE="747128859">
   <PARAM NAME="Size" VALUE="7267;882">
   <PARAM NAME="Value" VALUE="Enter text, select it, and drag it!">
   <PARAM NAME="FontCharSet" VALUE="0">
   <PARAM NAME="FontPitchAndFamily" VALUE="2">
   <PARAM NAME="FontWeight" VALUE="0">
</OBJECT>
```

That takes care of dragging (at least for selected text in text boxes and combo boxes). To drop, code needs to be added to two events for each control that is allowed to receive the drop.

Because all the controls in the example shown in Figure 11-10 work the same way, I'll just show you the combo box.

The BeforeDragOver event is fired as the first step of a drag-and-drop operation. Setting Cancel to True (False is the default) says the operation will be controlled with VBScript code. Setting Effect to 1 means that a copy of the dragged data will be dropped. (If Effect were set to 2, the data would be moved rather than dropped.) Here's an example:

```
Sub ComboBox1_BeforeDragOver(Cancel, Data, X, Y, DragState, Effect,
   Shift)
   Cancel.Value=TRUE
   Effect.Value=1
End Sub
```

The actual drop is handled in the BeforeDropOrPaste event. The Data parameter is a packaged data object containing the dragged information. Its GetText method is used to retrieve the string it contains. If the string is "doubleclick," the combo box's DoubleClick event is fired:

```
Sub ComboBox1_BeforeDropOrPaste(Cancel, Action, Data, X, Y, Effect,
   Shift)
   Cancel.Value=TRUE
   Effect.Value=1
      If LCase(Data.GetText)="doubleclick" Then
      ComboBox1_DoubleClick
   End If
   ComboBox1.AddItem Data.GetText
   ComboBox1.ListIndex = ComboBox1.ListCount - 1
```

```
End Sub

Sub ComboBox1_DoubleClick()
   MsgBox "I've been double clicked! Yippee and wow!",64, "Drag 'til
      U Drop"
End Sub
```

The best sources for explanations of the mechanics of the ComboBox control, and its properties, are the Visual Basic documentation and books about Visual Basic (for example, *Visual Basic 5 SECRETS*).

Images

There are two ways to include graphics within Layout controls. The graphic, or *image,* can be embedded in the Alx file, or it can be referenced. You reference images by placing their file location, expressed as a URL, in the PicturePath property of an Image control. (Officially, the intrinsic Image control is called the "Microsoft ActiveX Image Control 1.0.") Embedded images are referred to, logically enough, as "embedded"; referenced images are called "stand-alone."

There are a number of differences between the two approaches. To embed an image, set the Picture property of a CheckBox, CommandButton, Label, OptionButton, or ToggleButton control. Embedded images are physically included in the Alx file that corresponds to a Layout control. If you inspect the Alx file in a text editor, you'll see the embedded image information as a kind of text gobbledygook.

It's important to realize that you can only manipulate embedded images at design time. Once a control's Picture property has been set, at runtime that is that.

Stand-alones, on the other hand, can be manipulated dynamically at run time. However, the referenced file must be downloadable from the location that has been specified.

In other words, the big trade-off is that with embedded images, you create one larger Alx file; stand-alones generate numerous, smaller files. In addition, if you wish to change the images at runtime — perhaps in response to user actions — the images will have to be stand-alone.

Table 11-2 shows acceptable graphic formats for embedded and stand-alone images that can be included within a Layout control.

Table 11-2 Graphic Formats within a Layout Control

Image Type	*File Formats*
Embedded (included in an intrinsic control)	.Bmp, .Cur, .Gif, .Ico, .Jpg, .Wmf
Stand-alone (referenced in the PicturePath property of an Image control)	.Bmp, .Gif, .Jpg, .Wmf

Dynamic Image Control

To dynamically change a stand-alone image in response to a user's action you simply assign a PicturePath property in an event handler. For example, Figure 11-10 shows an ActiveX Web page with four Image controls. The Image controls have been set to the animals displayed initially by correctly assigning the image file's URL to the control at design time.

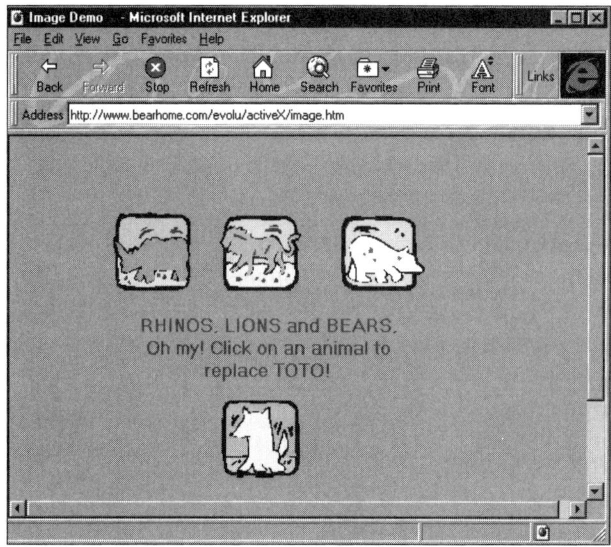

Figure 11-10: The user clicks on a Rhino, a Lion, or a Bear and replaces the dog with the selected image.

By clicking on any of the top three images, the user assigns the image that has been clicked to the Image control at the bottom of the page. Here's the VBScript code that accomplishes this:

```
<SCRIPT LANGUAGE="VBScript">
<!--
Sub Image4_MouseUp(Button, Shift, X, Y)
   Image1.PicturePath = "rhino.gif"
end sub

Sub Image3_MouseUp(Button, Shift, X, Y)
   Image1.PicturePath = "lion.gif"
end sub

Sub Image2_MouseUp(Button, Shift, X, Y)
   Image1.PicturePath = "bear.gif"
end sub
//-->
</SCRIPT>
```

TabStrips

The intrinsic TabStrip control provided with the Layout control is quite flexible and powerful. However, most of its properties must be configured in code (rather than at design time). Sticking with the Rhinos, Lions, and Bears theme, Figure 11-11 shows an intrinsic TabStrip control on an ActiveX Web page.

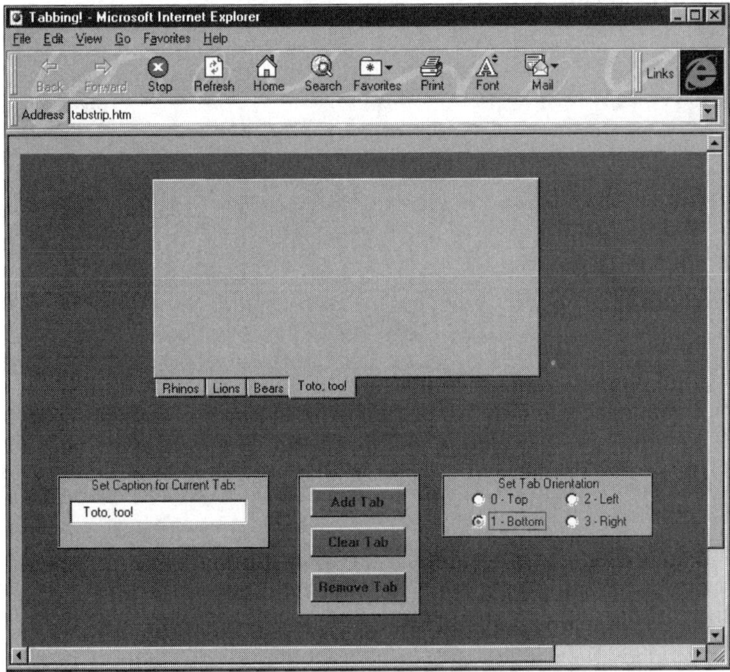

Figure 11-11: TabStrips can be scripted to interact with users.

The other controls that are part of the layout shown in Figure 11-11 allow the user to interactively configure the TabStrip by adding tabs, clearing all tabs, removing one tab, providing a caption for the current tab, and setting the tab orientation.

Here's the VBScript for adding a tab:

```
Sub CommandButton1_Click()
   TabStrip1.Tabs.Add()
end sub
```

To clear all tabs:

```
Sub CommandButton2_Click()
   TabStrip1.Tabs.Clear()
   TextBox1.Text = ""
end sub
```

To remove the current tab:

```
Sub CommandButton3_Click()
   Select Case TabStrip1.Tabs.Count
      Case 0
      Case 1
         call TabStrip1.Tabs.Clear()
         TextBox1.Text = ""
      Case Else
         TabStrip1.Tabs.Remove(TabStrip1.value)
   End Select
end sub
```

To set the caption of the current tab:

```
Sub TextBox1_Change()
   If TabStrip1.Tabs.Count <> 0 Then
      Tabstrip1.SelectedItem.Caption = Textbox1
   End If
end sub
```

As a matter of interface design, you should make sure to synchronize the current tab caption with the contents of the text box:

```
Sub TabStrip1_Click(Index)
    textbox1 = tabstrip1.selecteditem.caption
end sub
...
Sub TabStrip1_Change()
    textbox1 = tabstrip1.selecteditem.caption
end sub
```

To change the orientation of the tabs depending on which option button is clicked (and make sure the option buttons are set accordingly):

```
Sub OptionButton4_Click()
   OptionButton1.Value = 0
   OptionButton2.Value = 0
   OptionButton3.Value = 0
   OptionButton4.Value = -1
   TabStrip1.TabOrientation = 3
end sub

Sub OptionButton3_Click()
   OptionButton1.Value = 0
   OptionButton2.Value = 0
   OptionButton3.Value = -1
   OptionButton4.Value = 0
   TabStrip1.TabOrientation = 2
end sub

Sub OptionButton2_Click()
   OptionButton1.Value = 0
   OptionButton2.Value = -1
   OptionButton3.Value = 0
   OptionButton4.Value = 0
   TabStrip1.TabOrientation = 1
```

```
end sub

Sub OptionButton1_Click()
   OptionButton1.Value = -1
   OptionButton2.Value = 0
   OptionButton3.Value = 0
   OptionButton4.Value = 0
   TabStrip1.TabOrientation = 0
end sub
```

Summary

This chapter has covered the interaction of VBScript and ActiveX controls, particularly in the context of intrinsic ActiveX controls included with Microsoft's HTML Layout control.

Topics discussed included

- Using the HTML Layout control
- The **Codebase** parameter
- Downloading the Intrinsic Control Library
- The Layout control IDE
- The contents of the intrinsic control library
- Adding "extrinsic" controls
- Scripting with intrinsic ActiveX controls
- Dynamic labels
- Changing mouse pointers
- Programming drag and drop
- Working with images
- Using the TabStrip control

Part III

Adding Executable Content

Chapter 12

Using ActiveX in Web Applications

"No matter where you go, there you are."

— a plaque on the starship Excelsior in *Star Trek VI: The Undiscovered Country*

No matter where you go on the Web, exciting content involves sites that contain executables that are downloaded and then run on client machines.

Most of Part III of *Web Developer's SECRETS*, "Adding Executable Content," is about how to create your own Web executables — using Visual Basic 5, Visual C++, and Visual J++ to create ActiveX controls, and various Java environments (including J++) to create Java applets.

This chapter wraps up some unfinished business involving using VBScript to "control" ActiveX controls. It then covers creating exciting Web applications using existing ActiveX control libraries. An important topic: As you are probably aware, ActiveX (OCX) controls are the largest body of professional-quality, thoroughly tested components in the world today that are commercially available.

Using Nonintrinsic ActiveX Controls

Using the ActiveX Control Pad, you can add nonintrinsic ActiveX controls to an HTML page. (Nonintrinsic ActiveX controls are also known as *extrinsic* or *custom* controls.) As covered in Chapter 11, "VBScript and ActiveX," custom controls can also be added to an HTML layout. The resulting HTML code that inserts the control is the same as when the control is placed directly in an HTML page; the only difference is that it is placed in the layout's Alx file rather than in the HTML page.

Script that references a custom control should be placed in the Alx files if the control has been added to the layout and in the HTML file if it has been added directly to the Web page.

Of course, if you prefer, a third option is to add references to the control in code form using the HTML <OBJECT> tag and a text editor.

Adding the Custom Microsoft Label Control

The Microsoft Label control is an extended version of the intrinsic label control, meaning that it has an expanded property and method set compared to the intrinsic control.

You'll find a working sample of this control that you can download as part of the Microsoft ActiveX Control Gallery. The URL is *http://www.microsoft.com/activex/controls*.

To add the control directly to the HTML file using the ActiveX Control Pad, choose Insert ActiveX Control from the Edit menu. The Insert ActiveX Control dialog shown in Figure 12-1 appears. The control appears with the name that it used when registering in the CLSID section of the Windows Registry (in this case, Label Object).

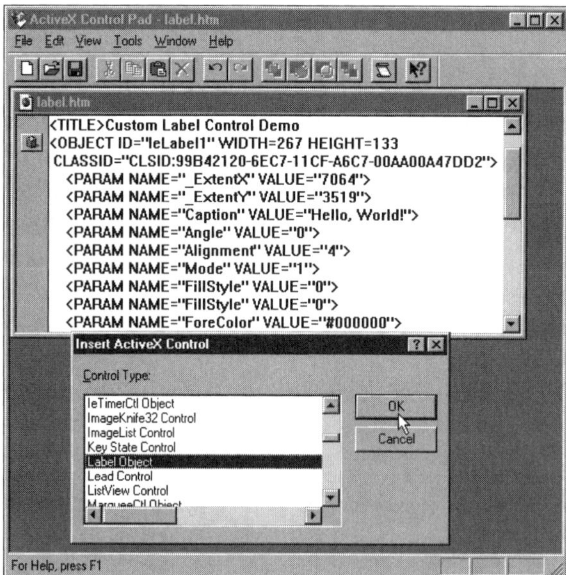

Figure 12-1: You use ActiveX Control Pad's Insert ActiveX Control dialog to add custom controls to an HTML page.

Adding custom controls to an HTML layout was covered in detail in Chapter 11, "VBScript and ActiveX." Although the dialog has a different name than the one you use when adding a custom control directly, the process and effect are the same.

To add a custom control to a layout (.alx) file, right-click in an empty area of the Toolbox. Choose Additional Controls from the pop-up menu. The

Additional Controls dialog appears, as shown in Figure 12-2. You can use this dialog to add ActiveX controls, or insertable OLE objects, to a layout.

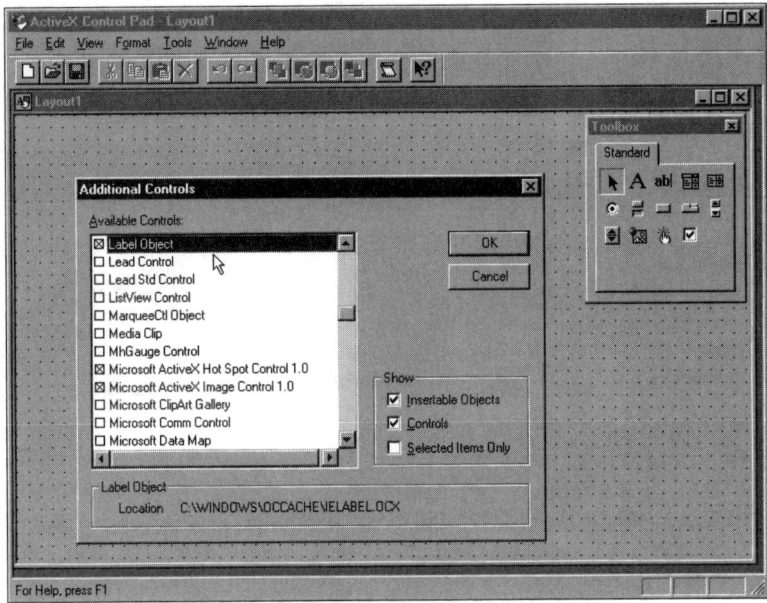

Figure 12-2: You use the Additional Controls dialog to add ActiveX controls and OLE objects to a layout.

In either case, the inserted HTML code is identical, using <OBJECT> and <PARAM> tags. It's certainly a viable approach to insert or edit this HTML by hand. As I'll show you, to create downloadable applications, you have to.

Roughly speaking, here's the HTML inserted by ActiveX Control Pad ("roughly," because it depends on the caption, size, and so on of the control):

```
<OBJECT ID="IeLabel1" WIDTH=267 HEIGHT=133
   CLASSID="CLSID:99B42120-6EC7-11CF-A6C7-00AA00A47DD2">
   <PARAM NAME="_ExtentX" VALUE="7064">
   <PARAM NAME="_ExtentY" VALUE="3519">
   <PARAM NAME="Caption" VALUE="Hello, World!">
   <PARAM NAME="Angle" VALUE="0">
   <PARAM NAME="Alignment" VALUE="4">
   <PARAM NAME="Mode" VALUE="1">
   <PARAM NAME="FillStyle" VALUE="0">
   <PARAM NAME="FillStyle" VALUE="0">
   <PARAM NAME="ForeColor" VALUE="#000000">
   <PARAM NAME="BackColor" VALUE="#C0C0C0">
   <PARAM NAME="FontName" VALUE="Arial">
   <PARAM NAME="FontSize" VALUE="12">
   <PARAM NAME="FontItalic" VALUE="0">
   <PARAM NAME="FontBold" VALUE="0">
   <PARAM NAME="FontUnderline" VALUE="0">
```

```
    <PARAM NAME="FontStrikeout" VALUE="0">
    <PARAM NAME="TopPoints" VALUE="0">
    <PARAM NAME="BotPoints" VALUE="0">
</OBJECT>
```

The syntax of the <OBJECT> tag is

```
<OBJECT parameters>
    <PARAM name=value>
</OBJECT>
```

<PARAM> is a subtag, embedded between <OBJECT> and </OBJECT> tags, that reflects the *property equals value* pairs of the ActiveX control. There is no limit to the number of <PARAM> tags that a given object can have.

Table 12-1 describes the important parameters of the <OBJECT> tag.

Table 12-1 The Parameters of the <OBJECT> Tag

Parameter	***Purpose***
ID	The internal name of the object. Used to refer to it in code within the HTML page / Web application.
ClassID	Specifies the class the object belongs to. For ActiveX controls, this is the class ID given to the control in the local system registry, which is supposed to be the same for all systems that have registered the control.
Codebase	Points to the location of the object's executable code. Only used if the object's executable file is not present on the local machine.
Type	Specifies the Internet MIME type to use. Type="application/x-oleobject" means an OLE object containing executable code.
Height	Size of object
Width	Size of object

To include the label control in an application intended for distribution, you'd want an <OBJECT> tag along these lines (rather than the one created by ActiveX Control Pad):

```
<OBJECT
    ID="myLabel"
    CLASSID="clsid:99B42120-6EC7-11CF-A6C7-00AA00A47DD2"
    CODEBASE="http://activex.microsoft.com/controls/
    iexplorer/ielabel.ocx#Version=4,70,0,1161"
    TYPE="application/x-oleobject"
    WIDTH=150
    HEIGHT=60
>
```

The **Codebase** and **Type** parameters allow an application to find and download the control, even if it is not present on a user's local machine.

It's not always easy to find the correct URL to specify in **Codebase** parameters (nor does knowing the location necessarily provide a license for distributing the control). Often, you'll have to do some digging.

The sample ActiveX applications included in Microsoft's ActiveX Control Gallery (discussed later in this chapter) include the correct **Codebase** URLs for controls that are included. To view this information, first find the page containing the source code by placing the mouse pointer over the hyperlink and using Explorer's status bar. When you've determined the URL for the page, open it, and use Explorer's View Source feature. (You cannot view its source code from the ActiveX Gallery because the Gallery is contained within frames.)

Making the Label Control Perform

Taking the custom label control that was added to either an HTML page or an Alx layout, it's easy to use its extended capabilities.

For instance, this label control includes an .angle property (not available in the intrinsic control). In its default position, the .angle property equals 0, and the label is — as we are used to seeing it — parallel to the bottom of the page.

You can allow the user to dynamically change the angle of the label, as shown in Figure 12-3.

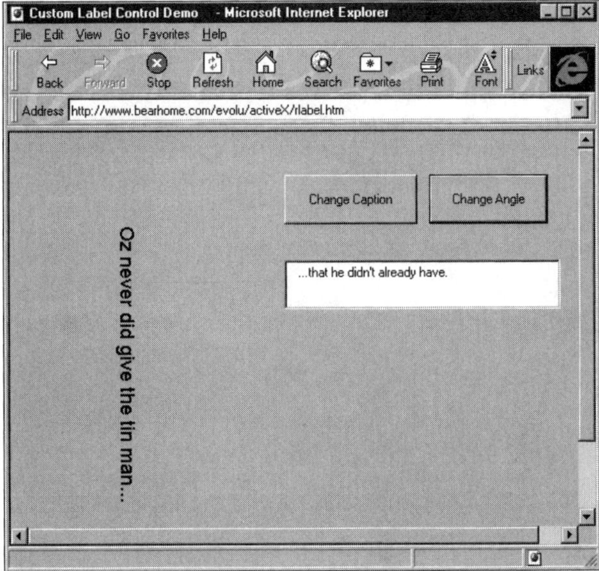

Figure 12-3: The ieLabel control allows dynamic rotations through its angle property.

Here's the underlying VBScript:

```
<SCRIPT LANGUAGE="VBScript">
<!--
Sub CommandButton1_Click()
   ieLabel1.caption = textbox1.text
end sub

Sub CommandButton2_Click()
   ieLabel1.angle = (ieLabel1.angle + 90) mod 360
end sub
-->
</SCRIPT>
```

This code only allows for a 90 degree clockwise rotation; you could easily alter it to anything you'd like.

Using Object Browsers

It can be pretty hard to determine information about an ActiveX control's properties, methods, and events using a text editor, or even the ActiveX Control Pad. One helpful technique is to use an external Object Browser. The Object Browser built into Visual Basic 5 works very well for this purpose.

First, use Visual Basic's Custom Control dialog to add the ActiveX control you wish to explore to the VB Toolbox. (The ActiveX Label control is listed as "IE Super Label.") Once the control is in the VB Toolbox, add it to a form (you can spot its icon in the Toolbox by its rakish angle).

Now, when you open VB's Object Browser, you'll find it displayed as shown in Figure 12-4. You can determine the expected data types of properties, and arguments that methods require. In addition, you can use Visual Basic event code scaffolding to determine the object's preset event handlers.

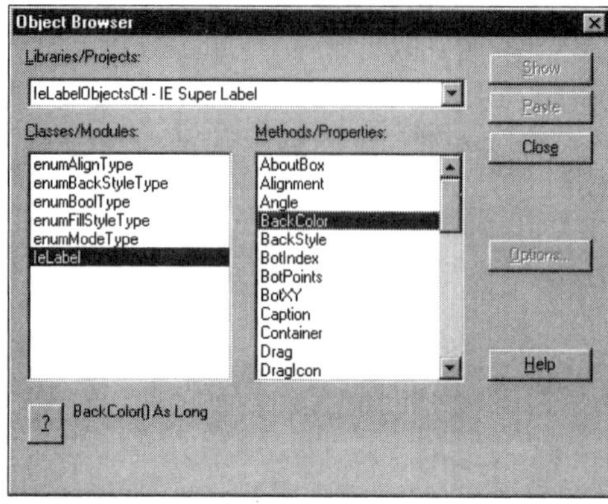

Figure 12-4: You can use Visual Basic's Object Browser to determine information about ActiveX controls.

Adding a Pop-Up Menu

It's easy to add context pop-up menus to ActiveX Web pages using Microsoft's Iemenu ActiveX control. Figure 12-5 shows a simple context menu application.

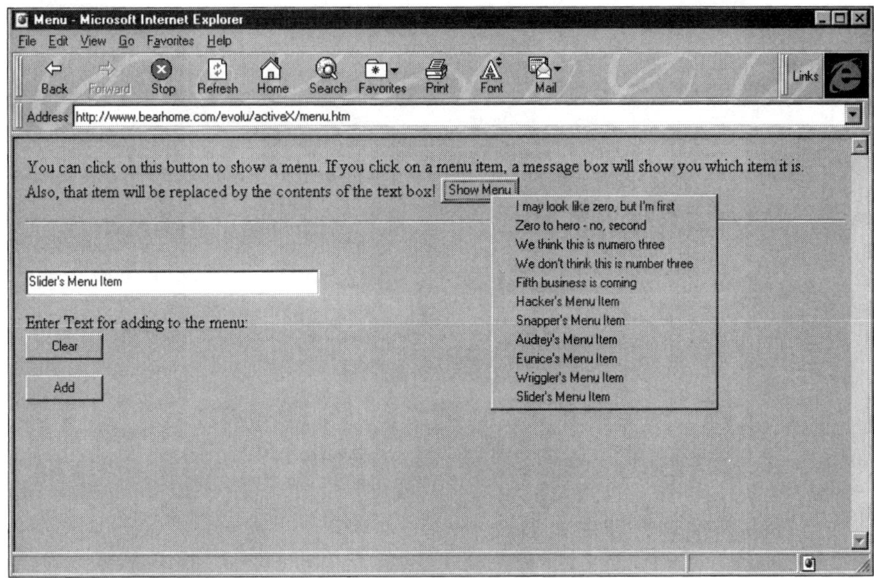

Figure 12-5: You can add pop-up menus to your Web pages using the Iemenu ActiveX control.

When the user clicks on the Show Menu button, a context menu is displayed. To start with, this menu contains five items that are loaded in code using <PARAM> tags. When the user clicks on a menu item, a message box displays the text of the item and its number on the pop-up menu. Then, the menu text is replaced with the contents of the text box.

New menu items can be added to the pop-up menu using the text box and Add button. The Clear button serves to delete the entire menu structure.

Inside Scoop

The buttons and text box are HTML form input elements, not intrinsic HTML Layout controls. This is worth emphasizing: This ActiveX Web page uses only one ActiveX control: the menu. Other user interactions are controlled using HTML and the object model of the browser, just as they conventionally are in JavaScript. The contents of the text box are accessed by instancing a copy of a form, itself a member of the Window.Document forms collection:

```
...
Dim thisForm
Set thisForm = Document.frmMenu
Iepop1.AddItem thisForm.txtMenu.value
...
```

Here's the <OBJECT> tag that adds the ActiveX control to the Web page (which is another way of saying that it loads the menu control):

```
<OBJECT
   ID="iepop1"
   CODEBASE="http://activex.microsoft.com/controls
   /iexplorer/iemenu.ocx#Version=4,70,0,1161"
   TYPE="application/x-oleobject"
   CLASSID="clsid:7823A620-9DD9-11CF-A662-00AA00C066D2"
   WIDTH=1
   HEIGHT=1>
    <PARAM NAME="Menuitem[0]" value="I may look like zero, but I'm
      first">
    <PARAM NAME="Menuitem[1]" value="Zero to hero - no, second">
    <PARAM NAME="Menuitem[2]" value="We think this is numero three">
    <PARAM NAME="Menuitem[3]" value="We don't think this is number
      three">
    <PARAM NAME="Menuitem[4]" value="Fifth business is coming">
</OBJECT>
```

Here's the HTML code that sets up the form:

```
<BODY>
   You can click on this button to show
   a menu. If you click on a menu item,
   a message box will show you which
   item it is. Also, that item will be replaced
   by the contents of the text box!
   <FORM name="frmMenu">
      <INPUT TYPE="button" NAME="ShowMenu" VALUE="Show Menu"
         ALIGN=RIGHT>
      <HR>
      <P>
      <BR>
      <INPUT Type="Text" Size=50 Value="Hacker's Menu Item"
         Name="txtMenu">
      <P>
      Enter Text for adding to the menu: <BR>
      <INPUT Type="Button" Value="Clear" Name="cmdClear">
      <P>
      <INPUT Type="Button" Value="Add" Name="cmdAdd">
   </FORM>
</BODY>
```

Finally, here's the VBScript code, placed in event handlers, that performs actions dynamically based on user input:

```
<SCRIPT Language="VBScript">
<!--
Sub Iepop1_Click(ByVal x)
   MsgBox "Menu click on item:  " & x &
      " ; replacing the menu item with contents of text box!"
   Iepop1.RemoveItem(x)
   Dim thisForm
   Set thisForm = Document.frmMenu
   call Iepop1.AddItem(thisForm.txtMenu.value, x)
```

```
End Sub

Sub ShowMenu_onClick
   Iepop1.PopUp
End Sub

Sub cmdClear_OnClick
   Iepop1.Clear
   MsgBox "The menu be gone!"
End Sub

Sub cmdAdd_OnClick
   Dim thisForm
   Set thisForm = Document.frmMenu
   Iepop1.AddItem thisForm.txtMenu.value
   MsgBox "The menu has been added!"
End Sub
//-->
</SCRIPT>
```

Explorer's Object Model

As the ActiveX menu example in the previous section suggests, Microsoft's Explorer is based on an object model. You can exploit this object model when constructing Web applications. In addition, you'll need to understand it to create many kinds of Web applications.

Unfortunately, Explorer's object model and syntax, although similar, are just different enough from Netscape's Navigator that you cannot use the same code (presumably, it would have to be JavaScript) to control the objects of each.

Table 12-2 shows Explorer's object hierarchy.

Table 12-2 Microsoft Internet Explorer Object Model

Object	***Contains/Events/Comments***
Window	This is the top-level object and is implied by a statement such as document.thisForm. Frame, History, Navigator, Location, Script, and Document objects are contained within the Window object. The Window object has two events, OnLoad and OnUnload. OnLoad is fired when a page is loaded. (You fire an OnLoad event when you refresh a page, as well as the first time you load it.) OnUnLoad is fired just before the page is unloaded.
Frame	The Frame object is an array of windows, one for each document in a frameset.

(continued)

Table 12-1 (Continued)

Object	*Contains/Events/Comments*
History	Contains Explorer's History list (where it has been).
Navigator	Contains information about the browser version.
Location	Changing Location properties causes pages to be loaded and unloaded.
Script	A collection of all the scripts in a page.
Document	Contains Anchor, Link, and Form objects.
	The Anchor object contains an array of all anchors on a page. The Link object contains an array of all hyperlinks on a page. Each hyperlink has a MouseMove, OnMouseOver, and OnClick event that code can be placed in. The Form object has one event, OnSubmit, and contains an array of the elements included in the form.

Controlling the Internet Explorer Object

Explorer is itself an OLE automation server. You can use the exposed methods and properties of the Explorer object to add Web browsing capabilities to your applications using any development environment that can control "foreign" OLE automation objects — for example, Delphi and Visual Basic.

Figure 12-6 shows a simple Visual Basic application that will open Explorer; go to the specified URL in Explorer; fire Explorer's Back, Forward, and Refresh methods; and, finally, close Explorer.

The first step in implementing the sample application shown in Figure 12-6 is to add Explorer's object library — listing its exposed properties and methods — to a VB project. You do this in the Custom Control dialog, which you open via the Tools menu. As shown in Figure 12-7, the name of Explorer's library is "Microsoft Internet Controls." It is stored in a dynamic link library (DLL file) named Shdocvw.Dll.

Once Explorer's object library has been added to the Visual Basic project, you can use VB's Object Browser to determine available methods and properties, as shown in Figure 12-8.

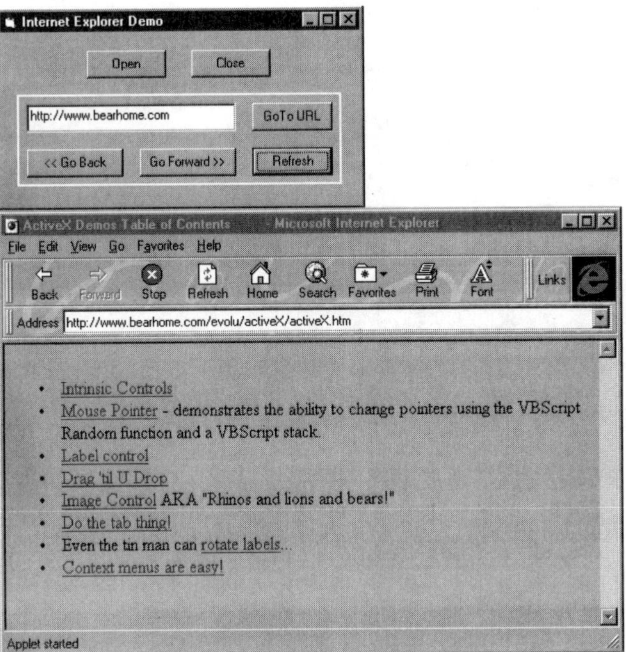

Figure 12-6: It's easy to use OLE automation to control an instance of Explorer.

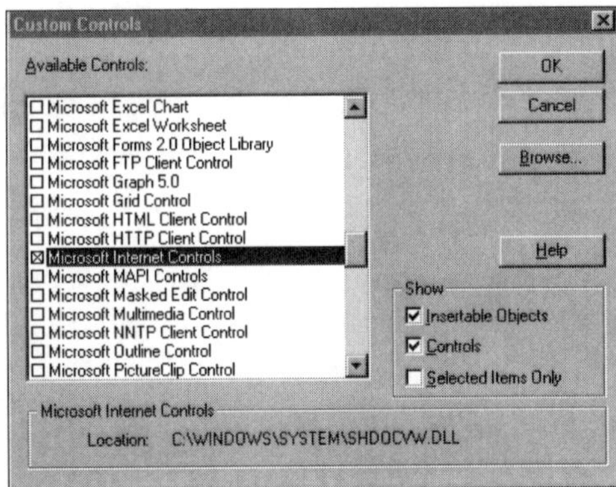

Figure 12-7: To add Explorer's object library to a Visual Basic project, make sure Microsoft Internet Controls is selected in the Custom Controls dialog.

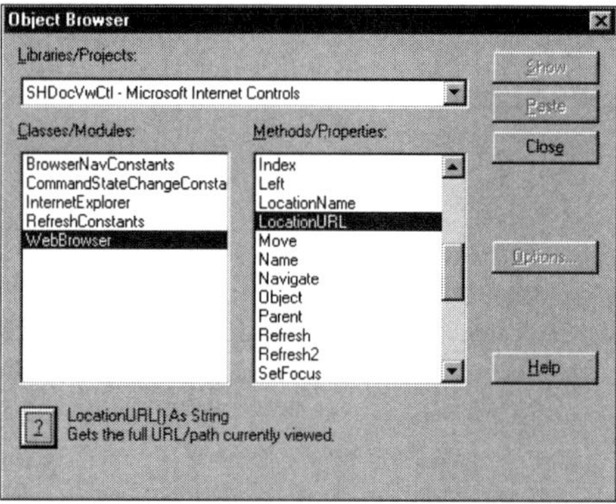

Figure 12-8: You can use Visual Basic's Object Browser to inspect available methods and properties included in Explorer's object library.

To add Explorer's functionality to the Visual Basic program, create an instance of the Explorer automation object using the New keyword:

```
Dim myBrowser As New InternetExplorer
```

Implementing the rest of the application's functionality is simply a matter of calling the automation object's methods:

```
Private Sub cmdOpen_Click()
   myBrowser.Visible = True
End Sub

Private Sub cmdClose_Click()
   myBrowser.Visible = False
End Sub

Private Sub cmdURL_Click()
   myBrowser.Navigate txtURL.Text
End Sub

Private Sub cmdBack_Click()
   myBrowser.GoBack
End Sub

Private Sub cmdForward_Click()
myBrowser.GoForward
End Sub

Private Sub cmdRefresh_Click()
   myBrowser.Refresh
End Sub
```

You should make sure to explicitly delete from memory the instance of the OLE automation object that you have created by setting to it nothing:

```
Private Sub Form_Unload(Cancel As Integer)
   myBrowser.Quit
```

```
   Set myBrowser = Nothing
End Sub
```

Microsoft's ActiveX Control Gallery

The ActiveX Control Gallery is located at *http://www.micorosoft.com/activex/controls*.

It contains numerous sample ActiveX controls available for download. The vendors involved range from first-tier software tools companies such as Adobe Systems, FarPoint Technologies, MicroHelp, Microsoft, and Seagate Technologies to aggressive, new Internet start-ups.

Although some of the controls in the galley are industrial strength, others are "lite" versions intended to entice developers. Each sample control is accompanied by a sample application and some documentation.

The controls can be used in ActiveX Web applications, or, for that matter, in stand-alone applications (use a development environment that can work with OLE components).

As noted earlier in this chapter, under "Adding the Label Control," it can take quite a bit of sleuthing to determine the URL for the **Codebase** parameter of a control's <OBJECT> tag. (You need this parameter to distribute an ActiveX control, unless you are prepared to distribute the control's code from your own server.)

It's also worth repeating that controls included in the gallery are not freeware. You can certainly download them and try them out, but you should contact the vendor for a license prior to distributing them as part of an application.

Table 12-3 shows the ActiveX controls that are currently available as part of the ActiveX Control Gallery.

Table 12-3 ActiveX Controls Available for Download That Are Included in Microsoft's ActiveX Gallery

Vendor	*ActiveX Control*
Adobe Systems, Inc.	Acrobat Control for ActiveX
Black Diamond Consulting, Inc.	Surround Video
Brilliance Labs, Inc.	QuantumChess CyberGO ActiveX Control
Citrix Systems, Inc.	Citrix WinFrame ICA control

(continued)

Table 12-3 *(Continued)*

Vendor	***ActiveX Control***
DameWare Development	Cal32 ChkList InfoTick NetList RasDial TapiDial
Data Dynamics, Ltd.	DynamiCube
Dimension X	Liquid Motion Player
Farallon Communciations, Inc.	Look@Me
FarPoint Technologies, Inc.	Boolean Currency Date Time Double Single Long Integer Mask Text
Fulcrum Technologies, Inc.	Fulcrum Document Viewer for ActiveX
FutureWave Software, Inc.	FutureSplash Player
InterCAP Graphics Systems, Inc.	ActiveCGM Viewer
LiveUpdate	Crescendo and Crescendo PLUS
mBED Software	mBED Player
Media Architects, Inc.	ImageKnife MediaKnife
MicroHelp, Inc.	Mh3dButn Mh3dCalendar Mh3dCheckbox Mh3dFile Mh3dFrame Mh3dGauge Mh3dGroup Mh3dKeyState Mh3dLabel Mh3dList Mh3dOptionButton Mh3dTextbox MhAlarm MhAvi MhCardDeck MhClock MhCommand MhDateInput

Vendor	ActiveX Control
	MhDial MhDice MhFileList MhHistograph MhInput MhIntegerInput MhMarquee MhMaskedInput MhMulti MhOddPic MhRealInput MhRollUp MhSlider MhTimeInput MhTimer
Microsoft	Animated Button Chart Gradient Label Marquee Menu Popup Menu Popup Window Preloader Stock Ticker Timer View Tracker
Outrider Systems	Outrider ButtonTool Outrider CheckList Outrider Enhanced SpinButton
ProtoView Development Co.	Button Control Calendar Control DataTable Grid Component DateEdit Control Dial Control Font Selection Control InterAct MultiButton Control Numeric Edit Control Percent Bar Control TimeEdit Control TreeView Control
Sax Software Corporation	Sax Canvas Control
Seagate Software	Crystal Reports Viewer Control
Software Publishing Corporation	ASAP Webshow

(continued)

Table 12-3 (Continued)

Vendor	*ActiveX Control*
Starfish Software, Inc.	EarthTime ActiveX Lite
Superscape VR Plc	Viscape for ActiveX
Template Graphics Software, Inc.	Visual 3Space Control
Totally Hip Software	Sizzler
Tumbleweed Software Corp.	Envoy Control for ActiveX
Vivo Software, Inc.	VivoActive Player for ActiveX
VREAM, Inc.	WIRL for ActiveX

The Internet Control Pack

The Internet Control Pack was jointly developed by Microsoft and NetManage, Inc. Also known as the *Internet ActiveX Controls*, it is a collection of ActiveX controls that can be added to applications in development environments that support OLE components (such as Access, Delphi, Visual Basic, and Visual C++).

You can download the Internet Control Pack from *http://microsoft.com/icp/*. Unlike the ActiveX Control Gallery, the Internet Control Pack is not a control-by-control installation. Rather, a large self-extracted executable is downloaded, which you then run to install the control pack.

Controls in the pack include

- Winsock ActiveX controls, which provide a high-level interface to the Winsock API.
- FTP ActiveX control, which encapsulates FTP file transfers. This control allows developers to easily integrate FTP clients into their applications, meaning that these applications can take advantage of the large installed base of FTP servers.
- NNTP ActiveX control, which lets developers give their applications access to Usenet news and other NNTP news sources. This control can be used to connect to a news server, retrieve a list of available newsgroups and their descriptions, enter a newsgroup, get lists of articles, and retrieve articles.
- SMTP/POP3 ActiveX control, which adds Internet mail functionality to an application.
- HTML ActiveX control, which adds Web parsing and display to applications (in other words, a Web browser).
- HTTP ActiveX control, which turns an application into a simple Web server.

Figure 12-9 shows a simple HTML browser that was created by adding the HTML ActiveX control to a Visual Basic form.

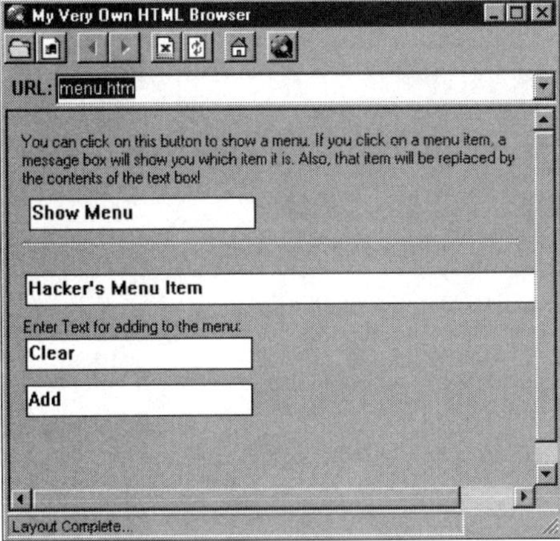

Figure 12-9: You can easily add customized HTML browsing and parsing facilities to your applications using the HTML ActiveX control.

The control opens an HTML page when its RequestDoc method is invoked, for example:

```
HTML1.RequestDoc (strURL)
```

Summary

This chapter covered a number of important topics related to integrating ActiveX control with your Web applications.

Topics covered included

- Using custom ActiveX controls
- The <OBJECT> tag
- The **Codebase** parameter
- Using Object Browsers
- Explorer's object model
- Using OLE to control Explorer
- Microsoft's ActiveX Control Gallery
- The Internet Control Pack

Chapter 13

Creating ActiveX Controls Using Visual Basic 5

"Everything in moderation — even moderation."

— Becca Brown

Visual Basic is the world's most popular programming environment. When all is said and done, the reason for this popularity is that it is relatively easy to use VB to harness the full power of Windows software development — almost.

The promise of version 5 of Visual Basic is to take the power of VB the final step forward. It's about time! Visual Basic developers will finally be able to create custom controls from the comfort of their Visual Basic environment. Furthermore, these ActiveX controls will "play" across the Internet — in any Explorer browser that has been equipped with the Visual Basic Virtual Machine (VM).

Thus, Visual Basic has been freed of its chains. VB developers can now compete with the "big boys" who create OLE-based ActiveX components in VC++. They can also hold their own with Java developers who, with the help of Java VMs, can download their applet-based executable content to any browser that has a Java VM. (My VM is better than your VM may be the spirit of this thing....)

Visual Basic 5 Custom Controls Edition (VB5CCE) is a subset of Visual Basic 5 that contains the VB5 mechanisms for ActiveX control creation. It's as though the relevant portions of VB5 were ripped out and distributed as a separate application whose sole purpose is the creation of ActiveX controls.

VB5CCE — and a tremendous amount of other software and information related to Visual Basic development — is available from Microsoft's VB site, *http://www.microsoft.com/vbasic/*.

Although this chapter is explicitly aimed to help you construct ActiveX controls using VB5CCE, you create ActiveX controls in the full version of VB5 in exactly the same fashion. In terms of creating ActiveX controls, there are essentially no differences between VB5CCE and the complete release of VB5.

In this chapter I'll show you how to use the new VB5 IDE. Next, I'll explain how to work with objects and classes in VB5. I'll show you how to subclass existing controls and build your own custom controls. I'll also demonstrate how to prepare your controls for download and how to integrate your custom controls with Web applications.

Note that the Visual Basic VM requires release 3.01 or later of Microsoft's Internet Explorer.

Traditionally, there have been two classes of developers: those who create components (for example, controls), and those who use the components to glue applications together. VB5CCE brings the possibility of true control creation to Visual Basic programmers. This promises to allow them to bridge the gap between those that glue and those that create controls.

Starting a New VB5CCE Project

VB5CCE allows you to create new projects that contain the source code for an ActiveX control, for a normal executable, or for a group of controls. Figure 13-1 shows the New Project dialog, with an icon representing each of these choices. (A variant of this dialog opens by default every time you start VB5CCE.)

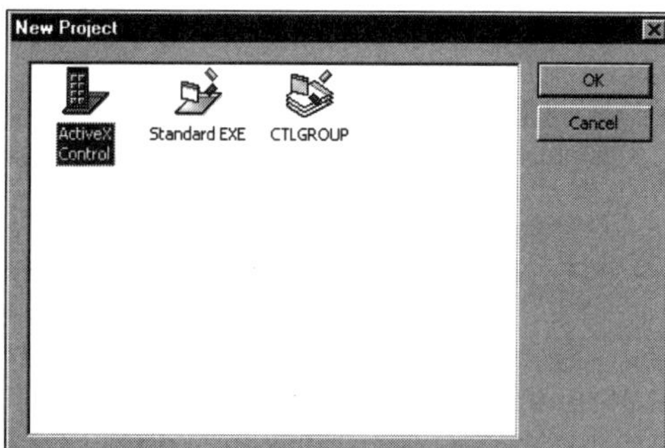

Figure 13-1: You can create projects in VB5CCE that constitute one ActiveX control, or contain a group of projects, or are a standard executable.

A couple of things about these project types bear some explaining.

The multiple project group — represented in Figure 13-1 by the icon labeled "CTLGROUP" — is a project type new to Visual Basic. The ASCII file that contains the information coordinating the various source files of a multiple project group is stored with a .Vbg extension (as opposed to normal Visual Basic project files, which end with .Vbp).

Why, might you ask, does the Visual Basic *Custom Control Edition* (emphasis mine) include the facility for creating normal executables. There are two reasons for this, and it's important to understand both of them.

Testing Controls

Developers need to be able to test their controls in a design-time environment. An ActiveX control — for example, an Ocx file — is not executable in and of itself. This means that if you create a project containing an ActiveX control, you cannot simply run it from within the VB5CCE environment to see if it works. You must first add the control to a container.

You do this by adding a standard executable project to the control's project (using Add Project on the File Menu) to form a project group. If all is well with its creation, the new ActiveX control will appear in the Toolbox. It can then be added to a VB container, which will serve as the container for the new control. (It's worth noting that VB forms are not the only containers available in VB. Some controls can themselves be OLE containers. For example, you can place controls on a frame control, which then becomes the container for the controls on it.)

Once the control has been added to a container, you can examine its *interface*. The interface of a control is defined as its exposed properties, methods, and events. If you have experience programming with Windows objects, these terms will no doubt be exceedingly familiar (and you can skip the brief explanations that follow).

An ActiveX control *exposes* its available properties, methods, and events in a standard manner. This means that any application — from Excel to Web scripting languages — that speaks this standard can use the exposed interface to communicate with and manipulate the ActiveX control.

Properties are used to set or retrieve values stored with the control.

Methods are functions that, when executed, cause the control to do something.

Events are code procedures (known as "event handlers") that an object causes to be executed ("fired") under certain conditions. They represent opportunities for users to add their own code to projects containing controls you created.

Later in this chapter, I'll show you how to work with and create custom properties, methods, and events — the control's interface. As you can see, "interface" used in this way does not mean the appearance of the control on the screen — although I'll cover that, too.

When you use VB5CCE to create ActiveX controls, the control, and its interface, can be entirely based on an existing control (or controls). This is called "subclassing." When you subclass another control, you can modify the behavior of its interface. Or, if you wish, you can start from scratch.

If the interface is what you designed it to be, you can run the executable project that contains the control — adding test code if needed — to make sure that it works at runtime.

It's important to understand that ActiveX controls will ultimately be used in two ways:

- By a developer when creating applications that use the control
- By the end user

These modes are fundamentally different. Developers need access to the interface of your control so that they can use it; end users do not need this access. The end user simply needs the control module to play its part in the functionality of the application as a whole.

There is a business issue involved here. Normally, the developer of a control distributes the control to other developers who use it at design time as a code module in their applications. These other developers then redistribute the control with their applications to the world at large. As a control developer, you probably do not want the world at large to be able to access your design-time interface (at least, not without paying you a licensing fee!).

VB5CCE contains a mechanism that allows a control to determine whether it is in design mode or run mode. I'll show you later in this chapter how to set controls up so that they require a license file to run in design mode (but do not require the file in run mode).

Packaging ActiveX Controls

Another reason that you can create standard executables in VB5CCE has to do with the scope of the ActiveX controls included in your project.

If you like, instead of distributing your ActiveX control in a separate Ocx file, you can include the source code in your one executable. The net effect of this is to make the ActiveX control private to the executable. As they sometimes say, the advantages of one are not the disadvantages of the other.

An ActiveX control in VB5CCE is contained in a UserControl source code module (the source file is saved with a .Ctl extension). The question of whether to compile this source code into an executable, or to compile it separately into an Ocx file that must be distributed, is one of *packaging*.

Public *controls* are controls that can be used by other applications. They must be compiled in an ActiveX control project (the Public property of the UserControl object must also be set to True). You make a control *private* by setting the Public property of the UserControl object to False. After the project is compiled, private controls cannot be used by other applications. They can be used only within the project in which they were compiled.

The Public property of a UserControl object cannot be set to True unless the UserControl is an ActiveX control project. If one of the controls in an ActiveX control project is only meant to be used by other controls within the project, you can set the Public property of the UserControl to False. External applications will not be able to use it but other controls in the project will.

Changing the Packaging

You can easily change the way a control you've created is packaged just by shifting the source files to a different type of project. For example, if you create some private controls that are part of a project, and you want to allow other applications to use them, you can add the Ctl files to an ActiveX control project and compile it into an ActiveX control. If you don't want to distribute a separate, compiled component, you can instead add the control's .Ctl file to the project for an application. When the application is compiled, the control is compiled into the executable.

The advantages of including a control as source code compiled into an executable are

- You don't need to distribute an external Ocx file.
- Testing and debugging the control is simpler, because you only have to worry about the way it is used in your application, not all possible uses of the control.
- You don't have to worry about future distributions of an updated control breaking your application, because the control code is completely compiled into the application.

Here are the disadvantages of including controls as source code:

- If you wish to update the control — or discover a bug in it that you need to fix — you can't just distribute the revised control. You must recompile the entire application, and redistribute the application.
- You may end up distributing the same code a number of times because multiple applications cannot share the control, and each application will require the source files that the control represents. This will lead to bigger applications that require more hard disk space on target systems.
- Version control becomes more difficult because source code used in separate applications inevitably gets changed. It may become hard to know what version of a control's source code is included in a given project.
- Sharing source code with other developers is more difficult, requiring more support effort than distributing a compiled component with a standard interface. By distributed source code rather than a compiled Ocx, you give up control over your source code.

The VB5CCE IDE

The VB5CCE is a very complex, full-featured development environment. Fortunately, much of it will seem familiar to developers who have worked in other versions of Visual Basic.

Once you've got VB5CCE fired up and loaded with a project, you'll find a number of windows that are tools designed to help you work with projects and objects (some are shown in Figure 13-2).

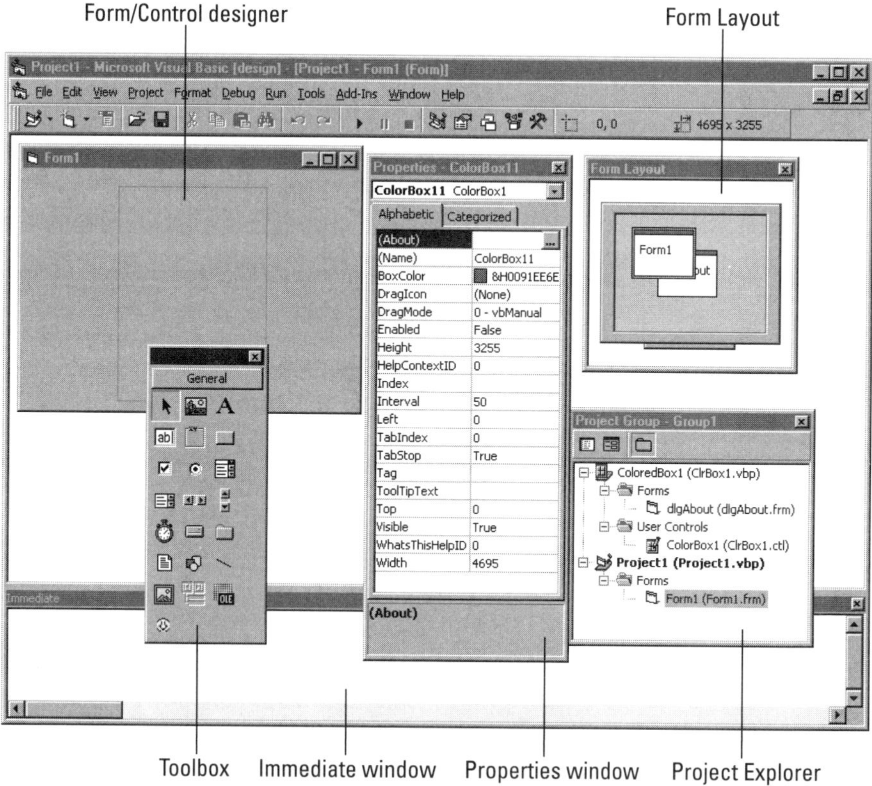

Figure 13-2: The VB5CCE environment contains many tools to help you work with projects and objects.

VB5CCE tools that are designed to ease the process of application and control design include the Project Explorer, the Toolbox, the Properties window, the Form Layout window, the Object Browser, the ActiveX Control Interface Wizard, and the Property Page Wizard.

The Project Explorer

The Project Explorer is a hierarchical view of all objects included in a project (or group of projects). You can use the Project Explorer to inspect the contents of a project and navigate between objects. Icons in the Explorer show you what an object is (for example, the Explorer in Figure 13-2 shows two form (.Frm) modules and one control (.Ctl) module.

The three buttons at the top of the Explorer open the code contained in modules for editing, open the module's interface for visual design, and toggle the hierarchy in the Explorer from expanded to contracted, respectively.

In addition, a context menu allows access, from within the Project Explorer, to most of the VB5CCE tools for creating objects.

The Toolbox

The Toolbox works in pretty much the way it does in VB4 and other Microsoft development tools (such as the ActiveX Control Pad discussed in Chapters 10 and 11). By default, when the Toolbox loads, it will contain the intrinsic VB5CCE controls.

You add controls to a container (such as a form or control module) either by dragging and dropping them to the display area of the container, or by double-clicking on the control in the Toolbox.

Any ActiveX control that is properly registered for design-time use on your system can be added to the Toolbox (from there, of course, it can be added to the container of your choice). To add a control to the Toolbox, open the Components dialog (shown in Figure 13-3) either by choosing Components from the Project menu or by right-clicking in the Toolbox and then choosing Components from the context menu.

Inside Scoop

If you create a control in an ActiveX project and then add a regular executable project (forming a project group), the bitmap for the ActiveX control will appear in the regular executable's Toolbox. Then you can test it without having to compile and recompile it.

The Properties Window

The Properties window, as shown in Figure 13-4, is basically a familiar animal. Developers use it at design time to set the properties of controls and forms. (The Properties window displays property names on the left and their values on the right.)

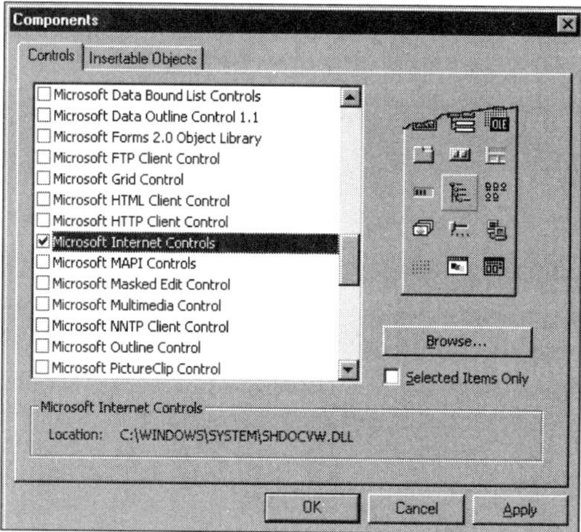

Figure 13-3: You can use the Components dialog to add controls to the Toolbox.

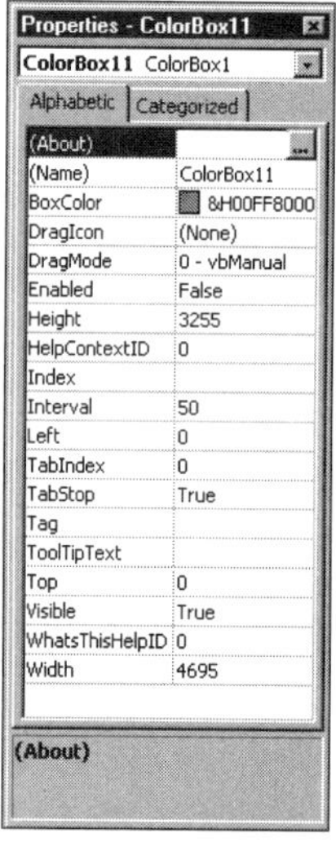

Figure 13-4: You can use the Properties window at design time to set the properties of controls and forms.

In Figure 13-4, notice that the first property displayed is "About," with a button on the right of its value field. Traditionally, control developers arrange to display a form that provides information about the control vendor when a developer using the control clicks the button. I'll show you how to easily add an About form to your controls later in this chapter.

The Form Layout Window

Figure 13-5 shows the Form Layout window. Unlike most visual programming environments, VB5CCE does not allow you to position forms directly by moving them around the screen. The Form Layout window is used to position forms on the screen by moving and positioning the form the way you want it.

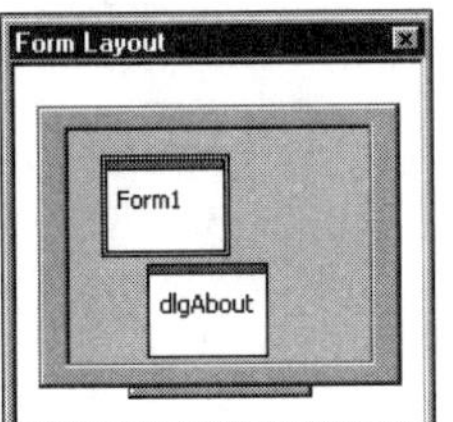

Figure 13-5: You can use the Form Layout window to position your forms on the screen.

The Object Browser

The VB5CCE Object Browser, shown in Figure 13-6, is a more powerful version of the Object Browser that was used in older Visual Basic versions. You can use it to find exposed properties, events, and methods of objects and object libraries (including user-defined objects).

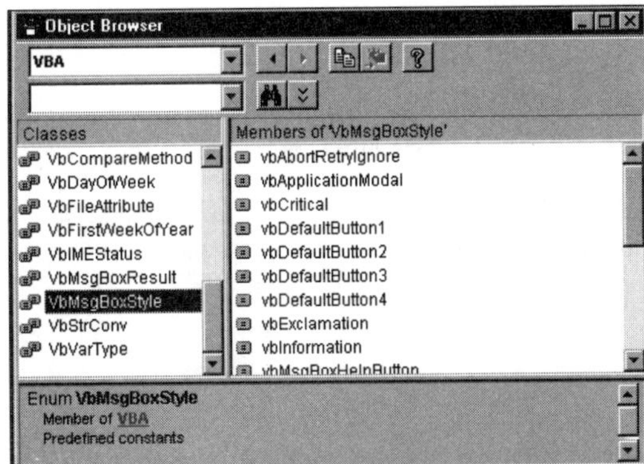

Figure 13-6: You can use the Object Browser to obtain very useful information about exposed properties, methods, and events of objects. (Here, for example, are the predefined constants from the VBA library that can be used with the MessageBox function.)

The ActiveX Control Interface Wizard

The ActiveX Control Interface Wizard is an add-in to VB5CCE that is intended, as the name implies, to simplify the creation of interfaces for basic ActiveX controls. (Add-ins are ActiveX server applications that interact with instances of the Visual Basic environment.)

You start the Wizard by selecting it from the Add-Ins menu. But first, before you start the Wizard, have an ActiveX control project open. Remember that the "interface" that the Wizard helps you create is *not* the appearance of the control on the screen but rather the exposed properties, events, and methods — also known as *members* — of the control as they show up in the Properties window and the event-handler code framework. This means that you can use graphics methods, such as Circle and Line, to draw your control or you can control its appearance with constituent controls.

As a demonstration, I'll create a control based on a command button that has some additional properties, methods, and events. It's nothing particularly fancy (or useful) but is enough to give you an idea of how to get started with the Wizard.

Start with a selected control named myTool.ctl in an ActiveX control project named myX.vbp. You'll find the source code for this project saved on the companion CD-ROM in the Ch13\Programs directory named as indicated in Table 13-1. This table also shows the new Visual Basic project structure in which multiple projects can be grouped in an overall Vbg project group.

Table 13-1 Filenames and Purposes (Mytool.Ocx)

Filename	*What It Contains*
myTool.ctl	ActiveX control module source code
myX.vbp	ActiveX control project
custom.pag	Custom property page source code module
myForm1.frm	Test form
myProj1.vbp	Test executable project
myGrp1.vbg	Project group file containing references to all the source files included in the project
mytool.ocx	Compiled ActiveX control

You can draw the command button (and other constituent controls that make up your ActiveX control) either before starting the Wizard or after the Wizard has completed. (If you need to use the Wizard to make modifications to your control, you can always run it later by selecting a control.)

It's important to realize that the Wizard does not implement members, except via the process of *delegation,* where one control inherits properties, methods, or events from constituent controls. This means that you are responsible for adding code that makes your user-defined members, termed *custom members*, work. Code added by the Wizard is essentially generic in nature. The example will be adding two custom properties, a custom method, and a custom event, as shown in Table 13-2.

Table 13-2 Custom Members in myTool.ctl

Member Name	*Type*	*Data Type*	*Default Value*
MessageEnabled	Property	Boolean	False
MessageText	Property	String	"Do you really want to click me?"
ShowMessage	Method	n/a	n/a
onShowMessage	Event	n/a	n/a

ShowMessage is a method which, if MessageEnabled is set to True, displays a message box containing the value of MessageText and then triggers the control's onShowMessage event.

Here's the difference between events that your control receives and that it triggers. (Events that a control causes are said to be *raised* by the control.) You can place code in the event-handler framework of your control to respond to events it receives; event-handler framework code is created for the use of developers using your control so they can respond to events it raises.

In the control module's code, once the Wizard finishes its work, you'll find property variables declared. For example:

```
'Property Variables:
Dim m_MessageText As String
Dim m_ForeColor As Long
Dim m_Enabled As Boolean
Dim m_Font As Font
Dim m_BackStyle As Integer
Dim m_BorderStyle As Integer
Dim m_MessageEnabled As Boolean
```

Constants are also initiated that contain the default values for the custom properties. For example:

```
'Default Property Values:
Const m_def_MessageText = "Do you really want to click me?"
...
Const m_def_MessageEnabled = 0
```

Custom events are declared as follows:

```
'Event Declarations:
Event onShowMessage()
```

Methods are implemented simply as public functions:

```
Public Function ShowMessage() As Variant
...
End Function
```

By default, the Wizard will preselect standard members for your control (as shown in Figure 13-7). You can use this dialog to remove these standard members or add others from a list of likely candidates.

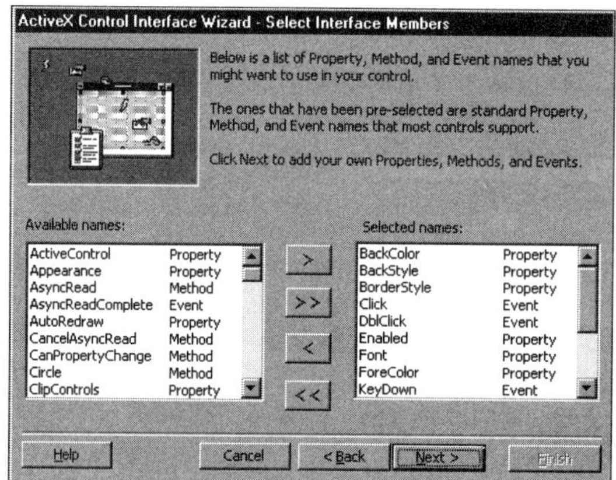

Figure 13-7: The Interface Wizard starts your control off with standard members.

The Wizard also allows you to add as many custom members as you'd like to your control (see Figures 13-8 and 13-9).

Finally, you'll need to set the attributes for each of your custom members. This sets the data type, the default value, descriptive text that will appear at the bottom of the Properties window, whether the member has full design-time and run-time access, and arguments if applicable. (Methods and events often have parameters.)

Figure 13-10 shows setting the attributes for the MessageEnabled custom property.

To create the template code for your control based on your choices within the Wizard, click on Finish. (Note that you can always come back and run the Wizard again if you prefer to make changes to your control using the Wizard interface rather than in code.)

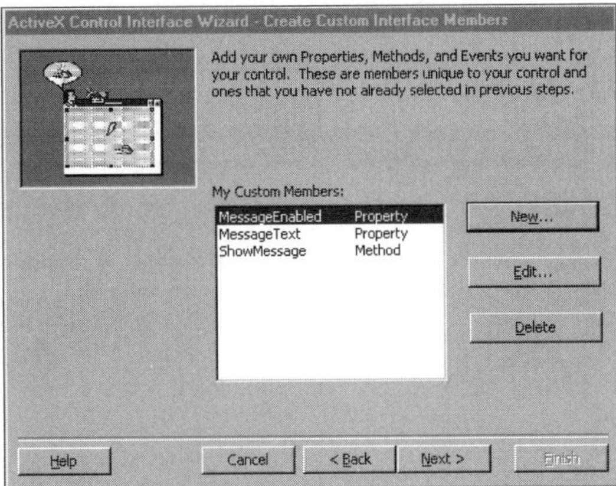

Figure 13-8: You can add custom members to your control using the Interface Wizard.

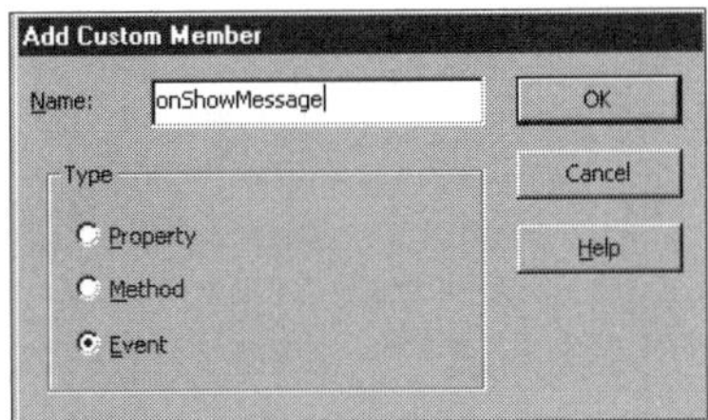

Figure 13-9: Members that you add can be custom properties, methods, or events.

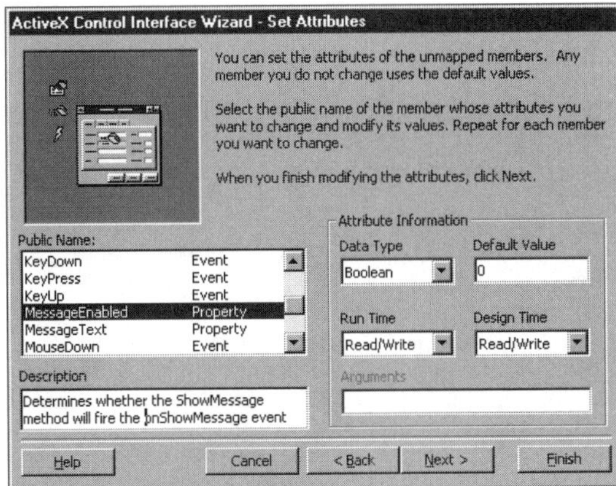

Figure 13-10: You can easily set the attributes for members of your control.

As a final act of charity to the struggling developer, the Interface Wizard displays a To Do list of steps required to complete the debugging of your control interface. You can save the list and then print it for later reference (a sample is saved in the Ch13\Programs directory on the companion CD-ROM as Ctlwiz.Txt).

Generally, you have to take the following steps, assuming that your control is part of an ActiveX project:

1. Save your control.
2. Close the control's *designer* — the window used for changing the appearance of the control. This places the control in run mode.
3. Add a standard executable project, using Add Project on the File menu. Save the combined projects as a project group (Vbg) file. The standard executable project is used to test your control in both design and run modes.
4. Double-click on your control's icon in the Toolbox to add it to the standard project's default form. If you haven't specified a Toolbox bitmap for the control, as explained in a moment, it will use a default icon.
5. Select your control on the form, and open the Properties window. Make sure you can see, and change, any properties you added to the control.
6. Change the value of one of your custom properties and close and open the form. Make sure that the changes to the value of your property were retained.
7. Open the Code window for your control, and make sure that any custom events you added to the control appear in the right-hand (Procedure) drop-down list.
8. At this point, you may want to go back to the control (rather than the instance of the control that is on the form) to add code and tweak existing code to make the control functional. Note that you should delete the instance of the control that is on the form and add a new instance once your modifications are complete.
9. Add some simple test code with the control on the form in design mode. For example, add a MsgBox statement to any events to make sure they are fired appropriately. Invoke methods to make sure they actually execute. Run the project, and make sure all is in order.

Adding a Toolbox Icon for Your Control

You can add a custom Toolbox icon for your control using the ToolboxBitmap property of the UserControl object. You can use the Properties window when your control is selected to set this property (the example uses a bitmap called myTool1.bmp).

Ideally, Toolbox bitmaps should be about 16 pixels high and 15 pixels wide. Conventional icons are the wrong size and should not be used for this purpose.

The Property Page Wizard

Property pages are an alternative interface that you can make available to developers who use your controls. They are accessed via a button in the value field of the (Custom) property that appears toward the top of the list of properties in the Properties window.

As a developer who has used ActiveX controls, you are probably familiar with property pages and their appearance; they consist of a tabbed set of dialogs, with one page per tab. Each page allows users of the control to set properties by using conventional controls (rather than by using the sometimes awkward Properties window).

The source code for each property page associated with a control is stored in a Pag file (the sample project's single property page is named Custom.Pag). These files are ASCII text files similar in structure to normal Visual Basic form module files (Frm files). This means that they contain internal references to encapsulated controls and their properties that, in theory, could be edited using a text editor. Each property page file becomes a node in the Property Pages folder under the control's project, as displayed in the Project Explorer.

It's quite straightforward to add a property page by choosing Add Property Page from the Project menu with the control selected. Controls are added, and the appearance of the page manipulated, using its designer — which works just the same as a form or control designer. Next you must add code to make the property page functional. Finally, you must connect the property page to the control using the Connect Property Pages dialog. (To access this dialog, make sure your control is selected, and then double-click the PropertyPages property in the Properties window.)

The Property Page Wizard, which you can start from the Add-Ins menu with your control selected, automates the process, although you may have to modify or add code once the Wizard has done its thing.

As you can see in Figure 13-11, the first step is to add the pages you want. The Wizard will generate property pages for each named page that is checked in the Select Property Pages dialog (shown in the background in Figure 13-11). By default, StandardColor and StandardFont pages will be created; if you do not want them, you must be sure to deselect them.

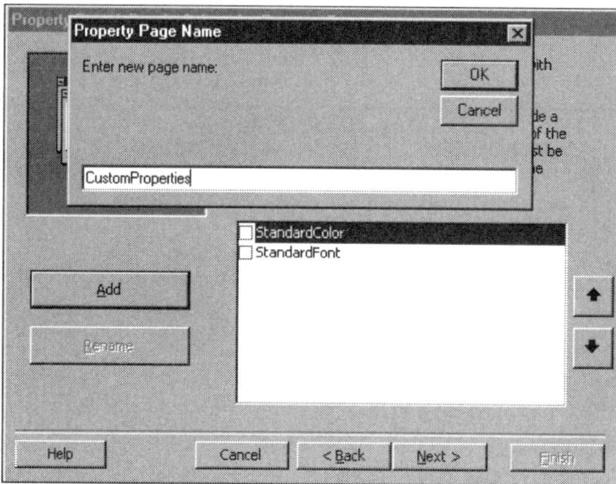

Figure 13-11: You can use the Select Property Pages dialog to easily add custom property pages.

The next step is to add the properties you want to the appropriate pages, as shown in Figure 13-12.

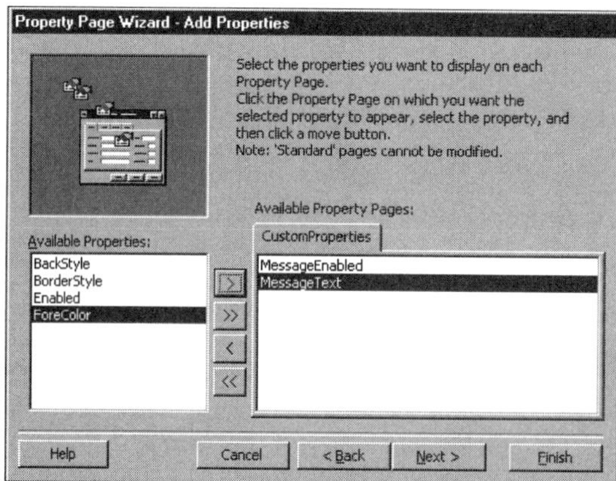

Figure 13-12: You can use the Add Properties dialog to add any available property to any available property page.

Based on the information you have provided, the Wizard generates your property page (or pages). A report of what you must still do to make the property pages functional is generated as its final step; generally this will consist of checking the code the Wizard has generated for comments labeled "TO DO" and following the directions contained in the comments. (For simple property pages, there even may be nothing further to do.)

It's a good idea to open your new property page in its designer and check whether you'd like to make any changes to its appearance. To do this, open the Project Explorer and select the property page, as shown in Figure 13-13. Its designer will open.

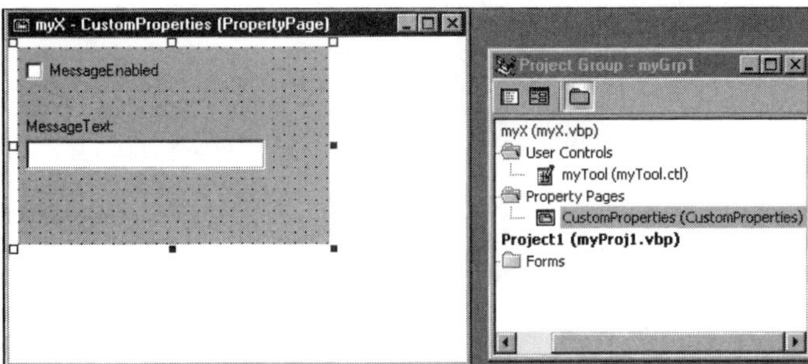

Figure 13-13: You can change the appearance of a custom property page using its designer.

After you make any changes (in the example, I made the page much smaller because it contains only two controls) it is a good time to save your work.

When you close the property page's designer (and the control's if necessary), and open the form containing the control, you'll find a (Custom) item at the top of the Properties window for the control. When you click on the button in the value field for this item, you'll see the custom property page you have created, as shown in Figure 13-14.

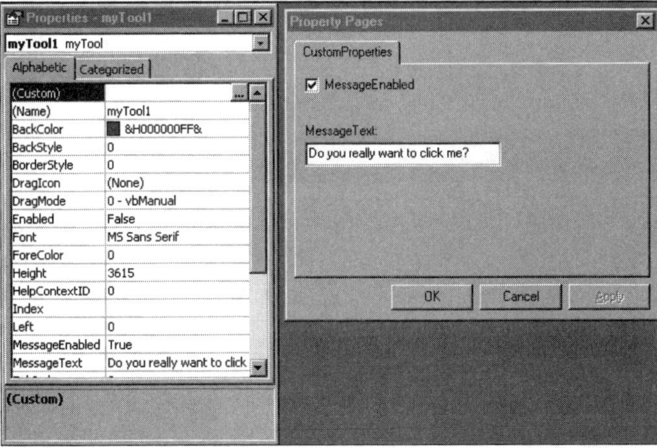

Figure 13-14: Property pages you have added to your control are accessed from the top item in the Properties window.

The code added to the property page's module to make it functional is not very extensive (see Listing 13-1).

Listing 13-1: Code required to make a custom property page functional

```
Option Explicit
Private Sub txtMessageText_Change()
   Changed = True
End Sub

Private Sub chkMessageEnabled_Click()
   Changed = True
End Sub

Private Sub PropertyPage_ApplyChanges()
   SelectedControls(0).MessageText = txtMessageText.Text
   SelectedControls(0).MessageEnabled = _
      (chkMessageEnabled.Value = vbChecked)
End Sub

Private Sub PropertyPage_SelectionChanged()
   txtMessageText.Text = SelectedControls(0).MessageText
   chkMessageEnabled.Value = _
      (SelectedControls(0).MessageEnabled And vbChecked)
End Sub
```

Obviously, the code shown in Listing 13-1 would need to be altered depending on the precise controls — and their names — placed on the property page (as well as the names of the properties involved).

You may prefer to create your property pages manually rather than using the Wizard. In that case, you could add code along the lines of what the Wizard would supply to make your pages functional.

Adding an About Dialog to Your Control

You can easily add a custom About box to your control. Developers using your control could access this dialog at design time by clicking on the button in the value field of the About property in the Properties window. You can use this dialog to provide contact, copyright, and authorship information for your control.

First create your About form, and add it to the ActiveX control project. (In the example, this form is named dlgAbout.) Next, open the code window for the UserControl object, and add the following procedure:

```
Public Sub ShowAbout()
   dlgAbout.Show vbModal
   Unload dlgAbout
   Set dlgAbout = Nothing
End Sub
```

With the code window still open, choose Procedure Attributes from the Tools menu. Click on the Advanced button to open the full Procedure Attributes dialog, as shown in Figure 13-15.

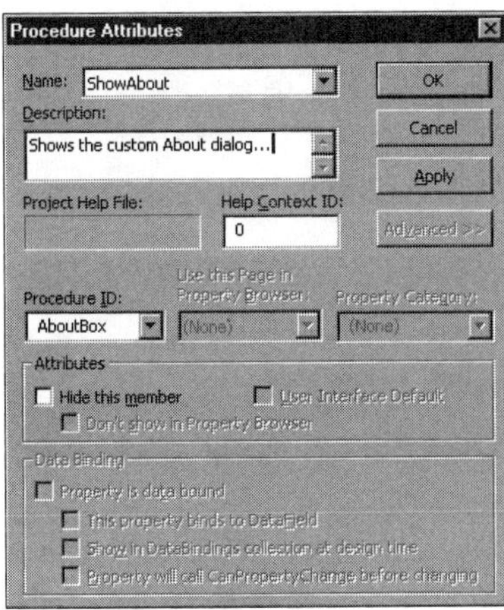

Figure 13-15: You can use the Procedures Attributes dialog to assign a procedure that shows an About box to an identifier that causes it to display in the Properties window.

Make sure ShowAbout is selected in the Name list box, and assign it to the AboutBox Procedure ID.

You can assign the same About box to as many controls as you'd like within a project.

If you open the standard project in design mode, and go to the Properties window with the myTool control selected, you'll now see an About field in the Properties window. Clicking on the button on the right of the About field displays the About box, as shown in Figure 13-16.

The About box used in this example (and shown in Figure 13-16) is reusable in the sense that it automatically loads the information it displays from the App object of the project that contains it.

To set the properties of an App object at design time, select the application in the Project Explorer window. Use the right-mouse context menu to access its tabbed Project Properties dialog, as shown in Figure 13-17.

For an explanation of how to code a reusable About box that uses the properties of the App object, see *Visual Basic 5 SECRETS* (same author, same publisher).

The sample About box uses Windows APIs to obtain system information. This may not be appropriate for ActiveX controls that are intended for Internet download. For a discussion of this and related issues, see "Making Controls Safe for Scripting" later in this chapter.

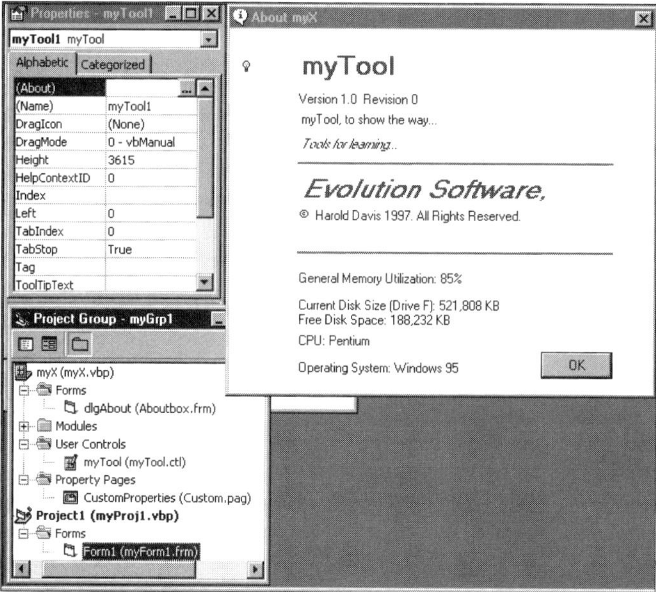

Figure 13-16: It's easy to add a professional finish to your controls with an About box.

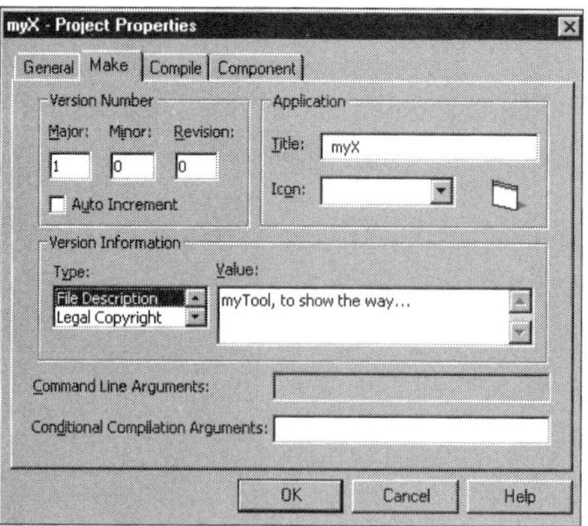

Figure 13-17: You can set the properties of an App object at design time using the Project Properties dialog.

Making the Control's Members Functional

You've now got a sample control whose interface is all present and accounted for! The interface looks the way it should. Custom properties show up in the Properties window and a new event, onShowMessage, appears in the code window as part of myTool's event-handler framework.

It's time to wire up the custom members of this control so that they perform as desired at runtime (in addition to working at design time, which they do now). Wiring up these puppies will take just a little bit of coding.

First of all, take a look at the internal UserControl mechanism for retrieving property values and changing property values:

```
Public Property Get MessageText() As String
   MessageText = m_MessageText
End Property

Public Property Let MessageText(ByVal New_MessageText As String)
   m_MessageText = New_MessageText
   PropertyChanged "MessageText"
End Property
```

Paired Property Gets and Lets are written into the UserControl's code for you by the Control Interface Wizard for every property that you've defined at the time the Wizard does its thing. Here's the pair for the custom MessageEnabled property, which has a different data type defined than the MessageText property (text as opposed to Boolean):

```
Public Property Get MessageEnabled() As Boolean
   MessageEnabled = m_MessageEnabled
End Property

Public Property Let MessageEnabled(ByVal New_MessageEnabled As
   Boolean)
      m_MessageEnabled = New_MessageEnabled
      PropertyChanged "MessageEnabled"
End Property
```

In addition to the Property Gets and Lets, which serve to retrieve and store property values during a designer's session with your control, your UserControl also needs a mechanism for saving changes to property values between sessions and for retrieving values that have previously been entered when it is opened. This is done using an object of the PropertyBag class.

As the name more-or-less implies, the purpose in life of a PropertyBag object is to store persistent property values across invocations of a control. The name of the PropertyBag class created by the Interface Wizard is PropBag. Here's the code — using the ReadProperty and WriteProperty methods of the PropertyBag object — that reads initial property values when the control is invoked and writes them when the instance of the control is closed. (I've left out all properties other than the custom ones defined in the example.)

```
'Load property values from storage
Private Sub UserControl_ReadProperties(PropBag As PropertyBag)
   ...
   m_MessageEnabled = PropBag.ReadProperty("MessageEnabled",_
      m_def_MessageEnabled)
   m_MessageText = PropBag.ReadProperty("MessageText",_
```

```
      m_def_MessageText)
End Sub
...
'Write property values to storage
Private Sub UserControl_WriteProperties(PropBag As PropertyBag)
   ...
   Call PropBag.WriteProperty("MessageEnabled", m_MessageEnabled,_
      m_def_MessageEnabled)
   Call PropBag.WriteProperty("MessageText", m_MessageText,_
      m_def_MessageText)
End Sub
```

The point of all this, of course, is that — like Dorothy and her friends in the *Wizard of Oz* — you don't really need a Wizard at all (at least to implement the interface of a UserControl object).

To summarize, you must add the following pieces of code to a UserControl's code for a property to show up and perform as expected in the control's interface (for example, Properties window):

1. Define a constant as the default property value, for example:

```
Const m_def_MessageText = "Do you really want to click me?"
```

2. Declare a variable of the appropriate type for the property, for instance:

```
Dim m_MessageText As String
```

3. Write Property Get and Property Let procedures for the property per the preceding examples.
4. Add ReadProperties and WriteProperties PropertyBag method calls using the methods of the UserControl object, as shown earlier.

This seems to me not much more difficult than using the Wizard.

Although the Interface Wizard pretty much handles the details of creating custom properties for you, it does no such thing for methods and events. A UserControl method is simply a public function. The Wizard does add the code framework for the function, along the lines of

```
Public Function ShowMessage() As Variant
...
End Function
```

It's up to you to add the code that makes the method tick. (The return type the Wizard creates for the function depends on what you entered in the Set Attributes dialog.)

As far as events go, the Interface Wizard adds an event declaration depending on events that you have included in the Select Interface Members and Create Custom Interface Members dialogs:

```
'Event Declarations:
...
Event MouseDown(Button As Integer, Shift As Integer, x As Single,_
```

```
   Y As Single)
...
Event onShowMessage()
```

This adds an event-handling framework for declared events when the control is added to a container (such as a form). Parameters that are displayed in the code window for the event handler depend on the arguments listed in the declaration, which can also be established in the Set Attributes dialog of the Wizard.

It's up to you to implement within the UserControl code module anything that triggers the event. (When the event is fired, the code that developers using your control entered in the event-handler framework is executed.)

To fire an event, the UserControl's RaiseEvent method is used:

```
RaiseEvent onShowMessage
```

There has been a lot of Control Interface water under the bridge since we started out with the myTool example of a UserControl, but — in case you've forgotten — here's what its custom members are supposed to do. (Not much, perhaps, but it is *our* UserControl.)

When a developer places an instance of the control on a form, it has two custom properties: MessageEnabled, a Boolean, and MessageText, a string. When the control is running, it responds to any invocations to the ShowMessage method placed in the control's click event by the developer using the control, depending on the value of MessageEnabled.

If MessageEnabled is False, a message saying that the Message feature is turned off should appear. Nothing else happens.

If MessageEnabled is True, when a user clicks on the control in run-time mode a message including the MessageText string is displayed. Next, the onShowMessage event is fired, and any code placed in the event-handler by the developer using the control is executed.

To implement this behavior, you'll need to recall that the command button placed on the UserControl has been programmed in the control's resize event to always be the size of the control. This means that when a user clicks on the control, the action will be received by the command button. You must add code to the UserControl module so that the event received by the command button is "passed along" to the UserControl. You do this by raising the UserControl's click event when the command button is clicked:

```
Private Sub Command1_Click()
   RaiseEvent Click 'pass it on to the control
End Sub
```

Remember, this is private code belonging to your control, whose sole purpose is to make sure that things happen as they should when a developer places code in myTool's click event.

It's worth emphasizing that your control — if it is made up of other controls — will only receive those events you choose to pass along to it.

Here's the code that implements the logic inherent in the ShowMessage method:

```
Public Function ShowMessage() As Variant
   If MessageEnabled Then
      MsgBox MessageText, vbInformation, "Like ActiveX, wow!"
      RaiseEvent onShowMessage
   Else
      MsgBox "The ShowMessage method must be enabled by setting" & _
         " the MessageEnabled property to true!", vbCritical, _
            "Like ActiveX, wow!"
   End If
End Function
```

To see this in action, you must return to the standard executable project that is part of the program group. With myTool added to the test form, add the following code to the myTool click event:

```
Private Sub myTool1_Click()
   myTool1.ShowMessage
End Sub
```

If you run the project and click on the control, you'll get a message box like the one shown in Figure 13-18.

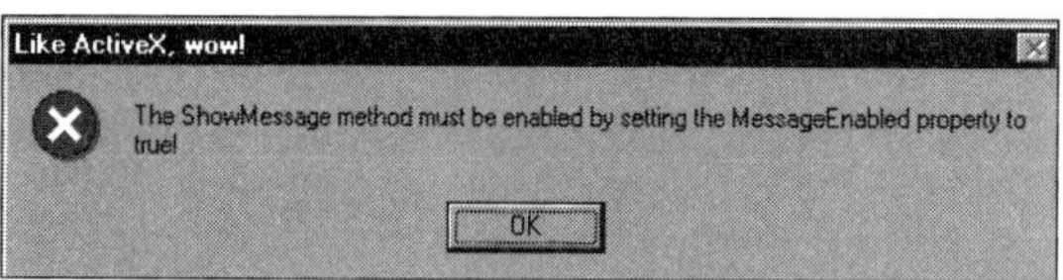

Figure 13-18: You can use message boxes to make sure that the inner logic of UserControl objects behaves as you want it to.

Ooops! Great. The control is functioning as specified at runtime. To get it to do more, you'll have to toggle the enabled property. In addition, you must add code along these lines to myTool's onShowMessage event:

```
Private Sub myTool1_onShowMessage()
  MsgBox "My onShowMessage event was fired!"
End Sub
```

If you run the project now, and click on the control, the value of the control's MessageText property will be displayed, as shown in Figure 13-19. After that, the "My onShowMessage..." message box will display, verifying that the event was indeed fired.

Figure 13-19: The message box displays the contents of the MessageText property, set in the Properties window.

As you can see, this control works as advertised. It's pretty easy to implement using VB5CCE, although you must keep three modes in mind at all times. They are

- Control design mode (you)
- Test application design mode (developer using your control)
- Test application run mode (end user)

Obviously, controls with more complex functionality will require more complex internal code implementation.

You can compile the control into a stand-alone Ocx file. To do this, open the ActiveX control project and choose Make from the File menu. Once it has been compiled, developers can use it in design mode in any environment that handles ActiveX controls — including, among others, the ActiveX Control Pad, Delphi, VB5, and VC++.

More about VB Controls and Objects

Obviously, there's a lot more to be said about creating ActiveX controls using VB5CCE. For one thing, to really create useful components in VB5CCE you'll need a good understanding of Visual Basic's object model and programming style.

In the remainder of this chapter, I'll provide at least an overview of what you'll need to know as a Web developer to create awesome controls in VB5CCE. (I do assume some Visual Basic programming experience.)

Objects and Classes in VB5

Objects, in Visual Basic, are instances of a class, meaning they are created — like a cookie from a cookie cutter — using the class as a template. The class defines an object's interface — that is, its properties, events, and methods. The class also determines whether the object is public or private, and under what circumstances an object based on the class can be created. Descriptions of classes are stored in *type libraries*, which you can view using an Object Browser such as the one in the VB IDE.

To use an object, you must place a reference to the object in a variable declared as an object, a variant, or a specific kind of object. For example:

```
Dim myObj as Object
Set myObj = CreateObject("SomeOLEClass")
```

or

```
Dim myForm As New dlgAbout
myForm.caption = "Casablanca"
```

The form of the declaration determines the kind of *binding* that the VB compiler uses to access objects. Binding determines when method code is assigned to method invocations. *Early binding*, the fastest kind, occurs when the object variable is strictly typed using the Dim...As syntax.

Objects can be contained in both static and dynamic arrays. This can be particularly useful with forms and control objects.

Collections are another helpful way to keep track of objects. Collections are themselves objects that provide a way to refer to and manipulate groups of objects. You can create your own collection objects in VB; in addition, many VB objects come with their own predefined collection objects. (For example, a form's controls collection contains all the controls on a form.)

Classes are implemented in VB using class modules (the source files are saved with a .Cls extension). Class modules contain properties — implemented with Property procedures, as in the myTool UserControl module explained earlier in this chapter. Methods are implemented, as in Ctl files, with a Public function. Events are implemented, as in Ctl modules, by declaring them with the event keyword and then firing them at the appropriate time. For example:

```
Event TeaTime (WhatToEat as String, WhatToDrink as string)
...
If AppropriateCircumstances Then
   RaiseEvent ("Crumpets and Honey", "Hot Tea")
End If
```

Class modules do not have a screen representation *per se*; however, you will often want to add classes to components. In older versions of Visual Basic, class modules were used to encapsulate the internal functioning of an application. Similarly, class modules are used to encapsulate the internal functionality of components in VB5CCE. Each public class you add to a control is the cookie-cutter template for an object that is part of your control.

The name you give a class module is appended to the name of your control to yield the class *progID,* or programmatic ID. For example, suppose you added a class module named myNewClass to the myTool control. The progID for the new class would be myTool.myNewClass.

The Instancing property of each class module defines how the class can be accessed. For ActiveX control projects, class module instancing must be either Private or PublicNotCreatable. Private means that outside applications cannot access type library information about the class and cannot create objects based upon it. PublicNotCreatable means that outside applications can only use instances of this class if your control has first created it. Objects based on PublicNotCreatable class module are termed *dependent*, because they must be created by their parent component before they can be used. If you want external applications to be able to create dependent objects, you have to provide a component method — such as .add — that creates an instance of the dependent object.

Controls and Containers

No control is an island unto itself. An instance of a control never exists by itself. It only has a life once it has been placed on a container. Classically, the container is a Visual Basic form, but it need not be. An Internet Explorer window is the up-and-coming candidate for container of the hour. For example, you cannot run an ActiveX control application in VB5CCE. You must add a standard executable application to your project group, and add the control to a container in that application before you can test your control.

Some of the interface members that appear to users of your control to be part of your control actually belong to the container object holding the control.

Your control is hosted by a container's *Extender* object. You can access the properties and methods of the container your control has been placed on through the Parent property of the container's Extender. In addition, a UserControl's Ambient object contains property information that you can use to make your control consistent with its background.

The Extender and Ambient objects are not available until a UserControl has been sited on a container. They are not available until InitProperties or ReadProperties has been fired, which is subsequent to the firing of the control's Initialize event.

Some ActiveX control features require support from the container they are placed on, and not every container supplies all possible feature support. Thus, depending on the container your control is attached to, some features may be disabled.

Visual Basic forms support the following features, which are not supported by some other containers:

- Transparent control background
- The ControlContainer property
- Alignable controls
- Modeless forms displayed by your control

Using the Container's Extender Object

If you place an instance of your control on a container, such as a form, and view its properties with the Properties window, you'll find quite a few properties you didn't create. These are the Extender object properties provided by the container object, although to a user of your control they appear to be a seamless extension of your control.

You can use the properties of the Extender object to set the properties of your control. For example, it's common to have the default value of the caption (or text) property of a control be the name given the control by the container object. Usually, this is the name of the control followed by a number indicating the number of instances of the control that have been placed on the container. Figure 13-20 shows a typical default caption — both on the control and in the Properties window — for myTool.

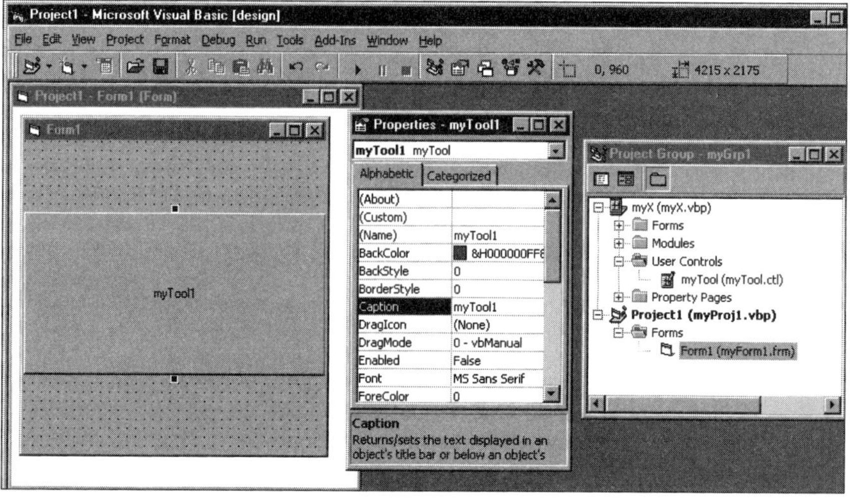

Figure 13-20: You can use the properties of the container's Extender object to set default values for your control's properties.

To implement this, first you'll need to add a caption property for myTool using the techniques explained earlier in this chapter. Next you'll need to add code to myTool's UserControl_InitProperties() event to let its caption be the default name of the control. Because the entire visible presence for this particular control is the constituent command button, you'll also need to add code that changes the command button's caption. (Without it, the default caption value in the Properties window would change, but not the text displayed on the control.)

```
Private Sub UserControl_InitProperties()
   ...
   m_Caption = Extender.Name
   Command1.Caption = m_Caption
End Sub
```

You'll also need to add a line of code in the UserControl module to the Caption's Property Let procedure to make sure that the caption displayed on the constituent command button is updated when the user changes the caption for the myTool instance in the Properties window:

```
Public Property Let Caption(ByVal New_Caption As String)
   m_Caption = New_Caption
   Command1.Caption = m_Caption 'Added for dynamic display change
   PropertyChanged "Caption"
End Property
```

Table 13-3 lists the extender properties that all containers are supposed to provide according to the ActiveX control specification.

Table 13-3 Mandatory Container Extender Properties

Property	*Data Type*	*Access*	*Meaning*
Name	String	Read	The name the user assigns to the control instance
Visible	Boolean	Read/Write	Indicates whether the control is visible
Parent	Object	Read	Returns the object that contains the control, such as a Visual Basic form
Cancel	Boolean	Read	True if the control is the Cancel button for the container
Default	Boolean	Read	True if the control is the default button for the container

The truth is that not all containers provide even these properties. You should use error trapping in code whenever referring to the Extender object of a control's container.

Many containers provide extender properties beyond those listed in Table 13-4, for example: Left, Top, Width, and Height properties.

To manipulate the visibility of your control at runtime — or to allow a developer using your control to do so — do not use the Extender object's visible property. Instead, use the UserControl object's InvisibleAtRuntime property.

You should know that if your control and its container's Extender object have properties with the same name, the Extender property will take precedence.

The Ambient Object's UserMode Property

You should know about the UserMode property of the Ambient object, which allows an instance of your control to determine whether it's running at design time (UserMode = False) or at runtime. The mnemonic for remembering what the value of UserMode means is that at design time a *developer,* not an end user, is working with your control. Because the control is not in "user" mode, UserMode = False.

For example, you could create a different container caption for developers and end users in myTool's resize event, as shown in Listing 13-2.

Listing 13-2: Using the Ambient object's UserMode property

```
Private Sub UserControl_Resize()
   ...
   If Ambient.UserMode Then
      Extender.Parent.Caption = "myTool says," + Chr(34) + _
         "Hi, end user!" + Chr(34)
   Else
      Extender.Parent.Caption = "Developer, thanks for" + _
         "using myTool!"
   End If
End Sub
```

Figure 13-21 shows an instance of myTool added to a form in design mode; Figure 13-22 shows the same instance of myTool and form in run mode.

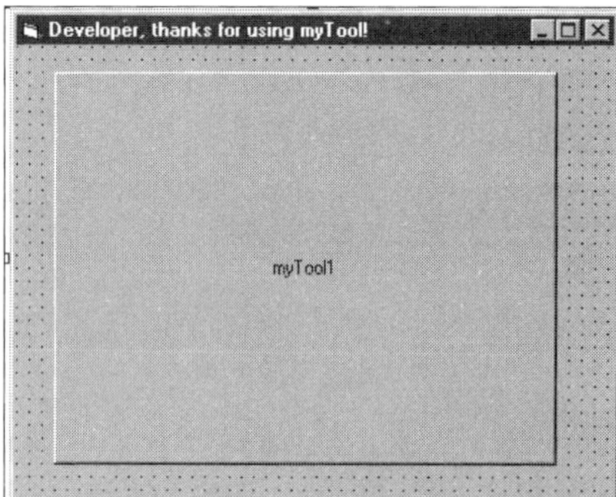

Figure 13-21: You can use the Ambient object's UserMode property to set the properties of the Extender object of the container for a control differently at design time...

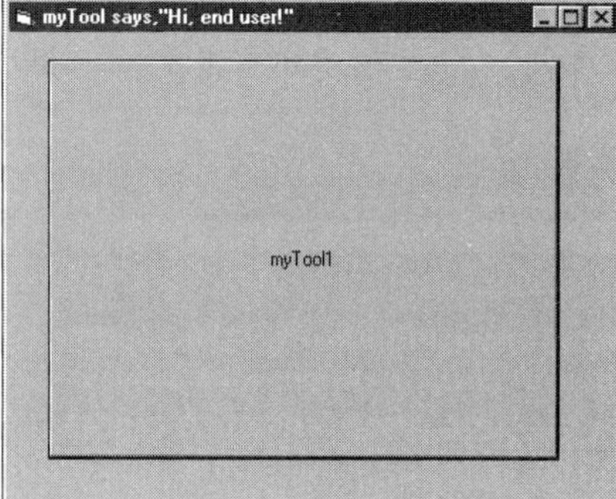

Figure 13-22: ...and at runtime.

User-Drawn Controls

In the myTool example, the appearance of myTool at both design time and runtime was determined by its constituent command button control. Another possible way to handle creation of the appearance of your controls is to *user-draw* them.

If you're creating a user-drawn control, you have to do all the drawing yourself. You should know when to draw your control, what state it's in (for example, clicked or unclicked), and whether you should draw a focus rectangle. (With controls made up of constituent controls most of these details are handled for you.)

When you're doing your own drawing, the only place you need to put drawing code is in the UserControl_Paint event handler. When the container repaints the area your control is located on, the UserControl object will receive a Paint event.

You can use the built-in graphics methods of the UserControl object, such as Line and Circle. In addition, the vast universe of Windows API calls are available to draw your control. Regardless of the drawing technique you use, the code goes in UserControl_Paint.

If your control has to change the way it looks based on user actions, such as users clicking on the control, you can raise the Paint event by calling the UserControl's Refresh method.

A Confetti Control

As an example of user-drawn controls, here's how you would create a Confetti control (pictured in Figure 13-23).

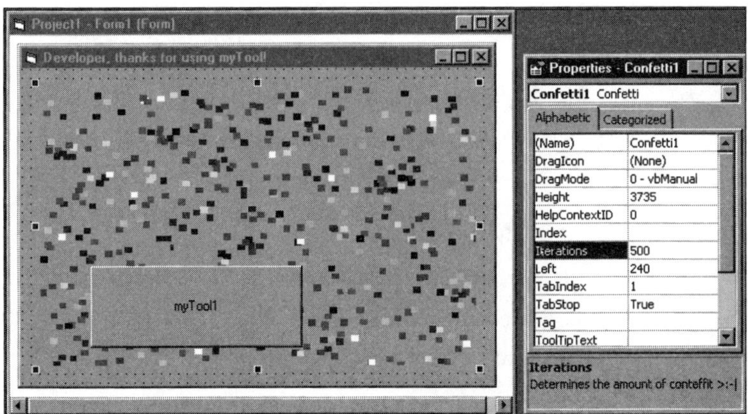

Figure 13-23: You can create user-drawn controls that handle their own screen appearance.

The Confetti control source code is on the companion CD-ROM in the Ch13\Programs directory. The control module is saved as Confetti.Ctl, and the ActiveX control project that includes it is Confetti.Vbp. Confetti.Vbp is part of the same project group as myTool, myGrp1.Vbg.

The Confetti control is very simple. It drops randomly colored confetti on its screen representation for the number of times specified in its Iterations property every time its Paint event is raised — for example, when the control is resized or initialized.

To set this up, first implement the Iterations property:

```
Option Explicit
'Default Property Values:
Const m_def_Iterations = 5000

'Property Variables:
Dim m_Iterations As Long

Public Property Get Iterations() As Long
   Iterations = m_Iterations
End Property

Public Property Let Iterations(ByVal New_Iterations As Long)
   m_Iterations = New_Iterations
   PropertyChanged "Iterations"
End Property

Private Sub UserControl_InitProperties()
   m_Iterations = m_def_Iterations
End Sub

Private Sub UserControl_ReadProperties(PropBag As PropertyBag)
   m_Iterations = PropBag.ReadProperty("Iterations",
      m_def_Iterations)
End Sub

Private Sub UserControl_WriteProperties(PropBag As PropertyBag)
   Call PropBag.WriteProperty("Iterations", m_Iterations,
      m_def_Iterations)
End Sub
```

Next, add the code that makes the confetti to the UserControl Paint event:

```
Private Sub UserControl_Paint()
 Dim I As Integer, X1 As Integer, Y1 As Integer, Color As Long
   Randomize
   For I = 1 To Iterations
      X1 = Rnd * ScaleWidth
      Y1 = Rnd * ScaleHeight
      Color = QBColor(Rnd * 15)
      Line (X1, Y1)-(X1 + 85, Y1 + 65), Color, BF
   Next I
End Sub
```

That's it! Now, when you add the control to a container, it will confetti away!

Inside Scoop

For an explanation of the Visual Basic graphics functions used in the Confetti control — and other interesting visual effects that you can easily achieve with Visual Basic — please see *Visual Basic 5 SECRETS,* also available from IDG Books.

A Day in the Life of a UserControl

It's important to understand that instances of your controls are constantly being created and destroyed — for example, when forms are opened and closed, when a control is added to a form from the Toolbox, and when you run the project. Creating or destroying an instance of a control means creating or destroying the instance of the UserControl object that it is based upon — and all constituent controls that are part of the UserControl.

For example, consider the myTool life cycle:

- A developer creates an instance of myTool by double-clicking on its bitmap in the Toolbox, or by opening a form on which an instance of myTool was previously placed.
- The constituent command button, part of myTool, is also created. Next, the UserControl object is created, and the command button is sited on it.
- The UserControl_Initialize event procedure is fired.
- The myTool control is sited on the form.
- If the user is placing a new myTool, the InitProperties event of the UserControl object is triggered, and the control's default property values are set. If an existing form is being opened, the ReadProperties event occurs instead, and the control retrieves its saved property values from the PropertyBag object.
- The UserControl_Resize event procedure fires next, and the command button is resized according to the size the user made the new control instance (or the size it was before form was closed).
- The Show and Paint events occur. If there are no constituent controls, the UserControl object draws itself.
- The user runs the project. VB5CCE closes the form.
- The UserControl object's WriteProperties event occurs, and the control's property values are saved to the PropertyBag.
- The control is unsited.
- The UserControl object's Terminate event is fired.
- The UserControl object and any constituent controls (in the case of myTool, the command button) are destroyed.

- Next, the run-time instance of the form is created, along with a run-time instance of the myTool control. When the user closes the form and returns once more to design mode, the instance of myTool is destroyed and re-created yet again.

Important UserControl Events

We all seek meaning in the seemingly random events that occur in our lives. Well, to a UserControl its life cycle is not a random walk. It knows what the events in its life cycle mean, and so should you if you are going to work with controls. Here are the meanings of the key events in the life of a UserControl object:

- The Initialize event occurs every time an instance of a control is created or re-created. It is always the first event in a control instance's lifetime.
- The InitProperties event occurs only in a control instance's first incarnation, when an instance of the control is placed on a form. In this event, you set the initial, or default, values of the control's properties.
- The ReadProperties event occurs the second and subsequent times a control instance is created. This event is used to retrieve the control instance's property values from the PropertyBag object.
- The Resize event occurs every time a control instance is re-created, and every time it is resized — whether in design mode, by the developer of a form, or at runtime, in code. If your UserControl object contains constituent controls, you arrange them in the event procedure for this event, thus providing your control's appearance.
- The Paint event occurs whenever the container tells the control to draw itself. This can occur at any time, even before the control receives its Show event — for example, if a hidden form paints itself. With user-drawn controls, the Paint event is where you draw your control's appearance.
- The WriteProperties event occurs just before a *design-time* instance of your control is destroyed, if at least one property value has changed. In this event, you should save to the PropertyBag object all the property values a developer has set for the control instance.
- The Terminate event occurs when the control is about to be destroyed.

To appear on the screen in Windows, a control must have a window. Before a control has been sited on a form, its window is not on the container. The UserControl object receives Show and Hide events when the control window is added and removed from the container.

While the control's window is on the form, the UserControl receives a Hide event when the control's Visible property changes to False and a Show event when it changes to True.

The UserControl object does *not* receive Hide and Show events if the form is hidden and then shown again, or if the form is minimized and then restored.

The control's window remains on the form during these operations, and its Visible property doesn't change.

If the control is being shown in Internet Explorer, a Hide event occurs when the page is moved to the history list, and a Show event occurs if the user returns to the page.

Controls on Web Pages

Unlike Visual Basic projects and compiled programs, HTML pages don't save design-time information. Therefore, a control on an HTML page always acts as though it's being created for the very first time, as Madonna might say. When the HTML is processed by a browser, a control on the page receives the Initialize, InitProperties, Resize, and Paint events — but not ReadProperties.

Property values specified with the *<param name = value>* tag — between the <OBJECT> and </OBJECT> tags that specify the control's place on the page — are assigned once the control is running.

UserControls Are Not Forms

UserControls are not forms. Some of the events you may be used to from working with forms never happen to a UserControl object. For example, there is no Activate or Deactivate event, because controls are not activated and deactivated (but forms are). In addition, the familiar Load, Unload, and QueryUnload events are missing from the lifestyle of a UserControl.

The UserControl object's Initialize and ReadProperties events provide the functionality of a form's Load event. The main difference between the two is that when the Initialize event occurs, the control has not been sited on its container, so the container's Extender and Ambient objects are not available. The control has been sited when InitProperties or ReadProperties occurs.

The UserControl event most like a form's Unload event is Terminate. The constituent controls still exist at this point, although you no longer have access to the container, because your control has been unsited. The WriteProperties event cannot be used in the place of Unload, because it occurs only at design time.

UserControl objects don't have QueryUnload events because controls are just parts of a form. Theirs is to do or die, and not to wonder why. It's not up to a control to decide whether the form that contains it should close. A control's duty is to destroy itself when it's told to. Said one UserControl to the other, "Pass the Koolaid, please!"

Spying on myTool

You can pretty quickly find out what's going on with a UserControl object by adding DeBug.Print commands to its key events, and then watching those events repeatedly being fired in the Immediate window.

For example, you could enter Debug statements as follows:

```
Private Sub UserControl_Initialize()
   Debug.Print "Initialize"
End Sub

Private Sub UserControl_InitProperties()
   Debug.Print "InitProperties"
End Sub

Private Sub UserControl_ReadProperties(PropBag As _
   PropertyBag)
   Debug.Print "ReadProperties"
End Sub

Private Sub UserControl_Resize()
   Debug.Print "Resize"
End Sub

Private Sub UserControl_WriteProperties(PropBag _
   As PropertyBag)
   Debug.Print "WriteProperties"
End Sub

Private Sub UserControl_Terminate()
   Debug.Print "Terminate"
End Sub
```

The results of adding these Debug statements will be along the lines of that shown in Figure 13-24.

Is myTool one hyperactive control? Does myTool need tranquilizers? Do all the Initialize events shown in Figure 13-24 actually come from one control?

The answer is that UserControls, by their very nature, have a frenetic pace of instancing and destruction. As in, "Live hard, drive fast, and die young!" While a user may put a control on a form, and thereafter think of the control as a permanent fixture of the form, from the control developer's viewpoint, controls are getting destroyed and re-created all the time. Welcome to fast times at UserControl High!

Requiring a License for Developer Use

If you create a UserControl that actually does something useful for other developers — say, a version of myTool that is the ultimate Web widget — you may wish to implement a licensing scheme for developer use.

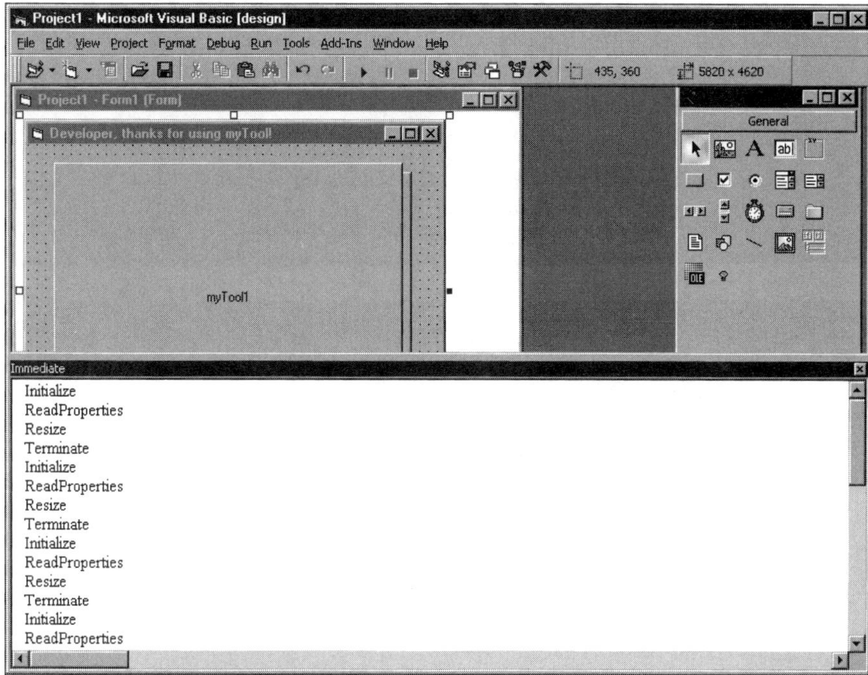

Figure 13-24: You can use Debug statements to gain an understanding of when UserControl events are fired.

There are some complex issues involved with this, because developers who use your control may themselves create controls that include yours. If you have required a design-time license for your control, and these subdevelopers have introduced a licensing scheme themselves, developer licenses will have to be present in the target Registry for both the subdeveloper's control and your control for the new control to open on the target system. One can foresee all kinds of chaos coming out of this, but, for the meantime here's the gist of how it works.

You can elect to include a licensing key for design-time use by making sure that the option Require License Key is checked in the Project Properties dialog before you make your Ocx (as shown in Figure 13-25).

After you've compiled your control, run the VB5CCE Application Setup Wizard. The resulting Setup program, when executed, will transfer the license key to another computer's Registry, allowing your controls to be used in design mode for development.

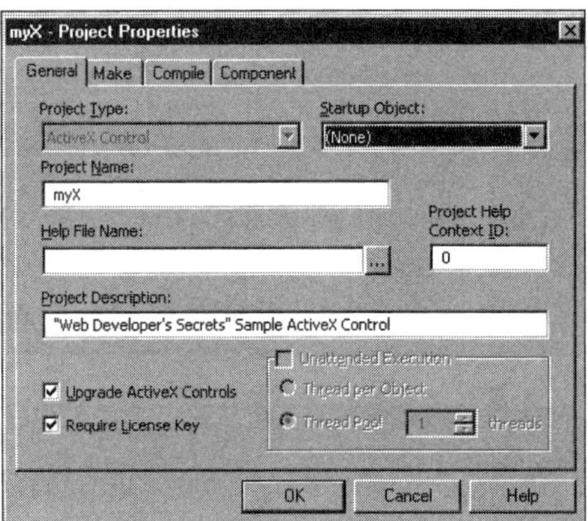

Figure 13-25: You can use the Project Property dialog to require a license key for your compiled UserControl.

Simply copying your Ocx file to another computer and then registering it will not transfer the license key. Without the license key, the control will only work in run-time mode and cannot be used by developers at design time! If a developer has a copy of your control, but not the registry key, the control cannot create instances of itself in the development environment.

Visual Basic creates a file with a .Vbl extension that contains the registry key that licenses your control. When you use the Setup Wizard to create Setup for your Ocx, the Vbl file is automatically included in the setup procedure.

Licensing and the Web

Licensed controls can be used on Web pages along with Internet Explorer. Both the control and the license key must be available to be downloaded to the browser accessing the Web page.

The downloaded license key is not added to the Registry. Instead, the browser asks the control to create a run-time instance of itself and passes it the downloaded license key.

The Web site that uses the control must be able to supply both control and license. If the license is not available, control creation will fail, and the browser will receive a standard control creation error.

Preparing Your Controls for Download

A control on an HTML page is specified using the HTML <OBJECT> and </OBJECT> tags. When the HTML is processed, the control is created and positioned. If the <OBJECT> tag includes any <PARAM NAME> attributes, the property values supplied with those attributes are passed to the control's InitProperties or ReadProperties event using the standard PropertyBag object. Once the HTML page is active, the control's property values may also be set by scripts attached to events that occur on the page.

The Setup Wizard that accompanies VB5CCE makes it easy to create an Internet setup for your control, with cabinet (Cab) files that can be automatically downloaded when a user opens an HTML page containing an instance of your control. If required support files — such as the Visual Basic VM (Msvbvm50.Dll) — already exist on the target machine, downloading time for the control can be very fast.

Making Controls Safe for Scripting

Making controls safe for scripting is one of those topics that sounds rhetorical, like making the world safe for democracy. Nonetheless, there are some issues you should consider.

The basic principle is that someone scripting your control should not be able to use it to read or write specific files or registry entries across the Web. (By specific files or registry entries, I mean ones selected by the person doing the scripting.) If a malicious person could gain these kinds of access through a Web ActiveX control, nothing on the systems that downloaded the control would be secure.

Because ActiveX controls that are downloaded across the Web do not come with whatever reassurance shrink-wrapped consumer packaging may provide, several mechanisms have been devised to reassure users.

Digital signatures create a path to you (through the company that authorized your certificate). You can incorporate your signature when you use Setup Wizard to create an Internet setup for your control component.

Obviously, if you go into commercial deployment of ActiveX controls on the Web, you'll need to obtain digital certificates — to placate potential customers, if for no other reason. In the meantime, the ActiveX SDK contains various test digital certificates you can use when debugging component downloads, as well as tools for obtaining your own certificate. The URL for the ActiveX SDK download is *http://www.microsoft.com/intdev/sdk/*.

You can mark your control as safe for scripting, which tells users that you believe a script on an HTML page cannot use your control to harm their computers, or to obtain information they haven't supplied willingly.

A control that permits a Web page designer to do any of the following is probably not safe for scripting:

- Create a file with a name supplied by a script
- Read a file from the user's hard drive with a name supplied by a script
- Insert information into the Windows Registry (or into an Ini file), using a key (or filename) supplied by a script
- Retrieve information from the Windows Registry (or from an Ini file), using a key (or filename) supplied by a script

- Execute a Windows API function using information supplied by a script
- Create or manipulate external objects using programmatic IDs (for example, "Excel.Application") that the script supplies

The line between safe and unsafe isn't necessarily obvious. For example, a control that uses the SaveSetting method to write information to its own registry key doesn't disqualify itself for safe scripting by doing so. On the other hand, a control that allows the registry key to be specified (by setting a property or invoking a method) is not safe.

A control that uses a temporary file may be safe for scripting. If the name of that temporary file can be controlled by a script, the control is not safe for scripting. Allowing a script to control the amount of information that goes into a temporary file will make the control unsafe for scripting, because a script could continue dumping information into the file until the user's hard disk overflowed.

As a final example, a control that uses API calls is not necessarily unsafe for scripting. Suppose, however, that the control allows a script to supply data that will be passed to an API and doesn't guard against oversize data overwriting memory, or invalid data corrupting memory. Such a control is not safe for scripting.

As an indication of the seriousness of scripting safety, note that VBScript itself does not include methods to access the registry, save files, or create objects.

You can mark your control as safe for initialization, which lets users know that you believe there's no way an HTML author can harm their computers by feeding your control invalid data when the page initializes it.

When you use Application Setup Wizard to create your Internet setup, you indicate that your control is marked in this fashion. If you don't, Internet Explorer by default will refuse to download your component.

Even if you mark your control as safe, the default setting in Explorer is to reject unsigned ActiveX components. To override this setting, in Explorer's Options dialog, select the Security tab, click on Advanced, and deselect the High Security setting.

Running the Application Setup Wizard

To have a customized automatic Web setup created for your ActiveX control, start the Application Setup Wizard. (It's a completely separate application with a menu shortcut that has been placed in the VB5CCE group.)

As Wizards are wont to do, the Application Setup Wizard presents a series of screens that require your input. You'll first have to tell the Wizard what component to set up. As an example, I've installed the Confetti ActiveX control, developed earlier in this chapter, on the Web.

To prepare a control for Internet component download, you must make sure that the option Create Internet Download Setup is selected, as shown in Figure 13-26.

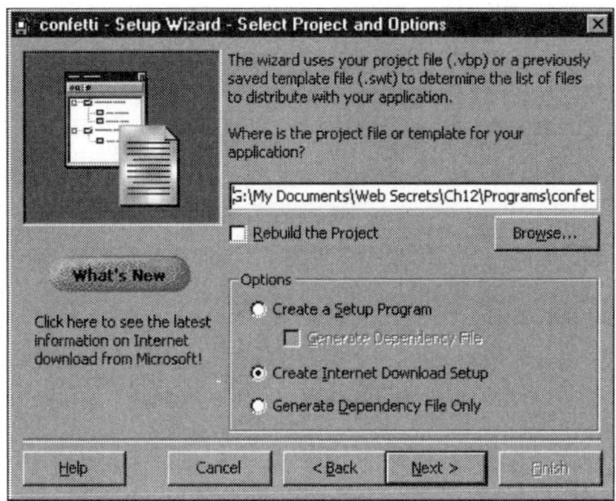

Figure 13-26: To set your control up for download across the Web, make sure that Create Internet Download Setup is selected.

You will not be able to use a setup routine that has been written for Internet component download for normal setup purposes. An Internet component download setup is intended for run-time usage and is therefore radically different from a conventional setup program, which is intended for design-time use.

You also need to specify a location for the Cab software installation file that the Wizard will create, and any supporting files that are required. Cab (cabinet) files are compressed in the standard Microsoft delivery format. For example, your Windows 95 or NT CD-ROM mainly contains Cab files.

It's a good idea to place all your Cab files in one directory on your Web site, for ease of administration.

Figure 13-27 shows the Wizard's Internet Distribution Location dialog.

The Internet Package dialog, which follows the Distribution Location dialog, is shown on the left-hand side of Figure 13-28. Use this dialog to specify whether Visual Basic run-time cabinet files should be downloaded from Microsoft's site or from an alternate location (if they are required).

Unless you are in an intranet setting with no outside Web access, you should download the Cab files from Microsoft (which is the default setting). Using Microsoft's site ensures that your users will get the latest versions of Microsoft-supplied support files and that the correct version for the target browser's operating system will be sent.

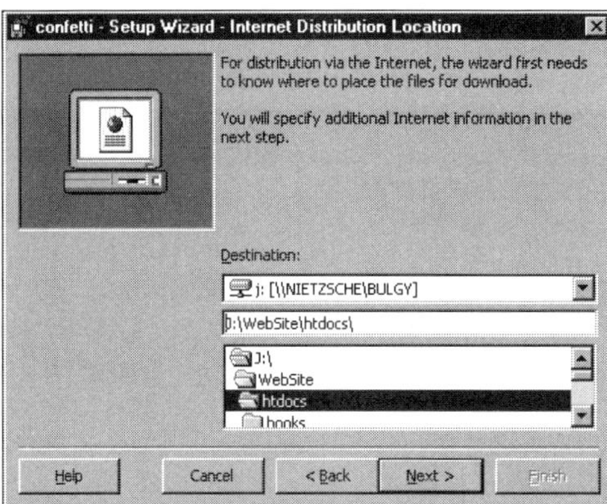

Figure 13-27: You must specify the target destination for your component setup files.

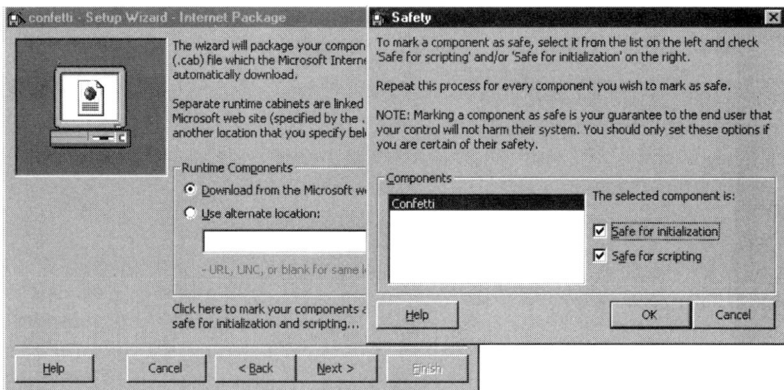

Figure 13-28: The Internet Package dialog allows you to specify support download file location and safety settings.

The following are the most commonly required support files, which have been digitally signed by Microsoft and are freely downloadable:

- Msvbvm5b.Cab, VB5 Virtual Machine, required for all VB5 built controls and applications
- CmCtlb32.Cab, VB5 Common controls, included TreeView, ListView, and so on
- Cmdlgb32.Cab, VB5 Common dialog control

If you are developing an intranet application, you should set up one standardized URL for support download to avoid versioning problems and administrative headaches.

Assuming that your component is safe for initialization and scripting, you should mark it as safe by clicking on the Safety button in the lower-right corner of the Internet Package dialog and checking the appropriate check boxes in the Safety dialog (shown on the right-hand side of Figure 13-28).

After checking for other files that your control may require, the Wizard completes its work and creates a number of files (and a folder):

- A cab file containing your control in the location you specified, Confetti.Cab
- An HTML file containing the <OBJECT> tag with CLSID reference for the confetti control, Confetti.Htm
- A *support* folder containing the input files for Confetti.Cab. The support folder contains the control, Confetti.Ocx; a setup information file, Confetti.Inf; and a project file for creating the Cab file, Confetti.Ddf.

More information on creating Cab files can be found at *http://www.micorosft.com/workshop/java/CAB-f.htm*.

Here's the partial contents of Confetti.Htm as generated by the Application Setup Wizard:

```
<HTML>
<OBJECT ID="Confetti" WIDTH=335 HEIGHT=269
    CLASSID="CLSID:42EE03EE-34EE-11D0-B8E8-0080C6026268"
    CODEBASE="confetti.CAB#version=1,0,0,0">
       <PARAM NAME="_ExtentX" VALUE="8864">
       <PARAM NAME="_ExtentY" VALUE="7117">
       <PARAM NAME="Iterations" VALUE="10000">
</OBJECT>
</HTML>
```

If you open this HTML page in Explorer, every time the Confetti ActiveX control's Paint event is fired you'll get the confetti effect with iterations set to the default, 10,000, as shown in Figure 13-29.

Each ActiveX control you create will have its own CLSID, which is theoretically unique to that control in the whole wide universe. In order to prevent multiple CLSIDs from being created for the same control, make sure to select Binary Compatibility in the VB5CCE Projects settings dialog for your project before "making" your control. (It's on the Component tab.)

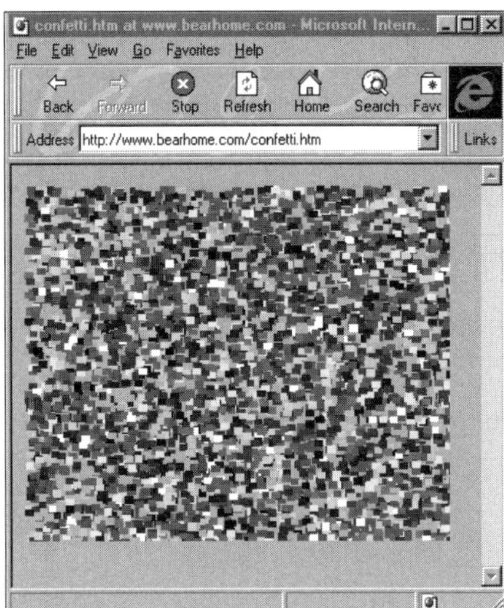

Figure 13-29: The Application Setup Wizard generates sample HTML code for you complete with an <OBJECT> tag and CLSID; if you open the HTML in a browser the control is activated.

Of course, you could modify the HTML page by using VBScript to make it interact with the Confetti ActiveX control (either by hand or using the ActiveX Control Pad):

```
<HTML>
<TITLE>
Confetti ActiveX Control
</TITLE>
<BODY>
<H4>
This ActiveX control was written in Visual Basic 5 using
VB5 Custom Controls Edition!
</H4>
<OBJECT ID="Confetti" WIDTH=335 HEIGHT=269
   CLASSID="CLSID:42EE03EE-34EE-11D0-B8E8-0080C6026268"
   CODEBASE="confetti.CAB#version=1,0,0,0">
      <PARAM NAME="_ExtentX" VALUE="8864">
      <PARAM NAME="_ExtentY" VALUE="7117">
      <PARAM NAME="Iterations" VALUE="10000">
</OBJECT>
Set Iterations (should be an integer value):
<INPUT TYPE=Text VALUE="5000" SIZE=10 NAME="txtNum">
<INPUT LANGUAGE="VBScript" TYPE=Button VALUE="Iterations"
   ONCLICK="Confetti.Iterations = txtNum.value"
   NAME="cmdIt">
</BODY>
</HTML>
```

When you open this revised page in Explorer, you'll be able to set the confetti iterations dynamically, as shown in Figure 13-30.

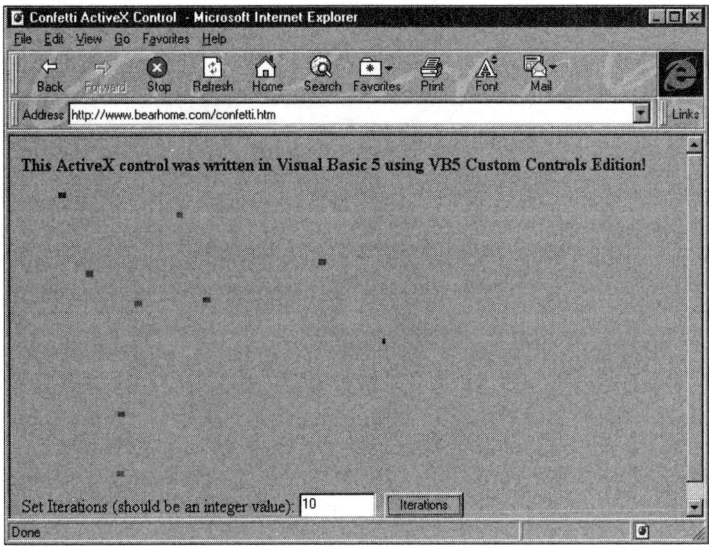

Figure 13-30: You can use script in HTML applications to interact with ActiveX controls created in VB5CCE.

Note that if you have your copy of Explorer's security level set to High, this Web page may appear to load, but the interactive content will have been broken. To load active content with the default security setting of High, you'll need to digitally sign your code.

Adding Internet Features to Controls

ActiveX controls created with VB5CCE are primed to support a variety of Internet-related features. (These features generally require that the control's container be Internet Explorer.) For example, UserControl objects can support asynchronous downloading of property values, such as Picture properties that may contain bitmaps. Through the Hyperlink property of the UserControl object, they can also request that a browser jump to a URL, or navigate through its history list.

If you design your controls normally to read and write property values using a PropertyBag object, these values will not persist between different loads of a Web page. You may want to design your control to support both normal loading of property values from a PropertyBag, which is not supported by browsers, and asynchronous downloading of property values.

One way to check that your ActiveX download setup actually works — and that you're not using a copy of the control previously registered on your machine — is to remove the control's registration entry and connect to the Web page that contains the control. It should then run correctly on your machine, which means that the Internet download is working.

To remove your Registry entry, run Regsvr32.Exe with the /u flag. For example:

```
Regsvr32 /u confetti.ocx
```

Summary

Obviously, there is a lot more to creating ActiveX controls with VB5CCE than this chapter can cover. Although VB5CCE does insulate control developers from having to understand lower-level COM and OLE concepts, creating OLE controls is still a very conceptually complex topic. But then again, it is tremendously exciting to be able to create ActiveX controls using Visual Basic. (The VB community has been waiting for this for years!) Furthermore, if it were easy everyone could do it, and where would your job security be? Besides, this chapter has given you enough details so that you should find Visual Basic ActiveX control creation a snap!

In this chapter I covered

- Starting a new control project
- ActiveX control projects, standard executable projects, and project groups
- Testing controls
- Packaging ActiveX controls
- The VB5CCE IDE
- The ActiveX Control Interface Wizard
- Creating a sample ActiveX control: myTool.Ocx
- The Property Page Wizard
- Adding an About dialog to your control
- Programming a control's members
- Objects and classes in VB5
- Controls and containers
- The Container's Extender object
- The Ambient object
- Creating a sample user-drawn control: Confetti.Ocx
- The UserControl life cycle
- UserControl events

- Developer licensing
- Preparing a control for download
- Practicing safe scripting
- Running the Application Setup Wizard
- Creating an interactive Web page that uses a sample ActiveX control created in VB5 (Confetti.Ocx)

Chapter 14

Adding Web Functionality to Visual Basic Applications

"A little pot and soon hot."

— Shakespeare, *The Rape of Lucrece*

Visual Basic is the stone soup of the Windows programming world! A pinch of this, a pinch of that, and pretty soon you have a marvelously functional application.

In this chapter I'll briefly review elements of the Visual Basic Integrated Development Environment (IDE) and VB's event framework. Next, I'll show you how to easily add Web functionality to applications written in Visual Basic 5.

Topics covered include

- Using Visual Basic
- Understanding ActiveX components and controls
- Using the Internet ActiveX Controls that ship with Visual Basic
- Controlling Internet Explorer using the WebBrowser control
- Web programming and the Office 97 suite

Using Visual Basic

Visual Basic 5 is the first entirely 32-bit version of Visual Basic and incorporates a number of features and ActiveX controls that make it particularly suitable for Web development. Before I get to them, a review of development using VB is in order.

Flavors of VB

In addition to the older versions of the Visual Basic IDE still in use, there are a number of variants of the Visual Basic language:

- VBScript, which is used for scripting ActiveX controls on the Web and other scripting activities. VBScript is covered in Chapter 10, "Doing It with VBScript," and Chapter 11, "VBScript and ActiveX."
- Visual Basic for Applications (VBA), which is the common macro language used by the Office 97 applications. (Note that the term "macro" hardly does VBA justice. Essentially, VBA is a full-fledged cross-application internal development environment. For more information, see "Web Programming with Visual Basic for Applications and Office 97" later in this chapter.)
- Visual Basic 5 Custom Control Edition (VB5CCE) is a subset of Visual Basic intended for use in creating ActiveX controls (see Chapter 13, "Creating ActiveX Controls Using Visual Basic 5").
- Visual Basic 5 (VB5), the world's most popular full-fledged development environment. VB5 comes in three flavors. The Learning Edition is a basic and inexpensive subset of Visual Basic. The Professional Edition is intended for heavy-duty development and includes the Internet ActiveX controls. Finally, the Enterprise Edition adds some collaborative tools — such as the Visual SourceSafe versioning program — to the mix.

The Visual Basic development environment is straightforward and easy to use. When you open a new project in Visual Basic, you'll see the New Project dialog shown in Figure 14-1.

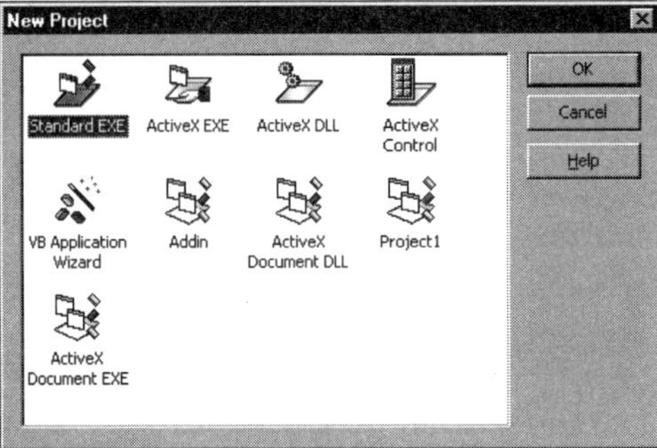

Figure 14-1: Visual Basic's New Project dialog allows you to select a project type or project template.

Projects that you add to Visual Basic's Templates\Project directory appear as template options in the New Project dialog. Templates appear in this dialog in addition to the built-in project types that are shown in Figure 14-1 and listed next.

The following generic project choices are available:

- Standard EXE is for creating a standard executable project.
- ActiveX EXE is for creating an out-of-process ActiveX component (OLE server application).

- ActiveX DLL is for creating an in-process ActiveX component (OLE server application).
- ActiveX Control is for creating an ActiveX control (see Chapter 13).
- VB Application Wizard guides you through the initial design choices regarding the interface of a standard application.
- Addin helps you to construct your own Visual Basic add-in (an ActiveX component that extends the VB environment).
- ActiveX Document DLL is for creating an in-process ActiveX document application (see Chapter 15, "ActiveX Document Applications and the Web").
- ActiveX Document EXE is for creating an out-of-process ActiveX document application (see Chapter 15).
- Any projects that you have created as templates, such as Project1 shown in Figure 14-1.

IDE Elements

Once you've opened a project in VB5, you'll see something along the lines of what is shown in Figure 14-2. (Note that you can configure the appearance of most IDE elements; your actual screen appearance will depend upon the settings you have selected and how you have arranged things.)

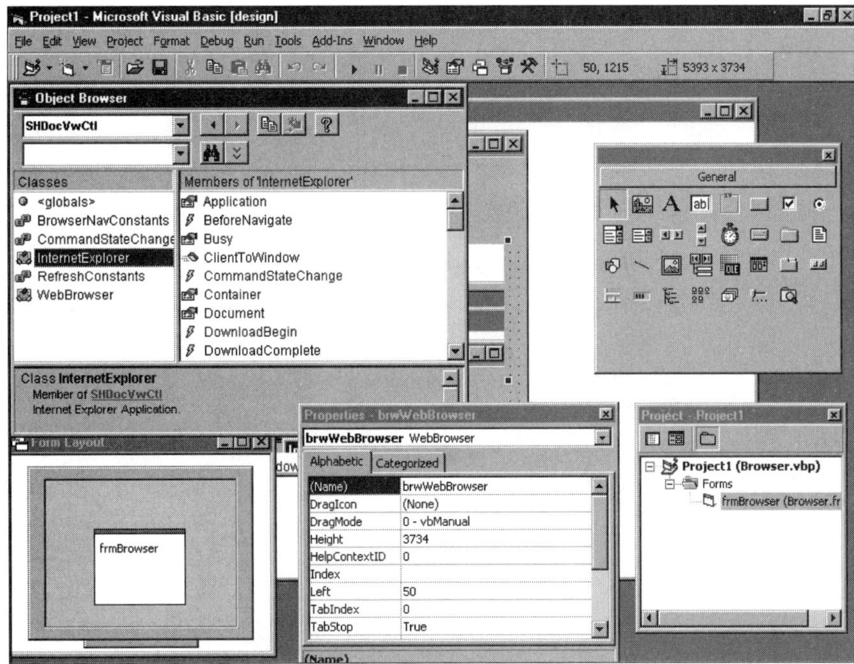

Figure 14-2: The VB5 IDE packs a lot of power, even before you start adding code.

At the top of the screen is the *title bar* (also called the *caption bar*), which displays the name of the open project and indicates whether you are working in design, run, or break mode.

Below the title bar is the *menu bar,* which gives you access to the commands for building your projects. The Visual Basic menu bar consists of the File, Edit, View, Project, Format, Debug, Run, Tools, Add-Ins, Window, and Help menus.

Below the menu bar is the *toolbar.* The toolbar contains buttons that let you quickly perform common programming tasks. These tasks include

- Adding a new project
- Adding a new module
- Opening the Menu Editor
- Opening an existing project
- Saving the current project
- Cutting, copying, pasting, finding, undoing, and redoing; starting, pausing, or stopping the execution of an application
- Showing the Project Explorer
- Showing the Properties window
- Showing the Form Layout window
- Showing the Object Browser
- Showing the Toolbox

Other IDE elements shown in Figure 14-2 include

- The Toolbox, which displays currently available ActiveX controls (and other objects that can be inserted in your VB form)
- The Immediate window, which is used in debugging to show information that results from debugging statements in your code, or that you request by typing commands interactively into the window
- The Project Explorer, which you can use to navigate between the modules in a project (and the projects in a project group)
- The Form Layout window, which you can use to position forms on the screen
- The Properties window, which you can use to set form and control properties at design time
- A Form Designer, which you can use to manipulate the appearance of a form

Event-Driven Programming

Events are procedures (subroutines) that are *fired* — meaning that if any code is in the event, the code is executed — in response to specific conditions. These conditions can be caused by the system, by another program, or by an action taken by a user.

All Windows programs are constructed around events, and Visual Basic applications are no exception. However, VB makes it very easy to program events and the response to these events.

Examples of familiar events include

- Clicking the mouse, which fires a VB Click event
- Using the keyboard to enter text, which fires KeyDown, KeyPress, and KeyUp events
- Closing a window, which fires a QueryUnload and then an UnLoad event

As these examples show, one event can — simply by firing — trigger other events. You should also know that many events are fired without user intervention. One event can fire a cascade of other events.

In traditional Windows programming, the internal scaffolding is something like a giant case statement where each option in the case selection responds to a possible Windows message. For example, selecting a menu item sends a WM_COMMAND message. Your case statement would have a branch for receipt of WM_COMMAND messages with a subbranch for the actual menu item selected.

What Visual Basic does is present template events with its forms and controls. You can create programmatic responses to events that have been fired simply by placing code within the template event handlers.

Inside Scoop

If you base a new project on the VB Application Wizard, it will build a great deal of the initial functionality of the user interface for you, based on the options you select. It will even add a Web Browser to your project!

An out-of-the-box form comes with many predefined events. Firing these events mostly doesn't *do* anything, however, unless you add code to them. If you open the code associated with one of these template events, you'll find a procedure beginning and end, and nothing in between. For example, here is the out-of-the-box template code for a Form_Click event:

```
Private Sub Form_Click()

End Sub
```

Event handlers by themselves don't do anything. In the simplest case, you could add code to an event handler to make it display a message using the MsgBox function:

```
Private Sub Form_Click()
   MsgBox "Come on and click me!"
End Sub
```

For complete information on the MsgBox function, your best bet is to look it up in VB's on-line help. You can also effectively use the Object Browser to find all possible values of an icon and return constants that you can use in the MsgBox function. Use the Object Browser to check under the VBA | Interactions library. Because these constants are predefined in VBA (Visual Basic for Applications) you can use the listed word equivalents without defining the description to be equal to the required numerical value.

To add this MsgBox statement to a form click event, open the Code window with the form active. Use the Object drop-down list in the upper-left corner of the Code window to select the form. Once you've selected the form, use the Procedure drop-down list in the upper-right side of the Code window to select the click event. When you select the click event, VB automatically creates template handler code:

```
Private Sub Form_Click()

End Sub
```

Add the MsgBox statement (or any other code you want) within the handler procedure:

```
Private Sub Form_Click()
   MsgBox "Forms love to be clicked!", vbExclamation, Me.Caption
End Sub
```

Now, when the user runs this sample program and clicks on the form, a message box will be displayed, as shown in Figure 14-3. (The Me.Caption keyword causes the caption of the current form to be displayed.)

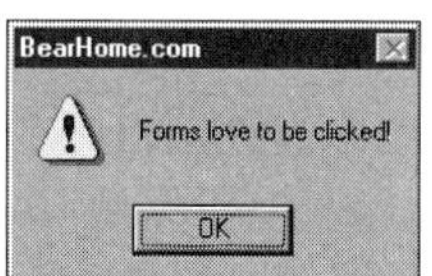

Figure 14-3: It's easy to add code to Visual Basic's predefined events.

Properties and Methods in Visual Basic

In addition to events, most Visual Basic objects — such as forms and controls — have properties and methods. Properties and methods are fundamental to the way objects work; they are the basic building blocks for working in VB.

Properties

A *property* is a setting that describes something about an object such as a form. Depending on the property, you can set it at design time using the Properties window and/or at runtime programmatically.

For example, to add a line of code to a form's double-click event at runtime, you could simply modify the event handler as follows:

```
Private Sub Form_DblClick()
   BackColor = &HFF& 'red
End Sub
```

You can set the same color change using the Properties window at design time. If you click on the BackColor property, you'll get a color palette like the one shown in Figure 14-4. (The appearance of this palette depends on your graphic device settings and the settings in your Windows Control Panel.)

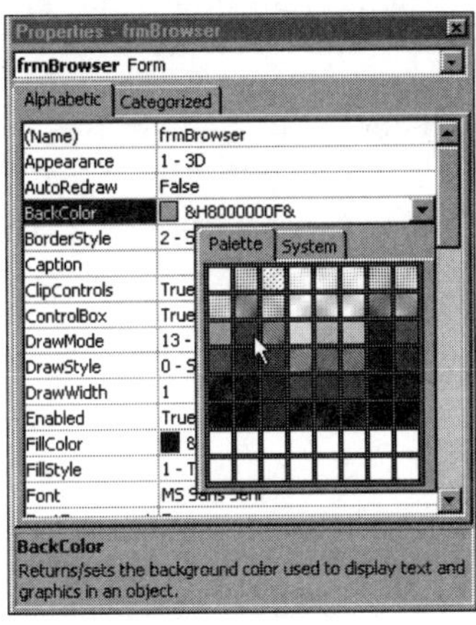

Figure 14-4: You can set a form's BackColor property using the Properties window.

Methods

Methods are procedures that act upon an object. (Internally, methods are written as functions.) They can only be executed at runtime, not at design time. Some examples of form methods are the Move method, which moves a form in two-dimensional space on the screen, and the ZOrder method, which positions the form in front of or behind other windows.

You invoke methods by naming the object whose method is being called, using the dot operator (.), and then listing the name of the method. Like routines, methods can take arguments. For example:

```
Form1.Zorder 0
```

Adding Code to Form and Control Events

Code attached to an event-handling procedure will often consist simply of procedure calls. The called procedures will in this case contain the actual executable code. One reason for designing a program in this fashion is that the same procedure can be called from many different event handlers, thus simplifying, shortening, and clarifying program architecture. A common technique is to pass a procedure called from an event handler a parameter indicating which handler has called it. Execution in the called procedure can then branch depending on which procedure called it (as determined by the parameter).

Here are the three ways to "reach" an event-handler procedure framework:

- Make sure the Project Explorer is open (if necessary, choose Project Explorer from the View menu). Select the form you wish to add event code to. (If you are adding an event to a control that has been placed on a form, select the form that is the control's "parent.") Click on the View Code button. (Alternatively, right-click on the form icon and choose View Code from the context menu that appears.)

  In the Object list box, select the form or other object (for example, a control) to which you want to add event code. Next, from the Procedure list box, select the event handler that you'll be adding code to. Note that event-handler procedures with code attached are boldfaced in the Procedure list box, whereas those with no code attached are not bold.
- Double-click on the form to which you want to add code. Make your selection from the Object list box and Procedure list box as just described.
- Right-click on the form. Choose View Code from the pop-up menu. Make your selection from the Object list box and Procedure list box as just described.

Understanding ActiveX Components and Controls

ActiveX is the technology formerly known to Visual Basic programmers as OLE. ActiveX components (created using VB ActiveX EXE and ActiveX DLL projects) used to be called OLE server applications.

ActiveX controls are ActiveX components designed with a particular interface and intended to be seated on another object such as a form or Web page (see Chapter 13 for details).

The easiest way to add Web functionality to your Visual Basic applications is to add appropriate Internet ActiveX controls to the forms in your projects. (See the section "Using the Internet Controls" later in this chapter.)

Visual Basic ActiveX Document applications represent a fascinating new way to add OLE compound storage applications to the Web. They are discussed further in Chapter 15.

The Active Group and the ActiveX Object Definition

An ActiveX object is defined as one that adheres to the Component Object Model (COM) originally defined by Microsoft. Microsoft has turned the definition of the specification over to a public industry group, the Active Group.

You can find more information about the Active Group on their Web site, at *http://www.activex.org*. The definitive resource for information on ActiveX is Microsoft's ActiveX Resource site, *http://www.microsoft.com/activex.*

A compliant ActiveX object has the following characteristics:

- The object is implemented as binary code. Therefore, it can be written in any source language.
- The object is encapsulated in an executable file or in a dynamic link library.
- The object contains data of two types: *presentation data,* which is required for screen display or printing, and *internal data*. You can think of both kinds of data as properties that are private to the object.
- The object also contains functions for manipulating its data.
- The object provides a standardized interface for other objects to communicate with it (described earlier).
- The object participates in *marshaling* — the process of passing function arguments and return values among processes and machines. Routines in the system file Compobj.Dll manage marshaling for Windows.

What an ActiveX Object Does

Mostly ActiveX objects — components and controls — sit around and wait to be used. However, ActiveX controls placed on a container are not quite so passive — they are constantly being created and destroyed along with their container, as described in Chapter 13.

In general, ActiveX objects are expected to support a number of protocols and provide a number of services:

- Objects are expected to provide an interface to their internal commands — termed automation — so that other objects can make the server object perform the specified operations on its data. Hence the phrase "OLE automation server."
- ActiveX applications are expected to support drag and drop. If the object windows, it should respond appropriately to data or objects dropped on it using the mouse.
- ActiveX objects support Uniform Data Transfer (UDT), which is a mechanism for handling the exchange of formatted data structures between applications. UDT transfers are made by conveying pointer information rather than the data itself, so that large amounts of data don't have to be read into memory.
- ActiveX objects are expected to participate in an OLE-defined architecture called structured storage, using an OLE service, *compound* files. Compound files define a way to share the contents of a file among components, using a mechanism that can be thought of as a file system

within a file system. VB implements OLE compound documents as ActiveX Document applications, which are covered in Chapter 15.

Working with ActiveX

Using Visual Basic, you can work with ActiveX objects in a number of different ways:

- You can install ActiveX controls in the VB Toolbox. You can then embed these tools into a form. You can set the control's properties in the Properties window or in code, you can invoke its methods in code, and you can place VB code in its published event handlers.
- You can work with exposed members of ActiveX servers within code after you instance the ActiveX object by using the Dim statement with the New keyword or the Set statement. Once you have instanced the object, you can invoke its properties and methods by using the object variable and the dot operator. You can use these techniques to include and manipulate, for example, Excel spreadsheets and Word documents within your VB applications.
- You can use the OLE control as a container for embedding objects on your form.
- You can use VB to create ActiveX server components. Your VB client objects can then invoke the exposed properties and methods of your servers.
- With Version 5 of Visual Basic, you can easily create ActiveX controls that can be hosted on the Web, as explained in Chapter 13.
- You can create ActiveX Document applications, which are applications that support OLE compound storage. By creating an ActiveX Document application, you can essentially turn VB forms into full-fledged Web applications. (See Chapter 15.)

Using the Internet Controls

Visual Basic 5 ships with three ActiveX controls that you can use to extend your VB applications by adding Internet-related technology. These controls are

- The WebBrowser control, which encapsulates an interface to many of the exposed objects of Microsoft Internet Explorer
- The Internet Transfer control, which encapsulates three Internet protocols
- The WinSock control, which allows the user to connect to a remote machine and exchange data

Adding Internet Features to Controls

One important way to add Internet capabilities to your VB5 applications is to write these capabilities into the controls you create. ActiveX controls created using Visual Basic 5 can support a variety of Internet-related features. (These features generally require that the control's container be Internet Explorer to work.) For example, UserControl objects can support asynchronous downloading of property values, such as Picture properties that may contain bitmaps. Through the Hyperlink property of the UserControl object, they can also request that a browser jump to a URL, or navigate through its history list.

If you normally design your controls to read and write property values using a PropertyBag object, these values will not persist between different loads of a Web page. You may want to design your control to support both normal loading of property values from a PropertyBag, which is not supported by browsers, and asynchronous downloading of property values.

The WebBrowser Control

Once you add the WebBrowser control to a form, you can quite easily add Web browsing capabilities to your applications. A sample project that contains the necessary code is saved on the companion CD-ROM as Browser.Vbp.

The first step toward adding the control and implementing Web browsing in your project is to add the control to your Toolbox using the Controls tab of the Components dialog. (Choosing Components from the VB Project menu opens this dialog.) With the Controls tab of the Component dialog open, the WebBrowser is listed as Microsoft Internet Controls, as shown in Figure 14-5.

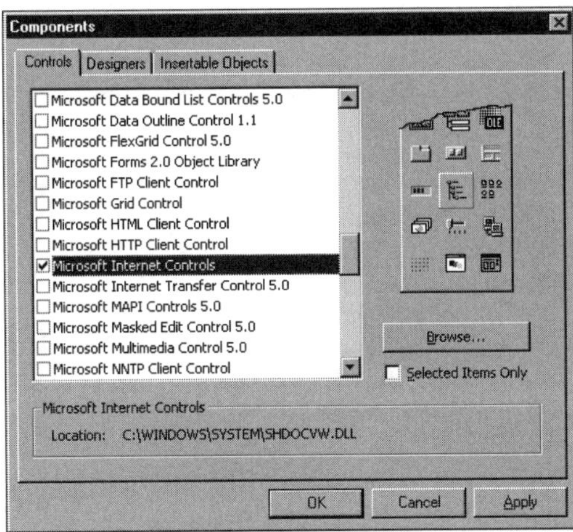

Figure 14-5: To add the WebBrowser control to your project, enable Microsoft Internet Controls on the Controls tab of the Components dialog.

To explore the members exposed by the WebBrowser control, select the SHDocVwCtl library in the Object Browser, as shown in Figure 14-6.

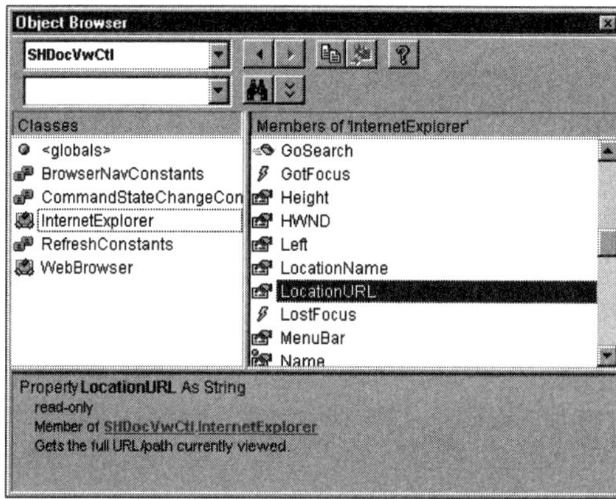

Figure 14-6: Once you've added the WebBrowser control to your project, you can view its members by selecting the SHDocVwCtl library in the Object Browser.

Browser.Frm in the sample project contains — in addition to the WebBrowser control — a Timer, a ComboBox, and a Toolbar control. When the browser form loads, the WebBrowser control needs to be sized and given a starting address:

```
Public StartingAddress As String
Private Sub Form_Load()
   On Error Resume Next
   Me.Show
   tbToolBar.Refresh
   Form_Resize
   StartingAddress = "http://www.bearhome.com"
   cboAddress.Move 50, lblAddress.Top + lblAddress.Height + 15
   If Len(StartingAddress) > 0 Then
      cboAddress.Text = StartingAddress
      cboAddress.AddItem cboAddress.Text
      'try to navigate to the starting address
      timTimer.Enabled = True
      brwWebBrowser.Navigate StartingAddress
   End If
End Sub
```

The form resize code handles sizing the WebBrowser:

```
Private Sub Form_Resize()
   cboAddress.Width = Me.ScaleWidth - 100
   brwWebBrowser.Width = Me.ScaleWidth - 100
   brwWebBrowser.Height = Me.ScaleHeight - _
      (picAddress.Top + picAddress.Height) - 100
End Sub
```

It's the job of the Timer control — once it has been enabled — to keep trying by firing its Timer event at short intervals until the WebBrowser connects to the specified address:

```
Private Sub timTimer_Timer()
   If brwWebBrowser.Busy = False Then
      timTimer.Enabled = False
      Me.Caption = brwWebBrowser.LocationName
   Else
      Me.Caption = "Working..."
   End If
End Sub
```

Assuming a working Internet connection and a valid address, this should work quite nicely. Figure 14-7 shows the WebBrowser control in the sample project with a Web page loaded.

Figure 14-7: It's easy to use the WebBrowser control to connect your projects to the Web.

Inside Scoop

The toolbar buttons, when clicked, are set to invoke methods of the WebBrowser object. For the most part, this works well. However, Home — which calls the GoHome method — and Search — which invokes the GoSearch method — are hard coded into Microsoft Internet Explorer settings. This makes more sense than it appears to at first, because the WebBrowser control is essentially an interface between your applications and the Internet Explorer object automation library. This means that if you want to control the effects of the Home or Search commands, you cannot use the built-in methods. You can substitute your own URLs using the control's Navigate method.

Here's the revised toolbar code:

```
Private Sub tbToolBar_ButtonClick(ByVal Button As Button)
   On Error Resume Next
   timTimer.Enabled = True
   Select Case Button.Key
      Case "Back"
         brwWebBrowser.GoBack
      Case "Forward"
         brwWebBrowser.GoForward
```

```
        Case "Refresh"
            brwWebBrowser.Refresh
        Case "Home"
            brwWebBrowser.Navigate StartingAddress 'GoHome
        Case "Search"
            brwWebBrowser.GoSearch
        Case "Stop"
            timTimer.Enabled = False
            brwWebBrowser.Stop
            Me.Caption = brwWebBrowser.LocationName
    End Select
End Sub
```

You can easily use the exposed methods and properties of the instance of the WebBrowser to implement a great variety of Web functionality. For example, you might want to allow users of your program to obtain stock quotes from the National Association of Security Dealers (Nasdaq) Web site. As a first step, you could add a suitable button to the application's toolbar. The Toolbar control is connected to an ImageList control: Before you can add a button to the toolbar you must add it to the ImageList using the ImageList custom Property Pages, as shown in Figure 14-8.

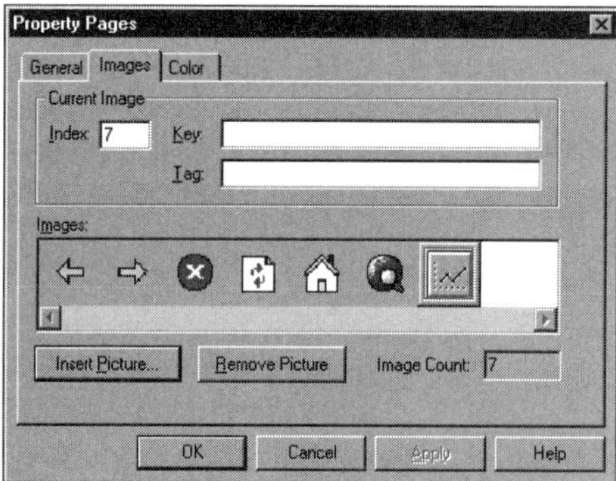

Figure 14-8: Before you can add a button to the toolbar, you must add it to the related ImageList control.

Once an appropriate button has been added to the ImageList, it can be connected to the toolbar using the Toolbar's custom Property Pages, as shown in Figure 14-9. A key is assigned that will be used to add appropriate code when the user clicks on the button.

Once you have added the button to the ImageList and Toolbar controls, you can add code to generate NASDAQ quote tables when the button is clicked (Listing 14-1):

Listing 14-1: Generating NASDAQ quotes

```
Private Sub tbToolBar_ButtonClick(ByVal Button As Button)
   On Error Resume Next
   timTimer.Enabled = True
```

```
   Select Case Button.Key
   ...
   Case "Quote"
      Dim QStr As String, NavStr As String
      QStr = InputBox("Enter ticker up to ten tickers using" & _
         "a plus sign (+) between them", "NASDAQ Quotes", _
         "ADBE+CHIR+COSFF+GANDF+INTC+KLAC+MSFT+SPAB+XOMA")
         NavStr = _
         "http://www.nasdaq.com/scripts/quote.dll?ver=3&symbol="
      NavStr = NavStr & QStr & "+&mode=Stock+Quotes"
      brwWebBrowser.Navigate NavStr
   ...
   End Select
End Sub
```

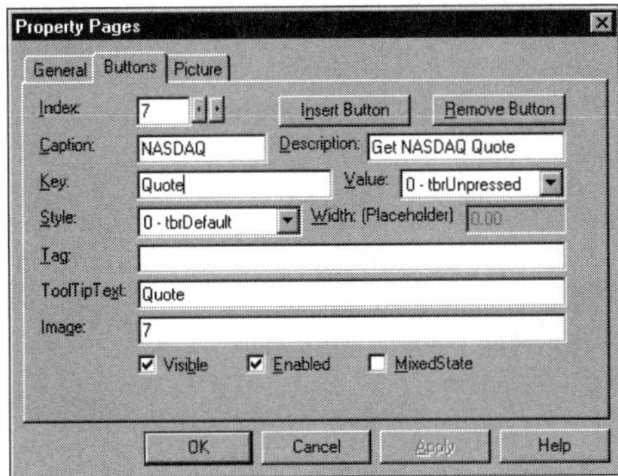

Figure 14-9: The Toolbar Property Pages are used to configure toolbar buttons.

The code within the Case "Quote" portion of the Select statement is activated when the Quote button's click event is fired. It accepts an input string of ticker symbols using the VB InputBox function shown in Figure 14-10.

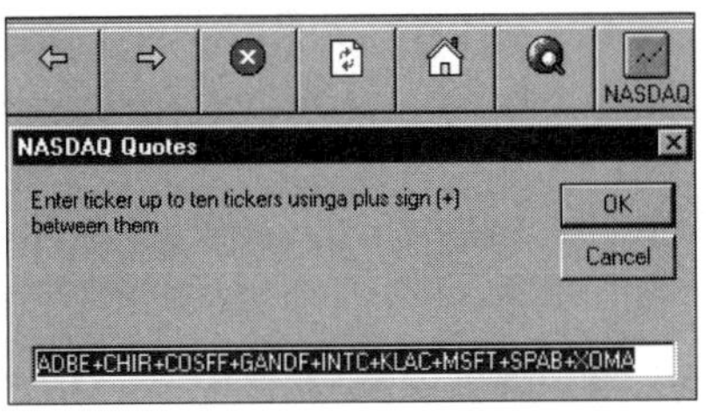

Figure 14-10: You can use the Visual Basic InputBox function to accept user input — for example, a string of stock ticker symbols.

The code then uses the variable NavStr to assemble a URL that complies with the requirements of the NASDAQ server for generating a quote table. The completed URL string is then used as an argument for the WebBrowser's Navigate method:

```
brwWebBrowser.Navigate NavStr
```

The results — a full page of expanded stock quotes — are quite attractive! I'd show them to you if I could, but copyright restrictions prevent me from reproducing the page. You'll just have to follow the example code, and see for yourself!

The Internet Transfer Control

The purpose of the Internet Transfer Control is to make it easier for your application to perform file transfers using standard Internet protocols.

To add the Internet Transfer Control to a project, select Microsoft Internet Transfer Control 5.0 in the Components dialog, as shown in Figure 14-11.

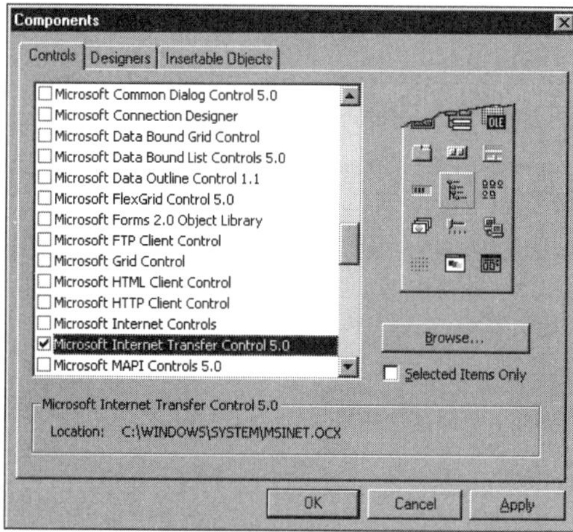

Figure 14-11: To add the Internet Transfer Control to a project, select it in the Components dialog.

The class name for this control as it appears in the Properties window is Inet. It appears in the Object Browser as InetCtlsObjects.Inet (see Figure 14-12).

Figure 14-13 shows the Custom Property Pages dialog for an instance of the Inet control. You select a protocol from the enumerated types shown in the Protocol drop-down list (FTP transfer protocol is shown selected in Figure 14-13).

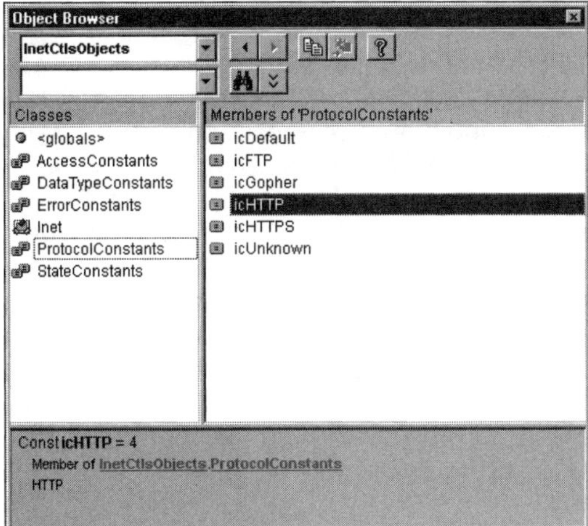

Figure 14-12: You can use the Object Browser to determine the members of InetCtlsObjects ("Inet" for short).

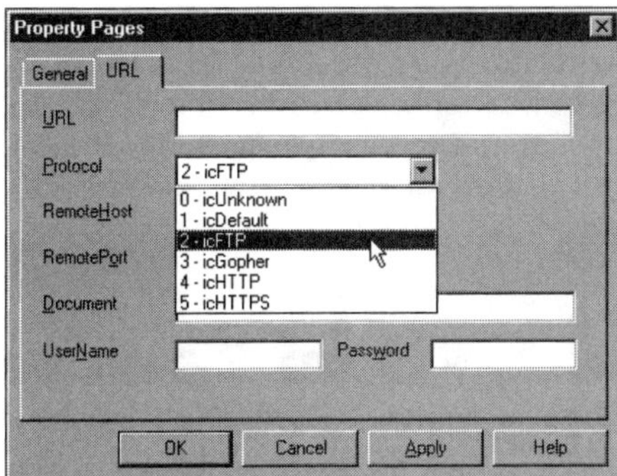

Figure 14-13: You use the Internet Transfer Control to implement file transfers using standard Internet protocols.

The WinSock Control

You add the WinSock control to your Toolbox by selecting Microsoft Winsock Control 5.0 in the Components dialog. Once you've added this control to your project, you can view its object library in the Object Browser (its name is MSWinsockLib).

The WinSock control, invisible to the user, provides an easy way to use TCP (transfer control protocol) and UDP (user datagram protocol) network services. By setting properties and invoking methods of the control, you can easily connect to a remote machine and exchange data in both directions. This is intended to help you create network client/server applications.

TCP Connections

TCP allows you to create and maintain a connection to a remote computer. Using the connection, both computers can stream data between each other. If you are creating a client application, you must know the server computer's name or IP address (RemoteHost property), as well as the port (RemotePort property) on which it will be "listening." After supplying values for these properties, you can invoke the control's Connect method. If you are creating a server application, set a port (LocalPort property) on which to listen, and invoke the Listen method. When the client computer requests a connection, the ConnectionRequest event will occur. To complete the connection, invoke the Accept method within the ConnectionRequest event. Once a connection has been made, either computer can send and receive data. To send data, invoke the SendData method. Whenever data is received, the DataArrival event occurs. Invoke the GetData method from within the DataArrival event to retrieve the data.

How UDP Works

UDP is a connectionless protocol. Unlike computers using TCP, computers using UDP do not first have to establish a connection. To transmit data, first set the client computer's LocalPort property. The server computer then only needs to set the RemoteHost to the Internet address of the client computer, set the RemotePort property to the same port as the client computer's LocalPort property, and invoke the SendData method to begin sending messages. The client computer uses the GetData method within the DataArrival event to retrieve the sent messages. UDP is faster than TCP; however, unlike TCP it does not guarantee delivery.

Web Programming with Visual Basic for Applications and Office 97

As you probably know, Office 97 applications contain numerous features that help users more easily integrate their work in a collaborative fashion over the Web. For example, Word will automatically create Internet links when you begin with a protocol such as http: — provided that the Internet and Network Paths with Hyperlinks option is selected in the AutoCorrect dialog, as shown in Figure 14-14.

Another example is that you can save any Office 97 document as a Web page simply by selecting Save as HTML from the File menu.

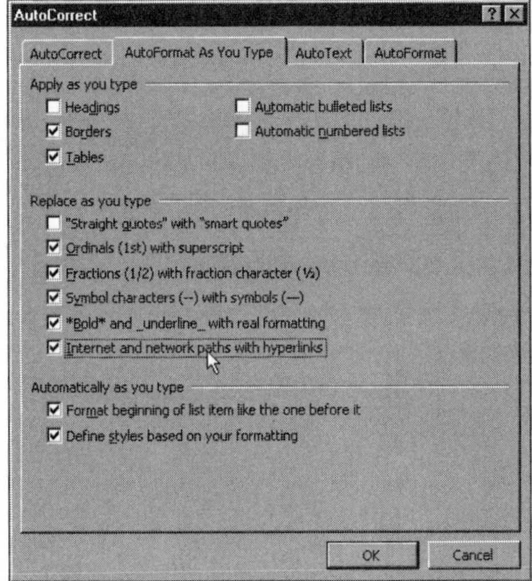

Figure 14-14: Word 97 includes many Internet features, such as the automatic hyperlink conversion option in the AutoCorrect dialog.

These two examples only touch the tip of the iceberg of Internet and Web features available to average users of Office 97. The features that will interest developers the most are

- Full-featured VBA development environment
- Ability to add and use ActiveX controls from within Office 97 applications
- Exposed nature of the members of the Office 97 object structure
- In Word and Excel, the ability to manipulate Hyperlink objects and members of the Hyperlinks collection

To start the VBA editing environment from an Office 97 application, choose Macro from the Tools menu and choose Visual Basic Editor from the submenu that appears. (The shortcut key combination that starts the VB IDE is Alt+F11.)

Figure 14-15 shows the Visual Basic for Applications Integrated Development Environment. I think you'll agree that it looks a lot like the full-fledged Visual Basic environment.

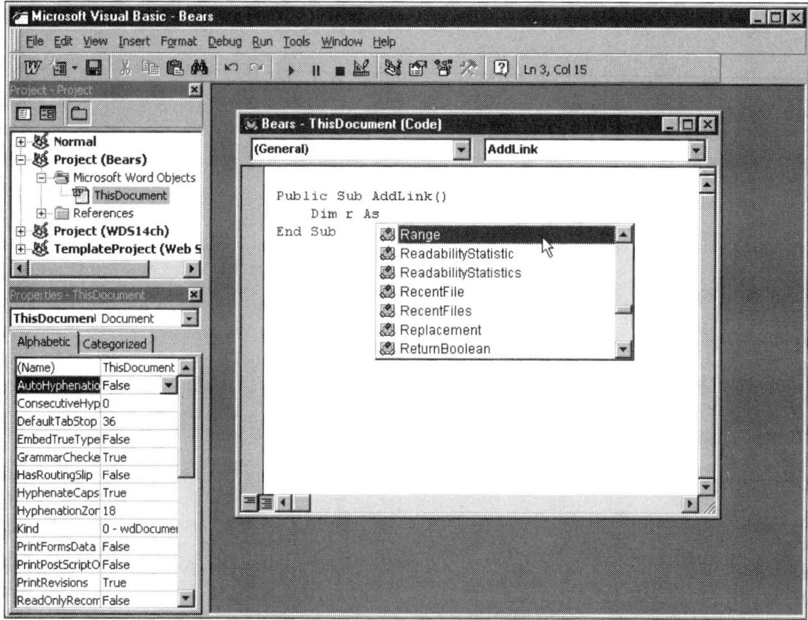

Figure 14-15: The Office 97 Visual Basic Editor looks a lot like the “big” VB environment.

You can easily create programs in the VB environment that use the objects exposed by Office 97. For example, the following procedure inserts the text “The Bear’s Web Site” at the beginning of the active document and then adds a hyperlink to the text that goes to *http://www.bearhome.com/* (see Figure 14-16):

```
Public Sub AddLink()
    Dim r As Range
    Set r = ActiveDocument.Range(Start:=0, End:=0)
    r.InsertBefore "The Bear's Web Site"
    Selection.MoveRight unit:=wdWord, Count:=4, Extend:=wdExtend
    ActiveDocument.Hyperlinks.Add Anchor:=Selection.Range, _
        Address:="http://www.bearhome.com/"
End Sub
```

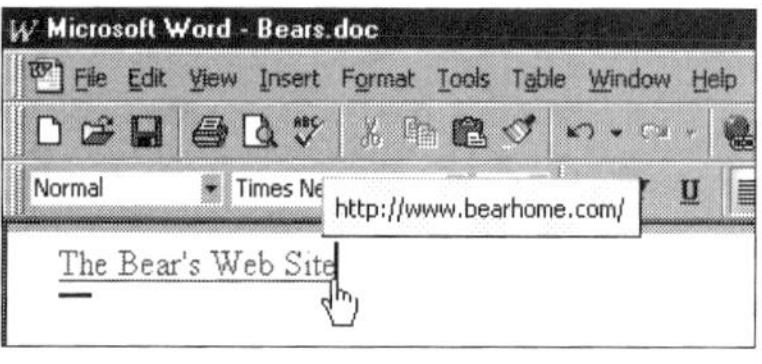

Figure 14-16: You can easily use the Visual Basic Editor to add hyperlinks to the active document.

The easiest way to learn about the Office object structure is to use the Object Browser. To start the Object Browser, choose it from the Visual Basic Editor View menu. All exposed Office 97 application members are available for inspection in the Object Browser (see Figure 14-17). With the information retrieved from the Object Browser, it isn't that difficult to manipulate the objects that are part of the Office applications.

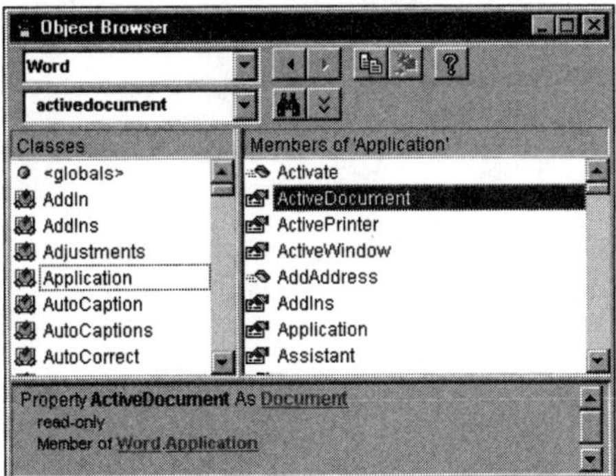

Figure 14-17: You can get information about exposed members of Office 97 applications using the Object Browser.

The following subroutine creates a beveled shape, adds the text "Setting free the bear..." to it, and then adds to the shape a hyperlink that goes to *http://www.bearhome.com/*:

```
Public Sub AddLinkShape()
   ActiveDocument.Shapes.AddShape(msoShapeBevel, _
      150, 150, 200, 100).Select
   With Selection
      .ShapeRange.TextFrame.TextRange.Select
      .Collapse
      .TypeText Text:="Setting free the bear..."
      .ShapeRange.Select
   End With
   ActiveDocument.Hyperlinks.Add Anchor:=Selection.ShapeRange, _
      Address:="http://www.bearhome.com/"
End Sub
```

Running the routine adds the shape (and link) to the active Word document, as shown in Figure 14-18.

Figure 14-18: You can use the exposed members and collections of the Office 97 applications to create fancy effects like the beveled shape containing a hyperlink shown here.

Summary

This chapter explained how to add Internet features into your applications using Microsoft's Internet controls that ship with Visual Basic 5.

Topics covered in this chapter included

- Different kinds of Visual Basic applications
- The Visual Basic IDE
- Event-driven programming
- Visual Basic properties and methods
- Understanding ActiveX components and controls
- The Active Group and the ActiveX object specification
- Working with ActiveX
- The Internet controls
- Using the WebBrowser control to add Web capabilities to your applications
- Generating a NASDAQ stock chart
- Understanding how the Internet Transfer controls and Winsock controls ork
- Office 97 and Visual Basic for Applications
- The VBA Editor
- Using VBA to create hyperlinks in an active document

Chapter 15

ActiveX Document Applications and the Web

"Your imagination is your preview of life's coming attractions."

— Albert Einstein

With Version 5 of Visual Basic, you can create a kind of application that is new to VB: an ActiveX document application. You can use ActiveX document projects to create complex applications that are hosted on the Web by Internet Explorer. It's particularly exciting that ActiveX document applications can customize data using OLE compound storage.

Understanding ActiveX Document Applications

ActiveX document applications represent a way for Visual Basic programmers to leverage their VB background and create sophisticated Internet applications.

ActiveX documents require a host application to run, much as ActiveX controls require a container. An ActiveX document application cannot exist on its own without the host, just as an ActiveX control cannot exist without a control container. The act of placing an ActiveX document in a host is referred to as *siting* the document. The properties of the document's parent only become available to it after it has been sited.

Possible ActiveX document application hosts include Microsoft Internet Explorer, Microsoft Office 97 Binder, and the Visual Basic 5 Tool Window. The chapter will concentrate on explaining how to use ActiveX document applications with Internet Explorer.

ActiveX document applications consist of ActiveX component automation servers and "documents." No, these are not really documents in the normal sense. These metaphoric "documents" call the automation server behind the

ActiveX document application in precisely the same way that Word documents call the exposed automation objects in the Word document server, Winword.Exe. How document-like they, in fact, are depends solely upon the implementations devised by the programmer who creates the ActiveX document application.

A Visual Basic document file (Vbd file) is created when you compile an ActiveX document application. The Vbd file uses OLE structured storage so that data in the document can be accessed and manipulated via standard OLE interfaces — just as Word and Excel documents do. In other words, an ActiveX document application consists of two conceptually distinct parts: ActiveX components that function as an OLE automation server and documents that are designed to interact with the server.

Compiling a Visual Basic document application creates both the document (a Vbd file) and the corresponding ActiveX server (an in-process Dll or an out-of-process Exe file). The Vbd file is to the ActiveX server as a Doc file is to Winword.Exe.

In addition to the normal considerations as to whether to make an ActiveX component server in-process or out-of-process, there is one other factor to consider with ActiveX document applications. If the ActiveX document server is out-of-process (an Exe file), then multiple clients — for example, if a suite of ActiveX documents were being used simultaneously by multiple instances of Internet Explorer — can overwrite global data.

Warning

Document applications compiled as Dlls are likely to run much faster than document applications compiled as Exes. However, when the ActiveX document host is Internet Explorer, you can't show a modeless form within an in-process server (Dll).

Creating an ActiveX Document Application

To create a new ActiveX document application, select ActiveX Document EXE or ActiveX Document DLL from the Visual Basic New Project dialog. Selecting an EXE project results in an out-of-process automation server, whereas selecting a DLL project produces an in-process server.

A default ActiveX document project contains a UserDocument object, much as a Standard EXE project is based on a form and a control project is based on a UserControl.

Controls are placed on the UserDocument, and modules and code are added to the project to achieve its desired functionality.

ActiveX document applications are compiled in Visual Basic's normal fashion. See the section "Using Visual Basic" in Chapter 14 for more information.

With the exceptions noted here, there are no general limits to the techniques you can use in creating ActiveX document applications. However, you should expect to take the time to get a feeling for how these applications work before you starting creating them.

An ActiveX document application cannot include the OLE Container control. Nor can an ActiveX document application include instances of embedded objects, such as Word or Excel documents.

ActiveX Documents and ActiveX Controls

ActiveX document applications are built around UserDocument objects in the same way that ActiveX control applications are constructed around UserControls (see Chapter 13, "Creating ActiveX Controls with Visual Basic 5," for more information on UserControls). UserDocuments are pretty similar in nature to UserControls.

In many ways, ActiveX document applications are akin to ActiveX control applications. Understanding that the two beasts are similarly structured can make learning to program ActiveX documents an easier chore. Similarities between ActiveX documents and ActiveX controls include the following

- ActiveX controls and ActiveX documents both require containers. They cannot independently execute with being sited on a container: (sometimes called a *host*).
- The creator of a control cannot know when the control is being written what development environment will host the control. (Possibilities include Visual Basic, Visual C++, FrontPage 97, the ActiveX Control Pad, and so on.) In the same way, the developer of an ActiveX document cannot know what container will be used to view the ActiveX document. As I'll show you later in this chapter, you can add code to your ActiveX documents to make sure that they can only be hosted by specific applications — such as Internet Explorer.
- Because UserDocuments are so much like UserControls, as you might expect, they share many of the same events, including Initialize, InitProperties, ReadProperties, WriteProperties, and Terminate. For more information on these events, see "A Day in the Life of a UserControl" in Chapter 13.

Vbd Files

When an ActiveX document project is compiled, in addition to the file containing the automation server, a Vbd file is created for each UserDocument in the application. Once an ActiveX Document application has been compiled, the Vbd files created by the compilation are opened by a host application, such as Internet Explorer.

Each Vbd file contains a reference to the class identifier of its automation server. It is also used by the application to store persistent data related to the document.

Inside Scoop

Once a Vbd file has been created, you don't have to keep the filename extension. You can rename the file with any extension you'd like. There's no technical reason not to change the name of MyDoc.Vbd to, say, MyDoc.Sad if that suits your mood.

Of course, in addition to being able to open ActiveX documents (Vbd files) locally, you can open ActiveX documents that have been placed on a server using Internet Explorer across the Web. For example, you could add a link to the document to an HTML list:

```
<UL>
...
<LI><A href="http://www.bearhome.com/evolu/activex/firstdoc.vbd">
   Sample ActiveX Document application!
</LI>
</UL>
```

For the ActiveX document to open properly, its related server needs to be registered with the system. Compiling an ActiveX component automatically registers it. But if you are placing ActiveX documents and servers on systems on which the server component has not been compiled you'll need to handle registering it. ActiveX component registration can be incorporated in Internet or standard installation routines. (For more information on packaging ActiveX applications for Internet installation, see "Running the Application Setup Wizard" in Chapter 13.)

You can also register an ActiveX component manually using the Regsvr32.Exe utility. This program ships with most Microsoft development tools — such as Visual Basic 5. For example:

```
regsvr32 C:\webdocs\evolu\activex\actxdoc.dll
```

Implementing ActiveX Documents

As I indicated earlier in this chapter, ActiveX document applications are created in Visual Basic 5 in pretty much the way that any application is created. An ActiveX document application contains one UserDocument for each eventual ActiveX document in the application (and a minimum of one UserDocument). In addition, you can add code, class, and form modules to the project. You can add code and ActiveX controls to the UserDocument or to forms included in the project.

Once all project elements are in place, you compile the document application normally by choosing Make from the File menu. An in-process server (Dll file) or an out-of-process server (Exe file) is created along with one ActiveX document for each UserDocument in the project.

Converting Existing Applications

Conceptually, ActiveX document applications are closer to ActiveX control applications than to normal projects. For one thing, both ActiveX documents and ActiveX controls must work with a container, or host. However, if you do want to convert an existing standard project, you may have some good candidates. The ActiveX Document Migration Wizard is a Visual Basic add-in that helps to convert standard projects into ActiveX document projects.

If you are creating an ActiveX document application for use with Internet Explorer, you can't really test it completely without running it in Explorer. Bear in mind that each time you recompile your project you should copy all Vbd files as well as the server to the location where tests will be run. The files all must go together; you cannot mix and match versions. Also, you should reregister your server each time you compile a new version.

You need to design projects with the ActiveX document conceptual framework in mind. You should approach these projects more like an ActiveX control project than a normal executable project.

Figure 15-1 shows a sample ActiveX document application open in the Visual Basic programming IDE. You can see VB's Project Explorer, a UserDocument, and the Code window.

The sample application shown in Figure 15-1 is saved on the *Web Developer's SECRETS* companion CD-ROM as ActXDoc.Vbp. The project is set to compile an in-process server, ActXDoc.Dll, and two ActiveX documents, FirstDoc.Vbd and SecndDoc.Vbd.

When FirstDoc.Vbd is loaded in Internet Explorer, the UserDocument shown in Figure 15-1 becomes the basis for the application shown in Explorer in Figure 15-2.

Using the HyperLink Object

When the user clicks on the Go Next button, Internet Explorer moves to a second ActiveX document, as shown in Figure 15-3. The second document is based on a second UserControl module included in the ActiveX document project.

If the host for the ActiveX document application is Internet Explorer, you can use the NavigateTo method of a UserDocument's HyperLink object to get from one document to another.

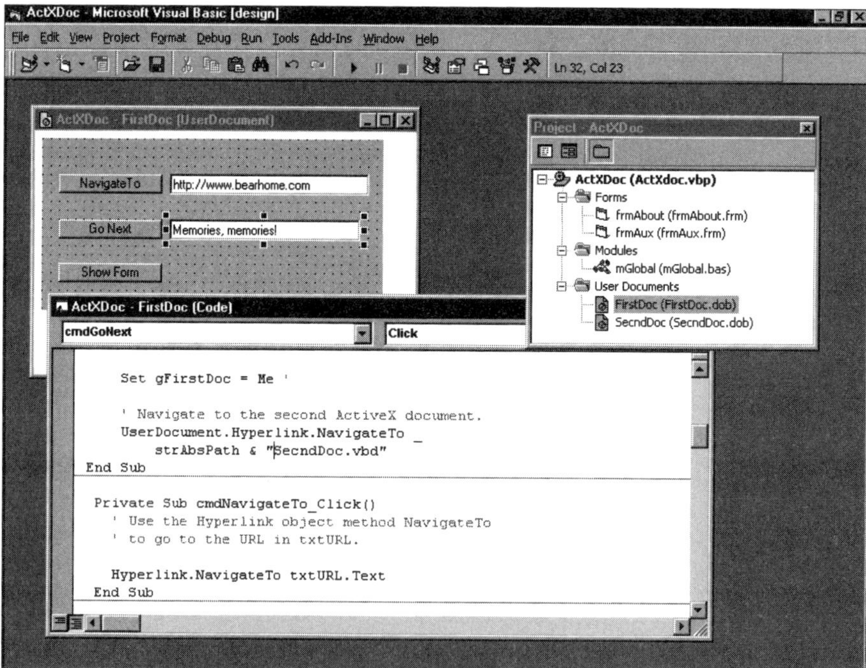

Figure 15-1: Creating ActiveX document applications in the Visual Basic IDE is pretty much like making a normal application.

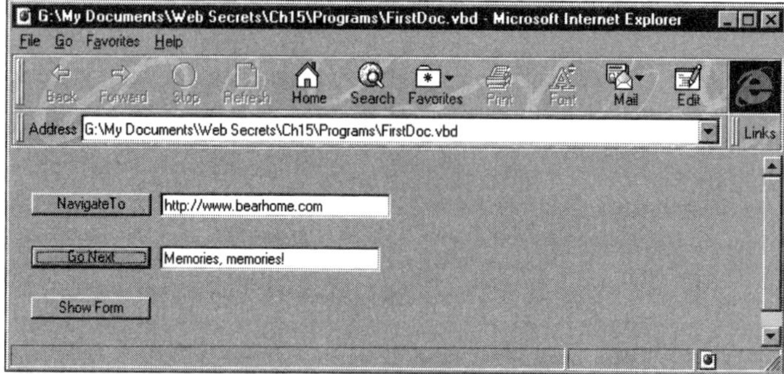

Figure 15-2: ActiveX documents form the basis for full-featured applications when they are opened in Explorer.

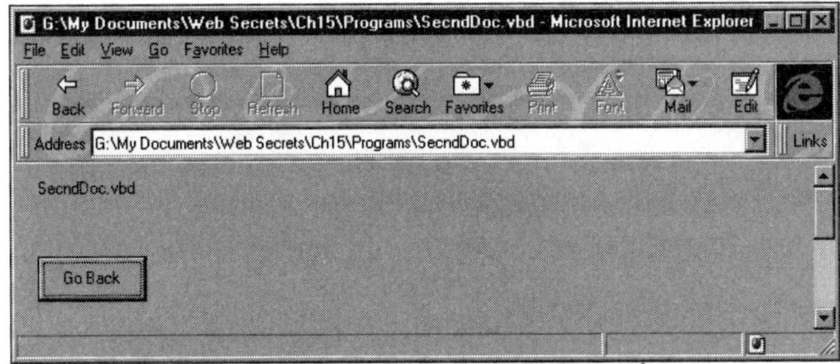

Figure 15-3: You can navigate ActiveX documents in an ActiveX document host (such as Explorer).

A UserDocument's Hyperlink object cannot be used until the UserDocument has been sited on Explorer. Hosts other than Explorer — such as the Office Binder — use different objects and methods to accomplish navigation between documents.

For example, to open a specific ActiveX document named West.Vbd in Explorer, you could use the following code:

```
UserDocument.Hyperlink.NavigateTo "file://c:\wicked\west.vbd"
```

The code that opens the second document in the sample application dynamically constructs the absolute path of the current document and then opens SecndDoc.Vbd in that location:

```
Private Sub cmdGoNext_Click()
   Dim strPath As String     ' String to be parsed
   Dim strAbsPath As String ' Result of parsing
   Dim intI As Integer       ' Character position counter

   ' Return the path of the current ActiveX document
   strPath = Trim$(UserDocument.Parent.LocationName)

   ' Find the position of the last separator character.
   For intI = Len(strPath) To 1 Step -1
      If Mid$(strPath, intI, 1) = "/" Or _
         Mid$(strPath, intI, 1) = "\" Then Exit For
   Next intI
   ' Strip the name of the current .vbd file.
   strAbsPath = Left$(strPath, intI)
   ' Set the global variable to Me, allowing
   ' the SecndDoc document to get any public
   ' properties, or call any public functions.

  Set gFirstDoc = Me 'Declared in code module

   ' Navigate to the second ActiveX document.
  UserDocument.Hyperlink.NavigateTo _
```

```
    strAbsPath & "SecndDoc.vbd"
End Sub
```

This routine assumes that the two ActiveX documents are located in the same directory.

Going back to the first document is simple:

```
Private Sub cmdGoBack_Click()
   UserDocument.Hyperlink.GoBack
End Sub
```

Determining the Container

You can programmatically determine an ActiveX document's container by using the TypeName statement with the Parent property of the UserDocument:

```
Dim strWhat As String
StrWhat = TypeName (UserDocument.Parent)
```

Table 15-1 shows three possible return strings. (Note: these *are* case sensitive!)

Table 15-1 Container Return Strings

Container	*String*
Binder	Section
Explorer	IwebBrowserApp
VB5 IDE Tool window	Window

The sample ActiveX document project determines its container in the UserDocument Show event (see Listing 15-1). If it is being opened in a host other than Explorer, it displays a warning message so the user knows that it won't function properly.

Listing 15-1: Determining an ActiveX document host programmatically

```
Private flgShow As Boolean 'Module level
...
Private Sub UserDocument_Show()
   If Not flgShow Then
      Dim strContainer As String
      strContainer = TypeName(UserDocument.Parent)
      Select Case strContainer
         Case "IWebBrowserApp"
         'Supported container, no problem
         Case Else
```

```
            MsgBox "Please use Internet Explorer!", , strContainer
        End Select
    flgShow = True
    End If
End Sub
```

This code goes in the UserDocument Show event, which occurs when the ActiveX document is sited on a container.

Because the Show event is fired again whenever the ActiveX document is shown — and to avoid erratic results — a module-level flag is added to the routine. This ensures that the container is only tested when the ActiveX document is first sited, not when it is subsequently shown.

Showing a Form

You display forms in an ActiveX document application using standard procedures. For example, you can easily show the auxiliary form in Figure 15-4 with the contents of the txtUrl Textbox from FirstDoc.Vbd:

```
Private Sub cmdShowForm_Click()
    ' Show the auxiliary form, and set the Text
    ' property of txtAux to the Text property
    ' of txtURL in the First Document.
    frmAux.txtAux.Text = txtURL.Text
    frmAux.Show vbModal
End Sub
```

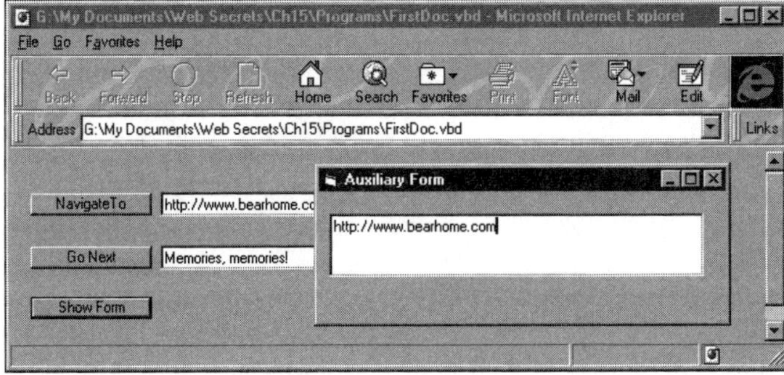

Figure 15-4: You can easily show any forms you have included in a project from an ActiveX document.

Persisting Document Information

You can manage persistent ActiveX document data in Internet Explorer using the PropertyBag object explained in detail in Chapter 13.

A text box that is part of the first ActiveX document, txtFirstDoc, illustrates data persistence in the sample application. The Text property of this control is initialized to "Memories, memories!" using the Property window.

Internally, textFirstDoc.Text is implemented using Property Get and Property Let procedures:

```
Public Property Get strDocProp() As String
   strDocProp = txtFirstDoc.Text
End Property

Public Property Let strDocProp(ByVal NewStrDocProp As String)
   txtFirstDoc.Text = NewStrDocProp
End Property
```

The ReadProperties event is used to retrieve stored values for the property from the PropertyBag object:

```
Private Sub UserDocument_ReadProperties(PropBag As PropertyBag)
   txtFirstDoc.Text = _
   PropBag.ReadProperty("StrDocProp", _
   "Memories")
End Sub
```

When the contents of txtFirstDoc change — because the user enters something new in the text box, for instance, "Roses are red, violets are blue..." — the PropertyChanged method of the UserControl is invoked:

```
Private Sub txtFirstDoc_Change()
   PropertyChanged
End Sub
```

Invoking this method notifies the container (Explorer) that a property has changed. The container is now "dirty" and this causes the WriteProperties event to be invoked before the container terminates. You can add implementation code to save changes to the PropertyBag object in the WriteProperties event:

```
Private Sub UserDocument_WriteProperties(PropBag As PropertyBag)
   PropBag.WriteProperty "StrDocProp", _
   txtFirstDoc.Text, "Memories"
End Sub
```

The txtFirstDoc field of the ActiveX document now functions as you would expect a document to behave. You can save it using the Save item on Explorer's File menu. If you attempt to close the document or exit Explorer without saving your changes, you'll get a message like the one shown in Figure 15-5.

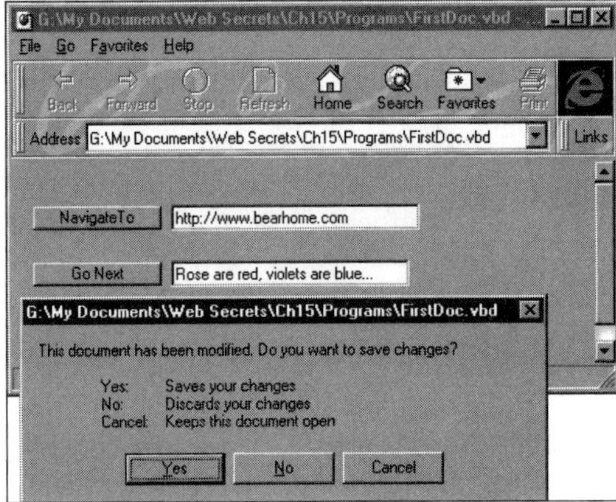

Figure 15-5: You can use the PropertyBag object to persist data when ActiveX documents are hosted by Internet Explorer.

Adding an About Box

It's easy to add an About box to an ActiveX document in the normal fashion:

```
Private Sub mnuAbout_Click()
   frmAbout.Show vbModal
End Sub
```

If the user clicks on the menu item, an About box appears, as shown in Figure 15-6.

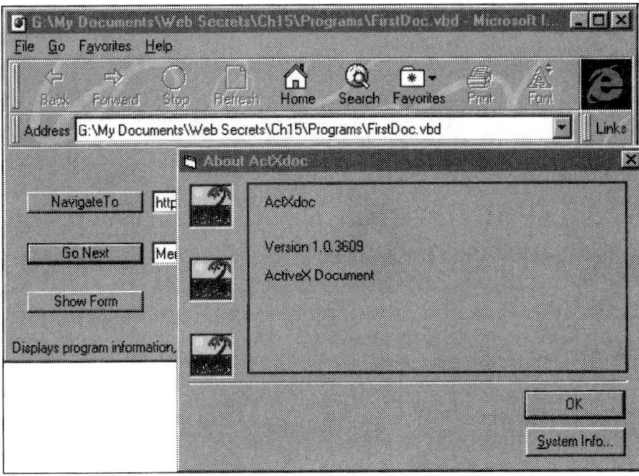

Figure 15-6: You can easily add About boxes to ActiveX documents.

Microsoft recommends adding an About box to every ActiveX document, so that users will understand what they have opened in a container such as Explorer. However, ActiveX documents engage in menu contention with their hosts. In addition, some hosts will not display document menus correctly unless the document merges a Help menu with the container's Help menu. The correct procedure, therefore, is to place the menu item that invokes the About box on a document menu captioned Help and named mnuHelp. You should handle contention by setting NegotiatePosition for mnuHelp to 3-Right.

Figure 15-7 shows the Visual Basic Menu Editor configured this way.

Figure 15-7: ActiveX documents should include an About box that users can reach through an item on the Help menu.

Summary

ActiveX document applications are an awesome way for Visual Basic programmers to leverage their knowledge and code base to produce applications that will play across the Web.

This chapter described the basics that you will need to produce an ActiveX document application that is hosted by Internet Explorer. You can successfully implement many kinds of projects as ActiveX documents — the only limit is your imagination and skill.

Topics covered in this chapter included

- Understanding ActiveX document applications
- Creating ActiveX document applications
- ActiveX controls and documents compared
- Vbd files
- Implementing ActiveX documents

- The HyperLink object
- Determining the container
- Showing a form
- About boxes and menu contention

Chapter 16

Creating ActiveX Controls in Visual C++

"One eye sees, the other feels."

— Paul Klee

The C language was developed by Dennis Ritchie at Bell Laboratories in the 1970s, originally for use with the UNIX operating system. C to a great degree combines high-level features — such as the ability to structure flow control — with low-level features — such as the ability to directly manipulate bits and registers.

C++ is an extension to the C language specified by Bjarne Stroustrop (also of Bell Labs) in the 1980s. In addition to being compatible with C, C++ includes object-oriented features such as classing. (It also provides more in the way of type checking than C.)

You should know that this chapter does not attempt to cover the basics of the C or C++ languages. Nor is the Visual C++ development environment covered — except as it relates to creating ActiveX controls.

Microsoft's Visual C++ (VC++) is the leading industrial-strength development environment for the Windows platform. True, it is not as easy to learn and cannot churn out projects as quickly as Rapid Application Development (RAD) systems such as Visual Basic or Delphi. Nor is it specifically geared for cross-platform Internet development, like Java (including Visual J++). But it's the traditional choice for robust, full-featured development of components such as ActiveX controls. Most of the ActiveX controls in use — and on the market — today have been written in Visual C++. (It's now easy to create ActiveX controls in Visual Basic. For more information, see Chapter 13, "Creating ActiveX Controls Using Visual Basic.")

If you've added ActiveX controls to an HTML page — for example, using ActiveX Control Pad (see Chapters 11 and 12) or FrontPage 97 (see Chapter 7) — it's quite likely that the controls you added were written in Visual C++.

VC++ is tightly integrated with Developer Studio, a front end that makes navigating through the complex VC++ development environment much easier.

Inside Scoop

Microsoft's Visual J++ — as well as some other Microsoft development tools, including upcoming releases of Visual Basic — are also integrated with Developer Studio. It's quite probable that most of Microsoft's development tools will eventually use Developer Studio as a front end.

With release 4.1 and 4.2 of VC++, Microsoft has included class libraries and Wizards that make it much easier to create ActiveX controls intended for use on the Internet. Although release 4.2 is more tightly integrated with tools that help you create Internet ActiveX controls, many developers have stuck with 4.1 — it will be the last release to support 16-bit development via the Win32s API as well as 32-bit development.

Inside Scoop

This chapter uses some object-oriented programming (OOP) terminology with the assumption that you understand at least the basics — for example, what properties, events, and methods are. OOP concepts and terminology are covered in more detail in Chapter 13.

The Microsoft Foundation Class (MFC) Libraries

The Microsoft Foundation Class (MFC) libraries are what's known as an *application framework* — a framework, or skeleton, that provides the basis for the structure and classes of a VC++ application and handles a great deal of tedious work for you.

Inside Scoop

MFC gives you a set of structured components that provide a ready-made basis for most Windows programs. Effectively, MFC is an abstraction over brute Windows development using C and the Windows SDK; the abstraction is intended to free you from having to handle trivial details.

MFC Notation and Terminology

MFC classes usually have names beginning with "C" — for example, CDocument and CView. The "C," of course, is short for "Class."

In C++, properties of a class are termed *data members* of the class and methods are called *function members* (or member functions). I'll be sticking to C-speak in this chapter — referring to "member functions" rather than "methods" and "data members" rather than "properties."

MFC data members are, by convention, prefixed with "m_," for example m_lpCmdLine.

It's conventional to name MFC variables, particularly those that originate in the Windows API, using the *Hungarian naming convention*.

The Hungarian naming convention was invented by Charles Simonyi. Hungarian names are made up of a base type followed by a prefix and a qualifier. Thus, m_lpCmdLine would indicate a data member of a class (because of the m_) that is of type pointer to a long.

When VC++ is started and you invoke the AppWizard to create a new application, as shown in Figure 16-1, the MFC library is automatically added to your application.

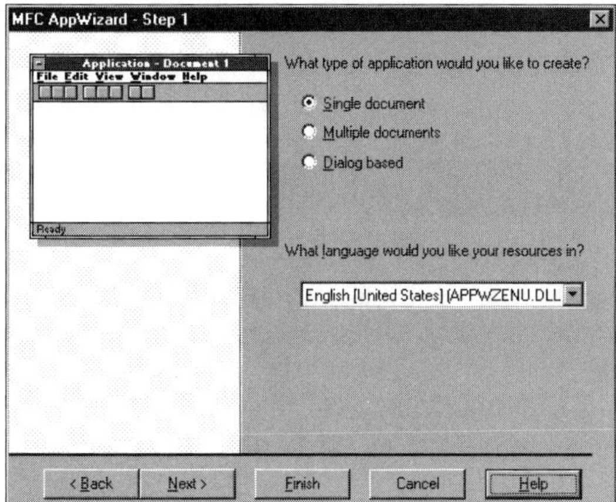

Figure 16-1: It's easy to use VC++'s AppWizard to create the framework for an MFC-based application.

The classes in the MFC make up the framework on which you build an application for Windows. This framework defines the skeleton of an application and supplies standard user interfaces that you can easily add to the skeleton.

If you're a developer working with MFC you must fill in the rest of the skeleton — things that are specific to your application. Your job in creating an application with the framework is to supply the application-specific source code and to connect the components by defining what messages and commands they respond to. You use the C++ language and standard C++ techniques to derive your own application-specific classes from those supplied by the class library and to override and augment the base class's behavior.

You can get help with these tasks by using Developer Studio's AppWizard to create the files for a starter application. You can use the VC++ resource editors to visually design user-interface elements. You use ClassWizard to connect those elements to code and the class library to implement your application-specific logic. In a similar fashion, the OLE ControlWizard ("ControlWizard") is generally used as the starting place for creating ActiveX controls. MFC is also added to a newly created project when you use the ControlWizard. Creating ActiveX controls using the ControlWizard (and MFC) is the primary focus of this chapter.

There is no doubt that MFC makes creating Windows applications — including OLE controls — much easier. The primary drawback to using it to create ActiveX controls that will be downloaded across the Internet is the size of the support files required. These files can either be compiled into your VC++ program or distributed separately. As usual, there are pluses and minuses each way. Including the Dlls in with your executable (or control) makes for programs that are much larger but will not break for lack of the proper library file. Programs that do not include the Dlls are smaller and thus more appropriate for Internet download. Several programs can share the libraries, but it's not as bulletproof an arrangement as compiling the libraries into the executable.

The required Dll files are shown in Table 16-1; they exceed one megabyte. (You might want to think of these Dll library files as similar to the run-time library needed by compiled Visual Basic 4.0 programs.)

Table 16-1 Run-Time Library Files Required by MFC Applications

File	*Description*
Ctl3d32.Dll	Support Dll for 3-D controls
Mfc*.Dll	MFC core code (Version, indicated by *, depends on version of VC++)
Msvcrt*.Dll	Shared Dll version of C-runtime (Version, indicated by *, depends on version of VC++)

In addition to creating ActiveX controls using MFC and the OLE ControlWizard, you can create them

- Using the ActiveX template library, although this requires a great deal of understanding of OLE, OLE containers, and how they communicate.
- With the ActiveX Software Development Kit (SDK) and a sample ActiveX SDK control called BaseCtl (this is also no straightforward exercise).
- Using Visual J++ (but currently limited to simple COM) objects. See Chapters 17, "Java Development and the Web," and 18, "Visual J++ Secrets" for details).

Using MFC and AppWizard

The general process for creating an application in VC++ using MFC and AppWizard involves the following steps (in addition to running AppWizard):

1. Design the application's user interface, using VC++ Resource Editors to create and refine it.
2. Create menus and define access keys.

3. Create dialogs. Test dialog boxes in the Dialog Editor.
4. Create and edit bitmaps, icons, and cursors. The default resource file created by AppWizard supplies models you can use as is — or edit — for many of the visual elements you will need.
5. Edit the toolbar supplied for you by AppWizard.
6. Map menus to handler functions. You can use ClassWizard or WizardBar to connect menus and accelerators to appropriate handler functions in your code. These tools insert message-map entries and empty function templates in the source files you specify and manage many coding tasks that you otherwise would have to do manually.
7. Write the actual handler code. You can use ClassWizard to jump directly to the empty handler function code in the source code editor.
8. Map toolbar buttons to commands by assigning the button an appropriate command ID.
9. Rebuild the program and use the built-in debugging tools to test that your handlers work correctly. You can step or trace through the code to see how your handlers are called. If you've filled out the handler code, the handlers carry out commands. The framework will automatically disable menu items and toolbar buttons that are not handled.
10. Add dialogs by using ClassWizard to create a dialog class and the code that handles the dialog for dialogs you've created in the Dialog Editor.
11. Test your dialogs and define how the dialog box's controls are to be initialized and validated. Use ClassWizard to add member variables to the dialog class and map them to dialog controls. Specify validation rules to be applied to each control as the user enters data.
12. Create additional classes. Use ClassWizard to create additional document, view, and frame-window classes beyond those created automatically by AppWizard. You can also create additional database recordset classes, dialog classes, and so on. ClassWizard adds these classes to your source files and helps you define their connections to any commands they handle.
13. Add ActiveX components to your application. You can use the Component Gallery to add a variety of controls to your application.
14. Implement application-specific classes, as required. Add member variables to hold data structures. Add member functions to provide an interface with the data. For example, if you want a form-based data-access application, derive a view class from CRecordView (for ODBC programming). The view works like a form view, but its controls are connected to the fields of a CRecordset object representing a database table. MFC moves data between the controls and the recordset for you.
15. Build, test, and debug your application.

The *application class* encapsulates an application's initialization, running, and termination under Windows. An application built using the MFC framework must have one — and only one — object of a class derived from the main window class, CWinApp.

Your application class constitutes your application's primary execution thread. Using Win32 API functions, you can also create secondary threads, which can also use MFC.

MFC supplies a WinMain function that is called when an application starts. WinMain performs standard services such as registering window classes. Then it calls member functions of the application object to initialize and run the application.

Here's how this sequence goes: To initialize the application, WinMain calls your application object's InitApplication and InitInstance member functions. To run the application's message loop — which determines response to user and other events — WinMain calls the Run member function. On termination, WinMain calls the application object's ExitInstance member function to clean up after the application.

CWinApp and AppWizard

When you use AppWizard to create a MFC skeleton application, AppWizard generates a file that contains the following:

- A message map for the application class
- An empty class constructor
- A variable that declares the one and only object of the class derived from CWinApp
- A standard implementation for your InitInstance member function

The application class is placed in the project header and main source files. The names of the class and files created are based on the project name you supply in AppWizard.

The easiest way to view the code for these classes is through the Class View in the Project Workspace window, as shown in Figure 16-2.

Control Registration

In the case of an ActiveX control, the InitInstance procedure contains the functions — DllRegisterServer and DllUnregisterServer — that are used to register the control (see Listing 16-1). The OLE ControlWizard will automatically add these functions; with them in place control registration can be handled with the standard Regsvr32.Exe utility.

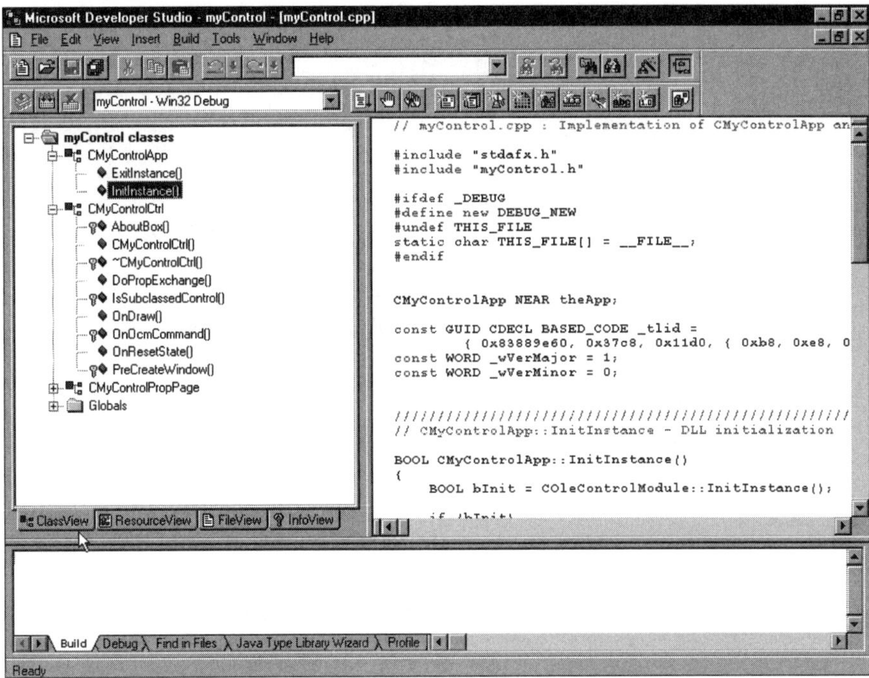

Figure 16-2: You can view code for classes created using MFC and AppWizard using Class View in Developer Studio.

Listing 16-1: Adding Server Registration code

```
////////////////////////////////////////////////////////////////////
///////
// DllRegisterServer - Adds entries to the system registry

STDAPI DllRegisterServer(void)
{
    AFX_MANAGE_STATE(_afxModuleAddrThis);

    if (!AfxOleRegisterTypeLib(AfxGetInstanceHandle(), _tlid))
          return ResultFromScode(SELFREG_E_TYPELIB);

    if (!COleObjectFactoryEx::UpdateRegistryAll(TRUE))
          return ResultFromScode(SELFREG_E_CLASS);

    return NOERROR;
}


////////////////////////////////////////////////////////////////////
///////
// DllUnregisterServer - Removes entries from the system registry

STDAPI DllUnregisterServer(void)
{
```

```
    AFX_MANAGE_STATE(_afxModuleAddrThis);

    if (!AfxOleUnregisterTypeLib(_tlid, _wVerMajor, _wVerMinor))
        return ResultFromScode(SELFREG_E_TYPELIB);

    if (!COleObjectFactoryEx::UpdateRegistryAll(FALSE))
        return ResultFromScode(SELFREG_E_CLASS);

    return NOERROR;
}
```

Regsvr32.Exe is a simple application that calls the DllRegisterServer entry point when you run it with an OLE server — such as an ActiveX control — as an argument:

```
regsvr32 mycontrol.ocx
```

Provided DllRegisterServer returns the success flag, you'll see the familiar dialog box shown in Figure 16-3. (RegOcx32 will also register ActiveX controls, but without returning a message upon success; it is primarily intended for use in installation routines.)

Figure 16-3: Regsvr32.Exe invokes a control's DLLRegisterServer function to register the control.

Overridable CWinApp Member Functions

To *override* a member function means to add your own implementation code to the member. CWinApp provides several important overridable member functions:

- InitInstance
- Run
- ExitInstance
- OnIdle

The standard InitInstance implementation created by AppWizard assumes a docu-centric application and performs the following tasks (which you can modify, or add to):

- As its central action, creates document templates that, in turn, create documents, views, and frame windows that are used to handle program information
- Loads standard file options from an Ini file or the Windows Registry, including the names of the most recently used files.

- Registers one or more document templates.
- For an MDI application, creates a main frame window.
- Processes the command line to open a document specified on the command line or to open a new, empty document.

The Run Member Function

Windows applications can be thought of as primarily constructed to respond to a huge number of potential messages. The Run member function of the CWinApp class is used to process this message loop; an MFC application spends the bulk of its time following initialization processing events in the Run member code.

The Run function cycles through a message loop, checking the message queue for incoming messages. If there is a message, the Run function sends it off — *dispatches* it — for action. If no messages need processing, the Run function calls OnIdle — a member function whose job is to sit on a porch sipping mint juleps with one hand and handling background chores until another message comes along.

The ExitInstance Member Function

The ExitInstance member function of the CWinApp class is called each time a copy of your application terminates, generally when a user quits the application.

Using ClassWizard

ClassWizard is designed to make it easier for you to accomplish certain routine tasks such as creating new classes; defining message handlers; and gathering user inputs from controls in a dialog box, form view, or record view.

ClassWizard lets you create classes derived from the MFC classes shown in Table 16-2.

Table 16-2 Types of MFC Classes Available Using ClassWizard

Class	*Description*
CAnimateCtrl	Windows common animation control.
CButton	Button control.
CCmdTarget	Base class for objects that can receive and respond to messages.
CColorDialog	Color-selection dialog.

(continued)

Table 16-2 *(Continued)*

Class	***Description***
CComboBox	Combo Box control.
CDaoRecordSet	A set of records selected from a data source. CDaoRecordSet objects are available in three forms: table-type recordsets, dynaset-type recordsets, and snapshot-type recordsets.
CDaoRecordView	Displays database records in controls. This form view is directly connected to a CDaoRecordset object.
CDialog	Dialog box.
CDocument	Class for managing program data.
CDragListBox	Windows list box that allows the user to move list box items within the list box.
CEdit	Rectangular child window used for text entry.
CEditView	Provides the functionality of a Windows edit control and can be used to implement simple text-editor features.
CFileDialog	Windows common file dialog control.
CFontDialog	Font-selection dialog box that displays a list of fonts that are currently installed in the system.
CFormView	Window that can contain dialog boxes.
CFrameWnd	Single document interface (SDI) frame window.
CHeaderCtrl	Provides the functionality of the Windows common header control.
CHotKeyCtrl	Provides the functionality of the Windows common hot key control.
CListBox	List box.
CListCtrl	Windows common list view control.
CListView	List control that simplifies use of CListCtrl.
CMDIChildWnd	Multiple document interface (MDI) child frame window.
COleDocument	Treats a document as a collection of CDocItem objects to handle OLE items. Both container and server applications require this architecture because their documents must be able to contain OLE items.
COleLinkingDoc	Base class for OLE container documents that support linking to the embedded items they contain.
COleServerDoc	Base class for OLE server documents.
CPrintDialog	Windows common print dialog.
CProgressCtrl	Windows common progress bar control.
CPropertyPage	An individual page of a property sheet.

Class	***Description***
CPropertySheet	Represents tabbed property sheets. A property sheet consists of a CPropertySheet object and one or more CpropertyPage objects.
CRecordset	Class for accessing a database table or query.
CRecordView	Window containing dialog box controls mapped to recordset fields.
CRichEditCtrl	Rich text edit control.
CRichEditDoc	Maintains the list of OLE client items that are in the CRichEditView class.
CRichEditView	Maintains the text and formatting characteristics of text.
CScrollBar	Scroll bar.
CScrollView	Scrolling window, derived from CView.
CSliderCtrl	Provides a window containing a slider and optional tick marks.
CSpinButtonCtrl	Provides a pair of arrow buttons that the user can click on to increment or decrement a value.
CStatic	A simple text field, box, or rectangle used to label, box, or separate other controls.
CStatusBarCtrl	Status bar.
CTabCtrl	Allows an application to display multiple pages in the same area of a window or dialog box.
CToolBarCtrl	Windows toolbar common control.
CToolTipCtrl	A "ToolTip" control, a small pop-up window that displays a single line of text describing the purpose of a control in an application.
CTreeCtrl	Displays a hierarchical list of items.
CTreeView	Tree control that simplifies the use of CTreeCtrl, the class that encapsulates tree-control functionality.
CView	Class for displaying program data.
CWinThread	Represents a thread of execution within an application.
CWnd	Custom window.

ClassWizard enables you to easily connect user-interface classes that are derived from the MFC library to the messages generated by the resources of your application. It uses *MFC message maps* to create this binding.

You can use ClassWizard in three ways to add MFC classes to a project:

- Click ClassWizard's Add Class menu button and choose the New command to create an entirely new class and add it to the ClassWizard database.
- Click ClassWizard's Add Class menu button and choose the From A File command to import an existing class from another project into the ClassWizard database.

- Click ClassWizard's Add Class menu button and choose the From An OLE TypeLib command to select elements from an OLE Type library, wrap them in an MFC C++ class, import the resulting class into a project, and add the class to the ClassWizard database.

In addition, you can use ClassWizard to establish an OLE control's interface. Figure 16-4 shows the MFC ClassWizard with an open OLE control project. You use the OLE Automation tab to add properties and methods to the control and the OLE Events tab to add events.

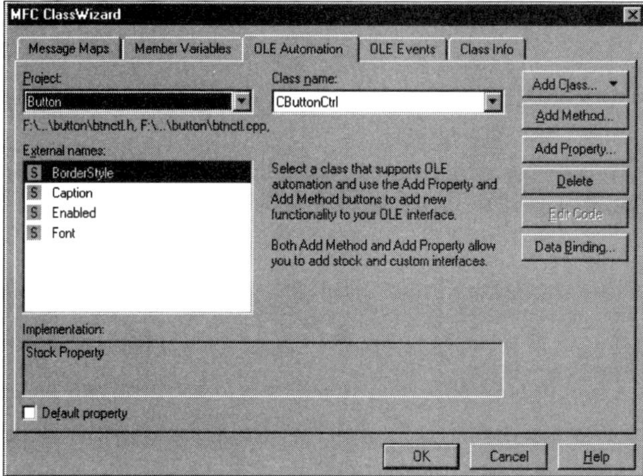

Figure 16-4: You can use the MFC ClassWizard to add classes to MFC projects — and to add properties, methods, and events to OLE controls.

Understanding OLE

OLE — short for "object linking and embedding" — has been defined by Microsoft OLE expert Kraig Brockschmidt:

> ***OLE is a unified environment of object-based services with the capability of both customizing those services and arbitrarily extending the architecture through custom services, with the overall purpose of enabling rich integration between components.***

In fact, the meaning of OLE has changed over time — and is still in transition. Early versions of OLE were primarily intended to facilitate embedding (or linking) objects and documents. (Remember DDE? Well, today's ActiveX is the great-grandchild of DDE and the child of OLE.)

As the technology has matured, it has been repositioned to enable and facilitate component interactions. In its Internet incarnation, OLE has become ActiveX — a way of delivering executable content across the Web.

From the viewpoint of the ActiveX developer, OLE provides a way to define an object with an interface whose members can be accessed in a standard fashion.

In other words, OLE provides a consistent standard that enables objects to *communicate* with one another for the purpose of using each other's code. The objects do not need to know in advance what object they will be communicating with, nor does their code need to be written in the same language.

OLE objects are conceptually divided into *servers* — objects that make their methods and properties available to others — and *clients* — applications that use exposed server objects, methods, and properties. (Clients are also called *containers*.) ActiveX controls are OLE servers of a special sort. Containers that communicate with ActiveX controls — either locally or across the Web — are OLE clients.

The Component Object Model (COM)

The *component object model* (COM) is a set of standard functions used for OLE communications, packaged in specific interfaces. You'll be pleased to know that when you create an ActiveX control using MFC and ControlWizard, you are effectively insulated from having to deal with the details of COM interfaces. Nevertheless, it's important to have a feeling for what is going on under the hood.

For each OLE server, at least one interface called IUnknown is always implemented. IUnknown contains three standard functions:

- *QueryInterface*, which tests whether a particular interface is supported by an object and returns a pointer to the interface if it is supported
- *AddRef*, which adds one to the count of clients using a server
- *Release*, which decrements the count of clients using a server; when the count is zero, the object can remove itself from memory

Using these three functions, you can access any interface that an object supports — provided you know about it.

OLE defines a set of standard interfaces, each identified an *Interface ID*, which can be accessed through a call to QueryInterface. In addition, objects can define custom interfaces — which are assigned unique Interface IDs.

COM involves several other interfaces besides IUnknown that handle chores such as data transfers and managing memory.

ActiveX Controls

An ActiveX — formerly known as Ocx, or OLE — control is a reusable software component that supports a wide variety of OLE functionality and can be customized to fit the needs of many different development projects.

These controls have been developed for many uses, including Internet interconnectivity, database access, data monitoring, graphing, and creating visual special effects.

By definition, an OLE control fully supports OLE Automation, which allows the control to expose persistent properties that can be set by the control user and a set of methods that can be called by the control user.

The OLE control classes in MFC are a set of C++ classes that can be used, in combination with some specialized tools, to develop ActiveX (OLE) controls.

The OLE control classes create a framework that supports OLE functionality — including in-place activation, OLE automation, and drag and drop — to create small, powerful custom controls that are also very portable. OLE controls are used in OLE control containers in current versions of Visual C++, Visual Basic, Delphi, and other products. You can use them in HTML Web pages by referencing their CLSID in <OBJECT> </OBJECT> tags.

Important features of OLE controls include

- The ability to fire events. Control events notify the control container that something important — such as a user mouse click — has happened. OLE controls can implement standard events, such as Click, or custom events unique to a control created (and raised) by the developer.
- Support for OLE automation through methods and properties that are accessible to any OLE control container. An OLE control should, in general, work properly in any OLE container in which it is placed.
- The ability to save the values of properties and methods between instances of the control.

Beginning with MFC 4.2, it is possible to create windowless OLE controls and controls that only create a window when they become active. Windowless controls speed up the display of your application and make it possible to have transparent and nonrectangular controls. With MFC versions 4.2 and later, you can also load OLE control properties asynchronously.

An OLE control is implemented as an in-process server — that is, in the same process space, or thread, as the application that uses the instance of the control. Although, in theory, OLE controls can be used in any OLE container, the full functionality of an OLE control is available only when used within an OLE container designed to be aware of OLE controls. A *control container* can operate an OLE control by using the control's properties and methods and receives notifications from the OLE control when events have been fired. In other words, there is a two-way communication going on between the control and its container. The container must initiate control methods calls, and the reading or writing of control properties. For its part, the control fires events, which the container can respond to.

What Goes into an ActiveX Control?

An ActiveX (OLE) control uses three programmatic elements to interact with a control container and with the developer using the finished control. These mechanisms are

- A feature set derived from the class COleControl
- Event-firing functions
- A dispatch map

The features derived from the MFC base class COleControl include OLE document object functionality, in-place activation, and OLE Automation logic. COleControl can provide the control object with the same functionality as an MFC window object, plus the ability to fire events. Alternatively, if you like, you can also use COleControl to create windowless controls, which rely on their container for help with some of the functionality a window provides (mouse capture, keyboard focus, scrolling, and so forth), but offer much faster display.

Because an MFC control class you create is based on COleControl, it inherits the capability to send messages, also known as "events," to the control container under certain conditions. These events notify the container when something important happens in the control. You can send additional information about an event to the control container by attaching parameters to the event — for example, the screen coordinates of the mouse when a click event is fired.

The third mechanism that makes up an OLE control is a *dispatch map*. A dispatch map is used to expose the control's interface to the control's user (usually a developer). The interface consists of methods — which, internally to the control, are functions — and attributes (called properties). (Internally to the control, properties are variables.) Properties allow the control container or the control user to manipulate the control in various ways. The user can change the appearance of the control, change certain values of the control, or make requests of the control, such as accessing a specific piece of data that the control maintains. The interface is created by the control developer and is most easily defined using ClassWizard.

Communication between Control and Container

A control and its container use two mechanisms to communicate:

- The control exposes properties and methods that the container can use.
- The control fires events that the container can respond to.

Both mechanisms for communication between the control and its container are buffered through the COleControl class contained within your specific control. To handle some of the container's requests, COleControl will call member functions (methods) that are implemented in the control class. All methods and some properties are handled in this way.

On the other side of the equation, events are fired when the control's class calls member functions of COleContainer.

States of an ActiveX Control

A control has two basic states: active and inactive. Traditionally, these states were distinguished by whether or not the control had a window. An active control had a window; an inactive control did not. With the introduction of windowless activation, this distinction is no longer universal but still applies to many controls.

When a windowless control becomes active, it invokes mouse capture, keyboard focus, scrolling, and other window services from its container. You can also provide mouse interaction to inactive controls, as well as create controls that wait until activated to create a window.

When a control with a window becomes active, it can interact fully with the control's container, the user, and the Windows operating system.

Persistence

Controls are said to have the ability to *serialize data*, which means that the control can write the value of its properties to persistent storage. Controls can then be re-created by reading the object's state from the storage.

A control is not responsible for handling this data storage. Instead, the control's container provides the control with a storage medium, which it can use at the appropriate times — when it is created and destroyed.

Using ControlWizard

The OLE ControlWizard can be used to create a framework — meaning a set of starter files — for an OLE control project. This set — which constitutes the files needed to build your control — includes source and header files, resource files, a module-definition file, a project file, and an object description language file. ControlWizard creates a core set of files for every control. Additional files may be created depending on the options you select when running ControlWizard.

Once you've generated your control's starter files using ControlWizard, you can switch over to ClassWizard to define your control's events, properties, and methods.

The OLE control framework created by ControlWizard includes a significant amount of functionality. The starter files include code to draw the control; serialize data; and define dispatch, event, and message maps that you can expand later in the development cycle.

To start the ControlWizard, open a New Project Workspace and select OLE ControlWizard, as shown in Figure 16-5.

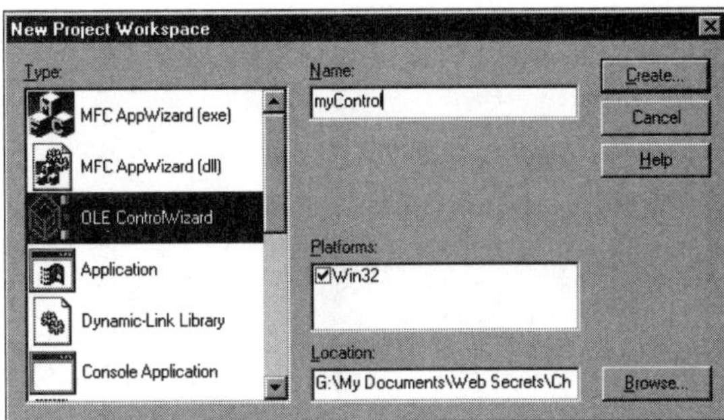

Figure 16-5: You create the framework for a new ActiveX control by running ControlWizard.

The first panel of the ControlWizard (Figure 16-6) lets you determine various development choices. As they say, it's more fun when you're having more than one. There's no limit to the number of ActiveX controls you can place in a single ControlWizard project.

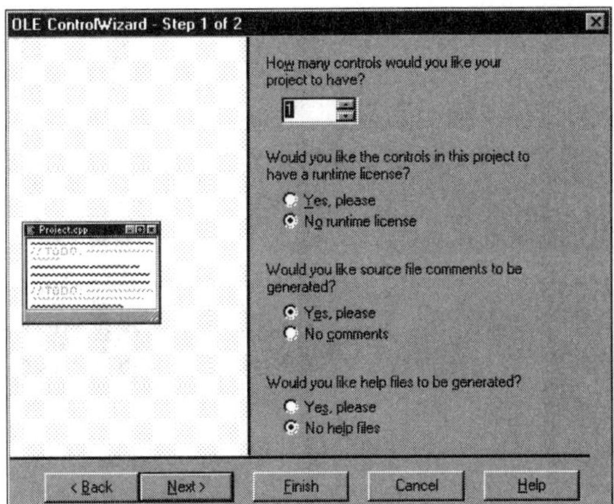

Figure 16-6: You use the first panel of the OLE ControlWizard to make choices about what the Wizard should do.

In addition to specifying the number of controls to be included in the project, this panel is where you decide whether the ControlWizard should

- Include a license file. If a license file is included, typically it must be present in the same directory as the control for an instance of the control to be created at design time — but it is not required by, or distributed to, an end user running the control.

- Include comments in the source code indicating things still to be done.
- Generate skeleton help files.

You use the second panel of the ControlWizard to select class and file names for the control, features included in the control project, and window control subclassing, as shown in Figure 16-7.

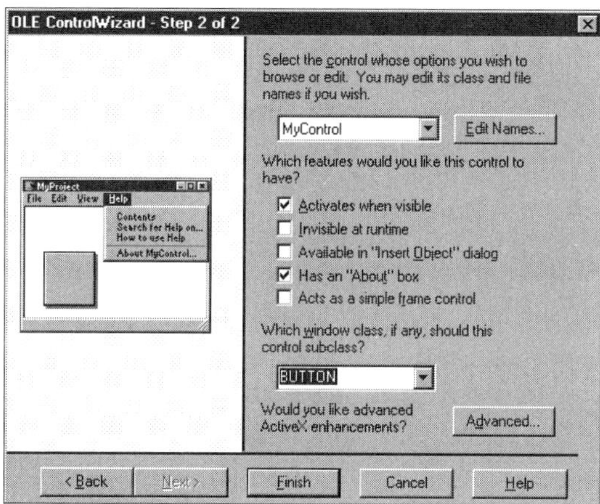

Figure 16-7: You use the second panel of the OLE ControlWizard to set the features included in your control.

To change default class and files names for your control, click on the Edit Names button shown in the upper-right corner of Figure 16-7. You can change any of the names used by the Wizard, as shown in Figure 16-8.

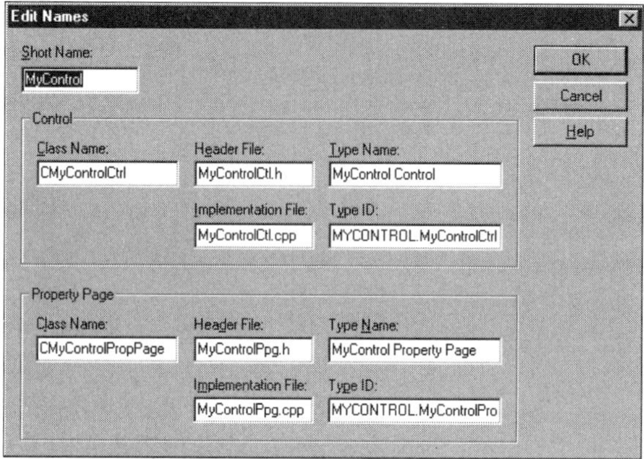

Figure 16-8: You can use the Edit Names dialog to change class and file names provided by ControlWizard.

Advanced ActiveX Features

The optional advanced ActiveX features offered by the ControlWizard are intended to accelerate the display and operation of controls you create.

Windowless Activation makes your control use the window services of its container. If a control does not need a window of its own, this speeds control creation and reduces code size. Windowless activation must be used for transparent or nonrectangular controls.

Unclipped Device Context disables tests for clipping, resulting in a small but detectable speed gain. You should only select this option if you are certain that your control doesn't paint outside its client rectangle. Note that a windowless control cannot also have its unclipped device context disabled.

Flicker-free Activation eliminates drawing operations and the accompanying visual flicker in transition between inactive and active states. Only select this option if the control draws itself identically in its inactive and active states. It is not available for windowless controls.

Mouse Pointer Notifications When Inactive allows your control to process WM_SETCURSOR and WM_MOUSEMOVE messages when the control is not active. The container delegates messages to IPointerInactive, which dispatches the messages through your control's message map. You process the messages like ordinary window messages, by adding the corresponding entries to the message map.

Optimized Drawing Code indicates that the control should perform optimized drawing if the container supports it.

Loads Properties Asynchronously specifies that your control can have properties that point to data that is loaded in the background — for example, across the Internet.

To include advanced ActiveX enhancements, click on the Advanced button shown in the lower-right corner of Figure 16-7. You can elect to include a feature on the Advanced ActiveX Feature list, as shown in Figure 16-9.

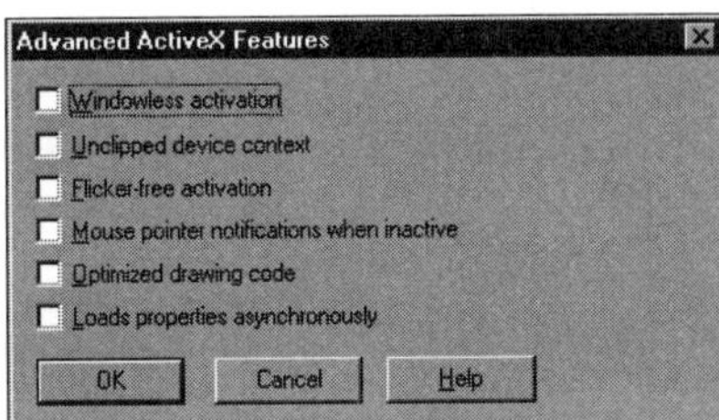

Figure 16-9: You can use the Advanced ActiveX Features dialog to select ActiveX enhancements that you'd like to include in your project.

After the ControlWizard has gathered the required information from you, it displays a project summary, as shown in Figure 16-10.

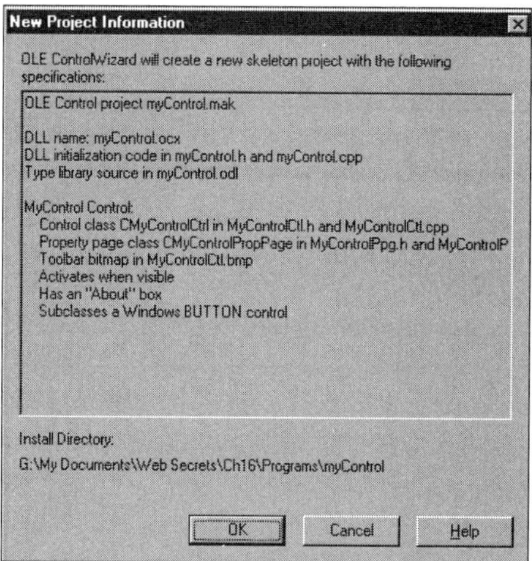

Figure 16-10: After gathering information from you, but before creating a project, ControlWizard displays a summary of what it is about to do.

Once ControlWizard has created your project, you can view the classes it has created by using the ClassView pane of the project workspace, as shown in Figure 16-11.

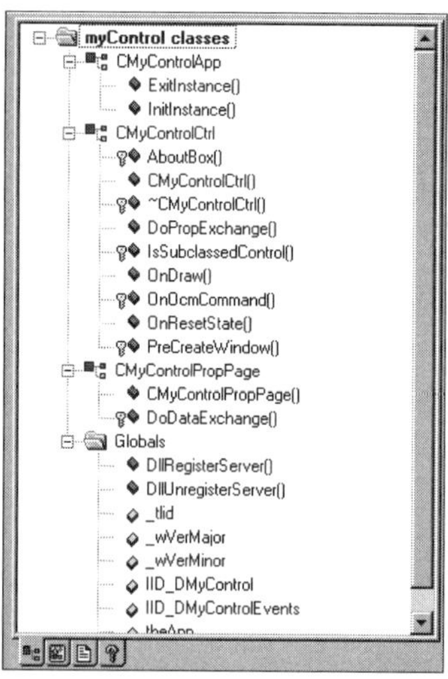

Figure 16-11: You can view the classes ControlWizard created for your control in the ClassView pane of your project's workspace.

The ControlWizard creates quite a few different files, both at the project and at the control level. Table 16-3 shows the standard project files ControlWizard creates for the myControl project.

Table 16-3 Standard Files ControlWizard Creates for the myControl project

File Name	*Purpose*
Readme.Txt	Lists all files created by ControlWizard.
myControl.mak	Visual C++ project makefile for building your OLE Control.
myControl.h	The main include file for your OLE Control Dll.
myControl.cpp	The main source file that contains code for Dll initialization, termination, and other internal housekeeping.
myControl.rc	A listing of the Microsoft Windows resources that the project uses. You can edit this file directly with the Visual C++ resource editor.
myControl.def	The module-definition file for the project. It provides the name and description of the control, as well as the size of the run-time heap.
myControl.clw	Contains information used by ClassWizard to edit existing classes or add new classes. ClassWizard also uses this file to store information needed to generate and edit message maps and dialog datamaps and to generate prototype member functions.
myControl.odl	Contains the Object Description Language (ODL) source code for the type library of your control. Visual C++ uses this file to generate a type library. The generated library exposes the control's interface to other OLE Automation clients.

Table 16-4 shows the control source code files created by the ControlWizard.

Table 16-4 Standard Files Created by ControlWizard for the myControl Project

File Name	*Purpose*
MyControlCtl.h	Contains the declaration of the CMyControlCtrl C++ class.
MyControlCtl.cpp	Contains the implementation of the CMyControlCtrl C++ class.
MyControlPpg.h	The declaration for the control's property page (CMyControlPropPage) C++ class.
MyControlPpg.cpp	Implementation of the CMyControlPropPage C++ class.
MyControlCtl.bmp	Bitmap used by the CMyControlCtrl control's container to represent the control in a Toolbox (or tool palette). This bitmap is included by the main resource file myControl.rc. The default bitmap supplied by ControlWizard shows the word "OCX."

In addition to files specific to a given control project, the ControlWizard adds standard VC++ files to the control project, as shown in Table 16-5.

Table 16-5 Standard Files VC++ Files Included in Projects by ControlWizard

File Name	Purpose
stdafx.h, stdafx.cpp	Files used to build a precompiled header (PCH) file named stdafx.pch and a precompiled types (PCT) file named stdafx.obj.
resource.h	The standard header file, which is used to define new resource IDs. The Visual C++ resource editor reads and makes changes to this file.

If you selected either the run-time license or help file generation options (see Figure 16-6) some other files will be created, as shown in Table 16-6.

Table 16-6 Files Added If License or Help Files Option Selected

File Name	Purpose
myControl.lic	If the run-time license option was selected, this user license file is created. This file must be present in the same directory as the control Dll to allow an instance of the control to be created in a design-time environment. Typically, you will distribute this file with your control to developers, but developers will not distribute it to end users.
makehelp.bat	Batch file used to create compiled Help file for myControl.
myControl.hpj	Help project file.
mycontrol.rtf	Help source file.
bullet.bmp	Bullet used for bulleted lists in the compiled help file.

Events

OLE controls use events to notify their containers that something has happened. From the viewpoint of the developer using the control, events may represent an opportunity to add code that responds to the "something."

Using MFC, there are two kinds of events: *stock* and *custom*. Stock events are those events that the class COleControl fires automatically whereas custom events are created by a control's developer and are specific to a particular control.

Table 16-7 shows the nine stock control events.

Table 16-7 Stock Control Events Included in COleClass

Event	*Firing Function*	*Comments*
Click	void FireClick( )	Fired when a mouse button is released over the control. The stock MouseDown and MouseUp events occur before this event. Event map entry: EVENT_STOCK_CLICK( )
DblClick	void FireDblClick( )	Similar to Click but fired when a BUTTONDBLCLK message is received. Event map entry: EVENT_STOCK_DBLCLICK( )
Error	void FireError(SCODE scode, LPCSTR lpszDescription, UINT nHelpID = 0)	Fired when an error occurs within your OLE control outside of the scope of a method call or property access. Event map entry: EVENT_STOCK_ERROR( )
KeyDown	void FireKeyDown(short nChar, short nShiftState)	Fired when a WM_SYSKEYDOWN or WM_KEYDOWN message is received. Event map entry: EVENT_STOCK_KEYDOWN( )
KeyPress	void FireKeyPress(short* pnChar)	Fired when a WM_CHAR message is received. Event map entry: EVENT_STOCK_KEYPRESS( )
KeyUp	void FireKeyUp(short nChar, short nShiftState)	Fired when a WM_SYSKEYUP or WM_KEYUP message is received. Event map entry: EVENT_STOCK_KEYUP( )
MouseDown	void FireMouseDown(short nButton, short nShiftState, float x, float y)	Fired if a BUTTONDOWN message (left, middle, or right) is received. Event map entry: EVENT_STOCK_MOUSEDOWN( )
MouseMove	void FireMouseMove(short nButton, short nShiftState, float x, float y)	Fired when a WM_MOUSEMOVE message is received. Event map entry: EVENT_STOCK_MOUSEMOVE( )
MouseUp	void FireMouseUp(short nButton, short nShiftState, float x, float y)	Fired if a BUTTONUP (left, middle, or right) message is received. Event map entry: EVENT_STOCK_MOUSEUP( )

For your control to properly fire events, your control class must map each event of the control to a member function that should be called when the related event occurs. This mapping mechanism (called an "event map") centralizes information about the event and allows ClassWizard to easily access and manipulate the control's events. This event map is declared by the following macro, located in the header (.h) file of the control class declaration:

```
DECLARE_EVENT_MAP()
```

Once the event map has been declared, it must be defined in your control's implementation (.Cpp) file. The following lines of code define the event map, allowing your control to fire specific events:

```
 BEGIN_EVENT_MAP(CSampleCtrl, COleControl)
//{{AFX_EVENT_MAP(CSampleCtrl)
   ...
//}}AFX_EVENT_MAP
END_EVENT_MAP()
```

If you use ControlWizard to create the project, it automatically adds these lines and you don't have to worry about them. If you do not use ControlWizard, you must add these lines manually.

Adding stock events involves less work than adding custom events because COleControl automatically handles the firing of the event for stock events. You yourself have to figure out when to fire it for custom events.

For controls created using ControlWizard, you can use ClassWizard — started from the Microsoft Developer Studio View menu — to add both stock and custom events.

The OLE Events tab — shown in Figure 16-12 — lists events and whether their implementation is stock or custom.

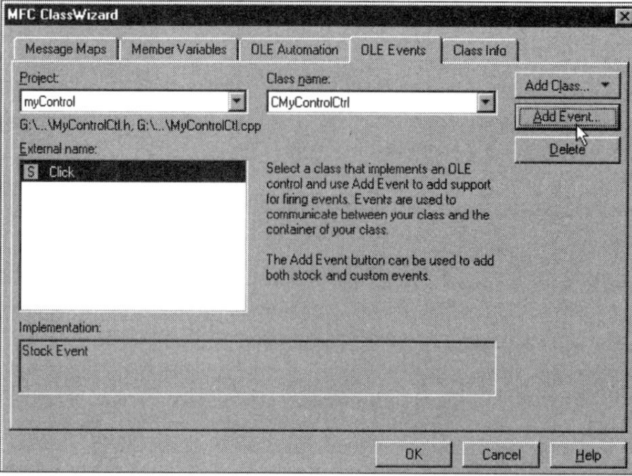

Figure 16-12: You use the OLE Events tab to list events and access the Add Event dialog.

If you click the Add Event button in the upper-right corner of the OLE Events tab (see Figure 16-12), the Add Event dialog (Figure 16-13) will open. You use this dialog to add stock or custom events to a control.

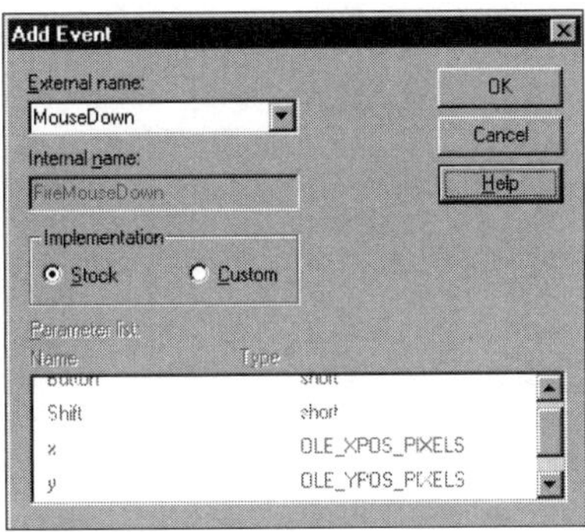

Figure 16-13: You use the Add Event dialog to add stock and custom events to a control (here a stock MouseDown event is being added).

Stock events are selected from the External Name drop-down list shown in Figure 16-13.

To add a custom event, enter a name for the event in the External Name drop-down list, as shown in Figure 16-14.

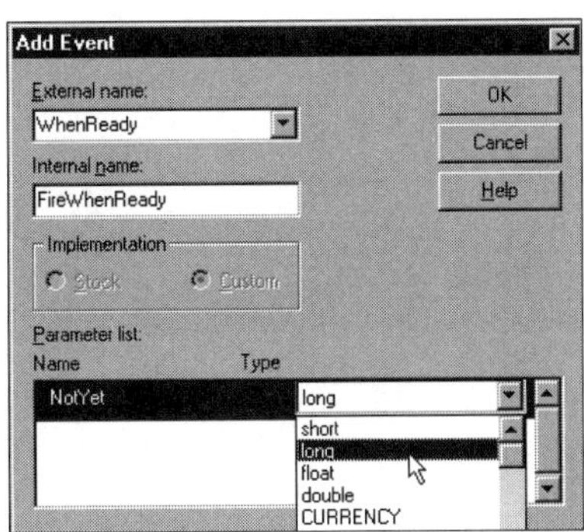

Figure 16-14: You can add custom events by entering a name for the event in the External name combo box.

By convention, the internal name for an event is the external name prefixed with "Fire." Thus, the event with the external name WhenReady is given the internal name FireWhenReady.

You can add parameters to your custom event using the Parameter list box shown at the bottom of Figure 16-14.

Custom events differ from stock events in that they are not automatically fired by COleControl. A custom event recognizes a certain action, determined by the control developer, as an event. The event map entries for custom events are represented by the EVENT_CUSTOM macro.

When you add a custom event, ClassWizard makes changes to the control class .h, .cpp, and .odl files.

For the WhenReady event, the following lines were added to the header (.h) file of the control class:

```
//{{AFX_EVENT(CMyControlCtrl)
   void FireWhenReady(BOOL NotYet)
      {FireEvent(eventidWhenReady,EVENT_PARAM(VTS_BOOL), NotYet);}
//}}AFX_EVENT
```

This code declares an in-line function called FireWhenReady that calls the COleControl function FireEvent with the WhenReady event — and any of its parameters, such as the Boolean NotYet, defined using ClassWizard — as parameters.

Next, the following line is added to the event map for the control, located in the implementation (.cpp) file of your control class:

```
EVENT_CUSTOM("WhenReady", FireWhenReady, VTS_BOOL)
```

This code maps the event WhenReady to the in-line function FireWhenReady, passing the parameters you defined using ClassWizard.

Finally, the following line is added to the control's Odl file:

```
[id(1)] void WhenReady(boolean NotYet);
```

This assigns the WhenReady event a specific ID number, taken from the event's position in the ClassWizard event list. The entry in the event list allows a container to anticipate the event. For example, it might provide handler code to be executed when the event is fired.

Calling a Custom Event

Now that the WhenReady custom event has been added, you must decide when this event is to be fired and actually fire it. You fire the event by calling FireWhenReady when the appropriate action occurs.

You use the Message Maps tab of the ClassWizard to create handlers for the messages associated with controls. You can add a message to a control, and then use the Message Maps tab of the ClassWizard to customize the message to add the call to FireWhenReady, as shown in Figure 16-15.

In the Messages box, select the message you want to handle — for example, OnClick. Choose the Add Function button — or double-click in the Messages list — to add the handler function to your application. Next, select the Edit Code button. The ClassWizard will bring up the appropriate message implementation. For example:

```
void CMyControlCtrl::OnClick(USHORT iButton)
{
   FireWhenReady (TRUE);
   COleControl::OnClick(iButton);
}
```

This should serve to fire the WhenReady event when the control's stock click event is fired.

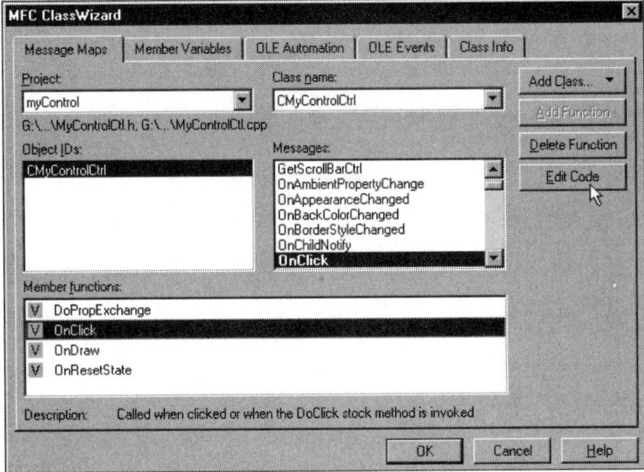

Figure 16-15: You can use the Message Maps tab of the ClassWizard to add handling code to control messages.

If you now compile the control, you can test that the custom event works by adding the control to a development environment capable of hosting ActiveX controls. In VB5, use the Components dialog and select MyControl. Once MyControl has been added to the project, you can use the Object Browser to find the custom event, as shown in Figure 16-16.

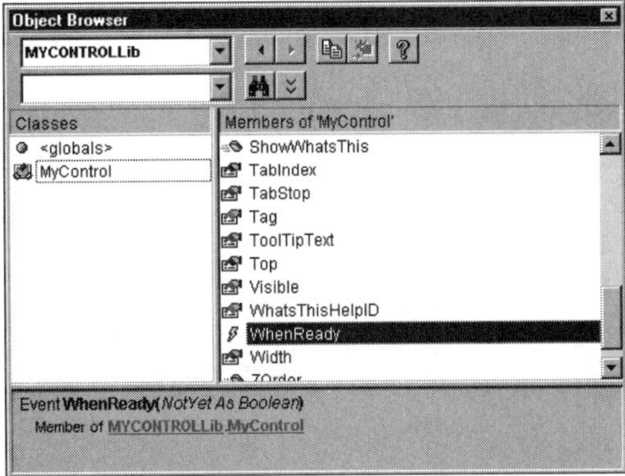

Figure 16-16: You can use the Visual Basic Object Browser to inspect custom control members.

You can also add the control to a form. With MyControl placed on a form, open the Code window. Scroll until you find MyControl's WhenReady event, and add code along these lines:

```
Private Sub MyControl1_WhenReady(ByVal NotYet As Boolean)
   MsgBox "I'm not ready to be fired!", vbExclamation, _
      "I'm all keyed up..."
End Sub
```

If you run the project and click on the instance of MyControl, you'll see a message like the one shown in Figure 16-17.

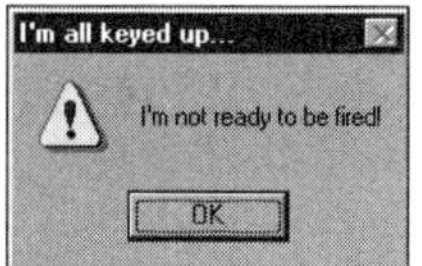

Figure 16-17: You can add code to control custom events to make sure they fire as intended.

Adding Properties

An ActiveX control fires events to communicate with its container. The container, in return, uses methods and properties to communicate with the control.

Methods and properties are similar in use and purpose to member functions and member variables of a C++ class. Properties are data members of the control, which are exposed to any container. In other words, properties provide an interface for applications that contain OLE controls.

Using ClassWizard, properties are added with Add Property dialog, which you open from the OLE Automation tab of ClassWizard.

Stock Properties

To add a stock property, simply select the property from the External Name drop-down list. Figure 16-18 shows the process of adding the stock Caption property to MyControl.

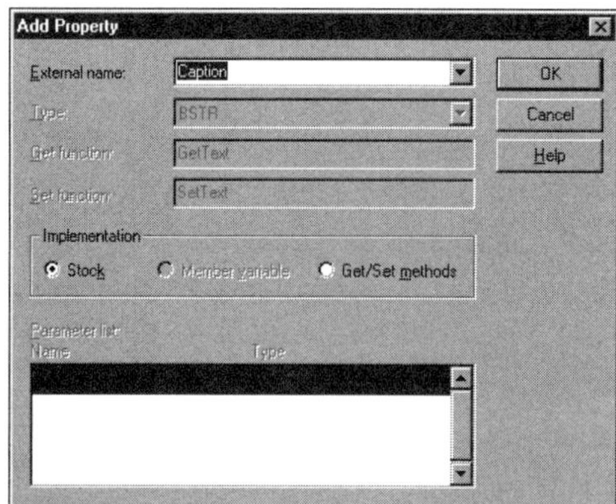

Figure 16-18: You can use ClassWizard's Add Property dialog to add stock properties — such as the Caption property shown here — to a control.

Once you click on OK to exit the Add Property dialog, and click on OK to exit ClassWizard, the stock property will be implemented.

Custom Properties

Custom properties are user-defined properties to which you give a name and a data type. You are responsible for adding code implementation for a custom property.

There are two kinds of custom property implementations:

- Member variable, which is implemented with direct access to a control variable.
- Get/set methods, which is used when you need to control access to the underlying property variable. Get/set methods are often used when user input needs to be validated before it is written to an internal property variable, or when a property value change has an impact on the user interface.

You create custom properties by entering the new custom property name in the External Name field of the Add Property dialog. Figure 16-19 shows adding a custom property named "frodo" that will be implemented as a Member variable.

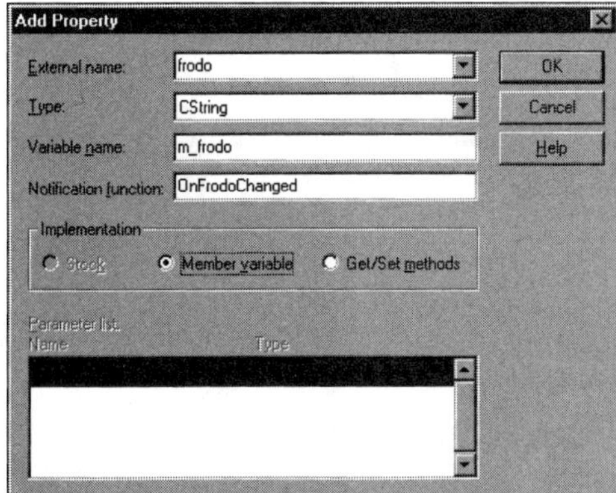

Figure 16-19: To create a new custom property, enter its name in the External Name field.

When the new property is created by ClassWizard, the following code is added to the control's Dispatch Maps:

```
// Dispatch maps
//{{AFX_DISPATCH(CMyControlCtrl)
   CString m_frodo;
   afx_msg void OnFrodoChanged();
   ...
```

Template code for the OnFrodoChanged function is also added:

```
void CMyControlCtrl::OnFrodoChanged()
{
   // TODO: Add notification handler code
```

```
   SetModifiedFlag();
}
```

This calls the SetModifiedFlag function when the value of m_Frodo is changed; it's up to you to add any other code required.

Inside Scoop

Calling SetModifiedFlag marks the control as modified. If a control has been modified, its new state will be saved when the container is saved. This function should be called whenever a property, saved as part of the control's persistent state, changes value.

If you added a custom property named "bilbo" and selected Get/Set methods implementation, you'd find additions to the Dispatch Maps:

```
afx_msg BSTR GetBilbo();
afx_msg void SetBilbo(LPCTSTR lpszNewValue);
```

ClassWizard would also add Get and Set property procedures for you:

```
BSTR CMyControlCtrl::GetBilbo()
{
   CString strResult;
   // TODO: Add your property handler here

   return strResult.AllocSysString();
}

void CMyControlCtrl::SetBilbo(LPCTSTR lpszNewValue)
{
   // TODO: Add your property handler here
   SetModifiedFlag();
}
```

It's up to you, of course, to add property implementations such as validation checking and assignment to an internal control variable.

For both properties, a Dispatch ID is added

```
// Dispatch and event IDs
public:
   enum {
   //{{AFX_DISP_ID(CMyControlCtrl)
   dispidFrodo = 1L,
   dispidBilbo = 2L,
   eventidWhenReady = 1L,
   //}}AFX_DISP_ID
   };
};
```

Methods

You can add template code for methods, which are member functions, using the Add Method dialog (see Figure 16-20), which you accessed via the ClassWizard OLE Automation tab.

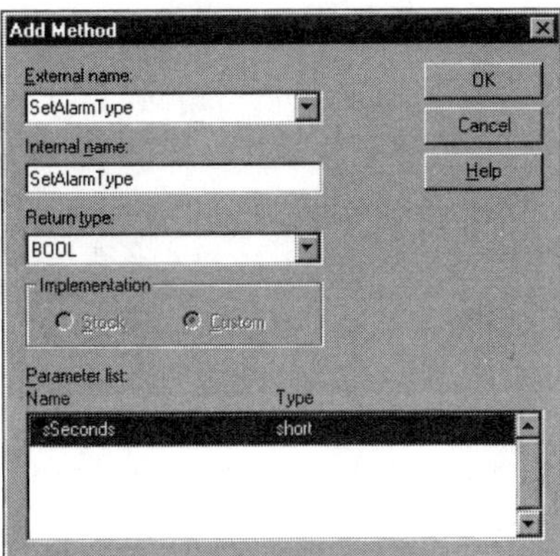

Figure 16-20: You can use the Add Method dialog to add methods to your controls.

Like properties, methods come in two flavors: stock and custom. You implement stock methods by selecting the method from the External name list in the Add Method dialog. Framework code for custom methods is created when you enter an external name for the method and supply an internal name, a return type, and parameters.

In this example, I'll show you how to add code that implements two custom methods and fires a custom event. SetAlarmType is a method that sets a timer to go off after the number of seconds specified. This method checks that the control has a valid handle and then calls the CWnd::SetTimer method with the number of seconds passed to the method:

```
#define TIMER_ID 100
...
BOOL CMyControlCtrl::SetAlarmType(short sSeconds)
{
   // TODO: Add your dispatch handler code here
   if ( GetHwnd() )
      return SetTimer (TIMER_ID, sSeconds * 1000, NULL );
   else
      return FALSE;
}
```

SetTimer expects time in milliseconds, hence the parameter passed to SetAlarmType is converted by multiplying by one thousand.

You could also add a custom method, StopAlarm, to turn the alarm off if the user changes her mind:

```
void CMyControlCtrl::StopAlarm()
{
   // TODO: Add your dispatch handler code here
   KillTimer ( TIMER_ID );
}
```

StopAlarm destroys the timer by calling CWnd::KillTimer.

The Windows timer mechanism produces a WM_TIMER message when the specified time period has elapsed. To trap this message, you'll need to add the WM_TIMER message to the control's message map using the Message Maps tab of ClassWizard. When you have done this, ClassWizard adds the following framework code:

```
void CMyControlCtrl::OnTimer(UINT nIDEvent)
{
   // TODO: Add your message handler code here and/or call default
   COleControl::OnTimer(nIDEvent);
}
```

To be able to inform control users that the alarm has been fired, you can add a custom event, AlarmWentOff. When the WM_TIMER message is received, the event is fired using the internal FireAlarmWentOff method, and the timer is destroyed so that it doesn't keep on firing:

```
void CMyControlCtrl::OnTimer(UINT nIDEvent)
{
   // TODO: Add your message handler code here and/or call default
   if (nIDEvent == TIMER_ID )
   {
      FireAlarmWentOff (nIDEvent);
      //kill the Timer
      KillTimer( TIMER_ID );
   }
   COleControl::OnTimer(nIDEvent);
}
```

After you rebuild the control, it's a good idea to try out these two new methods (and one new event) in a container to make sure that they work.

Figure 16-21 shows a test Visual Basic 5 application.

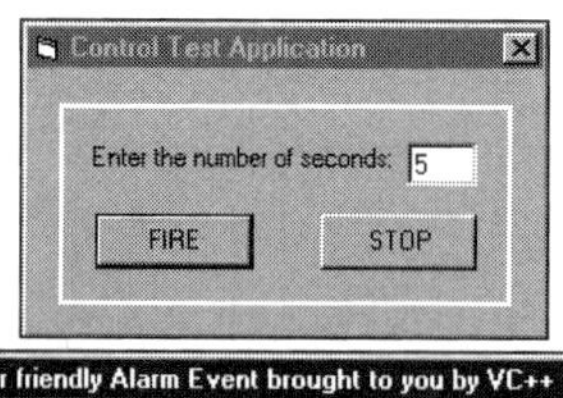

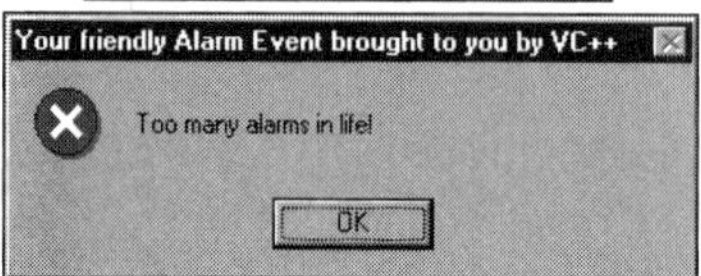

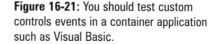

Figure 16-21: You should test custom controls events in a container application such as Visual Basic.

MyControl's SetAlarmType method is invoked in the cmdStart click event, using the number of seconds entered in Text1 as the duration for the alarm:

```
Private Sub cmdFire_Click()
   Call MyControl1.SetAlarmType(Text1)
End Sub
```

The MyControl.StopAlarm method is used to halt the alarm:

```
Private Sub cmdStop_Click()
   MyControl1.StopAlarm
End Sub
```

A MsgBox is added to the AlarmWentOff event handler so that we can see that the event is correctly fired (get out your stopwatches everyone!):

```
Private Sub MyControl1_AlarmWentOff(ByVal nTimerID As Long)
   MsgBox "Too many alarms in life!", vbCritical, _
      "Your friendly Alarm Event brought to you by VC++"
End Sub
```

Resources

If you select the Resource View tab in Developer Studio, you can access the resources — dialogs, strings, bitmaps, icons, and version information — that have been compiled into your control (see Figure 16-22).

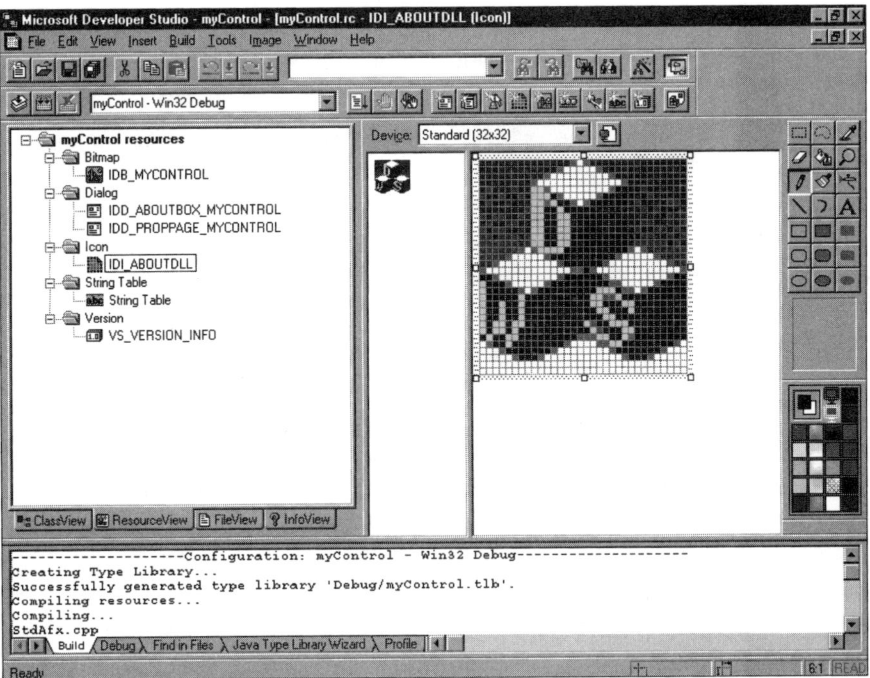

Figure 16-22: You can use the Resource View tab to view and edit the resources that have been compiled into your control project.

Depending on your selections in the ControlWizard, resources you'll see include

- IDB_MYCONTROL, a bitmap that represents the control in a container application Toolbox
- IDD_ABOUTBOX_MYCONTROL, an About box dialog
- IDD_PROPPAGE_MYCONTROL, a template dialog for a custom property page
- IDI_ABOUTDLL, an icon used in the About box
- String Table, strings used in the application that can be localized, if desired

Developer Studio provides tools to edit each kind of resource when it is opened. For example, the icon shown on the right of Figure 16-22 can be altered using the Toolbox and palette shown.

Viewing the Interface

You can use a container application to make sure that resources used in the control interface look all right and that control members have been implemented.

Figure 16-23 shows MyControl's Toolbox icon, custom About box, and Properties window interface in Visual Basic 5.

Using Visual Basic's Object Browser, you can make sure that all custom control members are properly defined (the AlarmWentOff event is shown highlighted in Figure 16-24).

You can also insert the new custom control in an HTML document, using an application such as ActiveX Control Pad or FrontPage 97.

Bear in mind that controls do not behave the same in all containers. A control will not necessarily work the same way in Visual Basic as it does in Internet Explorer. For a discussion of designing ActiveX controls with the Web and Internet Explorer in mind, and for information on preparing controls for use on the Web, see Chapter 13.

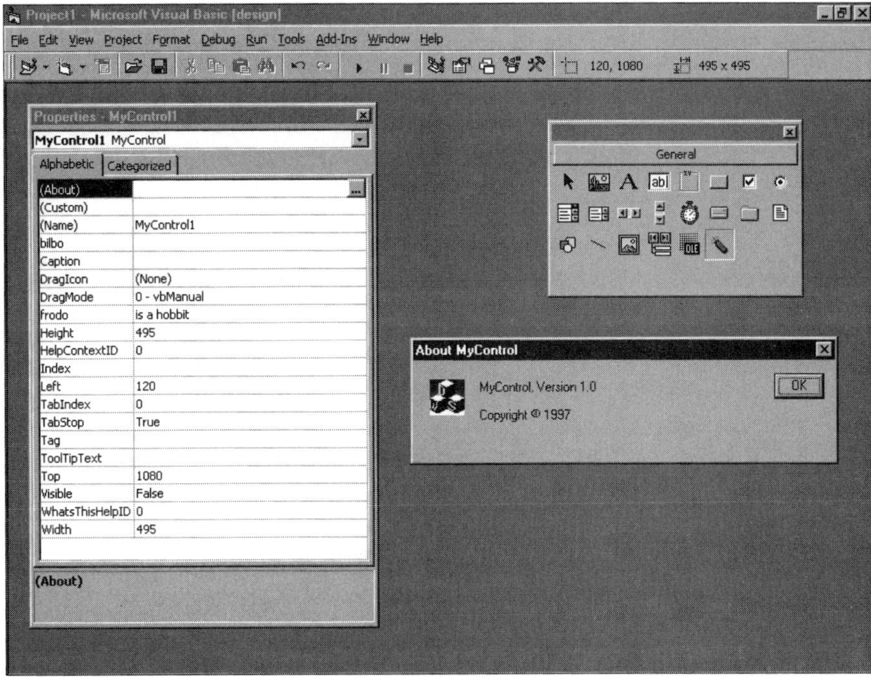

Figure 16-23: You can place a control on a container, such as a Visual Basic form, to make sure that the interface appears correctly.

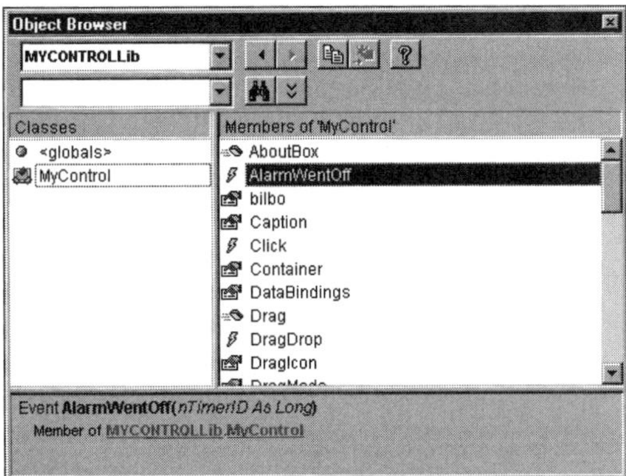

Figure 16-24: You can use Visual Basic's Object Browser to make sure that custom control members are correctly defined.

Figure 16-25 shows myControl placed in an HTML page using ActiveX Control Pad.

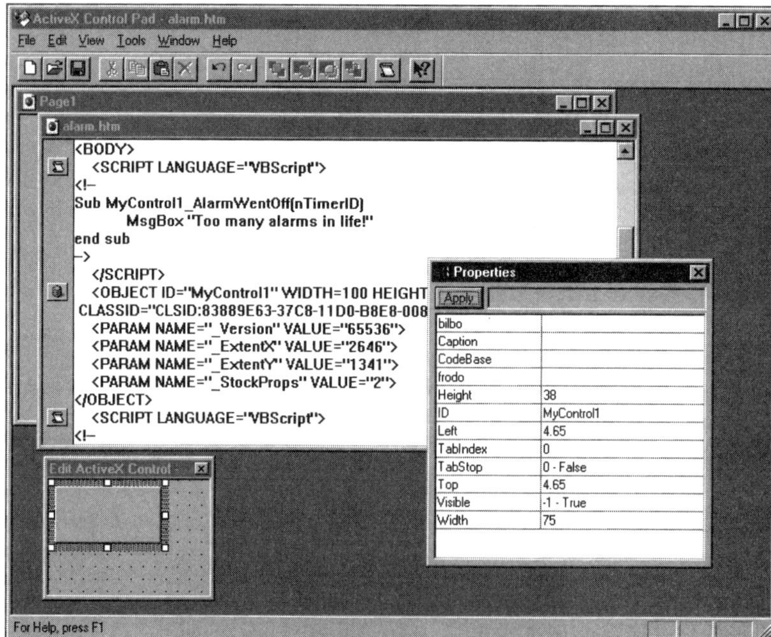

Figure 16-25: You can place custom ActiveX controls that you have created in VC++ on an HTML page using an application such as ActiveX Control Pad or FrontPage 97.

Here's the code underlying an HTML page that contains an instance of MyControl:

```
<HTML>
<HEAD>
<TITLE>MyControl Demo</TITLE>
</HEAD>
<BODY>
<SCRIPT LANGUAGE="VBScript">
<!--
Sub MyControl1_AlarmWentOff(nTimerID)
    MsgBox "Too many alarms in life!"
end sub
-->
</SCRIPT>
<OBJECT ID="MyControl1" WIDTH=100 HEIGHT=51
   CLASSID="CLSID:83889E63-37C8-11D0-B8E8-0080C6026268">
   <PARAM NAME="_Version" VALUE="65536">
   <PARAM NAME="_ExtentX" VALUE="2646">
   <PARAM NAME="_ExtentY" VALUE="1341">
   <PARAM NAME="_StockProps" VALUE="2">
</OBJECT>
```

```
<SCRIPT LANGUAGE="VBScript">
<!--
Sub CommandButton1_Click()
   call MyControl1.SetAlarmType(20)
    end sub
-->
</SCRIPT>
<OBJECT ID="CommandButton1" WIDTH=96 HEIGHT=32
   CLASSID="CLSID:D7053240-CE69-11CD-A777-00DD01143C57">
   <PARAM NAME="Caption" VALUE="Start that alarm">
   <PARAM NAME="Size" VALUE="2540;846">
   <PARAM NAME="FontCharSet" VALUE="0">
   <PARAM NAME="FontPitchAndFamily" VALUE="2">
   <PARAM NAME="ParagraphAlign" VALUE="3">
   <PARAM NAME="FontWeight" VALUE="0">
</OBJECT>
</BODY>
</HTML>
```

If you open this in Internet Explorer and click on the button that starts the alarm, the page that appears in the browser will be along the lines of the one shown in Figure 16-26.

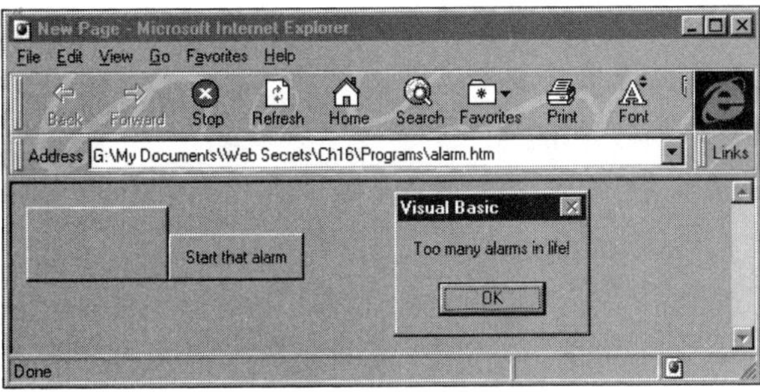

Figure 16-26: You can add custom ActiveX controls to HTML pages intended for use in Internet Explorer.

Summary

This chapter provided a guide for creating ActiveX Controls using Visual C++, MFC, the OLE ControlWizard, and ClassWizard. Obviously, I could say more on the topic. However, if you use the information in this chapter as an outline, there is no limit to the kinds of ActiveX controls you can design and implement — other than your knowledge of the relevant programming languages.

Topics covered in this chapter included

- Microsoft Foundation Classes (MFC) library
- Using the AppWizard
- CWinApp and the AppWizard

- Overridable CWinApp member functions
- The Run Member function
- Using ClassWizard
- MFC classes available with ClassWizard
- Understanding OLE
- The Component Object Model (COM)
- ActiveX controls
- What goes into an ActiveX control
- Communication between a control and a container
- States of a control
- Control persistence
- Using ControlWizard
- Advanced ActiveX features
- Standard files created by ControlWizard
- Adding stock and custom events to a control
- Adding stock and custom properties
- Methods
- Editing control resources
- Testing a control in Visual Basic
- Adding a custom control to a Web page

Chapter 17

Java Development and the Web

"O brave new world..."

— Shakespeare, "The Tempest"

If you're not an ostrich, you've heard of Java. In the scope of things, Java is a new programming language — it was officially introduced in January, 1996. It may be young, but it's already influential.

Why all the excitement about Java? First and foremost, Java is *the* universal language for developing executable content for the Web. Java is designed to let you create programs that can be compiled on any platform. These programs will execute on any system equipped with a Java interpreter. Java applets can be placed in a Web page and executed using a Web browser — and you don't have to be afraid that the Java code will attempt to illicitly access your computer. Java gives you access to network functions in an abstract, high-level fashion. You can use Java to create applications that multitask using threads. As if all this were not enough, Java is fully object-oriented, elegant, and easy to learn.

This chapter covers the following topics:

- Understanding Java
- Running a Java compiler
- Java applets and Java applications
- "Playing" an applet in a Web browser
- An overview of Java language and syntax
- An overview of important Java concepts

Understanding Java

Java was designed over a number of years by a team at Sun Microsystems led by James Gosling. The language was first officially released in January, 1996. The original purpose of the language was to control the relatively simple microprocessors that are the brains of home devices — such as multimedia entertainment devices. The designers of Java started with the object-oriented features of C++, simplified it, and made it easier to program and more elegant. Some of the features — such as pointers — that most often lead to programming errors in C++ were removed.

The story goes that the original working name for the language was "Oak." (Like many software innovations, "Oak" owed something to a research project at Xerox PARC — in this case code-named "Cedar/Mesa.")

However, "Oak" was already taken as a trademark. Supposedly, the developers came up with the name "Java" while taking a late-night break at a coffee shop. To my mind, "Java" has more of an energetic, perky rink than "Oak," which sounds solid and static. To some degree, the name "Java" may have helped with the incredible (and nearly instant) success of the language. But, obviously, it is a language and technology whose time has arrived.

The Java developers may originally have targeted a specific microprocessor. However, very early in the Java language development process they conceptualized a hypothetical computer — the Java Virtual Machine, or JVM — that Java would run on. The Java compiler was designed to produce binary code that executed on the JVM rather than on a specific machine. Of course, as the final step in this paradigm, JVMs had to be created for each platform that Java would run on.

These JVMs are Java interpreters that run on specific hardware under specific operating systems. They load and read the binary code created by compiled Java programs (Java byte code). The JVM translates Java byte code into target-specific functions and executes them. By now, there are JVM implementations for essentially all platforms and operating systems.

Sometime in 1994 or 1995, as Oak/Java neared completion, it became clear that Java was ideal for use on the Internet. Java programs embedded in Web pages could execute on any system that had a Java-enabled browser. Java programs that are embedded in Web pages are called *applets*. You can also create full-fledged applications using Java. For more information, see "Applications and Applets" later in this chapter.

To dream the impossible dream: operating system independence. Because all computers equipped with a JVM speak Java, Java development provides a ray of hope around the impossible Tower of Babel created by different, incompatible operating systems.

Java Compilers

Java visual development environments — such as Microsoft Visual J++, covered in Chapter 18, and Symantec's Visual Café, covered in Chapter 19 — are the best tools for quickly developing sophisticated Java programs. However, you don't need a fancy IDE to create Java programs; you just need a Java compiler and an ASCII text editor. Java compilers are included with the Java SDKs available from Sun Microsystems (the JDK) and Microsoft (the Java SDK).

Just What Is a Just In Time (JIT) Java Compiler?

A Just In Time (JIT) Java compiler — such as the one that ships with Microsoft Visual J++ — interprets Java byte code like a normal Java Virtual Machine. In addition, the JIT compiler translates the byte code into the local system's machine language. This means that code executed more than once — for example, in a loop — will be executed as native machine instructions, producing great performance improvements.

The Sun Microsystems JDK and related documents are on the *Web Developer's SECRETS* companion CD-ROM or can be downloaded from *http://java.sun.com/products/JDK/*. The Microsoft Java SDK can be downloaded from *http://www.microsoft.com/java/*.

In this chapter I'll show you how to create Java applets and applications using Sun's Java compiler and an ASCII text editor. I used version 1.02 of the Sun Java compiler to test the programs in the chapter. I chose the compiler because, after all, when it comes to Java, Sun is the "real McCoy."

To install the Sun Java compiler, after you have downloaded the self-extracting Exe file from Sun's Web site, simply run it:

```
JDC-1_0_2-win32-x86
```

The chapter uses a bare-bones text and command-line compilation because this makes it very easy to see what's going on. After you get the hang of Java, you'll probably want to graduate to development tools that make your job easier. That's fine! But the point of this chapter is to keep things as simple as possible.

Modifying Autoexec.Bat

You'll need to modify your Autoexec.Bat file so the system's PATH variable includes the Java\Bin directory. This directory contains — among other important programs — javac.exe, the Java compiler executable. You should add a statement along the following lines — depending on where you installed the JDK — to Autoexec.Bat:

```
Set PATH=%PATH%;c:\java\bin\;
```

Howdy, Pardner

All Java source files have a .java extension. If you create the file with a text editor, you should save Java source code files with this extension. For example, Figure 17-1 shows the Java source file created in Notepad and saved as Howdy.java.

Howdy.java - Notepad

File Edit Search Help

```
import java.awt.Graphics;
import java.awt.Color;
import java.awt.Font;
public class Howdy extends java.applet.Applet {
   Font f = new Font("Arial", Font.BOLD, 36);
   public void paint(Graphics g) {
      g.setColor(Color.red);
      g.setFont(f);
      g.drawString("Howdy, Pardner!", 20, 75);
   }
}
```

Figure 17-1: You can create Java source files with a text editor such as Notepad; you must save them with a .java extension.

Howdy.java is just a familiar "Hello, World" application, Java-style. Here's the source code:

```
import java.awt.Graphics;
import java.awt.Color;
import java.awt.Font;
public class Howdy extends java.applet.Applet {
   Font f = new Font("Arial", Font.BOLD, 36);
   public void paint(Graphics g) {
      g.setColor(Color.red);
      g.setFont(f);
      g.drawString("Howdy, Pardner!", 20, 75);
   }
}
```

The import statements let the applet use Java classes and methods. They are similar to #include directives in C.

Generally, applets with user interfaces will include java.awt.*. AWT is short for Abstract Windowing Toolkit (dubbed by some wags "Awful Window Toolkit" and even worse things). The AWT includes standard visual components and containers such as buttons, labels, dialogs, windows, and so on.

The statement

```
import java.awt.*;
```

automatically includes java.awt.Graphics, java.awt.Color, java.awt.Font, among other classes.

The class definition

```
public class Howdy extends java.applet.Applet
```

creates Howdy as a public class. In addition, all applet class definitions must extend java.applet.Applet.

Howdy inherits all members of the Applet class. The Applet class itself inherits from a long chain of classes. This means that Howdy can use variables and methods — including constructors, which are used to create an instance of a class — from java.lang.Object, java.awt.Component, java.awt.Container, and java.awt.Panel.

When writing an applet, you must always import java.applet.*. You will also usually want to import java.awt.* and java.lang.*.

The Font variable f is used to change the characteristics of the font used to display "Howdy, Partner!" The paint method overrides the paint method in Applet. It is invoked any time Howdy needs to be drawn on the screen.

Running the Java Compiler

To compile the Howdy applet, you'll need to go to the DOS command line and find the directory where the source code is located. Invoke the Java compiler on the command line with the source file as an argument, making sure to maintain the exact capitalization of the source file:

```
javac Howdy.java
```

If there are no syntax errors in your source file, it will successfully compile and generate a class file. This is a file with a .class extension, in this case Howdy.class.

Viewing the Applet in a Browser

Java applets (as opposed to Java Applications; see "Applications and Applets" later in the chapter) can be opened in a Web browser. You use the <APPLET> tag to reference the Java class file. For example, here's how you might open Howdy.class on a Web page:

```
<HTML>
   <HEAD>
      <TITLE>
      "Howdy, Pardner!" Applet Demo
      </TITLE>
   </HEAD>
   <BODY>
   <BR>
   <APPLET Code="Howdy.class" Width=350 Height=150>
      Java, can you see me?
   </APPLET>
   </BODY>
</HTML>
```

If you save this HTML as a file and open it in a Web browser that is Java-enabled, you'll see the "Howdy, Pardner" applet, as shown in Figure 17-2.

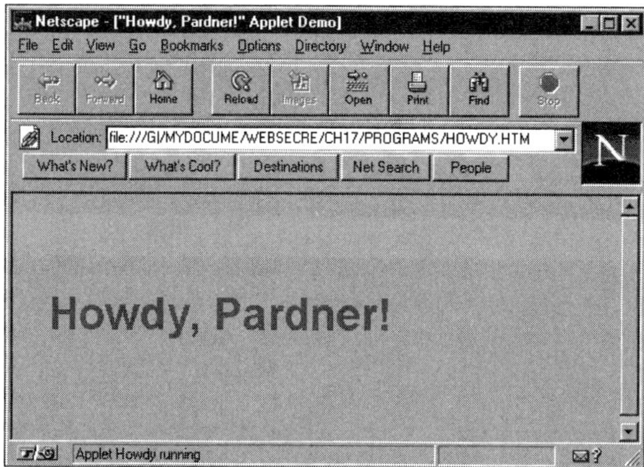

Figure 17-2: You open Java applets in a Web browser using the <APPLET> tag.

Browsers than don't "speak" Java will display the text included between the <APPLET> and </APPLET> tags — "Java, can you see me?" in the preceding example — instead of the applet.

Packages

If you are creating a program of any complexity, it's a good idea to break the source code for the program into separate files. You would then have a *package* of class source files, for example:

```
Klingon.class
Ferengi.class
Data.class
```

The code for each class should start with the package declaration:

```
package trek;
import java.awt.*;
public class Klingon extends Object {
...
```

Each compiled class file then goes in a folder named trek. You can reuse a package by invoking it using an import statement.

The Codebase Parameter

When you publish an applet on the Web, you may want to specify that the applet code (and package folder) is in a different location than the Web page. You do this using the Codebase parameter in the <APPLET> tags. For example:

```
<APPLET Codebase=http:\\www.bearhome.com\myapplet\
   Code="Howdy.class" Width=350 Height=150>
      Java, can you see me?
</APPLET>
```

Applet Viewer

Alternatively, Java applets can be viewed from the command line using the Applet Viewer program included in the JDK. You don't need to start a Web browser to view your applets.

You can run Applet Viewer from the command line (see Figure 17-3) to open an applet, for example:

```
appletviewer howdy.htm
```

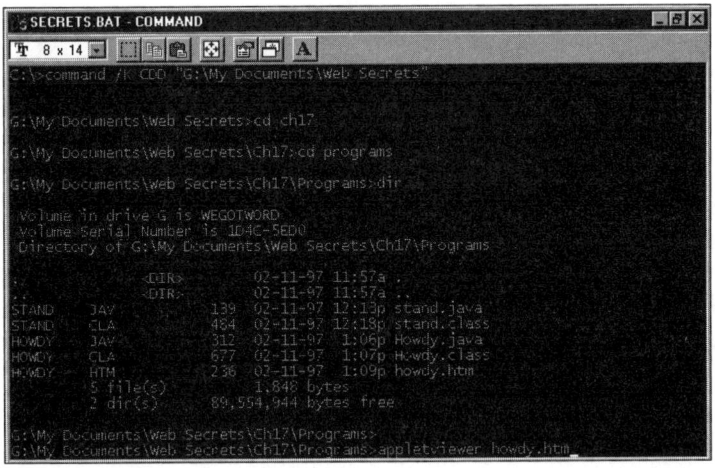

Figure 17-3: You can run Applet Viewer from the command line to view an applet without using a browser.

Applet Viewer displays the Java applet, as you can see in Figure 17-4.

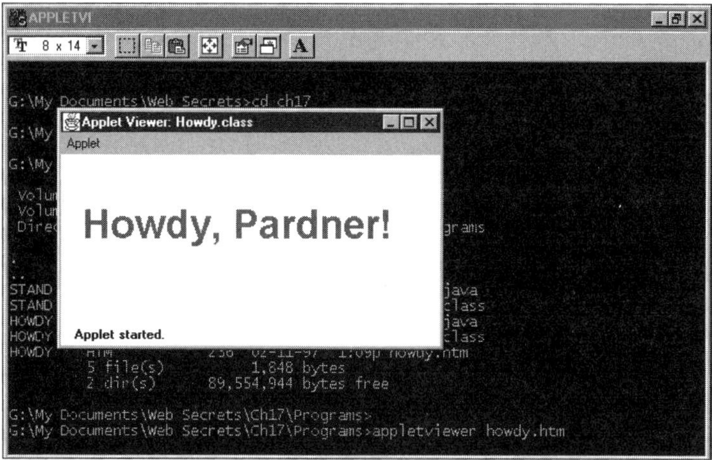

Figure 17-4: You use Applet Viewer to display Java classes.

Applications and Applets

Howdy.class is a Java applet, intended to be viewed in a Web browser. Applets are programs embedded in Web pages; they can only be run using a Web browser that is Java-aware (or appletviewer, as described a moment ago). You can also write Java applications that are stand-alone programs that run without a Web browser.

Java applets are designed for secure Internet downloading. They cannot

- Write information onto your hard drive unless you give them explicit access (Under Netscape Navigator 3.0 they cannot write to your disk no matter what.)
- Access specific memory locations
- Access memory outside of the Java address space
- Access resources on any other computer on your network, or elsewhere on the Internet, with the exception that they can open TCP/IP connections back to the Web server from which they were downloaded

These applet design restrictions give rise to a strictly limited universe that has been termed the "Java sandbox." It would truly be very difficult to construct a Java applet — such as a virus — that damaged machines downloading the applet. However, the restrictions mean that some important areas of functionality cannot be achieved using Java applets.

In contrast to applets, Java applications are full-featured programs that have full access to the resources of the computer they are running on. Java applications can read, write, create, and delete local files.

Here's a Java application that contains one line of executable code, which displays a message on the screen:

```
public class Stand {
   public static void main (String args[]){
      System.out.println("I am NOT an applet!");
   }
}
```

If this code were saved as a file named Stand.java, you'd compile it from the command line in the normal way:

```
javac Stand.java
```

This generates the file Stand.class. To execute the program, run the Java interpreter, specifying the file as an argument:

```
java Stand
```

The filename is case sensitive. When you're running the Java interpreter, you should not use the .class extension.

Figure 17-5 shows the Stand Java application's output.

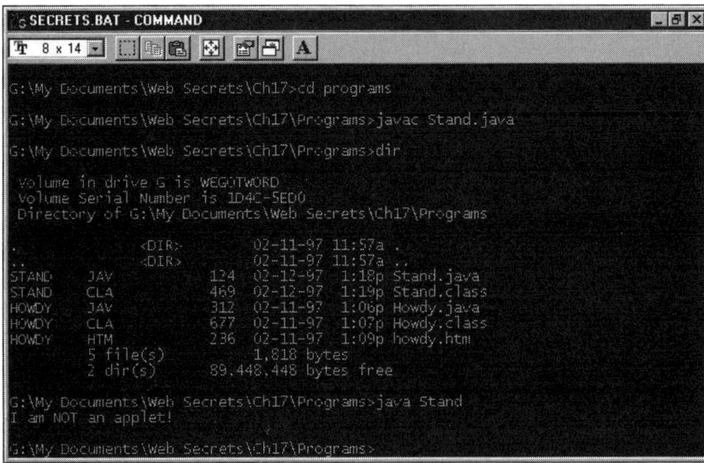

Figure 17-5: This Java application is definitely not an applet!

Going Both Ways

Actually, you don't have to decide whether you want your Java program to run as an applet or as a stand-alone application.

It's pretty easy to write code that will run as a stand-alone program when invoked from the command line. When invoked in a Web page with the <APPLET> tag, the code will run as an applet.

Listing 17-1 shows how to go about this.

Listing 17-1: Java source code that runs as an application or an applet

```
import java.awt.*;
import java.applet.*;
/* I go both ways. Run me as an applet or as an application! */
public class Both extends Applet {
   // applet code goes here
   Button button = new Button("Click me, please!");
   Label label = new Label("It's all right, press the button!");

   public void init() {
      add(button);
      add(label);
   }

   public boolean handleEvent(Event event) {
      if (event.target == button) {
         label.setText("Thanks for clicking, now take me home!");
         button.setLabel("Do it again!");
         return true;
      }
      else {
         return false;
      }
   }

   public static void main(String args[]) {
      //only called when run as an application
      TheFrame appletFrame = new TheFrame ("Both");
      Both newApplet = new Both();
      //make new instance of Both
      newApplet.init();
      newApplet.start();
      appletFrame.add("Center",newApplet);
      appletFrame.resize(600,200);
      appletFrame.show();
   }
}
/* TheFrame replaces the browser when this program
     is run as an application. */
class TheFrame extends Frame {
   public TheFrame(String str) {
      super(str);
   }
   public boolean handleEvent(Event event) {
      if (event.id == Event.WINDOW_DESTROY) {
         dispose();
         System.exit(0);
         return true;
      }
      else {
```

```
            return super.handleEvent(event);
        }
    }
}
```

The source file is saved as Both.java. After it's compiled, you can run it from the command line:

```
java Both
```

When you use the Java command to run the applet class rather than opening the applet from a Web page, the computer first executes the main method. The main method constructs a frame for the application to run in. It then constructs a new instance of the applet class, Both, that operates within the frame. This produces a Java application window, as shown in Figure 17-6.

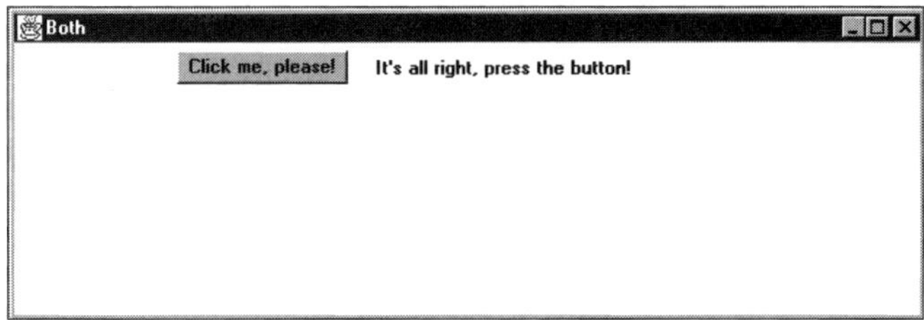

Figure 17-6: When the program is run as an application, main is invoked to construct a frame and an applet class instance.

You could, alternatively, embed the compiled Java file, Both.class, in an HTML page:

```
<HTML>
   <HEAD>
      <TITLE>
      "Both ways" Applet Demo
      </TITLE>
   </HEAD>
   <BODY>
   <BR>
   <APPLET Code="Both.class" Width=600 Height=200>
      Java, can you see me?
   </APPLET>
   </BODY>
</HTML>
```

In this case, the browser never gets to the main method. Instead, it calls the init and start methods of the applet, which does its thing within the browser, as shown in Figure 17-7.

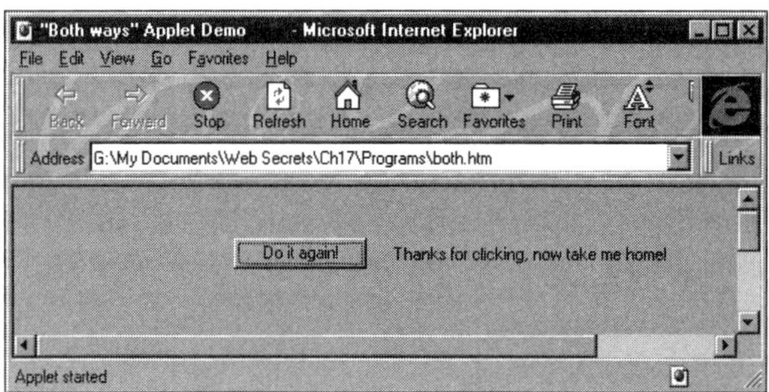

Figure 17-7: If the program is embedded in a Web page, when it is invoked by a browser the init and start methods of the applet are called.

Whether run as an applet or an application, this program of course doesn't do very much. When the user presses the applet's button, the button label is changed, as is the text of the applet's label.

Inside Scoop

The handleEvent method of TheFrame is used so the application can be closed by clicking on the window's Close button.

An Overview of Java Syntax

Java as a language is elegant and easy to learn.

Statements and Comments

Statements are case sensitive. Each statement ends with a semicolon (;). Because Java statements are not limited to a single line, there is no line continuation character.

You can indicate comments in two fashions:

- A line that begins with two forward slashes (//) is a comment.
- Any amount of code that starts with /* and ends with */ is a comment.

Here are some Java comments:

```
// I am a comment.
/* I'm a Java
   comment, too! */
```

Data Types

Table 17-1 shows the major Java data types.

Table 17-1 Java Data Types

Data Type	Contains
boolean	true or false
byte	signed 8-bit value
short	16-bit integer
int	32-bit integer
long	64-bit integer
float	32-bit floating point
double	64-bit floating point
char	16-bit character
String	16-bit characters

Variables

The first character of a variable must be a letter; otherwise, Java variables can be of any length and can be any combination of letters and numbers. Case is significant in Java, so these would all be different variables:

```
thisThing
ThisThing
THISTHING
```

Java variables must be declared. You can do these at the beginning of a procedure or when you use the variable. For example:

```
int x, y, z; // x,y and z are integers
```

or

```
int x = 3;
float y = x * martha;
```

You can implicitly convert between data types if the data being assigned has fewer bytes than the variable type it is being assigned to. For example:

```
float f; //f is a float
int i;   //i is an int
f = i;    //convert int to float
```

The other way around (converting the contents of a more-bytes variable to a less-bytes variable) requires casting — that is, putting the data type in parentheses and putting it in front of the variable you wish to convert:

```
i = (int)f; //convert float to integer
```

Boolean variables can only contain the values represented by true and false. You cannot assign a numeric value to a boolean, nor can you convert between booleans and other types.

It's common to assign values to a boolean variable based on comparisons and other operators. For example:

```
int i;
boolean  isless42;
isless42 = (i < 42); //true if i is less than 42
```

Operators

Table 17-2 shows the Java operators.

Table 17-2 Java Operators

<table>
<tr><th>Operator</th><th>Meaning</th></tr>
<tr><td>+</td><td>Addition, string concatenation</td></tr>
<tr><td>-</td><td>Subtraction, unary minus</td></tr>
<tr><td>*</td><td>Multiplication</td></tr>
<tr><td>/</td><td>Division</td></tr>
<tr><td>%</td><td>Modulo (remainder after integer division)</td></tr>
<tr><td>&</td><td>Bitwise And</td></tr>
<tr><td>|</td><td>Bitwise Or</td></tr>
<tr><td>^</td><td>Bitwise exclusive Or (Xor)</td></tr>
<tr><td>++</td><td>Increment</td></tr>
<tr><td>—</td><td>Decrement</td></tr>
<tr><td>></td><td>Greater than</td></tr>
<tr><td><</td><td>Less than</td></tr>
<tr><td>==</td><td>Is equal to (comparison)</td></tr>
<tr><td>!=</td><td>Is not equal to</td></tr>
<tr><td>>=</td><td>Greater than or equal to</td></tr>
<tr><td><=</td><td>Less than or equal to</td></tr>
<tr><td>&&</td><td>Logical And</td></tr>
<tr><td>||</td><td>Logical Or</td></tr>
<tr><td>~</td><td>Logical Not</td></tr>
</table>

You can combine arithmetic and assignment operators. For example, the following two statements both add 42 to x and store the result in the variable x:

```
x = x + 42;
x += 42; //combines addition and assignment operator
```

Making Decisions

If statements in Java have the following syntax:

```
if (condition) {
   statements
   }
else {
   statements
}
```

Obviously, the indentation and formatting are irrelevant to the compiler and up to you. But the condition must be enclosed within parentheses. If a list of statements is, in fact, only one statement, you can omit the curly braces ({}). Here's an example of a single-statement if, which, incidentally, has no else clause:

```
if ( isless42 )
   System.out.println("I'm less than 42!");
```

The switch statement is used to switch program execution where there are a number of possible choices. The form of this statement is

```
switch ( compare )
{
case m:
   statements;
   break;
case n:
   statements;
   break;
...
default:
   statements;
}
```

In this example, compare represents a variable that must be either of type int or type char.

Break means to exit the control structure. If the break statement is omitted, execution continues to the next case in the structure.

Looping

A while loop is executed as long as the condition within parentheses is true. For example:

```
j = 0;
while ( j < Borg.Count )
    {
    x = x + j++;
    }
// Call the reinforcements
GetTheKlingons.activate;
```

A do...while statement operates in pretty much the same way, except that it executes at least once because the condition test is at the bottom of the loop:

```
j = 0;
do
    {
    x = x + j++;
    }
while ( j < Borg.Count );
// Call the reinforcements
GetTheKlingons.activate;
```

The Java for loop contains three parts, separated by semicolons: an initializer, a condition, and an operation that takes place each time through the loop. The general syntax here is

```
for (initialization; expression; increment) {
    statements
}
```

Initialization is a statement that is executed the first time through the loop. *Expression* is a condition that is tested at the start of each trip through the loop. *Increment* is a statement that is executed at the end of each trip through the loop.

Consider, as an example:

```
for (i = 0; i < 42 ; i++) {
    x += i;
}
```

This loop initializes i to 0. It continues to loop as long as i is less than 42, incrementing i at each pass. The statement within the loop adds the value of i each time to the value already accumulated in x.

Doing Objects

As you surely must have realized by now, the heart, mind, and soul of Java lie in objects. Everything in Java is an object. Furthermore, programming through the creation, extension, and destruction of objects is enforced. It's essentially the only way to do it in Java.

As in any object-oriented language, it's important to keep in mind the difference between an object (or class) and an instance of the class. A good way to think of this is that classes are the cookie cutter, or blueprint, from which instances that you can actually use in programs are patterned.

Creating a Class Instance

The new operator is used in Java to create an instance of a class. For example, you could create an instance of the Button class:

```
Button myButton; //declare a button object
myButton = new Button("I'm a Button!"); /* create the new instance
                        of the button with "I'm a Button!" label */
```

Because you can declare variables as they are used, you could also write this as

```
Button myButton = new Button("I'm a Button!");
```

Constructors

As you probably know, if you define a class yourself, you usually need to include at least one constructor routine. The constructor is used to initialize class variables when an instance of the object is created. Here's the generalized syntax:

```
class name (type parameter1, type parameter2 ...) {
   setup statements;
}
```

Constructors have the same name as the class, are always public, and have no return value (not even void). The typed parameter list — sometimes referred to along with the class name as the constructor's *signature* — is the information required from the outside to set up an object of this type.

If you have more than one constructor, they must have different signatures (meaning, a different parameter list).

The code in the setup statements includes the necessary steps required to initialize the object. This code is executed every time an instance of the object is created.

Classes in a .java File

Java programs can consist of numerous .java files. But each .java file can contain only one public class, which must have the same name as the file itself. There can be additional classes within the file, but they cannot be declared as public (and are therefore normally only accessed by the public class within the file).

Public, Private, and Protected

A *public* method or variable can be accessed by any code inside or outside of the class.

A *private* method or variable can only be accessed by code within the class. A *private protected* method or variable can only be accessed within its class and classes derived from its class. A *protected* method or variable is accessible to classes in derived classes and to classes within its package. Methods and variables that are not marked as public, private, or protected are — by default — visible within the package, but not within derived classes.

Here's the constructor for TheFrame class from Listing 17-1:

```
class TheFrame extends Frame {
   public TheFrame(String str) {
      super(str);
   }
   ...
```

In this case, the invocation of the super() method calls the constructor in the base class, Frame. TheFrame's parent's constructor (for example, Frame) sets the title for TheFrame. (Note that if you use the super() method, it must be the first statement inside the constructor.) By the way, here's the constructor for the Frame class:

```
Frame myFrame = new Frame ("My Frame Title");
```

Class Data and Methods

In addition to its constructor(s), a class contains data and methods. Methods are functions. Both data and methods can be declared public or private. It is generally the best practice to declare data as private and create public access methods.

The keyword *extends* means that a class inherits the properties of another class (in addition to any you change or add).

The *instanceof* operator is used to determine whether an object is derived from a given class.

You can *override* — replace or modify — a method inherited from a super class.

Abstract classes are not intended to be instantiated. Rather, they are used as an organizing template for defining class methods. Note that classes derived from abstract classes must provide methods for every method defined in the abstract class. If you don't provide these methods, your new class will also be treated as abstract class, and you won't be able to instantiate it.

Events

The Event class customizes the way in which a Java program handles events such as user input. Essentially, the Event class is a wrapper for messages fired by the windows manager. For example — from Listing 17-1 — the following code fragment captures the WINDOW_DESTROY message:

```
public boolean handleEvent(Event event) {
   if (event.id == Event.WINDOW_DESTROY) {
      dispose();
      ...
```

To fire an event, you would create an instance of the Event object.

Obviously, there's a lot more to working with objects in Java than I've explained here. But from the start, Java has been conceptualized as a language of objects. This has led to an object syntax that is clear and intuitive. You'll find that programming objects in Java comes quite naturally.

Summary

Java is the most exciting new programming language to come along in quite some time. In addition, Java programs are the best way to implement cross-platform executable content on the Web.

This chapter has covered the basic concepts and information you need to know to get started with Java development.

The next two chapters explain how to use sophisticated development environments with the Java language. (Chapter 18 explains how to use Microsoft Visual J++ and Chapter 19 covers Symantec Visual Café.)

Topics covered in this chapter included

- Java and Java compilers
- Importing Java libraries
- Creating a simple applet
- Running the command-line Java compiler
- Viewing the applet in a browser
- Packages
- The Applet Viewer
- Java applets and Java applications
- Java language and syntax
- Objects in Java

Chapter 18

Visual J++ Secrets

"Ei! wie schmeckt der Kaffee süße,
lieblicher als tausend Küsse,
milder als Muskatenwein.
Kaffee, Kaffee muß ich haben,
und wenn jemand mich will laben,
ach, so schenkt mir Kaffee ein!"

— J.S. Bach, Kaffee Kantate, BWV 211

[Mm! how the coffee tastes,
more delicious than a thousand kisses,
mellower than Muscat wine.
Coffee, coffee I must have,
and if someone wishes to give me a treat,
ah, then pour me out some coffee!]

Microsoft's Visual J++ wraps the Java programming language in the Developer Studio development environment familiar from Visual C++. (For an overview of the Java language, see Chapter 17, "Java Development and the Web"; for information on Visual C++, see Chapter 16, "Creating ActiveX Controls in Visual C++.") Visual J++ thus tacks a modern visual front end — one that many developers are comfortable with — on the Java language.

This chapter explores how to use Visual J++ to quickly and easily create great Java applications.

Third-Party Goodies

The Visual J++ CD-ROM includes a variety of third-party Java source code and tools. This material includes the JAMBA graphics effects libraries from AimTech Corp., Liquid Motion animation tools from DimensionX, an E-mail Application Wizard from Neural Applications Corp., and JGL (a library of reusable data structures and algorithms) from ObjectSpace Corp.

The Visual J++ Web site at *http://www.microsoft.com/visualj* is a great source for current information on Visual J++.

A Simple Applet

Here's the procedure for creating a simple applet in Visual J++:

1. Start Developer Studio. Choose New from the File menu, and select Project Workspace from the New dialog as shown in Figure 18-1.

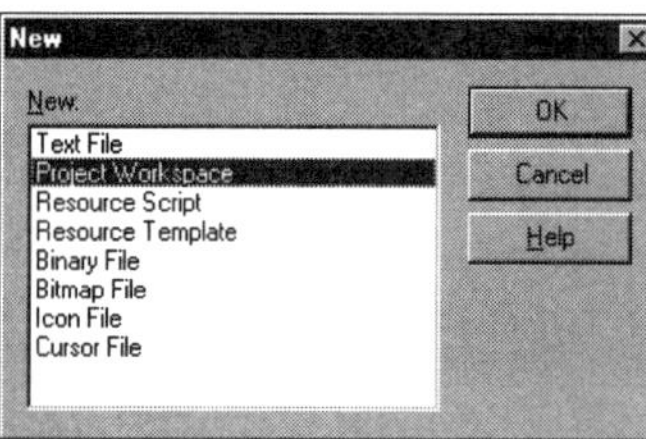

Figure 18-1: The first step in creating an applet is to start a new Project Workspace.

2. The New Project Workspace dialog will appear (Figure 18-2). Give your project a name and location, and Select Java Workspace. Make sure that Java Virtual Machine is checked as the target platform. Note that the project types appearing in this dialog depend on the Developer Studio applications that you have installed.

   All the Microsoft development languages installed on a system that use the Developer Studio interface share one instance of the environment. If Visual J++ and Visual C++ have both been installed on your system, numerous VC++ project types will be available in this dialog.

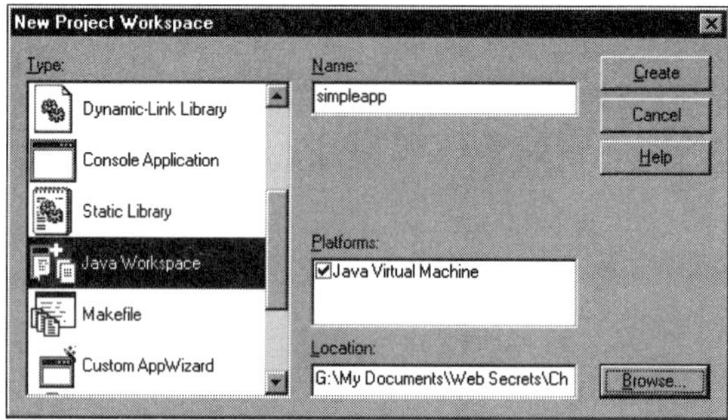

Figure 18-2: Make sure that Java Virtual Machine is selected as your target platform when you open a new Java Workspace.

3. Open a new text file (choose New from the File menu, and Text File from the New dialog).

4. Enter the code for a simple applet. For example, in the "Hello, World" mode:

```
import java.awt.Graphics;
class Bears extends java.applet.Applet
{
 public void paint( Graphics g )
 {
        g.drawString( "Bears love peace!", 50, 25 );
 }
}
```

5. Choose Save from the File menu. Note that Java is case sensitive. The file must have a .java extension and the exact same name as the class (in this case Bears.java).

6. Choose Files into Project from the Insert menu, and add Bears.java to your Java Workspace. If you have the left pane of Developer Studio set to Class view, your workspace should now look like that shown in Figure 18-3.

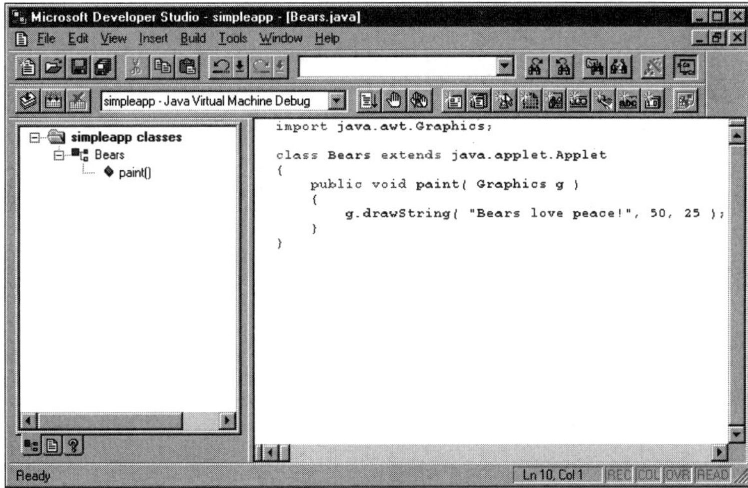

Figure 18-3: You can use the left pane of Developer Studio for viewing class hierarchies, while editing actual code in the right pane.

7. You can now run the applet directly from Developer Studio by choosing Execute from the Build menu. First Visual J++ compiles Bears.java into Bears.class. Next, the dialog shown in Figure 18-4 appears. You use this dialog to specify the class name and to select a viewer for the project.

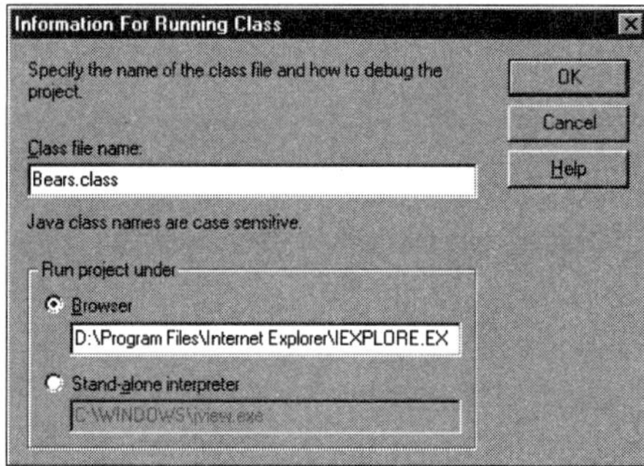

Figure 18-4: You use the Information For Running Class dialog to specify class, browser, and viewer preferences.

8. The applet loads in the selected viewer (it is shown in Explorer in Figure 18-5). Note that you could, alternatively, simply compile the Java source file and generate a Java class file. You could then have added an <APPLET> tag to an HTML page to start the applet.

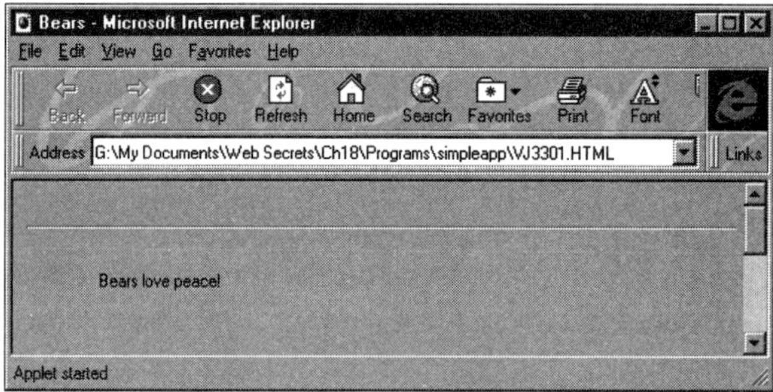

Figure 18-5: The Execute command allows you to view your applet in a browser without leaving the Developer Studio environment.

Creating a Stand-Alone Application

You can create a stand-alone application in pretty much the same way you'd create an applet. (The procedure outlined here differs from the simple applet in the order in which the Project Workspace is created. You can do this in either order.)

1. If a project is open, close the existing Workspace.
2. Open a new text file. Enter code along these lines:

```
class Bears2
{
```

```
public static void main( String args[] )
{
System.out.println( "We're happy to be big, brown bears!" );
}
}
```

3. Save the text file with the name Bears2.java.
4. Choose Build Bears2 from the Build menu. A dialog will ask whether you want to create a default Workspace. Click on Yes.
5. From the Build menu, choose Execute.
6. Enter **Bears2.class** and select Stand-alone interpreter in the Information for Running Class dialog.

The Applet Wizard

Visual J++ includes a tool for creating new Java applets that start out with a great deal of functionality: the Java Applet Wizard. Using the Applet Wizard can greatly speed the process of creating sophisticated Java applets.

To start the Applet Wizard, select it from the New Project Workspace dialog, as shown in Figure 18-6.

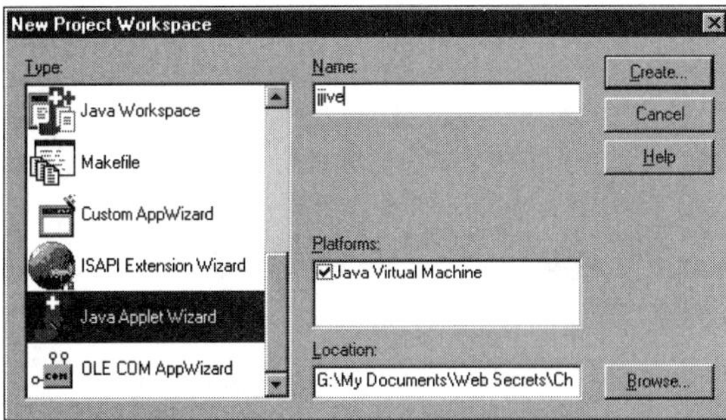

Figure 18-6: You select the Java Applet Wizard using the New Project Workspace dialog.

Depending on the options you select, the generic code generated by the Wizard can include

- The ability to run your project as an application or as an applet
- Comments in the source code that explain what the code is doing and what remains to be done
- A sample HTML page for running the applet
- Basic multithreading support

Source Code Differences Between an Applet and an Application

In terms of source code, the basic differences between an applet and an application are simple.

An applet must define a class derived from the Applet class. An application can do the same, but it is not required to do so.

An application must define a class with a method named main that controls its execution. An applet does not use a main method; its execution is controlled by various methods defined by the Applet class.

If you try running the program as an applet, you'll notice that it looks essentially the same as when it's run as an application. This is noteworthy because, by default, there's another fundamental difference between applets and applications: An applet automatically has a graphical user interface (a portion of the HTML page that contains it), whereas an application is text based by default.

The Applet Wizard has generated code to handle this difference, giving the program a graphical user interface even when it's run as an application. The Wizard does this by defining a class derived from the Frame class. This class, in conjunction with the program's Applet-derived class, provides a window for the application, allowing the same graphical user interface code to run. This frame window class is used only when the program is executed as a stand-alone application.

For more information, see "Applications and Applets" in Chapter 17.

- A sample animation that can be customized
- Handlers for mouse events
- Code for reading parameters from the HTML page
- Code for offering author and copyright information

The first panel of the Applet Wizard — shown in Figure 18-7 — lets you decide to include the application frame class so your program can run as a stand-alone. This panel is used to name your applet class. (The sample Java applet shown will be named jjive.class.) In addition, you can use this panel to have the Wizard insert comments in the code it generates.

You use the next Wizard panel to determine whether a sample HTML page should be generated, and, if so, what the initial size of the applet should be (see Figure 18-8).

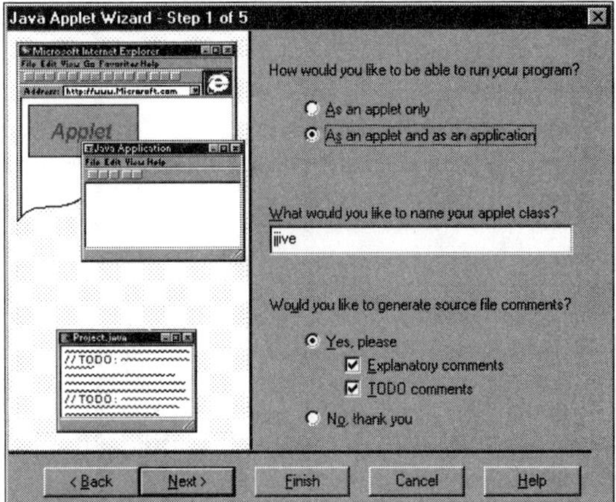

Figure 18-7: The first panel of the Java Applet Wizard lets you decide whether the applet will include code required to run it as a stand-alone, whether to name the applet class, and whether comments should be included.

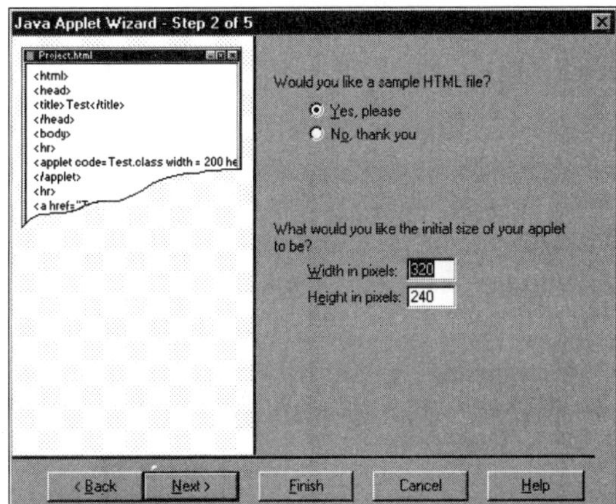

Figure 18-8: You use the second panel of the Java Applet Wizard to decide whether a sample HTML page should be generated.

Here's the HTML code generated for the jjive applet:

```
<html>
<head>
<title>jjive</title>
</head>
```

```
<body>
<hr>
<applet
    code=jjive.class
    id=jjive
    width=320
    height=240 >
    <param name=Frodo value="">
</applet>
<hr>
<a href="jjive.java">The source.</a>
</body>
</html>
```

You use the third Wizard panel to include multithreading, support for animation, and mouse event handlers (Figure 18-9).

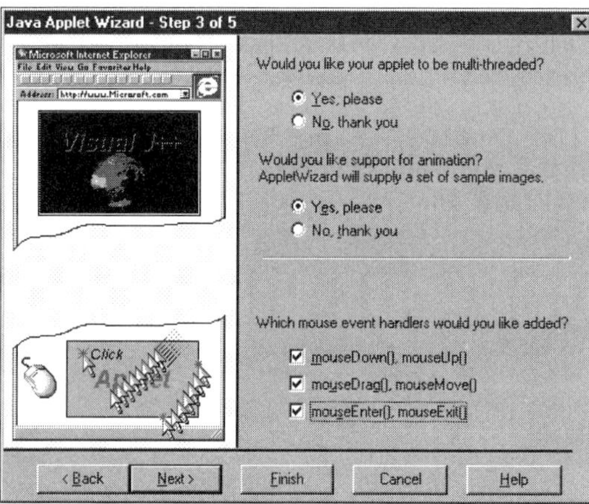

Figure 18-9: You can use the third panel of the Applet Wizard to include support for multithreading, animation, and mouse event handlers.

You use the fourth panel to add parameters that the applet will read from its host HTML page. (The variable Frodo, shown in Figure 18-10, becomes a parameter in the sample HTML code generated for the applet.)

You use the final Wizard panel, shown in Figure 18-11, to include author and copyright information that will be returned by the applet's getAppInfo method.

After you've made your choices in the five Wizard panels, a New Project Information summary screen is generated, as shown in Figure 18-12. At this point, if you're unhappy with any choices you've made, you can bail out and start over by clicking on Cancel.

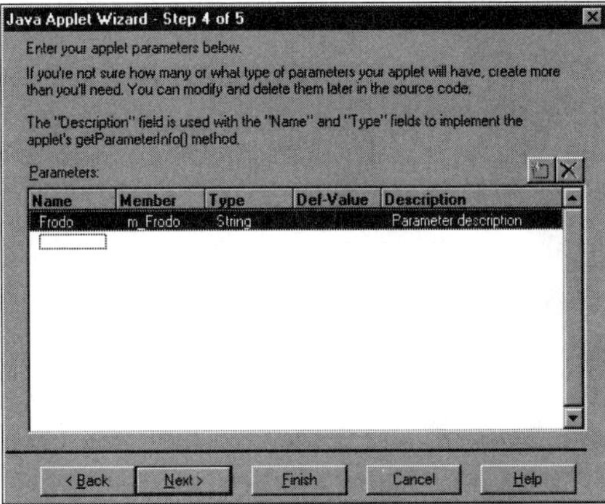

Figure 18-10: You can use this Wizard panel to include applet parameters.

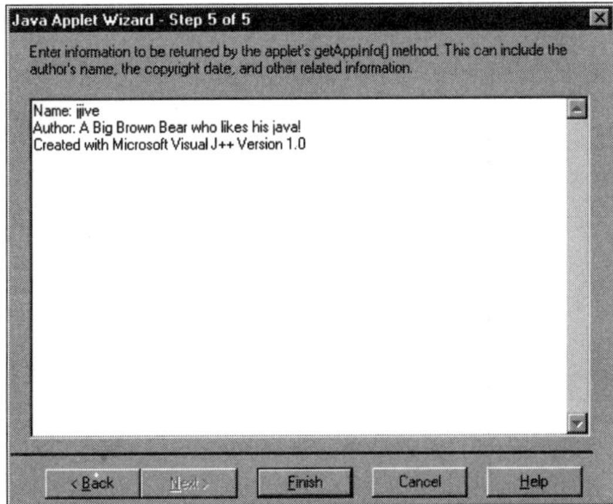

Figure 18-11: You use the final Wizard panel to enter identifying information for the applet.

When you click on OK on the summary screen, the Wizard generates your project files and Java code (we'll have a peek under the covers at what it actually does in a moment).

If you run the project that the Wizard generates — by choosing Execute from the Build menu — provided that you elected to include the sample animation in your applet, you'll see the earth spinning and spinning in your browser, as shown in Figure 18-13.

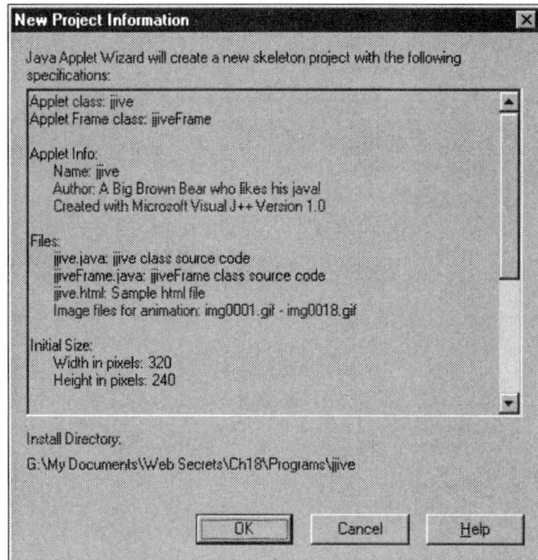

Figure 18-12: The New Project Information screen summarizes the choices you've made in the Java Applet Wizard.

Figure 18-13: If you included animation in your applet, an animated image of the earth will appear when you run it.

The Code Is in There

Shades of the slogan from the television show *The X-Files*: "The truth is out there." You click on some buttons on the Java Applet Wizard, it whirs and clicks and creates an applet. What has it actually done, and what code has it put in there? Let's have a look.

No surprises in the import statements (jjiveFrame is used to support the applet running as an application:

```
import java.applet.*;
import java.awt.*;
import jjiveFrame;
```

The declaration for the main class for the applet implements the Runnable interface, which means that it can be run in a thread by passing an instance of the class to a new thread object.

```
public class jjive extends Applet implements Runnable
{
    // THREAD SUPPORT:
    //          m_jjive is the Thread object for the applet
    //-----------------------------------------------------------
    Thread  m_jjive = null;
...
```

The start() method is called when the page containing the applet first appears on the screen. This is where execution of the applet's thread is started:

```
    public void start()
    {
        if (m_jjive == null)
        {
            m_jjive = new Thread(this);
            m_jjive.start();
        }
        // TODO: Place additional applet start code here
    }
```

The stop method is called when the page containing the applet is no longer on the screen. This is where the Applet Wizard's code stops execution of the thread:

```
public void stop()
    {
        if (m_jjive != null)
        {
            m_jjive.stop();
            m_jjive = null;
        }
        // TODO: Place additional applet stop code here
    }
```

Note that ongoing applet activities that do not require user input will probably be implemented in the applet's run method.

Here are the applet's animation declarations:

```
    // ANIMATION SUPPORT:
    //m_Graphics   used for storing the applet's Graphics context
    //m_Images[]   the array of Image objects for the animation
    //m_nCurrImage the index of the next image to be displayed
    //m_ImgWidth   width of each image
    //m_ImgHeight  height of each image
    //m_fAllLoaded indicates whether all images have been loaded
    //NUM_IMAGES   number of images used in the animation
    //-----------------------------------------------------------------
    private Graphics m_Graphics;
    private Image    m_Images[];
    private int      m_nCurrImage;
    private int      m_nImgWidth  = 0;
    private int      m_nImgHeight = 0;
    private boolean  m_fAllLoaded = false;
    private final int NUM_IMAGES = 18;
    ...
```

The animation code in the applet loads files from the images folder that the Wizard creates. For each image in the animation, a string is constructed containing the path to the image, and it is then loaded in the images array (m_Images[]). You could easily replace these images — and modify the applet code — to create a custom animation.

Parameters allow an HTML author to pass information to the applet (remember the variable Frodo entered in the Applet Wizard?):

```
//  Members for applet parameters
//  <type>       <MemberVar>    = <Default Value>
//-------------------------------------------------------------
private String m_Frodo = "";
// Parameter names.  To change a name of a parameter, you need only
// make a single change.  Simply modify the value of the parameter
// string below.
private final String PARAM_Frodo = "Frodo";
```

Code involving stand-alone application support follows. Applications can receive parameters on the command line, as opposed to applets, which receive them as part of the <APPLET> tag. Here's the code that implements retrieving <APPLET> parameters:

```
void GetParameters(String args[])
   {
    // Query values of all Parameters
    String param;
    // Frodo: Parameter description
    param = GetParameter(PARAM_Frodo, args);
       if (param != null)
          m_Frodo = param;
    }
```

If you wanted, you could easily display the value of the Frodo parameter:

```
g.drawString( m_Frodo, 50, 25 );
```

(For this to work, `g` must have been instantiated as a graphics object.)

Of course, to test this, you would have to add a value to the related HTML tag:

```
<hr>
<applet
    code=jjive.class
    id=jjive
    width=320
    height=240 >
    <param name=Frodo value="A Big Brown Bear who likes his java!">
</applet>
```

Figure 18-14 shows the results when you open the HTML.

Figure 18-14: You can use <APPLET> parameters in your applet; a parameter }value is displayed here.

Here's the code created with the author and copyright information entered in the Wizard:

```
public String getAppletInfo()
    {
    return "Name: jjive\r\n" +
           "Author: A Big Brown Bear who likes his java!\r\n" +
           "Created with Microsoft Visual J++ Version 1.0";
}
```

Here's the template code added for the mouseDown event:

```
public boolean mouseDown(Event evt, int x, int y)
    {
     // TODO: Place applet mouseDown code here
     return true;
     }
```

Adding a Class

You can use the Create New Class dialog shown in Figure 18-15 to add a class to your project.

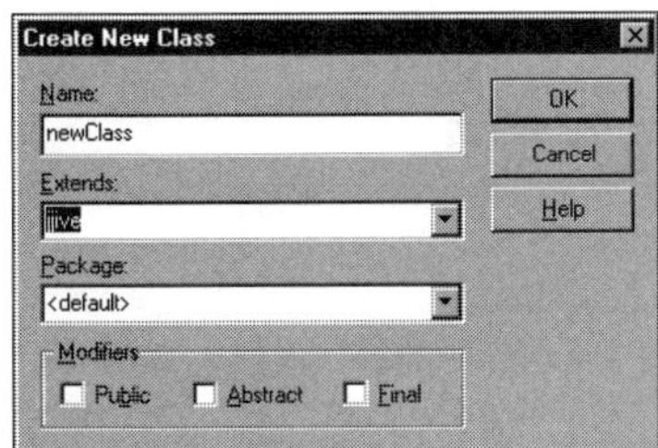

Figure 18-15: You can use the Create New Class dialog to add a class to your project.

You open the Create New Class dialog either by choosing New Java Class from the Insert menu or by using the context menu with a class selected in the Class view pane.

Figure 18-16 shows the jjive class structure with a new class added in the Class view pane.

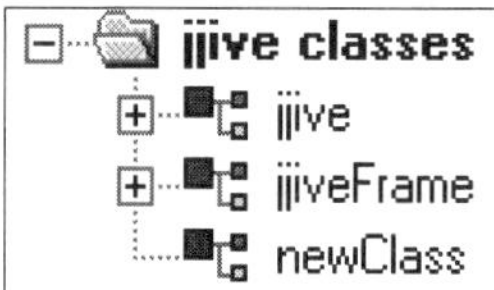

Figure 18-16: The hierarchy shown in Class view includes the newly added class.

Here's the code added to the project for newClass based on the selections in the Create New Class dialog:

```
import jjive;

/*
 *
 * newClass
 *
 */
class newClass extends jjive
{


}
```

Of course, there's no real need for fancy dialogs to add simple template code. If you prefer, you can just add it by hand by entering the code in a text file saved with the class name and inserting it in your project.

Adding a Method

You can use the Add Method dialog — shown in Figure 18-17 — to add a method to a class. To open the Add Method dialog, select the class that you want to add a method to in the Class view hierarchy. Choose Add Method from the context menu.

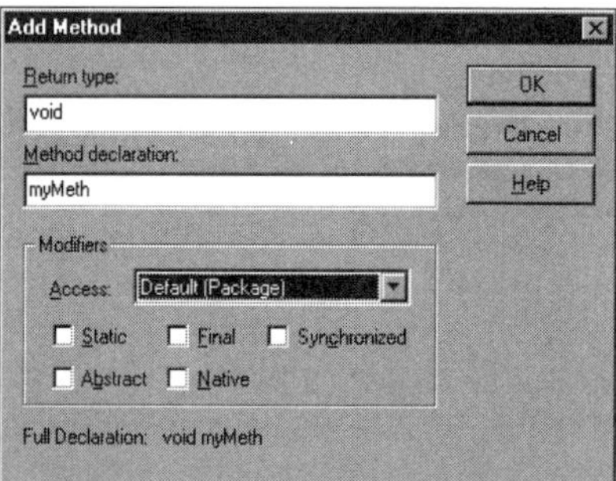

Figure 18-17: You can use the Add Method dialog to add a method to a class.

The function created by the Add Method dialog depends on your entries in the dialog. With the selections shown in Figure 18-17, here's the code that it adds:

```
void myMeth()
    {
    }
```

As with a class declaration, you could obviously add this code by hand if you preferred.

Adding a Variable

Adding a variable to a class works much like adding a method. You can select the Add Variable dialog (shown in Figure 18-18) from the Class view's context menu, as long as you have a particular class selected.

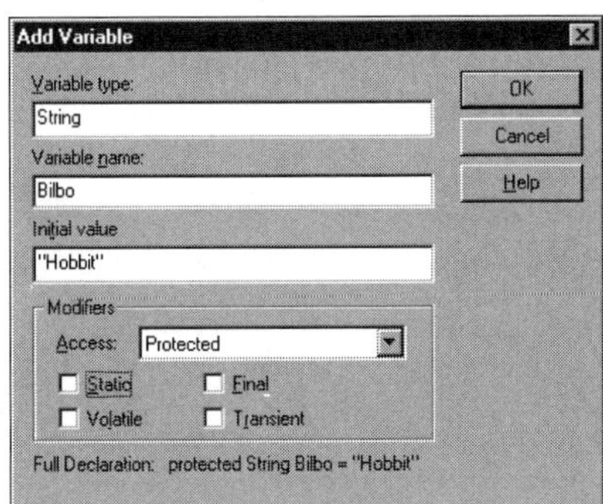

Figure 18-18: You can use the Add Variable dialog to add a variable to a class.

A declaration along these lines is added to the top of the selected class:

```
protected String Bilbo = "Hobbit";
```

Dialogs and Menus

In Visual C++, the user interface — dialogs and menus — are loaded from special resource files. These resource files are separate from the source code files. On the other hand, in Java, menus and dialogs must be created in the source code using classes and methods that are part of the Abstract Window Toolkit (AWT). (For more information on AWT, see Chapter 17.)

Visual J++ provides tools and techniques that constitute a bridge between these two worlds. To add user interface elements to a Java applet created in Visual J++, follow this procedure:

1. Design and create the dialogs and menus using the resource editors supplied with Developer Studio. Save the interface elements in a resource template (.Rct) file.

2. Run the Java Resource Wizard — accessed via the Tools menu — to convert the resource template into AWT-based elements. (You can also convert existing resource (.Res) files — perhaps created for use with a VC++ program — using the Wizard.)
3. Add code to your Java applet to implement the user interface items.

Creating the User Interface

To try this out, run the Java Applet Wizard to create the framework code for an applet. Make sure not to allow the program to run as an application and not to enable support for animation. (The sample applet project that is used in this section is saved on the companion CD-ROM as MenuR.)

Next, create the resource template file that the Resource Wizard will use as input by choosing New from the File menu and choosing Resource Template. From the Insert menu, choose Resource. The Insert Resource dialog appears, as shown in Figure 18-19.

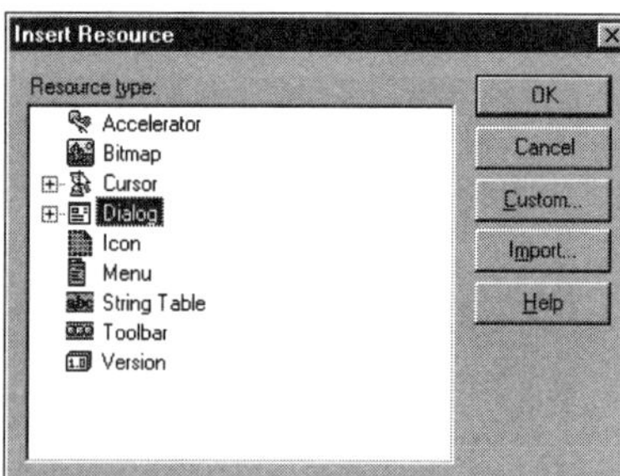

Figure 18-19: You use the Insert Resource dialog to add dialogs and menus to a resource template.

If you choose Dialog and click on OK, the dialog editing window appears, as shown in Figure 18-20.

Press Alt+Enter to open the property page for the dialog so you can change the ID (name) of the dialog. The ID in the demo applet is IDD_MyDialog. Add an edit box (sometimes called a text box), a static text control (sometimes called a label), and a command button to the dialog (see Figure 18-20).

You can add controls from your Toolbox to the dialog, but only controls that have an AWT analog will work in Java. Furthermore, controls that are converted to Java do not always function in exactly the same way as when they are placed on an ActiveX container.

Table 18-1 shows the controls that the Resource Wizard can successfully convert to Java.

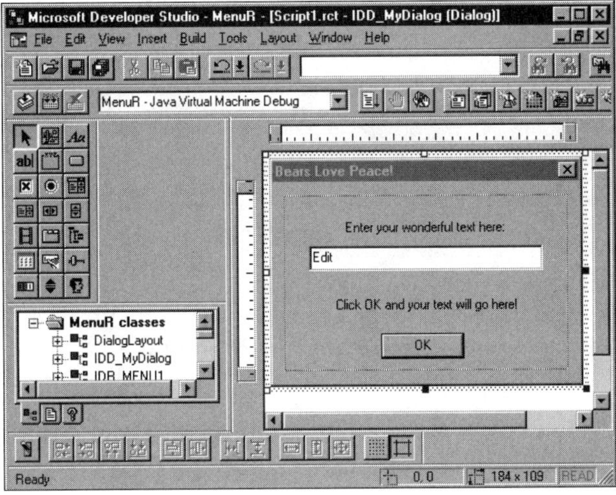

Figure 18-20: You use the dialog editing window to create the appearance of dialogs.

Table 18-1 Developer Studio Dialog Controls Supported by the Java Resource Wizard

Windows Resource	*Java Component (java.awt.*)*
Static Text control (Label)	Label class
Edit Box control (Text Box)	TextField class (or TextArea for multiline edit controls)
Button control	Button class
Check Box control	Checkbox class
Radio Button control	Checkbox (Resource Wizard generates and adds the control to a CheckboxGroup member)
List Box control	List class
Combo Box control	Choice class
Horizontal Scrollbar control	Scrollbar class (Resource Wizard sets the HORIZONTAL property)
Vertical Scrollbar control	Scrollbar class (Resource Wizard sets the VERTICAL property)

Once you have created the dialog to your satisfaction, close the dialog editing window, and use the Insert Resource dialog to create a menu. Create a menu with a few items on it captioned any way you'd like, as shown in Figure 18-21.

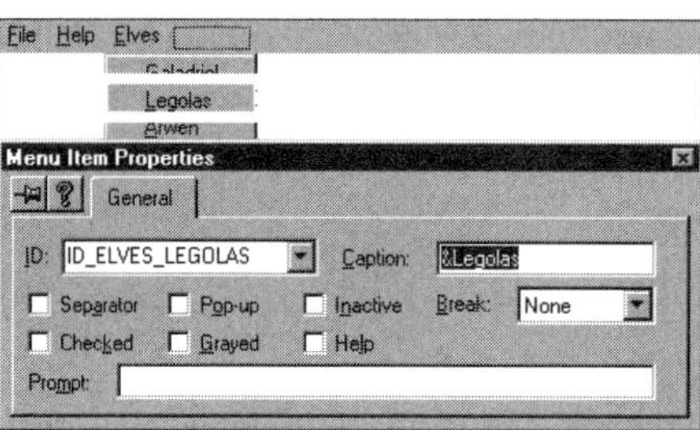

Figure 18-21: You use the Menu Editor to create menu resources.

Close the Menu Editor, and save the resource template file in the project directory. (The sample resource template file on the CD-ROM is named Script1.Rct.)

Running the Java Resource Wizard

The next step is to run the Java Resource Wizard, which you start from the Tools menu. The Resource Wizard first asks you to specify a resource file to convert (.Rct or .Res file). The second Wizard panel shows you the files it is going to create and their Java class names (see Figure 18-22). You can change the class names at this point if you'd like.

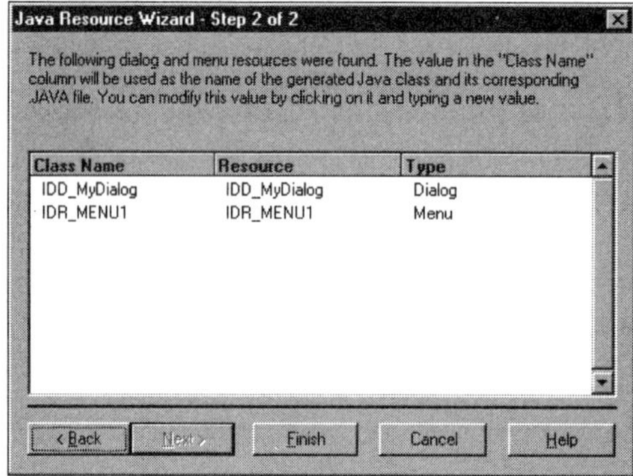

Figure 18-22: The Java Resource Wizard lets you change the class names it will use for your resources.

When you click on Finish, you'll see a dialog — shown in Figure 18-23 — listing the files that the Resource Wizard successfully created.

You can verify that these files have been added to your project using the File view pane in Developer Studio, as shown in Figure 18-24.

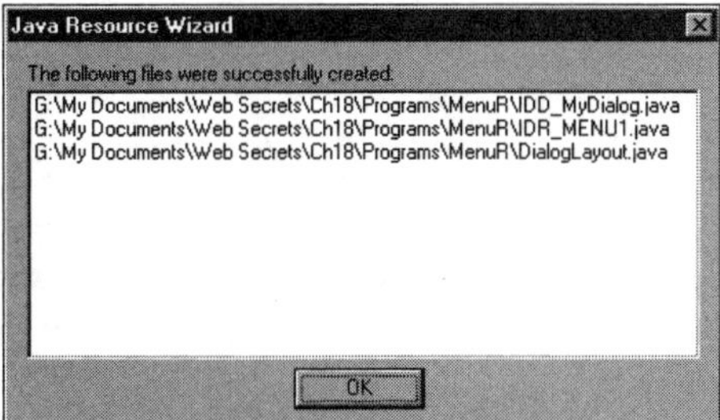

Figure 18-23: The Java Resource Wizard concludes with a list of the files it has successfully created.

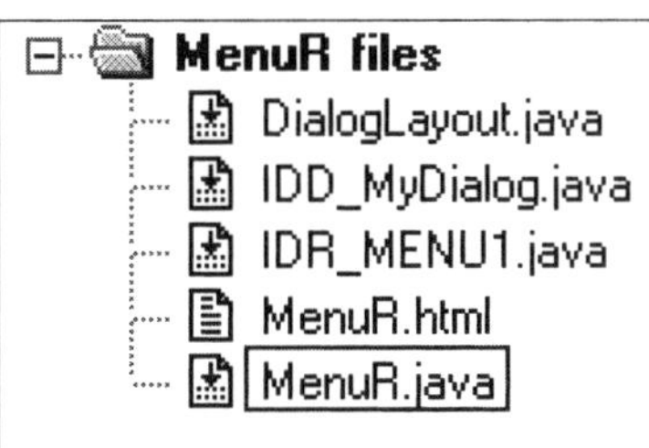

Figure 18-24: Files that the Java R esource Wizard added to a project appear in Developer Studio's File view pane.

For each dialog or menu in the resource template, the Java Resource Wizard creates a .java file containing a class whose name is the ID of the dialog or menu. In addition, when there are dialogs in the resource template, the Wizard creates a separate file for a DialogLayout class, which is used by the dialogs to manage the layout of controls.

The creators of Visual J++ assumed that developers would not modify the source code of the class files generated by the Wizard. Without speaking to the merits of this assumption, you should know that the easiest way to make changes to a dialog or menu is probably not to modify the Java source code. You can, instead, use the Menu and Dialog Editors and save the changes to the resource template file. Next, run the Resource Wizard to generate new Java class files.

Each time you run Resource Wizard, it overwrites the previous version of the source files it has created. As a result, any manual changes you make to the generated source code will be lost if you decide to run the Resource Wizard again.

Implementing the User Interface

In the Java AWT, user-interface controls can be placed on a variety of containers, such as panels, applets, windows, and dialogs. Because dialogs are not the only kind of container, the Resource Wizard does not generate a class derived from the AWT's Dialog class. Instead, a class is created that adds controls to an arbitrary container to make it resemble the dialog template. This way you can use Visual J++'s Dialog Editor to design the appearance not just of dialogs, but also of applets, panels, or windows.

The class generated by the Resource Wizard has two methods: a constructor that takes a Container object as an argument, and a CreateControls method. Resource Wizard also generates a class named DialogLayout, which implements the AWT LayoutManager interface. This class is a custom layout manager that allows the position of controls to be specified in the same way that Windows resource files do.

Inside Scoop

The files created by the Resource Wizard must be added to the project that will use them. Use the Files Into Project command on the Insert menu. (The example files generated by the Wizard are DialogLayout.java, IDD_MyDialog.java, and IDD_MENU1.java.)

Adding Dialogs

To use the dialogs in a Java applet, you'll have to add code that will reference the new classes. Open the applet source file (MenuR.java). Add the following import statement to the beginning of the file:

```
import IDD_MyDialog;
```

Near the beginning of the applet declaration, after the declaration of the Thread variable, add the following line:

```
IDD_MyDialog dlg;
```

In the applet's init method add the following lines:

```
dlg = new IDD_MyDialog( this );
dlg.CreateControls();
```

The first line allocates an instance of the IDD_MyDialog class, passing the this pointer to the constructor, which specifies the applet as the container. The second line calls the CreateControls method, which adds all the controls in the class to the applet.

Delete the line

```
g.drawString("Running: " + Math.random(), 10, 20);
```

from the applet's paint method.

At the bottom of the applet's source code, just before the final curly bracket (}), add the following code:

```
public boolean action( Event evt, Object arg )
{
   if ( evt.target instanceof Button )
   {
      String val = dlg.IDC_MyText.getText();
      dlg.IDC_STATIC1.setText( val );
      return true;
   }
   return false;
}
```

The action method responds to events generated by controls. In this example, the method checks whether the event's target was a Button object. (Because the dialog in this example has only one button, it's not necessary to test which button was clicked.) If so, the method reads the value of the TextField object (with the ID set to IDC_MyText) and uses it to set the value of the Label object (ID set to IDC_STATIC1). The names of the TextField and Label objects are the IDs originally set in the Developer Studio Dialog Editor.

Save the revised source code, and compile and run the project by choosing Execute from the Build menu. The applet loads, as shown in Figure 18-25. Whatever text is entered in the edit control is used as the caption of the label when the user clicks on OK.

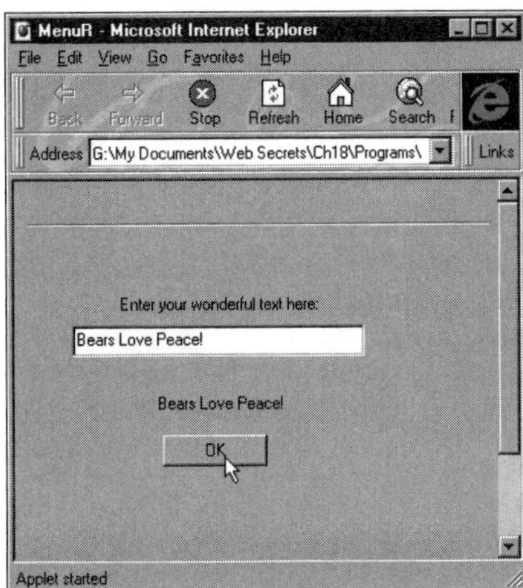

Figure 18-25: Dialogs converted by the Java Resource Wizard can easily be integrated into Java applets.

Adding Menus

In the Java AWT, menus must appear within a frame, described by the AWT's Frame class. The Resource Wizard generates a class that adds menus to a frame. This "menu creator" class generated by Resource Wizard has two methods: a constructor that takes a Frame object as an argument and a CreateMenu method. To implement the menu created in the Developer Studio editor, add an import statement to the beginning of the MenuR source code:

```
import IDR_MENU1;
```

Next, after the declaration of IDD_MyDialog, add the following lines to declare variables for using the IDR_MENU1 class:

```
IDR_MENU1 menu;
MyFrame frame;
```

In the init method, after the lines that create the dialog, add code as follows:

```
frame = new MyFrame( "Show that menu!" );
frame.resize( 100, 100 );
menu = new IDR_MENU1( frame );
```

```
menu.CreateMenu();
frame.show();
```

The MyFrame class will be defined in a moment. This code declares an instance of MyFrame, specifies it as the frame for an instance of the IDR_MENU1 class, initializes the menus, and displays the frame window.

The MyFrame class definition goes at the end of the applet's code, after the conclusion of the MenuR class definition (in other words, after the last curly brace):

```
class MyFrame extends Frame
{
    String text = new String(" ");
    MyFrame(String title)
        {
        super(title);
        }
    public void paint(Graphics g)
        {
        g.drawString(text, 10, 10);
        }
    public boolean action( Event evt, Object obj )
        {
        Object target = evt.target;
        if (target instanceof MenuItem)
        {
            text = (String)obj;
            repaint();
            return true;
        }
        return false;
    }
}
```

The MyFrame class extends the Frame class and declares a String variable. The override of the paint method displays the value of this string. The override of the action method responds to events generated within the frame. The method checks whether the event's target was a MenuItem object. If so, the method sets the text variable to the label of the menu item that was chosen, which is passed in the obj parameter. The method's action serves to display the caption of a menu when the menu item is selected by the user, as shown in Figure 18-26.

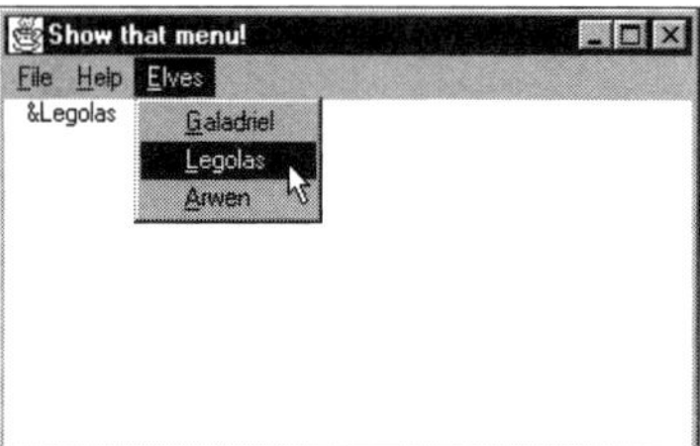

Figure 18-26: You can intercept menu events by overriding the action method of the menu's frame.

Note that the menu displays in its own frame after the applet loads. If you launched the MenuR applet from an HTML page, the menu frame would display a caption identifying it as a Java applet window, as shown in Figure 18-27.

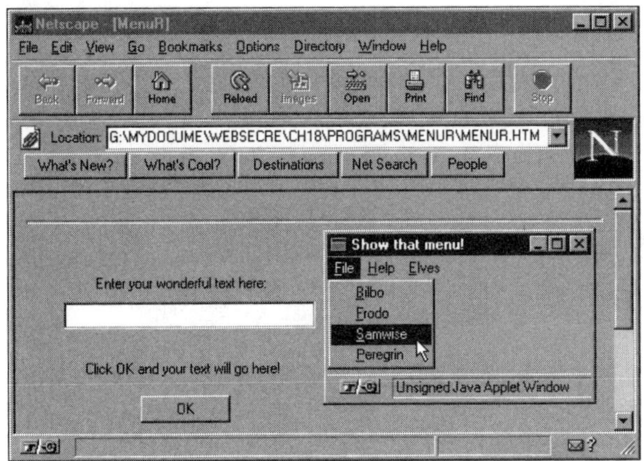

Figure 18-27: The frame containing the menu displays as a separate applet window.

Follow the Bouncing Ball

The Java Applet Wizard creates a code framework for your Visual J++ application. But, of course, you don't have to use it. Here's a sample Java project — the Java source code file is saved as mouseball.java and the J++ project file as Mouseball.Mdp — that J++ compiles to make a sort of proto-pinball game. The object is to hit the red ball by clicking on it. Of course, the object for the red ball is to not get hit! Figure 18-28 shows the mouseball applet "in action."

The source code imports java.lang.math so that it has access to a randomizer:

```
import java.awt.*;
import java.applet.*;
import java.lang.Math;
```

The paint method of the applet draws the ball and background using the methods of the Java graphics object. The location of the ball is picked at random:

```
public void paint(Graphics g) {
   g.drawRect(0, 0, size().width - 1, size().height - 1);
   g.setColor(Color.blue);
   g.fillRect(0, 0, size().width - 1, size().height - 1);
   mx = (int)(Math.random()*1000) % (size().width -
      (size().width/10));
```

```
    my = (int)(Math.random()*1000) % (size().height -
       (size().height/10));
    g.setColor(Color.black);
    g.drawOval(mx, my, (size().width/10) - 1,
       (size().height/10) - 1);
    g.setColor(Color.red);
    g.fillOval(mx, my, (size().width/10) - 1,
       (size().height/10) - 1);
}
```

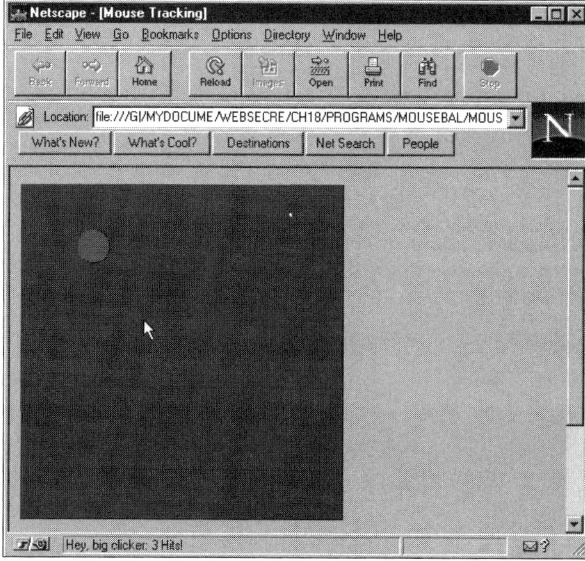

Figure 18-28: The idea of the mouseball applet is to click on the ball.

The mouseMove method uses the Java modulo operator (%) to make sure that the ball gets away some of the time:

```
public boolean mouseMove(java.awt.Event evt, int x, int y) {
     if((x % 3 == 0) && (y % 3 == 0))
        repaint();
     return true;
   }
```

The mouseDown method checks whether the user "got" the ball. An appropriate sound is played. (The getCodeBase method returns the current location of the applet.) The getAppletContext().showStatus method is used to add wise-guy comments to the browser's status bar:

```
public boolean mouseDown(java.awt.Event evt, int x, int y) {
     requestFocus();
     if((mx < x && x < mx+size().width/10-1) &&
      (my < y && y < my+size().height/10-1)) {
        if(onaroll > 0) {
```

```
            switch(onaroll%3) {
            case 0:
               play(getCodeBase(), "sounds/s1.au");
               break;
            case 1:
               play(getCodeBase(), "sounds/s2.au");
               break;
            case 2:
               play(getCodeBase(), "sounds/s3.au");
               break;
            }
            onaroll++;
            if(onaroll > 5)
               getAppletContext().showStatus(
               "You're on your way to THE JAVA BALL HALL OF FAME:"
                  + onaroll + "Hits!");
            else
               getAppletContext().showStatus
               ("Hey, big clicker: " + onaroll + " Hits!");
         }
         else {
            getAppletContext().showStatus("Do it one more time!");
            play(getCodeBase(), "sounds/s2.au");
            onaroll = 1;
         }
      }
      else {
         getAppletContext().showStatus("Try again! Nothing hit at ("
+
          x + ", " + y + "), exactly\n");
         play(getCodeBase(), "sounds/s1.au");
         onaroll = 0;
    }
repaint();
return true;
}
```

Java and Com

The Java Virtual Machine (VM) that is implemented in Internet Explorer supports integration between Java and the Component Object Model (COM), which is the protocol underlying ActiveX and Object Linking and Embedding (OLE).

To take full advantage of both Java and COM, you must use a development tool that supports this integration. Using Visual J++, you can give your Java program access to any of the software components that support COM, including thousands of ActiveX controls and ActiveX components.

This section discusses the following topics:

- Scripting a Java applet
- Using a COM object from Java

- Connecting a Java applet and an ActiveX control
- Exposing a Java applet as an ActiveX server

Scripting

Chapters 10, 11, and 12 explained how to embed ActiveX controls in Web pages and control them using VBScript. When a Java applet is running in Internet Explorer, all the public methods and variables of the applet automatically become available to VBScript. For example, take a Java applet with two methods, setText and resetText. (The source is saved as displaytext.class in the Script folder on the CD-ROM.) The setText method displays text passed as parameter, and resetText displays the original value:

```
public void setText(String string)
   {
   // set the display string
   m_phrase = string;
   // get the size of the display string
   Font font = getFont();
   Graphics g = getGraphics();
   g.setFont(font);
   FontMetrics fm = g.getFontMetrics();
   int height = fm.getHeight();
   int width = fm.stringWidth(m_phrase);

   // center the string (or left justify if it is too long)
   Dimension dim = size();
   m_x = ( dim.width - width) / 2;
   if (m_x < 0) m_x = 0;
   m_y = ( dim.height + height ) / 2
      - fm.getLeading() - fm.getDescent() / 2;
   if (m_y > dim.height) m_x = dim.height;
   // force a repaint of the applet
   repaint();
       }

    // Reset the display text to the initial value
    public void resetText()
    {
       setText(m_initialValue);
    }
```

To include such an applet in an HTML page, simply use the <APPLET> tag, assigning an ID attribute so that you can refer to the applet from the scripting language:

```
<APPLET
   code=displaytext.class
   id=TextDisplay
   width=600
   height=120 >
   <PARAM name=initialValue value="Make it so!">
</APPLET>
```

You can then define some controls that allow the user to control the applet. For example:

```
<INPUT name=Phrase value="Enter new text">
<INPUT type=button name=Set value="Set Display Text">
<INPUT type=button name=Reset value="Reset to Initial Value">
```

You can use the name attribute to refer to each control from the scripting language. In the scripting portion of your HTML page, you can define OnClick handlers for each button, making them manipulate the applet:

```
<script language=VBScript>
<!--
' Handle the click event for the Set button
sub Set_OnClick
   ' Call the applet setText method,
   ' with the value in the Phrase <input> box
   document.TextDisplay.setText Phrase.value
end sub

' Handle the click event for the Reset button
sub Reset_OnClick
   ' Call the applet resetText method
   document.TextDisplay.resetText
end sub
-->
</script>
```

Inside Scoop

When an applet is referenced from VBScript, its name — the ID assigned in the <APPLET> tag — is preceded with the identifier "document."

When a user clicks on a button on the Web page, the appropriate VB Script handler is invoked, which in turn manipulates the Java applet, as shown in Figure 18-29. The script can read and write the public variables of the applet, as well as call its public methods (including passing parameters and reading return values).

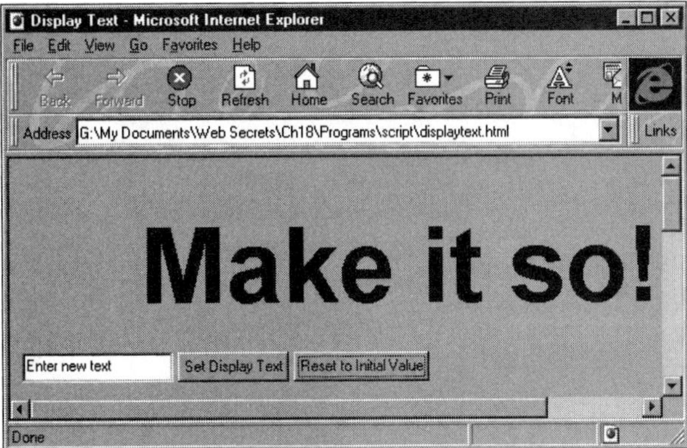

Figure 18-29: You can use VBScript to control Java applets in the same way that ActiveX controls are scripted.

Using a COM Object from Java

Using Visual J++, you can refer to COM objects — ActiveX controls and components — directly from your Java source code. Before you can use a COM class in Java, you must import it. To do this, you must create a Java class that represents the COM class from the viewpoint of Java. Essentially, the Java class is a wrapper for the exposed members of the COM object. The Visual J++ Java Type Library Wizard is a tool designed to automate this process.

Type libraries are a mechanism defined by COM to store type information; each type library contains complete type information about one or more COM entities, including its classes and interfaces. Each .class file generated by the Java Type Library Wizard contains a special attribute identifying it as a wrapper for a COM class. When the Java Support in Internet Explorer sees this attribute on a class, it translates all Java method invocations on the class into COM function invocations on the COM class.

To import a COM class for use in Java, choose Java Type Library Wizard from the Tools menu. The Java Type Library Wizard module displays all the type libraries registered on your machine, as shown in Figure 18-30.

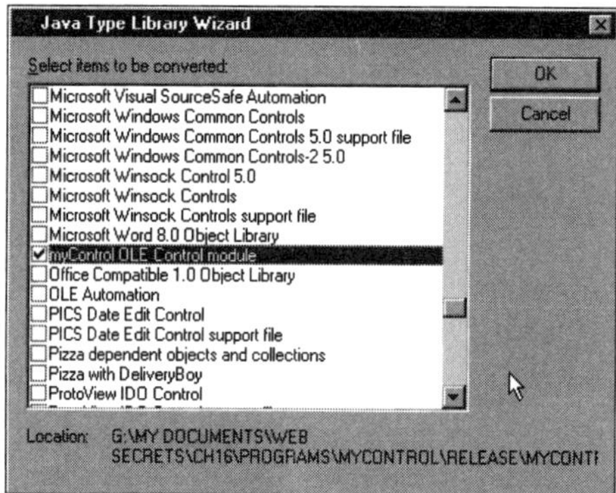

Figure 18-30: The Java Type Library Wizard displays all type libraries registered on your machine.

This list is generated using the entries beneath the \HKEY_CLASSES_ROOT\TypeLib key of the system registry.

Select the type library or libraries that describe the COM objects you'd like to convert, and click on OK. In the Output window, the Type Library Wizard prints the import statement(s) appropriate for each package it has created. You can use these import statements in your Java source code.

The Type Library Wizard also displays the complete path of a newly created file named Summary.Txt. By double-clicking on this line, you can open the text file in Developer Studio. This file lists the Java signatures of all the methods for the COM interfaces and classes described by the type library. You can call these methods from your Java program.

Connecting a Java Applet and an ActiveX Control

You can have a Java applet interact with an ActiveX control that resides on the same HTML page, using a combination of the techniques described earlier in this chapter.

There are two different ways of connecting a Java applet with an ActiveX control:

- You can forward events to the applet. This allows the applet to respond to events fired by the control. A Java applet cannot directly receive events fired by an ActiveX control. However, you can define VBScript methods that handle events fired by the control. These methods can then, in turn, call methods of the Java applet, as described earlier in this chapter in the section "Scripting."
- You can have the applet invoke control methods or set control properties. You do this by passing the control to the Java applet, using the techniques described in "Using a COM Object from Java."

You can use both types of connection to establish two-way communication between the applet and the control.

You cannot embed an ActiveX control directly into a Java applet the way you embed an AWT class. However, you can have your HTML page pass the ActiveX control as a parameter to a Java method and have your Java applet use it that way.

For your Java applet to know how to use an ActiveX control, you must first use the Java Type Library Wizard to import the ActiveX control — that is, to generate .class files that expose the control's functionality to Java programs.

In your Java source code, you should use one or more import statements to allow convenient references to the package associated with the OLE control. For example, if you had run the Java Type Library Wizard on the Msoutl32.Ocx control, you would use statements like this:

```
import msoutl32.*;
import olepro32.*;
```

There are two import statements because the type library inside Msoutl32.Ocx itself contains an importlib statement.

Then in your Java applet, define a public method that takes an Object as a parameter. For example:

```
public OutlineUser extends Applet
{
   // IOutlineCtrl interface defined in package MSOUTL32
   IOutlineCtrl m_outlineCtrl;
   public void setCtrl(Object oc)
   {
      m_outlineCtrl = (IOutlineCtrl)oc;
   }
```

```
    // other methods
    // ...
}
```

The setCtrl method casts the object to the IOutlineCtrl interface and stores a reference to that object. Because this method is public, it's accessible to the VBScript portion of the HTML page in which the applet resides. A VBScript function will use this function to pass an OLE control to the applet.

Once your Java applet has a reference to the object, in the form of an appropriate interface, you can call methods on the outline control. For example:

```
public String getText()
{
    return m_outlineCtrl.getText();
}
```

This Java method retrieves a property from the outline control.

Preparing the Java applet to receive the control is only half the work involved in letting the applet drive an ActiveX control. The other half is passing the control from VBScript.

First, add the ActiveX control to your HTML page using the <OBJECT> tag, as described in Chapters 11 and 12. Use the ID parameter of the <OBJECT> tag to provide a way to refer to the control, for example, ID="Outline1".

Then insert the Java applet on the HTML page using a tag like this:

```
<APPLET Code="OutlineUser.class" Name=user>
```

The ID parameter lets you refer to the applet using VBScript.

In the VBScript portion of your HTML page, define a window_onLoad function that passes a reference to the OLE control to the Java applet. For example:

```
<SCRIPT language="VBScript">
<!--
sub window_onLoad
    document.user.SetCtrl Outline1
end sub
-->
</SCRIPT>
```

The window_onLoad function is called as soon as the HTML page has finished loading. The VBScript code causes a reference to the outline control to be passed to the Java applet's setCtrl method. From that point forward, the Java applet can manipulate the outline control.

By both passing the control to the Java applet and forwarding events from the control to the applet, it's possible to establish two-way communication between the control and the applet.

Signing Applets

The cab&sign directory on the Visual J++ CD-ROM contains two tools: CabDevKit.Exe and CodeSignKit.Exe. Both of these are self-extracting executables that install the tools and documentation needed to, respectively, create a Cabinet (Cab) file, used for Internet download, and digitally sign a file.

These executables are not installed by the Visual J++ setup program. You need to copy them into their own directories and run them to extract their respective tool kits.

Exposing Java Applets as COM Objects

Besides allowing Java programs to use COM objects, the Java Support in Internet Explorer also allows Java programs to expose their functionality as COM services. This lets you use Java for developing component software without requiring that your clients use Java; your clients can use any language that is compatible with COM, such as Microsoft Visual Basic or C++.

To create your own COM object in Java, you must first write the COM object's Object Description Language (ODL) definition. This is a text file containing a description of the object's interface. ODL scripts are compiled into type libraries using the MkTypLib tool that is included with the ActiveX SDK. Next, you implement your object just like any other Java class.

When your code is compiled, Visual J++ realizes that the class is really a COM object because it finds the ODL file and automatically generates a Windows Dll with class factory and DllCreateClass() member functions and other required methods.

There's an excellent sample demonstration of creating COM components in Java on the Visual J++ CD-ROM in the Samples\Microsoft\COMCallingJava folder. The samples even include a Visual Basic client program.

The Microsoft Java SDK

The Microsoft Java SDK Version 1.5 includes many tools and utilities that are new or improved for this version:

- The Navigator Plugin utility lets you develop Java applications or applets that take advantage of the Microsoft VM for Java inside released versions of the Netscape Navigator browser.
- Cabarc.Exe is a compression utility for packaging Java applications and classes for Web distribution. Cabarc is a single tool for creating, viewing, and extracting cabinets and doesn't require complex scripts to create cabinets. It also supports wildcards and subdirectories.

- Script Debugger for Internet Explorer is the latest prerelease build of the script debugger, supported by the Microsoft VM for Java in this SDK. It allows developers using Internet Explorer to debug Java, JScript, VBScript, and HTML.
- JVC.Exe is the latest version of the Java compiler, which will be officially released with Microsoft Visual J++ 1.1.
- Javatlb.Exe is a utility to convert Ocx-type library files into Java classes; it will be released with the version of Microsoft Visual J++ 1.1.
- NT Service Package is a new set of Java classes that allows developers to write NT services in Java.
- AppletViewer.Exe is the Java applet viewer with internationalization enabled.
- ClassVue.Exe is a Java application designed to help developers to view and debug classes.
- Jexegen.Exe is a new version of a tool that converts stand-alone Java application into native executable binaries.

If you are interested in Java development — particularly with Visual J++ — make sure that you have Version 1.5 of the Microsoft Java SDK. You can download it from *http://www.microsoft.com/java/*.

Summary

Visual J++ is an industrial-strength Java development environment that uses the Microsoft's Developer Studio interface. It's a good choice for professional Java development for Web applications. If you want your Java applications to speak COM, the underlying protocol of ActiveX and much of Windows, Visual J++ is the only possible choice.

Topics covered in this chapter included

- Creating a simple applet in Visual J++
- Creating a stand-alone application in VJ++
- Using the Java Applet Wizard
- Code generated by the Applet Wizard
- Adding a class
- Adding a method
- Adding a variable
- Creating dialogs and menus
- The Java Resource Wizard
- Implementing the user interface
- Java and COM

- Scripting Java applets
- Using a COM object from Java
- The Java Type Library Wizard
- Connecting a Java applet and an ActiveX control
- Exposing a Java applet as a COM object
- What's new in version 1.5 of Microsoft's Java SDK

Chapter 19

Visual Café

"When I use a word," Humpty Dumpty said, in rather a scornful tone, "it means just what I choose it to mean — neither more nor less."

"The question is," said Alice, "whether you can make words mean so many different things."

"The question is," said Humpty Dumpty, "which is to be master, that's all."

— Lewis Carroll, *Through the Looking Glass*

Symantec Visual Café is a form-based Java development environment. This visual IDE is so easy to use that you can add event-handling code — termed "interactions" in Visual Café — without any programming. It's a complete snap in Visual Café to create powerful Java applets that add significant executable content to any Web site.

Visual Café is probably the best advanced development environment intended solely for Java programming on the 32-bit Windows platforms. However, the documentation that ships with the product is on the slim side. Fortunately, the environment is so intuitive that if you read this chapter you'll quickly be up to speed.

You can obtain Symantec product information from their Web site, *http://www.symantec.com*. The URL for Symantec's technical library on Java and Visual Café is *http://www.symantec.com/lit/dev/javaindex.html*.

Visual Café Versus Visual J++

Obviously, the choice of a programming environment is personal to each developer. As they say, there is no arguing one way or another with personal taste.

Visual J++ is Microsoft's powerful Java development IDE, discussed in detail in Chapter 18. It is incorporated in the Developer Studio environment used by Visual C++ and some other Microsoft development tools. If you are already familiar with Developer Studio, this is probably a Very Good Thing that will make life easier for you. On the other hand, if you don't know Developer Studio, Visual Café is almost certainly a more intuitive development environment, looking much like Rapid Application Development (RAD) tools such as Visual Basic or Delphi.

In Visual Café, as in most good RAD development environments, if you have some programming background you can start knocking out decent Java applets and applications in a matter of hours — if not minutes.

Inside Scoop

A word of caution is that Visual Café is not yet fully stable in this version. There seem to be some bugs involving synchronizing code between forms and code modules, and it's easy to lose code by mistake. No doubt subsequent releases will fix these minor problems. In the meantime, a word to the wise is to make frequent redundant backups of your work, particularly if you enter code by hand.

As technology columnist Nicholas Petreley has put it, "Visual Café continues to emulate a stereotypical Hollywood female spy: It's beautiful but treacherous."

It's worth noting that if your Java program needs to work with COM objects — for example, ActiveX controls — you should program in Visual J++. Visual J++ is the only Java programming environment that lets you work with COM objects, and it is the best choice for applications that will integrate with Windows.

Visual Café, on the other hand, comes in a Mac OS version as well as a 32-bit Windows version. It's likely that discrepancies between the Windows and Mac implementations of Java will be minimized if you develop in Visual Café.

The Visual Café IDE

The Visual Café development environment will seem familiar to anyone who has programmed in a visual development environment. Figure 19-1 shows the important elements of the Visual Café IDE.

The Visual Café window is the application's main interface. Closing it closes Visual Café. This main window includes menus, toolbars, and a Component Palette. The Palette contains a variety of Java components — visual objects, program modules, and form templates — that you can add to forms by clicking on the component and "drawing" it on the form.

The Form Designer is a visual tool for designing the appearance of your applet or application. This tool will be familiar to users of form-based development environments such as Delphi, Power Builder, or Visual Basic.

You use the Project window to create and manipulate the objects that make up an applet. This window has two panels:

- The Objects panel, which corresponds to a class view
- The Packages panel, which corresponds to a file view

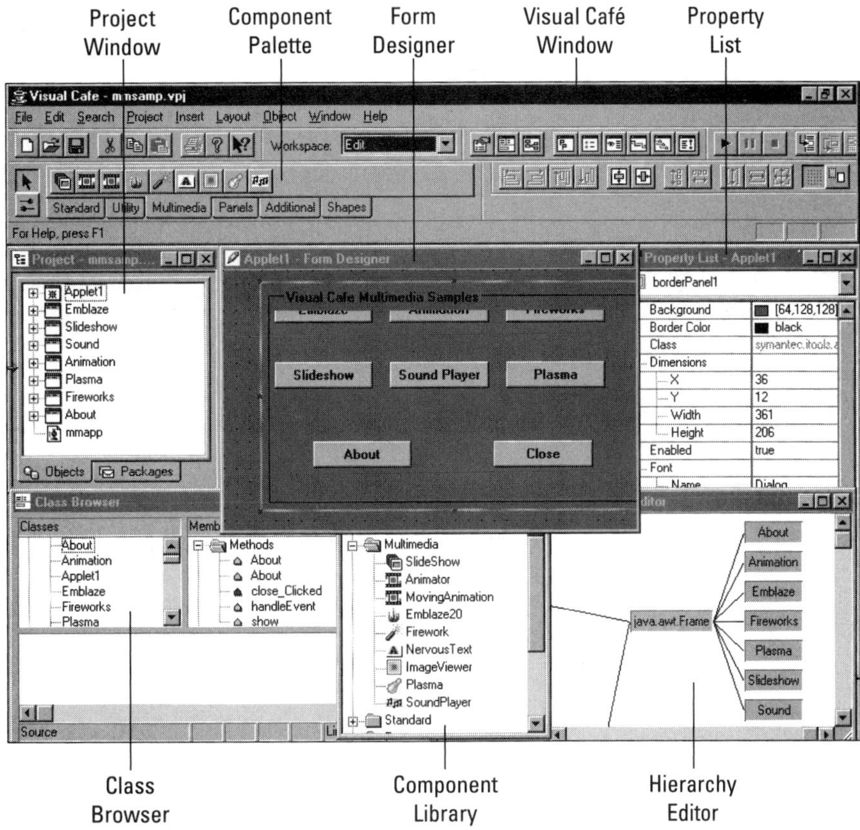

Figure 19-1: The Visual Café IDE will seem familiar to programmers who have worked in Visual development environments.

By using the context menu within the Project window, you can easily access important programming functionality. For example, you can open the Code window with the source code for a particular object loaded, or you can start the Interaction Wizard (for a description of the Interaction Wizard, see "A Simple Café Applet" later in this chapter).

The Class Browser — shown in Figure 19-2 — has three panes that list the classes in your project and the methods and members of each class. You can use the Class Browser to quickly navigate, edit, and add classes. In the Class Browser, you only see the methods and members for the selected class, and only the Java code for the selected member. This represents a different way of adding and editing source code than looking at the code belonging to an entire module in one lump. The Class Browser is a great tool for programming in an object-oriented fashion.

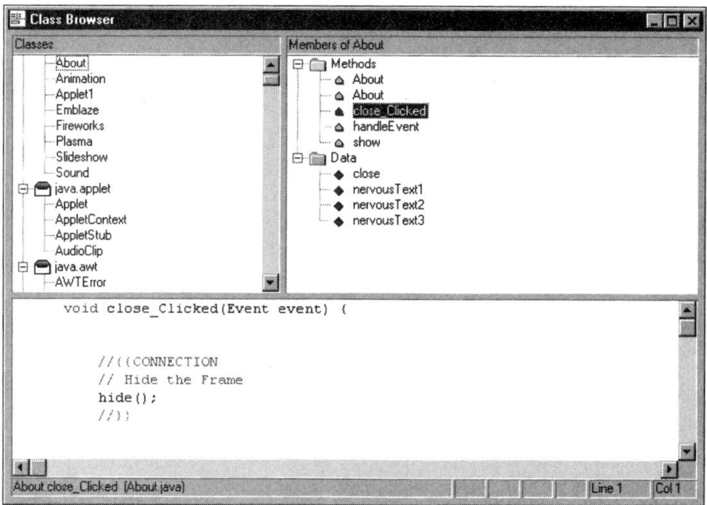

Figure 19-2: You can use the Class Browser as an object-oriented programming tool.

The Component Library, shown in Figure 19-3, is used to store, organize, and display project objects. The library can contain forms, windows, Visual Café components, third-party components, and applets that are accessible from all projects.

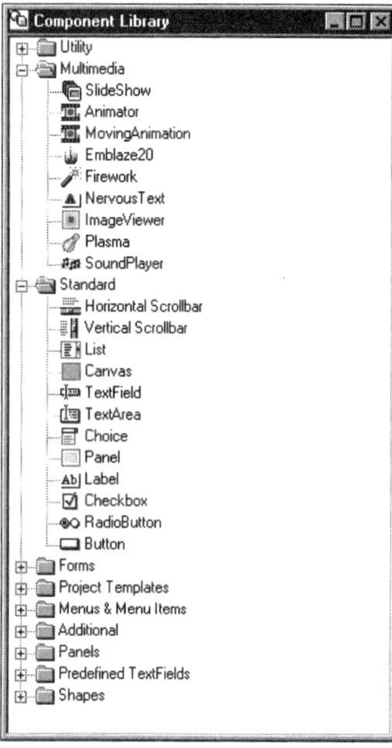

Figure 19-3: You can browse the Component Library to obtain information about Visual Café objects.

The Hierarchy Editor, shown in Figure 19-4, allows you to visually navigate and edit the relationships between the Java classes in your project. The editor displays a visual representation of the project's current classes and the classes that they inherit from. Changes you make here to classes or inheritance relationships are automatically changed in the underlying source code and in all open windows in the Visual Cafe environment.

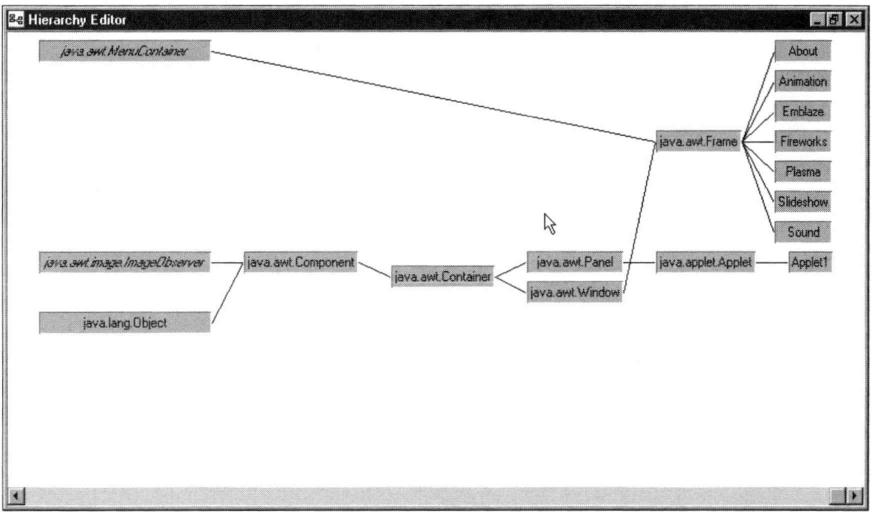

Figure 19-4: The Hierarchy Editor allows you to edit class relationships using drag and drop.

You can change an inheritance relationship by double-clicking on the line between a parent and child class and then dragging the line by its anchor to another parent class (see Figure 19-5).

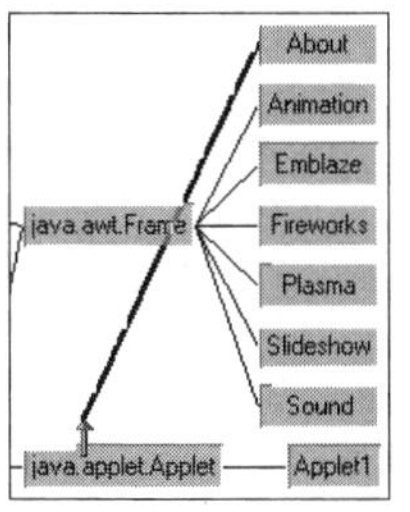

Figure 19-5: To change an inheritance relationship, double-click on the line between a parent and child class and drag the anchor using the arrow that appears.

If you double-click on the box representing a class, the Class Browser opens and you can edit the class.

You use the Property List, shown in Figure 19-6, to change the properties of the current component or form. You can select a component by using the Property List's drop-down list (at the top of the List). If a form is open in the Form Designer, any changes that you make using the Properties List are dynamically reflected on the form.

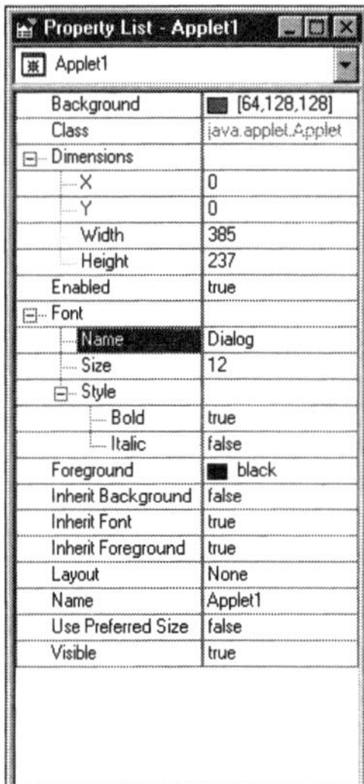

Figure 19-6: You can use the Property List to set component properties.

A Simple Café Applet

To demonstrate how easy it is to construct Java applets in Visual Café, I'll walk you through an example. This applet is called Simple, but it could also be called, "Look, ma, no code!" There's no need to open the Code Editor to add functionality.

Simple will take the text added to textField1 and add it to label1 when the user clicks on button1.

The first step is to start a new project. Provided that you have selected Create a New Project under On Startup on the General tab of the Environment Options dialog — as shown in Figure 19-7 — Visual Café will automatically open a new project when it loads. (You open the Environment Options dialog via the File menu.) If you haven't selected this option — or already have a project open — you can choose New Project from the File menu.

Next, use the Form Designer and Property List to create the user interface for the applet, as shown in Figure 19-8.

The process of designing the interface involves selecting components from the Component Palette, drawing them on the Form Designer, and setting their initial properties using the Property List.

The Simple form includes some components that will have nothing to do with the interactions that the applet will perform. These components — a panel and two extra labels — are there just to make the application look better.

To add the interactivity to the applet without having to write code, right-click on button1 in the Form Designer and choose Add Interaction from the context menu. The Interaction Wizard starts, as shown in Figure 19-9.

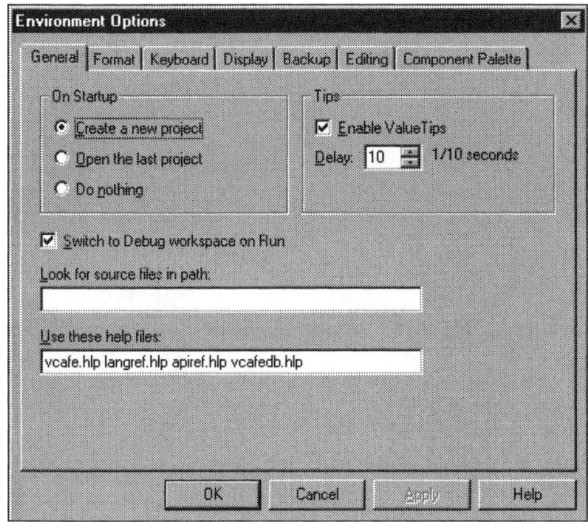

Figure 19-7: If you have selected Create a New Project under On Startup in the General tab of the Environment Options dialog, Visual Café automatically starts a new project when it loads.

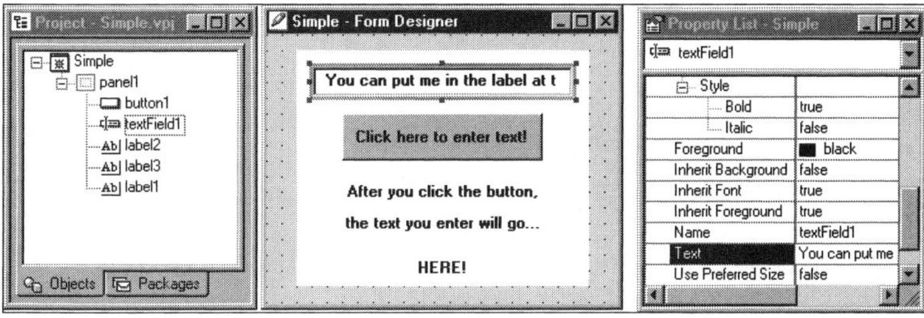

Figure 19-8: You can use the Form Designer and Property List to create the user interface for an applet.

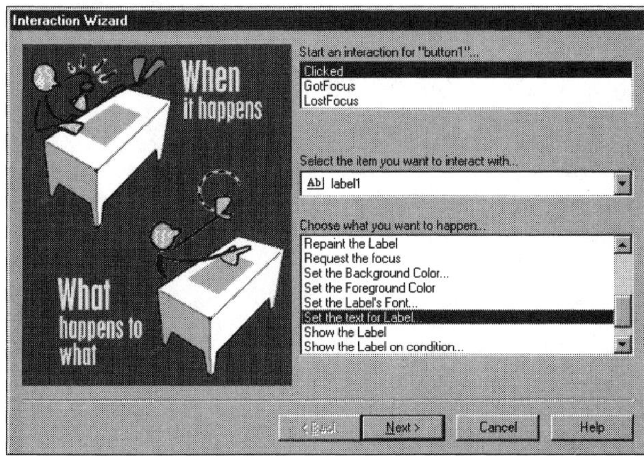

Figure 19-9: You can use the Interaction Wizard to add interactivity to components and forms without having to write code.

You use the topmost box to specify what object event triggers the interaction (in this case, when button1 is clicked). Next, you use a drop-down list to specify the object to interact with, in the example, label1. Finally, you choose what you want to happen from the bottom drop-down list (in the example, setting the text for the label).

In many cases, the Wizard doesn't need to gather more information. But if it does, as in this example, the Next button is enabled. When you click on the Next button, the second Interaction Wizard panel displays, as shown in Figure 19-10. You use this panel to collect additional information.

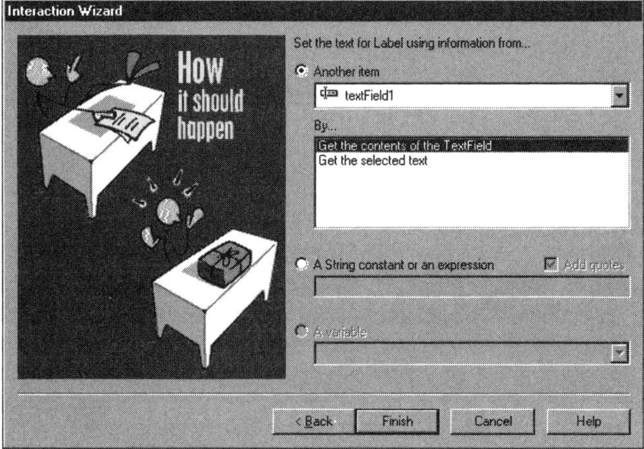

Figure 19-10: You use the second panel of the Interaction Wizard to specify additional parameter information.

In the example, you need to tell the Interaction Wizard where to get the new text (from textField1) and whether to use the entire contents of the TextField or only the selected text. You could also have used this panel to assign a string literal or a variable to label1.

Click on the Wizard's Finish button. There's nothing more to do. The appropriate code has been added to the applet.

In the Project Options dialog, which you open by choosing Options from the Project menu, make sure that Starter HTML is set to Automatic and that the option Execute Applet in Default HTML Viewer is selected (see Figure 19-11). This tells Visual Café to auto-generate an HTML page for the applet and run it in your default browser (rather than running the applet in the Applet Viewer utility).

Run the applet by choosing Execute from the Project menu. With the Simple applet running in your browser, if you enter text in the TextField and click on the button, the text will appear in the label at the bottom of the applet, as shown in Figure 19-12.

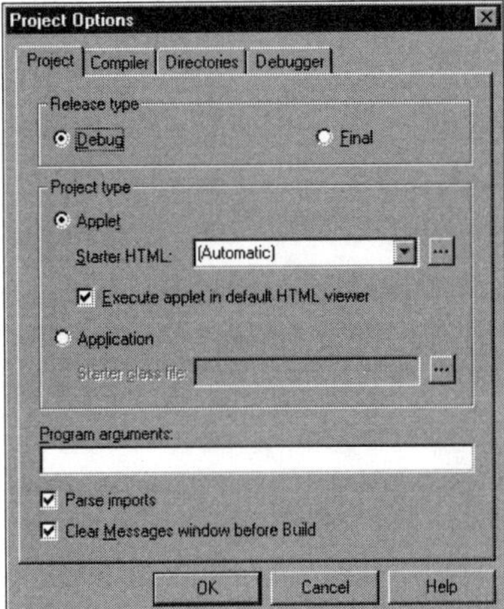

Figure 19-11: You use the Project tab of the Project Options dialog to auto-generate an HTML page for the applet and to run the applet from your default browser rather than in Applet Viewer.

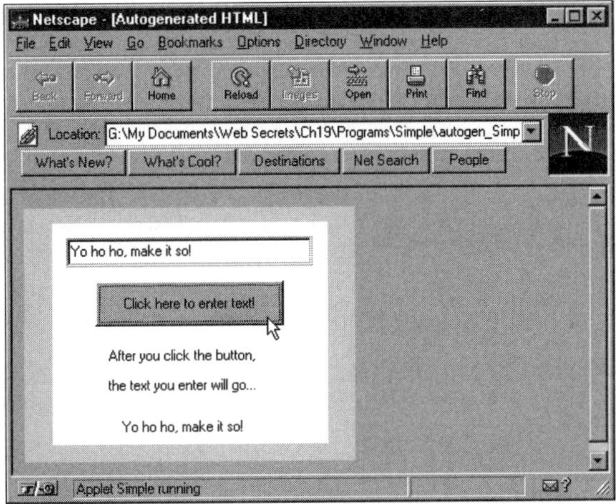

Figure 19-12: It's easy to use the Interaction Wizard to create applets that are fully functional when they run in a browser.

Files That Visual Café Generates

For each Visual Café project, a number of different file types are created, as shown in Table 19-1. If any of these files are missing, a Visual Café project will not open properly in the development environment. Visual Café project information is stored in a Vpj file, also called a *project* file; you can open a Visual Café project by double-clicking on its project file.

Table 19-1 Visual Café File Types

File Type and Extension	*Comments*
.vpj	A Visual Café project file
.cdb	Compiled database that Visual Café uses to track compilation dependencies
.class	A compiled version of a frame or applet .java file
.html	An HTML file (auto-generated for an applet if the IDE is set to do so)
.java	A component's Java source file; projects can, of course, have multiple .java files
.ve2	Secondary project information
.vep	Visual Café project options

The Code That Lies Beneath

This process of creating programs without handling code makes many programmers squeamish. Like scuba divers, we want to know not only the surface action of the waves, but the contours of the ocean floor that lies beneath.

To start with, here's the interaction code that Visual Café added to the button to set the label's text:

```
void button1_Clicked(Event event) {
      //{{CONNECTION
      // Set the text for Label... Get the contents of the TextField
      label1.setText(textField1.getText());
//}}
}
```

In addition, the Interaction Wizard added code to trap the event when the button was clicked:

```
public boolean handleEvent(Event event) {
   if (event.target == button1 && event.id == Event.ACTION_EVENT) {
      button1_Clicked(event);
      return true;
   }
   return super.handleEvent(event);
}
```

What about the rest of the applet? Mostly, you'll find component declarations. Here's the entire source code for Simple.java:

```
/*
      A basic extension of the java.applet.Applet class
*/
```

```
import java.awt.*;
import java.applet.*;
public class Simple extends Applet {
   public boolean handleEvent(Event event) {
   if (event.target == button1 && event.id == Event.ACTION_EVENT) {
   button1_Clicked(event);
   return true;
}
return super.handleEvent(event);
}
public void init() {
   super.init();
// Take out next line if you don't use
//symantec.itools.net.RelativeURL

//symantec.itools.lang.Context.setDocumentBase(getDocumentBase());

//{{INIT_CONTROLS
setLayout(null);
addNotify();
resize(275,206);
setBackground(new Color(65535));
panel1 = new java.awt.Panel();
panel1.setLayout(null);
panel1.reshape(24,12,228,180);
panel1.setBackground(new Color(16777215));
add(panel1);
button1 = new java.awt.Button("Click here to enter text!");
button1.reshape(36,48,156,36);
panel1.add(button1);
textField1 = new java.awt.TextField();
textField1.setText("You can put me in the label at the bottom!");
textField1.reshape(12,12,204,24);
textField1.setBackground(new Color(16777215));
panel1.add(textField1);
label2 = new java.awt.Label("After you click the
   button,",Label.CENTER);
label2.reshape(12,96,192,24);
panel1.add(label2);
label3 = new java.awt.Label("the text you enter will
   go...",Label.CENTER);
label3.reshape(12,120,192,23);
panel1.add(label3);
label1 = new java.awt.Label("HERE!",Label.CENTER);
label1.reshape(12,156,192,19);
label1.setForeground(new Color(0));
panel1.add(label1);
//}}
}
public boolean handleEvent(Event event) {
   if (event.target == button1 && event.id == Event.ACTION_EVENT) {
      button1_Clicked(event);
      return true;
   }
   return super.handleEvent(event);
```

```
}

//{{DECLARE_CONTROLS
java.awt.Panel panel1;
java.awt.Button button1;
java.awt.TextField textField1;
java.awt.Label label2;
java.awt.Label label3;
java.awt.Label label1;
//}}
}
```

Essentially, Java code is Java code. Visual Café acts as a wrapper on the Sun Java compiler. Source code modules could be compiled on the command line after they were generated in Visual Café. But why would you want to do this?

Running Outside the Visual Café IDE

The fancy Java components included in the Symantec Visual Café IDE — for example, the multimedia components discussed in the next section of this chapter — are not instanced from your generic just plain vanilla Java class libraries.

This creates no problems from within the Visual Café IDE. However, when you want to view your applet from outside the Visual Café environment, you'll have to make sure that Applet Viewer and/or your browser can find the custom classes included with Visual Café.

You can do this by adding a line to your Autoexec.Bat or Config.Sys file that points an environment variable to Symantec class libraries. For example, in Autoexec.Bat, depending on where you installed Visual Café:

```
SET CLASSPATH=C:\visualcafe\java\lib\symclass.zip.
```

The same issue arises in the context of the Web server that will display your applet. The Web server software needs to be able to find the Symantec Java classes. How to do this varies, depending on the server software.

If you are working with an Internet Service Provider (ISP) or other Web host, verify with them that the Symantec classes are present. If not, the ISP should explain how you can make them available.

If you are configuring your own server software, the classes in the Symclass.Zip file need to be in the server's classpath. If you can't find a way to set the server's classpath, a lowest common denominator solution that always works is to copy the contents of the \VisualCafe\Java\Lib\symantec directory — including subdirectories — to the location containing the applet.

The subdirectories of the symantec directory contain the Visual Café Java class libraries.

Adding Animations to an Applet

Visual Café includes a number of components on the Multimedia tab of the Component Palette that you can use to easily add multimedia and animated effects to any Web page.

Inside Scoop

Many Java applets have no function other than to jazz up Web pages with zippy multimedia effects. These can get old pretty quickly. Some people have even given this kind of applet a name — starting with a "cr" and ending with "applets." This kind of component usually has the following comment in the Symantec documentation: "This multimedia component is provided for novelty and programming convenience."

The point is not that you should never use multimedia effects in applets. Rather, go easy — and remember that Java is a programming language that can do great and powerful things on the Web. Don't trivialize it.

Table 19-2 describes the components on the Multimedia tab.

Table 19-2 Multimedia Tab of the Component Palette

Component	*Comments*
SlideShow	Displays a series of images, with or without captions.
Animator	Creates an animation by displaying a series of images in sequence. This component stays in one place on the form. You can specify images, and their order, using a URL. You can set looping. You can use the Interaction Wizard to start and stop the component.
MovingAnimation	Like the Animator, except that it can move on a form.
Emblaze	Displays Emblaze animation movies (.Blz files).
Firework	Creates an animated fireworks display.
NervousText	Creates an animated text display in which each letter moves independently of all other letters.
ImageViewer	Creates a platform-independent displayable image.
Plasma	Creates an animation along the lines of a lava lamp or 1960s light show. Visual Café documentation describes it as creating "...colored amorphous shapes, where colors gradually modulate as shapes merge and separate." Warning: this one is a video memory hog!
SoundPlayer	Plays an .au sound file.

Creating an Animated Applet

In this section, I'll show you how to put together an animated applet that you can add to a Web site. This source project for this applet, Fly.Vpj, has five components on its form (see Figure 19-13): a SoundPlayer, an Animator, a NervousText, and two buttons.

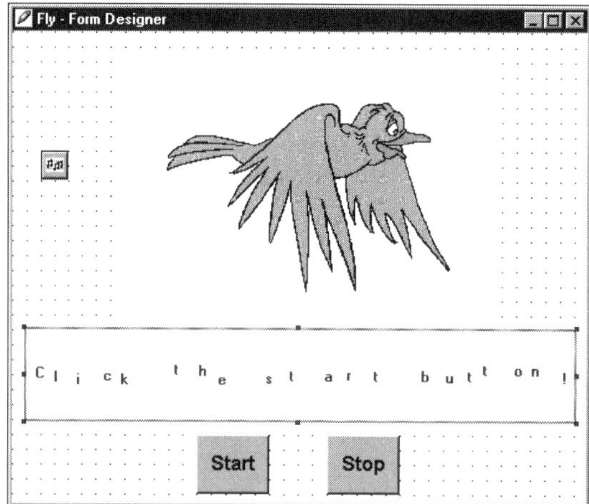

Figure 19-13: You can easily create animated applets by placing multimedia components on a form.

The Animator component works with Gif and Jpeg files. To add images to the Animator, use the Property List to select the component's URL List property. Selecting URL List opens the URL List dialog. Click on the Add button to locate the image files you want to add to the component. Note that the component will automatically add all files in a directory beginning with the same name — for example, bird.*, as shown in Figure 19-14.

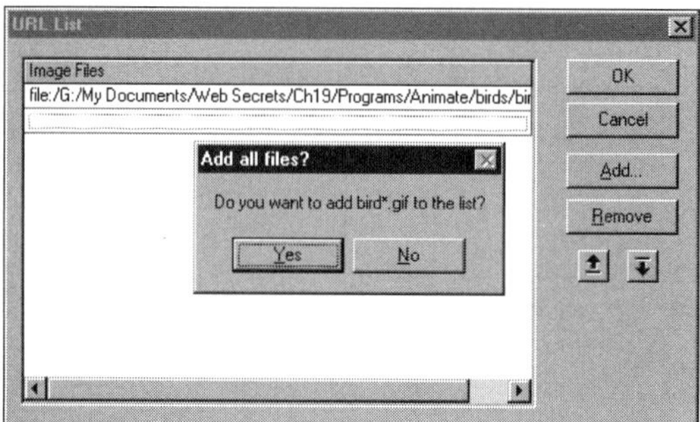

Figure 19-14: You can automatically add all files with the same beginning name in a directory to a URL List.

Once you've added all the image files (in the example, there are four, bird1.gif through bird4.gif), double-click on each image file in the URL List box to edit the file paths, as you can see in Figure 19-15. It's important to set this up so the images can be found if you move the Fly.class file away from its current location (for example, onto a server).

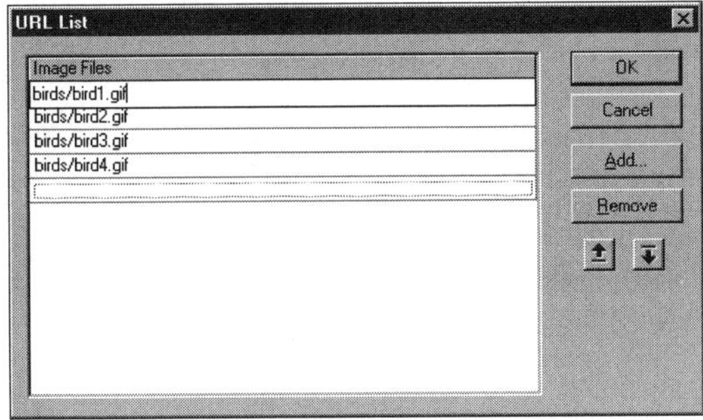

Figure 19-15: You can edit the file paths in a URL List dialog by double-clicking on each.

Set the animation to loop infinitely by setting the component's Loop Count property to -1.

Set the Visible property of the Animator component to False, so that it doesn't display until the user clicks on the Start button.

You configure the SoundPlayer component just as you configure the Animator — by using its URL List property to add sound files and setting its Loop Count property to -1.

The only sound format accepted by the SoundPlayer component is the .au file.

Next, use the Interaction Wizard to configure the Start and Stop buttons (see Figure 19-16). I added interactivity to the click event of the Start button that showed the Animator, started it, and started the SoundPlayer. The Stop button's click handler should be set to stop the Animator and SoundPlayer.

That's all there is to it! You can now run the applet in the Visual Café environment. If you'd like, you can also run it from a browser, or on a Web site, as shown in Figure 19-17. Users who download the applet can then happily watch the bird fly, if they don't have anything better to do.

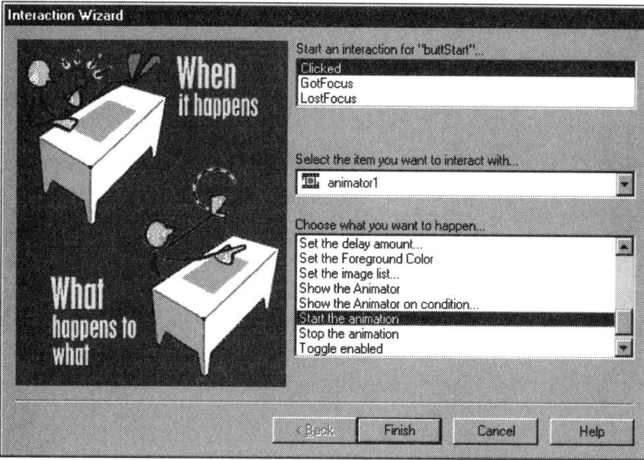

Figure 19-16: You can use the Interaction Wizard to add event-handling code to your applets (here the animation is being made to start when the Start button is clicked).

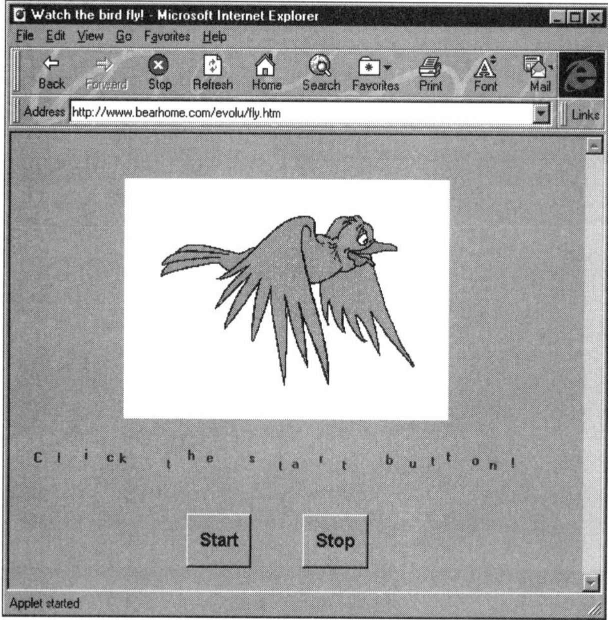

Figure 19-17: You can easily add to a Web site animated applets created in Visual Café.

Obviously, if you'd prefer to edit the source code manually instead of letting the Interaction Wizard do it, that's your prerogative — and not hard to do. Here's the code added by the Interaction Wizard:

```
public class Fly extends Applet {
   void buttStop_Clicked(Event event) {
   //{{CONNECTION
   // Stop the animation
      {
         animator1.stopAnimation();
       }
   //}}
   //{{CONNECTION
   // Stop the sound player after the specified delay...
      {
         soundPlayer1.stop(1);
}
   //}}
   }

   void buttStart_Clicked(Event event) {
      //{{CONNECTION
      // Start the animation
      {
         animator1.startAnimation();
      }
      //}}
          //{{CONNECTION
          // Show the Animator
             animator1.show();
      //}}
          //{{CONNECTION
          // Start the sound player
      {
        soundPlayer1.play();
       }
      //}}
}
...
public boolean handleEvent(Event event) {
            if (event.target == buttStart && event.id ==
Event.ACTION_EVENT) {
                        buttStart_Clicked(event);
                        return true;
            }
            if (event.target == buttStop && event.id ==
Event.ACTION_EVENT) {
                        buttStop_Clicked(event);
                        return true;
            }
            return super.handleEvent(event);
    }
...
```

A Matter of Degrees

Figure 19-19 shows an applet running in a Web page that converts temperatures entered in Fahrenheit to Celsius and Kelvin.

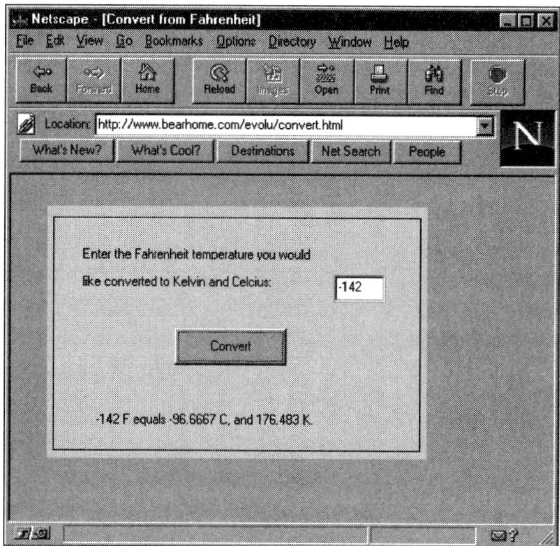

Figure 19-18: When the user clicks on the Convert button, the temperature input is converted.

It's easy to create applets with this kind of functionality using Visual Café.

First, create your interface using the Form Designer. Next, use the Interaction Wizard to get a jump start on creating code that handles the applet's events. This code will be tweaked manually.

In the case of the temperature converter, there really is only one event to handle, when the user clicks the button. As a starting place, tell the Wizard to place the contents of the input text field into the result label when the button is clicked.

The code generated by the Wizard will look something like this:

```
Result.setText(Input.getText());
```

You can manually edit the source code for the button click event to convert the input and format the results:

```
void button1_Clicked(Event event) {
   float degree;
   String tobeConvert;
   String returnString;
   tobeConvert = Input.getText();
   try {
      degree = (Float.valueOf(tobeConvert)).floatValue();
   } catch (NumberFormatException e) { return; }
   returnString = tobeConvert + " F equals " +
      String.valueOf ((degree-32.0)/1.8) + " C, and " +
      String.valueOf (((degree-32.0)/1.8) + 273.15) + " K.";
   Result.setText(returnString);
   }
```

Packages and Threads

Visual Café puts a great deal of powerful features at your fingertips. But to use these features, you must have information. (This is just another way of saying that knowledge is power!) Two of its powerful features are the way it organizes packages and allows you to control threads.

Browsing the Class Libraries

You may not have realized that you can use the Packages tab of the Visual Café Project dialog to easily browse the source code for all the current Java class libraries (see Figure 19-19).

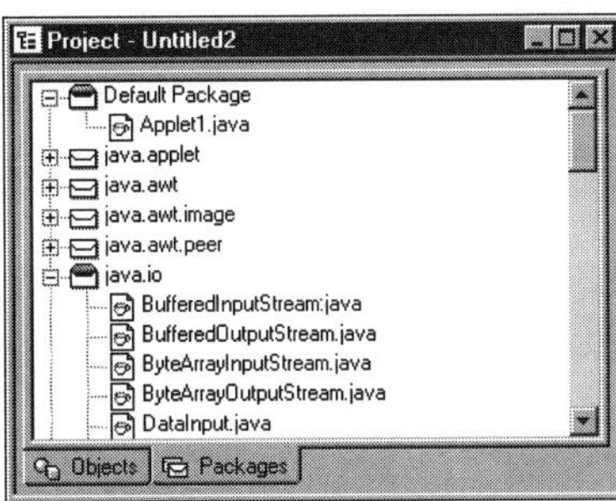

Figure 19-19: You can view the source code for the Java class libraries from the Packages tab of the Project dialog.

To open any of the Java class source files from the Packages tab, simply double-click on the .java file. For example, here's the definition of the Canvas object from canvas.java in the java.awt:

```
public class Canvas extends Component {
   /**
   *  Creates the peer of the canvas.  This peer allows you to
   *  change the user interface of the canvas without changing its
   *  functionality.
   */
   public synchronized void addNotify() {
      peer = getToolkit().createCanvas(this);
      super.addNotify();
   }
   /**
   *  Paints the canvas in the default background color.
   *  @param g the specified Graphics window
   */
   public void paint(Graphics g) {
     g.setColor(getBackground());
       g.fillRect(0, 0, width, height);
   }
}
```

Threads

The ability to create and control individual execution threads is one of the most powerful aspects of Java. Visual Café ships with a sample applet, Threadx.class, that demonstrates how to start and stop separate execution threads. As you can see in Figure 19-20, the application shows three polygons, each of which represents a separate execution thread.

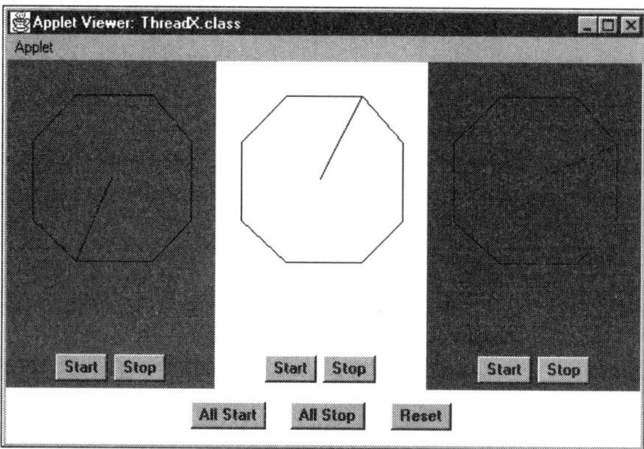

Figure 19-20: The Threadx sample applet that ships with Visual Café demonstrates how to control multiple threads in one Java applet.

Each thread's polygon contains a clock arm that sweeps around the polygon. At will, the user can start and stop each thread, which is verified by the sweeping clock arm.

Each polygon is an instance of the PolygonAnimation class. This class is a simple extension of the Canvas class that runs as its own thread (hence the implements Runnable statement in the class definition) and includes methods for creating, suspending, resuming, and destroying the thread. PolygonAnimation is also responsible for creating the sweep arm animation:

```
import java.awt.*;
class PolygonAnimation extends Canvas implements Runnable
{
    private Thread  myThread;
    private Polygon thePolygon;
    private int
       polyX[] = new int[9],  //The polygons X coordinates
       polyY[] = new int[9],  //The polygons Y coordinates
       position,              //The point on the polygon the line is
                              //drawn to
       delay = 100;

    public PolygonAnimation()
    {
       resize(130, 130);
       setupPolygon();
```

```
        thePolygon = new Polygon(polyX, polyY, 9);
        position = 0;
            myThread = new Thread(this);
        myThread.start();
    }

    public PolygonAnimation(int _delay)
    {
         this();
         if(_delay < 50) delay = 50;
         else if(_delay > 300) delay = 300;
         else delay = _delay;
    }

    public void reset() {position = 0;}

    public void resume() { myThread.resume(); }

    public void run()
    {
        while (true)
        {
            repaint();
            try{ Thread.sleep(delay); }
                catch(InterruptedException e) { this.stop(); }
            advance();
        }
    }

    public void stop() { myThread.suspend(); }

    public void destroy() { this.stop(); }

    //Draw the polygon and a line from the center to the
    //specified position.
    public void paint(Graphics g)
    {
         g.drawPolygon(thePolygon);
         g.drawLine(65, 65, polyX[position], polyY[position]);
    }

    private void advance()
    {
         if(position < 6) position++;
         else position = 0;
    }

    //Set up the two arrays with the X and Y coordinate values
    private void setupPolygon()
    {
         polyX[0] = 37;
         polyX[1] = 97;
         polyX[2] = 129;
         polyX[3] = 129;
         polyX[4] = 97;
         polyX[5] = 37;
```

```
            polyX[6] = 1;
            polyX[7] = 1;
            polyX[8] = 37;

            polyY[0] = 1;
            polyY[1] = 1;
            polyY[2] = 37;
            polyY[3] = 97;
            polyY[4] = 129;
            polyY[5] = 129;
            polyY[6] = 97;
            polyY[7] = 37;
            polyY[8] = 1;
        }
}
```

The main Threadx class creates instances of the three polygons based on the PolygonAnimation class:

```
PolygonAnimation pa1 = new PolygonAnimation(100);
PolygonAnimation pa2 = new PolygonAnimation(120);
PolygonAnimation pa3 = new PolygonAnimation(150);
```

The buttons on the Threadx applet form then manipulate each thread (meaning instance of the PolygonAnimation) when the appropriate click event is fired. For example:

```
...
void stop1_Clicked(Event event) {
   pa1.stop();
}
void start1_Clicked(Event event) {
   pa1.resume();
}
...
```

Summary

“Don’t hate me because I’m beautiful” might truly be Visual Café’s cry! This is an awesomely elegant and powerful Java development environment. Take it for a test spin, and you’ll probably get hooked.

Visual Café is indisputably still a little rough around the edges. But give it time. Most likely, by the time the next version is released, it will have the reliability that professional developers appreciate.

Topics covered in this chapter included

- Visual Café compared to Visual J++
- The Visual Café IDE
- A simple Café applet
- Files generated by Visual Café

- Placing Visual Café applets on a Web server
- Visual Café animation components
- Creating an animated applet
- Browsing the Java class libraries
- Implementing multiple threads in an application

Part IV

Client and Server on the Web

Chapter 20

Understanding the Client/Server Model and How It Applies to the Web

"May the force be with you!"

— Ben (Obi-Wan) Kenobi, *Star Wars*

The World Wide Web is the largest network of computers our world has ever known. There is no disputing its importance, or that it will continue to grow and mutate. It's important to understand that all computing on the Web — and all Web programming — follows the client/server model. Browsers, of course, are the clients. Connections between these clients and servers are weak and do not include easy means of persisting transaction information. A great deal of effort in Web development goes into creating mechanisms that allow clients to stay in touch with servers — and also allow users to follow that yellow-brick hyperlink that might lead over the rainbow.

Another difficulty revolves around the current state of browser scripting reliability. In a word, it's not. However, if all programming content is put on the server side, delays add up because information has to be passed to the server to be processed and then back to the client.

A related issue is that Web clients are actually much more universal than Web servers. There are only a few browsers in widespread use. But server-side solutions must be customized for each server and the operating system it is running on.

Inside Scoop

Experienced Web developers know that server-side programming is less prone to bugs than client-side solutions such as using JavaScript.

Execution of a program on the server is far more under the control of the developer than execution of a program on a client. Java applets, downloaded from the server and executed in the Java Virtual Machine on the client, represent a possible compromise. In many ways, Java is the closest thing yet to a universal programming language on the Web. But there are quite a few things that you cannot do gracefully from within the Java "sandbox."

As a Web developer you will have to grapple with these issues and the trade-offs involved. With the fast and furious pace of Web development, no doubt new techniques — and new problems — will come up. Probably, each major Web project you work on will have a unique solution, with its own blend of client and server.

Future developments — see, for example, the section on "Server Push" later in this chapter — will contort our current model of Web development, making it even more important to know where your projects stand in relationship to client/server development.

This chapter explains what you need to know to understand client and server on the Web before moving on to specific tools and techniques.

The HTTP Protocol

Hypertext Transfer Protocol (HTTP) is the underlying language used by clients and servers on the Web to communicate. You'll need to understand how HTTP works to build Common Gateway Interface (CGI) programs (see Chapter 21, "CGI Scripting"). In addition, if you understand HTTP, you'll be able to make sense of the error messages generated by Web servers from time to time.

Each HTTP client request and server response — sometimes termed a "transaction" — has three parts:

- A request or response line
- A header section
- The body of the transaction.

A client starts the transaction by contacting the server at a designated port (usually 80). It sends a document request using an HTTP method, followed by a document address, and an HTTP version number. For example:

```
GET /index.html HTTP/1.0
```

Next, the client sends header information consisting of configuration information about itself, and its document viewing preferences. Each topic of header information is contained on its own line, and the first blank line ends the header. For example:

```
Accept: image/gif, image/x-bitmap, image/jpeg, image/pjpeg, */*
User-Agent: Mozilla/2.0 (compatible;MSIE 3.0; Windows 95)
```

This User-Agent line identifies the client browser as a Windows 95 version of Internet Explorer 3. (For more information on using HTTP headers to obtain information about Web site browsers, see Chapter 4, "Different Browsers for Different Folk.")

After sending a blank line to end the header, the client may send additional information (usually created by CGI programs using the POST method).

Now it's up to the server to respond. The server's response starts with a status line containing the version number of HTTP the server is using, a status code indicating the result of the client's request, and an "English" description of the status code. For example,

```
HTTP/1.0 200 OK
```

means the server used version 1.0 of HTTP in its response and that the client's request was successful. In this case, the file or other data requested will be sent back to the client after the header.

Table 20-1 shows some other common HTTP server status codes.

Table 20-1 Some HTTP Server Status Codes

Code	*Meaning*
201	New URL created.
202	Request accepted but not acted on.
301	Moved permanently; the requested URL is no longer used by the server. The new location can be found in the Location item in the header.
400	Bad Request, meaning syntax error in the request.
403	Forbidden. The request was denied for reasons that the server cannot (or will not) explain.
404	Not Found. Document at the specified URL does not exist.
500	Internal Server Error. This usually means that part of the server — for example, a CGI program — has crashed.

After sending a status line, the server sends header information about itself and the document it is sending back to the client. For example:

```
Date: Fri, 20 Jun 1997 04:42:01 GMT
Server: NCSA/1.5.2
Last-modified: Mon, 16 Jun 1997 22:22:22 GMT
Content-type: text/html
Content-length: 4964
```

A blank line follows the header, and then comes the response to the client's request. This will often be a copy of a file (in the preceding example it is a 4964 bytes long HTML text file). Other times, it will be the output of a CGI program. This output will, itself, often be HTML, as explained later in this chapter in "Building HTML on the Fly," and in Chapter 21.

It's important to understand that HTTP is a stateless protocol. (No, this doesn't mean that it needs to apply for citizenship and a passport.) HTTP is a protocol under which state information does not persist. This means that each HTTP transaction starts from the beginning.

For information on using cookies to persist client/server information across the Web — even though HTTP connections are by nature not persistent — see Chapter 4.

HTTP Client Methods

The first line of an HTTP client request always contains an HTTP command, known as a *method*. There are three commonly used HTTP methods: GET, HEAD, and POST.

The GET Method

The GET method is a request for information located at a specific URL on the server.

Browsers use GET to retrieve HTML documents for viewing. The result passed back to the browser by the server can be a copy of a file available to the server, or it can be the output of a program, such as a CGI program.

GET is also used to send user HTML form input to a CGI program. The form input information is appended to the URL of the request.

When a <FORM> tag's **method** parameter specifies GET, for example,

```
<FORM method="GET">
```

name=value pairs corresponding to the input from the form are appended to the URL following a question mark (?). The name=value pairs are separated by an ampersand (&). For example,

```
GET http://commerce.corel.com/cgi-
bin/ImageSearch.exe?Disc=397000&Format=Terse HTTP/1.0
```

causes the ImageSearch program on the Corel Web site to execute with Disc 397000 as the argument in the Terse Format. Corel Corporation's Web site uses this technique to generate photo CD catalogs.

For more information on using the GET method with HTML forms and CGI scripts, see Chapter 21.

Note that you can easily cause a browser to execute a GET method request with whatever paired arguments you'd like just by entering them as a URL in a hyperlink. You don't need to use an HTML form to generate the GET method or the pairs.

Make sure to enter the arguments in the proper format using the question mark to start the name=value pairs and an ampersand to separate each parameter. For example:

```
<A href="http://commerce.corel.com/cgi-
bin/ImageSearch.exe?Disc=397000&Format=Terse">
Sierra Nevada Mountains CD-ROM by Harold Davis
</A>
```

It's interesting to realize that the program invoked does not have to be physically present on the Web server that is transacting. The only requirement is that the URL given is valid.

The HEAD Method

The HEAD method is like GET, except that no data is returned by the server. This method is used to find out information about a document on the server, not to retrieve it.

The POST Method

The POST method allows data to be sent to the server in a client request. The data is directed by the server to a CGI program. This technique can be used for a great many purposes, including implementing the interface for database operations.

The data sent by the browser — produced by an HTML form whose <FORM> tag uses the method="POST" attribute — is placed in the body of the HTTP request. As with the GET method, the data consists of name=value pairs that can be processed by a program on the server.

Generally, data sent in the body of a Web client request is converted using URL-encoding, a process that converts spaces and characters that have special meanings within a URL — for example, a slash (/) — to their hexadecimal equivalents. For more information on URL-encoding, see Chapter 21

An advantage to using the POST method compared to the GET method is that data sent using POST is not visible as a URL in the browser.

Building HTML on the Fly

Many — if not most — server-side Web programs output HTML that is displayed in the client browser. The HTML codes that are created usually depend in some fashion on client-side user inputs. Although creating these "on the fly" HTML documents is just an issue of string handling, things can get still get pretty complex. You might have to generate an HTML page that includes embedded quotes, hyperlinks, frames, and much, much more.

I've presented numerous examples of building HTML on the fly throughout *Web Developer's SECRETS*. For example, here's code from a Visual Basic program on the server that uses the O'Reilly Website Windows CGI model to return HTTP protocol and user information to the client:

```
Public Sub SendWhoRU()
    Dim Quote As String
    Const Terminator = "</BODY></HTML>"
    Quote = Chr(34)

    Send ("Content-type: text/html")
    Send ("")
    Send ("<HTML><HEAD>")
    Send ("<TITLE> We know who you are...</TITLE>")
    Send ("</HEAD><BODY><CENTER><H2>")
    Send ("Here is some of what we know about you:")
    Send ("<BR>")
    Send ("You are using the following protocol: " _
       & CGI_RequestProtocol)
    Send ("<BR>")
    If CGI_From <> "" Then
       Send ("Your e-mail address: " & CGI_From)
    Else
       Send ("Your e-mail address is not available!")
    End If
    Send ("<BR>")
    Send ("Your Hostname: " & CGI_RemoteHost)
    Send ("<BR>")
    Send ("Your Remote Host IP: " & CGI_RemoteAddr)
    Send ("</CENTER></H2>")
    Send ("Return to <A href=" & Quote & _
       "http://www.bearhome.com/evolu/evolu.htm" _
       & Quote & ">" & "Evolution Software" & "</A>")
    Send (Terminator)
End Sub
```

For a detailed explanation of this example, see "Using CGI to Obtain Client Information" in Chapter 4.

Creating a Standard Page

You can also write functions that standardize the generation of HTML pages. This might be a very useful thing to do on sites that require server generation of many pages. Here's a standard HTML page generator, written in Visual Basic:

```
Function StandardPage(szTitle As String, szBodyText As String, _
    Optional Description As Variant, _
    Optional Footer As Variant, _
    Optional BackgroundImage As Variant, _
    Optional LogoImage As Variant, _
    Optional LogoURL As Variant) As String

    ' Internal working copy of HTML page
    Dim szWorking           As String

    ' Flags for the optional arguments
    Dim nBackGroundImage    As Integer
```

```
    Dim nLogoImage           As Integer
    Dim nLogoURL             As Integer
    Dim nDescription         As Integer

    ' Set the argument flags
    nBackGroundImage = Not IsMissing(BackgroundImage)
    nLogoImage = Not IsMissing(LogoImage)
    nLogoURL = Not IsMissing(LogoURL)
    nDescription = Not IsMissing(Description)

    ' Start with the HTML header and title
    szWorking = "Content-Type: text/html" & vbCrLf & vbCrLf _
       & "<html><head><title>" & szTitle & "</title><body"

    ' Use background bitmap?
    If nBackGroundImage Then
       szWorking = szWorking & " background =" & _
          BackgroundImage & ">"
    Else
       szWorking = szWorking & ">"
    End If

    ' Logo image?
    If nLogoImage Then
       ' Is there a link in the image?
       If nLogoURL Then
          szWorking = szWorking & "<a href=" & LogoURL & ">"
       End If
       ' Here's the image itself
       szWorking = szWorking & "<img src=" & LogoImage & _
          " align=left " & "hspace=20 border=0>"
       ' If there's a link then close the anchor.
       If nLogoURL Then
          szWorking = szWorking & "</a>"
       End If
    End If

    ' Display the title
    szWorking = szWorking & "<H1>" & szTitle & "</H1>"

    ' Display the description text
    If nDescription Then
       szWorking = szWorking & Description
    End If

    ' Close off the top section
    szWorking = szWorking & "</head><br clear = left><hr size=7>"

    ' Display the content and the footer
    szWorking = szWorking & "<DL><DD>" & szBodyText & "</DL><p>" _
       & "<hr size=7><p>" & Footer & "</body>"

    ' Return the working copy
    StandardPage = szWorking
End Function
```

This is quite a generic HTML page! You can even use it to include a logo with a hyperlink back to your home page in every "served" page.

To generate an HTML page using this standard function, you'll need to invoke it with appropriate parameters. For example:

```
Public Function Action(ByRef environment() As String, _
   ByRef query() As String) As String
   Dim szTitle As String, szBody As String, szFooter As String, _
      szDescrip As String
   ' Create the title
   szTitle = "HTML on the fly!"

   ' Create the body of the page
   szBody = "You can customize the Standard Page function " & _
       "to return the HTML that is just right for your application!"

   ' Now the footer
   szFooter = "<center><font size=1>" & _
      "Bulgy Bears are Marshals of the Lists</font size=1></center>"

   ' Create the description
   szDescrip = "HTML generated using the StandardPage function."

    ' Invoke the StandardPage function and serve the page
   Action = StandardPage(szTitle, szBody, szDescrip, _
      szFooter, "http://www.bearhome.com/harold/invst-bk.gif", _
      "http://www.bearhome.com/welcome.gif", _
      "http://www.bearhome.com")
End Function
```

You'll need to use one of the many server-side mechanisms available (see Chapters 21 and 22 for the details) to get the auto-generated HTML back to the browser.

Of course, if your server-side programming is in a language other than Visual Basic, such as Perl, you'll have to modify the code to suit.

The example is written to be served using ClassTool's webAction ISAPI product (explained in Chapter 22). If you bring it up in a browser, you'll get the results shown in Figure 20-1.

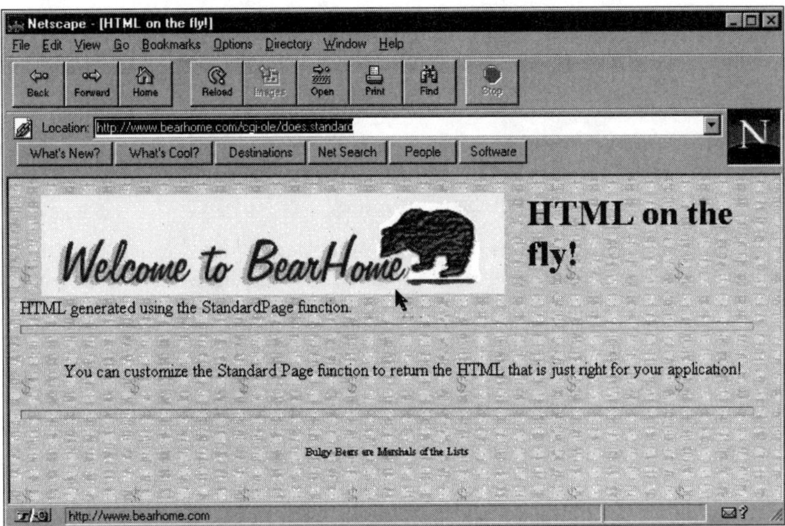

Figure 20-1: You can write routines that create standardized HTML pages on the fly that include fancy features such as image-based hyperlinks.

Server Push

Server "push" technology represents a new way to conceptualize client and server on the Web. The current idea is that browsers (clients) connect to Web sites (servers). When the client feels like it, she moves on to another server. With server push, information that can be viewed in a client is "pushed" over the Web. This is much more like broadcasting a channel than surfing a network. The client is no longer necessarily a browser. We've probably not yet found out the definite best idea for what kind of program should be a Web push client, but some current push clients include screen savers (PointCast) and e-mail clients (Netscape's InBox Direct).

According to Netscape technologist Marc Andreessen, "users need a blending of models — to pull down some information when you need it, and to have some information pushed to you so you don't have to seek it out."

Both Microsoft and Netscape will be integrating server push technologies further in future releases of their Web client products.

In the meantime, the following companies are key players in the move to Web server push:

- BackWeb Technologies, *http://www.backweb.com*, has an intranet/Internet client/server Channel Server package. The clients can subscribe to 30 public channels, in addition to publishing and subscribing to intranet channels.
- Intermind Corp., *http://www.intermind.com*, produces a free client, Communicator, which can subscribe to 140 Web channels. In addition, Intranet Publisher can publish channels within an intranet.

- Castanet, from Marimba, *http://www.marimba.com*, can be used to distribute programs across the Web to users with the Marimba Castanet Tuner client. Corel Corporation will soon be pushing its Office for Java product to users with this client.
- PointCast, Inc., *http://www.pointcast.com*, produces free clients in the form of screen savers, and I-Server, a product to allow the creation of server push PointCast channels.
- Incisa, from Wayfarer Communications, *http://www.wayfarer.com*, pushes on-screen rotating headlines, which can include a link to Web sites or databases.

Server Side Includes

Server Side Includes (SSI) are commands that you can place in an HTML document to execute other programs or to output data. Think of SSI as small macros that save you the trouble of writing server-side programs to generate small quantities of dynamic information.

Check the documentation of your particular server software to find out how to configure it for SSI and to determine which of the SSI commands are accepted by the server software.

All SSI directives have the format

```
<!–#command parameter(s)="argument"-->
```

Do not leave off the # sign, or your SSI commands will not work.

Table 20-2 lists the most important SSI commands and explains what they do.

Table 20-2 Standard SSI Commands

Command	*Syntax*	*Comments*
echo	<!--#echo var="env-var"-->	Inserts SSI variables and CGI environment variables
include	<!--#include file="path"-->	Inserts text of document into the current file
fsize	<!--#fsize file="path"-->	Inserts the size of the specified file into the current document
flastmod	<!--#flastmod file="path"-->	Inserts the last modification date and time for a file
exec	<!--#exec cmd="path/file"-->	Executes an external program and places output in the current document
config	<!--#config arg="string"-->	Used to modify SSI formatting

Table 20-3 shows the standard SSI environment variables (which can be used in SSI directives in addition to CGI environment variables).

Table 20-3 SSI Environment Variables

Variable	*Contains*
DOCUMENT_NAME	Name of the current file
DOCUMENT_URL	URL of the current file
DATE_LOCAL	Current date and time in the local time zone
DATE_GMT	Current date and time in Greenwich
LAST_MODIFIED	Date and time the current file was last modified

Summary

All development on the Web is, in some respects, client/server development. This chapter covered background information that you need to know before exploring detailed client/server solutions to Web development problems.

Topics covered in this chapter included

- Understanding the Web client/server model
- The HTTP protocol
- HTTP client methods
- Building HTML on the fly
- Server push
- Server Side Includes (SSI)

Chapter 21

CGI Scripting

"Common sense is not so common."

— Voltaire

The Common Gateway Interface (CGI) allows Web server software to communicate with other programs running on the server. Using CGI, the Web server can invoke an external program, passing it user input from an HTML form in a client browser. These external programs are often referred to as "scripts," which is not entirely accurate. In fact, they can be programs written in any language capable of reading the CGI environment variables and generating HTML on the fly. Most likely, the term "CGI script" comes from the fact that most CGI programming — particularly on UNIX servers — is done using Practical Extraction and Reporting Language (Perl), an interpreted scripting language.

Whatever the terminology (and development language) used, CGI programming is an important part of Web development. It's the closest thing to a universal methodology for publishing executable information from a Web server. You can use CGI programs to create a huge variety of Web applications, running the gamut from simple electronic guest books and counters to complex interactive financial programs.

Some Web server software has exciting proprietary ways to publish executable content. Microsoft's Active Server Pages (ASP) technology — also known as "Denali," and included with version 3 of Internet Information Server — will be explored in Chapter 22.

How It Works

Usually, CGI programs are invoked using the **action** parameter in an HTML <FORM> tag. As explained in Chapter 20, <FORM> information can be delivered to the server using either the GET or POST method (determined by the value of the <FORM> tag's **method** parameter). The HTTP protocol is used to transmit the request and related information to the Web server.

If you use the GET method, name=value user input pairs are placed in QUERY_STRING, a CGI environment variable, which is delivered as part of the URL.

If you use the POST method, instead of using an environment variable, the information is delivered as part of the standard input stream. Data sent using the POST method is identified using a special Multipurpose Internet Mail Extension (MIME) header, application/x-www-form-urlencoded.

Whichever method you use, the input data is formatted in the same way (see "URL Encoding" later in this chapter for more information). The server intercepts the client's HTTP request and directs it to the appropriate CGI program. (Of course, the program must be in the location indicated in the request, and the server software must have execute permission.) It's also the server's job to deliver the CGI environment variables and their values to the program.

The CGI program decodes the user input, either by parsing the CGI QUERY_STRING environment variable or by parsing the standard input stream. Next, the program performs any required actions. If database access is involved, a database interface may be invoked (see Chapter 23 for more information about using databases in Web applications). Finally, the program formats output.

CGI program output consists of two parts, a MIME header and the actual output. Typically, the CGI program generates HTML. In that case, the MIME header is

```
Content-type: text/html
```

Table 21-1 shows some common MIME content types.

Table 21-1 Common MIME Content Types

Content Type	*Meaning*
text/html	HTML pages
text/plain	Plain text pages
image/gif	Gif image files
image/jpeg	Jpeg image files
message/rfc822	E-mail message
video/mpeg	Mpeg image files
video/quicktime	QuickTime video files

The CGI program outputs both the MIME header information and the HTML it generates to the standard output stream.

In most languages, the default behavior of the Print statement is to direct content to the standard output stream.

The Web server software takes the CGI program's output and publishes it to the client that invoked the program.

To summarize, an HTML form action command causes an HTTP request to be sent to the server. The server send invokes the CGI program requested. The CGI program parses client input and processes it, invoking a database interface if necessary. Once its activity is complete, the CGI program creates a header and HTML as output. The server sends this back to the browser as a response. Figure 21-1 shows this process in overview.

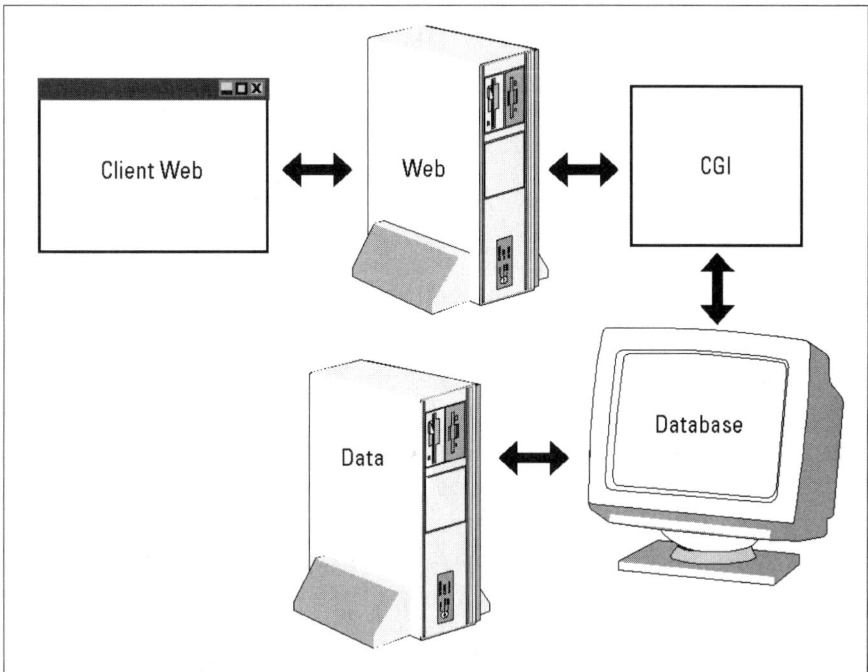

Figure 21-1: The Web server acts as an intermediary between the browser and the CGI program.

What Is ISAPI?

The Internet Server API (ISAPI) are tools that enable browsers to access programs running on Microsoft Internet Information Server (IIS). Essentially, ISAPI provides an alternative mechanism besides CGI for executing server-side programs. (Of course, because IIS is limited to the NT platform, so is ISAPI, while standard CGI programs can pretty much run on any server on any platform.)

ISAPI programs are in-process dynamic-link libraries (Dlls), as opposed to CGI programs, which are stand-alone executables. Because ISAPI programs run in the same process space as the Web server, they are potentially much faster than CGI programs.

Chapter 22 covers the details of creating ISAPI server-side programs.

Hello, Cousin Minnie

If you just want to execute a program on the server side — meaning that there is no custom user input to process — the usual way to invoke the program is to include its URL in a hyperlink.

Here's how you might invoke a "Hello, World" program named hello.pl and written in Perl:

```
<A href="http://www.bearhome.com/scripts/hello.pl>
   Say "Hello" to Minnie!
</A>
```

This assumes that

- A Perl interpreter has been installed on the server and associated with .pl files
- The server has been configured to grant Execute access to the .../scripts directory

See "Perl for Win32" later in this chapter for information on Perl. The section "Configuring IIS" later in the chapter also includes information on Internet Information Server, associating Perl scripts with the Perl interpreter under Window NT, virtual directories, and granting directory access.

The point of a "Hello, World" program, of course, is to do nothing other than execute, and send back something, so that you know that everything is correctly configured. I've taken the liberty of changing the message returned by hello.pl to an allusion to Cousin Minnie Pearl, the Grand Old Opry star. Listing 21-1 shows "Hello, World" à la Perl:

Listing 21-1: Hello, World in Perl

```
#Hello, Perl world!
print "Content-type: text/html", "\n\n";
```

```
print "<HTML>", "\n";
print "<HEAD><TITLE>Hello, Minnie!</TITLE></HEAD>", "\n";
print "<H1>Where's my cousin Minnie?</H1>", "\n";
print "</BODY></HTML>", "\n";
exit(0);
```

If you execute this CGI program from a browser, using its URL as I described, you'll get an HTML page returned to the browser, as shown in Figure 21-2.

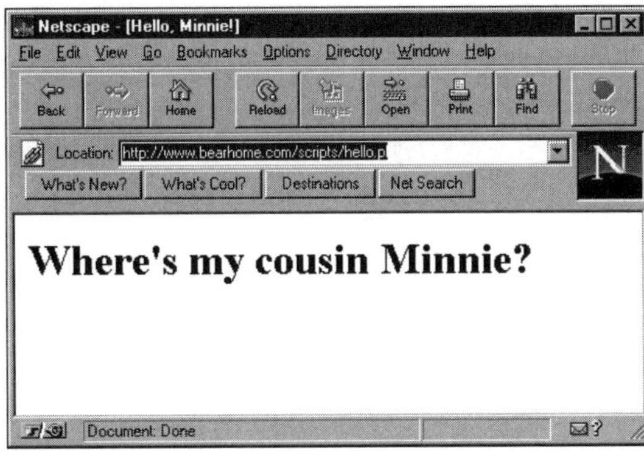

Figure 21-2: The output of a CGI program is usually HTML that is viewed in the browser that invoked the program.

When there is no user input to process, you can also invoke a server-side program using the #exec Server Side Include command. See the section "Server Side Includes" in Chapter 20 for more information.

CGI Programming Languages

Server-side Web programming has its roots in the UNIX operating systems. Therefore, CGI programs were originally written in UNIX-based languages, most commonly Perl and C or C++. Obviously, Perl — an interpreted scripting language known for its string manipulation and designed for ease of use — is very different in flavor than a compiled environment such as C (or its object-oriented super-charged child, C++).

As a general matter, being an interpreted rather than a compiled language is not a major drawback in the context of CGI programming (although you do have to have a Perl interpreter installed).

You'll find information on configuring Internet Information Server (IIS) to run Perl CGI scripts under "Configuring Internet Information Server (ISS)," later in this chapter. To read up on the Win32 Perl interpreter and the Perl language, consult the section "Perl for Win32."

Because Perl is the dominant cross-platform CGI language, with huge bodies of public-domain sample code available, I've emphasized it in this chapter. This is not to say that Perl is the best choice for you, or for your particular project. You can write CGI programs that work with Windows Web servers in any Windows programming language, including Delphi, Java, Visual Basic, and Visual C++.

Visual Basic programmers might be interested in the elegant CGI-Visual Basic interface created by O'Reilly for use with their Web servers: Website and Website Professional. For an example of how this works, see "Using CGI to Obtain Client Information" in Chapter 4.

Java is an up-and-coming contender for CGI programming language of choice. Java applications can be truly robust, as well as cross-platform in nature. (For more information on creating Web applications using Java, see Chapters 17 through 19.)

Although Java is in some respects a great CGI way to go, it does not, as of yet, have the body of CGI code available that Perl does.

Clearly, the choice of CGI programming language depends on a great many variables — not least of which are your familiarity with particular languages, and your comfort with the development styles dictated by these different languages.

CGI Environment Variables

The environment variables available to a server-side program depend on a number of factors, including the server software, the operating system, and the server's administration settings. However, the standard CGI environment variables listed in Table 21-2 are generally available.

Table 21-2 Standard CGI Environment Variables

Environment Variable	*Meaning*
CONTENT_LENGTH	The length of a body of an HTTP request (in characters or bytes), usually passed to a CGI program using the POST method.
CONTENT_TYPE	Media type of the request, for example, "text/html."
DOCUMENT_ROOT	The root directory from which Web documents are served.
GATEWAY_INTERFACE	Version of CGI used by the Web server.
HTTP_ACCEPT	Media types that the client can accept.
HTTP_REFERRER	The URL of the document that the browser had open before accessing the CGI program.

Environment Variable	*Meaning*
HTTP_USER_AGENT	Type of browser issuing the request. For example, "Mozilla/2.0 (compatible; MSIE 3.01;WindowsNT)" is Internet Explorer 3.01 running on NT.
PATH_INFO	Extra information that can be provided to a CGI program in its URL.
PATH_TRANSLATED	PATH_INFO appended to DOCUMENT_ROOT.
QUERY_STRING	Query information passed to the CGI program in name=value pairs.
REMOTE_ADDR	The remote IP address from which the client is making the HTTP request.
REMOTE_HOST	The remote host name from which the client is making the request.
SCRIPT_NAME	The virtual path of the program being executed, for example, */scripts/showserv.pl*.
SERVER_NAME	The server's host name.
SERVER_PORT	The port number on the host on which the server is running — usually 80.
SERVER_PROTOCOL	Name and revision of HTTP protocol of the request.
SERVER_SOFTWARE	The name and version of the server software that is answering the client request.

Displaying the Value of CGI Variables

In Perl, environment variables can be accessed using the ENV array. You could display specific environment variables in a browser, as shown in Listing 21-2.

Listing 21-2: Displaying specific environment variables in a browser

```
#Show CGI environment variables!
print "Content-type: text/html", "\n\n";
print "<HTML>", "\n";
print "<HEAD><TITLE>My server!</TITLE></HEAD>", "\n";
print "<BODY><H1>My server!</H1>", "\n";
print "Server Name:        ", $ENV{'SERVER_NAME'}, "<BR>", "\n";
print "Server Software:    ", $ENV{'SERVER_SOFTWARE'}, "<BR><HR>Called
From:<BR>", "\n";
print "Remote Address:     ", $ENV{'REMOTE_ADDR'}, "<BR>", "\n";
print "Remote Host:        ", $ENV{'REMOTE_HOST'}, "<BR>", "\n";
print "</BODY></HTML>", "\n";
exit(0);
```

If you use a browser to access the URL of this Perl script — for example, *http://www.bearhome.com/scripts/showserv.pl* — your browser will retrieve the named environment variables, as shown in Figure 21-3.

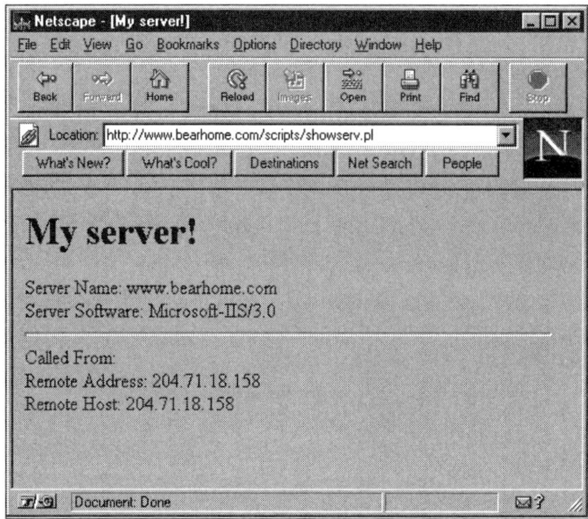

Figure 21-3: In Perl, the ENV array is used to access environment variables.

Alternatively, the script shown in Listing 21-3 displays all the available environment variables by cycling through the ENV array.

Listing 21-3: Displaying all environment variables

```
#Show CGI environment variables!
print "Content-type: text/html", "\n\n";
print "<HTML>", "\n";
print "<HEAD><TITLE>CGI Environment Variables</TITLE></HEAD><BODY>",
   "\n";
foreach $v (sort keys(%ENV))
    {print "$v: $ENV{$v}<BR>\n";}

print "</BODY></HTML>", "\n";
exit(0);
```

The results of running this script will vary, depending largely upon the Web server it is placed on. Figure 21-4 shows some of the environment variables provided by NT 4.0 and IIS 3.

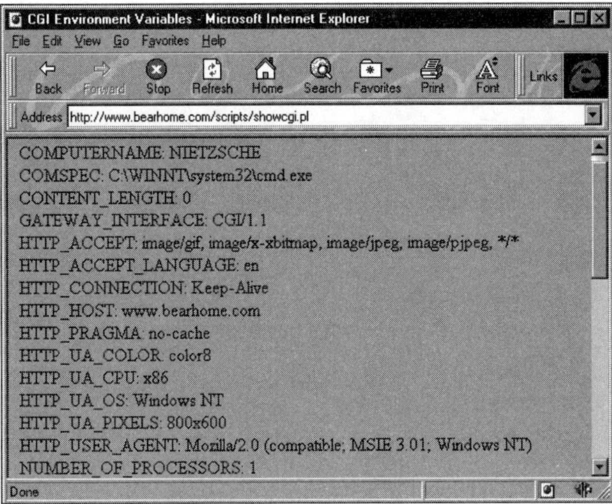

Figure 21-4: Using Perl, you can display all the environment variables by cycling through the ENV array.

HTML Form Tags

HTML forms consist of controls placed between <FORM> and </FORM> tags on an HTML page. User input into these forms is termed "form input."

As explained in the section "HTTP Client Methods" in Chapter 20, the **method** and **action** parameters of the <FORM> tag are used to send form input using the HTTP protocol to a CGI program residing on a Web server.

From the viewpoint of the CGI program, form input appears as URL encoded name=value pairs. In "URL Encoding" later in this chapter, I'll show you how to parse this information so that your CGI program can use it.

You use the <INPUT> tag within an HTML form to create many common form elements, including buttons, password fields, check boxes, radio buttons, reset buttons, and hidden fields. You specify the type of input form element using the **type** parameter of the <INPUT> tag. Each element, except for type="submit", must also be named using the <INPUT> tag's **name** parameter.

When the form is submitted, this name is passed to the CGI program as the name part of the name=value. As you'd expect, the value part of the pairing is the field value of the element, generally entered by the user.

The form is submitted — actually, as explained in Chapter 20, it is sent to the server as an HTTP request — when the user selects the submit button.

Table 21-3 provides a summary of the possible <INPUT> types. Note that the **value** parameter generally refers to the element's caption (or default text).

Table 21-3 <INPUT> Form Element Types

type=	*Parameters*	*Element*
"checkbox"	checked name value	Checkbox
"hidden"	maxlength name size value	Hidden text box.
"image"	align name src	Clickable image
"password"	maxlength name size value	Password text box
"radio"	checked name value	Radio (sometimes called option) button
"reset"	value	Clears the form
"submit"	name value	Submits the form
"text"	maxlength name size value	Text box

There are two other <FORM> tags besides <INPUT>: <SELECT> and <TEXTAREA>. <SELECT> is used in conjunction with <OPTION> tags to create drop-down list boxes. <TEXTAREA> creates a multiline text-entry area in the browser.

Here's the HTML for a very simple form, intended — in the due fullness of time — to demonstrate how your CGI programs can work with data sent to the server using the GET method:

```
<HTML>
   <HEAD>
      <TITLE>
      Form with an attitude!
```

```
      </TITLE>
   </HEAD>
   <BODY>
   <H1>
      Demonstrates a form using <BR>
      the GET method.
      <HR>
      Please fill in the form!
   </H1>
   <FORM method="GET" action="/scripts/getdemo.pl">
   Enter your first name:  <INPUT type="text" name="fname">
   Enter your last name:   <INPUT type="text" name="lname"><BR>
   <P>
   <HR>
   <INPUT type="submit"> <INPUT type="reset">
   </FORM>
   </BODY>
</HTML>
```

Figure 21-5 shows what this form looks like when it is open in a browser.

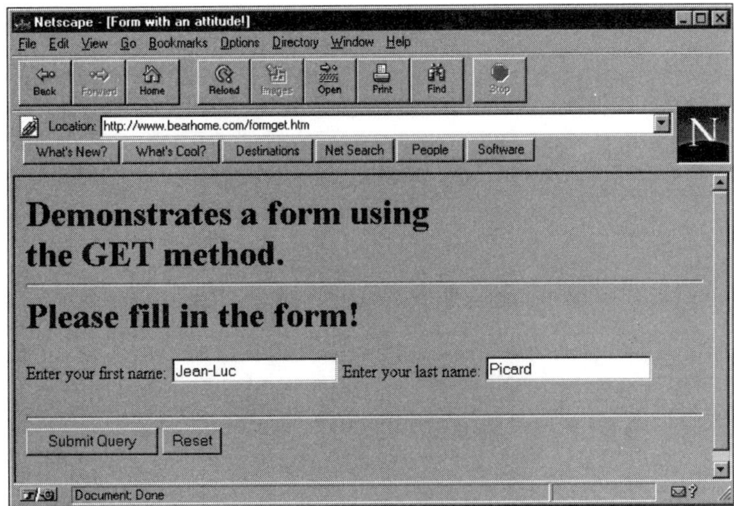

Figure 21-5: You can create HTML forms using <INPUT> tags.

URL Encoding

Before HTML form data is transmitted to the server, name=value pairs are created from the form. For example, in the case of the form shown in Figure 21-5, the pairs might be fname=Jean-Luc and lname=Picard.

These name=value pairs are separated with an ampersand (&), and, when the GET method is used, appended to the URL specified in the **action** parameter.

Because this information is being transferred as part of a URL, it cannot include spaces, characters that are not legal in URLs, or characters — such as slashes (/) — that have other meanings in URLs.

Inside Scoop

Although there is no technical reason that the same constraints would apply when you use the POST method, for the sake of consistency queries sent via the POST method are also URL encoded.

URL encoding, sometimes called hexadecimal encoding, is the process of replacing "illegal" characters in query strings with their hexadecimal equivalents. For example, the hexadecimal equivalent of a slash is %2F, and the space character is encoded as %20.

This means, of course, that before the CGI program at the server end of this process can use the values input, it needs to:

- Split the query string back into name=value pairs
- Reverse the URL encoding

Listing 21-4 shows how to retrieve the QUERY_STRING environment variable in Perl and break it up into an array of name=value pairs.

Listing 21-4: Retrieving the QUERY_STRING

```
# put the QUERY_STRING into a variable
$qs = $ENV{'QUERY_STRING'};

# split it up into an array using the '&' character
@qs = split(/&/,$qs);
```

Listing 21-5 shows reverse-engineering the URL encoding and breaking out individual variable values, which are then placed in an associative array.

Listing 21-5: Reverse-engineering the QUERY_STRING

```
foreach $i (0 .. $#qs)
    {
    # convert plus chars to spaces
    $qs[$i] =~ s/\+/ /g;

    # convert the hex characters
    $qs[$i] =~ s/%(..)/pack("c",hex($1))/ge;

    # split each one into name and value
    ($name, $value) = split(/=/,$qs[$i],2);

    # create the associative element
    $qs{$name} = $value;
    }
```

```
print "\nVariables:\n\n";

foreach $name (sort keys(%qs))
   { print "$name =", $qs{$name}, "\n" }
```

Using this code, it's pretty easy to create a demonstration response to the form sent to the server in Figure 21-5:

```
#!/scripts/getdemo.pl
#Show user input on the form

print "Content-type: text/html", "\n\n";
print "<HTML>", "\n";
print "<HEAD><TITLE>Parsing Query String
variables</TITLE></HEAD><BODY>", "\n";
print "<H1>Here's your form info!</H1>", "\n";

# put the QUERY_STRING into a variable
$qs = $ENV{'QUERY_STRING'};

# split it up into an array using the '&' character
@qs = split(/&/,$qs);

foreach $i (0 .. $#qs)
   {
   # convert plus chars to spaces
   $qs[$i] =~ s/\+/ /g;

   # convert the hex characters
   $qs[$i] =~ s/%(..)/pack("c",hex($1))/ge;

   # split each one into name and value
   ($name, $value) = split(/=/,$qs[$i],2);

   # create the associative element
   $qs{$name} = $value;
   }

print "\nVariables:\n\n<BR>";

foreach $name (sort keys(%qs))
   { print "$name =", $qs{$name}, "<BR>\n" }

print "<HR>Your first name is ", $qs{'fname'}, "<BR>\n";
print "<STRONG>That's sure a funny name!</STRONG><BR>";
print "<HR>Your last name is ", $qs{'lname'}, "<BR>\n";
print "<STRONG>I once knew a ",$qs{'lname'}, "!</STRONG>\n";
print "</BODY></HTML>", "\n";
exit(0);
```

The output is sent to the browser that made the GET request, as shown in Figure 21-6.

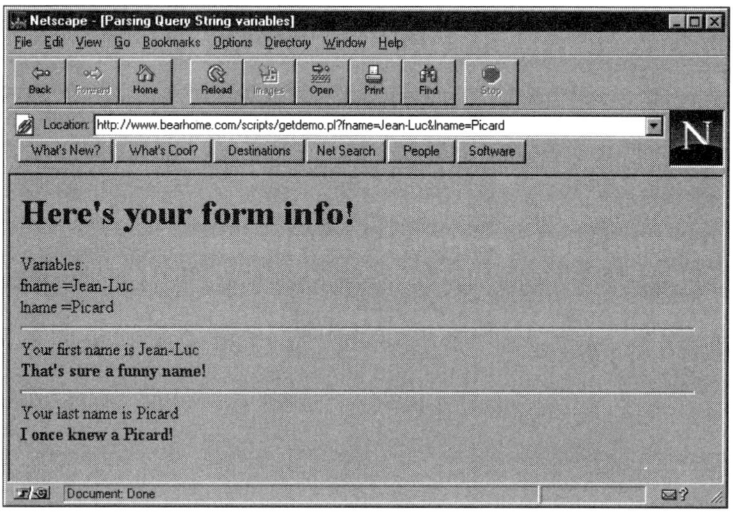

Figure 21-6: It's easy to write scripts that parse form information sent using the GET method.

Using Form Information in a CGI Program

The POST method works much like the GET method.

Note that — unlike the GET method, which is limited to the length of a URL — the POST method can be sent with an unlimited amount of information.

Here's the basic form from the GET example, modified slightly:

```
<HTML>
   <HEAD>
      <TITLE>
      Form with an attitude!
      </TITLE>
   </HEAD>
   <BODY>
   <H1>
      Demonstrates a form using <BR>
      the POST method.
      <HR>
      Please fill in the form!
   </H1>
   <FORM method="POST" action="/scripts/postdemo.pl">
   Enter your first name:  <INPUT type="text" name="fname">
   Enter your last name:   <INPUT type="text" name="lname"><BR>
   Enter something else:   <INPUT type="text" name="else"><BR>
   <P>
   <HR>
```

```
    <INPUT type="submit"> <INPUT type="reset">
    </FORM>
    </BODY>
</HTML>
```

Figure 21-7 shows this form.

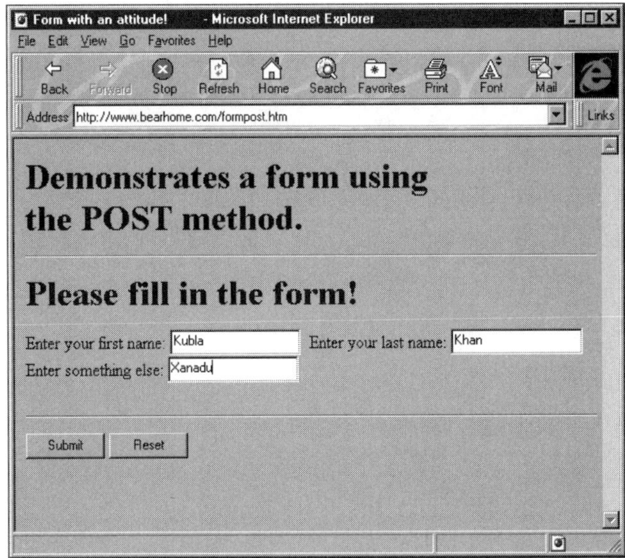

Figure 21-7: Forms submitted with the POST method can have an unlimited amount of information attached.

To retrieve and decode POST data, you must check the CONTENT_TYPE environment variable to make sure that the data has the correct MIME content type. The CONTENT_LENGTH environment variable is used to determine how much of the input stream to read. Listing 21-6 shows how to retrieve and decode POST data.

Listing 21-6: Retrieving and decoding POST data

```
$ct = $ENV{"CONTENT_TYPE"};
$cl = $ENV{"CONTENT_LENGTH"};

# check the content-type for validity
if($ct ne "application/x-www-form-urlencoded")
    {
    printf "I don't understand content-type: %s\n", $ct;
    exit 1;
    }

# put the data into a variable
read(STDIN, $qs, $cl);
```

```
# split it up into an array by the '&' character
@qs = split(/&/,$qs);

foreach $i (0 .. $#qs)
    {
    # convert plus chars to spaces
    $qs[$i] =~ s/\+/ /g;

    # convert hex tokens to characters
    $qs[$i] =~ s/%(..)/pack("c",hex($1))/ge;

    # split into names and values
    ($name, $value) = split(/=/,$qs[$i],2);

    # create the associative element
    # is there another value already (supports SELECT MULTIPLE)
    if($qs{$name}) { $qs{$name} .= ", $value" }
    else { $qs{$name} = $value; }
    }

print "\nVariables:\n\n";

foreach $name (sort keys(%qs))
    { print "$name = ", $qs{$name},"\n" }
```

You can use this as part of a script that relays the information back to the browser:

```
#/scripts/postdemo.pl
#Show user input on the form using GET

print "Content-type: text/html", "\n\n";
print "<HTML>", "\n";
print "<HEAD><TITLE>Retrieving and Decoding POST
data</TITLE></HEAD><BODY>", "\n";
print "<H1>Here's your form info!</H1>", "\n";

$ct = $ENV{"CONTENT_TYPE"};
$cl = $ENV{"CONTENT_LENGTH"};

# check the content-type for validity
if($ct ne "application/x-www-form-urlencoded")
    {
    printf "I don't understand content-type: %s\n", $ct;
    exit 1;
    }

# put the data into a variable
read(STDIN, $qs, $cl);

# split it up into an array by the '&' character
@qs = split(/&/,$qs);
```

```
foreach $i (0 .. $#qs)
   {
   # convert plus chars to spaces
   $qs[$i] =~ s/\+/ /g;

   # convert hex tokens to characters
   $qs[$i] =~ s/%(..)/pack("c",hex($1))/ge;

   # split into names and values
   ($name, $value) = split(/=/,$qs[$i],2);

   # create the associative element
   # is there another value already (supports SELECT MULTIPLE)
   if($qs{$name}) { $qs{$name} .= ", $value" }
   else { $qs{$name} = $value; }
   }

print "\nVariables:\n\n<BR>";

foreach $name (sort keys(%qs))
  { print "$name = ", $qs{$name},"<BR>\n" }

print "</BODY></HTML>", "\n";
exit(0);
```

The results are shown in Figure 21-8.

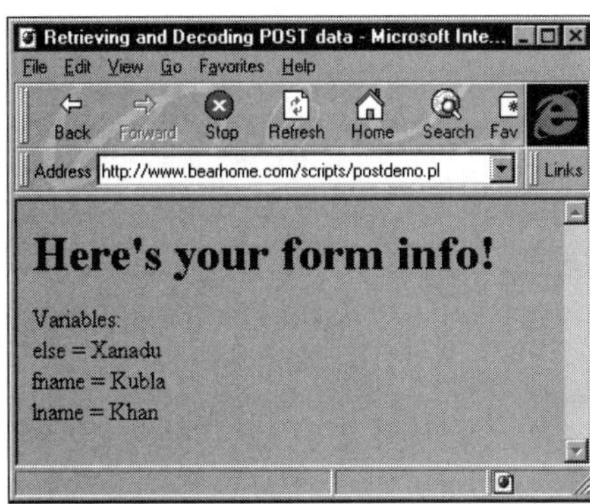

Figure 21-8: The CONTENT_LENGTH environment variable is used to determine how much of the input stream must be decoded.

You can use the same techniques to retrieve user input from more complex forms. Here's the HTML for a possible Web trading application ("WebStock...not Woodstock!"):

```
<HTML>
   <HEAD>
      <TITLE>
      WebStock On-Line Trading!
      </TITLE>
   </HEAD>
```

```
    <BODY>
    <TABLE>
       <TR>
          <TD>
             <H1>WebStock&#174&#153</H1>
          </TD>
          <TD>
             <IMG src="car.gif">
          </TD>
       </TR>
    </TABLE>
    WebStock&#174&#153...not Woodstock!<BR>
    This is not your father's trading vehicle.
    Welcome to the wide world of on-line trading.<BR>
    We at WebStock&#174&#153 promise you will have the most fun
    trading in real time.<HR>
    <FORM method="POST" action="/scripts/postdemo.pl">

Account Num:   <INPUT type="text" name="acct">
PIN:        <INPUT type="password" name="pin" size=8><BR>
Stock Symbol:     <INPUT type="text" name="ticker" size=11>
Transaction:      <SELECT name="transaction">
                      <OPTION SELECTED>Buy
                      <OPTION>Sell
                      <OPTION>Short Sell
                      </SELECT><BR>
    <INPUT type="radio" name="cash_or_margin" value="cash_true"
        checked>
      Transaction in cash account<BR>
    <INPUT type="radio" name="cash_or_margin" value="cash_false">
      Transaction in margin account<BR>
    Tell us what you think about WebStock&#174&#153!<BR>
    <TEXTAREA rows=3 cols=60 name="comments">
    </TEXTAREA><BR><BR>
    <INPUT type="submit"> <INPUT type="reset">
    </FORM>
    </BODY>
</HTML>
```

Figure 21-9 shows the WebStock form with some user input.

When the user clicks on the Submit button, the POST method is used to invoke the postdemo.pl Perl script used in the previous example. This script displays back to the browser all the variables and values entered in the form (see Figure 21-10).

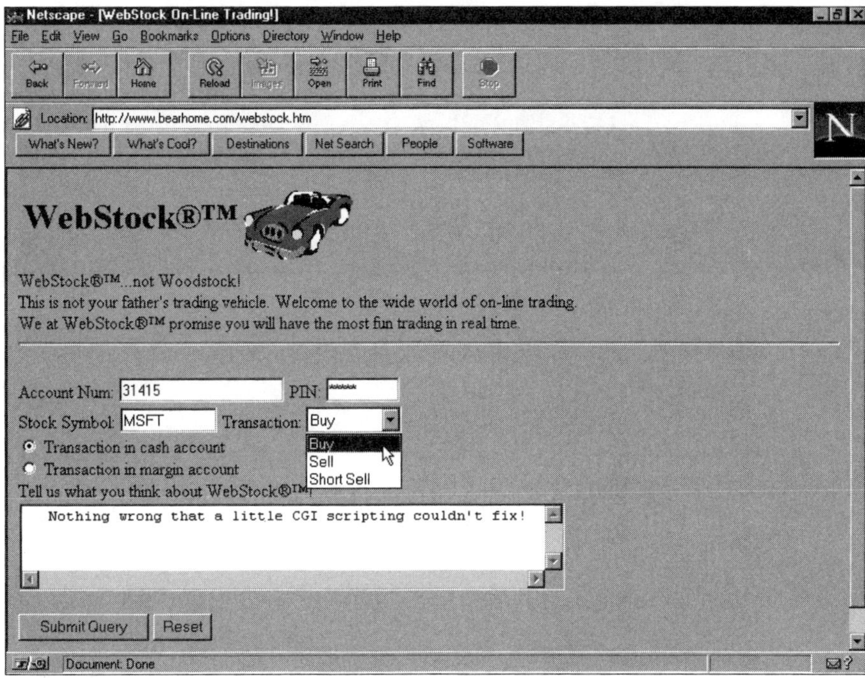

Figure 21-9: You can handle user input to complex forms using CGI programs.

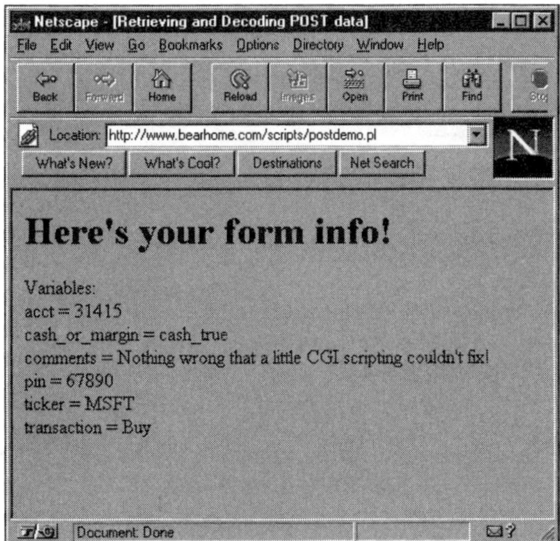

Figure 21-10: CGI programs such as the postdemo.pl Perl script can easily access user inputs.

Configuring Internet Information Server (IIS)

For the Perl CGI scripts shown so far in this chapter to work properly, the Web server software has to be configured so that

- A virtual directory for the scripts with Execute permission is established
- An attempt to execute the Perl script files automatically runs them through the Perl interpreter by associating the script file extension with the Perl interpreter

The examples in this chapter use a virtual script directory of /scripts; the Perl script files have an extension of .pl.

Inside Scoop

The configuration information provided in this section is specific to Internet Information Server (IIS) running on Windows NT 4.0. However the same basic concepts work with any NT Web server, including Netscape's and O'Reilly's, even though the specific interface may look different.

Using Service Manager to Set Virtual Directories

Microsoft Internet Information Server runs as a number of Windows NT 4.0 services. The Microsoft Internet Service Manager, shown in Figure 21-11, is an applet that can be used to configure these services.

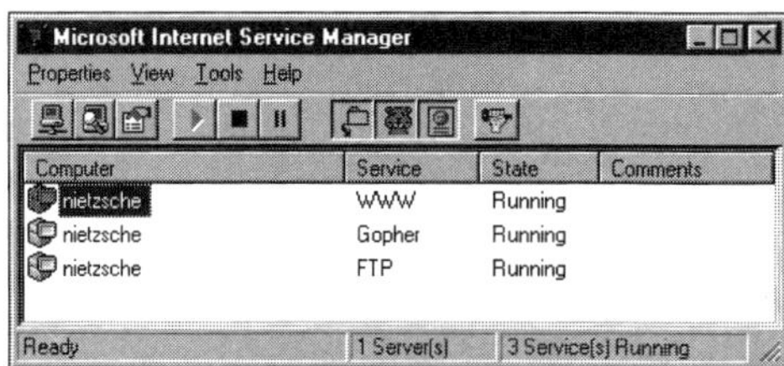

Figure 21-11: You can use the Microsoft Internet Service Manager to configure the services provided by IIS.

By the way, an HTTP version of the Internet Service Manager with an HTML interface is available with version 3 of IIS (see Figure 21-12). This is particularly handy for remote configuration of an IIS server.

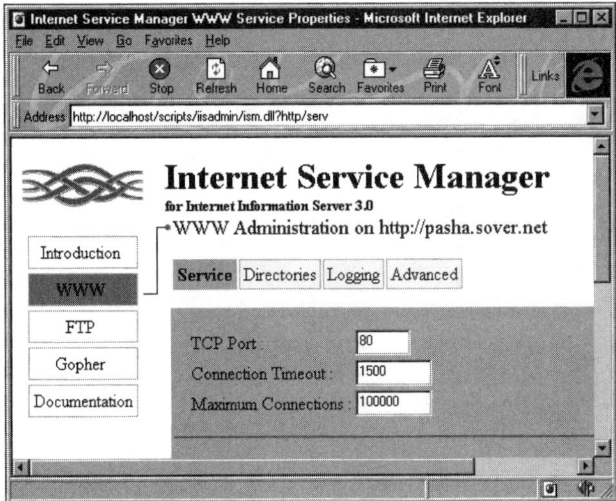

Figure 21-12: You can also use the HTTP version of Microsoft Internet Service Manager to remotely configure the services provided by IIS.

Using either version of the Internet Service Manager utility, to configure a virtual directory, open the Properties dialog for the WWW service. Using the Directories tab, you can add, remove, or set Directory properties (using the Directory Properties dialog shown in Figure 21-13).

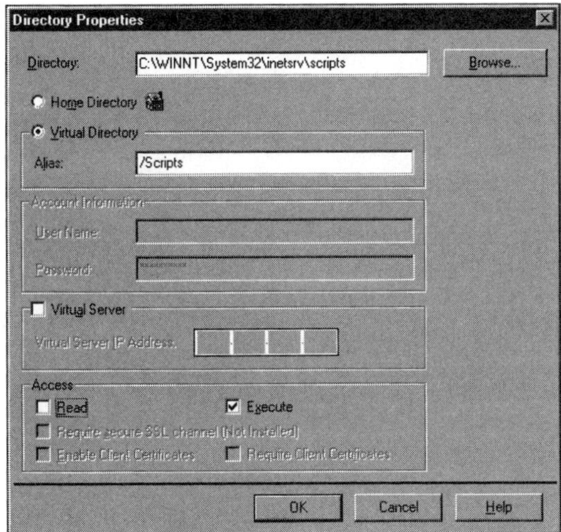

Figure 21-13: You use the Directory Properties dialog to assign a physical directory to a virtual path and to establish directory permissions.

A virtual directory (/Scripts is shown) needs to be established for CGI programs that will be invoked. This directory should be given Execute permission, so that programs in the directory can be run. HTTP requests that come in using the virtual path are now mapped into whatever physical directory contains the CGI programs.

Associating Interpreters with Applications

Perl is an interpreted language. For a Perl script to run, a Perl interpreter must be present on the server, and it must be invoked when the Perl script is executed.

Assuming you have a Perl interpreter on your system (Perl for Win32 is discussed in the next section), the mechanism for starting the interpreter is to use the Registry to associate the Perl script's filename extension (usually .pl) with the interpreter's executable file.

Internet Information Server comes with some predefined filename associations, as shown in Table 21-4.

Table 21-4 Predefined Filename Extension Associations

File Extension	*Default Associated Interpeter*
.bat, .cmd	Cmd.Exe
.idc	Httpodbc.dll
.exe, .com	System

CGI programs can be written in almost any language. (There's also no requirement that Perl scripts have the .pl extension.) This much flexibility has a downside: You'll have to figure out what associations you need and create them manually using Regedit.

The filename extension associations are located in the HKEY_LOCAL_ MACHINE\System\CurrentControlSet\Services\W3SVC\Parameters\Script Map branch of the Registry. Figure 21-14 shows adding an association for .pl files with the Perl executable.

Perl for Win32

ActiveWare Internet Corp. has been contracted by Microsoft to create a Win32 Perl interpreter. Recent builds of Perl for Win32 run under Windows 95 and NT 4.0.

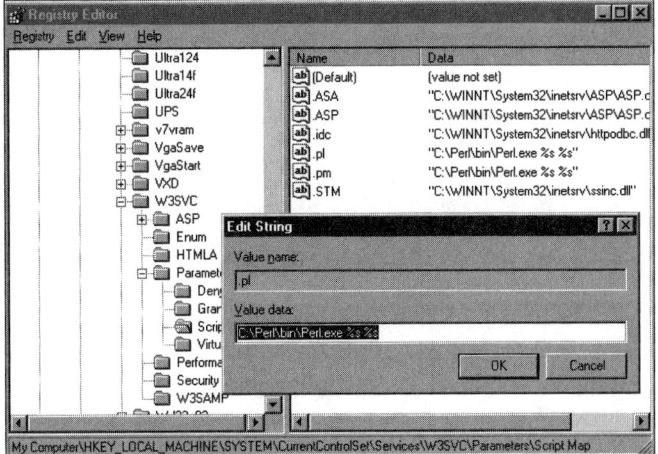

Figure 21-14: You can use the Registry to create an association between Perl scripts and the Perl interpreter.

Perl for Win32 is available for free download at *http://www.perl.hip.com/*. In addition to the Perl interpreter, which is available as a self-extracting WinZip archive, you can download PerlScript, a Perl-based scripting language used to create Active Server Pages under IIS 3 (see the section "PerlScript" that follows).

Perl Resources

There is a tremendous quantity of Perl information — and Perl source code — available on the Web.

For general Perl sites, with an emphasis on CGI scripting in PERL, you might start with

- The Perl Language Home Page, *http://www.perl.com/perl/index.html*
- O'Reilly's Perl page, *http//www.ora.com/www/info/perl/*
- *http://www.yahoo.com/Computer_and_Internet/Programming_Languages/Perl*

Sites that contain information particularly related to Perl for Win32 include

- Perl for Win32 Frequently Asked Questions (FAQ), *http://www.endcontsw.com/people/evangelo/Perl_for_Win32_FAQ.html*
- Robin Chatterjee's Perl for Win32 Page, *http://www.geocities.com/SiliconValley/Park/8312/*
- Aldo Calpini's Dada meets Perl!, *http://www.divinf.it/dada/perl*

- Perl for Win32 (Joseph L. Casadonte, Jr.), *http://www.netaxs.cpm/~joc/perlwin32.html*

PerlScript

You can use PerlScript to dish out, or publish, active server pages that can be viewed using most browsers. To run PerlScript on your server, you need to have Internet Information Server Version 3, and the Perl for Win32 and PerlScript executables installed.

Active server pages are explained in detail in Chapter 23.

Figure 21-15 shows an active server page generated using PerlScript. The code embedded in this page uses recursive function calls to generate the first 20 Fibonacci numbers.

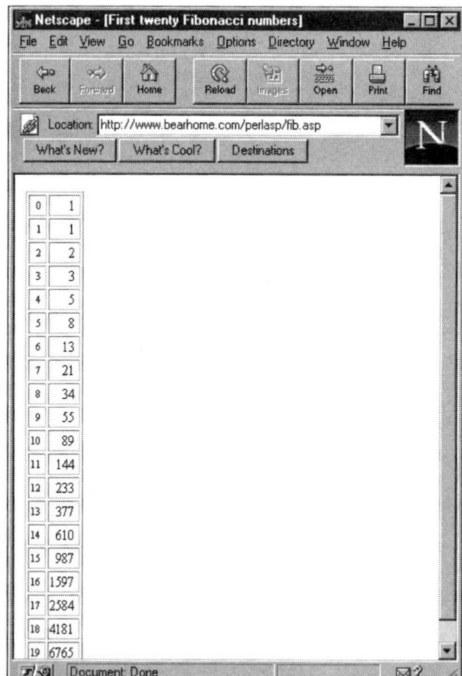

Figure 21-15: You can use PerlScript to create active server pages such as this list of Fibonacci numbers.

Here's the HTML for the Fibonacci page, which includes the embedded PerlScript:

```
<%@ LANGUAGE = PerlScript%>
<HTML>
<HEAD>
   <TITLE> First twenty Fibonacci numbers</TITLE>
</HEAD>
<BODY>
   <%$N = 20;%>
   <TABLE BORDER>
      <%for ($i = 0; $i<$N; $i++){%>
      <TR>
      <TD ALIGN=RIGHT><FONT SIZE=1> <%=$i%> </font></TD>
      <TD ALIGN=RIGHT><FONT SIZE=2>
      <%$Response->write(&Fibonacci($i));%> </font></TD>
   </TR>
      <%}%>
       </TABLE>

<%sub Fibonacci
{
   local $i=$_[0];
   local $fibA = 1;
   local $fibB = 1;
   if ($i == 0)
   {
      return $fibA;
   }
   elsif ($i == 1)
   {
      return $fibB;
   }
   elsif ($i > 1)
   {
      for ($j = 2; $j<=$i; $j++)
      {
         $fib = $fibA + $fibB ;
         $fibA = $fibB ;
         $fibB = $fib;
      }
      return $fib;
      }
} %>

</BODY>
</HTML>
```

Summary

Common Gateway Interface, or CGI, programming is the classical way to add executable content to Web applications. Once you get used to it, mastering the linkage between HTML forms and programs residing on your server is not that big a deal.

Topics covered in this chapter included

- How the Common Gateway Interface works
- MIME content types
- "Hello, World" in Perl
- CGI programming languages
- The CGI environment variables
- Displaying the value of the CGI environment variables
- HTML form tags
- URL encoding
- Using HTML form input in a CGI program
- Configuring Internet Information Server
- Virtual directories
- Associating Perl files in Windows NT with the Perl interpreter
- Perl for Win32
- Perl resources
- PerlScript

Chapter 22

The Internet Server API (ISAPI) and Active Server Pages (ASP)

"Dost thou not see my baby at my breast, That sucks the nurse asleep?"

— Cleopatra, from Shakespeare's *Anthony and Cleopatra*, V, ii, 311

This chapter covers some exciting techniques that you can use to interactively connect server-side programs running under Internet Information Server (IIS) with HTML Web pages.

First, I'll explain how the Internet Server API (ISAPI) works. Essentially, ISAPI — and its variants — is a replacement for CGI scripting that is specific to IIS. Programs written using ISAPI are dynamic-link libraries (DLLs). They execute in-process and have performance advantages over CGI programs.

Next, I'll demonstrate an exciting tool, webAction from classTools, that allows you to use Visual Basic to create ActiveX components that extend Internet Information Server and to interactively debug server-side programs.

Finally, you'll learn about Active Server Pages, or ASP — a technology formerly code-named Denali — which requires IIS version 3. These pages are generated when accessed from a browser. To achieve their extraordinary impact, ASP pages can include scripts — including VBScript, JScript (Microsoft's version of JavaScript), and PerlScript. They also can include active content: ActiveX controls and Java applets.

The Internet Server API (ISAPI)

An Internet Server Application (ISA) uses the Internet Server API (ISAPI) to provide server-side Web functionality under IIS.

These programs are written in Visual C++, although classTool's webAction allows you to create ISA-like applications using Delphi or Visual Basic (see "Using webAction" later in this chapter).

The communication paradigm between browser, server, and server-side program is different for ISA than for CGI applications. Figure 22-1 presents a high-level view of how this communication works for CGI programs (for more detailed information on CGI programs, see Chapter 21). Essentially, CGI environment variables are used to communicate back and forth between the server and the CGI program.

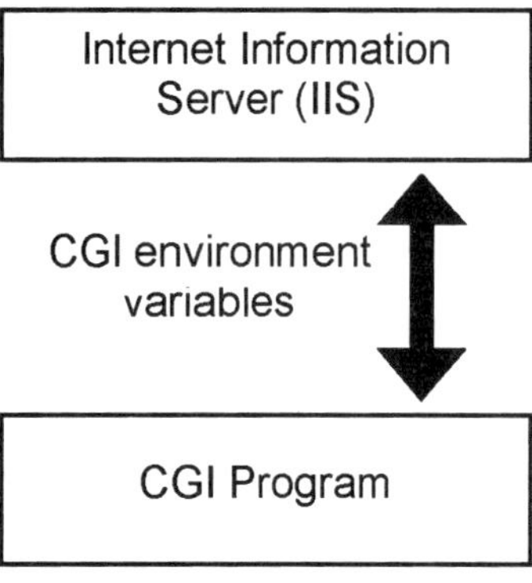

Figure 22-1: Environment variables are used to communicate between the web server and CGI program.

In contrast, communication between the web server and an ISA dynamic-link library is handled by a data structure known as the EXTENSION_CONTROL_BLOCK (ECB). This relationship is depicted in Figure 22-2.

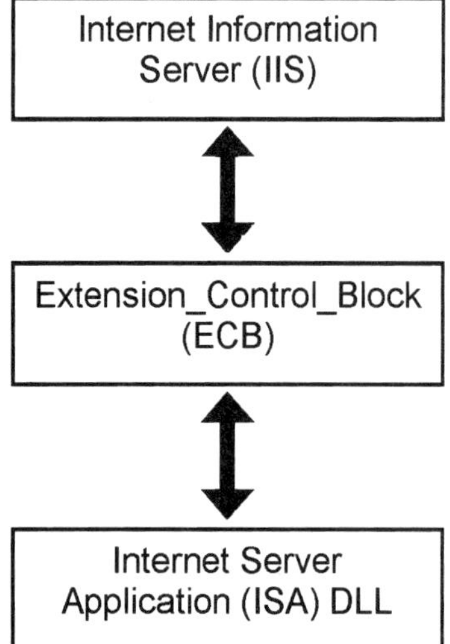

Figure 22-2: ISA applications use the EXTENSION_CONTROL_BLOCK data structure to communicate with the web server.

IIS can communicate with multiple ISA applications, each operating as an in-process Dll within the server's address space.

IIS allocates a block of memory in its address space for each ISA thread. This memory block is in the ECB format and usually referred to as an *ECB structure*. Here's the type definition for the structure:

```
typedef struct _EXTENSION_CONTROL_BLOCK {

   DWORD      cbSize;              //Size of this structure
   DWORD      dwVersion            //Version information of this spec
   HCONN      ConnID;
   DWORD      dwHttpStatusCode;
   CHAR       lpszLogData[HSE_LOG_BUFFER_LEN];
   LPSTR      lpszMethod;
   LPSTR      lpszQueryString;
   LPSTR      lpszPathInfo;
   LPSTR      lpszPathTranslated;
   DWORD      cbTotalBytes;
   DWORD      cbAvailable;
   LPBYTE     lpbData;
   LPSTR      lpszContentType;

      BOOL ( WINAPI * GetServerVariable )
     ( HCONN       hConn,
     LPSTR       lpszVariableName,
     LPVOID      lpvBuffer,
     LPDWORD     lpdwSize );

      BOOL ( WINAPI * WriteClient )
     ( HCONN       ConnID,
     LPVOID      Buffer,
     LPDWORD     lpdwBytes,
     DWORD       dwReserved );

      BOOL ( WINAPI * ReadClient )
     ( HCONN       ConnID,
     LPVOID      lpvBuffer,
     LPDWORD     lpdwSize );

      BOOL ( WINAPI * ServerSupportFunction )
     ( HCONN       hConn,
     DWORD       dwHSERRequest,
     LPVOID      lpvBuffer,
     LPDWORD     lpdwSize,
     LPDWORD     lpdwDataType );

}
```

Table 22-1 lists the fields in this structure that are likely to be significant to your ISA programs.

Table 22-1 Extension Control Block Fields Commonly Used in ISA Programs

Field	*Meaning*
connID	An unique connection ID assigned by IIS
lpszMethod	The method by which a request was made — for example, POST or GET

(continued)

Table 22-1 (Continued)

Field	*Meaning*
lpszQueryString	String containing the query string, or arguments, to be sent to the ISA application
lpszPathInfo	Extra path information provided by the browser
cbTotalBytes	The total number of bytes to expect from the browser
lpszContentType	The content type of the data sent by the browser
dwHttpStatusCode	The HTTP status code for the current transaction once the request is completed
lpszLogData	Text to be written to the IIS server log

There's documentation on writing ISA applications in the MSDN libraries. In addition, you can find up-to-the-minute information on the Microsoft site at *http://www.microsoft.com/win32dev/apiext/isapimrg.htm*.

Writing an Internet Server Application

You can generate template code for an ISA application using Visual C++ and Developer Studio. First, select the ISAPI Extension Wizard from the New Project Workspace dialog, as shown in Figure 22-3. The ISAPI Extension Wizard lets you create the basis for an ISA filter or an ISA application (see Figure 22-4). The ISA shown in Listing 22-1 is template code generated by the ISAPI Extension Wizard.

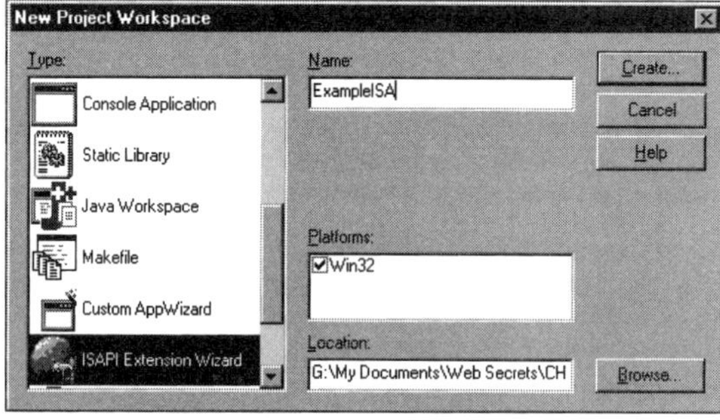

Figure 22-3: You can create template code for an ISA application using the ISAPI Extension Wizard.

ISA Filters

An ISA filter is an ISAPI-based dynamic-link library that processes requests before the web server receives them. Once a filter has been installed, it is invoked with every client request. In other words, filters modify the way IIS behaves, rather than answering specific client requests. For more information, see "Writing an ISAPI Filter" later in this chapter.

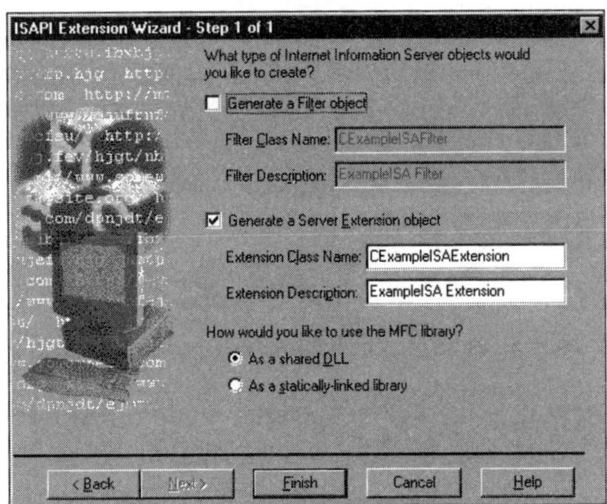

Figure 22-4: You can use the ISAPI Extension Wizard to create ISA filters or ISA applications.

Listing 22-1: Template code for a sample ISA

```
// EXAMPLEISA.CPP - Implementation file for your Internet Server
//    ExampleISA Extension

#include "stdafx.h"
#include "ExampleISA.h"

///////////////////////////////////////////////////////////////////////
//
// The one and only CWinApp object
// NOTE: You may remove this object if you alter your project to no
// longer use MFC in a DLL.

CWinApp theApp;

///////////////////////////////////////////////////////////////////////
//
// command-parsing map

BEGIN_PARSE_MAP(CExampleISAExtension, CHttpServer)
   // TODO: insert your ON_PARSE_COMMAND() and
```

```
   // ON_PARSE_COMMAND_PARAMS() here to hook up your commands.
   // For example:

   ON_PARSE_COMMAND(Default, CExampleISAExtension, ITS_EMPTY)
   DEFAULT_PARSE_COMMAND(Default, CExampleISAExtension)
END_PARSE_MAP(CExampleISAExtension)


///////////////////////////////////////////////////////////////////////////
/
// The one and only CExampleISAExtension object

CExampleISAExtension theExtension;


///////////////////////////////////////////////////////////////////////////
/
// CExampleISAExtension implementation

CExampleISAExtension::CExampleISAExtension()
{
}

CExampleISAExtension::~CExampleISAExtension()
{
}

BOOL CExampleISAExtension::GetExtensionVersion(HSE_VERSION_INFO*
pVer)
{
   // Call default implementation for initialization
   CHttpServer::GetExtensionVersion(pVer);

   // Load description string
   TCHAR sz[HSE_MAX_EXT_DLL_NAME_LEN+1];
   ISAPIVERIFY(::LoadString(AfxGetResourceHandle(),
      IDS_SERVER, sz, HSE_MAX_EXT_DLL_NAME_LEN));
   _tcscpy(pVer->lpszExtensionDesc, sz);
   return TRUE;
}

///////////////////////////////////////////////////////////////////////////
/
// CExampleISAExtension command handlers

void CExampleISAExtension::Default(CHttpServerContext* pCtxt)
{
   StartContent(pCtxt);
   WriteTitle(pCtxt);

*pCtxt << _T("This default message was produced by the Internet");
*pCtxt << _T(" Server DLL Wizard. Edit your
CExampleISAExtension::Default()");
*pCtxt << _T(" implementation to change it.\r\n");
```

```
    EndContent(pCtxt);
}

// Do not edit the following lines, which are needed by ClassWizard.
#if 0
BEGIN_MESSAGE_MAP(CExampleISAExtension, CHttpServer)
    //{{AFX_MSG_MAP(CExampleISAExtension)
    //}}AFX_MSG_MAP
END_MESSAGE_MAP()
#endif    // 0
```

You can invoke the ISA using a URL, for example:

```
http://www.bearhome.com/scripts/ExampleISA.Dll?
```

The virtual directory that the ISA is placed in should be given Execute rights. See "Using Service Manager to Set Virtual Directories" in Chapter 21 for more information.

You can use the command parsing map section of the code to establish members that can be invoked from a URL, for example:

```
http://www.bearhome.com/scripts/ExampleISA.Dll?DoIt
```

To implement this internally, you'd need to add a DoIt ON_PARSE_COMMAND statement to the command parsing map, as well as a related command handler. The parsing map for a particular command will also handle parameters passed with it via HTML form methods.

In the template code in Listing 22-1, the message sent back to the browser is plain text, created in the handler for the default command. Instead, you can send back HTML.

An ISA can retrieve the value of server variables — the analog to CGI environment variables — either by using the GetServerVariable ISAPI function or by reading the value directly from the fields in the ECB block.

Writing an ISAPI Filter

An ISAPI filter application is a dynamic-link library that IIS calls whenever there is an HTTP request. When the filter is first loaded, it communicates to the server what sort of events it will process. Whenever an appropriate event occurs, the server calls on the filter to process the transactions.

ISAPI filters are very powerful behind-the-scenes facilitators. You can use them for many purposes, including

- Authentication
- Compression
- Encryption
- Logging

- Web traffic analysis
- URL redirection

Provided that Filter is selected as the object type to be created by the ISAPI Extension Wizard, you can elect to include the notifications that your filter will process on the second Wizard panel (Figure 22-5).

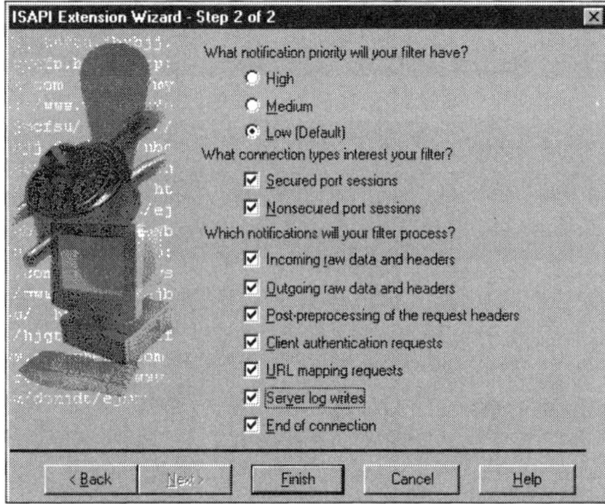

Figure 22-5: You can choose to include filter notifications in the template code generated.

Installing an ISA Filter

Once the filter has been compiled as a Dll, it should be placed in virtual directory with Execute rights.

Next, you'll need to inform IIS that the filter is present so that it will know to notify it when appropriate events occur. You do this by changing a Registry setting. First, use Internet Service Manager to stop the Web publishing services, as shown in Figure 22-6.

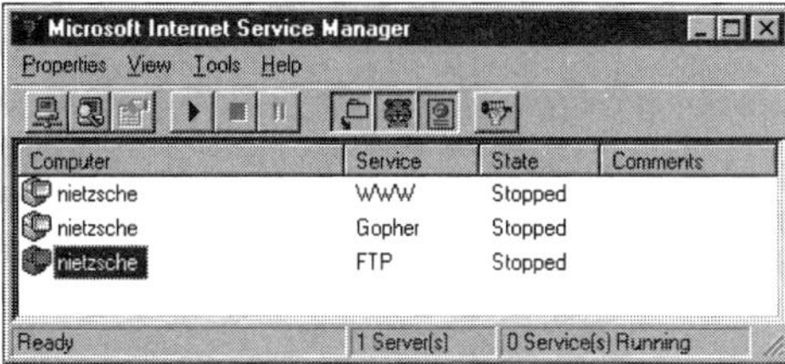

Figure 22-6: Before you change the Registry to reflect the presence of a new ISA filter, you must use Internet Service Manager to stop the Web services.

You should enter ISA filters in the Registry in a comma delimited list as the value for Filter DLLs key. Figure 22-7 shows how you might edit this value.

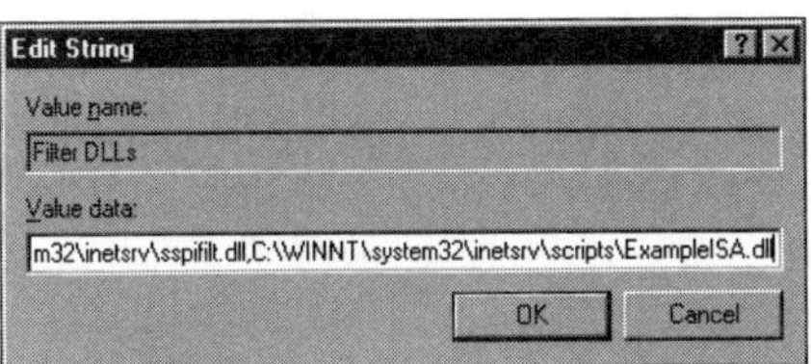

Figure 22-7: To add a new ISA filter, edit the Filter DLLs value in the Registry.

The order in which filters are invoked partially depends upon the order in which they are entered in the Filter DLLs value field (it also depends upon what notifications each filter is interested in).

The Filter DLLs key and value is located in the following branch of the Registry:

HKEY_LOCAL_MACHINE\SYSTEM\CurrentControlSet\Service\W3SVC\Parameters

Using webAction

The program webAction, published by classTools, Inc., provides an interface between web server software and ActiveX components (OLE servers) that you write.

There's a trial version of webAction on the *Web Developer's SECRETS* companion CD-ROM. For up-to-the-minute technical information on the product, you can contact classTools at *http://www.classtools.com/*.

Essentially, webAction is an ISAPI filter program that allows you to access ISAPI functionality using any language that can create OLE servers, including Visual Basic and Delphi.

In addition to Internet Information Server, webAction will work with O'Reilly's WebSite server software.

WebAction works by redirecting all calls within a fictitious URL, by default, *http://www.yourserver.com/cgi-ole/*. The cgi-ole directory doesn't really exist. Programs you write for use with webAction are invoked when your web server receives a URL consisting of the fictitious directory followed by a registered OLE server's classname — for example, ../cgi-ole/myServer.myclass.

The webAction product consists of two parts: the controller and a development toolset.

The controller uses ISAPI filtering techniques to look for requests from browsers that should be handled by your program. It then packages all of the information from a request in two simple arrays for use with your program. Finally, the controller sends your program's response back to the browser.

The toolset includes objects and methods to help display templates based on the contents of a database; generate HTML forms; post submitted information to a database; and control clients and HTTP interaction with cookies, redirection, and authentication.

In addition to supplying powerful tools for easy and fast server-side Web design, webAction offers great performance hits compared to normal CGI solutions.

Installing webAction

Installing webAction can be a bit complex. You'll have to do a fair amount of configuration (after you've installed the software by running the webAction setup program).

This discussion assumes that you already have Windows NT Server version 4.0, Build 1381, Service Pack 2, or later installed. You'll also need to have IIS up and running.

DCOM Access Permissions

After installing webAction, you need to set access and launch permissions for Distributed COM (DCOM). To set DCOM permissions, run the DCOM configuration utility, Dcomcnfg.Exe (see Figure 22-8), which you'll find in the C:\WINNT\system32 directory. You can launch it by choosing Run from the Windows Start menu and entering **dcomcnfg** in the resulting dialog box.

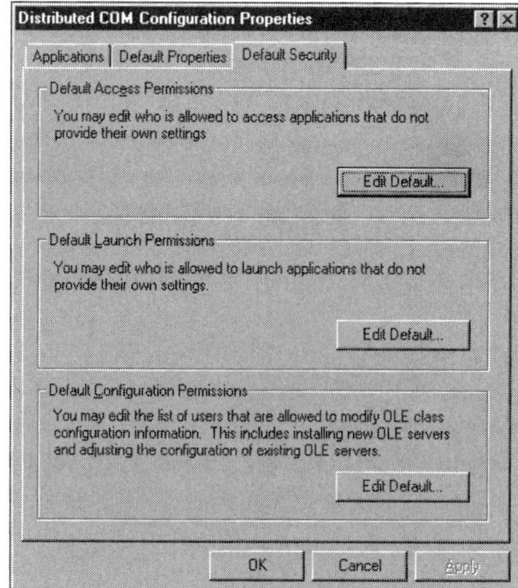

Figure 22-8: To use webAction, you need to set DCOM access and launch permissions.

Click on the Edit Default button for Default Access Permissions. This opens the Registry Value Permissions dialog for Default Access Permissions (see Figure 22-9). Choose Add, and select INTERACTIVE and SYSTEM.

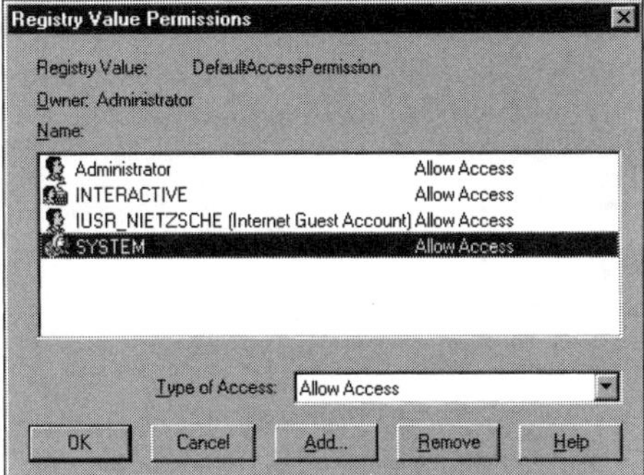

Figure 22-9: You should add INTERACTIVE and SYSTEM access permissions to the default.

Repeat this process for Default Launch Permissions, so that INTERACTIVE and SYSTEM launch permissions are added to the default.

IIS User Rights

To debug interactively with webAction, you need to grant three advanced user rights. These rights are not normally granted to a local account. To set these advanced rights, open the User Manager for Domains from NT's Administrative Tools group. The User Manager is shown in Figure 22-10.

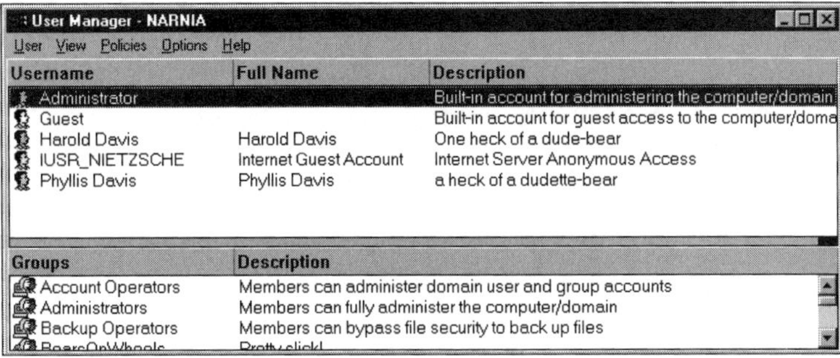

Figure 22-10: You use the User Manager to set rights you'll need to debug interactively with webAction.

Choose User Rights from the Policy menu, and make sure that the Show Advanced User Rights box is checked, as shown in Figure 22-11.

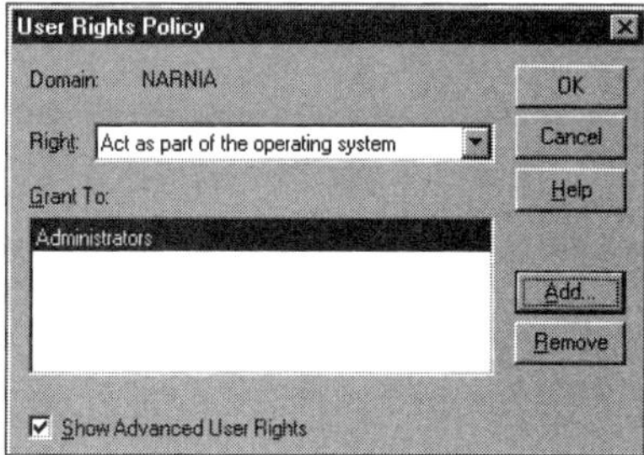

Figure 22-11: Make sure the Show Advanced User Rights box is checked in the User Rights Policy dialog.

Choose Act as Part of the Operating System from the drop-down list and click on Add. Choose a group you belong to, and select Members. Choose your account and click on Add. Click on OK twice to grant the right to you.

Repeat this process for the advanced rights named Generate Security Audits and Replace a Process Level Token. Log off and back on the system to have the rights take effect.

You Can Talk to Your Web Server

It's easy to create a "Hello, World" project that webAction will invoke for you. The example project will be invoked by the URL */cgi-ole/atest.SayHello.*

Using Visual Basic 5, start an ActiveX Exe or Dll project (meaning, an OLE server). Add a class module to the project, and change the name of the class module to SayHello. Make sure the module's Instancing property is set to 5-MultiUse, as shown in Figure 22-12.

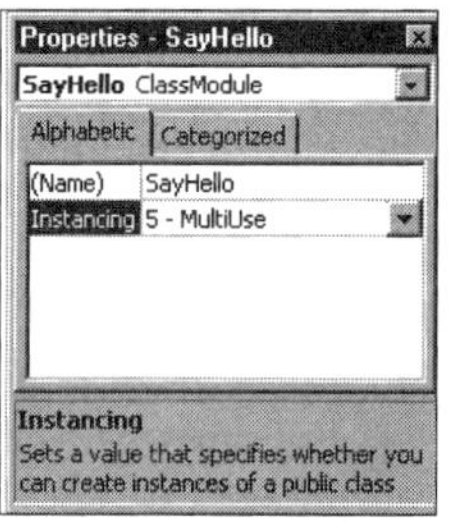

Figure 22-12: Make sure the class module's Instancing property is set to 5-MultiUse.

A function named Action is placed in the SayHello class module to return HTML to the browser invoking the program. For example:

```
Option Explicit
'Say Hello to webAction

Public Function Action(ByRef environment() As String, _
```

```
   ByRef query() As String) As String
   Dim strHTML As String
   Dim Quote As String
   Quote = Chr(34)
   strHTML = "<HTML><HEAD><TITLE>"
   strHTML = strHTML & "Coming up roses..."
   strHTML = strHTML & "</TITLE></HEAD><BODY bgcolor=" & Quote _
      & "#FF0000" & Quote & ">"
   strHTML = strHTML & "<H2>Roses are red, violets are blue <BR>"
   strHTML = strHTML & _
      "It's true, you can talk to your Web server, too!"
   strHTML = strHTML & "</H2></BODY></HTML>"
   Action = strHTML
End Function
```

Next, make sure the project has a standard code module (Bas file). Add a Sub Main to this standard module:

```
Public Sub Main()
   'Pro forma Sub Main for start
   'Global initialization code goes here
End Sub
```

As is true of OLE server applications in general, the project should be set to start from Sub Main. Sub Main need include no code, although it should include at least one comment to keep the compiler from removing it.

Open the Project Properties dialog — shown in Figure 22-13 — and make sure the startup object is Sub Main. Give the project the name, Atest, that will be used along with the name of the class module in the URL.

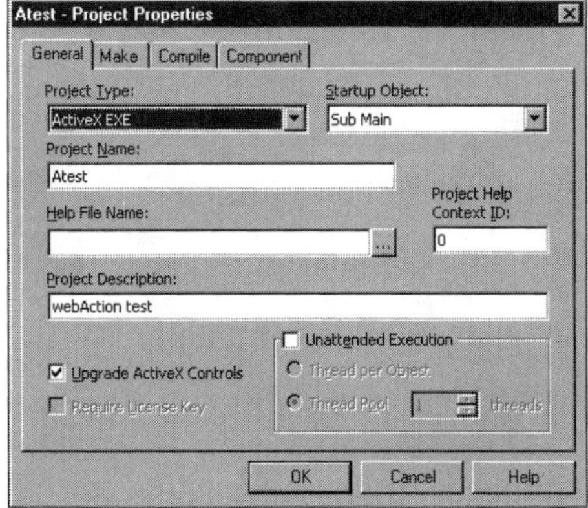

Figure 22-13: Use the Project Properties dialog to set the startup object and the project name.

You can compile the project, or, to run in debug mode, select Start With Full Compile in the Visual Basic IDE.

In either case, you can open the result of the class module's Action function (see Figure 22-14) by entering the fictitious virtual path in a browser, followed by the project's class name. For example:

```
http://www.bearhome.com/cgi-ole/atest.sayhello
```

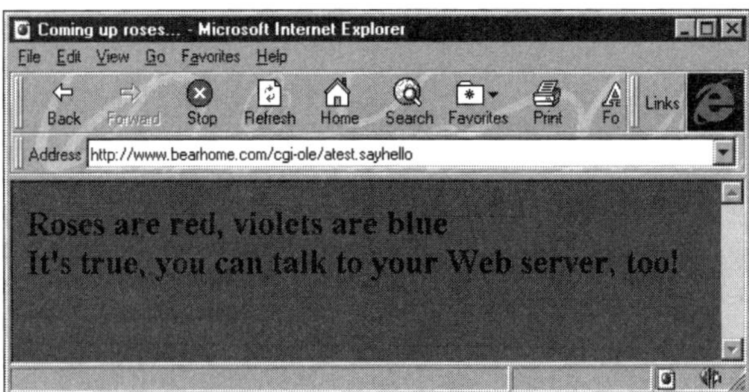

Figure 22-14: WebAction directs the output of the program to the browser that requested it.

It's important to understand that webAction finds programs based on their class names as entered in the Registry — not the physical location of the program on your system. If you want to move one of these programs, you'll have to unregister it first and then reregister it in the new location. See the sidebar "Using Regsvr32 and the /regserver Switch" for more information.

Using Regsvr32 and the /regserver Switch

To register an in-process server (Dll file), run the Regsvr32 program with the server as an argument, for example:

```
Regsvr32 C:\Samples\MyServer.Dll
```

To unregister an in-process server (Dll file), run the Regsvr32 program with the /u switch and the server as an argument, for example:

```
Regsvr32 /u C:\Samples\MyServer.Dll
```

To register an out-of-process server (Exe file), run the program using the /regserver switch, for example:

```
C:\Samples\MyServer.Exe /regserver
```

To unregister an out-of-process server (Exe file), run the program using the /unregserver switch, for example:

```
C:\Samples\MyServer.Exe /unregserver
```

OLE servers are automatically temporarily registered when they are running in a development environment such as VB or Delphi.

WebAction Properties

You can activate the webAction properties utility from the Windows Start menu. Once webAction is installed on your server, it can control IIS. You can use the Server tab of the webAction properties dialog, shown in Figure 22-15, to start and stop Web service on your server, and also to choose debug or normal mode.

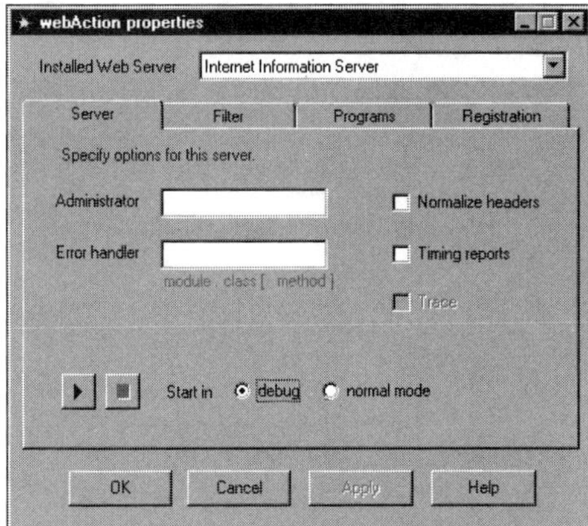

Figure 22-15: You can use webAction's Server tab to start and stop Web service and to select debug or normal mode.

If debug mode is selected, errors in programs running in their native IDEs will be trapped by the IDE. For example, if a server application is running in the Visual Basic development environment and webAction is running in debug mode, any errors will cause Visual Basic's error messages to be shown as they occur. This makes debugging a whole lot easier. In addition, you can set breakpoints in Visual Basic programs you are working on.

Because webAction works by filtering URL requests to a fictional directory, you can stop webAction from interacting with your web server without removing it from your system. You can use the Filter tab of the webAction properties dialog (shown in Figure 22-16) to make sure that no URLs, fictional or otherwise, are to be handled by webAction. When you are ready to use webAction again, simply add the appropriate filter to the Filter tab.

WebAction runs as a system service, and programs you write that are connected to your Web site using webAction run as server extensions. There are some limitations on what system services and server extensions can do:

- You cannot display a dialog or message box
- You cannot invoke a program that displays a dialog or message box
- Generally, you cannot access files or programs on other machines

The reason for the restriction regarding dialogs is that system services and server extensions are expected to run unattended. They must not create conditions — such as a dialog with an OK button — that require human intervention.

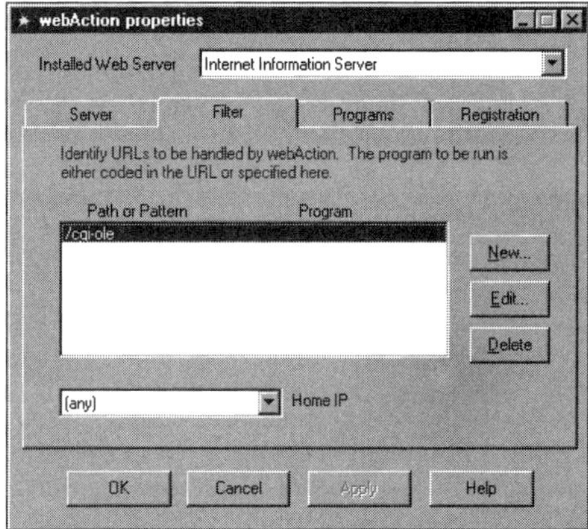

Figure 22-16: You use webAction's Filter tab to set the URLs — fictional or otherwise — that are intercepted.

HTML Forms

HTML form data can be sent to webAction (which sends it on to the appropriate program) using either the GET or POST method.

Form variables sent using GET will appear as part of the URL of the response; this information will not be shown in the Address field of the browser if you use the POST method.

WebAction captures form information for you and places it in a two-dimensional array named Query, which it passes to your program.

The first element of the array ranges from 0 to 1. The second element in the array ranges from 0 to n-1, where n is the number of name=value pairs in the form request. Thus, Query(0,x) is always a value, and Query(1,x) is always a name (provided in both cases that x is within bounds).

As an example, suppose that two name=value pairs were passed to a program via webAction using the GET method:

```
/cgi-ole/example.pairs?fname=bilbo&lname=baggins
```

Table 22-2 shows the — somewhat counterintuitive — way this works.

Table 22-2 WebAction Query Array and name=value Pairs

Name	*Value*
Query(0,0) fname	Query(1,0) bilbo
Query(0,1) lname	Query(1,1) baggins

Chapter 21 featured a CGI example that processed form data from a stock trading Web page ("WebStock...not Woodstock"). Here's the HTML form part of the Web page, modified to add a few fields:

```
...
<FORM method="GET" action="/cgi-ole/web.stock">

Account Num:    <INPUT type="text" name="acct">
PIN:        <INPUT type="password" name="pin" size=8><BR>
Stock Symbol:      <INPUT type="text" name="ticker" size=11>
Number of Shares: <INPUT type="text" name="quan" size=10>
Limit Price:       <INPUT type="text" name="limit" size=10>
Transaction:       <SELECT name="transaction">
                        <OPTION SELECTED>Buy
                        <OPTION>Sell
                        <OPTION>Short Sell
                        </SELECT><BR>
   <INPUT type="radio" name="cash_or_margin" value="cash_true"
   checked>
     Transaction in cash account<BR>
   <INPUT type="radio" name="cash_or_margin" value="cash_false">
     Transaction in margin account<BR>
   Tell us what you think about WebStock&#174&#153!<BR>
   <TEXTAREA rows=3 cols=60 name="comments">
   </TEXTAREA><BR><BR>
   <INPUT type="submit"> <INPUT type="reset">
```

Figure 22-17 shows the modified WebStock page in a browser.

The HTML form uses the GET method to a webAction OLE server named web.stock:

```
<FORM method="GET" action="/cgi-ole/web.stock">
```

To set up a program to respond to this request, you'd have to name the project web and include a class module named stock. Listing 22-2 shows the code required, if placed in the Request function of the class module, to return all form name=value pairs in plain text:

Listing 22-2: Returning all name=value pairs from the query array

```
Public Function Action(ByRef environment() As String, _
   ByRef query() As String) As String
   Dim i As Integer
```

```
    For i = LBound(query, 2) To UBound(query, 2)
      Action = Action & query(1, i) & " = " & _
        query(0, i) & vbCrLf
    Next i
End Function
```

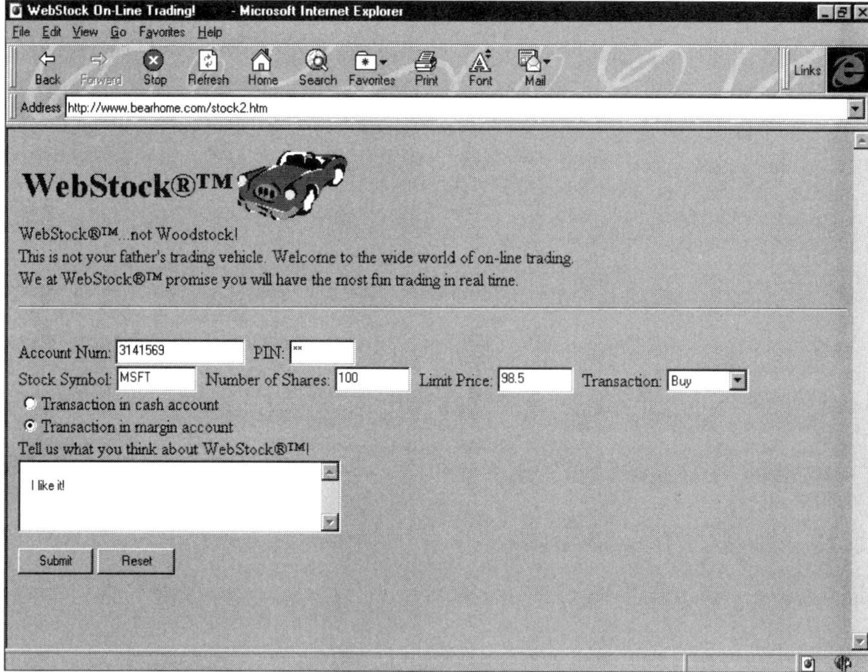

Figure 22-17: The WebStock page has been modified to include a number of new fields.

Figure 22-18 shows the results of submitting the WebStock form.

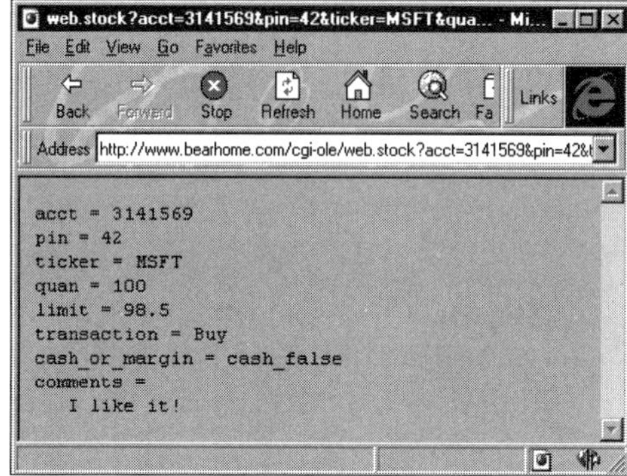

Figure 22-18: You can easily use the Query array in your program to return name=value pairs.

Inside Scoop

As you might expect, the Environment array is used in a similar fashion to retrieve environment variables.

Well, actually, perhaps the WebStock form should be processed a little more thoroughly. It would be a good idea, for example, to return a transaction confirmation!

If you attempt to modify the web.stock project, you'll find that you cannot compile a new version of the project — the original is being held in memory. (This is not a problem if you are running web.stock in debug mode from the VB IDE.)

To get webAction to release all OLE servers it is holding in memory, enter the following URL in your browser:

```
http://www.yourserver.com/webaction/free/all
```

Figure 22-19 shows the web.stock object being released.

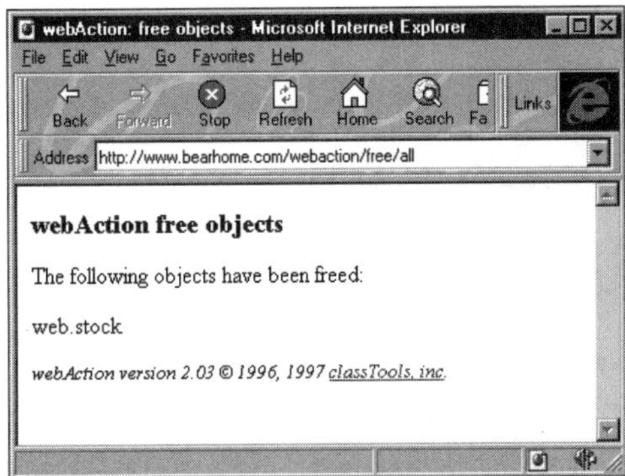

Figure 22-19: You can make webAction release all objects it is holding in memory.

First, why not modify the HTML form's method to POST, so that name=value pairs are not displaying all over the place.

Next, modify the code in the Stock class module to return an HTML transaction confirmation that has been generated on the fly:

```
Public Function Action(ByRef environment() As String, _
   ByRef query() As String) As String
   Dim strHTML As String
   Dim Quote As String
   Quote = Chr(34)
   strHTML = "<HTML><HEAD><TITLE>"
   strHTML = strHTML & "Transaction Confirmation"
   strHTML = strHTML & "</TITLE></HEAD><BODY bgcolor=" & Quote _
      & "#9966CC" & Quote & ">"
```

```
    If query(0, 6) = "cash_false" Then
       strHTML = strHTML & "<B>MARGIN ACCOUNT<BR><P>"
    Else
       strHTML = strHTML & "<B>CASH ACCOUNT<BR><P>"
    End If
    strHTML = strHTML & "Account Number: " & query(0, 0) & "<BR>"
    If UCase(query(0, 2)) = "MSFT" Then
       strHTML = strHTML & "Microsoft Corp.<BR>"
    Else
       strHTML = strHTML & "Ticker: " & query(0, 2) & "<BR>"
    End If
    strHTML = strHTML & "Quantity: " & query(0, 3) & "<BR>"
    strHTML = strHTML & "Limit Price: " & query(0, 4) & "<BR>"
    strHTML = strHTML & "Approximate order value is $" & _
       Format(Val(query(0, 3)) * Val(query(0, 4)), "##,##0.00")
    strHTML = strHTML & "<BR><P>Thanks for using WebStock" & _
       "(not Woodstock, and not your father's trading vehicle)!<BR>"
    strHTML = strHTML & "</B></BODY></HTML>"
    Action = strHTML
End Function
```

If you enter some information in the WebStock form, and submit it, you'll receive a transaction confirmation, as shown in Figure 22-20.

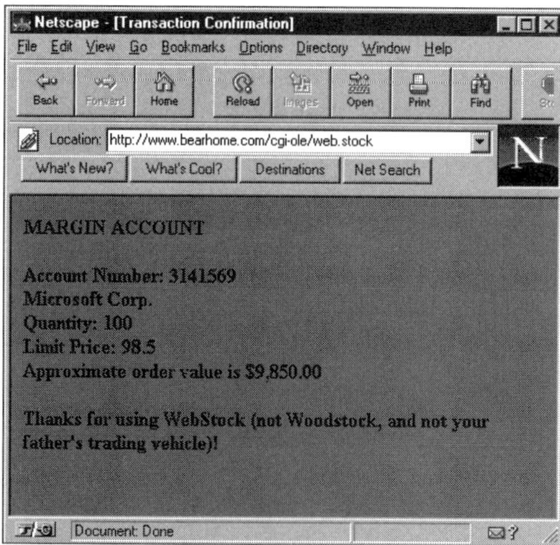

Figure 22-20: Using the Query array, it's easy to generate customized responses to HTML form information.

WebAction is an industrial-strength program used in numerous complex Web sites for server-side, on-the-fly HTML generation. For information on using webAction to facilitate Web database programming, see Chapter 23, "Databases on the Web."

OLEISAPI

Visual Basic programmers can create server-side executable content by writing ActiveX components (OLE automation servers) that interface with Oleisapi.Dll, an ISA application written (and supported) in his spare time by David Stutz, a Microsoft OLE expert.

Oleisapi is not officially supported by Microsoft in any way. A note of caution is that it is unlikely that the Oleisapi library is keeping pace with the changes in IIS.

In theory, Oleisapi works much like webAction. The Oleisapi.Dll is placed in a virtual directory with execute permissions, such as the /scripts directory. Oleisapi applications are registered as Dlls with Windows; Oleisapi.Dll acts as a transaction broker between the application and Internet Information Server.

For more information about Oleisapi, check out the OLEISAPI site, *http://www.datawide.com/oleisapi/*.

Climbing Denali

Denali, meaning "the great one" in native Athabascan, is the highest North American mountain. It dominates the surrounding Alaskan country side. It is also Microsoft's code name for the Active Server Page (ASP) technology (included in Internet Information Server 3).

Whatever name you use, ASP — or Denali — is an awesome server-side programming tool that allows you to generate HTML on the fly using scripting languages, ActiveX components, and Java applets. The ASP technology is extremely important because

- It incorporates and includes many existing Web development languages and techniques
- It makes it significantly easier to author interactive server content

Much of ASP scripting ends up being about connecting browsers with databases. Although this chapter focuses on the nuts and bolts of ASP development, Chapter 23 covers interactive database development using ASP.

There's a security bug that affects all current versions of IIS. If an ASP file is placed in a virtual directory, such as /scripts, that has Read as well as Execute permission, the source code for the script will display if the URL is entered in a browser with an extra period following the script name. This is potentially dangerous, because ASP scripts may contain confidential information, such as database passwords and server-side script logic. Be careful with the permissions settings for all virtual directories!

The shortcut installed by IIS to the ASP product documentation may not work on your system. If you have IIS version 3 installed on your server, you can view the ASP documentation by opening the following URL in Internet Explorer:

http://www.yourserver.com/iasdocs/aspdocs/roadmap.asp.

The Mechanics of ASP

The source code for an ASP file is an ASCII text file, just like a standard HTML page. You can create ASP pages using Notepad, or any other handy-dandy text editor. Saving the text file with an .asp file extension tells the server to process the file as an Active Server Page.

Active Server Pages (ASPs) must be saved with an .asp filename extension.

ASP script commands are included in the file between specialized delimiters, like this:

```
<% ASP Script Commands %>
```

Essentially, the mechanism works in a similar fashion to server-side includes (SSI), which also expand token delimited strings in HTML files (see Chapter 20 for more information on SSI).

In addition to ASP script commands, ASP files can contain any legal HTML commands.

Here's a simple ASP file:

```
<HTML>
<BODY>
<% For i = 1 To 7 %>
   <FONT SIZE=<% = i %>
   Cleopatra and her asp!<BR>
<% Next %>
</BODY>
</HTML>
```

The script code, indicated by the <% and %> tokens that surround it, iterates the text display seven times, each time making the font a size larger, with the results shown in Figure 22-21.

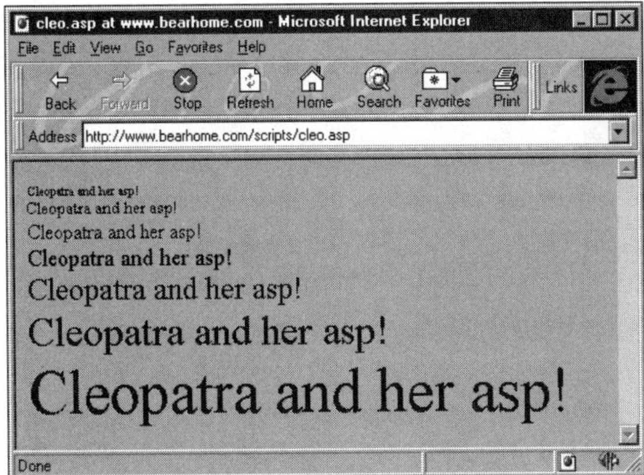

Figure 22-21: ASP sources files generate Web pages by expanding script entered between delimiters.

Active Script Languages

ASP is intended to be used "out of the box" with VBScript and JScript (Microsoft's version of JavaScript). To add more octane to your Web applications, you can, in addition, call ActiveX components (OLE servers) written in the language of your choice from within Active Script pages.

There are a number of third-party Active Script engines — for example, PerlScript, described in Chapter 21. Of course, you'll need to install the interpreter for the scripting language on your system.

VBScript is the default scripting language used in ASP files, meaning that the Active Server Pages interpreter will assume that the language between the ASP delimiters is VBScript unless you specify otherwise.

You can use multiple scripting languages in the same ASP page, provided that each is broken out into a separate procedure, with the language used indicated in the <SCRIPT> tag.

I'll use VBScript for the examples in this chapter because it is the most "native" to the Active Server Pages interpreter. For more information on VBScript, see Chapter 10, "Doing It with VBScript," and Chapter 11, "VBScript and ActiveX."

Creating a Form and a Response

As you might expect, you can use ASP pages to respond to HTML form submissions. The ASP response file is used as the argument for the **action** parameter of the <FORM> tag. For example

```
<FORM method="POST" action="/scripts/snake.asp">
```

sends the results of the form to the file Snake.Asp.

ASP response files contain HTML and code written in a delimited scripting language, as explained earlier. The Active Server Pages application processes the script commands and sends the expanded file back to the browser.

When a form request is transmitted to an ASP response file, the Forms collection of the Request object contains the values of the HTML form variables. To obtain the value of the form field, you'd use the following syntax:

```
Request.Form("formfieldname")
```

Here's an example of an HTML form used to obtain registration information for pet snakes:

```
<FORM method="POST" action="/scripts/snake.asp">

Serpent Name:   <INPUT type="text" name="name"><BR>
Serpent Type:     <INPUT type="text" name="type"><BR>
Characteristics:      <SELECT name="char">
                       <OPTION SELECTED>Friendly
                       <OPTION>Venomous
                       <OPTION>Nocturnal
                       <OPTION>Triangular Head
                       <OPTION>Rattles
                       </SELECT><BR>
   <INPUT type="radio" name="title" value="mr" checked>
     Mister Snake<BR>
   <INPUT type="radio" name="title" value="ms">
     Ms Snake<BR>
   <INPUT type="submit"> <INPUT type="reset">
</FORM>
```

Figure 22-22 shows the pet snake form in an HTML page.

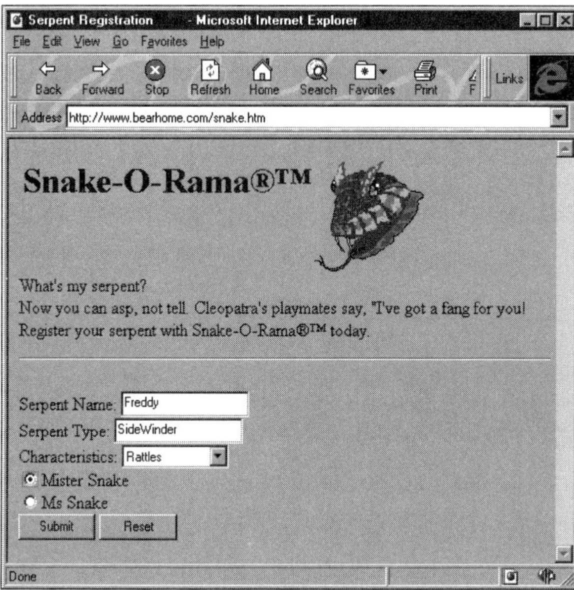

Figure 22-22: HTML forms can use the action parameter of the <FORM> tag to generate an active server response.

Snake.Asp, the Active Server Response file, is an HTML ASCII text file that obtains the form field values:

```
<%@ LANGUAGE = VBScript %>
<HTML>
   <HEAD>
      <TITLE>Serpent Registration Response
      </TITLE>
</HEAD>
<BODY BGCOLOR="#FFFFFF"><FONT FACE="ARIAL,HELVETICA">

   <H2><CENTER>What's Your Fang?</H2>
   <IMG src="http://www.bearhome.com/snake.gif"></CENTER>
   <P ALIGN=CENTER>
   Thank you for registering your snake! <BR>

   <%
   Title = Request.Form("title")
   Name = Request.Form("name")
   What = Request.Form("type")
   Char = Request.Form("char")
   If Title = "mr" Then
   %>
   Your serpent, Mister <%= Name %>
   <% ElseIf Title = "ms" Then %>
   Your serpent, Ms. <%= Name %>
   <%End If%>,
   is registered with Snake-O-Rama&#174&#153<BR>
   as a <%= What %>. Characteristics include: <%= Char %>.
   </P>
   </FONT>
</BODY>
</HTML>
```

Figure 22-23 shows a response to the form submission.

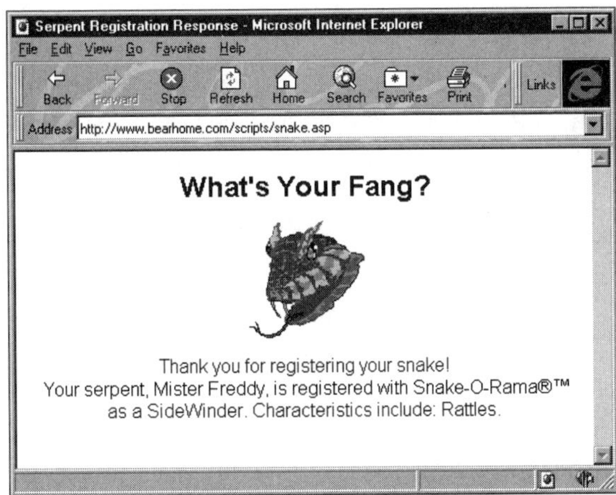

Figure 22-23: Active Server Response files can access form input values.

Note that the script in this ASP file checks whether "Mister" or "Ms" was selected in the original form and generates a different response accordingly. Obviously, you can readily accomplish much more complex parsing of user input, and appropriate response generation, using this technology.

The ASP Object Model

Conceptually, the Active Server Pages framework provides five built-in objects:

- Application
- Request
- Response
- Server
- Session

The Application Object

The Application object is used to share information among all users of a particular application. An ASP "application" is defined as all the ASP files in a virtual directory and its subdirectories.

The Request Object

The Request object is used to retrieve the values a browser sent to the server with an HTTP request. This information is stored in collections.

A collection contains a set of related objects. Usually, the collection provides methods for adding, editing, deleting, and retrieving values from the objects it contains.

The general syntax for accessing Request object collections is

```
Request.Collection.Variable
```

For example, Request.Form("name") was used to access an HTML form's name field in the Snake.Asp Active Server Response file explained in the previous section.

The Request object contains five collections:

- ClientCertificate, the values of client certificate fields sent in the HTTP request
- Cookies, the values of cookies sent in the HTTP request
- Form, the value of form elements in the HTPP request body generated when the POST method was used
- QueryString, the values of variables in the HTTP query string
- ServerVariables, the values of the environment variables

The Response Object

You can use the Response object to send output to the browser. You can use the Cookies collection of the Response object to set cookie values. In addition, the Response object has a number of properties and methods you can use, including

- ContentType, a property that specifies the HTTP content type for the response
- Expires, a property that specifies the length of time before a page cached on a browser expires
- Status, a property that sets the status line returned by the server
- AppendToLog, a method that adds a string to the web server log for the current transaction
- End, a method that stops processing the ASP file immediately, and returns the current result
- Redirect, a method that sends a redirect message to the browser, causing it to connect to a different URL
- Write, a method that writes a variable to the current HTTP output as a string

The Server Object

You use the Server object to provide access to server utility functions. These utilities are invoked as Server object method calls, for example,

```
Server.method
```

The Server object methods are

- CreateObject, which creates an instance of a server component (see "Using an ActiveX Component" later in this chapter)
- HTML Encode, which HTML-encodes the specified string
- MapPath, which translates a virtual path into a physical path
- URLEncode, which URL-encodes a string

The Session Object

The Session object is used to store information for a particular user session. In other words, this object is used to persist information when a user moves between pages in an ASP application.

IIS automatically creates a Session object when a Web page from the application is requested by a user who doesn't have a session; the server destroys the Session object when the session expires or is abandoned.

Inside Scoop

The Session object is an abstraction that uses cookies to do its dirty work. It will not persist information for browsers that do not support cookies.

You can store information about a user with the Session object, for example:

```
<%
   Session("name") = "Hacker Smith"
   Session("age")  = "18"
%>
```

Objects can also be stored in the Session object. If you use VBScript to do this, you must use the Set keyword:

```
<%Set Session("Obj") = Server.CreateObject("TheComponent") %>
```

The methods and properties of TheComponent can then be invoked as follows:

```
<%Session("Obj").TheMethod %>
```

Using an ActiveX Component

The power of ASP is greatly extended by the fact that it is easy to call ActiveX components — OLE servers — from within Active Server Pages. This enables you to use existing ActiveX components, or to reference components that you create in Visual Basic, Delphi, and other languages.

Writing your own ActiveX components is a great way to provide customized functionality for your ASP applications. Although there are some limitations on what you should place in an ActiveX component, creating your own components to interface with Active Server Pages provides "canned" functionality, reusability, and high-level development tools.

ActiveX components provide a simple, reusable way to access information. In Chapter 23, I'll show you how to use the Database Access component to query a database from an ASP script.

Quite a few useful ActiveX components ship with Active Server Pages. For example, the Ad Rotator component is an "ad flipper" that enables you to easily implement the Internet's ubiquitous changing advertisement banners.

Whether you're accessing a ready-made or a custom ActiveX component, you use the Server object's CreateObject method to create an instance of the component that you can use in your ASP application.

Creating the Component

First, I'll show you how to use Visual Basic 5 to create an ActiveX component that can be instanced from an ASP response file. The demonstration component provides one method, RoundNumber, that rounds off the number passed to it to the number of decimal places passed in the second method parameter. Although this functionality could be achieved in VBScript alone, it's certainly easier — and more reusable — to do it in "daddy" Visual Basic as an ActiveX component.

The process of creating an ActiveX component was covered earlier in this chapter in the section "Using WebAction." You'll also find a great deal of information on the topic in one of my other books, *Visual Basic 5 SECRETS*.

Start a new VB5 project. The project type selected should be ActiveX Exe or ActiveX Dll.

ActiveX components that are Dlls will run somewhat faster than ActiveX Exes because they use the same process space as IIS.

By definition, an ActiveX project contains "out of the box" a class module. Change its name to Number and its Instancing property to 5-MultiUse, as shown in Figure 22-24.

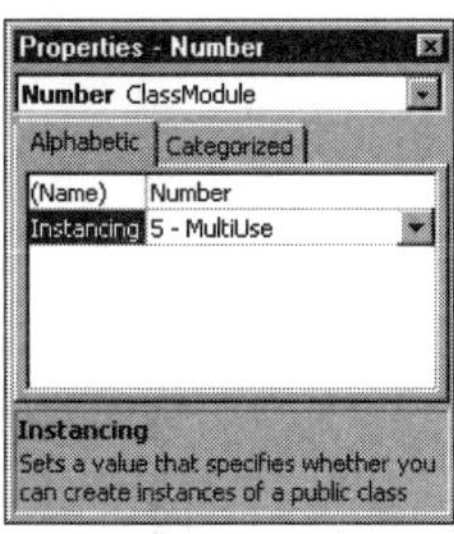

Figure 22-24: You should set the Instancing property of the ActiveX component's class module to 5-MultiUse.

Next, add the RoundNumber function that actually does the work to the class module. Note that this function has been declared Public:

```
'Number.cls - used to create the Round.Number object
Public Function RoundNumber(InNum, _
   DecimalPlaces)
   Dim Tmp As Double, DecShift As Long
   Tmp = CDbl(InNum)
   DecShift = 10 ^ DecimalPlaces
   RoundNumber = (Fix((Tmp + 0.5 / DecShift) * DecShift)) / DecShift
End Function
```

Make sure that explicit variable declaration is not required in the class module, by removing the Option Explicit statement if necessary. Parameters passed back and forth to Active Server Page component instances seem to work best if not typed in any way.

If there is no standard code module already in the project, add one now. Add a Sub Main to the standard module for component start-up. The Sub Main procedure should contain a comment so that the compiler does not delete it:

```
Public Sub Main()
   'Pro forma Sub Main for component start
End Sub
```

On the General tab of the Project Properties dialog — shown in Figure 22-25 — make sure the startup object is set to Sub Main. Name the project Round. The combination of the project name as entered in this dialog and the class name — Round.Number — will be used to identify the object when it is instanced in an Active Server Page.

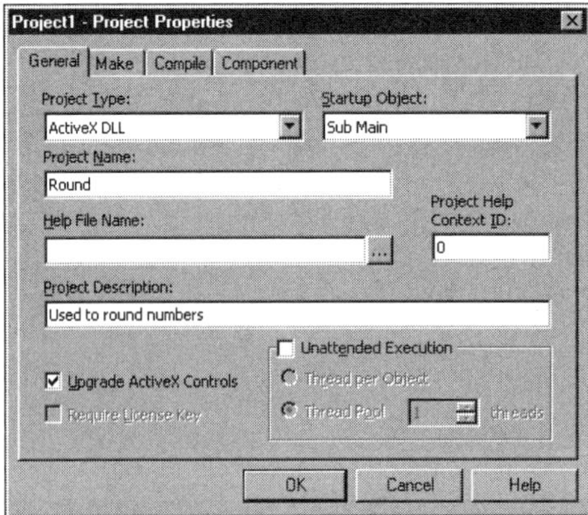

Figure 22-25: The name you give an ActiveX project in the Project Properties dialog is used with the class name to identify the object in an ASP response file.

Make sure that there are no syntax errors in the project by selecting Start With Full Compile. If the project runs without problems, you can stop it and proceed to compile it.

Compiling the ActiveX component registers it with your system. However, if you created it on a system different from the one on which IIS is running, plan to install it on different systems later, or need to move its physical location, you need to know how to manually register and unregister ActiveX components. For more information, see the sidebar "Using Regsvr32 and the /regserver Switch" earlier in this chapter.

Once an instance of your ActiveX component has been created in an ASP response script, it will be held in memory until the Internet Information Server's WWW service is shut down. This means that when you debug an ActiveX component you should be prepared to shut down — and restart — services using the Internet Service Manager.

Invoking the Component

Figure 22-26 shows the HTML form that will be used to invoke the ASP response file that creates the Round.Number object.

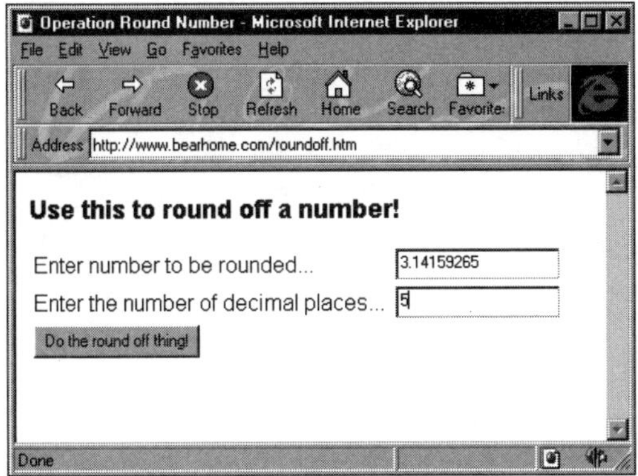

Figure 22-26: You can use an HTML form to invoke the Active Server Page response file that uses the Round.Number object.

Here's the HTML that creates the page shown in Figure 22-26:

```
<HTML>
<HEAD>
   <TITLE>
      Operation Round Number
   </TITLE>
</HEAD>
<BODY BGCOLOR="#FFFFFF"><FONT FACE="ARIAL,HELVETICA">
   <H3>Use this to round off a number!</H3>

   <FORM METHOD=POST ACTION="scripts/round.asp">
   <TABLE>
      <TR>
         <TD>Enter number to be rounded...
         <TD><INPUT TYPE=TEXT NAME=number>
      <TR>
         <TD>Enter the number of decimal places...
         <TD><INPUT TYPE=TEXT NAME=dec>
      <TR>
         <TD><INPUT TYPE=SUBMIT VALUE=" Do the round off thing! ">
   </TABLE>
   </FORM>
</FONT>
</BODY>
</HTML>
```

Here's Round.Asp, the Active Server Page response file:

```
<%@ LANGUAGE = VBScript %>
<HTML>
<HEAD><TITLE>Round Off Calculation</TITLE>
</HEAD>
```

```
<BODY BGCOLOR="#FFFFFF"><FONT FACE="ARIAL,HELVETICA">

<%
' Check to see if numbers entered

If IsNumeric(Request("number")) Then
   Number = (Request("number"))
Else
   Number = 0
End If

If IsNumeric(Request("dec")) Then
   Decimals = (Request("dec"))
Else
   Decimals = 0
End If

' Create an instance of the Rounding object
Set RN = Server.CreateObject("Round.Number")
' Use the instance of the Round Number object to
' calculate the rounded value
Result = RN.RoundNumber(Number, Decimals)
%>

<H3><% = Number %> rounded to <% =Decimals %>
decimal places equals
 <% = Result %>.</H3>

</FONT>
</BODY>
</HTML>
```

This code first checks whether both inputs were numeric. It then creates an instance of the Round.Number object. Finally, it calls the instance with the appropriate arguments and publishes the result, which is shown in Figure 22-27.

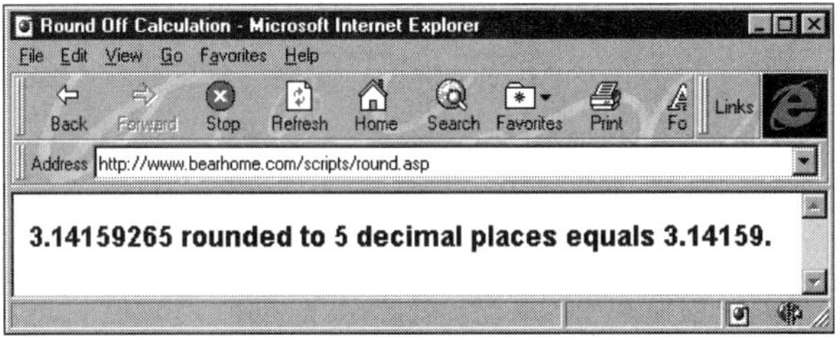

Figure 22-27: The Active Server Page response file uses an instance of the Round.Number object to publish the correct result.

Summary

Server-side programming is the only reliable, consistent way to deliver professional-level content to browsers. (But consider this: How can you serve compelling client-side content without being very familiar with client-side approaches?)

This chapter explained a number of alternatives for creating server-side content using Internet Information Server, the most widely used web server on the Windows NT platform.

Topics covered included

- The Internet Server API (ISAPI)
- Writing an Internet Server application
- Writing an ISAPI filter
- Using webAction
- Registering ActiveX components
- OLEISAPI
- Active Server Pages (Denali)
- The mechanics of ASP
- Creating a form and an ASP response file
- The ASP object model
- Using ActiveX components with ASP files
- Creating a custom ActiveX component for use with an ASP file

Chapter 23

Databases on the Web

"You will be assimilated into the Borg collective."

— Star Trek, *First Contact*

Databases, databases, databases! Every reasonably sized server-side Web application involves a database. This is obvious in the case of many Web sites: catalogs, Web commerce sites, and the like.

Database involvement is perhaps less obvious — but still true — for many other sites that do not apparently involve stereotypical database activities. These sites may well use databases to generate, store, and retrieve HTML libraries. One of the best examples of a Windows NT Web site of this sort is Silicon Investor, *http://www.techstocks.com*, which uses databases to store voluminous chat threads generated by its users.

The long and short of it is that any serious Web development involves linking your programs to databases. There are, of course, almost as many ways to go about this as there are programmers, programs, or stars in the sky. This chapter covers a number of approaches, with the focus on Internet Information Server, that the 32-bit Windows developer may find helpful.

Internet Database Connector (IDC)

Internet Database Connector (IDC) is an implementation of ISAPI. (For information on ISAPI, see Chapter 22.) IDC is designed to allow communication between an HTML front end and an ODBC (Open Database Connectivity) back end. The IDC ISAPI implementation is contained in a dynamic-link library file named Httpodbc.Dll. There are three kinds of ASCII text files involved with the IDC process: HTML forms, idc files, and htx files.

The IDC process is started when the **action** parameter of an HTML form invokes an Internet Database Connector (idc) file. The idc file extension is associated by default in the Registry with Httpodbc.Dll (see "Associating Interpreters with Applications" in Chapter 21 for more information). Httpodbc.Dll invokes the appropriate ODBC driver (depending on the ODBC data source designated in the idc file). Next, Httpodbc.Dll executes the SQL (structured query language) statement contained in the idc file against the designated ODBC data source. This SQL statement could update the database or retrieve information from the database. At this point, Httpodbc uses the htx file designated as the template in the idc file to generate HTML to be returned to the browser.

Figure 23-1 shows the logical flow of IDC requests.

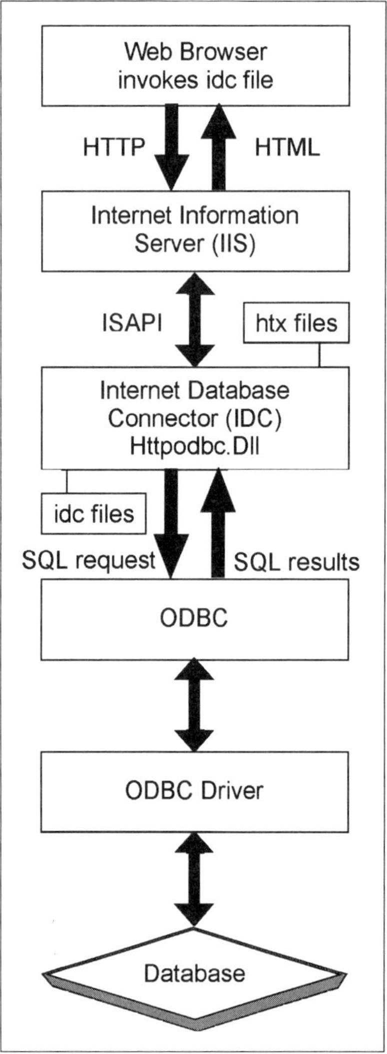

Figure 23-1: IDC is an ISAPI application that returns the results of SQL queries against ODBC data sources to a browser.

Table 23-1 summarizes the three kinds of files you will have to write to create IDC applications.

Table 23-1 IDC Files

File Type	*Contains*
HTML	Standard HTML file containing a form with an idc file specified in its **action** parameter
idc	Text file containing the ODBC data source; designating the htx template file; an SQL statement
htx	Template file for the HTML (including the results of the SQL statement) returned by Httpodbc.Dll

Configuring an ODBC Source

Internet Information Server provides the SQL Server ODBC driver — assuming that you elected to install it during IIS setup — but no other ODBC drivers. Generally, ODBC drivers are provided with database software, but you must configure them to work with a particular data source.

Inside Scoop

Remember that IDC is running as an ISAPI application, meaning that it is invoked by the WWW service. In general, services work only with system — as opposed to user — data sources. This applies to IDC, which will only work with ODBC data sources configured as system data sources.

You configure data sources with the ODBC Data Source Administrator, which you can open from the NT Control Panel. System data sources are configured using the System DSN tab of the ODBC Data Source Administrator dialog, shown in Figure 23-2.

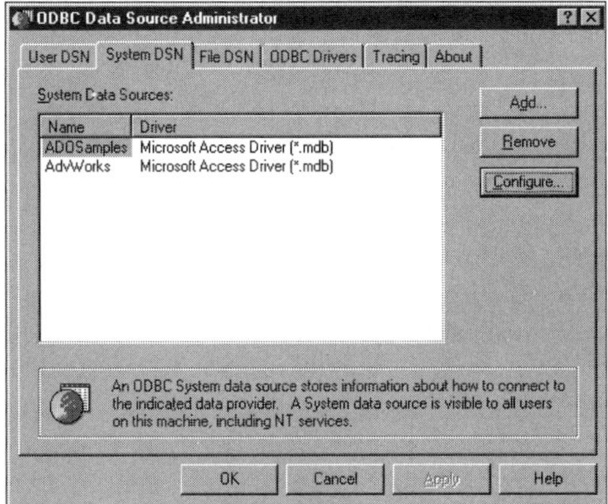

Figure 23-2: You use the System DSN tab of the ODBC Data Source Administrator dialog to configure system ODBC data sources.

Oh, what a sea of acronyms we live in! DSN — Data Source Names — should not be confused with DNS, Domain Name Server.

Click on the Add button on the System DSN tab to add a new data source. From the Create New Data Source dialog, shown in Figure 23-3, select a driver.

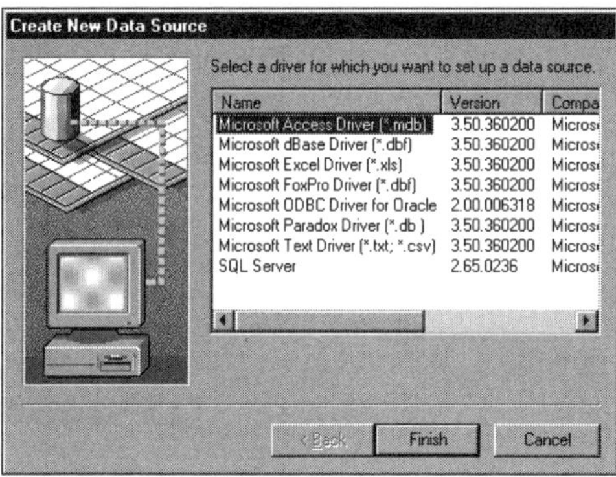

Figure 23-3: You use the Create New Data Source dialog to select an installed ODBC driver.

When you click on Finish in the Create New Data Source Dialog, the configuration dialog for the selected driver will appear. The configuration dialog for each driver is different. This configuration dialog is used to select a physical database and give it a name to make it easier to access. (This name will be used in idc files.) Figure 23-4 shows the ODBC setup dialog for Microsoft Access 97.

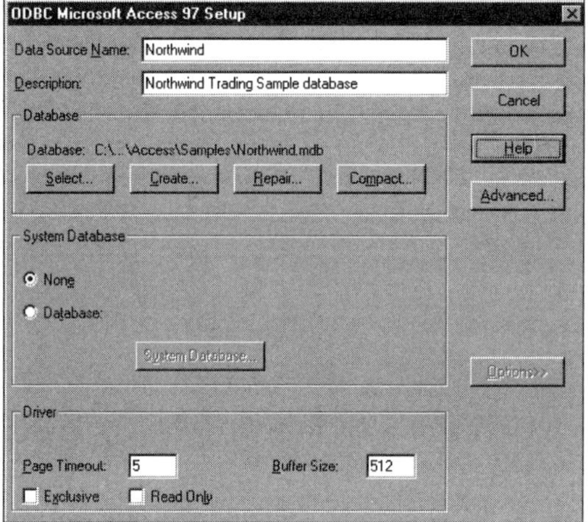

Figure 23-4: You use the ODBC Microsoft Access 97 Setup dialog to select a physical database and give it a name that will be used to reference it.

After you click on OK, the system data source is configured and ready to rock and roll.

A Sample IDC Application

This example IDC application uses the Access ODBC drivers to connect with the sample database for the Adventure Works outdoor equipment store. (This database ships with the Active Server Pages component of IIS.)

The internal name for the connection to the data source is AdvWorks. To use the sample code, you need to have installed on your server the database, Advworks.Mdb, and the Access 97 ODBC driver. In addition, you have to correctly configure the System DSN panel of the ODBC Data Source Administrator, as explained a moment ago under "Configuring an ODBC Source."

The example uses three files:

- Idc_demo.Htm, which contains the HTML query form that invokes the idc script
- Demo.idc, which contains the information needed by Httpodbc.Dll
- Demo.htx, which is the basis for the HTML returned to the browser

Figure 23-5 shows Idc_demo.Htm, the form used to invoke the query.

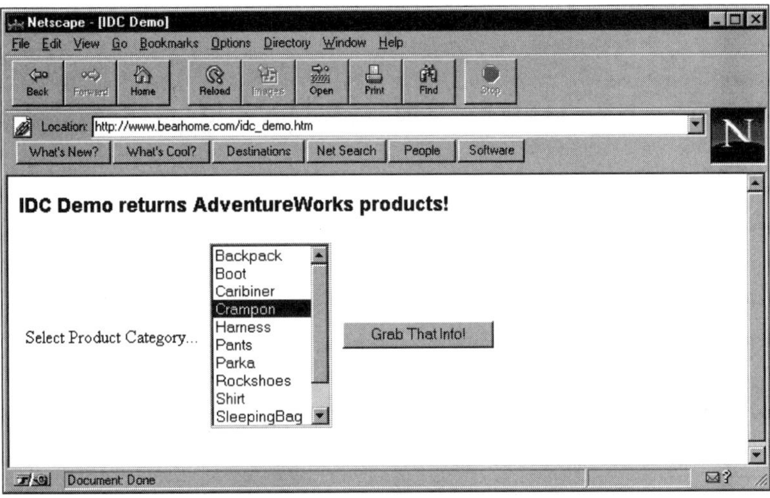

Figure 23-5: An idc file can be invoked in the **action** parameter of an HTML form.

Here's the HTML code that created the form shown in Figure 23-5:

```
<HTML>
   <HEAD>
      <TITLE>
         IDC Demo
      </TITLE>
   </HEAD>
   <BODY BGCOLOR="#FFFFFF"><FONT FACE="ARIAL,HELVETICA">
   <H3>IDC Demo returns AdventureWorks products!</H3>
   <FORM METHOD=POST ACTION="scripts/demo.idc">
      <TABLE>
      <TR>
         <TD>Select Product Category...
         <TD>
         <SELECT name="prodcat" size="10">
            <OPTION>Backpack
            <OPTION>Boot
            <OPTION>Caribiner
            <OPTION>Crampon
            <OPTION>Harness
            <OPTION>Pants
            <OPTION>Parka
            <OPTION>Rockshoes
            <OPTION>Shirt
            <OPTION>SleepingBag
            <OPTION>Supplies
            <OPTION>Tent
         </SELECT
      <TR>
         <TD><INPUT TYPE=SUBMIT VALUE=" Grab That Info! ">
      </TABLE>
   </FORM>
   </FONT>
   </BODY>
</HTML>
```

Demo.idc is invoked by the POST method call of this form. This file contains the name of the data source, the name of the template file for HTML output (Demo.htx), and an SQL query:

```
Datasource:AdvWorks
Template:demo.htx
SQLStatement:
+SELECT ProductName, ProductDescription
+FROM Products
+WHERE Products.ProductType='%prodcat%'
```

You can include named form variables in the SQL query by placing the variable name between % delimiters — for example, %prodcat%.

Once the results of the query have been obtained, the htx template file is invoked. HTML is returned to the browser based on the structure determined by the template. Here's Demo.htx:

```
<HTML>
<HEAD>
   <TITLE>
      IDC Demo Request Results
   </TITLE>
</HEAD>
<BODY BGCOLOR="#FFFFFF"><FONT FACE="ARIAL,HELVETICA">
<H3>These are the products you requested!</H3>
<P>
<CENTER>
<TABLE>
<%begindetail%>
   <TR>
      <TD>
         <%ProductName%>
      </TD>
      <TD>
         <%ProductDescription%>
      </TD>
    </TR>
<%enddetail%>
</TABLE>
</CENTER>
</BODY>
</HTML>
```

Figure 23-6 shows the results of the query (the product category selected to obtain this result is Crampon) returned to the browser.

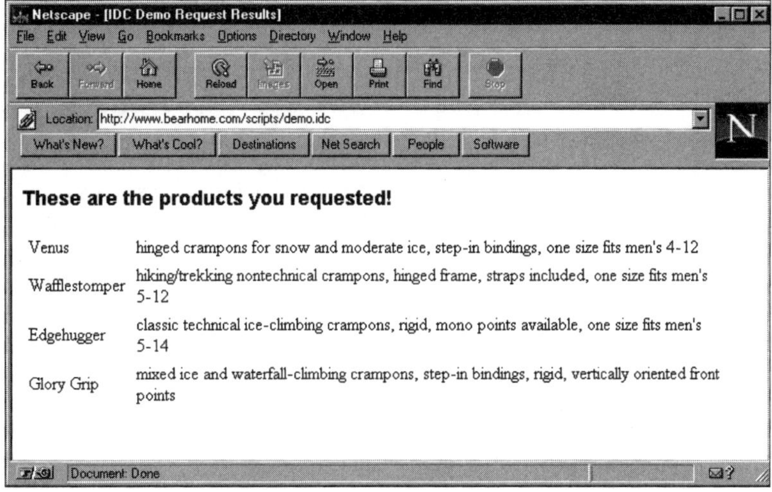

Figure 23-6: An htx file acts as a template for the HTML returned to the browser following a query.

The <%begindetail%> and <%enddetail%> tags are used to indicate a section of the HTML in which database information will be merged with the htx file. Within this section, database fields can be placed by naming the field within delimiters, for example, <%ProductDescription%>.

The percent character (%) is a wildcard character in SQL. You can use wildcards in an SQL query to search for elements in a table that contain specified characters. To prevent IDC from mistaking a percentage sign used as a wildcard with a percentage sign used as a delimiter, use two percentage signs together (%%) for the wildcard. For example:

```
SQLStatement
+SELECT co_name, price, price-earnings
+FROM stocks.nyse
+WHERE co_name like '%%%co_name%%%'
```

Fields in an IDC File

An IDC file must include some mandatory elements, which are shown in Table 23-2. In addition, there are a number of optional elements you can include.

Table 23-2 Required Fields in an IDC File

Field	*Comments*
Datasource	The name of the ODBC data source.
Template	The name of the htx template file that formats the data returned from the query.
SQLStatement	The SQL statement to execute. This SQL statement can contain parameter values passed from the HTML form, which must be enclosed within percent characters (%). The SQLStatement can span multiple lines. Following the SQLStatement field, each subsequent line beginning with a plus sign (+) is considered part of the SQLStatement field. Multiple SQLStatements can appear in the same file.

Table 23-3 lists optional idc file elements.

Table 23-3 Optional Fields in an IDC File

Field	*Comment*
Content-Type	A valid MIME type describing what will be returned to the client (usually "text/html").

Field	Comment
DefaultParameters	The parameter values, if any, that will be used in the IDC file if a parameter is not specified by the browser.
Expires	The number of seconds to wait before the database is required and the cached output page refreshed.
MaxFieldSize	The maximum size allocated by the IDC for each field. The default is 8192 bytes.
MaxRecords	The maximum number of records that the IDC will return for any one query. MaxRecords has no default value, meaning that in theory a query can return up to 4 billion records.
ODBCConnection	Used to add the connection to the connection pool.
Password	The password the user needs to access the database. If there is no password, this field can be omitted.
RequiredParameters	Used to ensure that specific parameters are passed to Httpodbc.Dll (for example, FirstName, LastName). Parameter names are separated with a comma. If the required parameters are not passed, IDC will return an error to the client.
Translationfile	The path to the file that maps non-English characters so that browsers can display them properly in HTML format.
Username	A valid user name to access the database.

Tags and Variables in an htx File

htx files — also called HTML extension files — support a specific syntax of keywords and variables that control how the output HTML file is constructed. Table 23-4 shows these elements.

Table 23-4 htx Tags and Variables

Keyword or Variable	Comment
<%begindetail%> <%enddetail%>	Tags used to delimit the portion of the htx file that you will use to merge data culled from the database.
<%*fieldname*%>	Replaced with information from the field indicated.
<%if%> <%else%> <%endif%>	Used with operators for conditional control in htx files.

(continued)

Table 23-4 (Continued)

Keyword or Variable	*Comment*
EQ LT GT CONTAINS	The only operators available for conditional control in htx files. EQ means equals, LT means less than, GT means greater than, and CONTAINS means contains the string.
CurrentRecord	Contains the number of times that the <%begindetail%> section has been processed. The first time through the database, its value is zero.
MaxRecords	Maximum number of records specified by the idc file. Can only be used with <%if%>.
Form input variables	Can be used provided they were used in the idc file. The syntax is <%idc.*variable*%>.

ASP Database Development

Active Server Pages are a technology included with Internet Information Server (IIS) version 3 that allow you to easily generate server-side HTML content. (You'll find information on ASP technology in Chapter 22.)

The Database Access component that ships with ASP uses a technology known as ActiveX Data Objects (ADO) to make it easy to access databases.

WebAction Templates

WebAction is an ISAPI filter application that diverts HTML form input to custom ActiveX components created in Visual Basic (or another suitable language). For more information on webAction, see Chapter 22.

You can use webAction to call a Visual Basic program that opens a database, generates an SQL statement, and serves appropriate HTML back to the browser. It goes without saying that it is easier to code complex database interactions in VB than in tools that are HTML-based. In addition, you can use webAction to create report templates using Visual Basic. This can effectively automate the process of returning formatted HTML output from a database.

Including the ADO Constants

To use ADO constants in your database connection scripts rather than the more cryptic numeric equivalents, you'll need to use a server-side include (SSI) in your ASP response file. The SSI directives include the constant definition files that ADO requires.

You should use a different include file based upon your primary scripting language. If you are mainly using VBScript, include Adovbs.Inc. If JScript is the primary scripting language, use Adojavas.Inc. By default, these files are placed in the virtual aspsamp/samples directory when ASP is installed.

The SSI directive, for VBScript, should look like:

```
<!--#include virtual="aspsamp/samples/adovbs.inc"-->
```

For JScript:

```
<!--#include virtual="aspsamp/samples/adojavas.inc"-->
```

Using the Data Access Component

The first step in using the Data Access Component is to make sure a System DSN source name is assigned to the ODBC data source your application will use. (For more information, see "Configuring an ODBC" earlier in this chapter.)

This section describes how to use the Data Access Component in the context of a sample application that ships with ASP. The sample application uses the Advworks.Mdb Access database (which is provided for learning purposes as part of ASP). The name given to the ODBC data source is AWTutorial.

Creating the Component Instance

Before you can use it, you need to create an instance of the ADO component. Here's the VBScript that creates the instance:

```
<%
Set OBJdbConnection = Server.CreateObject("ADODB.Connection")
...
```

Next, specify the ODBC data source:

```
OBJdbConnection.Open "AWTutorial"
```

Use the Database Access component's Execute method to issue a SQL query and store the returned records in a result set:

```
SQLQuery = "SELECT * FROM Customers"
Set RSCustomerList = OBJdbConnection.Execute(SQLQuery)
%>
```

It's easy to use a loop to display the result set information in a row in a table format:

```
<TABLE COLSPAN=8 CELLPADDING=5 BORDER=0>
...
<!--Column Head row goes here. -->
...
<% Do While Not RScustomerList.EOF %>
<TR>
   <TD BGCOLOR="f7efde" ALIGN=CENTER>
   <FONT STYLE="ARIAL NARROW" SIZE=1>
      <%= RSCustomerList("CompanyName")%>
   </FONT></TD>
   <TD BGCOLOR="f7efde" ALIGN=CENTER>
   <FONT STYLE="ARIAL NARROW" SIZE=1>
      <%= RScustomerList("ContactLastName") & ", " %>
      <%= RScustomerList("ContactFirstName") %>
   </FONT></TD>
   <TD BGCOLOR="f7efde" ALIGN=CENTER>
   <FONT STYLE="ARIAL NARROW" SIZE=1>
      <A HREF="mailto:">
      <%= RScustomerList("ContactLastName")%>
   </A></FONT></TD>
   <TD BGCOLOR="f7efde" ALIGN=CENTER>
   <FONT STYLE="ARIAL NARROW" SIZE=1>
      <%= RScustomerList("City")%>
   </FONT></TD>
   <TD BGCOLOR="f7efde" ALIGN=CENTER>
   <FONT STYLE="ARIAL NARROW" SIZE=1>
      <%= RScustomerList("StateOrProvince")%>
   </FONT></TD>
</TR>
...
```

To move to the next row, still within the loop, use the MoveNext method:

```
<%
RScustomerList.MoveNext
Loop
%>
</TABLE>
```

This causes each row to be placed in the table until the end of the file is reached.

The results served back to the browser appear in Figure 23-7.

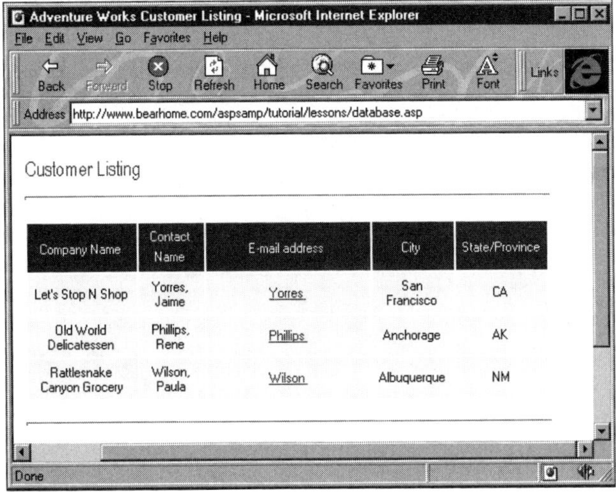

Figure 23-7: You can use ADO objects to easily manipulate ODBC data sources from ASP response files.

Summary

There are two givens in any serious Web development: HTML text files and database interaction. Indeed, database access is a theme that permeates the Web. In some sense, the entire universe of text-based Web pages is nothing more, and nothing less, than a common user interface to myriad isolated databases.

This chapter has explained some of the more palatable database development schemes if you are creating NT, Internet Information Server based server-side content. Topics covered included

- Internet Database Connector (IDC)
- Configuring an ODBC source
- Understanding Httpodbc.Dll
- idc files
- htx files
- ASP response files and database connectivity
- The ActiveX Data Objects (ADO) constants
- The Data Access component

Appendix A

Contents of the CD-ROM

The companion CD-ROM contains source files for the projects developed in *Web Developer's SECRETS*. Source code files and projects are organized by chapter. You'll find source code files that include HTML, JavaScript, VBScript, Visual Basic, Java, Visual C++, Visual J++, Visual Café, Perl for Win32, PerlScript, Active Server Pages, and more.

The source code on the companion CD-ROM allows you to follow projects developed as examples in the book. In addition, the primary purpose of this material is to let you copy and paste generic code without having to re-key it in.

The source code for some chapters is in WinZip library files. You must extract these archives using a utility such as WinZip that preserves long filenames.

I've made every effort to provide source code that is accurate and free of bugs. However, in the real world, there is no assurance that this is so. Neither I nor IDG Books Worldwide makes any representation or warranty regarding the code I have placed on the CD-ROM other than that I have done my best. I will not provide technical support for this code, but I am interested in learning about any significant bugs, or better ways to do something.

A number of leading vendors of Web development products have agreed to supply material for the CD-ROM. Each vendor's product has been placed in its own directory. In most cases, the vendors have supplied their own setup programs, which you should run to install the product on your system. In a few instances, you'll need to copy a zipped file to your hard drive and unzip it before you can run the product's installer.

Neither I nor IDG Books Worldwide provides any technical support for these products. Often, the vendor of the product will provide support, but only if you first purchase and register the software.

Web Development Products on the CD-ROM

This section describes the Web development products you'll find on the CD-ROM:

- ActiveX Control Pad: The ActiveX Control Pad, from Microsoft, is a complete VBScript and JavaScript editor, as well as an ActiveX Control editing tool. Using the ActiveX Control Pad, you can precisely align controls and other elements on an HTML page. For more information on the ActiveX Control Pad, see Chapters 11 and 12.

- Java Development Kit: The Sun Microsystem's JDK Version 1.1 is the fundamental tool needed by Java Web developers, including the one and only Sun Java virtual machine, the Sun Java class libraries and compiler, and much more. For more information on Sun's JDK, see Chapter 17.
- webAction: webAction, from classTools, Inc., is a powerful tool that extends your World Wide Web server with programs developed in Visual Basic, Delphi, or other languages. webAction works with O'Reilly WebSite and Microsoft Information Server. The developer version of the product on the CD-ROM is not limited in any way other than the number of simultaneous HTTP connections it allows. For more information on using webAction, see Chapter 22.

Index

Symbols & Numbers

A

B

C

(continued)

F

G

H

I

J

K

L

M

N

O

Q

R

S

T

U

(continued)

V

W

Z

IDG BOOKS WORLDWIDE, INC. END-USER LICENSE AGREEMENT

<u>READ THIS.</u> **You should carefully read these terms and conditions before opening the software packet(s) included with this book ("Book"). This is a license agreement ("Agreement") between you and IDG Books Worldwide, Inc. ("IDGB"). By opening the accompanying software packet(s), you acknowledge that you have read and accept the following terms and conditions. If you do not agree and do not want to be bound by such terms and conditions, promptly return the Book and the unopened software packet(s) to the place you obtained them for a full refund.**

1. **License Grant.** IDGB grants to you (either an individual or entity) a nonexclusive license to use one copy of the enclosed software program(s) (collectively, the "Software") solely for your own personal or business purposes on a single computer (whether a standard computer or a workstation component of a multiuser network). The Software is in use on a computer when it is loaded into temporary memory (RAM) or installed into permanent memory (hard disk, CD-ROM, or other storage device). IDGB reserves all rights not expressly granted herein.

2. **Ownership.** Author is the owner of all right, title, and interest, including copyright, in and to the compilation of the Software recorded on the disk(s) or CD-ROM ("Software Media"). Copyright to the individual programs recorded on the Software Media is owned by the author or other authorized copyright owner of each program. Ownership of the Software and all proprietary rights relating thereto remain with Author and its licensers.

3. **Restrictions On Use and Transfer.**

(a) You may only (i) make one copy of the Software for backup or archival purposes, or (ii) transfer the Software to a single hard disk, provided that you keep the original for backup or archival purposes. You may not (i) rent or lease the Software, (ii) copy or reproduce the Software through a LAN or other network system or through any computer subscriber system or bulletin-board system, or (iii) modify, adapt, or create derivative works based on the Software.

(b) You may not reverse engineer, decompile, or disassemble the Software. You may transfer the Software and user documentation on a permanent basis, provided that the transferee agrees to accept the terms and conditions of this Agreement and you retain no copies. If the Software is an update or has been updated, any transfer must include the most recent update and all prior versions.

4. **Restrictions On Use of Individual Programs.** You must follow the individual requirements and restrictions detailed for each individual program in the Appendix to this Book. These limitations are also contained in the individual license agreements recorded on the Software Media. These limitations may include a requirement that after using the program for a specified period of time, the user must pay a registration fee or discontinue use. By opening the Software packet(s), you will be agreeing to abide by the licenses and restrictions for these individual programs that are detailed in the Appendix to this book and on the Software Media. None of the material on this Software Media or listed in this Book may ever be redistributed, in original or modified form, for commercial purposes.

5. **Limited Warranty.**

(a) IDGB warrants that the Software and Software Media are free from defects in materials and workmanship under normal use for a period of sixty (60) days from the date of purchase of this Book. If IDGB receives notification within the warranty period of defects in materials or workmanship, IDGB will replace the defective Software Media.

(b) **IDGB AND THE AUTHOR OF THE BOOK DISCLAIM ALL OTHER WARRANTIES, EXPRESS OR IMPLIED, INCLUDING WITHOUT LIMITATION IMPLIED WARRANTIES OF MERCHANTABILITY AND FITNESS FOR A PARTICULAR PURPOSE, WITH RESPECT TO THE SOFTWARE, THE PROGRAMS, THE SOURCE CODE CONTAINED THEREIN, AND/OR THE TECHNIQUES DESCRIBED IN THIS BOOK. IDGB DOES NOT WARRANT THAT THE FUNCTIONS CONTAINED IN THE SOFTWARE WILL MEET YOUR REQUIREMENTS OR THAT THE OPERATION OF THE SOFTWARE WILL BE ERROR FREE.**

(c) This limited warranty gives you specific legal rights, and you may have other rights that vary from jurisdiction to jurisdiction.

6. **Remedies.**

(a) IDGB's entire liability and your exclusive remedy for defects in materials and workmanship shall be limited to replacement of the Software Media, which may be returned to IDGB with a copy of your receipt at the following address: Software Media Fulfillment Department, Attn.: *Web Developer's SECRETS*, IDG Books Worldwide, Inc., 7260 Shadeland Station, Ste. 100, Indianapolis, IN 46256, or call 1-800-762-2974. Please allow three to four weeks for delivery. This Limited Warranty is void if failure of the Software Media has resulted from accident, abuse, or misapplication. Any replacement Software Media will be warranted for the remainder of the original warranty period or thirty (30) days, whichever is longer.

(b) In no event shall IDGB or the author be liable for any damages whatsoever (including without limitation damages for loss of business profits, business interruption, loss of business information, or any other pecuniary loss) arising from the use of or inability to use the Book or the Software, even if IDGB has been advised of the possibility of such damages.

(c) Because some jurisdictions do not allow the exclusion or limitation of liability for consequential or incidental damages, the above limitation or exclusion may not apply to you.

7. **U.S. Government Restricted Rights.** Use, duplication, or disclosure of the Software by the U.S. Government is subject to restrictions stated in paragraph (c)(1)(ii) of the Rights in Technical Data and Computer Software clause of DFARS 252.227-7013, and in subparagraphs (a) through (d) of the Commercial Computer — Restricted Rights clause at FAR 52.227-19, and in similar clauses in the NASA FAR supplement, when applicable.

8. **General.** This Agreement constitutes the entire understanding of the parties and revokes and supersedes all prior agreements, oral or written, between them and may not be modified or amended except in writing signed by both parties hereto that specifically refers to this Agreement. This Agreement shall take precedence over any other documents that may be in conflict herewith. If any one or more

provisions contained in this Agreement are held by any court or tribunal to be invalid, illegal, or otherwise unenforceable, each and every other provision shall remain in full force and effect.

Java™ Development Kit Version 1.1.1 Binary Code License

This binary code license ("License") contains rights and restrictions associated with use of the accompanying software and documentation ("Software"). Read the License carefully before installing the Software. By installing the Software, you agree to the terms and conditions of the License.

1. **Limited License Grant.** Sun grants to you ("Licensee") a nonexclusive, nontransferable limited license to use the Software without fee for evaluation of the Software and for development of Java™ compatible applets and applications. Licensee may make one archival copy of the Software. Licensee may not redistribute the Software in whole or in part, either separately or included with a product. Refer to the Java Runtime Environment Version 1.1.1 binary code license (http://www.javasoft.com/products/JDK/1.1.1/index.html) for the availability of runtime code that may be distributed with Java compatible applets and applications.
2. **Java Platform Interface.** Licensee may not modify the Java Platform Interface ("JPI", identified as classes contained within the "java" package or any subpackages of the "java" package) by creating additional classes within the JPI or otherwise causing the addition to or modification of the classes in the JPI. In the event that Licensee creates any Java-related API and distributes such API to others for applet or application development, Licensee must promptly publish an accurate specification for such API for free use by all developers of Java-based software.
3. **Restrictions.** Software is confidential, copyrighted information of Sun and title to all copies is retained by Sun and/or its licensors. Licensee shall not modify, decompile, disassemble, decrypt, extract, or otherwise reverse engineer Software. Software may not be leased, assigned, or sublicensed, in whole or in part. Software is not designed or intended for use in online control of aircraft, air traffic, aircraft navigation, or aircraft communications; or in the design, construction, operation, or maintenance of any nuclear facility. Licensee warrants that it will not use or redistribute the Software for such purposes.
4. **Trademarks and Logos.** This License does not authorize Licensee to use any Sun name, trademark, or logo. Licensee acknowledges that Sun owns the Java trademark and all Java-related trademarks, logos, and icons including the Coffee Cup and Duke ("Java Marks") and agrees to: (i) to comply with the Java Trademark Guidelines at http://java.com/trademarks.html; (ii) not do anything harmful to or inconsistent with Sun's rights in the Java Marks; and (iii) assist Sun in protecting those rights, including assigning to Sun any rights acquired by Licensee in any Java Mark.
5. **Disclaimer of Warranty.** Software is provided "AS IS," without a warranty of any kind. ALL EXPRESS OR IMPLIED REPRESENTATIONS AND WARRANTIES, INCLUDING ANY IMPLIED WARRANTY OF MERCHANTABILITY, FITNESS FOR A PARTICULAR PURPOSE OR NONINFRINGEMENT, ARE HEREBY EXCLUDED.

6. **Limitation of Liability.** SUN AND ALL ITS LICNESORS SHALL NOT BE LIABLE FOR ANY DAMAGES SUFFERED BY LICENSEE OR ANY THIRD PARTY AS A RESULT OF USING OR DISTRIBUTING SOFTWARE. IN NO EVENT WILL SUN OR ITS LICENSORS BE LIABLE FOR ANY LOST REVENUE, PROFIT, OR DATA; OR FOR DIRECT, INDIRECT, SPECIAL, CONSEQUENTIAL, INCIDENTAL OR PUNITIVE DAMAGES, HOWEVER CAUSED AND REGARDLESS OF THE THEORY OF LIABILITY, ARISING OUT OF THE USE OF OR INABILITY TO USE SOFTWARE, EVEN IF SUN HAS BEEN ADVISED OF THE POSSIBLITY OF SUCH DAMAGES.
7. **Termination.** Licensee may terminate this License at any time by destroying all copies of Software. This License will terminate immediately without notice from Sun if Licensee fails to comply with any provision of this License. Upon such termination, Licensee must destroy all copies of Software.
8. **Export Regulations.** Software, including technical data, is subject to U.S. export control laws, including the U.S. Export Administration Act and its associated regulations, and may be subject to export or import regulations in other countries. Licensee agrees to comply strictly with all such regulations and acknowledges that it has the responsibility to obtain licenses to export, reexport, or import Software. Software may not be downloaded, or otherwise exported or reexported (i) into, or to a national or resident of, Cuba, Iraq, Iran, North Korea, Libya, Sudan, Syria, or any country to which the U.S. has embargoed goods; or (ii) to anyone on the U.S. Treasury Department's list of Specially Designated Nations or the U.S. Commerce Department's Table of Denial Orders.
9. **Restricted Rights.** Use, duplication or disclosure by the U.S. government is subject to the restrictions as set forth in the Rights in Technical Data and Computer Software Clauses in DFARS 252.227-7013(c)(1)(ii) and FAR 52.227-19(c) (2) as applicable.
10. **Governing Law.** Any action related to this License will be governed by California law and controlling U.S. federal law. No choice of law rules of any jurisdiction will apply.
11. **Severability.** If any of the above provisions are held to be in violation of applicable law, void, or unenforceable in any jurisdiction, then such provisions are herewith waived to the extent necessary for the License to be otherwise enforceable in such jurisdiction. However, if in Sun's opinion deletion of any provisions of the License by operation of this paragraph unreasonably compromises the rights or increase the liabilities of Sun or its licensors, Sun reserves the right to terminate the License and refund the fee paid by Licensee, if any, as Licensee's sole and exclusive remedy.

CD-ROM Installation Instructions

The companion CD-ROM contains source files for the projects developed in *Web Developer's SECRETS,* as well as powerful Web development tools from a number of leading vendors.

Source Code

Source code files and projects are organized by chapter. Some code is in WinZip library files. To get at it, you must first extract these archives using a utility such as WinZip that preserves long filenames.

Web Development Tools

Each vendor's product has been placed in its own directory. In most cases, the vendors have supplied their own setup programs, which you should run to install the product on your system. In a few instances, you'll first need to copy a zipped file to your hard drive and unzip it before you can run the product's installation program.

IDG
BOOKS
WORLDWIDE